LIFE AND DEATH IN IRON AGE IRELAND
IN THE LIGHT OF RECENT ARCHAEOLOGICAL EXCAVATIONS

Life and death in Iron Age Ireland
in the light of recent archaeological excavations

Christiaan Corlett and Michael Potterton

EDITORS

Wordwell

WORDWELL LTD
Published by
Wordwell Ltd
Unit 9, 78 Furze Road, Sandyford Industrial Estate, Dublin 18
www.wordwellbooks.com

First published 2012

ISBN 978 1 905569 72 4

The moral right of the authors has been asserted.

British Library Cataloguing-in-Publication Data.
A catalogue record for this book is available from the British Library.

Cover photograph: The Iron Age causeway at Annaholty Bog, Co. Tipperary.

Set in 10/13 Bembo
Typeset in Ireland by Wordwell Ltd
Printed by SPRINT-print Ltd, Ireland

Cover design: Nick Maxwell
Cover photograph: Hawkeye, courtesy of TVAS Ireland
Copy-editing: Emer Condit

Research papers in Irish archaeology, no. 4

Published in association with the Royal Society of Antiquaries of Ireland and the Discovery Programme.

This publication has received support from the Discovery Programme's Late Iron Age and Roman Ireland (LIARI) Project, the Environment Fund and the Heritage Council under the 2012 Heritage Education, Community and Outreach Scheme.

Contents

Abbreviations

AMS	Accelerator mass spectrometry	NGR	National Grid Reference
BP	Before present	NMI	National Museum of Ireland
DEHLG	Department of the	NRA	National Roads Authority
	Environment, Heritage and	OD	Ordnance Datum
	Local Government	OS	Ordnance Survey
DP	Diameter of perforation	Pl./Pls	Plate/Plates
ed.	Editor; edited by	prep.	Preparation
Excavations 1971 [etc.]	*Excavations 1971* [etc.]: *summary accounts of archaeological excavations in Ireland*, ed. T.G. Delaney (1971–6), Claire Cotter (1985–6), Isabel Bennett (1987–) [1977–84 incorporated in *Irish Journal of Archaeology*]	repr.	Reprint; reprinted
		RIA	Royal Irish Academy
		RMP	Record of Monuments and Places
		RSAI	Royal Society of Antiquaries of Ireland
		SEM	Scanning electron microscope
		ser.	Series
Fig./Figs	Figure/Figures	SMR	Sites and Monuments Record
LPRIA	Late pre-Roman Iron Age	UCD	University College Dublin
MS(S)	Manuscript(s)		

Foreword

The subtitle and chapter headings of Barry Raftery's indispensable survey of Iron Age Ireland, *Pagan Celtic Ireland: the enigma of the Irish Iron Age* (1994), speak to the agony and the ecstasy that accompanied a lifetime dedicated to the study of Iron Age Ireland. Chapter headings like 'The road to God knows where' and 'The invisible people' tell of an archaeological record that defies explanation, in much the same way as the Celts themselves remained enigmatic and unfathomable to their Mediterranean neighbours. Though less alarming, students of this period will not be lulled into a false sense of security by the other chapter titles. In fact, almost every one of them—'From bronzesmith to blacksmith', 'Hillforts', 'Technology and art', 'Beyond the empire', and so on—conceals an academic iceberg.

So much for the agony. The ecstasy resides in the fact that the pathos of the people of Iron Age Ireland seems so present, so familiar, so noble and heroic and yet so tragic that no one can be unmoved by it. We are all romanced by the past, and the Irish Iron Age is particularly seductive.

This book of essays takes up the challenge intrinsically present in Raftery's writings by assembling a new generation of scholars and arming them with data from a decade of unprecedented excavation activity that has the potential to bring about a quantum leap forward in knowledge about the Irish Iron Age. This will not happen overnight, and it will take quite a few more years of publication, discourse and synthesis before a new consensus is arrived at, but a critical first step is achieved here among essays that interrogate the analysis of Iron Age Ireland and introduce new science and new information.

A peculiarity of humanities research is that rather than solving age-old questions new data often simply refine or reformulate them. A quiet revolution in the approach to later Iron Age Ireland has been in train for about twenty years, building on a paradigm that embraces rather than eschews Roman influence. Notable successes have already been achieved, and this field of research has been given a major shot in the arm with the Discovery Programme's Late Iron Age and Roman Ireland (LIARI) project. In contrast, the beginning years of the Iron Age have remained impenetrable, despite being the focus of the first generation of Discovery Programme projects. 'Transition periods' have always been difficult, either because they never really existed except in the ordering minds of archaeologists, or because social flux plays havoc with the behavioural patterns that are the building blocks of the archaeological storyboard. Often it is our expectations that are at fault for being too simplistic or too optimistic: we may need our subjects to act rationally, to behave with consistency, but it is not always thus. Just as today, the coexistence of past and future in the human mind is what shapes the present, and epochs are rarely universal. As Julian Barnes writes in *The sense of an ending*, 'you may say, "But wasn't this the Sixties?" Yes, but only for some people, only in certain parts of the country' (2012, 23). Later he observes that 'most people didn't experience "the Sixties" until the Seventies'. One thinks here of the appearance of Hallstatt material in Ireland and the questions now being asked about its causality. Being a Celt was surely, first and foremost, a state of mind.

Complementing the LIARI project's focus on the later Iron Age, the Iron Age Ireland: Finding an Invisible People project is also systematically hoovering up the new and unpublished data. This is how the field will advance and is the principle behind INSTAR. As its name suggests, there is a focus in this second project on the quotidian, in an effort to counterbalance the impressive corpus of information about the 'royal' complexes like Tara, Emain Macha, Dún Ailinne, Rathcroghan and so on. Although these represent the success stories of archaeological investigation of the Iron Age, they are, in a way, exceptional. Day-to-day life was far more ephemeral, and more often than not radiocarbon dates are all there is to indicate Iron Age date. Against such a background, how did social identity, belongingness and cohesion arise? How can a people who left so slight a trace, whose footprints were so light that large parts of the very land around them returned from farmland to wilderness, have rallied to create great monuments and sublime works of art? Archaeology alone cannot provide answers to these questions, but with a sound theoretical footing, openness to interdisciplinarity and greater use of ethnographic comparanda we will begin to understand better the people of Iron Age Ireland and appreciate better the enormous contribution they made to the shaping of our island identity. Volumes such as this, that advance and challenge existing theory with a combination of new data and new synthesis, show how we can arrive at new knowledge.

Conor Newman
Chairman of the Heritage Council
16 August 2012

Introduction

Life and death in Iron Age Ireland in the light of recent archaeological excavations was the theme for a one-day seminar held in the Royal Society of Antiquaries of Ireland in Dublin on 2 February 2007. This volume brings together many of the papers presented on that day, as well as additional essays commissioned subsequently. It is also the fourth volume in the series 'Research papers in Irish archaeology'. The first, *Rural settlement in medieval Ireland*, was published in 2009; the second, *Death and burial in early medieval Ireland*, appeared in 2010; the third, *Settlement in early medieval Ireland*, came out in 2011. Work is under way on the fifth volume, on the church in early Ireland. The seminars aim to highlight the results of recent (and some not-so-recent) excavations, on a thematic basis, and to facilitate the dissemination and discussion of this information. By extension, the subsequent publications are a more permanent and accessible contribution to this process.

The Iron Age is without doubt the most enigmatic period in Irish archaeology. If there are more than 50,000 early medieval monuments known throughout Ireland, by contrast there are barely 50 monuments that one could point to and say definitively 'That's Iron Age'. The number of Iron Age artefacts is considerably higher, but pales into insignificance compared to the thousands of objects from either the Bronze Age or the early medieval period. Until recently it was thought that the Irish Iron Age was almost entirely absent from the excavation record. With hundreds of large-scale excavations throughout the country and newly discovered sites from every period, nothing jumped out and screamed *Iron Age*. When ^{14}C dates started coming back from many projects, however, it gradually became clear that the Iron Age has been there all along—typically unassuming and frequently masquerading as something from another period. The picture is still very murky, but what is obvious is that the textbook for the entire Iron Age in Ireland needs to be rewritten from start to finish. Preconceived ideas about the dating and significance of the artefactual record of the period are already being challenged. The new evidence from recent archaeological excavations has the potential to transform our new understanding of the Irish Iron Age and finally dispel the myths of Ireland's supposed dark age. The information contained in the 26 essays in this volume is a contribution to this process.

The editors are especially grateful to the Heritage Council, who, despite continued cutbacks to their own budget, have provided a substantial grant towards this publication. We would also like to acknowledge the financial support of the Environment Fund of the Department of Arts, Heritage and the Gaeltacht. This book would not have been published were it not for the additional funding supplied by the Late Iron Age and Roman Ireland (LIARI) Project of the Discovery Programme, Ireland's institute for advanced archaeological research. The LIARI Project aims to characterise the environment, settlement patterns, social structures and ritual practices of the people who lived and died in Ireland during the first five centuries AD. It is considering the nature of Ireland's interactions with the Roman Empire and especially with Roman Britain, with a view to reconstructing a more holistic and inclusive archaeological narrative for the later Irish Iron Age (AD 1–500). The project is directed by Jacqueline Cahill Wilson and she has contributed an essay to the current volume, on 'rethinking our approach to the archaeology of the later Iron Age'.

We would also like to thank those who participated in the seminar of February 2007, especially the late Barry Raftery (who introduced the proceedings), Tom Condit (who made the closing remarks) and the people who chaired sessions (Tiernan McGarry, Ann Lynch and Christina Fredengren). Papers were presented on the day by Richard Clutterbuck, Grace Fegan, James Eogan, Red Tobin, Frank Ryan, Margaret Keane, Eamonn Kelly, Cara Murray, Emmet Stafford, Cóilín Ó Drisceoil, Gerry Walsh, Sebastian Joubert, Holger Schweitzer and William O'Brien.

As well as papers on many of the sites discussed at the seminar, the present volume includes additional contributions by Katharina Becker, Michelle Brick, Laureen Buckley, Jacqueline Cahill Wilson, Tracy Collins, Jennie Coughlan, Tim Coughlan, Ed Danaher, Shane Delaney, Emma Devine, Katherine Eremin, William Frazer, Jonny Geber, Ellinor Larsson, Susan Lyons, Ciara McCarthy, Meriel McClatchie, Jim McKeon, Catherine McLoughlin, Siobhán McNamara, Melanie McQuade, Bernice Molloy, Charles Mount, Ellen OCarroll, Finola O'Carroll, Aidan O'Connell, Brian Ó Donnchadha, Maria O'Hare, Ian Russell, Alison Sheridan, Kate Taylor, Fintan Walsh and Yvonne Whitty. It is a pleasure to thank Conor Newman, who has been a stalwart supporter of this series and who penned the foreword to the present volume.

The preparation of this publication was facilitated by our friends and colleagues at the Royal Society of Antiquaries of Ireland and the Discovery Programme. The site location maps were prepared by Philip Behan. Others who have assisted in various ways and to whom we are very grateful are Michael Ann Bevivino, John Bradley, Gary Devlin, Colette Ellison, Stephen Johnston, Conor McDermott, Paul McMahon, Muiris Ó Conchúir, Amanda Ryan, Robert Shaw, Ingelise Stuijts, Fintan Walsh and Richard Warner.

Christiaan Corlett & Michael Potterton
Wicklow & Meath, 17 August 2012

Location of sites discussed in this volume.

1. Redefining the Irish Iron Age

Katharina Becker

Introduction

The large numbers of excavations conducted during the years of economic growth in Ireland have at last produced evidence of Iron Age settlement and industry. This paper sets the new record into its contemporary context and seeks to define the period in its broad chronological parameters, reviewing and assessing the previous discussion.

Rarely are archaeologists of our generation presented with the need or opportunity to define an entire archaeological period, more or less from scratch, in chronological, spatial and cultural terms. This is the unique challenge that presents itself to us today with regard to the Irish Iron Age, the important transition from prehistory to history. The conclusions and chronological scheme proposed here are considered only as a first step, but it is hoped that they capture the characteristics and change of the record appropriately to serve as the basis for future refinement.

The old Iron Age

Until recently, the archaeological record of the Irish Iron Age consisted of rather disparate and disjointed groups of artefacts and monuments, most of them datable to the last few centuries before and the first centuries after the birth of Christ. Ceremonial sites, linear earthworks, the trackways of the midlands, a small group of burial monuments and a small corpus of high-status metalwork primarily represent aspects of high-status and ceremonial life. On the other hand, they reveal little about everyday life in the Iron Age; domestic or industrial activity and evidence of the vernacular and the mundane have long remained elusive, with hardly any settlement evidence (see Armit 2007, 130–2; Raftery 1994, 112–46). This problem, encapsulated in the phrase 'the invisible people' (Raftery 1994, 112), has contributed to the enigmatic character of the period. Glimpses of everyday life can be caught in the archaeology of the wetlands, with its trackways and the wooden vessels and other mundane objects found as secondary deposits on these sites (see, for example, Raftery 1996; Moore 2008). Nevertheless, just as the palaeoenvironmental evidence from ceremonial high-status sites with evidence for feasting (see, for example, McCormick 2007, 95–7; 2002; 1997; Crabtree 2007) allows some insight into the agriculture of the period but cannot be read as an accurate reflection of subsistence patterns in the Irish Iron Age, these sites are not representative of

Fig. 1.1—Distribution of Iron Age La Tène metalwork and related material, excluding quernstones, up to 1984 (after Raftery 1983, map 23, with additions).

everyday life. In terms of both the activities and the social groups primarily thought to be involved in them, the archaeological record of Iron Age Ireland is thus curiously biased towards ceremonial and high-status activities. As a consequence, it is likely that not only certain aspects of life but also the majority of the population are not visible in the archaeological record (Raftery 1994, 112).

This is particularly apparent in the case of the metalwork. This material, with its clear typological affinities to Continental and British La Tène forms (see Raftery 1984; 1983), was for a long time synonymous with the 'Celtic Iron

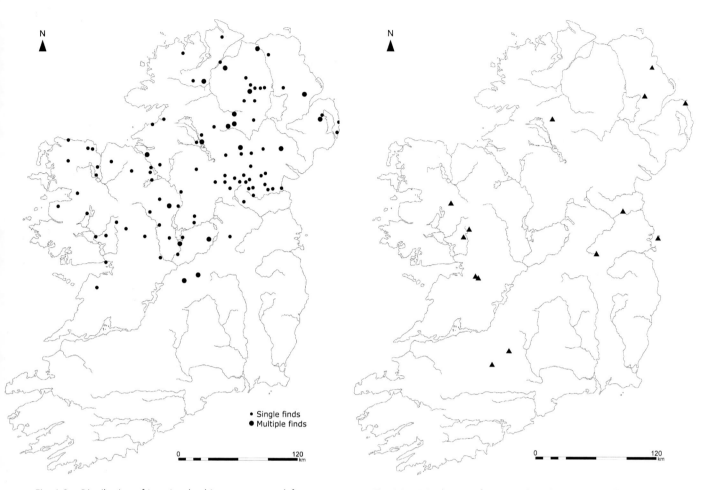

Fig. 1.2—Distribution of Iron Age beehive quernstones (after Warner 2002).

Fig. 1.3—Distribution of Iron Age burials recorded before 1983 (after Raftery 1983, map 23).

Age' in Ireland's prehistoric past. While these bronze, gold and probably contemporary stone artefacts constitute the main body of Irish Iron Age evidence, they clearly cannot be considered as representative of everyday life in the period. This is due to the fact that the range of artefacts is functionally biased, consisting largely of high-status items of a martial or ceremonial nature, with weaponry, horse gear and gold ornaments constituting some of the most prevalent find categories. These items reflect specialised activities and were probably only produced and utilised by a small stratum of society (see, for example, Raftery 1998b, 22).

In terms of its geographic distribution, too, the La Tène material has been revealed to be biased. One of the central issues in the discussion of the distribution of Iron Age evidence in Ireland has been the discrepancy between the north and the south of the country. Owing to the small number of settlement sites, the debate has focused primarily on the artefact record

(see, for example, Raftery 1976a; Warner 1998; Woodman 1998; Raftery 1998b). Artefacts that can be attributed to the La Tène complex are concentrated in the north of the country, especially in the province of Ulster (Fig. 1.1.),[1] but are rarely found in the south, a pattern that is particularly clear in the case of Iron Age quernstones (Fig. 1.2) (Warner 2002; Caulfield 1977). While there is a similar absence of burials in the south of the country, these are not very frequent in the north either (Fig. 1.3).[2] The few settlements known at the time and the ceremonial sites (the so-called 'royal sites': Navan Fort, Co. Armagh, Tara, Co. Meath, Knockaulin, Co. Kildare, and Rathcroghan, Co. Roscommon; Fig. 1.4) were also included on the map published by Raftery in 1983 (Raftery 1983, map 23) that, in subsequent research, provided a foundation for the debate on regionality in the Iron Age. These sites show, if anything, a predominantly eastern bias but their overall number is small. The uneven distribution of artefacts has been discussed

Fig. 1.4—Distribution of Iron Age ceremonial ('royal') sites and settlement (after Raftery 1983, map 23; 1994).

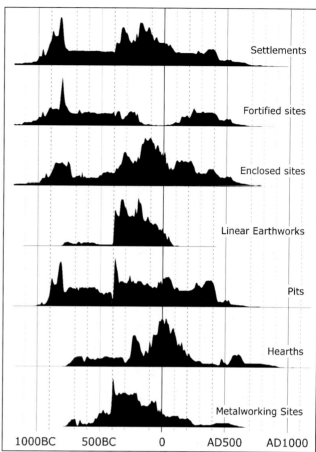

Fig. 1.5—Sum graphs of radiocarbon dates for different types of sites.

as representing the absence of an Iron Age, as evidence for the existence of a non-metal or a non-La Tène-using culture in the south (Raftery 1998b, 23; Warner 1998, 29) or as evidence for low population levels in these areas (Warner 1998, 29; but see Woodman 1998). The biases that clearly affect this particular part of the archaeological record make it clear that the body of La Tène and associated artefacts 'is not and was not representative of the majority of the population of Ireland in the centuries spanning the birth of Christ' (Raftery 1995b, 5). This obviously also had implications for the cultural interpretation of the period; consequently, the notion of Celtic invasions or immigrations into Ireland was widely abandoned as a relevant explanatory model and greater emphasis was put on the continuity between the Bronze Age and the Iron Age (see Armit 2007, 132; Cooney and Grogan 1994; Champion 1982; Ó Donnabháin 2000; Raftery 2006; 1998a; 1994; Waddell 1995; 1991).

The 'new' Iron Age

The lack of evidence for domestic and industrial activity made it impossible to replace the Celtic paradigm with a new framework or to examine the known high-status material within a contemporary everyday context. This only now becomes possible with the recent emergence of new archaeological information. The large numbers of excavations conducted within the context of recent private and public development have begun to bring to light the Iron Age settlement and industrial sites previously lacking in the archaeological record: they present Iron Age research in Ireland with a unique opportunity to address many of the issues raised by the previously known material. These new sites, most of which are still unpublished, are being collated and analysed in the project entitled 'Iron Age Ireland: finding an invisible people', the pilot phase of which was funded by the Irish Heritage Council in 2008 (Becker, Ó Néill et al.

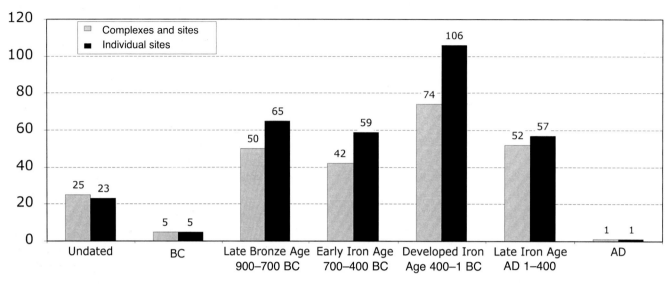

Fig. 1.6—Number of excavated late Bronze Age and Iron Age sites recorded in the project.

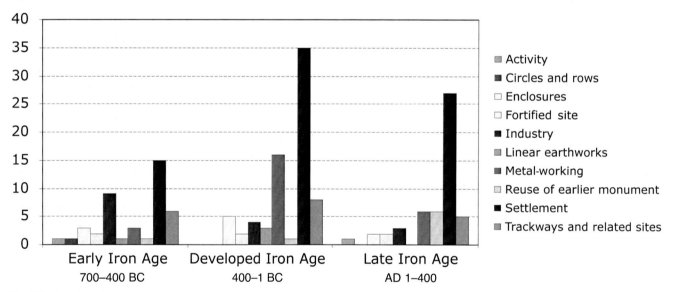

Fig. 1.7—Iron Age site types.

2008a; 2008b). All the sites excavated up to 2004 (the current cut-off date for the project) that have produced Iron Age dates (here defined as the period between the end of the Bronze Age, about 700 BC, and the beginning of the early medieval period around AD 400) were recorded in a database. In order to capture the transition from the late Bronze Age to the Iron Age, which is a particularly problematic issue in Ireland (see Raftery 1994, 17–37; 1976a; Champion 1989; 1971), it was decided to include sites dating from the later part of the late Bronze Age. Burials were not included because a comparable

study of those sites was conducted recently (McGarry 2007; 2005). Only securely dated sites were included. As securely datable artefacts are rare, radiocarbon and dendrochronological dates constitute the main source of dating evidence.

The dataset currently contains about 200 sites and complexes dating from the Iron Age. These include a variety of different forms of settlement and industrial sites, as well as the evidence from the 'royal sites' and the trackways and platforms in the bogs of the midlands (see also McDermott et al. 2009). A range of sites have been classified provisionally as evidence of settlement: these include unenclosed structures, enclosed sites, wetland sites and more ephemeral evidence such as pits, hearths and isolated post- or stake-holes that have been discovered in an area without a recognisable structure or enclosure. Such sites, in fact, make up a large portion of the dataset, while actual identifiable structures are relatively rare. As suspected on the basis of the few structures known from non-domestic sites such as Navan Fort, Co. Armagh (Waterman 1997), and Dún Ailinne, Co. Kildare (Johnston and Wailes 2007), the characteristic form of Iron Age structure seems to have been the roundhouse, which was also the characteristic type of structure prevalent in the preceding Bronze Age. Thirty such post or plank structures of either habitation or workshop character have so far been identified and have to be considered the exception to the rule. Occupation sites—sites without house structures—currently constitute the largest body of material from the period and are represented in all phases of the Iron Age (Fig. 1.7). It should be kept in mind, however, that, in addition to previously discussed building types such as tents (Raftery 1994, 113), a number of different construction methods for substantial houses may have been employed that leave no trace in the archaeological record (e.g. houses built of horizontal planking, on stone settings etc.). Iron-working sites constitute an important site category, but other craft activities such as bronze- and glass-working have also been found. Hillforts, which were expected to be Iron Age, have in fact proved to be a characteristic site type of the Bronze Age (see, for example, Raftery 1976b; Grogan 2005; Mallory 1995; Mallory and Warner 1988). In addition to these site types, *fulachta fiadh* can be shown to continue in use throughout the period, as can an increasing number of iron-working sites. Settlement and occupation sites (at times enclosed by ditches and palisades), kilns and other sites of as yet unknown function add to the evidence for significant levels of Iron Age activity. These are complemented by sites of enigmatic purpose (see, for example, Walsh 1987) and increasing numbers of burial sites (McGarry 2007; 2005), a good range of which are presented in the present volume.

The character of these newly excavated non-ritual and burial sites partly explains why it has only recently been possible to identify them. To a great extent this is a problem of recognisability: the lack of characteristic find assemblages has hindered the recognition of sites as being of Iron Age date. Already in the Bronze Age artefacts are rarely found on settlement sites, and in the Iron Age the problem is compounded by the fact that this period appears to have been aceramic (Raftery 1995a; see also Mallory 2009). Moreover, the lack of diagnostic site types and house forms has

contributed to the fact that these sites were not recognisable before the systematic application of radiocarbon and dendrochronological dating. In the case of individual features within scatters or clusters of features, these are often ephemeral and without stratigraphic associations, so that only the—at times random—radiocarbon or dendrochronological dates reveal these sites to be attributable to the Iron Age. As has emerged from the study, individual features on multiperiod sites often produce Iron Age dates, but these may not always be captured by radiocarbon-dating programmes, which tend to focus on recognisable structures. It can thus be suspected that similar ephemeral evidence for Iron Age activity will in many cases have gone unnoticed.

The sites recorded in this project completely change our understanding of the distribution of Iron Age activity in Ireland. As can be seen from Fig. 1.8, Iron Age sites can now be shown to have existed in all parts of the country, even if no sites can as yet be identified in some areas, e.g. along the south-eastern coast or in large parts of Connacht. This is in striking contrast to the small number of excavated sites recorded before 1994. The distribution of sites will have to be further examined in order to determine the degree to which it is the result of landscape types or modern land use. Clearly, recent development activity and its location influence the apparent distribution of Iron Age sites. Recent excavation activity has, for example, focused on the greater Dublin area, and the linear distribution of sites in Cork clearly shows how a single scheme can 'create' a regional cluster of Iron Age sites. Nevertheless, these clusters surely represent high levels of prehistoric reality, even if they do not preclude the existence of similar clusters in other areas not impinged on by recent building activity. The question of whether the apparent absence of sites at the locations of other schemes is an actual absence or is simply recovery-related will be addressed by comparison with datasets that were generated in similar circumstances and are thus subject to the same biases.

Defining the Iron Age

Until now, it has not been possible to develop a generally agreed chronological framework for the Irish Iron Age. A variety of conventions have been in use, which reflected the struggle not only with absolute- but also with broader relative-chronological issues (see, for example, Eogan 1964; Kelly 2002; Raftery 1994; Scott 1990; Waddell 2010; Warner 1976). The end of the late Bronze Age and the beginning of the Iron Age, in both absolute-chronological and cultural terms, have been the subject of much debate owing to the absence of burials, hoards and settlement assemblages between 700 BC and about 400/300 BC. The artefact record gives some indication of significant transitions occurring around 700 BC and in the late fourth century BC. While the earlier date signifies the end of the late Bronze Age (Dowris phase; Eogan 1964) and the later date that of the probable commencement of the La Tène metalwork traditions (Raftery 1984, 326), the period in between corresponds to what has been referred to as the Dark Age of the Irish Iron Age. While, after the end of the Bronze Age, Ireland was clearly populated to some degree until the beginning of the early medieval period, the size, location, cultural context and social structure of this population remained completely unknown and explanations along the lines of economic or social collapse were explored (see, for example, Mallory and McNeill 1991; Raftery 1976a; Warner 1974). After a small number of Hallstatt C imports and related artefacts (mainly local forms of Gündlingen swords), no objects with direct or indirect parallels to Continental styles of metalwork can be identified in the record. Neither Hallstatt D nor La Tène A-style objects have been found, and it is a small corpus of late La Tène B artefacts that marks the re-emergence of identifiable parallels with the Continent and, in fact, any artefact record at all (see Raftery 1984, 7–14). Few sites of peculiar, local, character were complemented by La Tène metalwork, which provided the only tenable link with a cultural phenomenon elsewhere—the later Iron Age on the Continent and in Britain. The newly excavated sites provide the backdrop of sites that demonstrate continuous occupation of the country throughout later prehistory. In addition, even at this early stage of data collection and interpretation, evidence for significant changes in site morphology is becoming visible and informs the phasing of the new Iron Age below. Reviewing, updating and augmenting previous discussions of chronological issues, it is here attempted to reconcile the newly excavated record and the conclusions that can be drawn from it with the artefact record.

The end of the Bronze Age
Traditionally, the lack of evidence for the period between the Dowris phase and the La Tène material—and, in the later (La Tène) period, the lack of artefact associations and stratigraphy of the few known sites—made both cultural and chronological definitions problematic. Naturally, both topics are intertwined, as they both depend on the identification of archaeological material. The prime example for the complications that arise from the lack of such evidence is the end of the Bronze Age. This, as represented by the Dowris metalwork, could not be dated, which allowed for speculation about its possible long duration in Ireland. This was a convenient scenario that seemed to account for some of the

Dark Age gap, in which the early Iron Age was assumed to occur. While the argument against this was already made by Champion (1971, 23), the legacy of such considerations can still be seen in chronology schemes that allowed for a long duration of the late Bronze Age, mainly in the form of Eogan's hypothetical Dowris C stage (see, for example, Eogan 1964, 320 and 339; see also Waddell 2010, 180, table 4, 279–83; Cooney and Grogan 1994, 183). The limited number of associations of Hallstatt C-type artefacts in late Bronze Age contexts, however, and their absence from post-800 BC contexts, complemented by radiocarbon dates for socketed spearheads, suggest that Dowris-style metalwork did not continue much after the eighth century BC (Becker, in press b.). More importantly, other major cultural markers also seem to end around the same time, namely the construction of hillforts and apparently the production of coarseware pottery.

An early Iron Age? The transitional period
The lack of identifiable material for the period between the end of the Dowris metal-working tradition and the onset of La Tène material has resulted not only in debates about the possibility of a cultural and economic collapse as an alternative explanation (see, for example, Raftery 1994, 35–7) but also in the question as to whether there is indeed an early Iron Age at all: how can the period between the late Bronze Age and the La Tène Iron Age be defined culturally? Raftery (1994, 220–1) considered the appearance of La Tène material as representing a true Iron Age, as opposed to that of the earlier rare Hallstatt or iron objects. This view is reflected in the use of the term 'early Iron Age' for this late material elsewhere (see, for example, Kelly 2002). Nevertheless, Raftery (1994, 36) stressed how unrelated Dowris material and La Tène material were, evidently separated by the radical cultural change taking place between them. Others, however, have pointed to the great degree of continuity of certain important cultural elements that speak against, for example, a new external group having formed the population of the La Tène Iron Age and instead suggest broad continuity between the late Bronze Age and the La Tène Iron Age. In particular, attention has been drawn to the similar patterns of deposition in both periods, even if hoards as such are missing (Cooney and Grogan 1994, 180–1). In addition, some sites enjoyed continued use (see, for example, Carrowmore 26; Cooney and Grogan 1994, 181), while there was morphological and potential functional continuity between the earlier and later phases at site B at Navan Fort, although this was not reflected in the radiocarbon dates (ibid., 185). Nevertheless, while this is certainly convincing as an argument against a complete disruption in terms of population and culture between the two periods and

there is widespread agreement on the late Bronze Age roots of certain elements, such as cremation burial in ring-ditches or barrows (see, for example, Raftery 1991, 29), putting too much emphasis on these elements of continuity means underestimating the significance of the elements of discontinuity, especially in cultural terms. The discontinuity of broad cultural phenomena, such as hillforts or pottery production, and the disruption of formal burial practices for several hundred years are meaningful.

One of the most striking results of the current project is that a significant number of sites can be assigned to the early Iron Age (Fig. 1.6), thus bridging the former gap between the end of the late Bronze Age and the Iron Age. The new evidence seems to suggest ongoing occupation of the country, albeit in a very changed character whereby, in contrast to the late Bronze Age, low-key sites dominate the record. Currently it is still defined more by what it is not than by what it is, and the next stages of the project will shed further light on the character of these rather ephemeral sites.

One particularly important element in the discussion of the Iron Age is obviously the use and production of iron. Owing to the limited number of examples that evidenced iron-working at the end of the Dowris period or contacts with the Hallstatt C world, Raftery saw this material as evidence for the beginning of an Iron Age in a late Bronze Age context that never took off. More optimistic was Scott, who devised an admittedly 'ferrocentric' chronology scheme that attempted to capture the development of iron-working technology phases represented in this meagre evidence of the earliest stages. His EIA A encapsulates the well-rehearsed range of Hallstatt C types and early Iron Age artefacts, which seemed to be either contemporary with or slightly later than the latest phase of the Dowris metalwork, representing the transition from bronze to iron technology in the centuries before the beginning of the La Tène Iron Age (Scott 1990, 6–9, 45–59). Some of the few artefacts that, besides their role as chronological markers, were seen as evidence of contacts with the iron-producing outside world and as indicators of early Iron Age aspects in Ireland have been recently revealed to be misdated, while others have to be considered with caution. A frequently cited piece of evidence for the association of Dowris and Hallstatt C material is the site of Rathtinaun (Raftery 1994, 32–5), where iron artefacts (one of them initially interpreted as a Hallstatt C swan's-neck pin), a shaft-hole axe, a three-pronged object and another iron artefact were associated with late Bronze Age material in what appears to be a late Bronze Age horizon on a crannog site. The artefacts in question, however, have been recently identified as being most likely of early medieval date and the site thus has

to be excluded from our list. The pin can now be identified as an early medieval crosier-headed stick-pin, examples of which have been found on several sites in Ireland and the Orkneys (Raftery, in press).

The Dunaverney flesh-hook, for a long time considered to be early Iron Age, was radiocarbon-dated to the late Bronze Age (Bowman and Needham 2007). A group of Gündlingen swords and chapes that may date from as early as 800 BC, contemporary with the earliest Hallstatt C, constitute the bulk of the relevant material. While Irish and British Gündlingen swords were traditionally seen as standing at the end of the series and as representative of Continental influence, recent research has shown that they probably originated in western Europe (see, for example, Gerloff 2004). An accordingly early date can be assigned to the Irish (*ibid.*) and British (O'Connor 2007, 72) examples. In Britain, these chapes and swords are part of the transitional Llyn Fawr horizon, which is currently seen as beginning around 800 BC, based on Continental dates for Hallstatt C and the Gündlingen swords (Needham 2007; O'Connor 2007). This fits with a cut-off point of Ewart Park traditions at about 800 BC, as indicated by radiocarbon dates (Needham 2007). The corpus of comparable transitional material in Ireland is relatively small, consisting of a few Gündlingen swords and Hallstatt C chapes (Gerloff 2004) and some seventeen bronze axes of southern British Sompting type (Eogan's class 14: Eogan 2000, 194–7). Like the British material, the majority of Hallstatt C finds—particularly the weaponry—is not found in association with late Bronze Age material. Gündlingen swords—Eogan's class 5 (Eogan 1965)— are not part of Dowris associations (*ibid.*, 21; Raftery 1984, 9). The only known hoard from Ireland with class 5 swords (Athlone, Co. Westmeath: Eogan 1983, 144–5) does not contain other types of artefacts. Some other Gündlingen swords may or may not have been part of the Cullen Bog find, which is not a secure closed find in itself (*ibid.*, 155–6). Boat-shaped and winged chapes of Hallstatt C type are also all stray finds (Waddell 2010, 281–2).

The lack of stratified sequences on the few known excavated sites contributes to this problem. A rare example of Hallstatt C finds from an excavated context is the winged chape from Navan Fort, Co. Armagh, which was found with late Bronze Age material in a third-century BC context (phase 3ii) and thus has to be considered residual (Warner 1997). The bar toggle from the site, originally interpreted as a late Bronze Age clothes-fastener (Raftery 1997), may also be connected to Continental Hallstatt forms of horse gear and, as such, may even be datable to Hallstatt D (Jochgurtverschlüsse: J. Koch, pers. comm.; see also Koch 2006, 164–8, particularly fig. 160, 2). The piece from Navan Fort, however, was found in a context belonging to the same phase of the site as the other artefacts mentioned and is thus not closely datable. An iron bridle-bit and a Hallstatt C bronze pin appear to have been found in a later Bronze Age context at Aughinish, Co. Limerick, as evidenced by their association with a late Bronze Age chisel and pottery (Kelly 1974) (the site of Aughinish will play a key role in future discussion but is excluded here pending full publication).

This leaves the skeuomorphs or technologically transitional items such as the Tulnacross, Lisdrumturk and Derrymacash cauldrons (Briggs 1987, 172–4; Scott 1990, 45). While the Derrymacash cauldron constructed of riveted sheet iron—a technology suitable for the working of sheet bronze but not for iron—may also be a copy of a Bronze Age type in a new material, the other two examples are bronze cauldrons with the iron repairs (possibly much later) in form of rivets (Waddell 2010, 284). The two socketed and looped iron axes from Lough Mourne and Toome Bar (Scott 1990, 48–52, pl. 3.3.1) that have also been discussed as skeuomorphs are undated, however. Similar pieces have been found in Britain and could be dated to the first half of the first millennium BC, although no precise dating evidence is available (Barclay et al. 2001; Needham 2007, 52). One of the two known simple unlooped socketed axes at Tara (Roche 2002, 29, 39 no. 31, 20; the other one comes from a not precisely dated context at Feerwore, Co. Galway: Raftery 1984, 240) suggests that at least transitional types like these were in use for a longer period of time and looped examples do not seem likely to have been produced at the transition. Shaft-hole axes, characteristic of the medieval period, may have been introduced already in the Iron Age. One example was found in association with some horse pendants (Y-shaped objects that belong to the general horizon of Irish La Tène material) at Kilbeg, Co. Westmeath. Indirect evidence for a change in axe type used in the seventh century BC may come from the worked timbers from Lisheen, Co. Tipperary, which may reflect the change from socketed bronze axes to iron axes (Ó Néill 2005, 337).

This limited evidence for iron-working taking place in a transitional horizon has to be considered with caution. This leaves the Kilmurry hoard as the only securely associated Hallstatt C item (Dowd, forthcoming; Eogan 1983, 93–4, no. 90). The earliest horizon of the Iron Age is notoriously badly represented elsewhere also (see, for example, O'Connor 2007), and so the body of identifiable Hallstatt C-related items is very small. Fortunately, the recent identification of early Iron Age iron spearheads as early as the seventh century BC serves to fill some of this gap. The recent radiocarbon dates obtained from organic materials in iron spearhead sockets (Halpin and Becker, in prep.) make it very likely that iron-working started in Ireland

in line with neighbouring countries in the eighth century BC, confirming the suspicion that typologically non-distinct iron types may fill this gap (Champion 1971, 23). The issue of preservation of iron objects that has frequently been raised in previous debates surely also plays a role in the absence of the deposition of bronze and gold objects. It is possible that iron artefacts took the place of bronzes in depositional practices and, considering the preservational issues attached to the deposition of single iron artefacts outside settlement and burial contexts, their general invisibility is not entirely surprising (see, for example, Champion 1971; Waddell 2010, 285–6).

Convincing evidence for the local production of iron has yet to be found, however. Some sites have been posited as providing early evidence (Carlin et al. 2008) but these have to be considered very problematic, as the dates associated with iron slag have very wide ranges. In one instance, however, it has been argued that the wide date range associated with a slag fragment can be narrowed down towards its earlier part owing to an association with coarse pottery. This is a problematic interpretation of a possibly redeposited very small fragment in

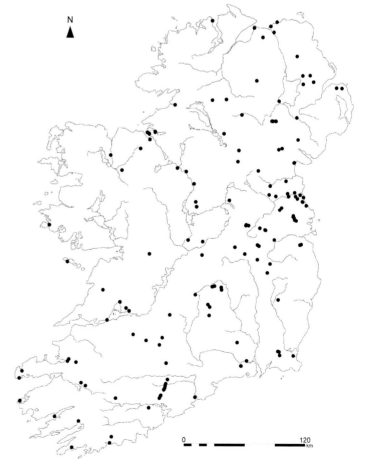

Fig. 1.8—Distribution of Iron Age sites.

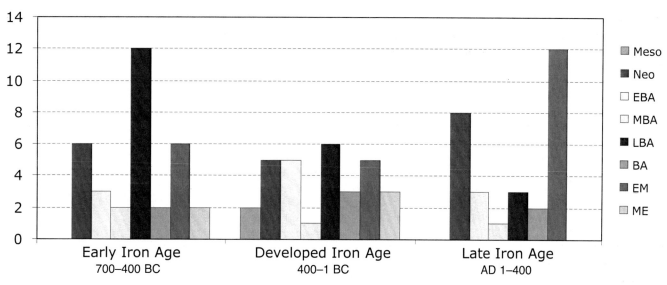

Fig. 1.9—Multiperiod sites that include the Iron Age, and their associated phases.

Date	Period	Pottery	Metal-working assemblage		Iron	Site types	Burial
500	Early medieval	Aceramic	La Tène	'Romanised'	Iron production	'Royal' sites Earthworks	Cremation with occasional grave-goods but no vessels
400							
300							
200	Late Iron Age						
100							
BC/AD							
100							
200	Developed Iron Age						
300							
400							
500						Iron use	
600	Late Bronze Age/ Iron Age transition						Cremation burial
700							
800							
900							
1000	Late Bronze Age	Coarseware	Dowris			Hillfort construction	Cremation with vessels
1150							

Fig. 1.10—Draft chronology for the Irish Iron Age. Absolute chronological dates only to be understood as a broad indication.

an ill-defined deposit. More importantly, it relies on an unprovable assumption that a single coarseware vessel could not have been produced, used or indeed deposited after 800 BC (see Becker, in press a). While the finding of secure evidence for iron production is perhaps just a matter of time, it is not on such individual finds that our interpretation of the period hinges. Neither the appearance nor the native manufacture of iron makes an Iron Age (Champion 1971, 20). Only the large-scale transition to iron as an established working material would justify the interpretation of this early phase but, on the basis of the current evidence, significant levels of iron production can only be evidenced from about 500 or 400 BC onwards (Fig. 1.10; Becker, in press a).

The developed Iron Age

The increase in the scale of iron technology coincides broadly with the appearance of the earliest La Tène-type metalwork, around 300 BC. Problematic in its dating, this material has so far resisted a coherent chronological systematisation. Broadly speaking, three different group styles or schools of decorative metalwork can be identified, and these have an unclear relationship with a larger body of undecorated or undiagnostic decorated artefacts. The three styles—the Irish scabbard style, the Loughcrew–Somerset style and the Petrie crown style—seem to represent major milestones in the development of an insular La Tène style and indeed appear to stand, according to current dating evidence, in a broad chronological sequence (Becker 2012; Raftery 1994; 1984; 1983). The small body of artefacts that can be assigned to these styles occupies a narrow chronological horizon within the period (c. 400 BC–AD 200), with the two earlier styles occupying broad horizons in the third and possibly the second century BC and the second and first centuries BC respectively, and the last one during the first two centuries AD. Scott saw the iron-working evidence from the earliest materials in the Lisnacrogher deposit up to the fifth century AD as standing in one technological tradition—his early Iron Age B (Scott 1990, 6–9, 61–98).

As stressed earlier, the artefact corpus of the Iron Age (and this goes for both the La Tène material and the Roman material) is 'culturally confined and numerically small' (Raftery 1995b, 5) and so it should not be what exclusively defines the period. With the recent discovery of new sites, a classification should be attempted that is meaningful in describing cultural coherency and change. The evidence for different types of site presented in this paper indicates significant changes in the material in the period after 400 BC (Fig. 1.5). In particular, the onset of certain new types of site can be observed around 400 or 300 BC, broadly corresponding with the emergence of La Tène-style

metalwork and the re-emergence of formal burial (McGarry 2007, 8–9). This is most clearly noticeable in the case of earthworks and metal-working sites. According to current dating evidence, the phase of the construction of the earthworks seems to have been restricted in the main to about 400–200 BC. The apparent increase in settlement sites and individual features such as hearths and pits should, for now, be considered with caution, as the dataset is likely to increase significantly with the inclusion of post-2004 sites. This period also sees the creation of enigmatic structures on 'royal sites'—monument types that are specific to Ireland, without parallels elsewhere—and an increased concern with divisions in the landscape. At the same time, contacts with the Continent are evidenced in the metalwork, even if the strongest link is to the UK, particularly Yorkshire and Scotland. The decidedly confident and sophisticated direction that the development of Irish La Tène art takes in this period underlines the independent development of the Iron Age in Ireland.

No Roman Iron Age—the Irish late Iron Age

Traditionally, La Tène metalwork has been set apart and treated separately from that of apparent Roman or Romano-British origins. Raftery's (1984; 1983) fundamental work on Irish Iron Age artefacts mainly considered those of La Tène stylistic derivation in detail. Using Bateson's catalogue, Warner (1976, 272) suggested a classification scheme based on the apparent presence of three phases, differentiating two early phases—R1 (up to the second century AD) and R2 (third to fifth century BC)—and stressing differences between the indigenous and Roman assemblages in terms of their cultural context. This distinction between La Tène and Roman material needs to be questioned. In fact, rather than the trappings of Romano-British invaders, traders or returning Irish mercenaries or royalty, these objects may have to be understood as deliberately employed by locals in the creation and display of new identities that draw on and cite connections with the Roman or Romano-British world in a similar way to the La Tène material previously (Armit 2007). The presence of these materials at places with long-standing local significance, as highlighted for Tara (Armit, forthcoming), or at Newgrange and elsewhere, may be an important hint that they are in fact embedded in, rather than randomly associated with, local tradition and practices. This also opens up the possibility that, like the La Tène material, some of these items were produced locally, and a revisitation of the corpus of 'Roman' artefacts in Ireland with an eye to their stylistic affiliations and the place of their manufacture is long overdue. Accompanied by the appearance of a new style of La Tène metalwork that includes some of the most famous items, such as the Monasterevin discs, as well as the Roman material in the first century AD, it seems that important changes are happening around this time. While no further earthworks are constructed and the use of the so-called 'royal sites' comes to an end, this is the phase into which some of the few Iron Age radiocarbon dates associated with the early phases of ringforts—usually from pre-fort levels—fall. Their relationship to the larger group of enclosed sites that were not followed by medieval occupation will be clarified in the next stages of the project (Armit, Becker *et al.*, in prep; Armit, Swindles *et al.*, 2012; Becker, Armit *et al.* 2011).

New agendas

While it is now possible to identify Iron Age activity in most parts of Ireland, the record still raises many questions. Although a variety of different site types have been found, it must be noted that actual houses or other structures are still rare, and agglomerations of the same are even rarer. The particular difficulties encountered in recognising Iron Age sites—as outlined above—make it likely that a large number of sites still go unrecognised. But, as noted elsewhere (Armit 2007, 135), the peculiar character of the evidence, which is often ephemeral and lacking in structures, stands in stark contrast to the high-status metalwork, to monumental structures such as the linear earthworks (see, for example, Lynn 1989; Walsh 1987) and to the so-called 'royal sites' of the period. This may imply that Iron Age society was rather mobile and that the construction of these monuments has to be considered as the representation of group identities on a regional scale (Armit 2007, 134–5). Mobility has been discussed in previous research as a possible explanation for the lack of settlement evidence (*ibid.*; Raftery 1994, 113) and, on the basis of the present evidence, can still be considered a possible model when attempting to reconcile the contrasting parts of the record. It also seems to be supported by the environmental record (see, for example, Plunkett 2007, 232–3, fig. 12.2). The study of the sites in their landscape setting and palaeoenvironmental evidence will thus play a central role in future studies of Iron Age settlement (Swindles *et al.*, in prep.). Comparisons with the preceding and following periods will be particularly relevant. Evidence of Iron Age activity has been found on sites that have yielded material indicating phases of earlier or later activity, thus demonstrating settlement continuity or the repeated use of certain landscapes throughout prehistory. Earlier use is surprisingly often Neolithic but, as is to be expected, many sites were also used in the late Bronze Age and the early medieval period (Fig. 1.9). The majority of sites appear to have only been used in the Iron Age, however, and the study of the similarities and differences between the various categories of site will also play a central role in any attempt to understand the changes that occurred during the course of later prehistory. Small-scale studies in particular will serve to elucidate regional responses to broader cultural processes (see, for example, O'Brien 2009a; 2009b), and more studies of this type are urgently needed. As research on the Iron Age will rely heavily on radiocarbon dates for the identification of sites, their appropriate interpretation is crucial (Armit, Swindles *et al.*, 2012; Becker, Armit *et al.*, 2011).

Conclusion

The fresh data not only provide new and significant information about settlement in the period but will also allow the contextualisation of previously disparate parts of the archaeological record. Most importantly, it is now possible to re-evaluate the distribution of La Tène artefacts. The distribution of Iron Age sites is relatively balanced throughout the island, a fact that stands in distinct contrast to the picture created by mapping the artefact record. Just as the functional range of artefacts cannot be considered representative of the artefacts in use during the period, the geographic distribution cannot be considered representative of the areas inhabited at that time. Most of the artefacts were found in natural places, mainly wet places such as bogs and rivers. As argued elsewhere, the type-specific deposition patterns visible in the record can be considered as a reflection of the symbolic relevance of these items (Becker 2011). This is clearly supported by the distribution of dated Iron Age sites, which shows a relatively even spread throughout the country and does not reflect the north–south bias visible in the artefact record. When compared with the settlement record, artefact deposition and the regionally restricted burial record are shown to be regional phenomena and a reflection of regionally restricted social practices.

It is now evident that most parts of the island were inhabited throughout the 'Dark Ages' and the later parts of the Iron Age. We see dramatic changes taking place at the end of the late Bronze Age, which probably led to a period of isolation or limited need for ostentatious display of external connections. The renewed desire for such displays in the developed Iron Age may be a sign of the re-emerging élites' need to define their identities. The introduction of Roman material in the early centuries AD, alongside probably the most elaborate form of insular La Tène art, can perhaps be understood as the archaeologically visible diversification of identities in this period, in which interactions with the Roman—or, rather, Romano-British—world were intense. The new data, by providing a vernacular backdrop for the formerly disjointed and specialised phenomena of La Tène and 'Roman' metalwork, ceremonial sites and trackways, will not only make the people of the Irish Iron Age visible but will also fundamentally change our understanding of this crucial period in Irish prehistory.

Bibliography

Armit, I. 2007 Social landscapes and identities in the Irish Iron Age. In C. Haselgrove and T. Moore (eds), *The later Iron Age in Britain and beyond*, 130–9. Oxford.

Armit, I. (forthcoming) Objects and ideas: Roman influences at Tara and beyond. In M. O'Sullivan, G. Cooney, C. Scarre and B. Cunliffe (eds), *Tara: from the past to the future*.

Armit, I., Swindles, G. and Becker, K. 2012 From dates to demography in later prehistoric Ireland? Experimental approaches to the meta-analysis of large ^{14}C data-sets. *Journal of Archaeological Science*, http://dx.doi.org/10.1016/j.jas.2012.08.039).

Armit, I., Becker, K. and Swindles, G. (in prep.) Mobility, climate and culture: re-modelling the Irish Iron Age. Journal of Archaeological Science (2012) (http://dx.doi.org/10.1016/j.jas.2012.08.039).

Barclay, A., Boyle, A. and Keevill, G.D. 2001 A prehistoric enclosure at Eynsham Abbey, Oxfordshire. *Oxoniensia* **66**, 105–62.

Becker, K. 2011 The Irish Iron Age: continuity, change and identity. In T. Moore and X. Armada (eds), *Atlantic Europe in the first millennium BC*, 449–67. Oxford.

Becker, K. 2012 The parallel La Tène. Kunst der vorrömischen Eisenzeit in Irland. In Archäologisches Landesmuseum Baden-Württemberg / Landesmuseum Württemberg / Landesamt für Denkmalpflege im Regierungs-präsidium Stuttgart (eds), *Die Welt der Kelten*, 501–7. Stuttgart.

Becker, K. (in press a) The introduction of ironworking to Ireland. In A. Kern and J. Koch (eds), *Technologieentwicklung und -transfer in der Eisenzeit. Tagungsbericht der AG Eisenzeit, Hallstatt 2009.* Beitäge zur Ur- und Frühgeschichte Mitteleuropas. Langenweissenbach.

Becker, K. (in press b.) The end of Dowris Late Bronze Age metalwork and the dating of Irish Late Bronze Age spearheads. *Journal of Irish Archaeology*.

Becker, K., Armit, I., Eogan, J. and Swindles, G. 2011 Later prehistoric radiocarbon dates from Ireland: an audit. *Journal of Irish Archaeology.* **20**, 19–26.

Becker, K., Armit, K. and Swindles, G. 2010 From data to knowledge: the new Irish Iron Age. *Archaeology Ireland* **24** (3), 13.

Becker, K., Armit, I., Swindles, G. and Batts, C. (in prep.) The new Irish Iron Age.

Becker, K., Ó Néill, J. and O'Flynn, L. 2008a Iron Age Ireland: finding an invisible people. *Archaeology Ireland* **22** (3), 5.

Becker, K., Ó Néill, J. and O'Flynn, L. 2008b Iron Age Ireland: finding an invisible people. Unpublished report prepared for the Heritage Council (project 16365).

Bowman, S. and Needham, S. 2007 The Dunaverney and Little Thetford flesh-hooks: history, technology and their position within the later Bronze Age Atlantic Zone feasting complex. *Antiquaries Journal* **87**, 53–108.

Briggs, C.S. 1987 Buckets and cauldrons in the late Bronze Age of north-west Europe; a review. *Actes du Colloque de Bronze de Lille*, 161–87. Paris.

Carlin, N., Ginn, V. and Kinsella, J. 2008 Ironworking and production. In N. Carlin, L. Clarke and F. Walsh (eds), *The archaeology of life and death in the Boyne floodplain: the linear landscape of the M4*, 87–112. Dublin.

Caulfield, S. 1977 The beehive quern in Ireland. *Journal of the Royal Society of Antiquaries of Ireland* **107**, 104–38.

Champion, T. 1971 The end of the Irish Bronze Age. *North Munster Antiquarian Journal* **14**, 17–24.

Champion, T. 1982 The myth of Iron Age invasions in Ireland. In B.G. Scott (ed.), *Studies on early Ireland: essays in honour of M.V. Duignan*, 39–44. Belfast.

Champion, T. 1989 From Bronze Age to Iron Age in Ireland. In M. Stig Sørenson and R. Thomas (eds), *The Bronze Age–Iron Age transition in Europe*, 287–303. British Archaeological Reports, International Series 483:2. Oxford.

Cooney, G. and Grogan, E. 1994 *Irish prehistory: a social perspective*. Bray.

Crabtree, P. 2007 Biological remains. In S.A. Johnston and B. Wailes, *Dún Ailinne: excavations at an Irish royal site, 1968–1975*, 157–69. Philadelphia.

Dowd, M. (forthcoming) *The archaeology of caves in Ireland*. Oxford.

Eogan, G. 1964 The later Bronze Age in Ireland in the light of recent research. *Proceedings of the Prehistoric Society* **30**, 268–351.

Eogan, G. 1965 *Catalogue of Irish bronze swords*. Dublin.

Eogan, G. 1983 *The hoards of the Irish later Bronze Age*. Dublin.

Eogan, G. 2000 *The socketed axes in Ireland*. Stuttgart.

Gerloff, S. 2004 Hallstatt fascination: 'Hallstatt' buckets, swords and chapes from Britain and Ireland. In H. Roche, E. Grogan, J. Bradley, J. Coles and B. Raftery (eds), *From megaliths to metal: essays in honour of George Eogan*, 124–54. Oxford.

Grogan, E. 2005 *The North Munster Project* (2 vols). Bray.

Halpin, A. and Becker, K. (in prep.) Irish iron spearheads.

Johnston, S.A. and Wailes, B. 2007 *Dún Ailinne: excavations at an Irish royal site, 1968–1975.* Philadelphia.

Kelly, E.P. 1974 Aughinish stone forts. *Excavations 1974*, 20–1. Belfast.

Kelly, E.P. 2002 The Iron Age. In P.F. Wallace and R. Ó Floinn (eds), *Treasures of the National Museum of Ireland*, 125–70. Dublin.

Koch, J.K. 2006 *Hochdorf VI. Der Wagen und das Pferdegeschirr aus dem späthallstattzeitlichen Fürstengrab von Eberdingen-Hochdorf, Kr. Ludwigsburg.* Stuttgart.

Lynn, C.J. 1989 An interpretation of the 'Dorsey'. *Emania* **6**, 5–10.

McCormick, F. 1997 The animal bones from site B. In D.M. Waterman, *Excavations at Navan, 1961–71* (ed. C.J. Lynn), 117–20. Belfast.

McCormick, F. 2002 The animal bones from Tara. *Discovery Programme Reports* **6**, 103–16.

McCormick, F. 2007 Mammal bone studies from prehistoric Irish sites. In E.M. Murphy and N.J. Whitehouse (eds), *Environmental archaeology in Ireland*, 77–101. Oxford.

McDermott, C., Moore, C., Murray, C., Plunkett, G. and Stanley, M. 2009 A colossus of roads: the Iron Age archaeology of Ireland's peatlands. In G. Cooney, K. Becker, J. Coles, M. Ryan and S. Sievers (eds), *Relics of old decency: archaeological studies in later prehistory*, 49–66. Bray.

McGarry, T. 2005 Identifying burials of the Irish Iron Age and transitional periods. *Trowel* **10**, 2–18.

McGarry, T. 2007 Irish late prehistoric burial practices: continuity, developments and influences. *Trowel* **11**, 1–25.

Mallory, J.P. 1995 Haughey's Fort and the Navan complex in the late Bronze Age. In J. Waddell and E. Shee Twohig (eds), *Ireland in the Bronze Age*, 73–86. Dublin.

Mallory, J.P. 2009 The conundrum of Iron Age ceramics: the evidence of language. In G. Cooney, K. Becker, J. Coles, M. Ryan and S. Sievers (eds), *Relics of old decency: archaeological studies in later prehistory*, 181–92. Bray.

Mallory, J.P. and McNeill, T.E. 1991 *The archaeology of Ulster.* Belfast.

Mallory, J.P. and Warner, R.B. 1988 The date of Haughey's Fort. *Emania* **5**, 36–40.

Moore, C. 2008 Old routes to new research: the Edercloon wetland excavations in County Longford. In J. O'Sullivan and M. Stanley (eds), *Roads, rediscovery and research*, 1–12. Bray.

Needham, S. 2007 800 BC: the great divide. In C. Haselgrove and R. Pope (eds), *The earlier Iron Age in Britain and the near continent*, 39–43. Oxford.

O'Brien, W. 2009a Hidden 'Celtic' Ireland: indigenous Iron Age settlement in the south-western peninsulas. In G. Cooney, K. Becker, J. Coles, M. Ryan and S. Sievers (eds), *Relics of old decency: archaeological studies in later prehistory*, 437–48. Bray.

O'Brien, W. 2009b *Local worlds: early settlement landscapes and upland farming in south-west Ireland.* Cork.

O'Connor, B. 2007 Llyn Fawr metalwork in Britain: a review. In C. Haselgrove and R. Pope (eds), *The earlier Iron Age in Britain and the near continent*, 64–79. Oxford.

Ó Donnabháin, B. 2000 An appalling vista? The Celts and the archaeology of later prehistoric Ireland. In A. Desmond, G. Johnson, M. McCarthy, J. Sheehan and E. Shee Twohig (eds), *New agendas in Irish prehistory: papers in commemoration of Liz Anderson*, 189–96. Bray.

Ó Néill, J. 2005 Worked wood. In M. Gowen, J. Ó Néill and M. Phillips (eds), *The Lisheen Mine Archaeological Project, 1996–8*, 329–40. Dublin.

Plunkett, G. 2007 Pollen analysis and archaeology in Ireland. In E.M. Murphy and N.J. Whitehouse (eds), *Environmental archaeology in Ireland*, 221–40. Oxford.

Raftery, B. 1976a Dowris, Hallstatt and La Tène in Ireland: problems of the transition from bronze to iron. In S.J. De Laet (ed.), *Acculturation and continuity in Atlantic Europe, mainly during the Neolithic period and the Bronze Age*, 189–97. Brügge/Ghent.

Raftery, B. 1976b Rathgall and Irish hillfort problems. In D.W. Harding (ed.), *Hillforts. Later prehistoric earthworks in Britain and Ireland*, 339–57. London.

Raftery, B. 1983 *A catalogue of Irish Iron Age antiquities* (2 vols). Marburg.

Raftery, B. 1984 *La Tène in Ireland: problems of origin and chronology.* Marburg.

Raftery, B. 1991 The Celtic Iron Age in Ireland: problems of origin. *Emania* **9**, 28–32.

Raftery, B. 1994 *Pagan Celtic Ireland: the enigma of the Irish Iron Age.* London.

Raftery, B. 1995a The conundrum of the Irish Iron Age pottery. In B. Raftery (ed.), *Sites and sights of the Iron Age: essays on fieldwork and museum research presented to Ian Mathieson Stead*, 149–56. Oxford.

Raftery, B. 1995b Pre- and protohistoric Ireland: problems of continuity and change. *Emania* **13**, 5–9.

Raftery, B. 1996 *Trackway excavations in the Mountdillon Bogs, Co. Longford, 1985–1991.* Dublin.

Raftery, B. 1997 Discussion of diagnostic finds. In D.M. Waterman, *Excavations at Navan Fort, 1961–71* (ed. C.J. Lynn), 90–5. Belfast.

Raftery, B. 1998a Kelten und Keltizismus in Irland: Die archäologischen Belege. In A. Müller-Karpe, H. Brandt,

H. Jöns, D. Krauße and A. Wigg (eds), *Studien zur Archäologie der Kelten, Römer und Germanen in Mittel- und Westeuropa*, 465–75. Rahden/Westfalen.

Raftery, B. 1998b Observations on the Iron Age in Munster. *Emania* **17**, 21–4.

Raftery, B. 2006 Celtic Ireland: problems of language, history and archaeology. *Acta Archaeologica Academiae Scientiarum Hungaricae* **57**, 273–9.

Raftery, B. (in press) The reliability of the alleged early Lough Gara iron. In L. Webster and A. Reynolds (eds), *Essays in honour of James-Graham Campbell*. Leiden.

Roche, H. 2002 Excavations at Ráith na Ríg, Tara, Co. Meath, 1997. *Discovery Programme Reports* **6**, 19–82.

Scott, B. 1990 *Early Irish ironworking*. Belfast.

Swindles, G., Armit, I. and Becker, K.. (in prep.) Rapid climate change in Ireland over the last 5,000 years: testing the regional coherency of terrestrial palaeoclimate records.

Waddell, J. 1991 The question of the Celticization of Ireland. *Emania* **9**, 5–16.

Waddell, J. 1995 Celts, Celticisation and the Irish Bronze Age. In J. Waddell and E. Shee Twohig (eds), *Ireland in the Bronze Age*, 158–69. Dublin.

Waddell, J. 2010 *The prehistoric archaeology of Ireland* (2nd edn). Bray.

Walsh, A. 1987 Excavating the Black Pig's Dyke. *Emania* **7**, 10–21.

Warner, R.B. 1974 The bronze/iron transition: a pessimistic view. *Irish Archaeological Research Forum* **1** (2), 41–2.

Warner, R.B. 1976 Some observations on the context and importation of exotic material in Ireland, from the first century BC to the second century AD. *Proceedings of the Royal Irish Academy* **76**C, 267–92.

Warner, R.B. 1997 The radiocarbon dates. In D.M. Waterman, *Excavations at Navan Fort, 1961–71* (ed. C.J. Lynn), 173–96. Belfast.

Warner, R.B. 1998 Is there an Iron Age in Munster? *Emania* **17**, 25–9.

Warner, R.B. 2002 Beehive querns and Irish 'La Tène' artefacts: a statistical test of their cultural relatedness. *Journal of Irish Archaeology* **11**, 125–30.

Waterman, D.M. 1997 *Excavations at Navan Fort, 1961–71* (ed. C.J. Lynn). Belfast.

Woodman, P.C. 1998 The early Iron Age of south Munster: not so different after all. *Emania* **17**, 13–19.

Notes

1.The map presented here is based on Raftery's 1983 inventory of finds with some additions, but requires updating to include more recent finds.

2. This map requires updating. Burials were not included in the project presented here but are the subject of a separate study (e.g. McGarry, this volume).

2. Lost in transcription: rethinking our approach to the archaeology of the later Iron Age

Jacqueline Cahill Wilson

As archaeologists we are charged with a responsibility to recreate meaning from the fragmentary remains of the past and, in so doing, our role is to offer insights that are (pre)historically situated and socially meaningful (Hodder 1997; 2008; Hodder and Hutson 2003). In endeavouring to be as objective as our training and our past experience will allow, we classify identifiable material culture or site morphology into that which is deemed to be diagnostic or characteristic within a given temporal period. Allowing the requisite time needed to think ourselves back into the past and to undertake the additional dating and scientific analyses that might contextualise the structural relations masking a range of localised social behaviour might be deemed an indulgence, especially given the speed with which commercial archaeology has carried out excavation over the past ten years. This paper will pose some questions and highlight some issues about whether we have abandoned a reflexive approach to archaeology in Ireland and have created an uncomfortable emphasis on essentialism and reductionism that has served to separate further and isolate the later Iron Age in Ireland from that which was happening outside (Shanks and Tilley 1992; Hodder 1997; Hodder and Hutson 2003; Armit 2007). It does not advocate the replacement of one normative line of investigation and enquiry with a singular methodological approach. Instead, it will attempt to demonstrate the value of taking the time to use multiple pathways of investigation fully incorporated within the archaeological interpretation.

This paper is based on the results of my doctoral research into Roman cultural influence in Ireland, the transformative nature of which has up to now been somewhat neglected in archaeological research despite being central to our understanding of the early medieval period in Ireland. It complements the recently published *Landscapes of cult and kingship* (Schot *et al.* 2011). This publication offers an entirely different approach to investigation, using a wide range of anthropological and theoretical models, and is an example of how we might approach Iron Age studies more generally in the future. There is much more to be gained, however, by the inclusion of contemporary scientific analysis, and this paper will demonstrate how theory and science can be used together to answer fundamental questions and suggest new lines of investigation.

I will begin by focusing on what I see as the inherent problems of chronology and classification endemic within the study of the later Iron Age to early medieval transition, and the problematic nature of reconciling 'foreign' or 'intrusive' material and burials within a 'Celtic' Iron Age, before moving to discuss my research on the monument known as Ráith na Senad (Rath of the Synods).

Local and 'intrusive' material in the later 'Irish' Iron Age

Some scholars working within Ireland have questioned the continued reluctance among Irish archaeologists to engage fully with the Anglo-American critical theoretical dialogues that have reshaped our approaches to archaeology over recent decades (see, for example, Tierney 1998, 193; J. O'Sullivan 1998, 179; Horning 2006; Newman 2005; Gavin and Newman 2007; 2011; Wallace 2008). It has been argued that this lack of engagement is due to the historical background within which the discipline of archaeology emerged, at the time when the new Free State government was struggling to create a new sense of nationhood, one which was divorced from that of Britain and offered an indigenous 'Celtic' past (J. O'Sullivan 1998; Tierney 1998; Wallace 2008, 169). That such an approach was adopted at that time is entirely understandable, but it does not explain the reluctance to include the considerable evidence of shared material culture and tangible socio-cultural signifiers between the islands of Ireland and Britain in 21st-century archaeological dialogues. The two 'Celtic' horizons in material culture of the earlier Iron Age—Hallstatt and La Tène—have long been recognised as an extension of that which was happening outside Ireland, but they have never been defined as 'foreign' or 'intrusive' within the 'Celtic' Irish Iron Age, and yet this is exactly how late pre-Roman Iron Age (from Britain) and Roman material and burials continue to be classified (J. Raftery 1972; O'Brien 1990; 2003; McGarry 2005; 2012; B. Raftery 2005; Lynn 2003; O'Sullivan 2004; Armit 2007).

Dialogues that seek to explore and explain social and cultural links between the neighbouring islands of Ireland and Britain in both the later Iron Age and the Roman period remain rare, with scholars both inside and outside Ireland raising questions about the lack of systematic research (Newman 2005; Hill 1995a; Mattingly 2006; Armit 2007). The 'missing' later Irish Iron Age—a period for which we have no beginning and as yet no consensus on its terminus—is concurrent with the Roman Iron Age in the western provinces (Raftery 2005; Ó Drisceoil 2007). Part of the problem may lie in our approaches to the archaeology rather than in a lack of evidence itself, because archaeologists working in both the Iron Age and the early medieval period continue to rely on a historiographical interpretation that is based on an approach to chronological classificatory systems and an emphasis on culture-historical models. At sites where there are no clearly diagnostic objects or where there appears to be conflicting evidence, the temptation is to generalise, resulting in some unsupportable hypotheses.[1] The existing typology of many 'diagnostic' artefacts or the 'characteristic' morphology at sites around Ireland was to a large extent devised over 70 years ago by Hencken and the Harvard Expedition Programme in Ireland (between 1930 and 1936). The objectives of the Harvard team, which had been agreed with the Irish government, were clearly stated within their research framework. The research was to inform an anthropological study based on 'sociological, racial and archaeological data'—a blueprint, as it were, for a 'single, unified anthropological history of Ireland' (Waddell 2005, 219). The aim was to create a chronology of early medieval sites based on the many references in the annals to Lagore crannog, which would become the principal site, the keystone, from which a relative chronology could be established. Central to this culture-historical model was Hencken's emphasis on the typology of the zoomorphic penannular brooch, an object which he believed to be a quintessentially indigenous Irish object and whose absence or presence would form the basis of his relative chronology (Johnson 1999).

Archaeological scholarship in Ireland has matured and Hencken's work has not gone unchallenged. Yet, despite the detailed arguments against the continued use of his work and the typology he devised made by scholars such as Joseph Raftery (1972), Barry Raftery (1972; 1994; 1996), Caulfield (1977; 1994), Ó Floinn (1999), Newman (1997; 2005) and Gavin and Newman (2007), Hencken's work continues to be used uncritically (see, for example, Lennon and O'Hara 2011) and, perhaps more worryingly, often inadvertently: see Crew and Rehren on glass-working at Ráith na Ríg in Roche 2002, using Guido 1978, which was based on Hencken's work at Lagore crannog (1950). The reason why it is important to recognise the problems inherent in Hencken's work is that his conclusions also feed into other works that are still used as primary reference sources (on early medieval Ireland see Edwards 1990; 2005; and see Guido 1978 for the classification of glass beads from British and Irish prehistoric and Roman sites). Guido's work, for example, is still referenced by authors

such as Roche (2002, 97) on Ráith na Ríg at Tara and Johnston and Wailes (2007) on Dún Ailinne. A range of new ^{14}C dates has confirmed that Hencken missed earlier phases of the site at Lagore, in keeping with Lynn's (1985) reassessment, and future work will offer a new interpretation of the array of late pre-Roman Iron Age (LPRIA), Roman and Germanic material that was deemed irrelevant by Hencken to the overall dating of the site (Hencken 1950; Lynn 1985; Fredengren, forthcoming). These new dates also raise considerable questions about the reliance on typological classifications of material or the use of a single absolute date at crannog sites especially, given the ease with which sherds of Samian ware and Roman objects have been dismissed from these sites as 'residual' or 'reliquary' (Warner 1985–6; J. O'Sullivan 1998).[2]

Decorated metalwork of the Iron Age and early medieval periods, such as horse-bits and Y-shaped pendants, ring-pins, hand pins and pseudo- and zoomorphic penannular brooches, continues to be treated as distinctively 'Irish', classified by the style and ornamentation of the objects (Raftery 1994; 2000). The problems with such an approach were discussed by Raftery in 1994 in relation to the La Tène-type Attymon horse-bit, a highly decorated snaffle-bit that had been dated to anywhere between the first century BC and the sixth century AD (Megaw and Megaw 1989; Raftery 1994). More recently, it has been argued that much of the decorated metalwork that has been classified as 'Irish' or 'Celtic' actually betrays Roman influence in its design, an argument that has been strengthened by finds of moulds for a range of these objects at sites in Scotland and northern Britain and examples of decorated pins in confirmed fourth- and fifth-century AD contexts in late Roman Britain (Ó Floinn 1999; Harding 2004; 2007). In his reassessment of the decorated metalwork from the massive stone cashel at Cahercommaun, Ó Floinn challenged the dates previously ascribed by Hencken (1938), suggesting that these were likely to be out by at least two centuries; nevertheless, in the summation of the site, the author chose to ignore this important clarification to the overall dating by suggesting that Hencken was 'not too far off the mark' (Ó Floinn 1999, 74; Cotter 1999, 82). This reclassification of material has been given additional weight by Gavin and Newman (2007), who have unequivocally demonstrated that decorated dress pins and hand pins classified as dating from the early medieval period are paralleled by finds in contexts that are at least two centuries earlier than previously considered and, more importantly, that those parallels are in late Roman contexts in Britain, which brings them back into the later Iron Age in Ireland. The importance of the dating of Cahercommaun may have escaped wider notice, but it is one of three sites, along with Lagore crannog and Ballinderry no. 2, used to create the absolute basis of all subsequent typology and chronology in the late Iron Age to early medieval transition period (Fowler 1960; 1963; Kilbride-Jones 1980; Newman 1997; Johns 1996). If such highly decorated and exceptional archaeological finds have proved so difficult to classify and date correctly, what else might we have missed, mis-classified or simply relegated to 'irrelevant' in our consideration of the essential Irishness of the later Iron Age?

In recent years there has been a growing recognition in published academic articles of the role that Roman cultural influence played in the first five centuries AD (O'Brien 1990; 2003; Swift 1997; Newman 1998; 2005; Dowling 2011; Gavin and Newman 2007; Ó Floinn 2000; Bhreathnach 2005; 2011), and two popular historical accounts have been published in the past ten years (Di Martino 2003; Leedham 2010). One interpretation that remains dominant within academic work is that Christianity was the catalyst for all subsequent social and economic changes evidenced throughout the early medieval period (see, for example, O'Donovan and Geber 2010; Charles-Edwards 2000; Cunliffe 2001; Edwards 2005). This too is problematic, not least because there is no incontrovertible evidence for widespread Christianity at this time in Ireland, and it reduces all earlier contact situations to episodic, harking back to classifications of Roman material within Irish contexts as 'random' and 'trifling' (Haverfield 1913, 3; Bateson 1973). The profound impact that the organisation and administration of the Christian church had on the people of Ireland from the seventh century AD is not disputed. There is, however, a wide and varied history of the origins and development of Christianity, firstly as an eastern cult closely related to the cult of Sol Invictus and only latterly as a recognised Roman imperial state religion under the reign of Constantine I between AD 306 and 337 (Henig 1984, 204), and these quite fundamental issues are rarely discussed or acknowledged in later Iron Age or early medieval studies. In the most recent research by Becker et al. (2008) for the Iron Age, and in the parallel work completed by O'Sullivan and Harney (2008) for the early medieval period, no attempt was made to assimilate material imports in either period (nor the important transitional overlapping temporal period) within a socio-cultural model that might have explored and explained the relationships between people on both sides of the Irish Sea. For the most part, imported material from the LPRIA, Romano-British period and Late Antiquity is treated as an adjunct to, rather than a part of, the narrative of this period.

The paradigm shift that has taken place within Roman archaeology in the past ten years has greatly altered our understanding of what it was to *be* a Roman within the Roman provinces, and it has opened up the study period to consider those who were outside the *territorium* of Rome but who were actively seeking to become as Roman as they *wished to be* within their communities (Mattingly 1997; 2004; 2006; 2010; Hingley 1995; 1997; 2005; 2010; Gosden 2004). Traditional approaches to Roman archaeology in Britain were framed around the reception of the Classical Histories, focusing on the impact of Roman conquest at the very apex of society—the élite—and stressing the eminently civilising influence of Roman occupation on the subjugated populations (Hingley 1997; 2010). There is a direct parallel between this Victorian attitude to what was seen as an essential single-point catalyst of change and that which we read within Irish archaeological approaches to the civilising role that Christianity played in ending the Iron Age. Multidisciplinary approaches taken to the archaeology emerging from Romano-British sites increasingly challenged this generalised perception of homogeneity in the 'Romanisation' of Britain to the extent that an influential post-colonial discourse, modelled on the concept of 'discrepant experience', has fundamentally altered the discipline (Mattingly 2010). This contemporary theoretical research has had a great impact on how Roman archaeology is interpreted today, as it allows us to consider the multiple ways people engaged with the Roman administration (read through the diversity of the archaeology rather than the history) and it recognises the role of individual agency and the inherently malleable nature of identities framed within individual or local circumstances. A lack of engagement with these and even more critical theoretical dialogues will ultimately limit interpretation of LPRIA and Roman material found in Ireland, because the inherent assumptions about what is 'native' and what is treated as 'intrusive' or 'foreign' is not just related to artefacts but is evident within all aspects of the materiality of the later Iron Age. Problems with assumptions about origin and ethnicity and relative dating are also noticeable in burial archaeology, whereby individual burials have been classified as local or 'intrusive' based on associations of 'foreign' or 'intrusive' material (close by or within the burial itself) and on the changes to burial practices themselves. More recently, individual burials have been classified as pagan or Christian, based entirely on assumptions about relative dates derived from these burial practices (see McGarry 2008; 2012). There is, however, an increasing corpus of burials of Iron Age date that do not fit the existing classifications, examples of which are discussed below.

In any attempt to understand and shed new light on the fragmentary remains that have been left to us, we cannot simply rely on the objects found within burials or sites; we have to reconstruct their meaning to the people who made, used and discarded them. It is only through a person's physical and emotional engagement with the conception, production and dispersal of artefacts, within and between the places and spaces of importance to them (in life and death), that we can offer meaning to our studies of *their* materiality. The consumption of material that we deem to be exotic does not require a singular or generalised explanation, as it may reflect a range of social practices and social classifications at a local level (Shanks and Tilley 1992). Multiple readings set within localised contexts allow for the manner in which objects themselves function within discrete communities to become part of our interpretation (Appadurai 1986, 29).

The problems of relying solely on typology in the later Iron Age are exemplified by one object in particular: the pseudo-penannular brooch, which has an origin in the second century AD in Roman Britain yet has become synonymous with Irish 'Celtic' culture. In keeping with Hencken's views, its origin in a Roman milieu is systematically ignored and it is regularly included within an existing typology of 'Irish' brooches that includes the highly decorated zoomorphic brooches of five or more centuries later (Hencken 1950; Kilbride-Jones 1980; Hawkes 1981; Warner 1995; forthcoming). In fixing an interpretation based on diagnostic objects, it has been argued that we need to

'develop approaches to typology which are concerned less with defining types and more with describing multi-dimensional surfaces of variability on which the "type" can be seen to vary with context [for as archaeologists] we tend to force material into type, style etc., preferring to ignore the random noise of individual variability' (Hodder and Hutson 2003, 208).

No one disputes the value of reliable chronological and typological frameworks, but the existing system in Irish archaeology for this period is creating too much random noise and has been shown to be incorrect too frequently to be relied upon as a principal dating method. If we are to offer a realistic reconsideration of non-local material in a localised context, then we need to look beyond the objects to explore the relevance of that material in the context of how and why it was adopted, adapted or consumed within existing or new social practices (Jones 2003). We must be cautious also that in moving from the artefact-centred approach that has dominated this period in past archaeological research we avoid replacing it with a new essentialist form of meta-narrative that catalogues all pits, kilns and enclosures as a collective in terms of morphology, form and function without the benefit of further scrutiny (see Becker *et al.* 2008). We must remember that it is we who have privileged artefacts as indicators of

status within the archaeology of this period, relegating the provision of animals for feasting or the inspiration for architectural or earthwork design as of lesser importance to our interpretation. We have to be able to recognise *differences* as well as similarities in the archaeological record, and if we cannot offer meaning then we need to continue to investigate, explore new avenues of enquiry, look for new parallels and apply new techniques, and be open to the possibility that in some cases we have got it wrong.

Local or 'intrusive' burial in the later 'Irish' Iron Age

The earliest form of indigenous burial practice in the Iron Age in Ireland appears to be that of unprotected cremation deposits in pits; often these are a central primary burial over which a small, shallow ring-barrow or embanked ditch was raised (McGarry 2008; O'Brien 2012). There are a few sites where multiple cremations have been located and which might suggest a permanent population group nearby. Such community cremation burials have been found at Kiltierney, Co. Fermanagh, Ballydavis, Co. Laois, Oranbeg, Co. Galway, Carbury Hill site A, Co. Kildare, and within the flat cemetery at Ráith na Senad at Tara, which pre-dates the activity at the site, considered below.

At some sites in Ireland there is evidence of a layer of charcoal and burnt bone dispersed widely across the site, such as at Grannagh, Co. Galway, where this was described as 'strewn in handfuls on the ground' (Macalister 1916–17, 509; O'Kelly 1989, 331; Ó Ríordáin 1945–8; Raftery 1994, 180). At Ballymacaward, Co. Donegal, the charcoal spread and cremated material found during excavation was dated to the second century AD and identified as a separate burial sequence at the site (O'Brien 1999). A blackened layer of bone and charcoal was also noted at Ráith na Senad at Tara but it was not dated separately (O'Brien 1990; Newman 1997). It is possible that what we are seeing at these sites is a further burial practice, the deliberate dispersal of cremated remains over an ancestral burial ground.

Burials that take the form of unprotected crouched inhumation in pits along with a few personal grave-goods appear to overlap chronologically with unprotected cremation deposits, and both are found either within low mounds or in the ditches of earlier monuments (both are evidenced at Ráith na Senad: O'Brien 1990; 2003; McGarry 2008). The crouched or foetal position is characterised by the knees being pulled tightly up to the chest, but it remains unclear whether the flexed position, with knees bent less tightly, is in fact a separate burial practice. It is entirely possible that some burials that have been recorded as crouched were in fact flexed, and this important detail may have simply been missed (Elizabeth

O'Brien, pers. comm.). Crouched burials appear to fall within a date range of the first century BC to the second century AD in Ireland. Although the quantities vary among the burials, there is a commonality of artefact found within them and these are often small personal items such as an iron or bronze knife, bronze or iron spiral rings, objects of worked stone and occasionally 'exotic' material, such as glass beads or Continental-type fibulae (Raftery 1994; O'Brien 1990; 2003; Keeley 1996; McGarry 2008). There is also commonality in location of cremations and crouched inhumations, as often they are found as a single burial inserted into the banks or within the ditches of much older mounds or monuments. This form of burial rite is evidenced from the first century AD in Britain and, as only a few have been radiocarbon-dated in Ireland, it has not yet been established whether what we are seeing is evidence of a single episode (the burial of a few non-local individuals) or a wider shift in burial customs (Elizabeth O'Brien, pers. comm.).

A transition in burial practice is more widely evidenced by the fourth century AD and it is characterised by extending the body into a supine position in an unlined grave (O'Brien 1990; McGarry 2005). The wider use of radiocarbon dating has demonstrated that the practice developed further by the fifth or sixth century AD, whereby the graves of these extended inhumations are either partially or wholly lined with stone. These are referred to in the literature as cist burials (O'Brien 1990; 2003; Raftery 1994; McGarry 2008). By the sixth century AD, protected extended supine inhumation in long stone cists is the most frequently identified burial practice in Ireland. Recent excavations have revealed multiple burials of this kind at sites such as Laytown and Colp West, Co. Meath, and in the far west at Owenbristy, Co. Galway (Eogan *et al.* 2012; Elizabeth O'Brien, pers. comm.).

In the original study of 'intrusive' burials in the Leinster region it was argued that some unusual burials might reflect intrusive burial practices in the later Iron Age (O'Brien 1990). The term 'intrusive' was qualified and set within the context of a discussion that outlined the significance of a change to such a deeply embedded social practice (Ucko 1969; Parker-Pearson 1982; 2003; Chapman 2003). Importantly, attention was drawn to the likely impact of cultural influences (and migration) from the LPRIA and Roman Britain (O'Brien 1990). The important distinction made between the classification of a burial practice as intrusive and its application to an individual and their origin appears to have been lost within subsequent debate, and the term, in keeping with its use in relation to artefacts, has become short-hand, a euphemism, for any burials that are deemed to be non-Irish or non-Christian (see McGarry 2008; 2012). Given the

frequency with which LPRIA material has been found within crouched inhumations and the rarity of these types of burials in Ireland, it is probable that these reflect non-local people using their own burial customs (O'Brien 2003; McGarry 2008).

Extended inhumations found alongside (the assumed) earlier burial practices of either cremation or crouched inhumation have been treated as 'intrusive' in the past and this is reflected in Grogan's summation of the phase 3 burials at Ráith na Senad, discussed below (Raftery 1994; O'Brien 2003; McGarry 2005; 2008; Grogan 2008). O'Brien has recently challenged McGarry's assertion that extended east–west burial is 'essentially Christian' and has argued that these burials are equally likely to reflect the changes in burial practices that took place in the Roman world in the latter part of the second century AD, as outlined in her work in 1990 (McGarry 2005; 2012; Eogan *et al.* 2012). Extended supine inhumation aligned east–west was a practice adopted by the Romans from an earlier Greek tradition (although this too was immensely variable: see Kurtz and Boardman 1971) and is distinct from the existing Roman practice of cremation described by Tacitus (*Annals*, xvi, 6; Grant 2003) as *Romanus mos* (that is, the Roman way). This shift in burial practice in the Roman world is usually explained by wider socio-cultural developments that took place under the Emperor Hadrian (Toynbee 1971), and O'Brien is correct in suggesting that some of these burials may date from the later second century AD or more likely the third century AD. In keeping with the overall theme of this paper, the archaeology in recent years has shown through more extensive use of ^{14}C dating that the reality is rather more complex, with a wide variety of burial practices evidenced throughout the Roman period, including evidence of extended, crouched and flexed inhumation (Philpott 1991). As there was no prescription regarding burial practices in Rome or its provinces, the variation and contemporaneity have been interpreted as evidence of the continuation and maintenance of existing local practices within a Roman cultural setting (see Whimster 1981 on continuation of LPRIA burial practices and Philpott 1991 for the range and diversity in local burial practices in the Roman period in Britain).

Against this background of complexity and diversity within the archaeological record in the later Iron Age in Ireland, a scientific analysis was undertaken as part of my doctoral research on examples of local and 'intrusive' burials of the period, using strontium and oxygen isotope analysis and some additional ^{14}C dating. The objective was to test whether the previous assumptions about the ethnicity, identity and origin of burials were correct (O'Brien 1990; 2003; Raftery

Fig. 2.1—LiDAR image of Ráith na Senad, Tara, with the location of animal remains overlaid.

1994; Mallory and Ó Donnabháin 1998; McGarry 2005). The sites chosen were Ráith na Senad, Carbury Hill site B, Rossnaree, Knowth and Betaghstown. The methodology devised by the University of Bristol and the Research Laboratory for Archaeology and the History of Art, Oxford University, will be published in full alongside the analysis and interpretation of Knowth and Rossnaree (Cahill Wilson *et al.*, forthcoming). The complete set of results will be published in a separate paper (Cahill Wilson and Pike, in prep.). For the purposes of this paper, I want to summarise and contextualise the findings for Ráith na Senad before offering an alternative interpretation of this site in line with my own research and the recently presented arguments that have challenged the existing interpretation (Dowling 2011; Bhreathnach 2011; Fenwick 2011; Warner, forthcoming).

Ráith na Senad, Tara

Seán P. Ó Ríordáin's excavations during the summers of 1952 and 1953 at Ráith na Senad on the Hill of Tara were finally published in 2008. In a detailed attempt at reconstruction of both the site and the finds, Grogan sought to create an account of activity there in the later Iron Age. No one would dispute that the evidence Grogan had to work with was complex, for Ó Ríordáin's excavations had attempted to make sense of a site whose stratigraphy had to a large extent been compromised through its destruction between 1899 and 1902 by a group known as the British-Israelites in their futile attempts to find the Ark of the Covenant (see Carew 2003 for a detailed account). Specialist appendices were included in Grogan's book to cover analysis of all the Roman material, with the ceramics, metalwork and glass considered separately by different authors. The faunal material from the site had been disposed of, although fortunately a record was included from Ó Ríordáin's notebooks of the types of faunal material discovered and its context and location within the areas excavated across the site. Notable from this record was the high proportion of ox, pig, dog and horse remains from this assemblage, as well as the structured deposition of this material in pits within the central area of the enclosure and its inclusion within the fill of the inner ditch (Fig. 2.1). The comprehensive series of ^{14}C dates from a range of contexts across the site were not received in time to be fully included within the main body of Grogan's text, but he commented in a separate note that they were broadly in keeping with his overall conclusions. In summation, it was concluded that the Roman finds and structures at the monument related to a 'high-status homestead of a native Irish group with familial ties in the region of Romano-Britain on the fringes of the empire, possibly in the Severn Valley' (Grogan 2008, 97).

In recent work, Grogan's overarching conclusions about Ráith na Senad have been eruditely critiqued and ably challenged (see Dowling 2011; Bhreathnach 2011; Fenwick 2011). Central to these critiques are the questions raised about the generalised assumptions that appear to have been based on the Roman artefacts from the site as well as the morphology of the site itself, a trivallate enclosure that encompassed an earlier extant barrow within its design. Two small, post-built rectangular structures were excavated in the centre of the site and it is from within these contexts that most of the Roman material was recovered. These structures and the material assemblage were interpreted as a 'native homestead' and later as a 'ringfort' (Grogan 2008, 91). In a forthcoming paper, Warner will put forward a detailed analysis that argues that the phasing as reconstructed is flawed (I am grateful to Richard Warner for making his paper available to me in advance of publication) and, so that Warner's article is not pre-empted here, I will focus on those aspects of my own research which give additional weight to the arguments against the existing interpretation of this remarkable site. These derive from a study of the burials classified as 'Phase 3: the Iron Age burials' in Grogan's interpretation.

Grogan's phase 3 'Iron Age burials', Ráith na Senad, Tara

In 2008, licences to alter and export faunal and human skeleton material from five sites around Ireland were granted to the author by the National Museum of Ireland (licence nos AL44 and 3983). Seven human males were sampled from Ráith na Senad, comprising three crouched burials (RnS B, RnS E, RnS I), three extended burials (RnS D, RnS H, RnS J) and one skull (RnS K); the skull came from Ó Ríordáin's extension of cutting 8 (cutting 23), which stretched from the inner ditch of Ráith na Senad to the outer ditch of Ráith na Ríg (Grogan 2008, 5), and, while not, strictly speaking, a burial, was sampled at Grogan's request. One faunal sample (RnS Pig), found near burial B, was also analysed (see below). The samples were examined and selected under the curatorial supervision of Laureen Buckley, a specialist osteologist, and in consultation with Grogan in advance of the publication of his monograph. The study itself focused on strontium and oxygen isotope evidence, the results of which are outlined below. A separate award of a grant from the Royal Irish Academy allowed for two of the human skeletons from the site to be dated, neither of which had been dated at the time the research was conducted (burials D and E). Two of the extended inhumations were subsequently ^{14}C-dated for Grogan's monograph: burial D to cal. AD 1252–1290 and burial H to cal. AD 898–1024. It is unfortunate that both

Grogan and I chose the same extended inhumation (burial D) for analysis, as the unnecessary duplication could have been avoided and a further individual dated. Nevertheless, burials D and H are separated by at least three centuries and both post-date the activity at the site in the second to fourth century AD. Burial D was found some distance from the rest of the group, closer to where the curtain wall of St Patrick's Church intrudes into the inner bank of the monument, and it seems likely that this burial is associated with the cemetery for the earlier church that once stood on the site, as the dates are comparable. Burial H dates from the tenth century AD and appears to have been placed extended and supine but unshrouded into an unprotected shallow grave.

Burial E, a crouched burial, was also dated as part of this research and the result (cal. AD 721–890; 1205±24 BP; UBA-11698) is completely at odds with the relative dating that had placed it in the first or second century AD (Raftery 1994; McGarry 2005; Grogan 2008). Although charcoal found near burial B returned a date of cal. AD 414–540 (UBA-8533; 1691±20 BP), the skeleton itself was not dated and, as with the other inhumations in this group, there is no certainty as to whether the charcoal was contemporary with the burial or is in fact from an earlier context which was disturbed during the insertion of the burial itself (Grogan 2008, 146).

Strontium and oxygen isotope analysis
In order to establish the first comparative dataset for strontium and oxygen isotope data in Ireland, the research focused on the five sites from an area of similar geology within a twenty-mile radius of the Hill of Tara. This allowed strontium and oxygen isotope values to be analysed on an inter- and intra-site basis.

The Hill of Tara rises to a height of about 155m above sea level. The geology is sedimentary, Carboniferous limestone, consisting of dark laminated calsilites, calcareous shales and some sandstone (McConnell et al. 2001). The River Boyne lies about 3km east, as it curves towards the hill on its route between the towns of Trim and Navan. The nearest older geology to Tara is the clearly defined area of Silurian/Ordovician age north of Knowth and Newgrange, both of which are about some 15km from Tara (ibid.; Newman 2005).

Tooth enamel is the most highly mineralised tissue in our bodies and while it is forming it records the chemical signatures of the geological and climatic environment in which people, and their livestock, lived. Unlike bone, which is completely remodelled within the body over approximately a ten-year cycle, once complete mineralisation of enamel has taken place (usually around twelve years of age) it does not alter in life or through diagenesis in a depositional context

(Budd et al. 2003; Montgomery et al. 2005; Cahill Wilson et al., forthcoming). Measuring the ratios of the various isotopes present in the tooth enamel can offer an indication of an individual's place of origin (see, for example, Dupras 2001; Schweissing and Grupe 2003; Budd et al. 2003; Bentley and Knipper 2005; Montgomery et al. 2005; Evans, Stoodley et al. 2006; Daux et al. 2008; Chenery et al. 2010; Cahill Wilson et al., forthcoming).

The strontium in teeth is derived from the geological environment through everything that we eat and drink and it consists of three stable isotopes and radiogenic isotope. It is the ratio of the radiogenic strontium ^{87}Sr assessed in relation to the stable ^{86}Sr (conventionally expressed as $^{87}Sr/^{86}Sr$) that varies with changing geology. Expected values for strontium isotopes can be calculated from knowledge of the geology. Young rock, or rock that has less rubidium, tends to give lower $^{87}Sr/^{86}Sr$ from around $^{87}Sr/^{86}Sr$ c. 0.706, whereas older, rubidium-rich and, it follows, more radiogenic rock tends to give much higher ratios of $^{87}Sr/^{86}Sr > 0.715$ (Evans, Stoodley et al. 2006). There is a difficulty in characterising a single geology, even within a relatively small geographical area, given that the soil may be derived from various sources or have been moved through natural geological/geomorphological events or even man-made processes (Chenery et al. 2010; Cahill Wilson et al., forthcoming). The mineralisation of enamel is also susceptible to the seasonality of precipitation, which may result in higher or lower ratios than could otherwise have been predicted (Bentley and Knipper 2005). We do not yet have a complete comparative dataset for the biologically available strontium isotope range in Ireland, and therefore the estimated range used here lies between the pure Carboniferous limestone range of 0.7075–0.7082 (McArthur et al. 2001) and more recent data based on measurements taken in England and north and central Wales by Evans, Montgomery et al. (2010), which give higher approximate values of 0.709–0.710 for Carboniferous limestone, 0.711–0.712 for the Silurian geology and 0.712–0.173 for Ordovician geology. As this was the first time multiple samples were being analysed on Irish material, wherever possible smaller mammals, which are not likely to have moved far from the local context of the burials, were used to establish a benchmark local signature for each site, as recommended by Bentley and Knipper (2005). It proved immensely difficult to locate any faunal material for Ráith na Senad, a fact now confirmed by Grogan's work (2008, appendix F), which noted that all of the material was disposed of at some date in the past. We did, however, locate a pig's tooth which was recorded as being found near burial B and this was sampled as part of the research.

The oxygen in teeth is derived from drinking water

Table 2.1—Ráith na Senad, Tara: radiocarbon dates. Errors are given at 2σ; oxygen results are reported as drinking water equivalents, typical error 0.2 per mil. [14]C dates have been calibrated using OxCal 4.1 and the IntCal09 calibration.

Lab ref.	Burial type	[87]Sr/[86]Sr	$\delta^{18}O_c$	$\delta^{18}O_{dw}$	[14]C dates cal. to 2σ
				SMOW per mil.	
RnS B	Juv. male, crouched	0.708641±0.000003	27.23	-6.46	★★
RnS D	Adult male, extended	0.708404±0.000003	26.47	-7.61	AD 1252–1290★
RnS E	Adult male, crouched	0.709104±0.000003	26.54	-7.51	AD 721–890★
RnS H	Adult male, extended	0.708600±0.000003	27.26	-6.42	AD 898–1024
RnS I	Adult male, crouched	0.709821±0.000004	27.31	-6.35	
RnS J	Adult ?, extended	0.709567±0.000003	26.52	-7.54	
RnS K	Adult skull	0.708862±0.000003	27.55	-5.99	
RnS Pig	(near burial B)	0.709625±0.000003	24.80	-10.22	

★These dates were funded under an award from the RIA and are shown in full within the discussion.

★★The published date for burial B was from a piece of charcoal found near the burial; the skeleton was not ^{14}C-dated and so is not included here.

sources and the mass differentiation of the isotopes (^{18}O, [17]O and ^{16}O) leads to relative enrichment or depletion (fractionation) by processes such as evaporation and precipitation that will vary according to climate, latitude, longitude and altitude (Budd *et al.* 2003; Cahill Wilson *et al.*, forthcoming). Conventionally, the differences in oxygen isotope ratios are expressed relative to a standard as $\delta^{18}O$. The [18]O isotope ratio within the carbonate of tooth enamel is derived from the local meteoric water sources, but the processes of metabolic fractionation are species-dependent and will vary across samples. The use of a paired system of strontium and oxygen allows us to reduce the range of possibilities across similar geology to a higher level of probability by cross-referencing the oxygen as a secondary indicator of geographical origin. Although the geochemistry is complex, the results have been used successfully to demonstrate population mobility and migration in prehistory (see, for example, Schweissing and Grupe 2003; Budd *et al.* 2003; Bentley and Knipper 2005; Montgomery *et al.* 2005; Evans, Stoodley *et al.* 2006).

The $\delta^{18}O$ on the samples used in this research was measured on the carbonate of the tooth enamel ($\delta^{18}O_c$) relative to PDB corrected to $\delta^{18}O_p$ in line with Iacumen *et al.* 1996, relative to standard mean ocean water (SMOW), and its meteoric water equivalent was converted to modern drinking water values ($\delta^{18}O_{dw}$) using the equations proposed by Longinelli (1984) for humans and cattle. The pig sample from Tara was modelled using Bentley and Knipper's (2005) variation of Longinelli 1984.

The strontium and oxygen results for the human skull (RnS K) are consistent with an origin at or near Tara. Only three of the burials are likely to have originated outside the immediate local area (burials D, E and J), and, given the $\delta^{18}O_{dw}$ result, this would be consistent with the area of older geology to the north, but notably not all on the same geology (Fig. 2.2). More importantly, there is no correlation between the strontium and oxygen analysis and the type of burial rite used and, as an origin for all of these burials can be offered within Ireland, they should no longer be classified as intrusive. Importantly, the crouched burial D, which has now been dated to centuries later than the relative date suggested, can be added to the growing corpus of burials that do not fit within the existing relative dating scheme. Furthermore, the analysis conducted on burials at Carbury Hill site B and Rossnaree, burials that had been classified as 'intrusive' based on exotic material found within the graves, suggests that these too were local individuals. Several burials at Betaghstown (demonstrating all of the known burial practices mentioned above) are a mix of local and non-local individuals, whose origin could not have been discerned based on the manner in which they were buried or the presence or absence of exotic grave-goods. One notable male flexed inhumation burial from Betaghstown, thought to be local and dated to cal. AD 356–622, had a remarkable result of $\delta^{18}O_{dw}$ = -2.96, suggesting an origin for him in southern Portugal or north Africa (Cahill Wilson and Pike, in prep.). At the very least, the results of the strontium and oxygen analysis and the new dates support O'Brien's recent argument that in the absence of absolute dating and additional scientific research the classification of an individual as 'Christian' or 'pagan'—or, indeed, as 'local' or 'intrusive'—is presumptive (Eogan *et al.* 2012, *contra* McGarry 2012).

The most depleted $\delta^{18}O_{dw}$ in the analysis was from the pig's tooth, which was recorded as coming from the area near

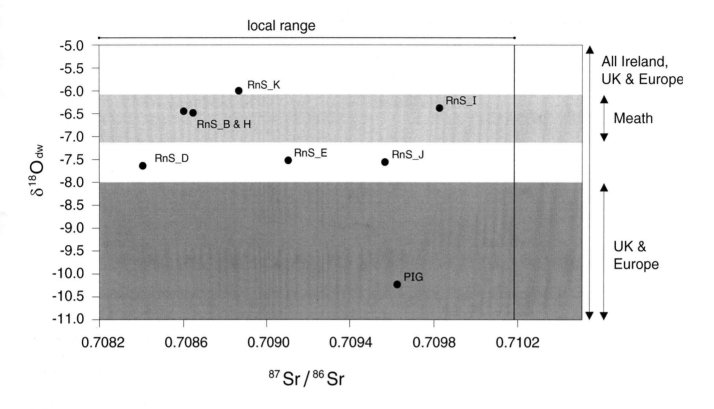

Fig. 2.2—Ráith na Senad, Tara: graph showing $\delta^{18}O_{dw}$ plotted against results for $^{87}Sr/^{86}Sr$. Expected local range for strontium and oxygen is plotted as highlighted rectangle. Arrows indicate geographic region consistent with level of depletion of $\delta^{18}O_{dw}$.

burial B. The result for this tooth is one of the most interesting of the research, as, at $\delta^{18}O_{dw}$ = -10.22, it is not local to the island of Ireland or Britain, or indeed most of Europe, but corresponds to values recorded in eastern Germany, Hungary and Romania as well as parts of Norway (http://wateriso.eas.purdue.edu: consulted 17/12/09; IAEA/WISER (2008) Global Network Isotope Project: consulted 17/12/09). Colleagues at the University of Bristol Veterinary School studied the pig's tooth (I am grateful to Kate Robson-Brown for initiating the analysis) and established that it is an upper molar from a female pig, around five years old. The result suggests the importation of pigs direct from Europe but, given the problems of stratigraphy and contexts at the site, an absolute date is needed before we could offer a link between it and related activity on the site.

Ritual and deposition at Ráith na Senad

The results of the strontium and oxygen analysis and the new ^{14}C dates, as summarised above, suggest that part of the existing phasing applied to the dating and classification of the burials at the site may be incorrect, and additional work will clarify whether any of the burials can be included within the

existing phase 3.

There are, however, further problems with the interpretation of both the site and its material assemblage as a 'domestic homestead' because, although such an interpretation is not supported by any other parallels in this period in Ireland, each and every aspect of the materiality of this site can find parallels within Roman Britain. The deposition of specific types of ceramic and glass drinking vessels (with an absence of coarsewares or even plates and platters, which are common on habitation sites in Roman Britain and elsewhere) was remarked upon by Evans (2008, 123), who noted that in the absence of a complete assemblage of what he would regard as of a 'domestic' character the evidence was suggestive of a ritualised activity on the site. The single example of a partial Roman fibula was highlighted by Allason-Jones (2008, 107) as problematic, and it formed an important element in her conclusion that these were not 'Roman' visitors at the site. This interpretation managed to occlude an alternative reading in favour of the essentialised treatment of the archaeological record: in this case, a subjective interpretation of what constituted correct Roman dress. She did, however, note the evidence for penannular brooches, multiple parts of which,

Table 2.2—Ráith na Senad, Tara: possible origin for individual burials based on the strontium and oxygen isotope analysis.

Lab ref.	Sex	Burial type	Classification based on relative dating method	Prior classification	14C date (where known)	Origin based on isotope analysis
RnS B	M	Crouched	First or second century AD	Local		Local
RnS D	M	Extended	Third or fourth century AD	Intrusive	Cal. AD 1252–1290	Southern midlands
RnS E	M	Crouched	First or second century AD	Local	Cal. AD 721–890	North midlands/ south Ulster
RnS H	M	Extended	Third or fourth century AD	Intrusive	Cal. AD 898–1024	Local
RnS I	M	Crouched	First or second century AD	Local		North midlands/ south Ulster
RnS J	M	Extended	Third or fourth century AD	Intrusive		North midlands/ south Ulster
RnS K		Skull	–	Intrusive		Local

along with one whole pseudo-penannular brooch, were catalogued among the many other fragments of jewellery and metalwork from the site. Parallels for these brooches in Irish contexts are found at Knowth and Newgrange, both sites for which we have assemblages of contemporary Roman material (Carson and O'Kelly 1977; Mulvin 2012a; 2012b; Warner, forthcoming). Interestingly, Allason-Jones offered a further example of a parallel with a brooch from Cahercommaun, which supports Ó Floinn's redating of that site, the importance of which was outlined above (Ó Floinn 2000). Given the sheer numbers of similar penannular brooches from Roman temple sites in Britain, such as Lydney (Bathurst 1972), Uley (Woodward and Leach 1993) and Nettleton (Wedlake 1982), one could argue that the brooches from Ráith na Senad fit well within the characteristics of deposition at a Romano-British rural shrine or temple.

Even if we did not have the remarkably rich archaeological evidence from millennia of activity at the Hill of Tara, Ráith na Senad would still be exceptional. That it is positioned beside the large, internally ditched enclosure of Ráith na Ríg makes it even more extraordinary. In recent work, Dowling (2006; 2011) has argued cogently for the need to recognise the chthonic nature inherent in the manner in which a *space* is delineated to create a place imbued with ritual and sacral significance, and he draws convincing attention to the importance of symbolism inherent within the triplication in the ditch and bank construction at Ráith na Senad. He is rightly cautious, however, in explicitly stating that not all sites with multiple enclosing banks and ditches should be read in the same way, ensuring that we adhere to the concept of the specificity of ritual practice in this localised context (Dowling

2011). Furthermore, he has argued that we cannot ignore the interrelationship between Ráith na Senad and Ráith na Ríg and the structured deposition of an important child burial, which was accompanied by a dog, especially given that we can now demonstrate contemporary activities at both sites (Roche 2002; Dowling 2006). More recent work has further undermined much of the interpretation of both the morphology and the phasing of the site and has questioned the interpolation of discrete features, pits and post-holes, as presented within Grogan's work (Fenwick 2011; Dowling 2011; Bhreathnach 2011).

If a more convincing argument is needed to demonstrate the importance of the ritual and sacral nature of this site, then we should explore further the evidence for intentionality in the deposition of specific animal remains in pits within the central enclosure of Ráith na Senad and within the ditches at both Ráith na Senad and Ráith na Ríg, as highlighted by Dowling (2006). There is a growing body of literature within academic research on the nature of structured deposition in both late Iron Age and Roman contexts, and it has been convincingly demonstrated that, despite social and economic changes brought about in the wake of conquest, local cultic and ritual practices were maintained (Henig 1984; Hill 1995b; Fulford 2001; King 2005; Mattingly 2006; Haynes, forthcoming). Often the earliest evidence for Roman cultural influence at these sites in Britain is single coins and small items of jewellery such as those found at Wanborough in Surrey, Hayling Island in Hampshire, Ivy Chimneys in Essex and Uley in Gloucestershire (Lewis 1966; Woodward and Leach 1993; Jones and Mattingly 1990; King 2005). In addition, the most notable change in what we know of pre-Roman Iron Age cultic practices in the western Roman provinces is the move from using entirely open-air sanctuaries enclosed within an outer *temenos* to the inclusion of an area of enclosed space, the *cella* or sacred area, often small, rectangular post-built structures, such as those evident at Ráith na Senad. A close parallel for those excavated at Ráith na Senad is the late Iron Age/early Roman phases at the temple of Dean Hall in the Forest of Dean (Jones and Mattingly 1990). Here, small, rectangular post-built structures offer the earliest evidence of an LPRIA shrine, along with some contemporary coins, with a development towards more formal (permanent) enclosure in the mid- to late first century AD, whereby the shrine was enclosed within a timber construction including walls of wattle and daub (*ibid.*, 292). The association of these post-built rectangular shrines with extant barrows is also evident at sites such as Slonk Hill in Sussex, Irthlingborough in Northamptonshire and Fryston Ferry in Yorkshire, where in each case the barrows appear to have been a focal point and were deliberately included within the demarcated sacred space (*ibid.*; Orton 2007). Individual coins deposited separately and multiple coins placed in containers are evidenced from shrines and temples in both urban and rural contexts in Roman Britain (Lewis 1966; Fulford 2001; King 2005), and we have good parallels for such deposition from the site of Newgrange (Carson and O'Kelly 1977). A hoard of fifteen 'copper' coins of Constantine I (AD 306–37) was found within the inner ditch of the enclosure at Ráith na Senad during the excavation by the British-Israelites between 1899 and 1902 (Carew 2003; Grogan 2008). The hoard, although rejected in a paper by Dolley (1968) and similarly dismissed by Bateson (1973), was regarded as genuine by Grogan, who argued that there was no evidence to doubt the presence of a fourth-century coin hoard, particularly given all the rest of the fourth-century activity and Roman finds from the site (Grogan 2008, 120).

As mentioned previously, the faunal material from Ráith na Senad is no longer available for study and, given the Sr and O isotope result for the pig, we can only regret its loss. What we do know is that from within the pits near the rectangular structures and from the inner ditch of the site significant quantities of faunal material were recovered, the relative proportions of which are enlightening (Fig. 2.1). Notable are the records relating to ox jaws (not cattle), pig, dog and horse. The ox is an animal that has been deliberately altered by human hands through castration and it was an important propitiatory offering to the god Mars in all his forms; dogs and/or hounds are animals that are known to have been both guardians and door-keepers of the Otherworld in Irish mythology and are the familiars of the goddess Diana; pigs are also associated with the Otherworld and are known to have

been the food of choice for feasting both in Irish mythology and in Roman accounts; and horses were imbued with sacred resonance at Tara through the mythology of the investiture of sacral kingship and are also associated with Mars in the Roman world. Preferential choices in deposition of both the animal species and the types of animal remains are evidenced within both the later Iron Age and the Roman period, and are clearly an important underlying aspect of the rituals performed in both local and Roman contexts (Haynes, forthcoming).

At shrines and temples in the Roman provinces, the assemblages of animal remains often reflect feasting at the site and consist of the types of animals that would have been eaten in a domestic context (King 2005). Many sites of the mid- to late first century AD and second century AD, however, demonstrate clear choices in specific types of animals and in these cases the evidence has been interpreted as relating to specific ritual or cult practices linked to certain deities (at Uley in Gloucestershire, for example, the evidence for a high proportion of goat and domestic fowl was interpreted as relating to the god Mercury, and this was confirmed by inscriptions at the site). At Vertault in Gaul, and at Folly Lane (Gosbecks), the relatively high numbers of horse and dog remains dating from the mid- to later first century AD have been linked to rituals relating to the 'divine hunt' and the role of the goddess Diana as both celestial moon goddess and huntress, linked to concepts of fertility, death and rebirth (King 2005, 360). Furthermore, a direct parallel can be offered between the deposition of a horse within the outer ditch of Ráith na Ríg and a similarly placed horse within the outer ditch of the enclosure at Folly Lane (Grogan 2008; King 2005). When all of the evidence is considered from both Ráith na Senad and Ráith na Ríg, it suggests that the ritual and votive practices carried out on the Hill of Tara between the second and fourth centuries AD reflect both local and Roman influences (Henig 1984; Hill 1995b; Fulford 2001; Ó hÓgáin 2001; King 2005; Newman 2011; Dowling 2011; Haynes, forthcoming).

The parallels with Roman cult sites are strengthened further by another site in Ireland that has long been associated with a possible Roman shrine. At Freestone Hill, Co. Kilkenny, the votive deposition of Roman jewellery, a bifurcate toilet implement and Romano-British pottery, alongside the structured deposition of oxen, pigs and dogs, was interpreted as reflecting cult practice within an area with a relatively high concentration of Roman material (Ó Floinn 1999; 2000). The two Romano-British ceramic sherds found at Freestone Hill have proved difficult to identify in the past (see Raftery 1994; Ó Floinn 2000). The sherds were viewed by the author in 2009 and they belong to two separate small drinking vessels, one of which is Nene Valley colour-coated ware and the other Severn Valley ware. Both are contemporary with the coin of Constantine I (minted at Trier and dated to AD 337–40) and the jewellery evidence from Freestone Hill, and they offer a parallel with the discrete types of ceramic drinking vessels and the absence of any coarsewares in the assemblage found at Ráith na Senad. Furthermore, although the faunal material from Freestone Hill is no longer available to study, it is clear from the published accounts that oxen, dog and horses were deposited around the central area on the crown of the hill (Raftery 1994; Ó Floinn 2000).

The distinctive set of ritual practices at Ráith na Senad and Freestone Hill can be paralleled in both Roman and local contexts in the western Roman provinces, and in Roman studies they are interpreted using the concept known as 'interpretatio Romana'. Tacitus's notion of interpretatio Romana, as first recounted in the Germania (43.4) (Mattingly 1970), is generally believed to be his attempt at the translation of a practice of religious syncretism and cultural negotiation that he witnessed (or was made aware of) within and beyond the Roman provinces. Although scholars have questioned how we should use such a literary construct (Ando 2008), interpretatio is widely accepted as one of a series of politically astute methods of exercising social control through a process of syncretism, a shared value system, often in unstable periods of post-conquest upheaval, or, importantly for these two Irish sites, a process by which encounters through cultural contact can be eased or reconciled within existing practices (Gosden 2004; Haynes, forthcoming). Continuity in religious practice and conflation of local deities with those of the pantheon of Rome would have enabled areas of commonality to be created within the most fundamental of lived human experiences— the relationship between the sense of self and the divine. The deposition of faunal remains, whether from ritual feasting or associated with expiation or propitiatory offerings, can be likened to similarly placed deposits at late Iron Age sacral sites, the favissae in Roman cult practices or the bothros of ancient Greece, and they are of equal if not greater importance than any of the artefacts themselves (Hill 1995b; Hodder and Hutson 2003; Haynes, forthcoming). Even if some remain reluctant to apply such a Roman interpretation to material and sites in Ireland, and there will be many who will argue strongly against that presented here, we must at least recognise that, in instances where communities were engaging with Roman social or religious practices, theirs was a different, a discrepant experience of being 'Irish' in this period (Mattingly 2004; 2006; 2010).

In order to move to a new narrative for the later Iron Age (one that is inclusive), we need to recognise the importance of these differences within the local archaeological record. We can no longer use the dichotomous terms 'native' and 'intrusive' or 'Celtic' and 'Roman' to typify both material and burials found in Ireland. This separatory and isolatory construct is rooted in an essentialist archaeology that is replete with predetermined assumptions about the origin and identities of the people of the later Iron Age, their material culture and their belief systems. If the archaeology of this period has proved so difficult to understand, perhaps we need to alter how we have viewed the later Iron Age through a lens of essential Irishness, ignoring the growing body of 'foreign' evidence that does not fit within it. Similarly, we should no longer rely on relative dating alone for burial practices in Ireland and we must not assume that burials are 'intrusive' or 'local' or, indeed, 'Christian', as we can now demonstrate that some of the burials that we have thought of as intrusive appear to be of local people, such as those at Ráith na Senad, while some of those we thought of as local people appear to have an origin outside Ireland, such as BTS XII at Betaghstown (see above). Contemporary methods of dating and scientific investigation highlight the immensely fluid and changing nature of people's identities, and these have to be situated within both local social, religious and funerary practices and exposure to cultural influences and population immigration in this period. We must be open to the possibility that the people worshipping at both Freestone Hill and Ráith na Senad had adopted aspects of Roman socio-cultural practices—and in this case a set of definable religious practices—that can be directly paralleled in the western Roman provinces, notably at rural shrines and temples in Roman Britain. Theoretical dialogues and scientific analyses have to be incorporated fully within archaeological interpretation, otherwise the people of the past become lost in an archaeological record that is merely a 'manifestation of pre-defined entities or units and their interactions' (Shanks and Tilley 1992, 259), and, in the case of Ráith na Senad, the extraordinary will remain lost to the ordinary within an essentialist transcription.

Bibliography

Allason-Jones, L. 2008 Appendix A: The small finds. In E. Grogan, The Rath of the Synods, Tara, Co. Meath: excavations by Seán P. Ó Ríordáin, 107–12. Bray.

Ando, C. 2008 The matter of the gods: religion and the Roman Empire. Berkeley, CA.

Appadurai, A. 1986 Introduction: commodities and the politics of value. In A. Appadurai (ed.), The social life of things: commodities in cultural perspective, 3–63. Cambridge.

Armit, I. 2007 Social landscapes and identities in the Irish

Iron Age. In C. Haselgrove and T. Moore (eds), *The later Iron Age in Britain and beyond*, 130–9. Oxford.

Bateson, J.D. 1973 Roman material from Ireland: a re-consideration. *Proceedings of the Royal Irish Academy* **73**C, 21–97.

Bateson, J.D. 1976 Further finds of Roman material from Ireland. *Proceedings of the Royal Irish Academy* **76**C, 171–80.

Bathurst, W.H. 1972 *Roman antiquities at Lydney Park*. London.

Becker, K., Ó Néill, J. and O'Flynn, L. 2008 Iron Age Ireland: finding an invisible people. Unpublished report prepared for the Heritage Council (project 16365).

Bentley, R.A. and Knipper, C. 2005 Geographical patterns in biologically available strontium, carbon and oxygen isotope signatures in prehistoric south-west Germany. *Archaeometry* **47**, 629–44.

Bentley, R.A., Krause, R., Price, T.D. and Kaufmann, B. 2003 Human mobility at the early Neolithic settlement of Vahingen, Germany: evidence from strontium isotope analysis. *Archaeometry* **45**, 471–86.

Bhreathnach, E. 2002 Observations on the occurrence of dog and horse bones at Tara. In H. Roche, 'Excavations at Ráith na Ríg, Tara, Co. Meath, 1997'. *Discovery Programme Reports* **6**, 117–22.

Bhreathnach, E. 2005 The medieval kingdom of Brega. In E. Bhreathnach (ed.), *The kingship and landscape of Tara*, 410–21. Dublin.

Bhreathnach, E. 2011 Transforming kingship and cult: the provincial ceremonial capitals in early medieval Ireland. In R. Schot, C. Newman and E. Bhreathnach (eds), *Landscapes of cult and kingship*, 126–49. Dublin.

Bradley, R. 2003 A life less ordinary: the ritualization of the domestic sphere in later prehistoric Europe. *Cambridge Archaeological Journal* **13** (1), 5–23.

Brubaker, R. and Cooper, F. 2000 Beyond 'identity'. *Theory and Society* **29** (1), 1–47.

Budd, P., Chenery, C., Montgomery, J. and Evans, J. 2003 You are where you ate: isotopic analysis in the reconstruction of prehistoric residency. In M. Parker-Pearson (ed.), *Food, culture and identity in the Neolithic and early Bronze Age*, 69–78. British Archaeological Reports, International Series 1117. Oxford.

Burton, J.H., Price, T.D., Cahue, L. and Wright, L.E. 2003 The use of barium and strontium abundances in human skeletal tissues to determine geographic origins. *International Journal of Osteoarchaeology* **13**, 88–95.

Cahill Wilson, J. 2010 Becoming Irish: the materiality of transcultural identities in the later Irish Iron Age.

Unpublished Ph.D thesis, University of Bristol.

Cahill Wilson, J. and Pike, A.W.G. (in prep.) Comparative data for strontium and oxygen isotope analysis from sites in Ireland.

Cahill Wilson, J., Usborne, H., Taylor, C.A., Ditchfield, P. and Pike, A.W.G. 2012 Strontium and oxygen isotope analysis on Iron Age and early historic burials around the Great Mound at Knowth, Co. Meath. Appendix 5. In G. Eogan, *Excavations at Knowth 5: the archaeology of Knowth in the first and second millennia AD*, 775–87. Dublin.

Carew, M. 2003 *Tara and the Ark of the Covenant: a search for the Ark of the Covenant by British-Israelites on the Hill of Tara, 1899–1902*. Dublin.

Carson, R.A.G. and O'Kelly, C. 1977 A catalogue of the Roman finds from Newgrange, County Meath. *Proceedings of the Royal Irish Academy* **77**C, 35–55.

Caulfield, S. 1977 The beehive quern in Ireland. *Journal of the Royal Society of Antiquaries of Ireland* **107**, 104–38.

Caulfield, S. 1994 Some Celtic problems in the Irish Iron Age. In D. Ó Corráin (ed.), *Irish antiquity: essays and studies presented to Professor M.J. O'Kelly*, 205–15. Dublin.

Chapman, R. 2003 Death, society and archaeology: the social dimensions of mortuary practices. *Mortality* **8** (3), 305–12.

Charles-Edwards, T.M. 2000 *Early Christian Ireland*. Cambridge.

Chenery, C., Muldner, G., Evans, J., Eckardt, H. and Lewis, M. 2010 Strontium and stable isotope evidence for diet and mobility in Roman Gloucester, UK. *Journal of Archaeological Science* **37**, 150–63.

Cotter, C. 1999 *Western Stone Forts Project: Cahercommaun Fort, County Clare: a reassessment of its cultural context*. Dublin.

Crew, P. and Rehren, T. 2002 High-temperature workshop residues from Tara: iron, bronze and glass. In H. Roche, 'Excavations at Ráith na Ríg, Tara, Co. Meath, 1997'. *Discovery Programme Reports* **6**, 83–102.

Cunliffe, B. 2001 *Facing the ocean: the Atlantic and its peoples, 8000 BC–AD 1500*. Oxford.

Daux, V., Lécuyer, C., Héran, M. *et al.* 2008 Oxygen isotope fractionation between human phosphate and water revisited. *Journal of Human Evolution* **55**, 1138–47.

Di Martino, V. 2003 *Roman Ireland*. Cork.

Diefendorf, A.F. and Patterson, W.P. 2005 Survey of stable isotope values in Irish surface waters. *Journal of Paleolimnology* **34**, 257–69.

Dolley, R.H.M. 1968 Two numismatic notes. *Journal of the Royal Society of Antiquaries of Ireland* **92**, 62–5.

Dowling, G. 2006 The liminal boundary: an analysis of the

sacral potency of the ditch at Ráith na Ríg, Tara, Co. Meath. *Journal of Irish Archaeology* **15**, 15–37.

Dowling, G. 2011 The architecture of power: an exploration of the origins of closely-spaced multivallate monuments in Ireland. In R. Schot, C. Newman and E. Bhreathnach (eds), *Landscapes of cult and kingship*, 213–32. Dublin.

Dupras, T.L. 2001 Strangers in a strange land: stable isotope evidence for human migration in the Dakhleh Oasis, Egypt. *Journal of Archaeological Science* **28**, 1199–208.

Edwards, N. 1990 *The archaeology of early medieval Ireland*. London.

Edwards, N. 2005 The archaeology of early medieval Ireland, *c.* 400–1169: settlement and economy. In D. Ó Cróinín (ed.), *A new history of Ireland: prehistory and early Ireland*, 235–300. Oxford.

Eogan, G. with contributions by O'Brien, E. and Weekes, B. 2012 Burials and enclosures of the seventh to ninth centuries AD. In G. Eogan, *Excavations at Knowth 5: the archaeology of Knowth in the first and second millennia AD*, 45–83. Dublin.

Evans, J. 2008 Appendix G: the Roman pottery from the Rath of the Synods. In E. Grogan, *The Rath of the Synods, Tara, Co. Meath: excavations by Seán P. Ó Ríordáin*, 123–6. Bray.

Evans, J., Montgomery, J., Wildman, G. and Bouton, N. 2010 Special variations in biosphere $^{87}Sr/^{86}Sr$ in Britain. *Journal of the Geological Society* **167**, 1–4.

Evans, J., Stoodley, N. and Chenery, C. 2006 A strontium and oxygen isotope assessment of a possible fourth-century immigrant population in a Hampshire cemetery, southern England. *Journal of Archaeological Science* **33**, 265–72.

Fenwick, J. 2011 Review of '*The Rath of the Synods, Tara, Co. Meath: excavations by Seán P. Ó Ríordáin*' by Eoin Grogan. *Ríocht na Midhe* **22**, 280–5.

Fowler, E. 1960 The origins and development of the penannular brooch in Europe. *Proceedings of the Prehistoric Society* **26**, 14–177.

Fowler, E. 1963 Celtic metalwork of the fifth and sixth centuries AD. *Archaeological Journal* **120**, 98–160.

Fredengren, C. (forthcoming) *The isles of the dead*. Discovery Programme.

Fulford, M.G. 2001 Links with the past: pervasive 'ritual' behaviour in Roman Britain. *Britannia* **32**, 199–218.

Gavin, F. and Newman, C. 2007 Notes on Insular silver in the 'military style'. *Journal of Irish Archaeology* **16**, 1–10.

Gosden, C. 2004 *Archaeology and colonialism: cultural contact from 5000 BC to the present*. Cambridge.

Grant, M. (trans.) 2003 *Tacitus: The Annals of Imperial Rome*.

London.

Grogan, E. 2008 *The Rath of the Synods, Tara, Co. Meath: excavations by Seán P. Ó Ríordáin*. Bray.

Guido, M. 1978 *The glass beads of the prehistoric and Roman periods in Britain and Ireland*. London.

Harding, D.W. 2004 *The Iron Age in northern Britain: Celts and Romans, natives and invaders*. London and New York.

Harding, D.W. 2006 Redefining the northern British Iron Age. *Oxford Journal of Archaeology* **25** (1), 61–82.

Harding, D.W. 2007 *The archaeology of Celtic art*. London and New York.

Hartridge, R. 1978 Excavations at the prehistoric and Romano-British site on Slonk Hill, Shoreham, Sussex. *Journal of the Sussex Archaeological Society* **116**, 69–141.

Haverfield, F. 1913 Ancient Rome and Ireland. *English Historical Review* **28**, 1–12.

Hawkes, C.F.C. 1981 The wearing of the brooch: Iron Age dress among the Irish. In B.G. Scott (ed.), *Studies on early Ireland: essays in honour of M.V. Duignan*, 51–73. Belfast.

Haynes, I. (forthcoming) Advancing the systematic study of ritual deposition in the Greco-Roman world. In G. Lindstrom, A. Schaefer and M. Witteyer (eds), *Rituelle Deponierungen in Heligtumern der hellenistisch-romischen Welt*, 47–59. Cologne.

Hencken, H. O'Neill 1938 Cahercommaun: a stone fort in County Clare. *Journal of the Royal Society of Antiquaries of Ireland* **38**, 1–82.

Hencken, H. O'Neill 1938–9 Unpublished excavation notes for Lagore crannog. Topographical files, National Museum of Ireland.

Hencken, H. O'Neill 1942 Ballinderry Crannog no. 2. *Proceedings of the Royal Irish Academy* **47**C, 1–76.

Hencken, H. O'Neill 1950 Lagore Crannog: an Irish royal residence of the 7th to 10th centuries AD. *Proceedings of the Royal Irish Academy* **53**C, 1–247.

Henig, M. 1984 *Religion in Roman Britain*. London.

Hill, J.D. 1995a The pre-Roman Iron Age in Britain and Ireland (*c.* 800 BC to AD 100): an overview. *Journal of World Prehistory* **9** (1), 47–98.

Hill, J.D. 1995b *Ritual and rubbish in the Iron Age of Wessex*. British Archaeological Reports, British Series 242. Oxford.

Hingley, R. 1995 Britannia: origin myths and the British Empire. In S. Cottam, D. Dungworth, S. Scott and J. Taylor (eds), *TRAC: the proceedings of the fourth annual Theoretical Roman Archaeology Conference*, 11–23. Oxford.

Hingley, R. 1997 Resistance and domination: social change in Roman Britain. In D.J. Mattingly (ed.), *Dialogues in*

Roman imperialism: power, discourse and discrepant experience in the Roman Empire, 81–102. *Journal of Roman Archaeology*, Supplementary Series 23.

Hingley, R. 2005 *Globalising Roman culture: unity, diversity and empire*. London and New York.

Hingley, R. 2010 Cultural diversity and unity: empire and Rome. In S. Hales and T. Hodos (eds), *Material culture and social identities in the ancient world*, 54–75. Cambridge.

Hodder, I. 1982 Theoretical archaeology: a reactionary view. In I. Hodder (ed.), *Symbolic and structural archaeology*, 1–16. Cambridge.

Hodder, I. 1997 Always momentary, fluid and flexible: towards a self-reflexive excavation methodology. *Antiquity* **71**, 691–700.

Hodder, I. 1999 *The archaeological process*. London.

Hodder, I. 2008 Multivocality and social archaeology. In J. Habu, C. Fawcett and J.M. Matsunaga (eds), *Evaluating multiple narratives: beyond nationalist, colonialist, imperial archaeologies*, 196–200. New York.

Hodder, I. and Hutson, S. 2003 *Reading the past: current approaches to interpretation in archaeology* (3rd edn). Cambridge.

Hodos, T. 2010 Local and global perspectives in the study of social and cultural identities. In S. Hales and T. Hodos (eds), *Material culture and social identities in the ancient world*, 3–31. Cambridge.

Horning, A.J. 2006 Archaeology, conflict and contemporary identity in the north of Ireland: implications for theory and practice in comparative archaeologies of colonialism. *Archaeological Dialogues* **13** (2), 183–200.

Iacumen, P., Bocherens, H., Mariotti, A. and Longinelli, A. 1996 Oxygen isotope analyses of co-existing carbonate and phosphate in biogenic apatite: a way to monitor diagenetic alteration of bone phosphate? *Earth and Planetary Science Letters* **142**, 1–6.

Janaway, R.C. 1997 The decay of buried human remains and their associated materials. In J. Hunter, C.A. Roberts and A. Martin (eds), *Studies in crime: introduction to forensic archaeology*, 58–85. London.

Johns, C. 1996 *The jewellery of Roman Britain: Celtic and classical traditions*. London.

Johnson, R. 1999 Ballinderry Crannog no. 1: a reinterpretation. *Proceedings of the Royal Irish Academy* **99**C, 23–71.

Johnston, S.A. and Wailes, B. 2007 *Dún Ailinne: excavations at the royal site, 1968–1975*. Philadelphia.

Jones, A. 2003 Technologies of remembrance. In H. Williams (ed.), *Archaeologies of remembrance: death and memory in past societies*, 65–88. New York.

Jones, B. and Mattingly, D. 1990 *An atlas of Roman Britain*. Oxford.

Keeley, V. 1996 Excavations at Ballydavis, Co. Laois. *IAPA Newsletter* **22**, 11.

Kilbride-Jones, H.E. 1980 *Zoomorphic penannular brooches*. London.

King, A. 2005 Animal remains from temples in Roman Britain. *Britannia* **36**, 329–69.

Koch, P.L., Tuross, N. and Fogel, M.L. 1997 The effects of sample treatment and diagenesis on the isotopic integrity of carbonate in biogenic hydroxylapatite. *Journal of Archaeological Science* **24**, 417–29.

Kurtz, D.C. and Boardman, J. 1971 *Greek burial customs*. London.

Leedham, D. 2010 *The limits of the habitable world: Ireland and the conquest of Britain*. Chester.

Lennon, A.-M. and O'Hara, R. 2011 Archaeological excavation of an early medieval enclosure at Leggetsrath West, Co. Kilkenny. In C. Corlett and M. Potterton (eds), *Settlement in early medieval Ireland in the light of recent archaeological investigations*, 223–38. Bray.

Lewis, M.J.T. 1966 *Temples in Roman Britain*. Cambridge.

Longinelli, A. 1984 Oxygen isotopes in mammal bone phosphate: a new tool for paleohydrological and paleoclimatological research? *Geochimica et Cosmochimica Acta* **48**, 385–90.

Lynn, C.J. 1983 Some 'early' ring-forts and crannogs. *Journal of Irish Archaeology* **1**, 47–58.

Lynn, C.J. 1985 Lagore, County Meath, and Ballinderry no. 1, County Westmeath, crannogs: some possible structural reinterpretations. *Journal of Irish Archaeology* **3**, 69–73.

Lynn, C.J. 2003 *Navan Fort: archaeology and myth*. Dublin.

Macalister, R.A.S. 1916–17 A report on some excavations recently conducted in Co. Galway. *Proceedings of the Royal Irish Academy* **33**C, 505–10.

McArthur, J.M., Howarth, R.J. and Bailey, T.R. 2001 Strontium isotope stratigraphy: LOWESS Version 3: best fit to the marine Sr isotope curve for 0–509 Ma and accompanying look-up table for deriving numerical age. *Journal of Geology* **109**, 155–70.

McConnell, B., Philcox, M.E. and Geraghty, M. 2001 *Geology of Meath: a geological description to accompany the bedrock geology 1:100,000 scale map Sheet 13, Meath*. Dublin.

McCormick, F. 2002 The animal bones from Tara. In H. Roche (ed.), 'Excavations at Ráith na Ríg, Tara, Co. Meath, 1997'. *Discovery Programme Reports* **6**, 103–14.

McGarry, T. 2005 Identifying burials of the Irish Iron Age and transitional periods, c. 800 BC–AD 600. *Trowel* **10**, 2–18.

McGarry, T. 2008 Some exotic evidence amidst Irish late

prehistoric burials. In O.P. Davis, N.M. Sharples and K. Waddington (eds), *Changing perspectives on the first millennium*, 215–34. Oxford.

McGarry, T. 2012 The Knowth Iron Age burials in an Irish and wider context. In G. Eogan, *Excavations at Knowth 5: the archaeology of Knowth in the first and second millennia AD*, 689–94. Dublin.

Mallory, J.P. and Ó Donnabháin, B. 1998 The origins of the population of Ireland: a survey of putative immigrations in Irish prehistory and history. *Emania* **17**, 47–71.

Mattingly, D. (ed.) 1997 *Dialogues in Roman imperialism: power, discourse and discrepant experience in the Roman Empire*. Journal of Roman Archaeology, Supplementary Series 23.

Mattingly, D. 2004 Being Roman: expressing identity in a provincial setting. *Journal of Roman Archaeology* **17**, 5–25.

Mattingly, D. 2006 *An imperial possession: Britain in the Roman Empire*. London.

Mattingly, D. 2010 Cultural crossovers: global and local identities in the classical world. In S. Hales and T. Hodos (eds), *Material culture and social identities in the ancient world*, 283–95. Cambridge.

Mattingly, H. (trans.) 1970 *Tacitus: The Agricola and The Germania* (revised by S.A. Handford). London.

Megaw, J.V.S. and Megaw, M.R. 1989 *Celtic art: from its beginnings to the Book of Kells*. London and New York.

Montgomery, J. and Grimes, V. 2010 Report of the isotope analysis of a burial from Ratoath, Co. Meath. In C. Corlett and M. Potterton (eds), *Death and burial in early medieval Ireland in the light of recent archaeological investigations*, 309–11. Bray.

Montgomery, J., Evans, J. and Chenery, C. 2005 Report of the lead, strontium and oxygen isotope analysis of the Iron Age burial from Rath, Ireland. Unpublished report for CRDS.

Mulvin, L. 2012a Toilet items: Roman toilet items. In G. Eogan, *Excavations at Knowth 5: the archaeology of Knowth in the first and second millennia AD*, 390–1. Dublin.

Mulvin, L. 2012b Pottery vessels: Roman pottery. In G. Eogan, *Excavations at Knowth 5: the archaeology of Knowth in the first and second millennia AD*, 440–2. Dublin.

Newman, C. 1997 *Tara: an archaeological survey*. Dublin.

Newman, C. 1998 Reflections on the making of a 'royal site' in early Ireland. *World Archaeology* **30**, 127–41.

Newman, C. 2005 Recomposing the landscape of Tara. In E. Bhreathnach (ed.), *The kingship and landscape of Tara*, 361–82. Dublin.

Newman, C. 2011 The sacral landscape of Tara: a preliminary exploration. In R. Schot, C. Newman and E. Bhreathnach (eds), *Landscapes of cult and kingship*, 22–44.

Dublin.

O'Brien, E. 1990 Iron Age burial practices in Leinster: continuity and change. *Emania* **7**, 37–42.

O'Brien, E. 1999 Excavations of a multi-period burial site at Ballymacaward, Ballyshannon, County Donegal. *Journal of the Donegal Historical Society* **51**, 56–61.

O'Brien, E. 2003 Burial practices in Ireland: first to seventh centuries AD. In J. Downes and A. Ritchie (eds), *Sea change: Orkney and northern Europe in the later Iron Age, AD 300–800*, 62–72. Balgavies.

O'Brien, E. 2009 Pagan or Christian? Burial in Ireland during the 5th to 8th centuries AD. In N. Edwards (ed.), *The archaeology of the early medieval Celtic churches*, 135–54. London.

Ó Donovan, E. and Geber, J. 2010 Excavations on Mount Gamble Hill, Swords, Co. Dublin. In C. Corlett and M. Potterton (eds), *Death and burial in early medieval Ireland in the light of recent archaeological investigations*, 227–38. Bray.

Ó Drisceoil, C. 2007 Life and death in the Iron Age at Carrickmines Great, County Dublin. *Journal of the Royal Society of Antiquaries of Ireland* **137**, 5–28.

Ó Floinn, R. 1999 The date of some metalwork from Cahercommaun reassessed. In C. Cotter, *Cahercommaun Fort, Co. Clare: a reassessment of its cultural context*, 73–9. Bray.

Ó Floinn, R. 2000 Freestone Hill, Co. Kilkenny: a reassessment. In A. Smyth (ed.), *Seanchas: studies in early and medieval Irish archaeology, history and literature in honour of Francis J. Byrne*, 12–29. Dublin.

O'Kelly, M.J. 1989 *Early Ireland: an introduction to Irish prehistory*. Cambridge.

Ó hÓgáin, D. 2001 *The sacred isle: belief and religion in pre-Christian Ireland*. Woodbridge, Suffolk.

Ó Ríordáin, S.P. 1945–8 Roman material in Ireland. *Proceedings of the Royal Irish Academy* **51**C, 35–82.

O'Sullivan, A. 1998 *The archaeology of lake settlement in Ireland*. Dublin.

O'Sullivan, A. and Harney, L. 2008 *Early Medieval Archaeology Project: investigating the character of early medieval archaeological excavations, 1970–2002*. Report for the Heritage Council, published on-line.

O'Sullivan, J. 1998 Nationalists, archaeologists and the myth of the Golden Age. In M. Monk and J. Sheehan (eds), *Early medieval Munster: archaeology, history and society*, 178–99. Cork.

O'Sullivan, M. 2004 *Duma na nGiall: the Mound of the Hostages, Tara*. Bray.

Orton, D. 2007 A local barrow for local people: the Fryston Ferry cattle in context. In S. Cottam, D. Dungworth, S.

Scott and J. Taylor (eds), *TRAC: the proceedings of the fourth annual Theoretical Roman Archaeology Conference*, 77–91. London.

Parker-Pearson, M. 1982 Mortuary practices, society and ideology: an ethno-archaeological study. In I. Hodder (ed.), *Symbolic and structural archaeology*, 99–114. Cambridge.

Parker-Pearson, M. 2003 *The archaeology of death and burial*. Stroud.

Philpott, R. 1991 *Burial practices in Roman Britain: a survey of grave treatment and furnishings, AD 43–410*. British Archaeological Reports, British Series 219. Oxford.

Raftery, B. 1969 Freestone Hill, Co. Kilkenny: an Iron Age hillfort and Bronze Age cairn. *Proceedings of the Royal Irish Academy* **68**C, 1–108.

Raftery, B. 1972 Irish hillforts. In C. Thomas (ed.), *The Iron Age in the Irish Sea province*, 37–59. London.

Raftery, B. 1981 Iron Age burials in Ireland. In D. Ó Corráin (ed.), *Irish antiquity: essays and studies presented to Professor M.J. O'Kelly*, 173–204. Dublin.

Raftery, B. 1994 *Pagan Celtic Ireland: the enigma of the Irish Iron Age*. London.

Raftery, B. 1996 Iron Age studies in Ireland: some recent developments. In T.C. Champion and J.R. Collis (eds), *The Iron Age in Britain and Ireland: recent trends*, 155–61. Sheffield.

Raftery, B. 2000. A bit too far: Ireland's Transylvanian link in the later Iron Age. In A.P. Smyth (ed.), *Seanchas: studies in early and medieval Irish archaeology, history and literature in honour of Francis J. Byrne*, 1–11. Dublin.

Raftery, B. 2005 The Iron Age in Ireland. In D. Ó Cróinín (ed.), *A new history of Ireland*, 134–81. Oxford.

Raftery, J. 1940 A suggested chronology for the Irish Iron Age. In J. Ryan (ed.), *Féilsgríbhinn Éoin Mhic Néill*, 272–81. Dublin.

Raftery, J. 1972 Iron Age and Irish Sea: problems for research. In C. Thomas (ed.), *The Iron Age in the Irish Sea province*, 1–10. London.

Raftery, J. 1981 Concerning chronology. In D. Ó Corráin (ed.), *Irish antiquity: essays and studies presented to Professor M.J. O'Kelly*, 82–90. Dublin.

Roche, H. 2002 Excavations at Ráith na Ríg, Tara, Co. Meath, 1997. *Discovery Programme Reports* **6**, 19–82.

Schot, R., Newman, C. and Bhreathnach, E. (eds) 2011 *Landscapes of cult and kingship*. Dublin.

Schweissing, M.M. and Grupe, G. 2003 Stable strontium isotopes in human teeth and bone: a key to migration events of the late Roman period in Bavaria. *Journal of Archaeological Science* **30**, 1373–83.

Shanks, M. and Tilley, C. 1992 *Re-constructing archaeology: theory and practice*. London.

Stout, G. 2002 *Newgrange and the Bend of the Boyne*. Cork.

Swift, C. 1997 *Ogam stones and the earliest Irish Christians*. Maynooth.

Tierney, M. 1998 Theory and politics in early medieval Irish archaeology. In M. Monk and J. Sheehan (eds), *Early medieval Munster: archaeology, history and society*, 190–9. Cork.

Toynbee, J.M.C. 1971 *Death and burial in the Roman world*. London.

Ucko, P.J. 1969 Ethnography and archaeological interpretation of funerary remains. *World Archaeology* **1** (2), 262–80.

Waddell, J. 2005 *Foundation myths: the beginnings of Irish archaeology*. Bray.

Wallace, P.F. 2008 Irish archaeology and the recognition of ethnic difference in Viking Dublin. In J. Habu, C. Fawcett and J.M. Matsunaga (eds), *Evaluating multiple narratives: beyond nationalist, colonialist, imperial archaeologies*, 166–83. New York.

Warner, R.B. 1985–6 The date of the start of Lagore. *Journal of Irish Archaeology* **3**, 75–7.

Warner, R.B. 1995 *Tuathal Techtmar*: a myth or ancient literary evidence for a Roman invasion? *Emania* **13**, 23–32.

Warner, R.B. (forthcoming) Some notes on Tara and its hinterland during the later Iron Age. In M. O'Sullivan, G. Cooney, C. Scarre and B. Cunliffe (eds), *Tara: from the past to the future*.

Wedlake, W.J. 1982 *The excavation of the shrine of Apollo at Nettleton, Wiltshire, 1956–1971*. London.

Whimster, R. 1981 *Burial practices in Iron Age Britain: a discussion and gazetteer of the evidence, c. 700 BC–AD 42*. British Archaeological Reports, British Series 90. Oxford.

Woodward, A. and Leach, P. 1993 *The Uley Shrines: excavation of a ritual complex on West Hill, Uley, Gloucestershire, 1977–9*. London.

Wylie, A. 2008 The integrity of narrative: deliberate practice, pluralism and multivocality. In J. Habu, C. Fawcett and J.M. Matsunaga (eds), *Evaluating multiple narratives: beyond nationalist, colonialist, imperial archaeologies*, 201–12. New York.

Young, R. 1995 *Colonial desire: hybridity in theory, culture and race*. London and New York.

Notes

1. See A. O'Sullivan's (1998) suggestions relating to finds of Samian ware at crannog sites across Ireland.

2. Roman sherds and Roman objects have been found at Lagore, Ballinderry no. 2, Island McHugh, Lough Faughan and Cloonfinlough crannogs (Bateson 1973; Cotter 1999; A. O'Sullivan 1998).

3. Iron Age ritual and settlement at Cookstown, Co. Meath

Richard Clutterbuck with a contribution by Susan Lyons

Introduction

Excavations in Cookstown for the N2 Finglas to Ashbourne Road Scheme identified settlement and ritual activity from the late Neolithic to the modern period, revealing over 5,000 years of history in one hectare (Clutterbuck 2006; FitzGerald 2006; Clutterbuck 2008; 2009; O'Carroll, forthcoming).[1] The archaeological site at Cookstown, situated 1km north-west of Ashbourne town, was discovered in three pasture fields beside a modern farmstead on a knoll overlooking the Broad Meadow River some 150m to the south (Figs 3.1 and 3.2). The site's Iron Age horizon consisted of a pair of narrow, shallow, concentric ring-ditches surrounded by burnt pits, interpreted as a local ritual enclosure or shrine, and a further sequence of burnt pits which appear to have been corn-drying kilns. This paper describes these discoveries and discusses their significance for our evolving understanding of settlement, agriculture and ritual in the Irish Iron Age.

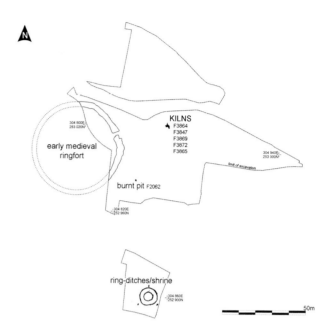

Fig. 3.2—Cookstown: Iron Age features and early medieval ringfort.

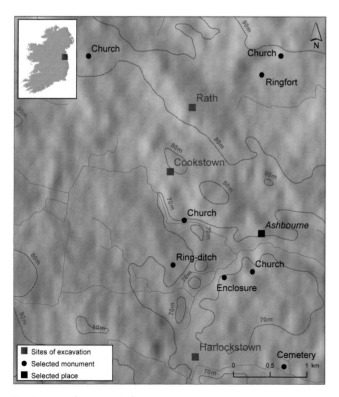

Fig. 3.1—Cookstown: site location.

Kilns

Five overlapping burnt pits were exposed near the centre of the site (Figs 3.2–3.4). The earliest pit in this sequence (F3865 in Fig. 3.3) measured 2.68m by 0.8m by 0.12m deep and contained a single fill of mixed clay, ash and occasional unidentifiable burnt animal bone.[2] A second, smaller pit (F3872), measuring 0.7–1m in diameter and *c.* 0.2m deep, cut across the first. It had four fills: a primary fill of burnt clay beneath fills of charcoal-rich clays containing burnt barley (Appendix 3.1). Willow charcoal from these layers was radiocarbon-dated to 170 BC–AD 1 (2-sigma; Wk-18210; Table 3.1). The final fill of this pit contained burnt barley, wheat and hazel. Cut into this was a third small pit (F3869; 0.17m by 0.14m by 0.04m deep) with a single charcoal-rich fill. A fourth long, shallow cut (F3874), measuring 4m long, 0.08m wide and 0.25m deep, cut north–south across the second and third pits. This contained a single fill of charcoal-rich clay with the remains of wheat, barley, oats and *Raphanus* or radish. The fifth pit (F3864), and the last in stratigraphic sequence, measured 0.6m by 0.5m by 0.25m deep and contained three fills: a primary fill with moderate charcoal inclusions containing barley (F3863), a second, heavily burnt

35

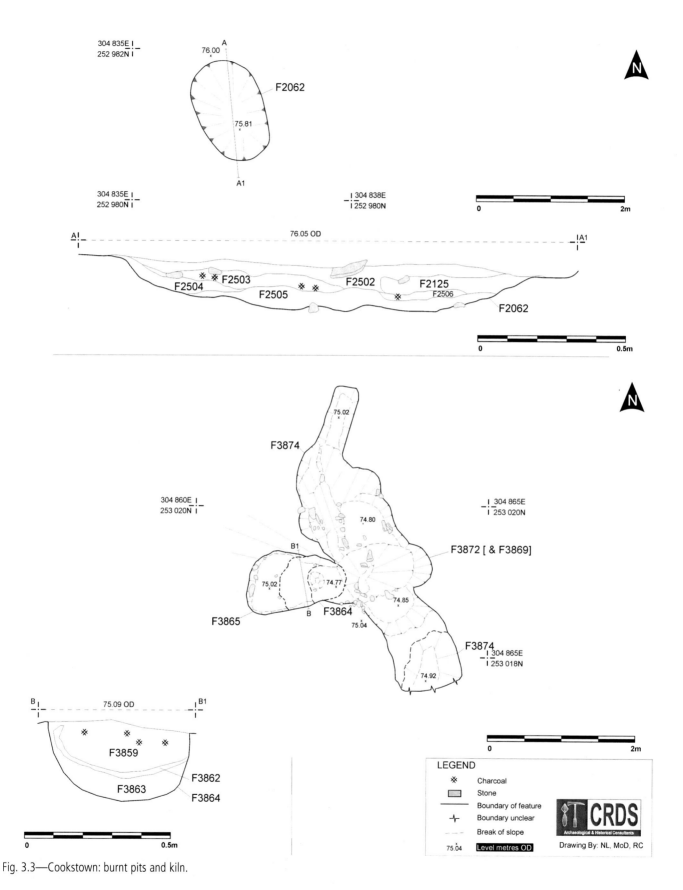

Fig. 3.3—Cookstown: burnt pits and kiln.

Table 3.1—Cookstown: Iron Age radiocarbon dates from site 25 (01E1252).

Lab no.	Sample	Feature	¹⁴C BP date	¹⁴C 1σ date	¹⁴C 2σ date
Wk-16313	104	4005	2148±47	360–100 BC	360–50 BC
Wk-16314	105	4005	2192±40	360–190 BC	360–160 BC
Wk-17937	60	3151	2620±60	900–660 BC	920–540 BC
Wk-17939	67	1085	1555±41	AD 430–550	AD 410–600
Wk-17940	195	4033	1904±42	AD 20–140	AD 1–230
Wk-18210	434	3871	2066±33	160–20 BC	170 BC–AD 1
Wk-18211	286	2503	1896±33	AD 60–210	AD 20–220
Wk-18213	351	2512	1937±30	AD 25–125	AD 1–130

Fig. 3.4—Cookstown: Iron Age corn-drying kilns (F3864, F3865, F3869, F3872, F3874).

fill with oak charcoal and poorly preserved barley and wheat grains (F3862), and a final fill (F3859) of charcoal-rich fire-reddened clay containing barley.

A single shallow burnt pit (F2062) was discovered 58m south-east of the other burnt pits (Fig. 3.2). This oval pit measured 1.48m by 0.86m, was 0.23m deep and contained six fills (Fig. 3.3). The primary fill of the pit appeared to be burnt. Secondary fills of the pit contained barley, wheat and *Chenopodium* or goosefoot (Appendix 3.1). A radiocarbon date

from a barley grain, of AD 20–220 (2-sigma; Wk-18211; Table 3.1), dates this feature to the later Iron Age.

Ring-ditches

Two concentric shallow ring-ditches (Figs 3.2 and 3.5) were discovered 115m south of the kilns on the gentle south-facing slope of a pasture field overlooking the Broad Meadow River. These features had no surface expression; all that survived was cut into subsoil. In plan, the ring-ditches had slightly flattened

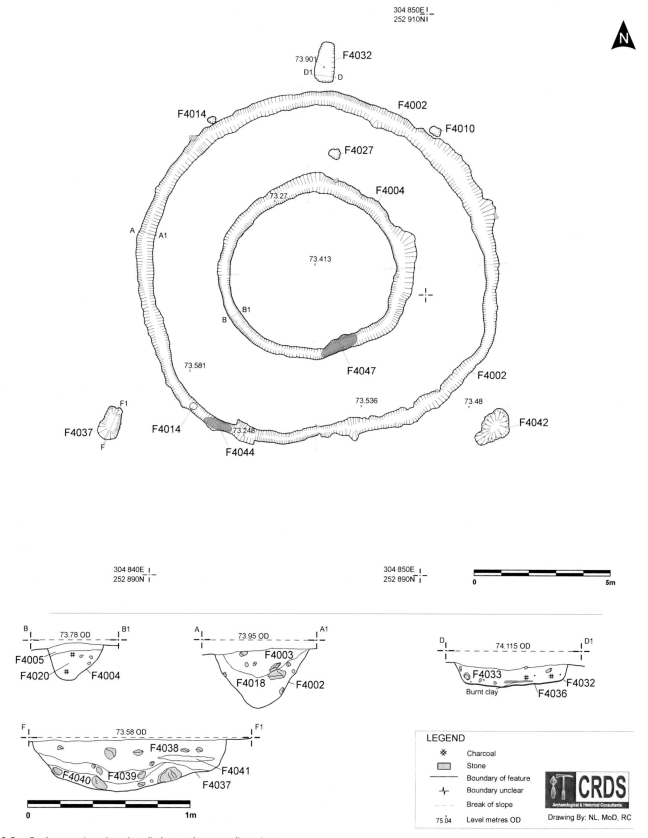

Fig. 3.5—Cookstown: Iron Age ring-ditches and surrounding pits.

Table 3.2—Cookstown: summary table of animal bone from the Iron Age features (after Murray 2008).

		Cattle	Sheep/ goat	Pig	Horse
Pit fill	F3145	1	–	–	–
Ditch fill	F4002	5	2	1	–
Ditch fill	F4004	3	2	–	1
	Total	9	4	1	1

southern quadrants. Their concentric arrangement and shape, in particular the similarly distorted southern quadrants, suggest that both ditches were contemporary. The outer ditch (F4002) was 0.4m wide and between 12.8m and 13.45m in diameter; the inner ditch (F4004) was 0.54m wide and between 6.25m and 7.29m in diameter. The inner and outer ditches were separated by 2.3–3.1m. The inner ditch was shallower (maximum 0.27m) than the outer ditch (maximum 0.45m). The outer ring-ditch (F4002) contained six fills. A primary fill (F4003 in Fig. 3.5) contained inclusions of charcoal, unidentified burnt bone, cattle, sheep/goat and pig bone and cereal grain of indeterminate species (see Table 3.2 and Appendix 3.1). The lower fills of the outer ditch (F4018) had a higher silt composition, suggesting that the ditch had filled up gradually. A more compact fill (F4044 in Fig. 3.5) in the southern quadrant, however, appears to have been inserted to create a 1.7m-wide entrance into the interior of the ring-ditch.

The inner ditch (F4004) contained five fills with charcoal inclusions from unidentified species, occasional cattle, sheep/goat and horse bone inclusions and unidentified burnt bone. As with the outer ring-ditch, a compact 'entrance feature' (F4047 in Fig. 3.5) occupied a *c.* 1.5m-long section of the southern quadrant of the inner ditch but was slightly offset from the outer ring-ditch 'entrance', suggesting a more complex use of the ring-ditch's interior space (discussed further below). Charcoal from the tertiary fill (F4005 in Fig. 3.5) of the inner ring-ditch produced two radiocarbon dates: 360–50 cal. BC and 360–160 cal. BC (2-sigma; Wk-16313 and Wk-16314; see Table 3.1).

Three artefacts were recovered from the fills of the two ring-ditches. A fragment of a glass bracelet (4003:0001;[3] Fig. 3.6) was found in the outer ring-ditch. This toffee-brown or amber-coloured bracelet or bangle has a D-shaped section. Its original internal diameter was approximately 60mm. The interior surface is slightly rough, most likely from the metal or ceramic form around which the bangle was originally made. This form also appears to have been tapered, perhaps to more easily remove the newly made glass object. Although the piece

is of one colour, the bands of glass layers from its manufacture are clearly visible. A pitted surface shows that the quality of the glass used to make the object was poor and this probably contributed to its breakage in prehistory. Raftery (1983, vol.1, 175–6) identified five examples of Iron Age glass armlets from Ireland. These were all of a single colour, either deep purple, blue or yellow, in contrast to the Scottish and northern English examples, which tend to be more highly decorated with a number of colours (Kilbride-Jones 1938; Stevenson 1954). Multicoloured glass bracelets or bangles in Ireland, mostly blue, white and yellow, are more commonly associated with the early medieval period (Carroll 2001). Two first-century BC amber-coloured glass bracelets were discovered at the Knockaulin or Dún Ailinne ceremonial sites (Johnston and Wailes 2007, 120). Amber-coloured glass also appears to be relatively rare in British examples and was derived from adding a mixture of sulphur or a carbon compound, sometimes horse manure, to the glass mixture (Stevenson 1954, 215, 217–18). Irish armlets made of various materials, catalogued by Raftery, ranged in size from 20mm to 61mm in internal diameter. The Cookstown example, at *c.* 60mm in internal diameter, is towards the higher end of this range. Most were D-shaped in section, similar to the Cookstown example. Three of the five glass armlets examined by Raftery were found in burial deposits: one from Dunadry, Co. Antrim, and two from Loughey, Co. Down. Two came from occupation sites: Feerwore, Co. Galway, and Freestone Hill, Co. Kilkenny. Their function is not completely understood but they may have served as bracelets or armlets, although their small diameter would have made them difficult to wear; anything less than 55mm in diameter could only have been worn by a child. Alternatively, the objects could have been worn strung on torcs, as found on the Continent, worn singly as a pendant or used as hair-rings (Johns 1996, 123; Carroll 2001, 101–3).

A sherd of abraded domestic Beaker pottery was also recovered from this fill of the outer ring-ditch (F4003:2), although this appears to be a residual find from an earlier Beaker phase of occupation on the site (Clutterbuck 2008

Fig. 3.6—Cookstown: Iron Age glass bracelet (4003:1); scale 2cm (photograph by John Sunderland).

Fig. 3.7—Cookstown: Iron Age bronze penannular ring (4005:2) (photograph by John Sunderland).

Vol. 1, 17; Roche and Grogan 2008). In the inner ring-ditch a single object was recovered from the upper fill: a penannular bronze spiral ring (4005:2; Fig. 3.7) made of a single piece of bronze wire. Bronze spiral rings were also found at Knockaulin or Dún Ailinne, Co. Kildare (Johnston and Wailes 2007, 106–8). Raftery (1983, vol. 1, 179–84) identified 21 similar examples. Most were found in bogs or in burial contexts. These rings ranged in size from 11mm to 32.5mm in diameter and from 2mm to 5mm in thickness; the Cookstown spiral ring was 19.2mm in diameter and 1.8mm thick. Fine ribbing or herringbone hatch form the most common decoration on these objects; Cookstown's spiral ring had fine ribbing similar to an example from the Lisnacrogher hoard (Raftery 1983, vol. 2, 181, fig. 150, no. 484).

The only archaeological feature inside the ring-ditches was a small shallow pit (F4027 in Fig. 3.5) between the northern quadrants of the inner and outer ring-ditches. The pit measured 0.25–0.29m in diameter and 0.13m deep, with a fill of sandy clay with frequent charcoal inclusions and occasional burnt bone but no artefacts. Another possible truncated post-hole (F4010 in Fig. 3.5) was discovered immediately *outside* the outer ring-ditch's north-eastern quadrant. This contained a single silty sand fill with occasional charcoal inclusions and a single reworked chert flake (4011:1). A second possible post-hole (F4014 in Fig. 3.5) was truncated by the south-western quadrant of the outer ring-ditch.

Three burnt pits (F4032, F4037 and F4042 in Fig. 3.5)

were found outside the ring-ditches' northern, south-eastern and south-western quadrants. They ranged in size from 0.68m by 1.42m to 1m by 1.52m wide and from 0.1m to 0.34m deep. The base of each pit was burnt and their fills contained charcoal inclusions and burnt barley. The upper fill of the south-western pit contained fragments of alder, charcoal, barley and indeterminate cereal grain (Appendix 3.1). All of the fills in the south-western pit contained inclusions of bone or flecks of burnt bone, as did one of the fills of the northern pit. Unfortunately, the burnt bone from these features was too poorly preserved to identify. The only find recovered from the three pits was a flint flake from the upper fill of the northern pit. Blackthorn and alder charcoal from the pits suggests that both wood types may have been used for fuel, although alder makes poor, slow-burning firewood (Nelson and Walsh 1993, 49–52; Stuijts 2005, 139). Blackthorn charcoal recovered from the upper fill of the northern pit yielded a radiocarbon date of cal. AD 1–230 (2-sigma; Wk-17940; Table 3.1). Assuming that the three surrounding pits are contemporary, this makes the pits significantly younger than the ring-ditches. The position of the pits suggests that the ring-ditches were still visible, if not still in use, and that the pits were placed around the ring-ditches. If this was the case, it would mean that the ring-ditch complex was in use, perhaps with some modifications, over several centuries.

Discussion

The Irish Iron Age has been characterised as something of an enigma, with significant gaps in our understanding of settlement, agriculture and domestic material culture (Raftery 1994). In recent years important Iron Age horizons have been identified on archaeological sites across Ireland, helping to fill these gaps in our knowledge (Becker *et al.* 2008; McLaughlin and Conran 2008; Taylor 2008; O'Connell 2007). The results of excavations at Cookstown provide some further insights into Iron Age settlement, agriculture and ritual.

There was no direct evidence for Iron Age settlement at Cookstown (no structures or settlement enclosure ditch), but the presence of kilns used over an extended period of time indicates the existence of a nearby agricultural settlement. Carbonised grain in these kilns dated from the second and first centuries BC. The small single-event burnt pit to the south of these kilns, radiocarbon-dated to several hundred years later, suggests continued occupation of the site later into the Iron Age. Cereal was dried in kilns to harden the grains prior to threshing and grinding, to dry corn seed prior to sowing, to roast sprouted grain to produce malt for beer, to fumigate for destructive insects and to reduce the grain's moisture content prior to storage (Monk 1981, 217–18; Monk and Kelleher

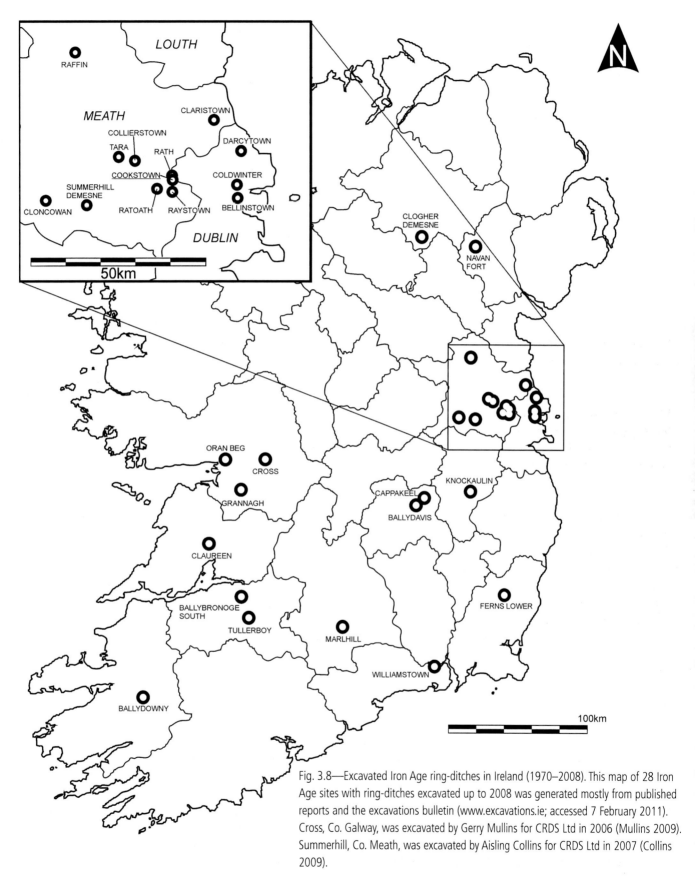

Fig. 3.8—Excavated Iron Age ring-ditches in Ireland (1970–2008). This map of 28 Iron Age sites with ring-ditches excavated up to 2008 was generated mostly from published reports and the excavations bulletin (www.excavations.ie; accessed 7 February 2011). Cross, Co. Galway, was excavated by Gerry Mullins for CRDS Ltd in 2006 (Mullins 2009). Summerhill, Co. Meath, was excavated by Aisling Collins for CRDS Ltd in 2007 (Collins 2009).

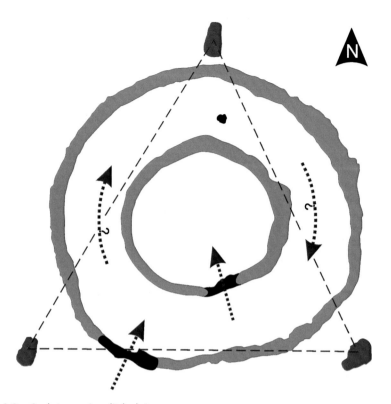

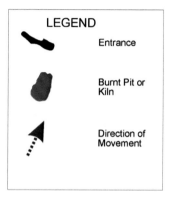

LEGEND

Entrance

Burnt Pit or Kiln

Direction of Movement

Fig. 3.9—Cookstown: ring-ditch shrine.

2005). Relatively few assemblages of cereals from Iron Age sites have been published (Monk 1986; McClatchie 2007, 210). Grain-milling appears to have been carried out using hand-powered rotary quernstones (Caulfield 1977). Pollen diagrams illustrate a decline in cereals and a regrowth of woodland in the later Bronze Age and early Iron Age, corresponding with deterioration in the climate (Mitchell 1965; Mitchell and Ryan 1997, 237). There is, however, some evidence at Kerloge, Co. Wexford, that the range of cereals actually expanded in the Iron Age (McClatchie 2007, 210). At Waterunder, Co. Louth, where sixteen Iron Age kilns were excavated, mostly figure-of-eight in plan, an analysis of the cereal remains identified barley, wheat and cultivated oats (McQuade 2005, 41–2). Barley was also prevalent in the two Iron Age kilns excavated by Linnane in Rath-Healy, Co. Cork, although here small quantities of oats were also identified.[4] The use of individual pits at Cookstown rather than larger composite kilns suggests that the grain-processing here was carried out on a much smaller scale. The presence of burnt bone and radish in the pit fills may also suggest refuse disposal.

The concentric ring-ditches at Cookstown appear to have been a focus of ritual activity. There appear to be few Irish parallels to the Cookstown ring-ditches. The Record of Monuments and Places identifies a 20m-diameter 'ring-ditch'

crop-mark 950m south of Cookstown, in Killegland townland (ME045:002), while Bronze Age ring-ditches were excavated in Ballybin (600m south of Cookstown), in Rath (1.35km north-north-east; O'Carroll, forthcoming) and in Killegland (Frazer 2007), 1.4km south-south-east of Cookstown (Fig. 3.1). A significant number of Iron Age ring-ditches have been discovered in north Dublin and Meath (Fig. 3.8). Most Iron Age ring-ditches are associated with burial (O'Brien 1990, 37; 2003, 63; Clarke and Carlin 2006). The diameter of these monuments ranges from 2.95m (Rath, Co. Meath; see Schweitzer 2005) to 16m (Ballydavis, Co. Laois; see Keeley 1996; 1999), with an average of about 7.7m. The width of the ditches ranges from 0.4m to 2m, with an average of about 1m—significantly wider than the ditches at Cookstown. It is likely that a number of these features are truncated barrows. None of the bone recovered from the Cookstown ring-ditches or its pits could be identified as human and so it is not possible to be sure that this was a site associated with mortuary ritual.

A number of Iron Age sites have concentric circular ditches that have been interpreted as structural. Navan Fort site B contained a sequence of structures ranging in diameter from 10.7m to 13.1m, with the remains of burnt daub in their fill (Waterman 1997, 17, 150–1; Lynn 2000). Similar remains

Fig. 3.10—Cookstown: oblique photograph of ring-ditches.

at Knockaulin consisted of a sequence of concentric slot-trenches for a 38m-diameter enclosure and a 21m annexe (Johnston and Wailes 2007, 13–14). In both cases the remains are interpreted as those of significant structures: a house annexed to an enclosure at Navan B; a large enclosure and a walled open-air structure in Navan A/C; and a viewing platform annexed to an enclosure at Knockaulin. Navan Fort B's concentric alignment has been interpreted as evidence that the walls of the house were replaced twice (Waterman 1997, 150–1). Excavations at Raffin, Co. Meath, uncovered the remains of up to three circular buildings (A, B and C), built in slot-trenches and ranging in size from 5m (building C) to 13m (building A). The larger building was interpreted as a ritual structure and it was surrounded by six free-standing posts; the smaller structure (structure C) appears to have been domestic (Newman 1992; 1993; 1994). Concentric structural trenches were also identified at the Rath of the Synods, Tara, Co. Meath (Grogan 2008). Significantly, each of these was a high-status ritual or 'royal' site.

The Cookstown ring-ditches were not foundation slots but rather appear to have been the remains of open ditches which silted up gradually. The deformation apparent in the southern side of both ring-ditches at Cookstown suggests that they were contemporary, or at least that one was built relatively soon after the other. Considering that the ditches constituted no physical barrier to movement into the

monument's interior, it is likely that they were associated with some form of ritual (Fig. 3.9). Bounded space formed a significant element of Irish Iron Age ritual sites (Dowling 2006). Comparisons for Cookstown may be drawn with the Iron Age sanctuaries and temples such as Hayling Island in Hampshire, England, or the Romano-Gallo temple at St Maur in France, where the internal 'shrines' were surrounded by enclosures, creating an ambulatory and separating spaces of different levels of sacredness (Cunliffe 2004, 112; Dowling 2006, 19–20). While these sites incorporated structures, at Cookstown the interior 'sacred space' was open and visible. Even so, the ring-ditches at Cookstown may still be interpreted as separating space and controlling movement. The slightly offset arrangement of the entrances into the Cookstown ring-ditch suggests the movement of people into and between the ring-ditches. Furthermore, the creation of entrances into the interior of the ring-ditches, which were originally created as complete circles, hints at changes in the nature of ritual on the site over time. If, as their position indicates, the surrounding pits were associated with the ritual nature of the ring-ditches, radiocarbon dates indicate that the whole complex may have been in use for several centuries, perhaps with a shift in ritual focus from the ring-ditches to the surrounding pits.

Each of the three pits outside the ring-ditches contained charred barley grains. McClatchie (2007, 211) speculated that cereal foodstuffs may have played a part in ceremonial activities in the structure at Kerloge. This may also have been the case at Cookstown. Dowling (2006, 24) noted that lighting fires in and around sacred boundary ditches may have acted to 'cleanse the boundary of malignant influences and revitalise the protective strength of the perimeter zone'. While there is no evidence at Cookstown for *in situ* burning in either of the ring-ditches, it is possible that the three surrounding pits served this ritual purpose.

Iron Age ditches, often places of deposition, particularly at entrances, can themselves be viewed as sacred spaces (Dowling 2006). Cookstown, however, did not contain significant volumes of deposited material. The primary fills of the ring-ditch contained flecks of burnt bone too poorly preserved to identify. Animal bone inclusions in the ditches were from large domesticates only—cattle, sheep/goat, pig and horse—and this is similar to the range of species identified at Iron Age sites such as Knockaulin (Crabtree 1990), but in much smaller quantities. Neither the glass bracelet nor the bronze spiral ring were found close to the 'entrance' features in the ring-ditches. The nature of ritual activity at Cookstown was much more modest than at the 'royal sites' such as Tara or Knockaulin. In fact, Cookstown's ring-ditch complex may be characterised as a small-scale 'shrine' of local significance, perhaps only used by the adjacent settlement.

Conclusion

Ireland's high-status Iron Age ritual sites have maintained their position in folklore and popular culture and have been the focus of archaeological investigations for some time. Little is known, however, about the smaller, local ritual sites such as the example described here. As at the high-status ritual sites, the builders of the site at Cookstown used concentric circular enclosures, but on a much smaller scale. Whereas the high-status Iron Age sites like Tara were prominently situated at locations that were already infused with ritual significance and incorporated often impressive structures, earthworks and older monuments, Cookstown's ritual site was discreet, low-key, probably adjacent to an agricultural settlement and involved the use of low-level earthworks rather than monumental upstanding structures. Cookstown's Iron Age ritual complex appears to have been in use for several centuries, perhaps with a shift in focus from the ring-ditches to the surrounding pits. Only a very few objects were deposited as votive offerings in the ditches at Cookstown, in contrast to high-status ritual sites. Perhaps foodstuffs, the remains of which were found both in the ring-ditches and in the surrounding pits, were the most significant, or the most appropriate, ritual offerings for an agricultural community to make in their local shrine.

Acknowledgements

This paper was prepared following a short presentation at a one-day conference on the Iron Age in Ireland in 2007, at the invitation of Chris Corlett and Michael Potterton. The archaeological excavation at Cookstown was directed by the author for CRDS Ltd on behalf of Meath County Council and was funded by the National Roads Authority. I would like to express my gratitude to Finola O'Carroll, CRDS Project Manager, and Maria Fitzgerald, Meath County Council Project Archaeologist, and in particular to the excavation and post-excavation team and the specialists who worked with me on this site. Donal Fallon offered constructive advice on drafts of this paper but any mistakes or omissions are my own.

Bibliography

Becker, K., Ó Néill, J. and O'Flynn, L. 2008 Iron Age Ireland: finding an invisible people. Unpublished report prepared for the Heritage Council (project 16365).

Carroll, J. 2001 Glass bangles as a regional development in early medieval Ireland. In M. Redknap (ed.), *Pattern and purpose in Insular art*, 101–14. Oxford.

Caulfield, S. 1977 The beehive quern in Ireland. *Journal of the Royal Society of Antiquaries of Ireland* **107**, 104–38.

Clarke, L. and Carlin, N. 2006 Life and death in County Meath. *Archaeology Ireland* **21** (3), 22–5.

Clutterbuck, R. 2006 Wretched beyond description: the excavation of a cottier's cabin in Cookstown, Co. Meath. *Seanda* **1**, 46–7.

Clutterbuck, R. 2008 Report on archaeological excavation of Site 25, Cookstown, County Meath. Unpublished report prepared for the National Roads Authority and Meath County Council (3 vols).

Clutterbuck, R. 2009 Cookstown, Co. Meath: a medieval rural settlement. In C. Corlett and M. Potterton (eds), *Rural settlement in medieval Ireland in the light of recent archaeological excavations*, 27–47. Bray.

Collins, A. 2009 R158 Realignment scheme, Summerhill to Kilcock road improvement scheme: final report licence 07E0164, Site 2: Summerhill Demesne, Co. Meath. Unpublished report prepared for the National Monuments Service, DEHLG, Dublin.

Crabtree, P. 1990 Subsistence and ritual: the faunal remains from Dún Ailinne, Co. Kildare, Ireland. *Emania* **7**, 22–5.

Cunliffe, B. 2004 *Iron Age Britain*. Bath.

Dowling, G. 2006 The liminal boundary: an analysis of the sacral potency of the ditch at Ráith na Ríg, Tara, Co. Meath. *Journal of Irish Archaeology* **15**, 15–38.

FitzGerald, M. 2006 Archaeological discoveries on a new section of the N2 in counties Meath and Dublin. In J.

O'Sullivan and M. Stanley (eds), *Settlement, industry and ritual*, 29–42. Dublin.

Frazer, W. 2007 Ashbourne Town Centre. *Excavations 2004*, 283–4. Bray.

Grogan, E. 2008 *The Rath of the Synods, Tara, Co. Meath: excavations by Seán P. Ó Ríordáin*. Bray.

Johns, C. 1996 *The jewellery of Roman Britain: Celtic and classical traditions*. Ann Arbor, MI.

Johnston, S.A. and Wailes, B. 2007 *Dún Ailinne: excavations at an Irish royal site, 1968–1975*. Philadelphia.

Keeley, V.J. 1996 Ballydavis. *Excavations 1995*, 51–2. Bray.

Keeley, V.J. 1999 Iron Age discoveries at Ballydavis. In P.G. Lane and W. Nolan (eds), *Laois: history and society*, 25–34. Dublin.

Kilbride-Jones, H.E. 1938 Glass armlets in Britain. *Proceedings of the Society of Antiquaries of Scotland* **72**, 366–95.

Lynn, C. 2000 Navan Fort Site C excavations, June 1999. *Emania* **18**, 5–16.

McClatchie, M. 2007 The study of non-wood plant macro-remains: investigating past societies and landscapes. In E.M. Murphy and N.J. Whitehouse (eds), *Environmental archaeology in Ireland*, 194–220. Oxford.

McLaughlin, M. and Conran, S. 2008 The emerging Iron Age of south Munster. *Seanda* **3**, 51–3.

McQuade, M. 2005 Archaeological excavation of a multi-period prehistoric settlement at Waterunder, Mell, Co. Louth. *County Louth Archaeological and Historical Journal* **26** (1), 31–66.

Mitchell, G.F. 1965 Littleton Bog: an Irish agricultural record. *Journal of the Royal Society of Antiquaries of Ireland* **95**, 121–32.

Mitchell, G.F. and Ryan, M. 1997 *Reading the Irish landscape* (3rd edn). Dublin.

Monk, M.A. 1981 Post-Roman drying kilns and the problems of function: a preliminary statement. In D. Ó Corráin (ed.), *Irish antiquity: essays and studies presented to Professor M.J. O'Kelly*, 216–30. Dublin.

Monk, M.A. 1986 Evidence from macroscopic plant remains for crop husbandry in prehistoric and early historic Ireland: a review. *Journal of Irish Archaeology* **3**, 31–6.

Monk, M.A. and Kelleher, E. 2005 An assessment of the archaeological evidence for Irish corn-drying kilns in the light of the results of archaeological experiments and archaeo-botanical studies. *Journal of Irish Archaeology* **14**, 77–114.

Mullins, G. 2009 N6 Galway to east Ballinasloe PPP scheme: archaeological contract 3, phase 2: final report: ministerial direction A024; excavation registration E2069: Cross, Co. Galway, cemetery site, ring-barrow,

cremations and extended inhumations. Unpublished report prepared for the National Roads Authority.

Murray, E. 2008 Animal bone report. In R. Clutterbuck, 'Report on archaeological excavation of Site 25, Cookstown, County Meath', vol. III, 128–45. Unpublished report prepared for the National Roads Authority and Meath County Council.

National Roads Authority Archaeological Database: www.nra.ie/Archaeology/NRAArchaeologicalDatabase.

Nelson, C. and Walsh, W. 1993 *The trees of Ireland*. Dublin.

Newman, C. 1992 Raffin Fort, Raffin, Co. Meath. *Excavations 1991*, no. 107. Bray.

Newman, C. 1993 Raffin Fort, Raffin, Co. Meath. *Excavations 1992*, no. 153. Bray.

Newman, C. 1994 Raffin Fort, Raffin, Co. Meath. *Excavations 1993*, no. 183. Bray.

Newman, C. 1997 *Tara: an archaeological survey*. Dublin.

O'Brien, E. 1990 Iron Age burial practices in Leinster: continuity and change. *Emania* **7**, 37–42.

O'Brien, E. 2003 Burial practices in Ireland: first to seventh centuries AD. In J. Downes and A. Ritchie (eds), *Sea change: Orkney and northern Europe in the later Iron Age, AD 300–800*, 62–72. Balgavies.

O'Carroll, F. (forthcoming) Archaeological excavations on the N2 Finglas to Ashbourne road scheme. Dublin.

O'Connell, A. 2007 The elusive Iron Age: a rare and exciting site type is uncovered at Lismullin, Co. Meath. *Seanda* **2**, 52–4.

Raftery, B. 1983 *A catalogue of Irish Iron Age antiquities* (2 vols). Marburg.

Raftery, B. 1994 *Pagan Celtic Ireland: the enigma of the Irish Iron Age*. London.

Roche, H. and Grogan, E. 2008 Prehistoric pottery report. In R. Clutterbuck, 'Report on archaeological excavation of Site 25, Cookstown, County Meath', vol. III, 30–1. Unpublished report prepared for the National Roads Authority and Meath County Council.

Schweitzer, H. 2005 Iron Age toe-rings from Rath, County Meath, on the N2 Finglas–Ashbourne road scheme. In J. O'Sullivan and M. Stanley (eds), *Recent archaeological discoveries on national road schemes 2004*, 93–8. Bray.

Stevenson, R.B.K. 1954 Native bangles and Roman glass. *Proceedings of the Society of Antiquaries of Scotland* **88**, 208–21.

Stuijts, I. 2005 Wood and charcoal identification. In M. Gowen, J. Ó Néill and M. Phillips (eds), *The Lisheen Mine Archaeological Project, 1996–8*, 137–85. Bray.

Taylor, K. 2008 At home on the road: two Iron Age sites in County Tipperary. *Seanda* **3**, 54–5.

Waterman, D.M. 1997 *Excavations at Navan Fort, 1961–71* (ed. C.J. Lynn). Belfast.

APPENDIX 3.1: A REVIEW OF THE PLANT MACROFOSSIL ANALYSIS FROM IRON AGE DEPOSITS (Susan Lyons)

Introduction

This report discusses the archaeobotanical assemblage recorded specifically from Iron Age deposits associated with the archaeological excavations at Cookstown, Co. Meath (03E1252). Archaeobotany is the study of plant remains from archaeological sites and can help in understanding the economic use of plants and the local flora that may have surrounded a site. The identification and analysis of domesticated plant remains and wild taxa can highlight the role of arable farming on a site, agricultural techniques and changes to crop regimes over time.

Sample strategy

An on-site soil-sampling strategy was implemented at Cookstown, and features and deposits deemed archaeologically significant were sampled. A total of 3,293 litres of bulk soil samples were taken from primary, secondary and tertiary deposits of all known features associated with occupational activity. These were processed by CRDS Ltd. Seventeen samples were directly associated with Iron Age features and the results of these samples form the basis for this report. These features include pits F2062, F3864, F3872, F3874, F4032, F4037 and F4042 and ditches F4002 and F4004.

Methodology and results

The soil samples were subjected to a system of flotation.[5] The processed flot samples were viewed under a low-powered binocular microscope (magnification x0.8 to x5) and plant remains were recorded using an abundance key to highlight the concentrations/quantities of material identified from each sample: + = rare (1–10); ++ = occasional (11–50); +++ = common (51–100); and ++++ = abundant (>100). Plant species determinations are made using the author's seed collection and standard seed atlases and references.[6] The results are summarised in Table 3.3 and arranged according to feature type. All plant remains were preserved by carbonisation.

Wood charcoal

Charcoal was recorded as small fragments (<50mm in length) and fibres from all samples. The most notable charcoal concentrations (+++) were recorded from pits F2062 (F2503

and F2504), F3864 (F3862), F3872 (F3861 and F3872) and F3874 (F3867).

Carbonised cereal remains

Carbonised cereal grains were recorded in relatively low concentrations (+ and ++) from pits F2062 (F2502, F2503 and F2504), F3864 (F3859, F3862 and F3863), F3874 (F3867) and F4037 (F4038) and ditch F4002 (F4003). The highest concentration of grain was identified from pit F2062, F3872 (F3872), pit F4032 and pit F4042. All grains were in a poor state of preservation and this hindered further species identification in many cases.

Barley (*Hordeum* sp.) dominated the crop assemblage and was recorded from all of these features. Wheat (*Triticum* sp.) grains, many of which were tentatively identified as bread/club wheat (*T. aestivum/compactum*), were recorded from F2062, F3864, F3872 and F3874. Oat (*Avena* sp.) grains were identified from F3874, but the abraded nature of the grain and the absence of chaff components prevented any definitive species identification. Carbonised cereal grains that were in a poor state of preservation appear in the table as indeterminate cereal grain (cereal indet.). These grains are difficult to identify to species level and can become vesicular and eroded as a result of charring at high temperatures, the burning of damp grain or degradation owing to redeposition and/or exposure.

Carbonised wild taxa

The remains of wild radish (*Raphanus raphanistrum*) in the form of fragmented siliqua pods or seed capsules were identified from pit F3874. The seeds of goosefoot (*Chenopodium* sp.) were also recorded in low concentrations from pits F2062 and F4042.

Carbonised nut shell

The fragmented remains of hazelnut shell were identified from pit F3872. Nut shell recorded from archaeological sites is usually interpreted as:

- the waste debris of gathered foodstuffs that have been discarded onto fires;
- the remnants of drying or parching hazelnuts near or over a fire; or
- material collected with wood for fuel or kindling.

Since the nut shell from F3872 was such a small amount, its origins here are uncertain.

Discussion

Carbonisation of plant remains

Charred plant remains are those which have been heated to more than *c.* 200°C but where there was not enough oxygen

Table 3.3—Cookstown: composition of plant remains from Iron Age features (key: + = rare (1–10); ++ = occasional (11–50); +++ = common (51–100); and ++++ = abundant (>100)).

Feature	Feature	Sample	Feature type	Approx. vol. (ml)	Charcoal	Carbonised cereal grain	Carbonised wild taxa	Carbonised hazelnut shell	Comments
Pit (F2062)	2502	285	The upper fill of pit	20ml	++	++	+		Barley ++ / Wheat + (poor preservation)
	2503	286	Fill of a pit	50ml	+++	++			Barley ++ / Wheat ++ (poor preservation)
	2504	287	Fill of pit	100ml	+++	+	+		cf. Wheat + (poor preservation) / Chenopodium sp. +
Pit (F3864)	3859	409	Upper fill of pit	20ml	++	++			Barley ++ (poor preservation)
	3862	405	Layer of charcoal, burnt wood and fire-reddened clay	50ml	+++	++			Barley + / Wheat + (poor preservation) / Oak charcoal noted
	3863	406	Base fill of a pit	20ml	++	++			Barley ++ (very poor preservation)
Pit (F3872)	3861	432	Almost pure ash fill of a pit	50ml	+++	+		+	Barley + / Wheat indet. + / Hazelnut shell +
	3872	433	Fill of pit	50ml	+++	+++			Barley +++ (poor preservation, but hulled variety identified)
Pit (F3874)	3867	407	Fill of pit	20ml	+++	++			Wheat ++ / Barley + / Oat + / Raphanus raphanistrum + / Animal bone ++
Ditch (F4002)	4003	113	One of the primary fills of the outer ring-ditch	10ml	++				Charcoal only
	4003	94	One of the primary fills of the outer ring-ditch	10ml	++				Charcoal only
	4003	95	One of the primary fills of the outer ring-ditch	20ml	++				Charcoal only
	4003	125	One of the primary fills of the outer ring-ditch	10ml	+	+			Cereal indet. (2)
Ditch (F4004)	4005	105	The upper fill of the inner ditch	10ml	+				
Pit (F4032)	4033	195	The fill of the pit to the north of the outer ring-ditch	100ml	++	+++			Barley +++ / Cereal indet. ++
Pit (F4037)	4038	213	Upper fill of a pit	30ml	++	++			Barley + / Cereal indet. ++
Pit (F4042)	4046	217	Lower or primary fill of a pit found outside the south-eastern quadrant of the outer ring-ditch (F4002)	100ml	++	+++	+		Barley +++ (poor preservation) / Chenopodium sp. +

to complete the burning process. Instead, the organic components are converted to a more carbon-rich resilient material or to carbon itself rather than to ash (Boardman and Jones 1990). Despite being subjected to high temperatures, many charred remains retain a morphology or exterior detail that can aid plant identification to genus or even species level. The carbonisation process obviously affects different species and plant components in different ways, where finer, lighter material can be destroyed more easily than larger elements. It must be noted, therefore, that the charred plant remains recovered from archaeological features can reflect the results of the carbonisation process as much as how and what plant remains were used on a site.

Plant remains from Iron Age deposits

The majority of the samples contained the remains of charcoal, which is a common indicator of occupational and domestic activity on archaeological sites. The presence of charcoal usually reflects (a) the use of hearths/kilns and firing activities in and around the site and/or (b) the cleaning out and dumping of this burnt debris into nearby open features.

Carbonised cereal grain from archaeological sites is interpreted as the residual debris from corn-drying events. The cereal assemblage from Iron Age deposits at Cookstown, albeit small, was made up of barley and wheat, which were both cultivated in Ireland from the prehistoric period (Monk 1986, 32). Oat, which was recorded from pit F3874, is generally considered to have been cultivated from the early medieval period in Ireland (*ibid.*, 33) and little is known about its use in the prehistoric Irish economy and agriculture. It has been surmised that oats recovered from a prehistoric context are either intrusive components of a later date or wild oats (*Avena fatua*), a common field weed, which may have grown among other cultivated crops at the time (Godwin 1975, 404; Fairweather and Ralston 1993).

To date, the archaeobotanical evidence in Ireland for Iron Age arable agriculture is quite patchy (Monk 1986, 33; McClatchie 2007, 210). The emergence of beehive querns during this period (Caulfield 1977), however, suggests that crop husbandry was being practised at some level. The analysis of carbonised plant remains from sites excavated as part of the Gas Pipeline to the West project (Johnston 2007) highlighted the chronological changes in cereal crop use from the Neolithic to the Iron Age. The study showed a decline in wheat from the middle Bronze Age, with barley becoming the predominant crop during the later Bronze Age and Iron Age (*ibid.*, 70). Oats, too, began to emerge during this time, becoming much more common in the early historic period (*ibid.*). This trend coincided with the beginning of the historic

period, where cereal assemblages are dominated by barley and oats, with a much lesser occurrence of wheat (Monk 1991). Barley, oats and wheat were also identified from Iron Age sites at Kerloge, Co. Wexford (McClatchie 2007, 210), and Waterunder, Co. Louth (McQuade 2005, 41), and from later Bronze Age/Iron Age assemblages from sites excavated along the N8, especially Shanballyduff and Kilemly, Co. Tipperary, and Brackbraun, Co. Limerick (Halwas *et al.* 2009). Barley was also present in eight pits associated with the excavations at the Haughey's Fort complex (Weir and Conway 1988, 30). Archaeobotanical investigations carried out by Helbæk (1952) on cereal grain imprints from Britain highlighted the prominence of barley in the south of England from the late Bronze Age into the Iron Age. The presence of wild oats was also reported from British Iron Age sites at Maiden Castle and Fifield Bavant (Jessen and Helbæk 1944; Helbæk 1952, 229) and at Aldwick, Barley, near Royston in Hertfordshire (Renfrew 1965; Renfrew 1973, 89).

It is also important to note that climatic change and localised environmental conditions would have played a part in crop cultivation. Wheat favours dry conditions and mineral-rich soils and may have been rarely grown in damper climates (Renfrew 1973, 66). In contrast, barley and oats are more versatile crops that can grow in wetter climates and can be cultivated on most soils (Monk *et al.* 1998). Barley is tolerant of saline and alkaline soils (Leonard and Martin 1963, 500), while oats are less sensitive to acidity than barley and wheat (Martin and Leonard 1967, 480) and grow well in the humid, wet Irish climate, tolerating poorer soils where other crop types may not thrive (Clarke 1991, 173). This, together with the fact that they are used both for human consumption and as animal fodder, may account for their high frequency on later prehistoric sites and may contribute to their preponderance on Iron Age sites in Ireland.

The weed seed assemblage recorded from Cookstown was very small and confined to F2062, F3874 and F4062. After a harvest, the cultivated crop goes through a series of processing procedures in which the product (grain) and the various by-products (chaff, straw and weed seeds) are separated from each other (van der Veen 1989). The absence of weeds and chaff from a carbonised cereal assemblage can indicate that cereals were being prepared for either long-term storage or grinding and milling (*ibid.*). Grains would require full processing (removal of chaff and weeds) prior to storage to prevent spoilage of the crop.

Goosefoot (*Chenopodium* sp.) is a typical weed of disturbed areas and the margins of arable fields. This material is likely to have been brought to the site with the gathered crop and entered kilns inadvertently or was used as a fuel component (Hillman 1981). Wild radish (*Raphanus raphanistrum*) capsules or siliqua pods are quite large and can be more difficult to extract during the initial crop-processing procedures. As a result, this material can enter and be kilned with a pure grain assemblage. It has also been suggested that wild radish may have been commonly eaten as a supplement to cereals in times of bad harvests (Geraghty 1996, 32), which may also account for this material within F3874. A larger cache of this species would be required for any definitive interpretation to be made. The carbonisation process can also play a part in misinterpreting an assemblage. Inevitably, finer elements of the cereal and weed components will become charred and disintegrate more quickly than others, which will also alter the original assemblage and make interpretations more difficult (van der Veen 1989, 305).

Distribution of plant remains

The carbonised plant remains recorded at Cookstown were concentrated within three main areas:

- a cluster of pits at the centre of the site (F3864, F3874 and F3872);
- a single shallow burnt pit (F2062) 58m to the south-east;
- the concentric ring-ditches (F4002 and F4004) 115m south of the pit cluster, with three burnt pits (F4032, F4037 and F4042) immediately outside.

Pits (F3864, F3874 and F3872)

F3864 and F3872 displayed evidence for *in situ* burning in the form of reddened clay, which suggests that these features were associated with crop-drying, perhaps functioning as kilns. Crop-drying was an essential yet hazardous domestic and industrial process carried out for a number of reasons, such as drying crops to aid threshing, de-husking and removing the awns of hulled grain, improving the storage quality of the grain, removing excess moisture, killing germination and pests like the grain weevil (*Sitophilus granaries*), and preparing the grain for grinding or milling (Scott 1951; Monk 1981).

While barley is the dominant cereal recorded from F3864 and F3872, wheat was also identified, albeit in lower concentrations. That the grain was left *in situ* could be because (a) these kilns had burnt down but were not properly cleaned before being reused or (b) the grain represented a build-up of material that had accumulated in the bowl of the kiln during several dryings. All grains from these deposits were also very abraded, which would support the interpretation of kiln reuse, where the grain would have been consistently exposed to extreme heat during several drying episodes. It is difficult to establish whether both barley and wheat were being dried together at the time of the conflagrations or whether they represent different phases of kiln use. While barley is the dominant crop in the assemblage, it is tempting to suggest that this was the last crop being dried. The barley, wheat and oats together from nearby F3874, however, may also represent the remains of multiple drying events from previous drying episodes, the remains of which were not cleaned out but became mixed over time with later deposits.

The lack of any obvious *in situ* burning and the presence of a mixed cereal assemblage (wheat, barley and oats) from F3874 suggest that this pit functioned as a dumping ground or refuse pit. The animal bone recorded in this feature (Holden and Lyons 2006) also supports this interpretation. Nearby corn-drying kilns (F3864 and F3872) would have required regular cleaning out (Monk 1981) and therefore charcoal and charred grain debris would have been dumped into nearby open features or into purposely dug dumping pits. The only evidence for oats at the site was recorded from F3874. In the absence of a larger cache of grain, however, it is difficult to put forward any interpretations about its role in the arable economy of the site or to say whether it was associated with the Iron Age activity.

Burnt pit (F2062)

Based on the carbonised cereal grain identified, together with evidence for *in situ* burning, F2062 was also interpreted as a corn-drying kiln. Barley was again present in this feature, but there was a higher occurrence of wheat grains. Radiocarbon dating of this feature indicates that it is later than the cluster of pits previously discussed. Despite this, the composition of the grain assemblage remains relatively unchanged and the higher incidence of wheat could just represent the localised remains of the cereal assemblage being dried within F2062 rather than a shift in crop use at the site.

Ring-ditch (F4002 and F4004) and burnt pits (F4032, F4037 and F4042)

F4032, F4037 and F4042 all contained evidence of *in situ* burning, along with carbonised cereal grains, which implies that these features were most probably related to crop-drying or kiln activity. F4032 and F4042 contained the highest number of cereal grains, in the form of barley, with some grains of indeterminate species. Barley was the only definitive grain recorded from here, suggesting that it was the last or only crop being dried within these features or in this area of the site. Whether all three features are contemporary is difficult to ascertain based on the cereal assemblage alone. The radiocarbon date for F4032 (cal. AD 1–230) puts it much later than the neighbouring ring-ditch F4004 (360–50 cal. BC). As a result, it is very unlikely that F4032 and perhaps the other two pits were associated with the activities surrounding the ring-ditches. The indeterminate cereal grains from F4002 are likely to be the redeposited charred remains from earlier drying events, which entered the ditch when it was open. Little more information can be deduced based on such a small assemblage. Whether the cereal grain component from this part of the site was associated with ritual activity, as speculated (Clutterbuck 2008), is difficult to ascertain based on a small assemblage of grain. Carbonised cereal grain has been identified from ritual deposits dating from the middle Bronze Age and into the later prehistoric period (Johnston 2007, 75) in Ireland, but whether the grains recovered are stray finds or deliberate acts of deposition is still open to debate.

Summary

The archaeobotanical assemblage recorded from Iron Age features at Cookstown represents corn-drying. It is difficult to ascertain whether this was associated with domestic, industrial or ritual activities. The assemblage contained primarily carbonised barley grain, with much lesser incidences of wheat, oats and wild plant remains. Whether this preponderance of barley is following the archaeobotanical pattern already beginning to emerge from other Irish Iron Age sites or just reflects the localised use of barley in this area at this time is difficult to establish definitively. Overall, the cereal assemblage from Cookstown was relatively small, considering the number of possible kiln features recorded (F2062, F3864, F3872, F4032, F4037 and F4042). The absence of burnt grain from archaeological sites and features can reflect the results of the carbonisation process, which is a method of destruction, as much as how and what plant remains were used on a site. It must also be noted that a successful crop-drying episode would result in few or no charred remains to analyse. The absence of cereal chaff and weed seeds could be interpreted as evidence for long-term storage or for grinding and milling, but this is speculative and a much larger assemblage would be required for any definitive interpretations to be reached.

It is difficult to postulate from the cereal grain assemblage whether there was a shift in crop regimes over time at Cookstown or whether barley was the dominant cereal type being processed or dried during the Iron Age use of the site. In the absence of a more substantial grain assemblage and cereal chaff, it is difficult to establish what level of arable agriculture was practised, or indeed whether such activities were directly associated with the features recorded. It must be remembered, however, that this assemblage represents just a snapshot of the grain destroyed during drying activities and does not reflect earlier and later crop-drying events, so all interpretations are based only on the plants that have survived.

Bibliography

Beijerinck, W. 1976 *Zadenatlas der Nederlandsche Flora*. Amsterdam.

Boardman, S. and Jones, G. 1990 Experiments of the effects of charring on cereal plant components. *Journal of Archaeological Science* **12**, 1–11.

Cappers, R.T.J., Bekker, R.M. and Jans, J.E.A. 2006 *Digital seed atlas of the Netherlands*. Groningen.

Caulfield, S. 1977 The beehive quern in Ireland. *Journal of the Royal Society of Antiquaries of Ireland* **107**, 104–38.

Clapham, A.R., Tutin, T.G. and Warburg, E.F. 1957 *Flora of the British Isles*. Cambridge.

Clarke, A. 1991 The Irish economy, 1600–60. In T.W. Moody, F.X. Martin and F.J. Byrne (eds), *Early modern Ireland, 1534–1691*, 168–86. New York.

Clutterbuck, R. 2008 Report on archaeological excavation of Site 25, Cookstown, County Meath. Unpublished report prepared for the National Roads Authority and Meath County Council (3 vols).

Fairweather, A. and Ralston, I. 1993 The Neolithic timber hall at Balbridie, Grampian Region, Scotland: the building, the date, the plant macrofossils. *Antiquity*, **67** (255), 313–23.

Geraghty, S. 1996 *Viking Dublin: botanical evidence from Fishamble Street*. Dublin.

Godwin, H. 1975 *History of the British flora: a factual basis for phytogeography* (2nd edn). Cambridge.

Halwas, S., O'Donnell, L. and Geber, J. 2009 The environmental and faunal remains. In M. McQuade, B. Molloy and C. Moriarty, *In the shadow of the Galtees: archaeological excavations along the N8 Cashel to Mitchelstown road scheme*, 262–75. Dublin.

Helbæk, H. 1952 Early crops in southern England. *Proceedings of the Prehistoric Society* **18**, 194–233.

Hillman, G. 1981 Reconstructing crop husbandry practices from charred remains of crops. In R. Mercer (ed.), *Farming practices in British prehistory* (2nd edn), 123–62. Edinburgh.

Holden, T. and Lyons, S. 2006 Soil sample assessment for Site 25: Cookstown, Co. Meath. Unpublished report for CRDS Ltd.

Institute of Archaeologists of Ireland 2007 Environmental sampling guidelines for archaeologists (www.iai.ie/Publications_Files/IAIEnvironmentalSampl ingGuidelinesFINAL.pdf).

Jessen, K. and Helbæk, H. 1944 *Cereal in Great Britain and Ireland in prehistoric and early historic times*. Det Kongelige Danske Videnskabernes Selskab, Biologiske Skrifter 3 (2). Copenhagen.

Johnston, P. 2007 Environmental archaeology: identifying patterns of exploitation in the Bronze Age. In E. Grogan, L. O'Donnell and P. Johnston, *The Bronze Age landscapes of the Pipeline to the West: an integrated archaeological and environmental assessment*, 70–7. Bray.

Leonard, W.H. and Martin, J.H. 1963 *Cereal crops*. New York and London.

McClatchie, M. 2007 The study of non-wood plant macro-remains: investigating past societies and landscapes. In E.M. Murphy and N.J. Whitehouse (eds), *Environmental archaeology in Ireland*, 194–220. Oxford.

McQuade, M. 2005 Archaeological excavation of a multi-period prehistoric settlement at Waterunder, Mell, Co. Louth. *County Louth Archaeological and Historical Journal* **26** (1), 31–66.

Martin, J.H. and Leonard, W.H. 1967 *Principles of field crop production*. New York and London.

Monk, M. 1981 Post-Roman drying kilns and the problem of function: a preliminary statement. In D. Ó Corráin (ed.), *Irish antiquity: essays and studies presented to Professor M.J. O'Kelly*, 216–30. Dublin.

Monk, M.A. 1986 Evidence from macroscopic plant remains for crop husbandry in prehistoric and early historic Ireland: a review. *Journal of Irish Archaeology* **3**, 31–6.

Monk, M. 1991 Archaeo-botanical evidence for field crop plants in early historic Ireland. In J. Renfrew (ed.), *New light on farming: recent developments in palaeo-ethnobotany*, 315–28. Edinburgh.

Monk, M.A., Tierney, J. and Hannon, M. 1998 Archaeo-botanical studies and early medieval Munster. In M.A. Monk and J. Sheehan (eds), *Early medieval Munster: archaeology, history and society*, 65–75. Cork.

Pearsall, D. 2000 *Palaeo-ethnobotany: handbook of procedures* (2nd edn). San Diego.

Renfrew, J.M. 1965 Appendix IV: Grain impressions from the Iron Age sites at Wandleburg and Barley. In M.D. Cras'ter, 'Aldwick, Barley: recent work on the Iron Age site'. *Proceedings of the Cambridge Antiquarian Society* **58**, 1–11.

Renfrew, J.M. 1973 *Palaeo-ethnobotany: the prehistoric food plants of the Near East and Europe*. London.

Scott, L. 1951 Corn-drying kilns. *Antiquity* **20**, 196–208.

Stace, C. 1997 *New flora of the British Isles* (2nd edn). Cambridge.

Van der Veen, M. 1989 Charred grain assemblages from Roman-period corn-dryers in Britain. *Archaeological Journal* **146**, 302–19.

Weir, D.A. and Conway, M. 1988 Haughey's Fort: a preliminary palaeo-botanical analysis. *Emania* **4**, 28–31.

Notes

1. Excavations at Cookstown (03E1252) were funded by the National Roads Authority through Meath County Council. The centre of the site is located at NGR 304860/253000.

2. Only feature numbers illustrated in the accompanying figures are quoted in the text. The fully referenced descriptions and list of feature numbers are available in the final excavation report for Cookstown (Clutterbuck 2008; O'Carroll, forthcoming).

3. The full find number, following the conventions of the National Museum of Ireland, consists of the excavation number, the feature number and the number of the find from that feature; for example, 03E1252:4003:0001 is the first archaeological find from feature F4003 on excavation 03E1252. For the purposes of this paper, however, this system has been abbreviated by leaving out the excavation number. The full description of finds is available in the site's final excavation report (Clutterbuck 2008; O'Carroll, forthcoming).

4. NRA Archaeological Database: www.nra.ie/Archaeology/NRAArchaeologicalDatabase/; accessed 6 March 2009.

5. Soil samples were processed according to the standards and guidelines outlined in Institute of Archaeologists of Ireland 2007 and Pearsall 2000.

6. Clapham *et al.* 1957; Beijerinck 1976; Stace 1997; Cappers *et al.* 2006.

4. Week at the knees: the discovery of partial human remains in a badger sett at Ballysimon, Co. Limerick

Tracy Collins

Introduction

This essay details the archaeological excavation of the isolated partial remains of a human skeleton identified during archaeological works as part of the construction of the Southern Limerick Ring Road Phase 1 in 2000. On 22 December that year, the survey, recording and systematic destruction of a badger sett in a large field, locally known as the 'camp field', at Ballysimon, Co. Limerick, were undertaken by Chris Small and wildlife ranger Seamus Hassett. This systematic destruction was carried out with a mechanical digger, and the work was monitored by an archaeologist. The human remains, which are the subject of this paper, were discovered by the archaeologist. The badger sett was demolished and recorded because it was within the road-take. The badgers were safely relocated.

The sett was located approximately 3km south-east of Limerick city, on the northern right bank of the River Groody, about 100m to the north-west of a medieval ringwork, which was also excavated as part of this road project

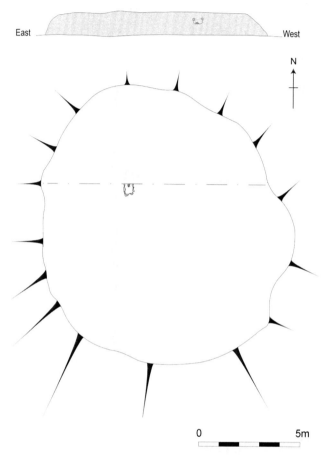

Fig. 4.2—Ballysimon: plan and section of site.

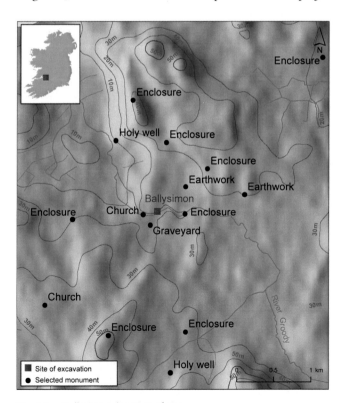

Fig. 4.1—Ballysimon: location of site.

(Collins and Cummins 2001) (Fig. 4.1). The sett (NGR 161948/155123) was in the townland of Ballysimon, in the parish of Kilmurry and the barony of Clanwilliam.

The sett had been stripped of vegetation prior to its demolition. When the scrub cover was removed, the site was revealed as a slightly irregular but fairly circular low mound, measuring approximately 12m in diameter with a maximum height of 1m, and sloping slightly to the lower ground beside the river. There was no trace of an enclosing ditch. Because of its general similarity to a barrow, which had the potential to be archaeological in nature, it was suggested by Aegis Archaeology Ltd (archaeological contractors for Limerick

County Council on the Limerick Southern Ring Road construction) that the destruction of the sett should be archaeologically supervised, as part of the ongoing archaeological works for the project, in case of archaeological remains being uncovered.

It was during this archaeological supervision that portions of two leg bones and two patellae were uncovered, projecting from the section face, as the badger sett was being dismantled. When these bones were revealed, all work ceased. The spoil created was examined but no bones were recovered, indicating that the entire archaeological feature had been discovered. On examination, it was obvious that the remains were human and articulated. It was possible to see the upper leg bones (femora) protruding from the section face where the bones were first discovered (Fig. 4.2). It was supposed from the site of the bones and their condition that they were of archaeological rather than forensic interest. The Gardaí at Roxboro, Limerick, were informed of the discovery and insisted that the removed bones be passed to John Harbison, then state pathologist, for forensic analysis. The writer subsequently received notice from the police that the bones were not of forensic interest and that the archaeological excavation could proceed. A licence to excavate was applied for, but owing to the foot-and-mouth crisis of spring 2001 excavation was not undertaken until June 2001. The excavation of the site was undertaken by the writer over the course of five days under licence 01E0030.

The excavation

Portions of leg bones and two kneecaps had been recovered in December 2000 during the demolition of the badger sett. It was thought at the time that the remainder of the skeleton would be present, but upon excavation it became apparent that only the upper portions of the lower legs were left *in situ*. It was clear from the remains that they had been cut in antiquity and post-mortem. The skeletal remains were found *c.* 15cm below the surface ground level of the badger sett and did not appear to have been disturbed by animal activity beneath. They were covered with a light mid-brown silty loam deposit and were surrounded by, and rested on, a very similar material. A badger tunnel was immediately below the human remains but had not interfered with them.

The human remains had been surrounded by a setting of twelve stones (Fig. 4.3). Despite the fact that it appeared as though the leg bones had been cut in antiquity, with the upper body and both lower legs and feet missing, the stone setting itself seemed to be an original feature, apparently contemporary with the interment of the bones. This setting, aligned north–south, was composed of limestone and some

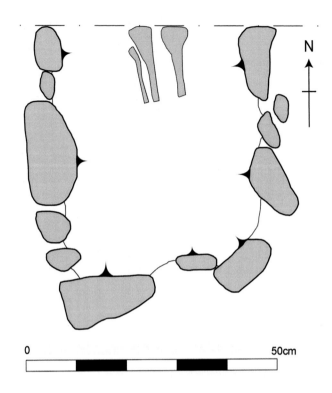

Fig. 4.3—Ballysimon: plan of excavated features.

sandstone/mudstone. It measured 60cm north–south, 40cm east–west and a maximum of 20cm in depth. The leg bones had also been aligned north–south, with the upper portions (the head end, had it been present) to the north.

The human remains

The human remains were excavated with the assistance of Linda Lynch, osteoarchaeologist with Aegis Archaeology Ltd. The setting was first removed to investigate whether it and the burial had been inserted into a cut. There was no evidence for this, and the layer below the setting and burial was archaeologically sterile and greatly disturbed by the badger tunnel beneath. There was no surface evidence of the burial and there are no known records of burials in this area. No grave-goods were recovered with the remains and there were no archaeological features or monuments in the immediate area to which the burial might have been related.

The bones that were recovered represented the diaphyses and metaphyses of the right and left femora and the right and left patellae. The proximal halves of the tibiae and the right fibula were present, while the left fibula was represented by fragments of the proximal diaphysis only. The bones represented an adult, as the epiphyses of the bones had completely fused to the metaphyses. It was not possible to determine accurately the sex of this individual.

Despite the poor preservation of the skeletal remains a number of pathological lesions were observed, suggestive of periostitis. This is a painful condition, sometimes caused by excessive physical activity, and occurs when the fibrous layer (the periosteum) directly overlying the bone becomes infected. Owing to the accumulation of fluids and pus, it becomes inflamed and a new layer of bone can form underneath (Ortner 2003, 206). It is probable that the lesions represented quite a severe condition but one from which the individual had recovered.

In addition, the right tibia appeared to have ante-mortem pathological lesions, as there were traces of at least three fracture lines on the bone. The lines were smooth and healed, indicating that the fractures had occurred some time prior to death. The lesions may have resulted from a trauma to the right knee joint. They resulted from a compressive stress, so the individual may have fallen quite sharply on the knee. There were no indications of subsequent infection, however. It seemed likely, as noted in the osteoarchaeological report (Lynch 2001), that the periostitis noted in the right tibia was actually related to the fracture. A bony growth, called an exostosis, was present on the right fibula and may have resulted from a muscle strain. An exostosis occurs when a muscle is torn and the subsequent bleeding into the tear ossifies into a bony growth. It is probable, therefore, that this exostosis was related to the healed fracture.

The surviving leg bones appeared to have been articulated when interred. The articulated tibiae and fibulae were lying north–south, with the proximal ends to the north. The distal halves of the bones and the feet appeared to have been removed in antiquity. The tibiae and fibulae were articulated, supine and extended, indicating that the individual was buried in a supine extended position with the head to the north (assuming that an entire body was originally buried; it is possible that this was a full inhumation that was truncated sometime later, though the archaeological evidence does not illustrate this event). In addition, the tibiae were in contact with each other, and it is possible that the body was very tightly bound in some type of cloth or that the knees themselves were tied prior to burial.

In summary, this individual had suffered from a quite serious non-specific infection in her/his lifetime but had recovered by the time of death. There appeared to have been a traumatic fracture of the right knee and this again had healed well before the time of death. In addition, there may have been slight degeneration of the left knee joint.

Discussion and conclusions

The radiocarbon determination (AMS) returned a date for the human remains in the latter half of the Irish Iron Age (Beta-192433, 2-sigma, cal. AD 230–460 and cal. AD 480–520). The burial and its Iron Age date present a number of interesting questions. Why, for example, was a person buried in this location, and why was (possibly) only a portion of the person interred? The Iron Age date and its north–south alignment suggest that the burial is unlikely to be Christian, as Christian tradition dictates an east–west alignment for burial. Isolated human burials, such as the one represented by the Ballysimon example, are not wholly uncommon, and from time to time isolated human remains are uncovered, some of which yield unexpected dates. For instance, an extended burial uncovered near Nenagh, Co. Tipperary (Collins and Lynch 2006), returned a date of cal. AD 660–910 (2-sigma calibration, Beta-192432). Another example is that of a complete burial found near Kildimo, Co. Limerick, which returned a date of cal. AD 400–570 (2-sigma calibration, Beta-214238) (L.G. Lynch, pers. comm.).

Known Iron Age burials were quite rare in the Irish archaeological record, but in the light of recent discoveries they are becoming increasingly less so. It appears, from the information available to date, that both inhumation and cremation were practised, and a wide variety of burial forms are found (O'Brien 1992; 1999; McGarry 2005). There are also particularly unusual burial practices, such as that recorded at Cloghermore, near Tralee, Co. Kerry, where the bones of a sub-adult dating from cal. AD 430–645 (Beta-137052) were excavated in a cave that had been used as a burial place over a long period of time, with the dating of human remains ranging from the fifth to the eleventh century AD (Connolly and Coyne 2005, 165).

Indeed, many Iron Age inhumation burials are difficult to distinguish in the field from those of other periods, such as the Bronze Age or the early medieval period, especially when grave-goods are lacking. Some scholars suppose that there was some continuity of burial practice between the periods. Native Irish burials of the Iron Age have been classified by Raftery (1981) into four distinct groups: type I, earthen monuments (ring-barrows, mounds with or without ditch); type II, secondary burials in earlier mounds; type III, cremations in simple pits; and type IV, inhumations (unprotected, protected, single or in cemeteries). The Ballysimon badger-sett burial would fit into Raftery's type II or type IV categories.

Many burials dating from the Iron Age have been found interred in older monuments (type II). At Carrowbeg North, Co. Galway, two mounds of early to mid-Bronze Age date were excavated and found to contain secondary Iron Age burials (Willmott 1939). These consisted of four inhumations, interred in the fill of the ditch of one of the mounds. Three were extended (like the one at Ballysimon) and the last was partially flexed. They were not contained in cists and were aligned north-west to south-east. Another site, excavated in the 1990s, which has superficial similarities to the Ballysimon example is at Kiltullagh Hill, Co. Roscommon. Human remains representing four people were found during quarrying and produced radiocarbon dates between AD 269 and 480, while an area around a standing stone on the hill contained a cremation and a male inhumation, radiocarbon-dated to the late Iron Age or the early medieval period. A ring-barrow, 11m in diameter, was also partially excavated. It had been extensively damaged on its northern side by quarrying. A central grave consisted of a pit containing disarticulated bones from a number of people, with the only *in situ* bones being those of a human foot (Coombs and Maude 1997).

More common are the type IV Iron Age burials. According to Raftery (1981, 191), extended inhumations in long stone cists are the most frequent. For instance, at Knowth, Co. Meath, an impressive Neolithic passage tomb in its own right, there were 27 later inhumed burials. Two of those were unprotected inhumations and four were extended skeletons in long stone cists. The majority of the burials were in a flexed position (Eogan 1974, 68–70; Raftery 1981, 191).

The AMS dating of the human remains at Ballysimon places the burial in the latter half of the Irish Iron Age. The skeletal material was buried in an existing mound. If the people who buried this individual thought that the mound was an earlier burial monument, sited as it was beside a river, with a convincing (though natural) barrow shape, then the burial would fit neatly into Raftery's type II burials. It is also possible, however, that the skeleton is a burial of type IV (single inhumations with or without stone cists), which was a much more common burial type in the Iron Age. The stone setting associated with the skeleton was very crude in construction and could not be considered a cist. Despite this, however, the stones did appear to be deliberately set and so at least it can be said that some form of protection was afforded to the remains. Perhaps, therefore, the people who interred these remains thought that they were reusing an existing burial monument and mistook a natural mound for a ring-barrow. Reuse of an existing monument is not unusual in the Iron Age, as there does not appear to have been a definitive burial monument peculiar to the period.

This discovery at Ballysimon on the bank of the River Groody represents a clearly deliberate interment, which indicates that some care was taken during the burial. Indeed, apart from the orientation this burial is similar to many Christian burials, with a noticeable lack of grave-goods. As

part of the road project, extensive areas of topsoil were stripped from the large field surrounding this burial but no further burial evidence was uncovered. This suggests that the example at Ballysimon is an isolated burial. Its truncated nature was very unusual. While it is possible that a full body was originally buried, it appeared from the analysis that the skeleton was severed midway along the legs and upper thighs, post-mortem but in antiquity. These portions may have been interred separately, in an articulated state. There is no obvious explanation for this second interpretation and direct parallels for this treatment are yet to be found by the writer.

To conclude, these human remains are unusual in a number of ways. They are severely truncated and isolated, interred beside the River Groody in a natural mound, which was later used by badgers. An entire body may have been buried or the legs may have been buried separately in the correct anatomical arrangement. The remains appear not to have had associations with any other burials—or, indeed, any other monument. Therefore it is possible that when these bones were interred in the later Iron Age they were intended as a token burial, erroneously inserted into a natural mound in the mistaken belief that it was a barrow-type burial monument.

Bibliography

Collins, T. 2001 Archaeological excavation of an isolated skeleton and isolated features at Ballysimon, County Limerick: 01E0030. Unpublished Aegis Archaeology report for client.

Collins, T. and Cummins, A. 2001 *Excavation of a medieval ringwork at Ballysimon, Co. Limerick*. Limerick.

Collins, T. and Lynch, L.G. 2006 Excavation of human remains at St Conlan's Road, Nenagh, Co. Tipperary. *Tipperary Historical Journal* (2006), 7–14.

Connolly, M. and Coyne, F. 2005 *Underworld: death and burial in Cloghermore Cave, Co. Kerry*. Bray.

Coombs, D.G. and Maude, K. 1997 Kiltullagh Hill, Kiltullagh. *Excavations 1996*, 95. Bray.

Eogan, G. 1974 Report on the excavations of some passage graves, unprotected inhumation burials and a settlement site at Knowth, Co. Meath. *Proceedings of the Royal Irish Academy* **74**C, 11–112.

Lynch, L. 2001 Analysis of human remains. In T. Collins, 'Archaeological excavation of an isolated skeleton and isolated features at Ballysimon, County Limerick: 01E0030', 26–30. Unpublished Aegis Archaeology report for client.

McGarry, T. 2005 Identifying burials of the Irish Iron Age and transitional periods, *c*. 800 BC–AD 600. *Trowel* **10**, 2–18.

O'Brien, E. 1992 Pagan and Christian burial in Ireland during the first millennium AD: continuity and change. In N. Edwards and A. Lane (eds), *The early church in Wales and the West*, 130–7. Oxford.

O'Brien, E. 1999 *Post-Roman Britain to Anglo-Saxon England: burial practices reviewed*. British Archaeological Reports, British Series 289. Oxford.

Ortner, D.J. 2003 *Identification of pathological conditions in human skeletal remains* (2nd edn). Washington DC.

Raftery, B. 1981 Iron Age burials in Ireland. In D. Ó Corráin (ed.), *Irish antiquity: essays and studies presented to Professor M.J. O'Kelly*, 173–204. Dublin.

Willmot, G.F. 1939 Two Bronze Age burials at Carrowbeg North, Belclare, County Galway. *Journal of the Galway Archaeological and Historical Society* **18**, 121–40.

5. 'Follow me up to Carlow': an outline of the Iron Age sites found along the M9/N10 route from Knocktopher, Co. Kilkenny, to Powerstown, Co. Carlow

Tim Coughlan with a contribution by Michelle Brick

Introduction

A number of Iron Age sites were discovered in counties Kilkenny and Carlow during excavations by IAC Ltd on the route of the M9/N10 Knocktopher to Powerstown: Phase 4 road. These sites demonstrate a continuity of settlement from the Bronze Age in this area, where a complex landscape with habitation, funerary and ritual activity is evident (Fig. 5.1).[1]

The existing Iron Age landscape (COMPILED BY MICHELLE BRICK)

Direct evidence of Iron Age activity in the landscape at the southern end of the M9/N10 Phase 4 is limited (Fig. 5.2). There is a marked absence of hillforts from south Kilkenny but this does not necessarily infer absence of settlement (Gibbons 1990, 20). A possible Iron Age hillfort is located at Cotterellsrath to the west of the route. To the north-east of this

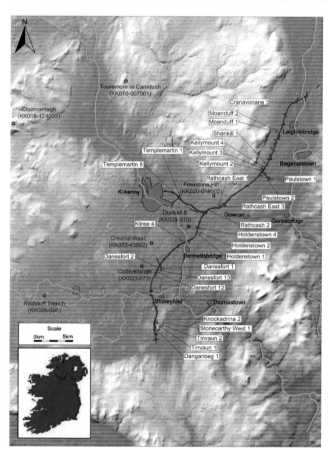

Fig. 5.1—General location map of scheme with sites annotated.

site and four miles south of Kilkenny city are the remains of a linear earthwork at Grevine West (*ibid.*), also indicating an Iron Age presence in the region. In the centre of the scheme, Iron Age activity is represented by the hillfort at Freestone Hill, where in late prehistory a defensive hillfort and inner enclosure were built encircling the hilltop (*ibid.*, 18), reusing the site of an earlier burial cairn. The site was then reoccupied *c.* AD 300 (Raftery 1969). The hill has steep slopes on all sides and a gently rounded summit, and is located in a strategic position overlooking the adjacent portions of the valleys of the rivers Nore and Barrow to the west and east, as well as the undulating lowland watershed between them to the south. The site also affords control over the upland valleys to the north as well as a view over the lower reaches of the Dinin/Douglas valleys to the north-west. Additionally, excavations were carried out at two ringforts in the townland of Dunbell, Co. Kilkenny—Dunbell 6 in 1972 and Dunbell 5 in 1990 (Foley 1974; 2006; Cassidy 1991). The ringfort settlement at Dunbell 5 in particular produced dates from the Bronze Age to the eighth and tenth centuries AD, including evidence of Iron Age occupation. Two more hillforts are located in the north of Kilkenny. Clomantagh overlooks Johnstown in north-west Kilkenny and, like Freestone Hill, the site was originally used in the Bronze Age as a funerary complex (Gibbons 1990, 18). A linear earthwork has also been recorded at Woodsgift (*ibid.*, 20) and is located directly to the south of this site. The other possible hillfort in the region is recorded at Tooremore or Carndubh to the east (*ibid.*). This site is on Corrandhu Hill, two miles east of Ballyragget, straddling the townland boundary between Toore More and Donaghmore (Condit and Gibbons 1988, 49). In addition to these sites is a linear earthwork known as the Rathduff Trench, located along the Kilkenny–Carlow border. It extends for over three miles from the River Barrow at Duninga in a north-westerly direction to the foothills of the Castlecomer plateau above Shankill (Gibbons 1990, 20). A portion of this linear earthwork was excavated at Shankill 1 as part of the M9/N10 Phase 4 and consisted of a U-shaped bank with a ditch.

Of the important late prehistoric hillfort sites in north Kilkenny, only Freestone Hill has been excavated (Raftery 1969). Current research suggests that hillforts were most active during the late Bronze Age (Grogan 2005; Raftery 1994; Mallory 1995) and many of these sites were probably in use

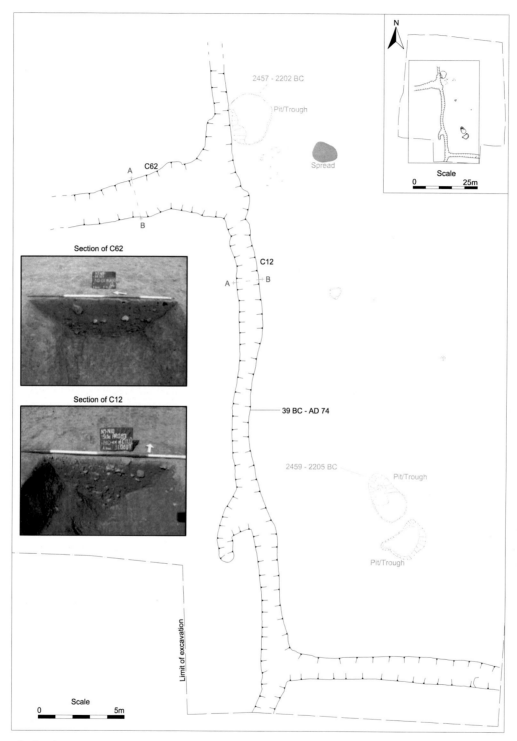

Fig. 5.2—Tinvaun 1: site plan.

during the Iron Age. These sites were in prominent and strategic locations. Hillforts have been seen as indicators of territories, functioning as central places for communities with separate and distinct identities (Grogan 2005). As such, they may have been specifically placed in locations of potential confrontation, but it is also possible that they may be interrelated, providing control over a wider landscape. The location of the hillforts within the landscape of the scheme shows the importance and value of the area in terms of agriculture and the significance of the Nore and Barrow river systems as routeways through it.

Near the south-east of the scheme is Stoneyford, where in 1832 a Roman cremation burial was discovered. The cremation was in a glass urn and was accompanied by a glass bottle of Roman style, a cosmetic-holder and a bronze disc-holder. These grave-goods and the style of the burial were typical of a Roman middle-class burial of the first and second centuries AD (Bourke 1989, 56; 1994) and may attest to a Roman presence in Kilkenny.

Settlement

There is a scattering of dates that testify to a potential Iron Age domestic presence within the area of the M9/N10 road-take, although no definitive domestic structures with Iron Age dates were identified. In the south of the scheme, a number of Iron Age dates were obtained from features possibly related to domestic activity at Danganbeg, Moanduff, Rathcash and Tinvaun. Excavations identified a complex Bronze Age landscape in the Danesfort area, including clear evidence of domestic settlement, so it would have been expected that a continuity of settlement would be identified, particularly as there are many early medieval sites in this area, the majority of which are ringforts and enclosure sites.

Danganbeg, Co. Kilkenny
A cluster of post-holes with no discernible pattern but with a possible north-east/south-west linear orientation extending for 12m were excavated at Danganbeg 1 (Devine and Coughlan 2011b), and they may represent the line of a fence or boundary. A small fragment of hazelnut shell from one of the post-holes was dated to the middle Iron Age (356–117 BC). One post-hole contained packing material and a post-pipe; the post appeared to have rotted *in situ*—its packing stone and soil were still intact. The other post-holes, however, were quite shallow, contained silts with some charcoal inclusions and appeared to have filled by natural deposition. Fragments of charcoal of hazel (*Corylus avellana*), ash (*Fraxinus excelsior*), pomaceous fruitwoods (Maloideae spp), blackthorn (*Prunus spinosa*), oak (*Quercus* sp.), yew (*Taxus baccata*) and elm

Fig. 5.3—Danganbeg 1: slot-trench with stone packing.

(*Ulmus* sp.) were identified from the fills of the post-holes. The wide variety of species identified suggests that the charcoal is not the remains of burnt posts *in situ* but rather represents general on-site burning. It should be noted, however, that a further cluster of post-holes and pits nearby to the north produced a late Bronze Age date and domestic pottery usually associated with the later Bronze Age. Therefore some of the interpreted Iron Age cluster may be associated with the Bronze Age activity, and vice versa.

Also at Danganbeg 1, on slightly raised ground overlooking the Danganbeg wetlands to the south, a number of other features were identified, including a slot-trench with post-holes, pits and a small burnt spread. A fragment of hazel charcoal from a nearby hearth/kiln has been dated to the middle Iron Age (41 BC–AD 55) and it is suggested that the activity was probably all broadly contemporary. The slot-trench (1.97m long, 0.35m wide and 0.24m deep) ran north-east/south-west and contained four post-holes that had all been heavily packed with stone and may have supported a

Fig. 5.4—Danganbeg 1: post-holes.

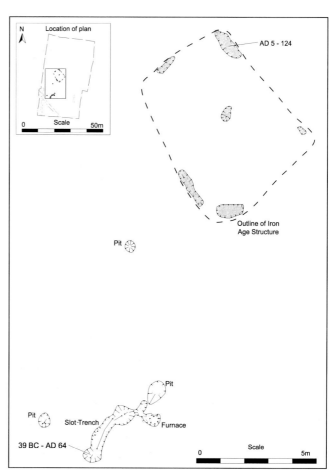

Fig. 5.5—Tinvaun 2: site plan.

shelter of sorts (Fig. 5.3). The posts had all been removed and the holes were sealed with charcoal-rich silts. Charcoal from the slot-trench was identified as oak, possibly indicative of the structural wood. The nature of the slot-trench with the inset post-holes suggests that it was associated with a structure of some kind, although the lack of any other similar features could indicate that this was a short fence or windbreak rather than an enclosed or roofed building. It should be noted, however, that the slot-trench was located in close proximity to a large post-medieval ditch, which may have disturbed further related deposits. Adjacent to the slot-trench, on its northern side, were two intercutting pits. The earlier pit (0.85m by 0.7m across and 0.14m deep) was cut and backfilled with a stony silty clay. The second pit (0.75m by 0.65m across and 0.14m deep) was then cut and was deliberately backfilled with burnt mound-type material, consisting of heat-shattered stone.

A hearth/kiln was located 10m south-west of the slot-trench and pits. It was oval, measuring 1.2m by 0.89m across and 0.23m deep, and displayed evidence of oxidisation along the base and sides of the cut, indicative of exposure to

considerable heat. Two charcoal-rich layers had built up on the base, possible evidence that the hearth/kiln had been used at least twice. Charcoal was retrieved from the basal fill and was identified to species. Hazel and pomaceous fruitwoods were the primary species burnt in the hearth. A variety of charred cereal grains were retrieved from the hearth/kiln, including barley grains (*Hordeum vulgare* L.), wheat grains (*Triticum* L. species), wheat/rye grains (*Triticum/Secale*), indeterminate cereal grains, indeterminate grass seeds (Poaceae) and indeterminate seeds from the knotgrass family (Polygonaceae). The presence of charred seeds may indicate an association with cereal-drying, probably as part of a kiln, and a fragment of hazel charcoal was dated to 41 BC–AD 55.

Tinvaun, Co. Kilkenny

A ditch at Tinvaun 1 (Fig. 5.2) had been interpreted as post-medieval prior to dating, although nothing diagnostic was recovered. It extended for 30m across the length of the excavation, continuing to the north and south of the site. It was 1.3m wide by 0.8m deep and had a broad V-shaped

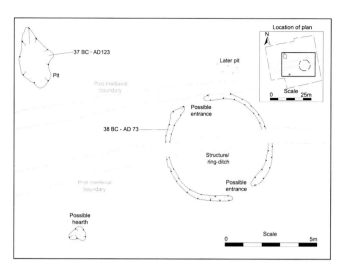

Fig. 5.6—Rathcash East 1: plan

profile. A sample of blackthorn charcoal from the fill of the ditch was dated to 39 BC–AD 74 (Lyne and Coughlan 2011). A second ditch extended west for 12m from the first one and also continued beyond the excavation limit. The identification of similarly dated features at the nearby site of Tinvaun 2 to the north suggests that this possible field system is indeed middle Iron Age. The possible hut structure at Tinvaun 2 (Fig. 5.5) consisted of four truncated slot-trench-like pits, a post-hole and a shallow, roughly central pit from which a fragment of ash charcoal was dated to AD 5–124. Besides ash, a large number of hazel and willow (*Salix* sp.) charcoal fragments were also identified. The lack of any obvious *in situ* burning in the pit suggests that this material was either redeposited from another source or dumped charred debris. The slot-trenches were quite evenly spaced. A small number of hazel charcoal fragments were recovered from the slot-trench fill. There was no evidence of a hearth, flooring or obvious entrance. The subrectangular structure measured 6.5m by 5m and was aligned north-west/south-east.

In addition to the hut, a possible furnace was recorded approximately 6m to the south, from which young oak charcoal was dated to 39 BC–AD 64. The presence of small slag spheres indicates that primary or bloom-smithing may have been carried out at the site. These features collectively could indicate activities associated with a small farmstead.

Rathcash East, Co. Kilkenny

A possible ring-ditch recorded at Rathcash East 1 (Coughlan and Bailey 2011c) consisted of two very shallow curvilinear cuts, forming an incomplete circle with a diameter of 6m and potential openings or entrances (1.45m wide) at the south-eastern and north-western sides (Fig. 5.6). The ditches were a

maximum of 0.57m wide and 0.2m deep. The fill of one of the cuts produced a single sample of charcoal, identified as oak and holly; the latter produced an Iron Age date of 38 BC–AD 73. Activity nearby included a hearth and a possible refuse pit containing charcoal, burnt and unburnt animal bone, a charred hazelnut shell and a piece of slag, all representing possible domestic waste. Animal bone retrieved from the pit has been identified as representing four species: cow, pig, sheep/goat and deer. A high incidence of cow bone indicates that cattle husbandry dominated at Rathcash East 1. The type and location of recorded butchery marks indicate that activities such as disarticulation, skinning and filleting of cattle carcasses were being undertaken in the vicinity. A single piece of metallurgical debris was recovered from the pit. Radiocarbon analysis of blackthorn charcoal from this pit returned a date (37 BC–AD 123) similar to that of the ring-ditch. It is possible that this activity was related to funerary practices associated with the ring-ditch; it is also possible, however, that the ring-ditch represents a domestic structure, based on the lack of associated burial activity and the nearby domestic waste.

Fig. 5.7—Templemartin 5: aerial view of site (photograph by Gavin Duffy, Airshots).

Templemartin, Co. Kilkenny

Another possible domestic ring-ditch was recorded at Templemartin 5 (Devine and Coughlan 2012a) (Fig. 5.7). This penannular ditch was located on the site of an earlier Bronze Age flat cemetery. Five other ring-ditches suggest that the ring-ditches are a continuation of the ritual tradition into the Iron Age. Ring-ditch 5 was the only penannular ring-ditch, however, and also contained a roughly central hearth (dated to 369–203 BC). Furthermore, the lack of funerary evidence may indicate a domestic function for ring-ditch 5.

Fig. 5.8—Moanduff 1: palisade.

Moanduff, Co. Carlow

Moanduff 1 was a particularly interesting site. The primary activity consisted of an early Bronze Age burnt mound. The site was reoccupied in the late Iron Age in the form of a palisaded enclosure. Eighteen post- or stake-holes formed the north-eastern corner of a possible subrectangular palisade (Fig. 5.8). The area within the confines of the site that was enclosed by the palisade was approximately 110m², although it is probable that this represented only one quadrant and that the full extent of the palisade enclosed an area in excess of 400m², as the palisade extended beyond the site limits to the south and west. The post/stake-holes were positioned 0.3–0.8m apart. The posts varied in diameter from 0.29m to 0.08m (with the majority being about 0.12m across), and varied in depth from 0.1m to 0.36m. A fragment of hazel charcoal from the fill of one of the post-holes was dated to AD 215–376 (Lynch and Coughlan 2011). Although some of the palisade was sealed by the early Bronze Age burnt mound deposit, it is felt likely that this is a result of post-medieval or modern agricultural disturbance of the original mound. Originally the mound would probably have been confined within the limits of the palisade, and it is possible that the existence of a low mound may have been the attraction for the location of a later enclosing palisade.

There may have been an entrance in the north-eastern corner of the palisade, evidenced by a noticeable gap in the spacing between post/stake-holes, but there was some later disturbance in this area that may have removed some elements of the palisade. The features represent the holes created by posts that were driven into the ground. A number of undated pits both inside and outside the palisade may be related, although subsequent activity on the site in the form of a pit

and another burnt mound trough have been dated to the early medieval and medieval period respectively.

Burial

The funerary evidence from the M9/N10 scheme was apparently distinct from the domestic—perhaps owing to the lack of definitive domestic settlement evidence. The evidence for funerary activity consisted of several ring-ditches, principally from the central area of the scheme. No sites in the south of the scheme produced evidence for Iron Age funerary activity. In the central area there were three clusters of funerary activity noted at Danesfort, Kilree/Holdenstown and Templemartin 5. Also in the central area, a possible ring-ditch was recorded at Rathcash East 1, which was outlined above as a possible domestic site, and one of the six ring-ditches at Templemartin 5 may also have represented a domestic ring-ditch (see above).

Fig. 5.9—Danesfort 12: aerial view of site (photograph by Gavin Duffy, Airshots).

Fig. 5.10—Danesfort 13: aerial view of site (photograph by Gavin Duffy, Airshots).

Fig. 5.11—Danesfort 1: aerial view of site (photograph by Gavin Duffy, Airshots).

Danesfort, Co. Kilkenny

Danesfort was the focus of quite intense activity in the Bronze Age, and sites in the area included evidence for domestic settlement, burial and burnt mound activity. The burial tradition clearly continued into the Iron Age. At Danesfort 13 (Fig. 5.10) the primary fill of a ring-ditch returned a radiocarbon date of 503–384 BC from a fragment of charred hazelnut (Jennings and Coughlan 2011e). The ring-ditch was 2.2m wide, 0.68m deep and enclosed an area 5.8m in diameter. An area of metal-working was identified at Danesfort 13, which included an Iron Age smelting furnace (0.85m by 0.38m by 0.25m deep) and an associated smithing hearth (1.2m by 0.75m by 0.12m deep), a metalled surface and three possible waste pits in an area of approximately 15m by 10m. The furnace contained evidence of scorching and large chunks of charcoal and slag, and returned a date of AD 7–125 from a charred hazelnut. The majority of the metallurgical residues from the furnace consisted of relatively small drippy slags characteristic of smelting. The quantity suggests a small-scale smelting operation. A scatter of iron slag and lumps of burnt clay lay over the metalled surface and within the fills of adjacent pits. It is possible that the metalled surface was a working platform. A fine blue glass bead of probable Iron Age date was found within a pit to the north of the metal-working area. The pit also contained iron slag in three of its fills and its slightly keyhole shape resembled that of a kiln, though there was no evidence to suggest that it ever functioned as one.

Two ring-ditches were excavated at the adjacent site of Danesfort 12 (Jennings and Coughlan 2011d) (Fig. 5.9), one of which was Bronze Age. The second ring-ditch measured 5.2m across and was defined by a ditch 0.9m wide and 0.3m deep.

An indeterminate seed from the ditch fill was dated to the Iron Age (88 BC–AD 54). Other Iron Age activity at Danesfort 12 included a possible cereal-drying kiln that was dated to 162 BC–AD 2 from a sample of charred barley seed. The oval kiln measured 1.25m by 0.8m across and 0.3m deep. Hulled barley and indeterminate cereal grains were recorded in its fill. A nearby furnace had reddened sides and a blackened rim. The primary fill contained large quantities of charcoal and occasional pieces of slag. Burnt clay pieces, possibly from a clay superstructure, were recovered in the middle fills, together with large concentrations of slag. The furnace was not radiocarbon-dated but may date from 400 BC–AD 700, based on the morphology and quantity of material. Residues from this site were predominantly distinctive small drippy slags characteristic of iron-smelting. The quantity of slag (12.45kg) indicates one prolonged smelting episode, and the site cannot be seen as a major iron-working centre.

A ring-ditch at Danesfort 1 (Fig. 5.11) also produced an Iron Age date from a charred hazelnut shell: AD 28–214 (Jennings and Coughlan 2011c). Cremated animal bone was found in the middle of its three fills, at opposite sides of the ditch. The burnt animal bone fragments (114.61g) recovered from the ditch represented cow, horse, pig, sheep/goat, rodent and domestic fowl. It is possible that they represent token or ceremonial depositions within the ditch. The ring-ditch had a total external diameter of 11.8m and an internal diameter of 7.8m. The U-shaped ditch was 2.8m wide and 0.75m deep. It was almost perfectly circular except for a kink at the south, the reason for which is unclear.

Kilree, Co. Kilkenny

Adjacent to the west bank of the River Nore, on flat, gravelly ground that overlooked the river and its floodplain, was Kilree

Fig. 5.12—Kilree 4: aerial view of site (photograph by Gavin Duffy, Airshots).

4, which consisted of a probable token cremation burial in a small pit (0.8m by 0.64m by 0.37m) within a double ring-ditch (Coughlan and Lynch 2012) (Fig. 5.12). The small cremation pit was dated to the Bronze Age from a sample of unidentified burnt bone. A total of 73g (seventeen fragments) of burnt bone was identified within the pit; while it was not possible to identify most of this to species, two fragments were identified as human skull fragments. The inner ditch was circular with an internal diameter of 10.4m. It measured 1.45m wide and 0.62m deep but was undated; a sample of cow phalange from the fill was forwarded for dating but the sample failed. The outer ditch was circular in plan with an internal diameter of 19.8m north–south; it was 1.02m wide and 0.52m deep. The lower fill of the outer ditch was dated to 171 BC–AD 4 from a sample of willow charcoal. There was no evidence for a bank, either internal or external, and no evidence for any recuts within either the inner or the outer ditch. A field boundary truncated the eastern edge of both ring-ditches, particularly the outer ditch. It appears, therefore, that the outer ditch represents the reuse during the Iron Age of a Bronze Age ring-ditch.

The site also contained a keyhole-shaped cereal-drying kiln approximately 20m south-west of the ring-ditch (in addition to later activity consisting of a medieval moated enclosure). The kiln measured 3.67m by 1.6m by 0.8m. Charred grains of free-threshing wheat (*Triticum* cf. *aestivum* L./*turgidum* Desf./*durum* L.) were recovered and the kiln has been dated to AD 139–336 from a sample of oak brushwood charcoal. An undated kiln and two further kilns dated to the medieval period were also found on the site. While the site at Kilree 4 was located at the bottom of the Nore Valley, the Iron Age sites at Holdenstown 1 were situated prominently at the top of the valley and overlooked the river from the east (see Whitty, this volume).

Templemartin, Co. Kilkenny
The remaining site demonstrating Iron Age funerary activity was Templemartin 5 (Fig. 5.7), which was located just to the east of Kilkenny city along the Kilkenny Link Road (Devine and Coughlan 2012a). Two pits from this multiphased site contained cremations in Neolithic Grooved Ware vessels, and three of the pits returned middle Bronze Age radiocarbon dates. There were also six ring-ditches that are interpreted as later than the Grooved Ware cremation pits. The ring-ditches formed the main concentration of funerary activity, focused on a gravel ridge overlooked by Freestone Hill. A geophysical survey carried out in the adjacent field to the east of the site did not identify additional ring-ditches. Of the six ring-ditches, it is felt that ring-ditch 5 (5.2m in diameter, 1.2m

wide and 0.37m deep) was the earliest, not least because it was partially truncated by ring-ditch 4 (5m in diameter, 0.77m wide and 0.4m deep). It was also the only one that was penannular, which could indicate that it represented a domestic structure rather than a burial monument. While ring-ditch 5 was undated, a hearth close to the centre of the enclosed area was dated to 369–203 BC from a sample of hazel charcoal. This central hearth could also suggest a domestic enclosure rather than burial, as no evidence for human cremated bone was recovered. Ring-ditch 1 (11.9m in diameter, 2.1m wide and 0.35m deep) was the only one actually dated and it returned a middle Iron Age date of 41 BC–AD 60. Ring-ditch 3 consisted of another large ring-ditch of similar dimensions to ring-ditch 1, while ring-ditches 2 and 6 were smaller, similar to ring-ditches 4 and 5. Further Iron Age activity on the site was identified in a pit which had truncated two earlier Bronze Age cremations. The pit was dated to 40 BC–AD 60. While not all of the ring-ditches were dated, it is likely that they are broadly contemporary, representing an Iron Age continuity of an earlier Bronze Age ceremonial site.

Metal-working and kilns
Evidence of small-scale industrial or agricultural activity such as metal-working and cereal-drying was uncovered at a number of sites. For example, at Tinvaun 2, Co. Kilkenny, an oval furnace had a small flue extending from the south-east corner and was dated to 750–416 BC (Devine and Coughlan 2011c). It contained a simple dumped deposit of burnt clay, charcoal and other waste. At Knockadrina 2, Co. Kilkenny, a suboval cereal-drying kiln was identified (51 BC–AD 78) with a small number of indeterminate charred grains (Kyle and Coughlan 2012b). At Kellymount 4, Co. Kilkenny, there was a small oval cereal-drying kiln and a post-hole/small pit (Wierzbicki and Coughlan 2011c). A large quantity of charred seeds identified as barley (*Hordeum vulgare*) and indeterminate grains were recorded, and the kiln was dated to 91 BC–AD 50 (willow charcoal). At Paulstown, Co. Kilkenny, contemporary kilns were identified, and both were located on sites with significant Bronze Age activity. Paulstown 1 (Elliott and Coughlan 2012a) was a roughly keyhole-shaped kiln that was dated to 36 BC–AD 118 (willow charcoal). A sample of hazel charcoal from the kiln at nearby Paulstown 2 was dated to 46 BC–AD 53 and was associated with an adjacent waste pit containing charred seeds (Elliott and Coughlan 2012b). Seeds from the kiln were identified as barley (*Hordeum vulgare*) and wheat (*Triticum* L. species). The similarity of the dates from kilns at these adjacent sites suggests that this was a significant area of cereal production in the middle Iron Age. An isolated

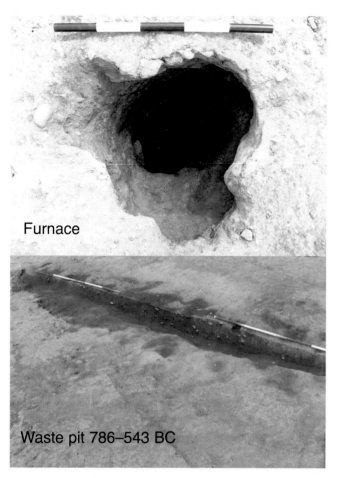

Furnace

Waste pit 786–543 BC

Fig. 5.13—Danesfort 5: furnace and waste pit (786–543 BC).

Fig. 5.14—Danesfort 5: kiln.

pit at Moanduff 2, Co. Carlow, contained a significant amount of iron slag. A sample of young oak charcoal was dated to AD 140–385 (Phelan and Coughlan 2012). The site also produced a number of features that, although undated, may also be associated with Iron Age metal-working. A small Iron Age oval cereal-drying kiln was also recorded at Cranavanone 3, Co. Carlow, and had a sample of hazel charcoal dated to 104 BC–AD 50 (O'Carroll and Coughlan 2011).

Danesfort, Co. Kilkenny

The metallurgical activity at Danesfort 12 and 13 has been described above in relation to the contemporary ring-ditches on both sites. At the multiperiod site of Danesfort 5 (Devine and Coughlan 2011a) there was evidence of quite extensive Iron Age metal-working. This activity was focused on an iron-smelting furnace (Fig. 5.13), and in her analysis of the slags Angela Wallace has identified that the residues have morphological characteristics of iron-smelting slags. The furnace was undated but other features in the vicinity returned Iron Age dates. The furnace consisted of a circular cut, 0.49m in diameter and 0.67m deep. A number of other pits may represent waste pits, and post-holes and stake-holes may indicate a windbreak or shelter. The residues recovered from some of the pits consisted of small pieces of slag, fragments of baked clay and a small, rounded nodule of hammerscale that may also point to smithing activity being carried out at various locations around the site over time. The furnace was undated but other slag-rich pits in the south of the site returned Iron Age dates. One of the pits that contained slag residues returned a date of 786–543 BC from ash charcoal. This date for the pit could point to the iron-smelting activity on the site being exceptionally early and this would indicate that the site is very significant in terms of the evolution of Irish early iron-working technology (Wallace 2010). The evidence from the dated pit suggests that it was a refuse pit and the date may not reflect the date of the metallurgical activity. Stone discs were recovered from the pits and deposits associated with the metal-working activity, as well as a variety of artefacts including a possible rubbing stone and metal fragments.

One keyhole-shaped kiln was also identified at Danesfort 5 and was dated to the Iron Age (Fig. 5.14). It was 2.45m long and the bowl had a maximum width of 1.2m and was 0.4m deep. A number of dates were returned from different deposits within the kiln, as it was felt that it may have been reused over time. Collectively, they indicate a date ranging from 169 BC to AD 1 (there were three different dates, each from a different context, all using charcoal: cherry, 110 BC–AD 50; hazel, 169–44 BC; ash, 161 BC–AD 1). Cereal grains were recovered from the kiln fills and were identified mostly as barley

Fig. 5.15—Holdenstown 2: kiln 1.

Fig. 5.16—Holdenstown 2: kiln 5.

(*Hordeum vulgare* L.) grains, hulled and indeterminate cereal grains, with small quantities of wheat/barley (*Triticum/Hordeum*) grains, sloe (*Prunus spinosa* L.) stones, possible rye (cf. *Secale cereale*) grains and hazelnut (*Corylus avellana* L.) shell fragments.

At Danesfort 10, four probable cereal-drying kilns were discovered in the vicinity of a 10m² pond (Jennings and Coughlan 2011a). The pond was 2m deep and, although silted up, may have been open in prehistory, as a small patch of burnt stone was discovered near its base. The kilns all showed evidence of intense burning *in situ* and were either circular or oval. The largest measured 2.1m by 1.6m by 0.26m, while the smallest measured 1.6m by 1.1m by 0.15m. Seeds recovered from the kiln fills were identified as barley (*Hordeum vulgare* L.) grains and indeterminate cereal. A sample of charred barley seed from one of the kilns was sent for radiocarbon dating and returned a date of 184 BC–AD 56. The similarity of the dates from the kilns at Danesfort 5 and 10 could indicate that a larger permanent settlement site/farmstead dating from the Iron Age was located nearby.

Holdenstown, Co. Kilkenny

At Holdenstown 2, a total of five Iron Age kilns were identified. One may represent a furnace rather than a kiln (Whitty and Coughlan 2012a). Three of these were located on the flat ground to the south of the subsequent early medieval burial area and one was truncated by a burial at the eastern limits of the burial ground. Kilns 1 and 2 contained charred cereal remains and appear to represent cereal-drying kilns. Kiln 1 was keyhole-shaped (3.06m by 1.6m by 1.16m) and was dated to AD 258–409 (Fig. 5.15). Cereal remains consisted of barley (*Hordeum vulgare*), emmer (*Triticum dicoccum* L.) and wheat (*Triticum* L. species) grains, as well as indeterminate cereal grains, emmer (*Triticum dicoccum*) spikelet forks and emmer/bread wheat (*Triticum dicoccum* L./*aestivum* L./*turgidum* Desf./*durum* L.). Chaff was recovered from three samples and in all cases was identified as emmer wheat, a primitive hulled wheat that is one of the earliest types of cultivated wheat. Emmer is usually replaced by bread wheat in later deposits; the recovery of this primitive type from kiln deposits is therefore quite unusual but not unknown. Kiln 2 was suboval and

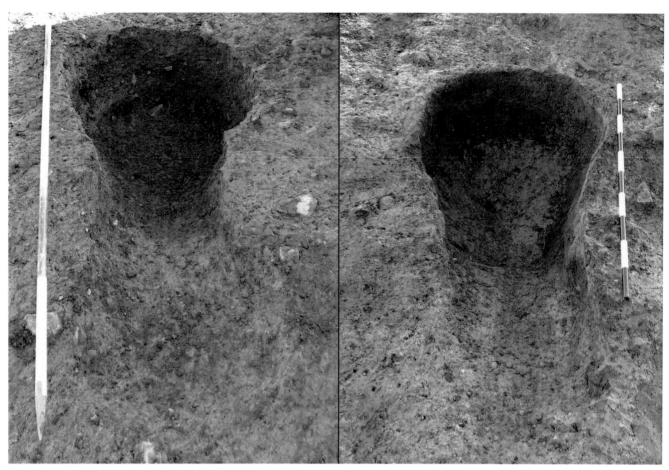

Fig. 5.17—Templemartin 1: kilns.

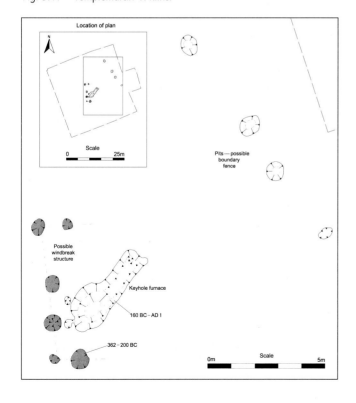

undated and measured 1.75m by 1.58m by 0.8m. Cereals recovered from kiln 2 consisted of barley (*Hordeum vulgare*), wheat (*Triticum* L. species) and indeterminate cereal grains. Kiln 3 was suboval and measured 2.81m by 1.59m across by 1.3m deep. The lower fills contained barley (*Hordeum vulgare*) grains of naked, hulled and indeterminate varieties. Kiln 4 had vertical sides and a flat base and measured 1.5m by 1.4m by 0.32m deep. A possible grinding stone recovered from the primary fill was probably associated with cereal-processing activities conducted at the site. Kiln 4 was truncated by a later burial but was nevertheless dated to 372–203 BC by a fragment of charred hazelnut shell. Kiln 5 was a large, keyhole-shaped kiln (3.8m by 1.24m by 0.07m). It did not contain charred cereals but its shape suggests that it had a cereal-drying function (Fig. 5.16). It did contain a small piece of slag, however, so it may have been associated with some other industrial activity or may simply have been used for dumping domestic waste after its

Fig. 5.18—Rathcash East 3: plan.

abandonment as a kiln. Two of the kilns were dated to the Iron Age and the other three remain undated, but it could be that they are all Iron Age, despite the significant activity on the site in the early medieval period in the form of a cemetery. An additional Iron Age date was returned from a possible sixth cereal-drying kiln, as grains of wheat (*Triticum* L. species) and possible wheat (cf. *Triticum* species) were recovered from the fills of a small hearth. The suboval hearth/kiln measured 1.78m by 0.85m by 0.35m and was dated to AD 21–203. It was not adjacent to any of the identified kilns, but these were all randomly scattered across the site.

Templemartin and Rathcash East, Co. Kilkenny

Two keyhole-shaped kilns, 3m apart, were identified at Templemartin 1 (Devine and Coughlan 2011d); they measured 1.54m by 0.7m by 0.45m deep and 1.85m by 1.28m by 0.45m deep respectively (Fig. 5.17). Large quantities of charred seeds—grains of barley (*Hordeum vulgare*), wheat (*Triticum* L. species), free-threshing wheat (*Triticum* cf. *aestivum* L./*turgidum* Desf./*durum* L.) and indeterminate cereal—in one of the kilns suggest that it may have caught fire and was subsequently abandoned. A sample of hazel charcoal from one of the kilns was dated to the late Iron Age (AD 259–430), and their similarity in shape and their relative proximity suggest that they were contemporary.

The site at Rathcash East 3 (Coughlan and Bailey 2011b) contained a large keyhole-shaped furnace (5.24m by 2.04m by 0.72m) and seven pits, possibly post-pits, aligned north–south in two adjacent rows (Fig. 5.18). The large furnace had eighteen fills, with the majority containing significant amounts of charcoal and frequent slag (almost 14kg). The bulk of the material consisted of small to medium-sized irregular-shaped nodules, some with drippy morphology (5–60mm across) indicative of smelting. There were also several larger lumps and blocky pieces, ranging from 60mm to 20mm, as well as fragments of baked and vitrified clay material. The morphology of the feature, the combination of scorched soil and significant quantities of residues are indicative of at least a single smelt being carried out within this furnace. The furnace was dated to 160 BC–AD 1 from a sample of oak charcoal, as only oak charcoal was identified. The seven pits were almost circular or oval, with the largest being 0.95m in diameter and 0.44m deep and the smallest being 0.4m in diameter and 0.12m deep. The lack of evidence for *in situ* burning and the relatively small quantities of slag recovered would suggest that they were not used as 'bowl furnaces'. Instead, they were more likely used to hold posts for a shelter over the furnace, or wooden posts used as anvils. One of the post-pits returned a radiocarbon date of 362–200 BC, also from oak charcoal.

Burnt mound activity

A large number of burnt mounds (*fulachta fiadh*) were recorded along the route of the M9/N10, usually (but not exclusively) in the more marginal and wetter areas of the landscape. The majority of these sites were dated to the Bronze Age, but several produced dates in the Iron Age.

Danganbeg, Co. Kilkenny

An Iron Age burnt mound was located at the southern end of Danganbeg 1. The focal point of the activity was a trough or well, two further possible troughs, a number of pits and a scatter of post-holes to the north of the well and east of the burnt mound deposit, which was quite small and may have been ploughed out or disturbed. The large primary trough/well measured 1.9m by 1.43m and was 0.75m deep. As troughs associated with burnt mounds can have an average depth of 0.4–0.5m, the greater depth identified at Danganbeg may indicate a feature that was used for water storage rather than water-heating. The post-holes formed no discernible pattern or plan, but the fill from one of the larger ones in the centre of the cluster returned a date of 762–416 BC from a charred hazelnut. The site was immediately north of the Danganbeg wetlands, which were probably a focus of activity throughout prehistory.

Danesfort, Co. Kilkenny

At Danesfort 2 a complex of burnt mound activity was identified, with a variety of features including troughs, pits, post-holes and a very large pit or possible 'water-hole' (Fig. 5.19). One of the troughs and the possible water-hole were dated to the early Bronze Age, although they were not contemporary. Other possible Bronze Age troughs and pits in the centre of the site were truncated by early Iron Age features, including a subrectangular unlined trough that measured 2.25m by 1.6m across and 0.75m deep. A charcoal sample (*Prunus*) was dated to 744–407 BC. A large pit immediately west of the trough appears to have been directly related, possibly as a secondary trough, and measured 2.9m by 2.7m by 0.7m. Two possible structures were identified, the first of which (A) consisted of a number of circular post-pits in a horseshoe-shaped formation around the east of the trough. While the pits did not seem deep enough to support substantial structural posts, the regular arrangement may have supported a platform erected on shorter posts around the trough. Some small stake-holes appear to have augmented the structure. At a distance of 5m to the east of structure A was structure B. This consisted of two parallel lines of four post-holes and may have been the location for a small platform (1.5m by 0.5m). One of the post-holes of structure B was

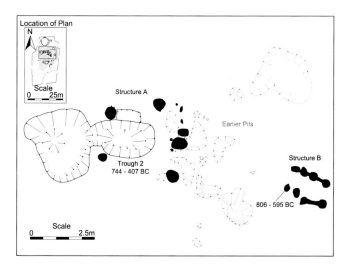

Fig. 5.19—Danesfort 2: plan.

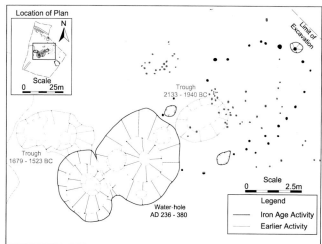

Fig. 5.20—Kellymount 2: plan.

Fig. 5.21—Kellymount 2: water-hole.

dated from a sample of cherry charcoal to 806–595 BC, making them broadly contemporary with the trough.

Holdenstown, Co. Kilkenny

At Holdenstown 4, a large burnt mound deposit sealed a trough and other pits (Whitty and Coughlan 2011). The large, suboval trough was aligned east–west and was filled with deposits that were dated to 765–420 BC by a sample of ash charcoal. These deposits were similar to the overlying burnt mound material. The trough measured 3.86m by 2.8m across by 0.22m deep and there was no evidence that it was lined. To the west of the main area of the trough, a step was evident on the western side. This effectively reduced the ground level of a slightly higher ridge of subsoil. This western edge was not as pronounced as the main cut and was more irregular in plan. Its function may have been to provide better access to the trough or to reduce the depth/step of the cut at this western end, where the subsoil was slightly raised.

Rathcash, Co. Kilkenny

At Rathcash 2, burnt mound activity was dated to the Bronze Age (Coughlan and Bailey 2011a). A subsequent Iron Age phase was identified by a large pit/trough. The possible trough contained a total of nine fills, possibly indicating that it was used for a long period or was subject to more activity. Some grey clay was deposited at the base of the trough, but the majority of the fills were characterised by the presence of charcoal and heat-affected stones. Degraded and unidentified wooden rods were also present within the lower fills of this feature, indicating that it may originally have contained a wicker lining. The pit/trough was particularly deep, measuring 3.38m by 2m with a maximum depth of 1.3m. It was dated to

Fig. 5.22—Kellymount 3: troughs with post-holes.

344–55 BC by a sample of hazel charcoal. Given the depth of the cut, and the volume of water that would have been contained within it, it is possible that this feature was used for water storage rather than heating.

Kellymount, Co. Kilkenny

Two burnt mound sites west of Paulstown in north Kilkenny produced evidence of Iron Age activity. At Kellymount 2, a very large spread of burnt mound material sealed pits, troughs and stake-hole scatters (Fig. 5.20). One of the troughs and a pit were dated to the early and middle Bronze Age respectively. The centre of the site contained a very substantial, roughly circular pit that was 4m in diameter and 2m deep. It was interpreted as a possible water-hole/reservoir (Fig. 5.21). One of its lower fills was dated to AD 236–380. A second large pit was located immediately to the south-west. A series of stake-holes extended in a horseshoe shape from the north-east of the water-hole, possibly representing an area enclosed by a small fence. A fragment of an amber bead was recovered from the lower fills of the water-hole. Three large pits/post-holes were located within the area of the cut of the water-hole but external to its base, and these may have supported a light structure or possible roof. Given the size and depth of the water-hole, it is unlikely that the volume of water within it was being heated to a temperature suitable for cooking, which could imply that this was a bathing place, and the presence of a fragment of personal ornament may support this.

Kellymount 3 lay only a few hundred metres north-east of Kellymount 2. Again, multiphased burnt mound activity was evident, with the earliest trough dated to the early Bronze Age. This site also had a large water-hole feature, similar to Kellymount 2, that measured 7m by 6.2m at the top. The upper level of the cut sloped gently for a depth of 1.5m, below which the cut became almost vertical, with a diameter of approximately 3m. The total depth of the pit was approximately 6m. The water-hole was not dated but adjacent to it were two troughs. One was subcircular, and evidence from the many stake-holes around the perimeter of the base suggest that it was originally wicker-lined. The second trough was rectangular (2.38m by 1.56m by 0.2m deep) and it too had multiple stake-holes in its base, suggesting that it was also lined (Fig. 5.22). This trough was dated to 751–409 BC by ash charcoal. To the west of the water-hole and trough, ten post-holes possibly represent a small enclosing fence. Collectively, the features again suggest a possible bathing place. To the north of the main concentration of activity was an isolated pit, 0.8m in diameter and 0.19m deep, with burnt mound-type fill from which a sample of holly charcoal was dated to 362–196 BC. It is thought that this may represent a pot-boiler or roasting pit,

as there was no obvious overlying mound material. What is interesting about the two Kellymount burnt mounds is that they represent burnt mound activity in one small area at either end of the Iron Age, although they retain very similar features. The fact that they could both represent bathing sites may indicate that there was a tradition of bathing in this particular area, possibly indicating the presence of a larger domestic settlement in the wider landscape.

Stonecarthy West, Co. Kilkenny

Stonecarthy West 1 was the site of multiphased burnt mound activity dating from the early–middle Bronze Age and the early Iron Age (Kyle and Coughlan 2012a), and was located in a drier, more upland area than the wet marginal landscapes usually associated with burnt mounds. The earliest phase of activity consisted of an oval slot-trench that contained vertical

Fig. 5.23—Stonecarthy West Iron Age trough (highlighted). Note the post-holes in the corners.

Fig. 5.24—Stonecarthy West: detail of slot-trench with packing stones.

packing stones in places, suggesting that it had supported vertical timber walls, possibly planks (Figs 5.23 and 5.24). The slot-trench, 0.23m wide and a maximum of 0.36m deep, may represent the walls of a small domestic structure or possibly a sweat-house, given the associated burnt mound deposits. Its fill was dated to 1757–1616 BC from a sample of ash charcoal. The internal area enclosed by the slot-trench had been lowered, possibly to form a shallow, enclosed trough measuring 3m by 2m. A large water-hole-type feature filled with interleaved layers of burnt mound material was recorded nearby and was dated to 1440–1315 BC, indicating a probable second phase of activity on the site. Iron Age activity was related to a rectangular trough (2.45m by 1.45m by 0.2m deep) that truncated the earlier slot-trench structure. Post-holes were recorded in three of the corners of the trough, with the possible remnants of another identified in the area of the fourth corner. The posts they held are believed to have supported a wooden trough lining, although no lining survived. The fill of the trough was dated to 771–539 BC by a sample of ash charcoal. An undated bowl furnace and related pits around the periphery of the site could indicate further activity in the Iron Age, as the site is located *c.* 300m to the north of the middle Iron Age settlement activity recorded at Tinvaun 1 and 2.

Bibliography

Armit, I. and Ginn, V. 2007 Beyond the grave: human remains

Table 5.1—Iron Age radiocarbon dates from the M9/N10 Phase 4.

Site name	Context	Lab no.	Uncal. date	Cal. date	Sample
Ballinvally 1	C15; fill of possible waste pit	UBA-15411	2053±28	109–2 BC, 1-sigma 166 BC–AD 15, 2-sigma	Young oak
Baysrath 2	C13; fill of post-hole	UBA-10984	2052±27	107–2 BC, 1-sigma 165 BC–AD 16, 2-sigma	Alder
Cranavanone 3	C6, 7, 8, 9; fills of kiln	UBA-12251	2028±24	52 BC–AD 16, 1-sigma 104 BC–AD 50, 2-sigma	Hazel
Cranavanone 3	C10; fill of pit	UBA-12252	2122±24	196–111 BC, 1-sigma 341–54 BC, 2-sigma	Ash
Danesfort 1	C4; fill of ring-ditch	UB-15556	1900±31	AD 68–130, 1-sigma AD 28–214, 2-sigma	Hazelnut shell
Danesfort 10	C12; fill of pit	UB-15559	2048±49	155 BC–AD 3, 1-sigma 184 BC–AD 56, 2-sigma	Barley
Danesfort 12	C48; fill of pit	UB-15546	2052±22	102–3 BC, 1-sigma 162 BC–AD 2, 2-sigma	Barley
Danesfort 12	C52; fill of ring-ditch	UB-15550	2015±24	44 BC–AD 17, 1-sigma 88 BC–AD 54, 2-sigma	Seed, indeterminate
Danesfort 13	C108; basal fill of ring-ditch	UBA-10999	2350±21	406–394 BC, 1-sigma 503–384 BC, 2-sigma	Charred hazelnut
Danesfort 13	C51; bottom fill of furnace	UB-15552	1939±24	AD 26–84, 1-sigma AD 7–125, 2-sigma	Hazelnut
Danesfort 2	C105; fill of pit	UBA-11000	2434±20	703–414 BC, 1-sigma 744–407 BC, 2-sigma	*Prunus* spp
Danesfort 2	C122; fill of post-hole	UB-15554	2571±25	797–769 BC, 1-sigma 806–595 BC, 2-sigma	Cherry
Danesfort 5	C294; fill of kiln	UBA-12189	2031±24	84 BC–AD 4, 1-sigma 110 BC–AD 50, 2-sigma	*Prunus*
Danesfort 5	C304; fill of kiln	UBA-12190	2079±22	152–51 BC, 1-sigma 169–44 BC, 2-sigma	Hazel
Danesfort 5	C298; fill of kiln	UBA-12191	2054±22	106–4 BC, 1-sigma 162 BC–AD 1, 2-sigma	Ash
Danesfort 5	C38; fill of pit	UBA-12192	2514±23	770–563 BC, 1-sigma 786–543 BC, 2-sigma	Ash

Table 5.1 (cnt.)

Site name	Context	Lab no.	Uncal. date	Cal. date	Sample
Danganbeg 1	C16; fill of post-hole	UB-14021	2163±22	349–173 BC, 1-sigma 356–117 BC, 2-sigma	Charred hazelnut
Danganbeg 1	C291; basal fill of hearth	UB-14024	1992±19	37 BC–AD 28, 1-sigma 41 BC–AD 55, 2-sigma	Hazel
Danganbeg 1	C211; fill of post-hole	UB-14025	2471±25	751–522 BC, 1-sigma 762–416 BC, 2-sigma	Charred hazelnut
Danganbeg 3	C9; fill of pit/furnace	UB-14026	2443±24	730–416 BC, 1-sigma 750–408 BC, 2-sigma	Pomoideae
Garryduff 1	C85; fill of post- and stake-holes	UBA-15413	2251±26	385–234 BC, 1-sigma 392–209 BC, 2-sigma	Hazel
Garryduff 1	C18; fill of pit	UBA-15416	2416±30	522–407 BC, 1-sigma 746–400 BC, 2-sigma	Ash
Holdenstown 1	C77; primary fill of possible ring-ditch	UBA-13108	2068±22	146–45 BC, 1-sigma 168–3 BC, 2-sigma	Hazelnut shell
Holdenstown 1	C59; lower grave fill of burial 1	UB-15561	2418±31	537–407 BC, 1-sigma 1748–400 BC, 2-sigma	Pomoideae
Holdenstown 1	C21; basal fill of ring-ditch	UBA-15401	2119±25	192–110 BC, 1-sigma 203–53 BC, 2-sigma	Hazel
Holdenstown 1	C12; fill of ditch	UBA-15403	2046±23	92–1 BC, 1-sigma 160 BC–AD 18, 2-sigma	Wild/bird cherry
Holdenstown 1	C56; basal fill of ring-ditch	UBA-15404	1728±22	AD 256–344, 1-sigma AD 250–383, 2-sigma	Alder
Holdenstown 1	C6; lower fill of enclosure	UBA-15405	2019±25	46 BC–AD 17, 1-sigma 91 BC–AD 53, 2-sigma	Hazel
Holdenstown 2	C44; fill of post-hole	UBA-13109	1910±24	AD 70–125, 1-sigma AD 25–135, 2-sigma	Hazelnut shell
Holdenstown 2	C464; fill of hearth	UBA-13111	1913±26	AD 67–125, 1-sigma AD 21–203, 2-sigma	Hazelnut shell
Holdenstown 2	C182; fill of kiln	UBA-15407	1699±23	AD 264–390, 1-sigma AD 258–409, 2-sigma	Charred barley
Holdenstown 2	C515; fill of kiln	UBA-15408	2214±22	359–208 BC, 1-sigma 372–203 BC, 2-sigma	Hazelnut
Holdenstown 4	C23; secondary fill of trough	UBA-13114	2477±22	753–539 BC, 1-sigma 765–420 BC, 2-sigma	Ash
Jordanstown 1	C25; basal fill of shallow pit	UBA-12233	2227±20	365–211 BC, 1-sigma 382–206 BC, 2-sigma	Hazel
Kellymount 2	C82; lower fill of pit	UB-14041	1746±23	AD 249–331, 1-sigma AD 236–380, 2-sigma	Hazel brushwood
Kellymount 3	C5; fill of trough	UB-14043	2446±25	733–416 BC, 1-sigma 751–409 BC, 2-sigma	Ash
Kellymount 3	C172; basal fill of pit	UB-14045	2195±22	354–203 BC, 1-sigma 362–196 BC, 2-sigma	Holly
Kellymount 4	C7; middle fill of kiln	UB-14046	2023±22	47 BC–AD 4, 1-sigma 91 BC–AD 50, 2-sigma	Willow
Kilree 4	C105; basal fill of outer ring-ditch	UB-15563	2059±31	155–4 BC, 1-sigma 171 BC–AD 4, 2-sigma	Willow

Table 5.1 (cnt.)

Site name	Context	Lab no.	Uncal. date	Cal. date	Sample
Kilree 4	C271; bottom fill/burnt post of kiln	UBA-15398	1777±22	AD 226–322, 1-sigma AD 139–336, 2-sigma	Oak brushwood
Knockadrina 2	C329; fill of linear feature	UBA-12178	1989±32	37 BC–AD 52, 1-sigma 51 BC–AD 78, 2-sigma	Pomoideae
Moanduff 1	C142; fill of stake-hole	UBA-13124	1762±22	AD 240–323, 1-sigma AD 215–376, 2-sigma	Hazel
Moanduff 2	C285; fill of pit	UBA-12260	1759±19	AD 236–335, 1-sigma AD 140–385, 2-sigma	Young oak
Paulstown 1	C192; fill of trough	UBA-15418	2408±24	510–407 BC, 1-sigma 727–401 BC, 2-sigma	Ash
Paulstown 1	C400; fill of kiln	UBA-15427	1957±22	AD 23–70, 1-sigma 36 BC–AD 118, 2-sigma	Willow
Paulstown 2	C374; fill of kiln	UBA-15432	2003±22	39 BC–AD 21, 1-sigma 46 BC–AD 53, 2-sigma	Hazel
Rathcash 2	C53; fill of trough	UBA-12219	2125±25	198–111 BC, 1-sigma 344–55 BC, 2-sigma	Hazel
Rathcash East 1	C10; fill of pit	UBA-12220	1954±28	AD 18–77, 1-sigma 37 BC–AD 123, 2-sigma	Blackthorn
Rathcash East 1	C20; fill of curvilinear feature	UBA-12221	1973±21	AD 4–57, 1-sigma 38 BC–AD 73, 2-sigma	Holly
Rathcash East 3	C30; fill of furnace	UBA-14032	2054±19	100–5 BC, 1-sigma 160 BC–AD 1, 2-sigma	Oak
Rathcash East 3	C22; fill of bowl furnace	UBA-14033	2201±21	357–204 BC, 1-sigma 362–200 BC, 2-sigma	Oak
Shankill 5	C34; fill of pit	UBA-15417	2527±24	784–593 BC, 1-sigma 791–547 BC, 2-sigma	Hazel
Stonecarthy West 1	C76; primary fill of trough	UBA-12174	2498±22	760–551 BC, 1-sigma 771–539 BC, 2-sigma	Ash
Templemartin 1	C5; mid-fill of kiln	UB-14057	1669±29	AD 345–415, 1-sigma AD 259–430, 2-sigma	Hazel
Templemartin 5	C75; lining of hearth	UBA-15441	2213±22	359–208 BC, 1-sigma 369–203 BC, 2-sigma	Hazel
Templemartin 5	C144; fill of pit	UBA-15442	1987±21	20 BC–AD 52, 1-sigma 40 BC–AD 60, 2-sigma	Pomoideae brushwood, 6yrs
Templemartin 5	C128; fill of ring-ditch	UBA-15444	1989±22	36 BC–AD 51, 1-sigma 41 BC–AD 60, 2-sigma	Ash and birch
Tinvaun 1	C80; fill of ditch	UBA-10993	1973±24	AD 3–59, 1-sigma 39 BC–AD 74, 2-sigma	Prunus spp
Tinvaun 2	C15; primary fill of pit	UBA-12169	1941±22	AD 26–81, 1-sigma AD 5–124, 2-sigma	Ash
Tinvaun 2	C43; basal fill of furnace	UB-14028	1983±21	17 BC–AD 54, 1-sigma 39 BC–AD 64, 2-sigma	Young oak

from domestic contexts in Atlantic Scotland. *Proceedings of the Prehistoric Society* **73**, 113–34.

Bourke, E. 1989 Stoneyford: a first-century Roman burial from Ireland. *Archaeology Ireland* **3** (2), 56–7.

Bourke, E. 1994 Glass vessels of the first nine centuries AD in Ireland. *Journal of the Royal Society of Antiquaries of Ireland* **124**, 163–209.

Cassidy, B. 1991 Digging at Dunbell. *Archaeology Ireland* **5** (2), 18–20.

Condit, T. and Gibbons, M. 1988 Two little-known hillforts in Co. Kilkenny. *Decies* **37**, 47–53.

Coughlan, T. and Bailey, F. 2011a E3860 Rathcash 2: final report. Unpublished report prepared for the National Monuments Service, DEHLG, Dublin.

Coughlan, T. and Bailey, F. 2011b E3861 Rathcash East 3: final report. Unpublished report prepared for the National Monuments Service, DEHLG, Dublin.

Coughlan, T. and Bailey, F. 2011c E3892 Rathcash East 1: final report. Unpublished report prepared for the National Monuments Service, DEHLG, Dublin.

Coughlan, T. and Lynch, P. 2012 E3730 Kilree 4: final report. Unpublished report prepared for the National Monuments Service, DEHLG, Dublin.

Devine, E. and Coughlan, T. 2011a E3456 Danesfort 5: final report. Unpublished report prepared for the National Monuments Service, DEHLG, Dublin.

Devine, E. and Coughlan, T. 2011b E3606 Danganbeg 1: final report. Unpublished report prepared for the National Monuments Service, DEHLG, Dublin.

Devine, E. and Coughlan, T. 2011c E3671 Danganbeg 3: final report. Unpublished report prepared for the National Monuments Service, DEHLG, Dublin.

Devine, E. and Coughlan, T. 2011d E3849 Templemartin 1: final report. Unpublished report prepared for the National Monuments Service, DEHLG, Dublin.

Devine, E. and Coughlan, T. 2012a E3846 Templemartin 5: final report. Unpublished report prepared for the National Monuments Service, DEHLG, Dublin.

Devine, E. and Coughlan, T. 2012b E3852 Garryduff 1: final report. Unpublished report prepared for the National Monuments Service, DEHLG, Dublin.

Devine, E. and Ó Drisceoil, C. 2007 Preliminary stratigraphic report on findings from excavations at Highhays, Kilkenny city. Unpublished report for the National Monuments Service, DEHLG, Dublin..

Elliott, R. and Coughlan, T. 2012a E3642 Paulstown 1: final report. Unpublished report prepared for the National Monuments Service, DEHLG, Dublin.

Elliott, R. and Coughlan, T. 2012b E3632 Paulstown 2: final

report. Unpublished report prepared for the National Monuments Service, DEHLG, Dublin.

ENVision: Environmental Protection Agency Soil Maps of Ireland (www.epa.ie/InternetMapViewer/mapviewer.aspx).

Foley, C. 1974 Précis of excavation results, 1973. National Monuments files F94/1781/1.

Foley, C. 2006 Excavation of a ringfort at Dunbell Big, Co. Kilkenny. *Journal of the Royal Society of Antiquaries of Ireland* **136**, 5–22.

Gibbons, M. 1990 The archaeology of early settlement in County Kilkenny. In W. Nolan and K. Whelan (eds), *Kilkenny: history and society*, 1–32. Dublin.

Grogan, E. 2005 *The North Munster Project, vol. 2. The prehistoric landscape of north Munster*. Dublin.

Jennings, R. and Coughlan, T. 2011a E3459 Danesfort 10: final report. Unpublished report prepared for the National Monuments Service, DEHLG, Dublin.

Jennings, R. and Coughlan, T. 2011b E3540 Danesfort 2: final report. Unpublished report prepared for the National Monuments Service, DEHLG, Dublin.

Jennings, R. and Coughlan, T. 2011c E3541 Danesfort 1: final report. Unpublished report prepared for the National Monuments Service, DEHLG, Dublin.

Jennings, R. and Coughlan, T. 2011d E3616 Danesfort 12: final report. Unpublished report prepared for the National Monuments Service, DEHLG, Dublin.

Jennings, R. and Coughlan, T. 2011e E3617 Danesfort 13: final report. Unpublished report prepared for the National Monuments Service, DEHLG, Dublin.

Kyle, J. and Coughlan, T. 2011 E3680 Tinvaun 2: final report. Unpublished report prepared for the National Monuments Service, DEHLG, Dublin.

Kyle, J. and Coughlan, T. 2012a E3610 Stonecarthy West 1: final report. Unpublished report prepared for the National Monuments Service, DEHLG, Dublin.

Kyle, J. and Coughlan, T. 2012b E3611 Knockadrina 2: final report. Unpublished report prepared for the National Monuments Service, DEHLG, Dublin.

Lynch, R.P. and Coughlan, T. 2011 E3839 Moanduff 1: final report. Unpublished report prepared for the National Monuments Service, DEHLG, Dublin.

Lyne, E. and Coughlan, T. 2011 E3678 Tinvaun 1: final report. Unpublished report prepared for the National Monuments Service, DEHLG, Dublin.

Lyng, T. 1984 *Castlecomer connections: exploring history, geography and social evolution in north Kilkenny environs*. Castlecomer.

McCutcheon, S. 2007 The small stone artefacts. In M. Clyne (ed.), *Kells Priory, Co. Kilkenny: archaeological excavations by*

T. Fanning and M. Clyne, 424–33. Dublin.

Mallory, J.P. 1995 Haughey's Fort and the Navan complex in the late Bronze Age. In J. Waddell and E. Twohig (eds), *Ireland in the Bronze Age*, 73–86. Dublin.

O'Carroll, E. and Coughlan, T. 2011 Cranavonane 3 E3731: final report. Unpublished report prepared for the National Monuments Service, DEHLG, Dublin.

Phelan, S. and Coughlan, T. 2012 E3735 Moanduff 2: final report. Unpublished report prepared for the National Monuments Service, DEHLG, Dublin.

Raftery, B. 1969 Freestone Hill, Co. Kilkenny: an Iron Age hillfort and Bronze Age cairn. *Proceedings of the Royal Irish Academy* **68**C, 1–108.

Raftery, B. 1994 *Pagan Celtic Ireland: the enigma of the Irish Iron Age*. London.

Wallace, A. 2010 Report on archaeo-metallurgical residues from Danesfort 5 E3456 AR082, Co. Kilkenny. N9/N10 Kilcullen to Waterford Scheme Phase 4: Knocktopher to Powerstown. Unpublished report on behalf of Irish Archaeological Consultancy Ltd.

Whitty, Y. and Coughlan, T. 2011 E3682 Holdenstown 4: final report. Unpublished report prepared for the National Monuments Service, DEHLG, Dublin.

Whitty, Y. and Coughlan, T. 2012a E3630 Holdenstown 2: final report. Unpublished report prepared for the National Monuments Service, DEHLG, Dublin.

Whitty, Y. and Coughlan, T. 2012b E3681 Holdenstown 1: final report. Unpublished report prepared for the National Monuments Service, DEHLG, Dublin.

Wierzbicki, P. and Coughlan, T. 2011a E3757 Kellymount 2: final report. Unpublished report prepared for the National Monuments Service, DEHLG, Dublin.

Wierzbicki, P. and Coughlan, T. 2011b E3856 Kellymount 3: final report. Unpublished report prepared for the National Monuments Service, DEHLG, Dublin.

Wierzbicki, P. and Coughlan, T. 2011c E3857 Kellymount 4: final report. Unpublished report prepared for the National Monuments Service, DEHLG, Dublin.

Note

1. All radiocarbon dates listed here are calibrated to 2-sigma.

6. A possible Iron Age homestead at Ballinaspig More, Co. Cork
Ed Danaher

Introduction

The excavation at Ballinaspig More 5 was carried out as part of the resolution phase on the N22 Ballincollig Bypass during the summer of 2002. An area measuring roughly 160m east–west by 40m north–south was exposed under licence number 02E1033. This revealed a multiphased site with remnants of human activity dating from the Neolithic onwards. The early Neolithic, Iron Age and post-medieval were the best-represented periods and many of the features within the site were associated with structural and domestic evidence. The Neolithic phase produced clusters of pits and post-holes, the Iron Age levels contained two timber structures, and the post-medieval was represented by a vernacular cottage with associated yard as well as a series of field drains and cultivation furrows. Traces of final Neolithic/early Bronze Age as well as middle Bronze Age activity, including hearths and pits containing diagnostic pottery, were also uncovered. A number of these features were located in the vicinity of the smaller of the two Iron Age

structures. Analysis of environmental samples from the site revealed charred cereal grains, mainly seeds of barley and wheat, and a wide variety of wood species. The finds assemblage from the site consisted of prehistoric pottery, both Neolithic and Bronze Age, chipped and ground stone artefacts, as well as various post-medieval items. Radiocarbon dating of seven samples returned four Neolithic, a Bronze Age and two Iron Age dates.

Ballinaspig More 5 was one of seven archaeological sites discovered within this townland. Ballinaspig More 1, 2, 3, 6 and 7 were all associated with burnt mound activity, while Ballinaspig More 4 was separated from Ballinaspig More 5 by the Twopot River and would have shared some of its occupational history. This essay will focus on the Iron Age phase of Ballinaspig More 5 (BM5), consisting of the remains of two timber structures.

Location

The site is located on a slight ridge at a height of about 22m OD, 3.5km south-east of the village of Ballincollig (NGR 162860/069150; Figs 6.1–6.4). It is in an area of good agricultural soil, which at the time of excavation was under cultivation. The Twopot River traverses the area, separating Ballinaspig More 4 (02E0947), to the east, and Ballinaspig More 5, and is the boundary between two farms in this townland. The location of the river may have been one of the contributory factors to making this area a favourable location for settlement since the early Neolithic. Evidence of early medieval activity is present in the form of a ringfort, which is situated just south of the road-take. North of the site, the ridge on which BM5 was located gives way to marginal low-lying fields where five *fulachta fiadh* were discovered (BM6 and BM7) and subsequently excavated in association with this development. Agricultural activity had a major impact on the site throughout the last century, while the construction of the 1885 railway line also appears to have had a significant impact on the landscape in the area.

Ballinaspig More 5 was located in a prominent position, commanding views of Bishopstown and the surrounding countryside. Although factors such as topography and local resource availability were undoubtedly taken into account by the various inhabitants of this site in determining the choice of settlement location, the proximity to good agricultural land

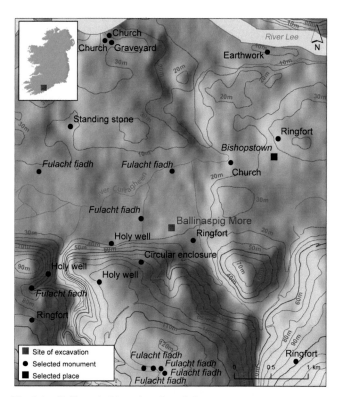

Fig. 6.1—Ballinaspig More: location of site.

Fig. 6.2—Ballinaspig More: site location of Ballinaspig More 1–7 and Curraheen 1 and 4.

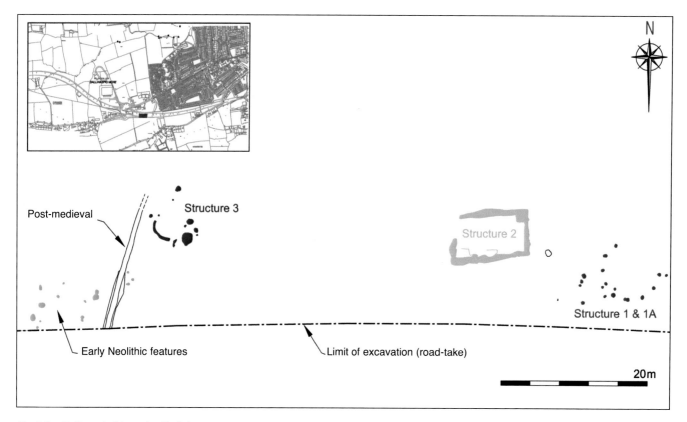

Fig. 6.3—Ballinaspig More: detail of site.

Fig. 6.4—Ballinaspig More: view of surrounding landscape taken from site (cherry-picker), looking south-east. Structure 1 is visible as a series of dots towards the centre of the photograph.

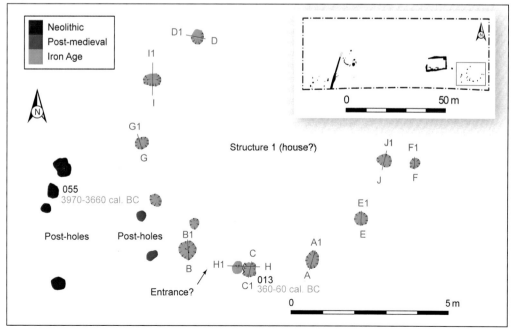

Fig. 6.5—Ballinaspig More: post-excavation plan of structure 1.

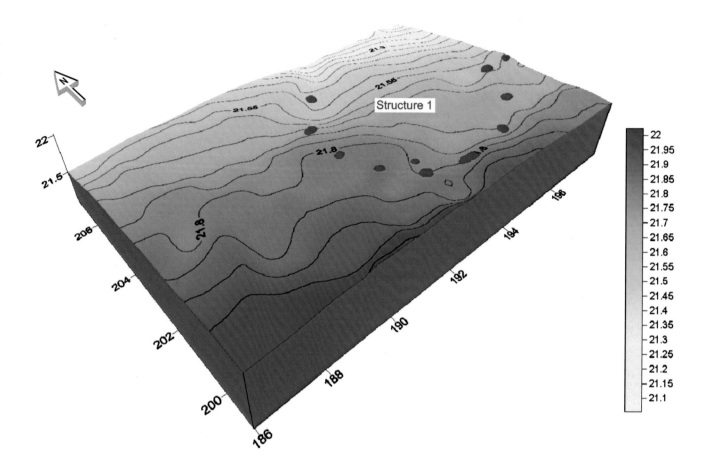

Fig. 6.6—Ballinaspig More: topographical survey of location of structure 1.

Fig. 6.7—Ballinaspig More: post-excavation view of structure 1 from north-west.

Fig. 6.8—Ballinaspig More: post-excavation view of C13 and C52 from north.

and a nearby water source would have been of prime importance.

The excavation

The Iron Age structures

This phase of the site is represented by two structures. The larger of these, structure 1, was situated to the east of the site close to its southern edge. It was C-shaped in plan and consisted of a discontinuous circular arrangement of post-holes with a diameter of 7.4m (Figs 6.3–6.10). These post-holes had an average diameter of 0.4m and depth of 0.36m and appear to have contained relatively stout posts. They were spaced at regular intervals, with the distance between each falling between 1.4m and 1.6m. Although only twelve survived, there may originally have been up to sixteen, and the others could have been removed by later erosion.

No hearth, occupational layers or internal features were uncovered during the excavation of this structure, which suggests that either they were truncated over time or the structure may not have been used as a dwelling. The absence of internal features does not, however, exclude a domestic interpretation for this building. If the structure was a dwelling, the lack of any internal posts would suggest that the excavated posts as well as being the outer walls were also the main structural supports for the roof. Alternatively, the incomplete ring of post-holes may have provided the internal roof supports of a larger building, with the external wall consisting of either a sod or wattle and daub wall, of which no trace survived. In this instance, however, this is unlikely (see discussion below).

Excavation of posts C51 and C13 to the south of the structure suggests that the former was a bracing post for C13, implying that this was not a stand-alone post but rather a load-bearing one (Fig. 6.8). Charcoal (ash) from the main fill (C12) of this feature was dated to 360–280 cal. BC (Beta-178205). In addition to some unidentifiable burnt bone fragments, a grain of wheat and a possible slag fragment were the only other finds associated with structure 1. A number of unrelated post-holes and pits were located to the west of the structure, but a post-hole (C33) to the east of it tentatively suggests that

Fig. 6.9—Ballinaspig More: post-excavation view of C30/31 from west.

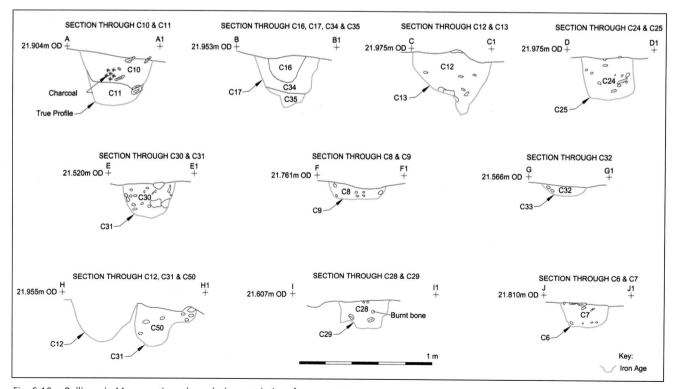

Fig. 6.10—Ballinaspig More: sections through the post-holes of structure 1.

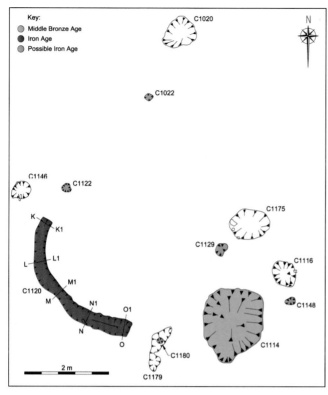

Fig. 6.11—Ballinaspig More: detail of structure 3.

this structure may have had an entrance porch (Figs 6.5–6.7). If so, the entrance would have been to the east: the corresponding entrance post-hole would have been to the north-east of the structure and may have been removed through natural erosion as discussed below (Figs 6.5–6.7).

The second Iron Age structure, designated structure 3 during excavation (structure 2 was a post-medieval building; Fig. 6.3), was of different construction and of smaller scale (Figs 6.11–6.16). Situated *c.* 60m north-west of the former structure, it had a diameter of less than 4m. It was roughly circular and defined by a small slot-trench (C1120), which held split planks, and four (possibly) associated post-holes (C1122, C1146, C1180 and C1148). The curvilinear slot-trench was 3.9m in length and varied between 0.24m and 0.4m in width, with a depth of 0.21m. It contained the charred remains of upright split-timber planking (wall), packed with a relatively sterile deposit. Radiocarbon analysis of charcoal (oak) from this trench returned a date of 790–390 cal. BC (Beta-178209). The trench was located along the south-west of this possible structure and would have given shelter from the prevailing south-westerly winds. Following the alignment of this slot-trench, combined with the three post-holes, a roughly circular shape was discernible. The remaining walls of the structure may have been composed of

Fig. 6.12—Ballinaspig More: pre-excavation view of slot-trench of structure 3, from south.

wattle and daub screening, with stake-hole C1125 possibly acting as support for a light roof. Charred seeds of wheat and barley were retrieved from the fill of the slot-trench.

A concentration of other features were located in the vicinity of the undated post-holes discussed above, some of which contained middle Bronze Age pottery, with at least one dating from this period (Fig. 6.11). It is possible that these post-holes relate to this middle Bronze Age activity and not to the Iron Age slot-trench. If so, this latter feature may simply have been a stand-alone structure such as a windbreak associated with some sort of workstation/area.

Discussion

The Iron Age landscape

The Iron Age is probably the most obscure period in Irish prehistory and, despite the recent boom in development-led archaeology, it continues to be so. Knowledge of this period is sketchy at best and is predominantly based on a limited artefact record, mainly from the north of the country, a small number of prestigious monuments referred to as the 'royal sites', some hillforts and a restricted burial record. Although many new sites dating from this period have been discovered

in recent years, there has been no meaningful or widespread assessment of these new data. Consequently, little is known about settlement and society during this period.

The structures excavated at Ballinaspig More are two of only a small number of Iron Age structures excavated in Cork, with others being discovered at Muckridge and possibly Conva. At present there is little evidence of a significant Iron Age presence in the Cork region. Settlement sites are few and far between, as well as being difficult to identify (Woodman 2000), while the material culture of this period, which has been used to indicate Iron Age activity in other regions of the country, is almost non-existent. Only a few traces of Iron Age activity were revealed within the N22 Ballincollig development. Apart from the two structures at Ballinaspig More 5, only a small number of pits dating from this period were discovered. These were located at Curraheen 1 (two pits, one a possible bowl furnace) and Curraheen 5 (a pit associated with burnt mound activity). The low number of Iron Age sites from the Ballincollig Bypass is echoed across all of the other recent road schemes within Cork, including the N8 Rathcormac to Fermoy, the N8 Fermoy to Mitchelstown and the N8 Glanmire to Watergrasshill. Iron Age activity along all

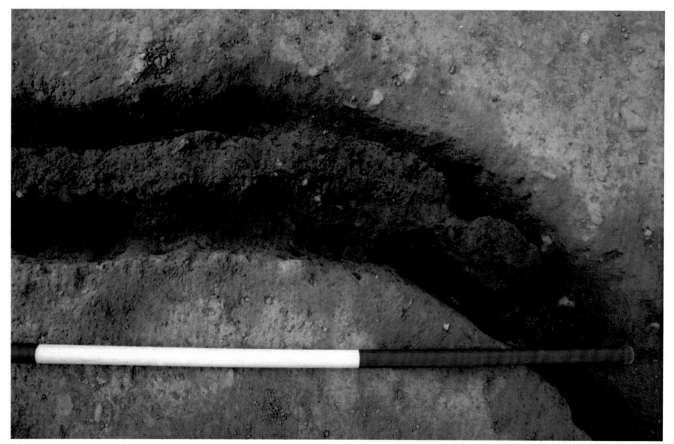

Fig. 6.13—Ballinaspig More: slot-trench containing burnt remains of timber planking, from east.

Fig. 6.14—Ballinaspig More: post-excavation view of slot-trench C1120.

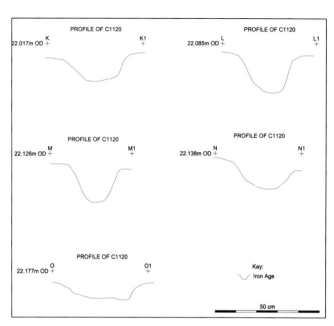

Fig. 6.16—Ballinaspig More: profiles through slot-trench of structure 3.

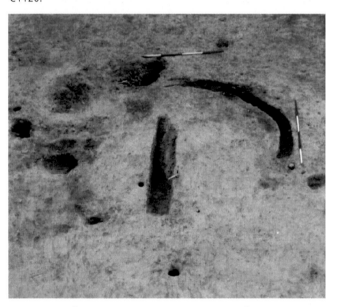

Fig. 6.15—Ballinaspig More: post-excavation view of structure 3, from north.

of these road schemes was predominantly represented by pits, frequently isolated and mostly interpreted as possible bowl furnaces; no structures dating from this period were discovered (Ken Hanley, pers. comm.). Despite these low numbers, however, the combined presence of these features, together with the recent discoveries of Iron Age sites elsewhere in the country, is of major significance. A recent survey of the sites excavated on all NRA road schemes indicates that 10% of

them have produced Iron Age dates, though not surprisingly many consist of ephemeral features and isolated pits. McLaughlin and Conran (2008) have indicated that in recent years 30 new Iron Age sites have been discovered on National Roads Authority schemes in Munster. These include burial, ssettlement and industrial activities; interestingly, all 30 sites were confirmed as Iron Age on the basis of radiocarbon dating. Very few of the sites had contemporary artefacts, with the exception of blue glass beads from Muckridge, Co. Cork, Knockcommane, Co. Limerick, and Knockgraffon, Co. Tipperary, while at Marlhill, Co. Tipperary, blue glass beads, nail shanks and fragments of copper alloy were discovered.

Evidence from the pollen record from around the country suggests that there was a significant decrease in agricultural activity during the Iron Age. The opposite, however, was true in the early medieval period, which saw an intensification of agriculture. Pollen diagrams from the Beara Peninsula, Co. Cork (Lynch 1981), appear to support this trend, while, in contrast, the pollen record from the Mizen Peninsula, Co. Cork (O'Brien 1999), suggests that agricultural activity and woodland clearance continued into the early medieval period.

The Iron Age settlement
The Iron Age, as mentioned earlier, is one of the least understood periods of Irish prehistory, particularly in the south-west (Raftery 1994). Therefore the discovery of any features dating from this period is welcome in trying to piece together this elusive age. Radiocarbon analysis of charcoal

derived from a post-hole associated with structure 1 and from the slot-trench of structure 3 returned Iron Age dates (360–280/240–60 cal. BC, Beta-178205; 790–390 cal. BC, Beta-178209). As the area around structure 1 was heavily degraded, predominantly as a result of soil erosion and to a lesser extent of agricultural activity, interpretation of this structure has proved difficult. Further difficulties were caused by the possible removal of any potential occupational layers or deposits.

Structure 1 consisted of a C-shaped alignment of post-holes, which may originally have formed a complete circle. The post-holes to the north-east of the structure were shallower than elsewhere, mainly owing to their precarious position on the ridge, where soil erosion had a greater impact. No post-holes were evident to the extreme north-east of the structure, and it is possible that they were completely destroyed, with a difference in ground level of 0.5m between this area of the structure and the south-west (Fig. 6.6). Soil erosion cannot, however, explain the absence of any internal roof supports.

As it was difficult to determine the exact function of this structure, a number of options have been explored; although a domestic interpretation is preferred, other alternatives are also considered, albeit in less detail. The first interpretation suggests that this is the remnants of an Iron Age roundhouse. Many houses were constructed by using large upright posts to support the roof. Ring-beams or plates rested on top of the upright posts, which would have taken the weight of the rafters, lessening the need for an internal roof support. These rafters met in the centre, creating a conical roof. The frame of the roof would then be constructed by securing cross-ties or battens on which a roof covering would be placed. This could have been of turf or, more probably, thatch. The main timbers used in construction ranged from ash and elm to birch and oak. Ash was identified from one of the posts associated with this structure. Various types of joint, such as mortise-and-tenon and scarf-and-lap, would have been used to strengthen the structure, although simple ties could have been used. Walls were made by weaving lengths of wood between upright stakes to produce wattle screens, which were then covered in mud, clay, dung or a mixture of all three to produce a solid wall (www.gangsterno1.co.uk/history/timeteam/ironage.html).

A post-hole to the east of the structure tentatively implies that the building may have included an entrance porch, which would further corroborate a domestic function (Figs 6.5–6.7). Iron Age domestic houses are extremely elusive in Ireland and many excavated sites of this date contain no traces of domestic structures. Finding parallels to structure 1 is therefore difficult in the extreme, though one such example

was discovered during archaeological works on the Youghal Bypass. This structure was located at Muckridge, Co. Cork, and has been dated to cal. AD 20–350. It consisted of a circular arrangement of ten post-holes, with a diameter of 6m. As with structure 1 at Ballinaspig More, these posts would have formed the main structural components of a timber roundhouse. A hearth at the centre of the Muckridge house consisted of a circular, bowl-shaped cut, which contained a blue glass bead fragment. An oval, stone-lined storage pit, which may have been used to store grain or other foodstuffs, was located close to the hearth (Noonan 2004).

Recent excavations along the route of the N8 Cashel to Mitchelstown road revealed six Iron Age settlement sites, all of which were dated by means of radiocarbon analysis. Structural remains included three subcircular buildings at Ballydrehid, Co. Tipperary, while at Killemly, Co. Tipperary, a scatter of pits and post-holes were found. Isolated and ephemeral features may represent domestic activity at Ballylegan and Shanballyduff, Co. Tipperary, while an enclosed circular building was discovered at Knockcommane, Co. Limerick (see below) (McQuade et al. 2009).

At Ballydrehid there appeared to have been continuity of activity, with evidence for settlement from all phases of the Bronze Age. It has been suggested that the three subcircular structures and associated features were all contemporary, as they were located in close proximity to each other, had similar ground-plans and walls defined by post-holes (McQuade et al. 2009). Like structure 1 at Ballinaspig More, these three structures have been interpreted as domestic buildings, although none contained hearths. Only one of the structures was dated, with charcoal from an oak post producing a date of cal. AD 240–392 (UB-7221).

At Moneylawn Lower, Co. Wexford, a structure of Iron Age date formed part of a multiphased site: it consisted of two C-shaped slot-trenches, an inner and outer ring. Although these trenches were incomplete, the excavator believes that they are likely to have formed more complete circles originally. A modern field boundary truncated the structure along its south-eastern side (McKinstry 2008). The diameter of the outer slot-trench has been estimated at c. 6.1m and the inner one at c. 4.8m. Several pits, post-holes and hearths were enclosed by these slot-trenches, and it is not known whether the slot-trenches were contemporary. It is possible that one of the slot-trenches represents a phase of repair or rebuilding, or alternatively the inner slot-trench may denote an internal division. Charcoal from a possible hearth within this structure was dated to 349–308 cal. BC (UBA-8222).

At Baysrath, Co. Kilkenny, a large multiphased site has been excavated recently, and initial radiocarbon analysis indicates that it contains a considerable quantity of Iron Age settlement evidence, including pits, post-holes, furnaces and hearths, as well as indications of funerary activity. The site includes evidence for a number of roundhouses, although a definitive Iron Age date has not yet been established (Channing 2008).

While the majority of the sites mentioned above do not appear to have been enclosed, evidence for enclosed settlement has also been identified recently. As noted, Knockcommane, Co. Limerick, was defined by a circuit of four discontinuous gullies or ditch segments, 15m in diameter, which enclosed the remains of a possible structure. A blue glass bead was recovered from one of the gullies, while hazel charcoal from this feature was dated to 357–47 cal. BC (UB-7842). A circular structure 8.5m in diameter and consisting of a slot-trench and five post-holes was identified within the enclosure. A bowl furnace and associated smelting waste located within this building provided evidence for iron production at the site, while charred oak sapwood from this furnace was dated to 375–182 cal. BC (UB-7239) (McQuade et al. 2009). Fills from the outer gullies contained waste from the furnace, suggesting that they were contemporary; industrial activity may therefore have been associated with the domestic structure.

Alternatively, rather than being a dwelling, structure 1 at Ballinaspig More may have had a ceremonial/non-secular role, with similar functions being ascribed to a number of post-built structures dating from this period. It is also possible that structure 1 may never have been roofed, basically consisting of a 'C' or circular arrangement of large timber uprights, somewhat reminiscent of the timber circles of the Neolithic or the stone circles of the Bronze Age. Condit and Simpson (1998) refer to two timber circles that have been placed firmly in the Iron Age. The building of a multiringed timber circle at Navan Fort has been dated to 98 BC, while the timber circle from Dún Ailinne also originated during this period. Two phases of timber circle construction in Ireland have now been documented: one in the late Neolithic and the other in the Iron Age. Gibson (2000, 11–14) has pointed out that there is 'an increasingly recognised phenomenon in Irish archaeology that if a monument resembles a type of monument found in Neolithic Britain, then the Irish example is more likely to be Iron Age!' This is particularly true of ritual sites. In the case of timber circles with millennia separating the demise of the final Neolithic and the advent of the Iron Age, we can only speculate as to what facilitated the reincarnation of this tradition, especially when no physical trace of the timber circles would have survived centuries, let alone millennia. Gibson believes that stories of the late Neolithic timber circles

may have persisted in the Iron Age oral traditions.

As noted above, structure 3 at Ballinaspig More consisted of a combination of a wall-slot and post-holes. At Magheraboy, Co. Sligo, a small circular structure with a diameter of c. 4m was excavated. This structure was defined by a penannular foundation trench with a possible entrance situated to the north-east. Charred split-oak planks lined the base of the trench and one of these was dated to 370–30 cal. BC (Beta-86485). While the function of this structure was uncertain, it is possible that it consisted of a light timber frame covered either by hides or thatch. This building would have functioned adequately as a store, shelter or hut (Danaher 2007). Recent excavations around the country have revealed similar structures, which are currently awaiting radiocarbon dating. For instance, a structure of similar shape and dimensions was unearthed at Morett 4, Co. Laois. A gully defined the circular structure, which measured 4.4m in diameter. The north-western section of this gully was U-shaped in profile and measured 0.6m wide by 0.26m deep, while the western and south-western sections of the gully had a V-shaped profile with an average width of 0.74m and an average depth of 0.34m (J. Dempsey, pers. comm.).

In terms of morphology, comparisons can be made with hut structures of the late Bronze Age, many of which contained footing trenches and were of similar dimensions (Doody 2000). Both structure 3 and the Magheraboy structure dated from the middle Iron Age, suggesting that there may have been a continuation of building styles from the late Bronze Age through to the Iron Age, particularly in terms of small huts with a footing trench. When excavated, many of these structures reveal no trace of an associated/diagnostic finds assemblage. The current archaeological literature identifies a large number of middle to late Bronze Age structures and consequently many sites are assumed, during excavation, to date from this period. It is only through radiocarbon analysis, however, that their true dates emerge. Therefore the dearth of Iron Age structures in the Irish archaeological record may be partially due to the automatic designation of similar structures as late Bronze Age, without considering a later date for them. As with structure 1, the only finds associated with structure 3 were cereal grains and a piece of possible metal slag. Of the charred cereal grains, barley predominated, with some wheat also present. The purpose of structure 3 is debatable. Its light timber frame may indicate that it was a store or shelter (hence the cereal grains), but its functionality as a house would have to be questioned. Owing to the mishmash of features dating from various prehistoric periods within the vicinity of the slot-trench, the footprint of this structure (3) was not immediately discernible. Only the

Fig. 6.17—Ballinaspig More: visualisation of structure 1 (drawing by John Hodgson).

slot-trench was dated to this period.

Charcoal from this slot-trench was identified as oak, with radiocarbon analysis returning a date of 790–390 cal. BC (Beta-78209), while a sample of charcoal (identified as ash) from structure 1 was dated to between 360–280 cal. BC and 240–60 cal. BC (Beta-178205). Although these dates do not appear to be contemporary, the 'old wood effect' should be taken into consideration. As oak can live for 300–400 years, this could add the same number of years onto structure 3, particularly if heartwood from an old tree was used in the construction of this building. Assuming that the oak used in the construction of structure 3 was old, then the likelihood is that both structures are broadly contemporary. In terms of understanding these two structures, they have proved as elusive as the period from which they originated, but it is probable that they represent a homestead consisting of at least a

domestic structure and outbuilding. Unfortunately, the presence of cereal grains from these structures only came to light after they had been dated.

From the scant evidence for Irish Iron Age houses, it appears that the settlement pattern for this period was one of small, dispersed farmsteads. Interestingly, few if any of these houses date from the early Iron Age, with the majority occurring in the middle Iron Age between c. 400 BC and 100 BC. In contrast to the meagre evidence for Iron Age domestic structures in Ireland, a large number are known from Britain; these span the entire period and, in stark contrast to the Irish evidence, there are numerous early Iron Age examples (Eoin Grogan, pers. comm.).

Conclusion

The excavation revealed a multiphased site that spanned almost six millennia, from the early Neolithic through the final Neolithic/early Bronze Age, the middle Bronze Age, the Iron Age and the post-medieval period. An indication of what the surrounding landscape could have looked like in antiquity may be garnered from some of the other excavations that were carried out in the vicinity of the site. Ballinaspig More 4, to the east of the Twopot River, contained early Neolithic and post-medieval features and, like the site at BM5, BM4 was sited on good agricultural land. The elevated ridge on which BM5 was located gives way to marginal low-lying fields to the north, with a height difference of 9m separating the two. Within this latter area, five *fulachta fiadh*, which are usually located close to water, were discovered and subsequently excavated (Murphy 2003; Danaher 2004). A number of these occurred within recently reclaimed land. The presence of these features indicates that a marshy environment may have prevailed during prehistory. Curraheen 1 and 4, the other sites containing Iron Age activity within the route of the N22 Ballincollig Bypass, were situated over 2.5km to the west of this site.

Excavation of BM5 revealed that many of the features were located along and close to the southern excavation limits of the site. This suggests that the archaeological remains identified may be positioned on the periphery of the larger settlement areas, with the core settlement locations being sited to the south of BM5. It is feasible, therefore, that a number of the features encountered within this site were outliers of the main settlement concentration. In particular, this may apply to the Neolithic and Bronze Age phases.

This essay has focused on two Iron Age structures and, although their exact function is uncertain, a domestic interpretation is preferred, with structure 1 being the remains of a roundhouse and structure 3 representing a store. Unfortunately, no artefacts were found in connection with these buildings that could shed further light on their role.

Despite the number of recently constructed roads and other developments transecting diverse landscapes, very little coherent Iron Age evidence has been discovered in Ireland; nevertheless, the features that have been found make a significant contribution to our understanding of this enigmatic period. The settlement pattern appears to be one of small, dispersed farmsteads. While the evidence for the architecture of the period is for the most part informative, many of the roundhouses that have been discovered have been badly truncated. With increasing numbers of Iron Age roundhouses emerging, it is becoming clear that there are interesting differences between individual structures. The footprint of some is defined by a ring of evenly spaced post-holes; others are defined by penannular foundation trenches, and a few by a combination of post-holes and foundation trenches. Internal features noted at some houses indicate internal divisions, while structure 1 at BM5 may have had a porch. Interestingly, few, if any, of the sites mentioned in this text contained evidence for external fences or boundaries. The potential entrance to structure 1 at BM5 was to the east, while the structure at Magheraboy, Co. Sligo, had a north-eastern entrance. As with many Bronze Age roundhouses, this may have been a conscious attempt by the builders to denote the direction of the rising sun. The remains of most of the structures discussed above suggest that there was a continuation of the structural styles established in the Bronze Age. At multiphased sites where numerous structures are present, often the first indication of an Iron Age presence at these locations comes on receipt of the radiocarbon dates, and this is particularly true when the material culture of this period is absent, which it frequently is. At multiphased sites where numerous roundhouses of similar construction have been identified, only one or two may be dated and the rest assumed to be contemporary. Consequently, it is conceivable that structures of Iron Age date may lie undetected within these sites. In order to address this potential problem, future excavation of any multiphased settlement site should rely on clearly defined dating strategies to distinguish between roundhouses, particularly in the absence of any associated material culture. Though by no means comprehensive, our understanding of Iron Age settlement and society is becoming more illuminated with each new discovery.

Bibliography

Channing, J. 2008 Sites 53 and 54, Baysrath, Co. Kilkenny (E2517 A032). Unpublished preliminary report prepared for the DEHLG.

Condit, T. and Simpson, D. 1998 Irish hengiform enclosures and related monuments: a review. In A. Gibson and D. Simpson (eds), *Prehistoric ritual and religion*, 45–61. Stroud.

Cooney, G. 2000 Recognising regionality in the Irish Neolithic. In A. Desmond, G. Johnson, M. McCarthy, J. Sheehan and E. Shee Twohig (eds), *New agendas in Irish prehistory: papers in commemoration of Liz Anderson*, 49–60. Bray.

Cooney, G. and Grogan, E. 1999 *Irish prehistory: a social perspective*. Bray.

Danaher, E. 2004 *Fulachta fiadh* at Ballinaspig More, Ballincollig, Co. Cork (02E1230 & 02E1233). Unpublished report prepared for Dúchas: the Heritage Service.

Danaher, E. 2007 *Monumental beginnings: the archaeology of the N4 Sligo inner relief road*. Dublin.

Doody, M. 2000 Bronze Age houses in Ireland. In A. Desmond, G. Johnson, M. McCarthy, J. Sheehan and E. Shee Twohig (eds), *New agendas in Irish prehistory: papers in commemoration of Liz Anderson*, 135–60. Bray.

Gibson, A. 2000 Circles and henges: reincarnations of past traditions? *Archaeology Ireland* **51**, 11–14.

Lynch, A. 1981 *Man and environment in south-west Ireland*. British Archaeological Reports, British Series 85. Oxford.

McKinstry, L. 2008 Site 13, Moneylawn Lower, Co. Wexford (E3478 A003/015). Unpublished preliminary report prepared for the DEHLG.

McLaughlin, M. and Conran, S. 2008 The emerging Iron Age of south Munster. *Seanda* **3**, 51–3.

McQuade, M., Molloy, B. and Moriarty, C. 2009 *In the shadow of the Galtees: archaeological excavations along the N8 Cashel to Mitchelstown road scheme*. Dublin.

Murphy, D. 2003 Ballinaspig More 1, 2 and 3. *Excavations 2001*, 26. Bray.

Noonan, D. 2004 Muckridge, Co. Cork. Unpublished report prepared for Dúchas: the Heritage Service.

O'Brien, W. 1999 *Sacred ground: megalithic tombs in coastal south-west Ireland*, 1–59. Galway.

Raftery, B. 1994 *Pagan Celtic Ireland: the enigma of the Irish Iron Age*. London.

Woodman, P.C. 2000 Hammers and shoeboxes: new agendas for prehistory. In A. Desmond, G. Johnson, M. McCarthy, J. Sheehan and E. Shee Twohig (eds), *New agendas in Irish prehistory: papers in commemoration of Liz Anderson*, 1–10. Bray.

7. Two Iron Age ring-ditches in Ballyboy, Co. Galway

Shane Delaney, Jim McKeon and Siobhán McNamara

Introduction

A long, whale-backed gravel ridge rises above surrounding bogs, about 5km south of the town of Gort, in the townland of Ballyboy, Co. Galway. The elevated ridge of well-drained, good arable land is exactly the type of topographical feature where one might expect to find evidence of prehistoric activity. The ridge in Ballyboy did not disappoint. Two ring-ditches containing cremation burials and a large assemblage of artefacts—mainly glass and amber beads—were discovered *c.* 1km apart near the brow (Ballyboy 1) and on the eastern flank (Ballyboy 2) of the ridge during excavations in advance of the construction of the M18 Gort to Crusheen road (Figs 7.1 and 7.2). Radiocarbon dating of the human remains, in addition to comparable burial practices and artefactual assemblages, indicates that the two ring-ditches were broadly contemporary and in use between the final century BC and the first century AD.

The Iron Age ring-ditches were two of 35 archaeological sites excavated within the footprint of the new M18 (25 of

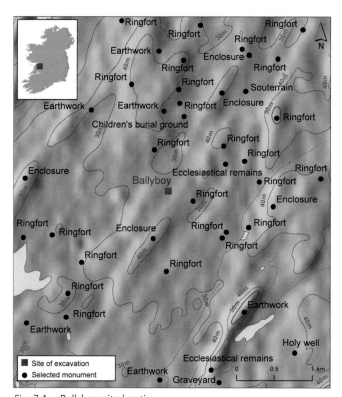

Fig. 7.1—Ballyboy: site location.

which were burnt mounds or *fulachta fiadh*). The road passes through the modern and ancient boundary between Connacht and Munster (formerly Thomond). It is 22km long and traverses 23 townlands, from just north of Gort, Co. Galway, to just south of Crusheen, Co. Clare, where it ties in to the Ennis Bypass. The archaeological investigations were conducted by Irish Archaeological Consultancy (IAC) Ltd on behalf of Galway County Council and the National Roads Authority.

Site typology: ring-ditches

Ring-ditches are one of the monument types classified under the general 'barrow' label and generally consist of a single ditch enclosing a roughly circular area. Examples with two and even three enclosing ditches have been noted, such as at Tankardstown, Co. Limerick (Gowen and Tarbett 1988, 156), and Creevy, Co. Donegal (Waddell 2010, 366, fig. 182.3). The incorporation of an entrance into the enclosed area—generally a simple undug causeway—appears to be more common in later examples. Ring-ditches are generally located on higher ground and are often found in close proximity to streams or rivers. Sites may be clustered—along with other barrow types—to form barrow cemeteries.

Ring-ditches may contain central cremation pits or cremated bone/funeral pyre debris, either in or beneath a mound or in the fill of the enclosing ditch. Sometimes there is no direct funerary evidence associated with the ring-ditch, but in such examples the monuments are commonly located within a prehistoric cemetery complex (Daly and Grogan 1993). It is often unclear whether ring-ditches formed stand-alone funerary monuments or whether they are the remnants of flattened barrows. It is also possible that those examples lacking associated burials represent cemetery-markers or even non-funerary structures.

The manner in which human remains were deposited in the ring-ditch varies from site to site. Both inhumation and cremation burials have been noted, but cremation appears to have been the dominant rite. Human remains were most commonly buried in simple unlined pits but were also interred in cists and stone-lined pits. The interior burial space was usually defined by the ring-ditch, but in some cases burials can be found outside this enclosed area. It is also common to find cremated deposits in simple spreads within the interior or

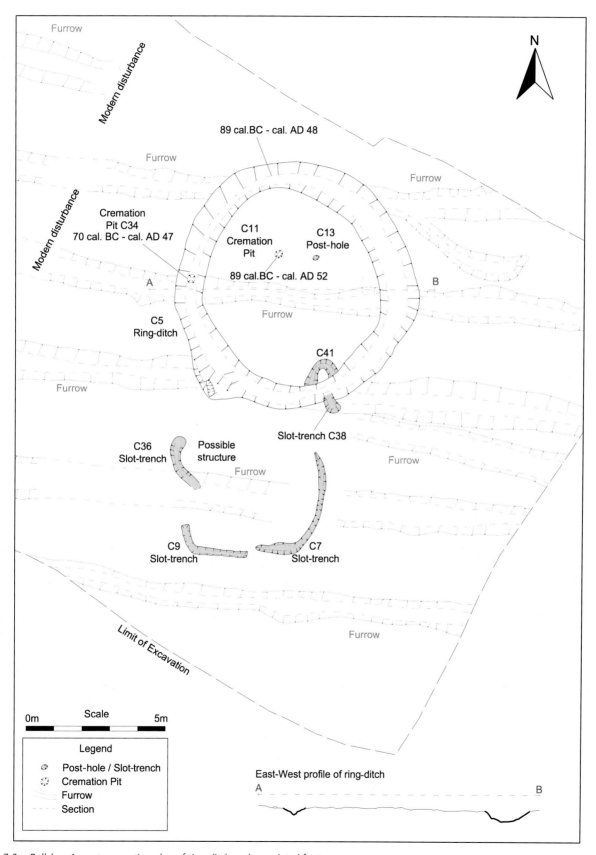

Fig. 7.2—Ballyboy 1: post-excavation plan of ring-ditch and associated features.

Fig. 7.3—Ballyboy 1: aerial view of ring-ditch, showing topographical setting; note slot-trench to right of ring-ditch and later cultivation furrows that cross the site.

in the enclosing ditch. In many cases a variety of burial forms are found in one ring-ditch. In general, the burials represent only a small proportion of the population and, given the type of artefacts that often accompany the remains, they probably represent the treatment of high-ranking individuals.

In general, ring-ditches date from the Bronze Age, with the earlier examples being simpler in form and later ones incorporating entrances and a wider range of burial practices. Ring-ditches continued to be built—or earlier monuments reused—during the Iron Age and early medieval period. Iron Age ring-ditches were excavated at Ardsallagh, Co. Meath (Clarke 2007), Cherrywood, Co. Dublin (O'Neill 2000, 54), and Knockcommane, Co. Limerick (McQuade *et al.* 2009, 163–5), while two early medieval examples were excavated in Cross, Co. Galway (Mullins and Bermingham, forthcoming).

Ballyboy 1: ring-ditch and cremation burials[1]
This ring-ditch was discovered in the townland of Ballyboy, *c.* 4.5km south of Gort and approximately 200m east of the Gort

to Tubber road. The ring-ditch was situated in an elevated, hedge-bound pasture field just below the crest of a long, east-facing ridge, with good views to east and west (Fig. 7.3). Three human cremations were identified within the ring-ditch, bone from which produced Iron Age radiocarbon dates. The earth-cut remains of a later structure were also found, and artefacts included decorated beads and an antler die.

The ring-ditch was 28.5m in circumference and enclosed a space measuring 6.4m by 6.2m, with a maximum external diameter of 8.6m (Fig. 7.2). The ditch was 1.65m wide and 0.46m deep (max.). The primary fill of the ditch comprised silty clay with occasional charcoal (birch, crab-apple and ash) and cremated bone. A cremation pit (C34), 0.29m long by 0.14m deep, was cut into this fill in the western arc of the ring-ditch. The cremated human remains of a single adult were recovered from the pit. A radiocarbon date of cal. 90 BC–AD 47 (UBA-13026) was returned for a sampled bone. A decorated antler gaming piece (Fig. 7.7) and six water-rolled stones were included in the deposit, along with charcoal

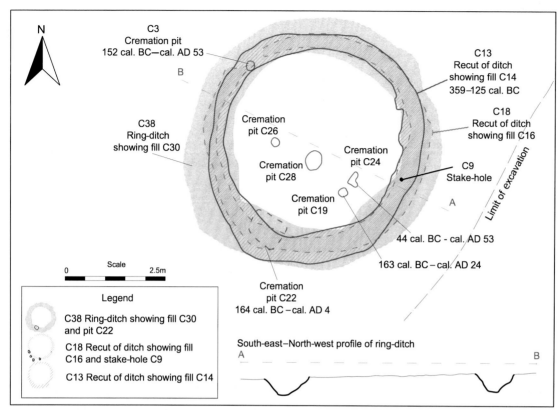

Fig. 7.4—Ballyboy 2: plan of ring-ditch, showing cremation pits and ditch recuts.

Fig. 7.5—Ballyboy 2: post-excavation view of ring-ditch during final stages of recording.

Fig. 7.6—Ballyboy 1 and 2: glass and amber beads. (a) Type A, small, light blue-green, translucent glass bead; (b) type B, plain, dark blue, annular glass bead; (c) multicoloured glass bead; (d) glass toggle bead; (e) heat-affected fragment of multicoloured glass bead; (f) large clear glass bead; (g) amber bead; (h) amber toggle bead.

Fig. 7.7—Ballyboy 1: parallelepiped antler/bone die, front and reverse.

Fig. 7.8—Ballyboy 2: glass and amber beads.

fragments of ash and Maloideae species (hawthorn, rowan and crab-apple).

The ditch had been recut above the cremation pit. The shallow recut was deliberately filled (C4) with black, silty clay, rich in charcoal (hazel, birch, oak, ash and Maloideae) and cremated human bone from at least one adult. A sample of the bone returned a radiocarbon date of cal. 89 BC–AD 48 (UBA-13024). Seven glass beads and one of amber were recovered from the top of this fill, along with two pieces of corroded iron.

Another small cremation pit (C11) in the north-western quadrant of the ring-ditch—towards the centre—measured 0.34m by 0.3m by 0.27m deep (Fig. 7.2). The position of this pit suggests that it was the primary burial and the focus of the ring-ditch. The cremated remains of an adult female returned a radiocarbon date of cal. 89 BC–AD 52 (UBA-13025). Charcoal of hazel, ash, crab-apple and hawthorn was included in the pit, and a post-hole (C13) was identified *c.* 1m to the east.

A subrectangular structure was cut into the top of the ring-ditch, at its southern edge (Figs 7.2 and 7.3). The remains consisted principally of three L-shaped trenches (C7, C9 and C36) with well-defined cuts and V-shaped cross-sections. The fragmentary remains of two other possible slot-trenches formed the rest of the structure (C41 and C38), but these were heavily disturbed by a series of east/west cultivation furrows of later date. Together the slot-trenches defined an area measuring 6m north–south by 4.8m east–west. No datable material was recovered from the trenches but the structure post-dated the ring-ditch and pre-dated the furrows. There is no positive evidence that it had any relationship to the ring-ditch or that it is of early date.

Ballyboy 2: ring-ditch and cremation burials[2]

This ring-ditch was approximately 5.5km south of Gort, on the lower eastern flank of the same ridge as the ring-ditch at Ballyboy 1 but *c.* 1km to the south-south-west. Ballyboy 2 lay in a pasture field enclosed by hedgerows on stony embanked field dykes, with a low-lying bog to the south (Fig. 7.5). Unlike Ballyboy 1, the views from the site were restricted owing to its low-lying aspect. The site included a number of cremation burials and a rich artefactual assemblage, including 69 glass and 24 amber beads (Figs 7.6 and 7.8) as well as pieces of copper alloy. The surface of the ring-ditch was crossed by later cultivation furrows.

The ring-ditch at Ballyboy 2 (C38) measured 19.5m in circumference (Fig. 7.4). The ditch—1.27m wide by 0.55m deep (max.)—defined an area of roughly 4.15m by 4.2m and had an average external diameter of 6.2m. Four cremation pits were identified in the interior of the ring-ditch (C19, C24, C26 and C28), all of similar size (max. 0.49m by 0.42m by 0.02m deep) and fills. The pits were arranged along a roughly west/east line, just south of the middle of the interior, and may have been the primary focus of activity on the site (Fig. 7.4). Charcoal from the pits included birch, oak and ash, and cremated human bone provided radiocarbon date ranges of cal. 163 BC–AD 24 (UBA-13030) and cal. 44 BC–AD 53 (UBA-13031).

The primary fill of the ditch (C30) contained fragmentary charred timbers, as well as bone fragments and charcoal of alder/hazel, birch, oak, ash, elm and poplar. A large cremation pit (C22)—1m by 0.7m and 0.28m deep—was cut into the primary fill of the ditch and contained charcoal and adult human bone (35–64 years of age at death). The

cremation pit was substantially larger than the others identified in the ring-ditch and was marked with stones. Cremated bone from the pit returned a radiocarbon date of cal. 164 BC–AD 4 (UBA-13032).

The ring-ditch was recut (C18) on either side of the cremation pit (C22) and deliberately filled with sandy silt containing charcoal, bone and stones. This fill (C17) contained the largest deposit of cremated bone (189g); while it was recovered from throughout the entire ditch, it was identified as belonging to one adult individual (18–44 years). Charcoal from the fill included hazel/alder, birch, oak, ash, hawthorn and some carbonised hazelnut shell. The fill was homogeneous apart from one lens of sandy silt that contained stones, charcoal and the cremated remains of a juvenile (12–17 years). The fill of the recut and the cremation pit (C22) were covered by a layer of stones—one of these stones was positioned directly over the cremation pit. A sealing layer, including charcoal and bone, was then deposited on top of the ring-ditch. A stake-hole within this layer may have held a marker.

At a later stage the ditch was recut again (C13) and refilled with dark, sandy silt with charcoal, bone and stone inclusions (C14). A fragment of cremated human bone yielded a radiocarbon date of 359–125 cal. BC (UBA-13028), which pre-dates the stratigraphically earlier cremation (C22). This indicates that the later deposit was contaminated with earlier material. An area of oxidisation—or heat-scorching—was noted at the base of the second recut ditch. A charcoal-rich layer with cremated human bone on this scorched area may represent an *in situ* cremation, possibly conducted immediately prior to the backfilling of the recut ditch. A small cremation pit was cut into the top fill of the recut. Burnt human bone from the pit returned a radiocarbon date of cal. 152 BC–AD 53 (UBA-13027) and came from a juvenile aged 12–18 years at death.

Chronology

The radiocarbon dates from Ballyboy indicate that the ring-ditches were broadly contemporary, though the earliest activity may have occurred at Ballyboy 2. The three cremations at Ballyboy 1 dated from between 90 cal. BC and cal. AD 52, while the radiocarbon dates recorded at Ballyboy 2 spanned the years between 164 cal. BC and cal. AD 53. Bone from the cremation pit (C22) that cut the primary ditch fill of Ballyboy 2 returned a radiocarbon date of cal. 164 BC–AD 4 (UBA-13032), however, providing a *terminus ante quem* of AD 4 for the initial construction of the ring-ditch. While cremated bone in the second recut ditch at Ballyboy 2 returned an earlier radiocarbon date—359–125 cal. BC (UBA-13028)—this was at odds with the stratigraphical evidence and must represent residual material. It does, however, reveal earlier Iron Age funerary activity in the immediate vicinity.

At both sites it is argued that the cremation pits within the ring-ditch interiors represented the primary focus of activity. At Ballyboy 1 this consisted of a single burial, while at Ballyboy 2 four cremations were identified. No real chronological distinction was revealed between the radiocarbon dates returned for the burials in the interiors and those in the enclosing ditches, however, suggesting that little time separated those funerary events.

Cremated human remains

Three cremation burials were found in the ring-ditch at Ballyboy 1. These contained the remains of adult individuals, of which at least one is likely to have been a female and one a male (Geber 2010a). One burial was located in a cremation pit (C11) almost in the centre of the ring-ditch interior (Fig. 7.2). It contained almost 500g of well-cremated, but fragmented, clean bones, comprising over 2,200 fragments. About 33% of the weight could be identified to skeletal elements, and these included bones from all four anatomical regions (skull, axial, upper and lower limbs). Age at death was estimated to have been between eighteen and 44 years, and the sex was determined as probably female based on a fragment of a mastoid process of a temporal bone, as this anatomical landmark is smaller and less marked in females than in males (*ibid.*). A second burial (C4) contained nearly 900 fragments of cremated bone, weighing almost 80g. It was deposited within the cut of the ring-ditch. The bones were well preserved but had suffered considerable fragmentation. A minimum of one individual was identified, of indeterminate sex. Bones from all anatomical regions of the body were present, indicating that a complete body was cremated. The final burial was interred within a pit (C34), which in turn cut the principal fill of the ring-ditch. Almost 564g of cremated bone was found in this feature, comprising about 2,400 fragments. Again, bones from all four anatomical body regions were identified. The age at death was estimated at between eighteen and 44 years (*ibid.*). The sex of the individual is likely to have been male, based on an assessment of the mastoid process of a temporal bone.

Eighteen deposits of cremated bone from Ballyboy 2 were analysed. Six cremation pit burials were identified (Fig. 7.4), all of which contained adult remains with one possible exception (C28), which might constitute the remains of an adolescent (Geber 2010b). Twelve depositions of cremated human bone were found within the ring-ditch. The largest deposit (189g) derived from an adult individual aged 18–44 years at the time of death. The remaining deposits were very small, ranging from only 0.07g to 18.24g. Unfortunately,

severe fragmentation of the bones hindered much of the age and sex estimation of the cremated individuals. As a result there is no evidence that the difference in burial contexts could have been related to social factors such as age and sex.

Artefacts

The artefactual assemblage from the Ballyboy ring-ditches is dominated by glass and amber beads. Other significant finds include Neolithic worked stone tools, a decorated antler/bone die, and copper-alloy fragments that probably represent clothes-fasteners or jewellery.

Worked stone

Nine pieces of worked chert were recovered from topsoil and from the fills of later cultivation furrows at Ballyboy 1: one bifacial blade core, four flakes, one piece of débitage and two convex end scrapers. The worked lithics are typologically and technologically diagnostic and date from the middle Neolithic (Sternke 2010). There is evidence of *in situ* flint-knapping/tool-resharpening at this site in the form of cores and débitage. The artefacts recovered are most likely associated with domestic tasks carried out in and around the environs of a possible nearby Neolithic settlement. Six small natural water-rolled pebbles (manuports) of sandstone, limestone and chert were recovered from the fill of a cremation pit (C34). The inclusion of small water-rolled pebbles, often made of quartz, with cremation and inhumation burials occurs frequently throughout prehistory and the early historic period.

Beads

A minimum of 105 beads made from glass (77) and amber (28) were recovered from cremation deposits in the ring-ditch (ditch and interior) at Ballyboy 2, while nine glass beads and one amber bead were found in the upper fills of the ditch at Ballyboy 1 (Carroll 2010a; 2010b) (Figs 7.6 and 7.8). The glass beads comprised two main types. Type A was a very small, light blue-green, translucent annular glass bead (though some were opaque). There were 38 of these from Ballyboy 2 and five from Ballyboy 1, which were almost all between 1.75mm and 2.5mm in diameter and 1mm thick (Fig. 7.6, a). The chalky, opaque surface of some of these beads appears to be due to heat damage or deterioration of the antimonite (tin or lead) components of the glass. Type B was a plain, dark blue annular bead, mainly of translucent glass, and is the most common type of bead found on Iron Age burial sites. At Ballyboy 2 there were 28 examples between 2mm and 3.5mm in diameter, and a further eight ranging from 3.6mm to 9mm in diameter (Fig. 7.6, b). Three (fused together) examples were found at Ballyboy 1, measuring 2–3.4mm in diameter.

There were three further glass beads at Ballyboy 2. One was roughly circular, dark red/red-brown, with a marvered brown and white twisted cable decoration in the form of an elongated 'S' placed laterally around its outer surface (Fig. 7.6, c). A toggle/dumb-bell bead was also found, composed of two translucent, pale blue-green spheres with a heavily pitted surface (Fig. 7.6, d). Finally, four small sherds of opaque blue glass with marvered red linear decoration are probably parts of one large decorated annular bead that split in the heat of the cremation pyre (Fig. 7.6, e). At Ballyboy 1 there was one almost spherical bead that measured 12.75mm by 12mm and had slightly flattened ends. It was pale blue-green and clear to translucent, with bubbles in its interior (Fig. 7.6, f).

At least 28 amber beads were recovered at Ballyboy 2—one small group (1–3 beads) had melted owing to exposure to intense heat and the number of beads was unclear. Most of the amber beads were larger than the glass beads. They ranged from 5mm to 6.5mm in diameter and were roughly 3.5mm thick (Fig. 7.6, g). The single amber example from Ballyboy 1 was a large toggle/dumb-bell bead, 14mm long and 9–10mm thick (Fig. 7.6, h). It was dark yellow-brown and had been heat-damaged/distorted.

In summary, the beads were mostly small, annular and monochrome. There were only three (including four glass fragments making up one bead) decorated with a second colour or motif, and only one bead from each site (toggle beads) that deviated from the annular, spherical or tub-shaped varieties. A large number of the beads were heat-affected, and in several cases were fused together. The melting and carbonisation of the beads, as well as the linear fusing of groups of beads that retain the shape of the perforation for the string throughout, indicate that the beads were lying horizontally in some cases as they were exposed to heat, probably as a consequence of being strung together and worn on the corpse in a pyre.

Antler/bone die
An antler/bone gaming piece recovered from the cremation pit (C34) at Ballyboy 1 has been identified as a parallelepiped die of flat rectangular form (Riddler and Trzaska-Nartowski 2010) (Fig. 7.7). It measures 26.3mm long by 15.1mm wide by 5.4mm thick and weighs 1.9g. The incomplete antler/bone die lacks a part of both of its broad faces, less than half of one of which now survives. It has been intensely burnt to a light grey colour and most of the inner tissue no longer survives. The extent of the burning can be clearly seen on the broader faces, where the triple ring-and-dot motifs, originally inscribed as circular patterns, are now oval. The die has been reduced in size by heat along its length and to a greater extent

across its width. The original parallelepiped form of the die is evident, however, despite its subsequent history, and it was originally rectangular and noticeably flat, the narrow sides being scarcely wide enough to accommodate the ring-and-dot patterning.

The sequence of ring-and-dot designs allows the numbering of the die to be reconstructed. The broad faces were originally incised with five and six motifs. One of the longer sides is complete and has three motifs, while both of the short sides have two motifs. On a conventional six-sided die the number 4 would be expected to fill the remaining space, but it appears that on this die the number 5 is repeated. The other long side has three motifs surviving, crowded towards one end, and could have accommodated four awkwardly spaced motifs originally, or as many as five in a more orderly arrangement, as noted below. The numbering sequence was almost certainly 3–5–5–6–2–2 (Riddler and Trzaska-Nartowski 2010).

The antler/bone parallelepiped die from Ballyboy 1 conforms to a small group of similar gaming pieces known from Iron Age contexts in Ireland, including examples from Mentrim Lough crannog and Lough Crew, Co. Meath, and Cush, Co. Limerick (Raftery 1984, 248–50). The majority of Irish rectangular dice—both this flat type and those of square section—are dated to the first few centuries AD based on parallels from Britain. The flat series—to which the Ballyboy example belongs—is thought to be a little earlier, dating from between the late first century BC and the first century AD (Raftery 1997).

Metal
Fifteen fragments of copper alloy were recovered from Ballyboy 2. These were mostly unidentified pieces from the ring-ditch and a cremation pit (C22). Seven of the copper-alloy objects are thin, curved fragments of wire. One is bent in a ring, with overlapping ends and a subrectangular section. Other pieces are thin, curved wire fragments with an oval/rectangular section, possibly from a single spiral-ringed object. This suggests a parallel with small spiral rings from early medieval pins (Fanning 1994, 13–15). Two fragments are flat and curved, possibly from small copper-alloy washers or flat beads. A small rivet is still encased in a fragment of folded sheet metal. Two items are roughly L-shaped with protrusions and are possibly terminals or feet from the same unidentified object. The remaining copper-alloy objects remain unidentified. The metal artefacts were found in association with the glass/amber beads and it is probable that, collectively, the objects are fragments of jewellery or clothes-fasteners that were on the body when it was cremated (MacDermott 2010).

Discussion

The ring-ditches at Ballyboy can be added to a number of Iron Age funerary monuments identified in the south Galway/north Clare region, many of which have been excavated in advance of recent infrastructural/road projects. A concentration of funerary barrows to the north of the Gort–Crusheen scheme (to the east and north-east of Ardrahan) may date from the Iron Age. One excavated example at Grannagh, Co. Galway, consisted of a ring-ditch containing pockets of cremated bone and a variety of finds, including glass and dumb-bell-shaped beads and bone pins (Waddell 2010, 367). Another ring-ditch, complete with cremation deposits, was excavated at Oran Beg, near Oranmore, Co. Galway (Rynne 1970). Over 80 glass beads were recovered during the excavation and, like many of those from Ballyboy, some appeared to have been fused in the cremation pyre. South of the Gort–Crusheen road scheme, evidence for Iron Age funerary activity was identified during excavations along the N18 Ennis Bypass and the N85 Western Relief Road. At Manusmore, Co. Clare, 27 burial pits returned radiocarbon dates spanning the Neolithic to the Iron Age, although the later pits contained burnt animal bone that may not be specifically related to the cremations (Hull 2006a). Another Iron Age pit burial was located nearby (Hull 2006b). At Killow, Co. Clare, a cremation pit was dated to the very early Iron Age and a wooden bowl found in nearby peat returned a similar date (Taylor 2006). An Iron Age ring-ditch was also excavated on the Ennis Bypass scheme, at Claureen, Co. Clare (Hull 2006c). That ring-ditch was 6m in diameter and, although it had been disturbed, yielded cremated bone deposits and finds including glass beads and fragments of quartz. Most of the Iron Age sites identified in close proximity to the new road relate to the funerary deposition of cremated bone, either in ring-ditches or in pits.

The bones in the cremation burials at Ballyboy 1 and 2 were all well incinerated, indicating that the cremations were successful and reached temperatures exceeding 650°C (Geber 2010a; 2010b). All the bones were clean, which suggests that they were collected and sorted immediately after burning, as soot-staining on the bones would have indicated that they were left in a smouldering pyre for some time before collection (Gevjall 1948, 155; Lisowski 1968, 78). The cremation of an average adult individual would generate around 1,000–2,400g of bone (McKinley 1993, 285). At Ballyboy 1 the largest deposit amounted to 563.22g (C34), while at Ballyboy 2 the largest deposit contained only 189g. The obvious absence of bone is indicative of token burial practice; since collecting the bones from the spent pyre would have been a time-consuming task, it may be an indicator of the high social status of the deceased (McKinley 1997, 142). Like the ring-ditches at Ballyboy, evidence from most of the excavated Iron Age funerary sites in the region (see above) reveals that the bone recovered from human cremation burials commonly does not represent complete individuals. This indicates that the practice of placing token deposits within pits and monuments was a common characteristic of Iron Age burials in the region.

The successful cremation of an average human requires about one ton of fuel, and, in common with other prehistoric cremation sites in Ireland, the local community of Ballyboy appear to have specifically selected wood—such as oak, hazel and ash—which burns slowly at high temperatures in order to optimise the cremation process and minimise the amount of fuel required (Cobain 2010; Grogan et al. 2007, 48–9). Again, as noted elsewhere, the presence of charcoal from the Maloideae family—particularly crab-apple, which has an aromatic scent when burnt—may indicate a conscious decision also to select fuels that would help to mask the smell of burning human remains (Grogan et al. 2007, 112).

The Ballyboy beads add to our knowledge of Iron Age bead assemblages and of Iron Age burial practices. Glass and amber bead assemblages from this period are increasingly found in cremation burial sites from between the latter centuries BC and the first century AD, and it is possible that in the future we will be able to refine their dates and identify the trade and importation of particular bead types. It is of great interest that bead assemblages are closely comparable and that a number of different bead types constantly recur between Iron Age burial sites where they are found. Strings of very small coloured beads seem to have been particularly popular in opaque yellow, translucent and opaque dark blue and a translucent blue-green, almost turquoise colour. Larger coloured beads seem to have been common in ones and twos. A string of beads typically may have held a small number of decorated beads, interspaced by small monochrome beads that formed most of the necklace (or bracelet).

The origin of many of the beads of this period is likely to have been in Britain rather than the European mainland, and the beads may have been sourced from factories such as that at Meare in Somerset (Guido 1978, 65–75). There is no evidence for similar bead-production factories in Ireland, and the fact that the majority of sites at which beads are found are coastal, or fairly close to main rivers, increases the likelihood that they were traded from abroad by water. The Ballyboy beads can be closely paralleled by bead assemblages from along the east coast of Ireland such as those from Donacarney, Co. Meath (Carroll 2010c), Balrothery, Co. Dublin (Ryan 2008), Loughey, Co. Down (Jope and Wilson 1957, 84), and Ferns and Ask, Co. Wexford (Carroll 2000; 2007). Ballyboy is not far from the mouth of the Shannon and the west coast of Ireland, and is close to Grannagh and Derrybrien, Co. Galway. A toggle bead comparable with the Ballyboy 2 example was found at Grannagh (Raftery 1984, 202), while a spectacular amber necklace of 500 strung beads was recovered from an Iron Age context in a bog at Derrybrien (O'Kelly 2005, 133). Trade links between these and several other sites producing similar beads at a similar time may very well be worth exploring in the future.

The fragmented copper-alloy objects from Ballyboy 2 were mostly unidentified pieces found in association with the glass and amber beads in the ring-ditch and a cremation pit (C22). They included curved pieces of wire, possible washers and rivets, folded sheet metal and L-shaped terminals or feet. Their material, form and provenance would suggest that—along with the decorative beads—they represent fragments of jewellery or clothes-fasteners that were on the body when it was cremated.

The antler/bone gaming piece found at Ballyboy 1 can be interpreted as a parallelepiped die of flat rectangular form and it is part of a small group of these gaming pieces known from Iron Age contexts in Ireland (Riddler and Trzaska-Nartowski 2010). Raftery (1984, 248–50) drew attention to similar 'rectangular plaques' from Mentrim Lough crannog, Co. Meath, and Cush, Co. Limerick, and an unfinished strip of bone from Lough Crew, Co. Meath, can also be added to this group. The Cush die, although more elaborate in its decoration, nonetheless includes five triple ring-and-dot motifs on one broad face and six on the other, as is the case with the Ballyboy example. One of the long sides has three motifs and two survive on the other, fragmentary long side, where there may originally have been four or five (Ó Ríordáin 1940, fig. 38; Raftery 1984, fig. 122.2). The identification of the Cush implement as a die was confirmed with the publication of a comparable die of Iron Age date from Navan Fort, Co. Armagh (Raftery 1997). This is a rectangular antler or bone strip of a simple type, without any elaboration of its single ring-and-dot markings. Both this die and another of the flat die series from Kilcurrivard, Co. Galway, include motifs representing the numbers five and six on the broad faces, with three and five on the long sides.

There appears to be some consistency in the numbering arrangements across all of the dice of this flat die series. They have five and six motifs on the broad faces, and three and five motifs on the long narrow sides. Interestingly, however, the short narrow faces are different. The Navan die has one motif at either end, while Ballyboy 1 has two; Cush has no motifs on these sides. The Mentrim Lough strip is more problematic,

being considerably larger than the other members of this class, with three and four motifs on the long narrow sides, six on one broad face but only two apparent on the other (Raftery 1984, fig. 122.1). The dice from Cush, Navan and Ballyboy 1 are all less than 30mm in length and 12–16mm in width, while the Mentrim Lough strip is 64mm by 27mm.

Raftery (1997) argued that the majority of Irish rectangular dice—both the flat type and those of square section—should be dated to the first few centuries AD on the basis of parallels from Scotland and England. The flat series, to which the Ballyboy die belongs, is thought to be a little earlier, dating from the late first century BC to the first century AD. The Scottish series of parallelepiped dice were catalogued by Clarke (1970), and subsequent discoveries have been noted by Hall (2007, 9 and fig. 18). The earliest Scottish dice date from the late first century BC and extend well into the first millennium AD, a dating scheme that matches the Irish evidence. The English series also consists of both flat rectangular dice and those of square section. The former group includes examples from Cadbury Castle and Maiden Castle, of late Iron Age to early Roman date (Gray 1966, 296; Wheeler 1943, 310–11 and fig. 106.5–6). While there can be some differences in numbering arrangements, flat rectangular dice from England generally come from contexts of the late first century BC to the first century AD—the same dating that Raftery proposed for the Irish series.

Summary

The ring-ditches at Ballyboy represent small funerary monuments that were used for a period between the first century BC and the first century AD. The radiocarbon dates for both sites, in addition to the comparable burial practices and artefactual assemblages, indicate that Ballyboy 1 and 2 were contemporary or nearly contemporary. The sites were used for multiple burials—comprising token cremations—over a relatively short period of time. Owing to the fragmented nature of the burnt bone, the diagnostic traits for sexing and aging were mostly absent; most age groups were noted in those remains that could be identified, however. The funerary activity at the sites was represented by pit burials and also by the deposition of cremated material in the enclosing ditches, perhaps as a ritual clearing of the non-specific pyre material. The recovery of a large assemblage of imported glass and amber beads (often heat-affected) and the remnants of possible copper-alloy dress-fasteners at Ballyboy 2 indicates that at least some of the bodies were cremated clothed and presumably in their finery. The artefacts recovered from the sites and the funerary rites revealed, combined with the specific dating of the burials, have furthered our knowledge of

Iron Age funerary monuments and practices both locally and on a national level. The ring-ditches at Ballyboy compare well with a number of other Iron Age funerary monuments identified in the south Connacht/north Munster area and beyond, with regard to their form, date, use and artefactual assemblages. The antler/bone die, in particular, represents a significant find, as it joins only a small group of similar objects recorded in the country.

On a final note, the anomalous radiocarbon date (359–125 BC) for cremated human bone at Ballyboy 2 reveals earlier Iron Age funerary activity in the immediate vicinity, and the diagnostically Neolithic chert tools and débitage from Ballyboy 1 push the human story of the townland even further back.

Acknowledgements

The archaeological excavations at Ballyboy 1 and 2, Co. Galway, were carried out on behalf of Galway County Council and the National Roads Authority in advance of the construction of the M18 Gort to Crusheen road. Sincere thanks are due to all the field and office staff at IAC and to Jerry O'Sullivan, NRA Archaeologist, who acted as project archaeologist on the scheme for Galway County Council.

Bibliography

Carroll, J. 2000 Report on the glass beads from a ring-ditch at Ferns, Co. Wexford. In F. Ryan, 'Excavation of a ring-ditch at Ferns, Co. Wexford'. Unpublished report prepared for the National Monuments Service, DEHLG, Dublin.

Carroll, J. 2007 Glass bead report. In P. Stevens, 'Preliminary report on archaeological excavation at Ask, Co. Wexford, Site 42–44 (A003/020)'. Unpublished report prepared for the National Monuments Service, DEHLG, Dublin.

Carroll, J. 2010a The glass and amber beads from Ballyboy 1. In S. McNamara, 'N18 Gort to Crusheen road scheme, Ballyboy 1: final report'. Unpublished report by IAC Ltd for Galway County Council.

Carroll, J. 2010b The glass and amber beads from Ballyboy 2. In S. McNamara, 'N18 Gort to Crusheen road scheme, Ballyboy 2: final report'. Unpublished final report by IAC Ltd for Galway County Council.

Carroll, J. 2010c Report on the glass beads from a ring-ditch at Donacarney Great, Co. Meath. In A. Giacometti, 'Excavation of a ring-ditch at Donacarney Great, Co. Meath (09E0451)'. Unpublished report prepared for the National Monuments Service, DEHLG, Dublin.

Clarke, D.V. 1970 Bone dice and the Scottish Iron Age. *Proceedings of the Prehistoric Society* **36**, 214–32.

Clarke, L. 2007 Interim excavation report of Ardsallagh 2, Co. Meath. Unpublished excavation report for Archaeological Consultancy Services Ltd.

Cobain, S. 2010 The charcoal remains from N18 Gort to Crusheen: Ballyboy 2. In S. McNamara, 'N18 Gort to Crusheen road scheme, Ballyboy 2: final report'. Unpublished report by IAC Ltd for Galway County Council.

Daly, A. and Grogan, E. 1993 Excavations of four barrows in Mitchelstowndown West, Knocklong, County Limerick. *Discovery Programme Reports* **1**, 44–60.

Fanning, T. 1994 *Viking Age ringed pins from Dublin*. Dublin.

Geber, J. 2010a Osteological report on cremation burials, Ballyboy 1. In S. McNamara, 'N18 Gort to Crusheen road scheme, Ballyboy 1: final report'. Unpublished report by IAC Ltd for Galway County Council.

Geber, J. 2010b Osteological report on cremation burials, Ballyboy 2. In S. McNamara, 'N18 Gort to Crusheen road scheme, Ballyboy 2: final report'. Unpublished report by IAC Ltd for Galway County Council.

Gevjall, N.-G. 1948 Bestämning av de brända benen från gravarna i Horn. In K.E. Sahlström and N.-G. Gejvall (eds), *Gravfältet på kyrkbacken i Horns socken, Västergötland*, 153–99. Stockholm.

Gowen, M. and Tarbett, C. 1988 A third season at Tankardstown. *Archaeology Ireland* **8**, 156.

Gray, H. St G. 1966 *The Meare lake village: a full description of the excavations and relics from the eastern half of the west village, 1910–1933*, vol. III. Taunton.

Grogan, E., O'Donnell, L. and Johnston, P. 2007 *The Bronze Age landscapes of the Pipeline to the West: an integrated archaeological and environmental assessment*. Bray.

Guido, M. 1978 *The glass beads of prehistoric and Roman Britain and Ireland*. London.

Hall, M. 2007 *Playtime in Pictland: the material culture of gaming in early medieval Scotland*. Rosemarkie.

Hull, G. 2006a N18 Ennis bypass and western relief road: Site AR100, Manusmore, Co. Clare. Unpublished excavation report by TVAS Ireland for Clare County Council.

Hull, G. 2006b N18 Ennis bypass and western relief road: Site AR102, Manusmore, Co. Clare. Unpublished excavation report by TVAS Ireland for Clare County Council.

Hull, G. 2006c N18 Ennis bypass and western relief road: Site AR131, Claureen, Co. Clare. Unpublished excavation report by TVAS Ireland for Clare County Council.

Jope, E.M. and Wilson, B.C.S. 1957 A burial group of the first century AD at Loughey near Donaghadee, Co. Down. *Ulster Journal of Archaeology* **20**, 72–95.

Lisowski, F.P. 1968 The investigation of human cremations.

In T. Bielicki and K. Saller (eds), *Anthropologie und Humangenetik*, 76–83. Stuttgart.

MacDermott, J. 2010 The metal finds from Ballyboy 2. In S. McNamara, 'N18 Gort to Crusheen road scheme, Ballyboy 2: final report'. Unpublished report by IAC Ltd for Galway County Council.

McKinley, J.I. 1993 Bone fragment size and weight of bone from modern British cremations and the implications for the interpretation of archaeological cremations. *International Journal of Osteoarchaeology* **3**, 283–7.

McKinley, J.I. 1997 Bronze Age 'barrows' and funerary rites and rituals of cremation. *Proceedings of the Prehistoric Society* **63**, 129–45.

McNamara, S. 2010a N18 Gort to Crusheen road scheme, Ballyboy 1: final report. Unpublished report by IAC Ltd for Galway County Council.

McNamara, S. 2010b N18 Gort to Crusheen road scheme, Ballyboy 2: final report. Unpublished report by IAC Ltd for Galway County Council.

McQuade, M., Molloy, B. and Moriarty, C. 2009 *In the shadow of the Galtees: archaeological excavations along the N8 Cashel to Mitchelstown road scheme*. Dublin.

Mullins, G. and Bermingham, N. (forthcoming) Ring-ditches with cremations and inhumations at Cross. In J. McKeon and J. O'Sullivan (eds), *The quiet landscape: archaeological excavations between Galway City and Ballinasloe in advance of the M6 PPP motorway*. Dublin.

O'Kelly, M.J. 2005 Bronze Age Ireland. In D. Ó Cróinín (ed.), *A new history of Ireland*, vol. I, 98–133. Oxford.

Ó Néill, J. 2000 Cherrywood Science and Technology Park, Co. Dublin. *Excavations 1999*, 54–6. Bray.

Ó Ríordáin, S.P. 1940 Excavations at Cush, County Limerick. *Proceedings of the Royal Irish Academy* **45**C, 83–181.

Raftery, B. 1984 *La Tène in Ireland: problems of origin and chronology*. Marburg.

Raftery, B. 1997 The die. In D.M. Waterman, *Excavations at Navan Fort, 1961–71* (ed. C.J. Lynn), 95. Belfast.

Riddler, I. and Trzaska-Nartowski, N. 2010 Report on worked bone gaming piece from Ballyboy 1. In S. McNamara, 'N18 Gort to Crusheen road scheme, Ballyboy 1: final report'. Unpublished report by IAC Ltd for Galway County Council.

Ryan, F. 2008 Excavation of Iron Age ring-ditches, cist burials and features relating to habitation at Glebe South. In J. Carroll, F. Ryan and K. Wiggins, *Archaeological excavations at Glebe South and Darcystown, Balrothery, Co. Dublin*, 107–38. Dublin.

Rynne, E. 1970 Oran Beg ring-barrow. *Excavations 1970*, 10. Belfast.

Sternke, F. 2010 Lithic finds report. In S. McNamara, 'N18 Gort to Crusheen road scheme, Ballyboy 1: final report'. Unpublished report by IAC Ltd for Galway County Council.

Taylor, K. 2006 N18 Ennis bypass and western relief road: Site AR104, Killow, Co. Clare. Unpublished excavation report by TVAS Ireland for Clare County Council.

Waddell, J. 2010 *The prehistoric archaeology of Ireland* (2nd edn). Bray.

Wheeler, R.E.M. 1943 *Maiden Castle, Dorset*. London.

Notes

1. Excavation E3719; director Siobhán McNamara; NGR 143125 197976; height 39m OD; parish of Beagh, barony of Kiltartan, Co. Galway.

2. Excavation E3718; director Siobhán McNamara; NGR 142802 197359; height 33m OD; parish of Beagh, barony of Kiltartan, Co. Galway.

8. An Iron Age penannular ring-ditch at Ballybronoge South, Co. Limerick

James Eogan with a contribution by Laureen Buckley

Introduction

A ring-ditch was discovered in Ballybronoge South townland, Co. Limerick, during the monitoring of topsoil clearance in advance of construction of the Adare to Annacotty N20/N21 road improvement scheme in July 1999. The ring-ditch was found at the northern end of the townland,[1] approximately 1.5km south of the village of Patrickswell (Fig. 8.1). It was situated on the crest of a low ridge (35m OD) in a field most recently used for pasture, with clear views in all directions.

There was no surface indication of the existence of the site. Initially, three subcircular spreads of charcoal-rich soil containing burnt bone were identified. These features were cordoned off and the remaining topsoil was removed by hand. This led to the discovery of the penannular ring-ditch. Unfortunately, an engineering test-pit had been dug through part of the site prior to the commencement of topsoil clearance in the area, without archaeological supervision; this had truncated the north-eastern ditch terminal and had removed a substantial portion of the enclosed area.

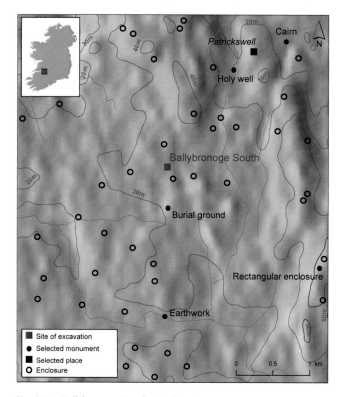

Fig. 8.1—Ballybronoge South: site location map.

The excavation

Ring-ditch

A penannular ditch (F9), 1–1.4m wide, was the main feature discovered. It had a U-shaped profile and a maximum depth of 0.5m. The maximum diameter of the area enclosed was 5m. The maximum external diameter of the ring-ditch was 7m (Fig. 8.2).

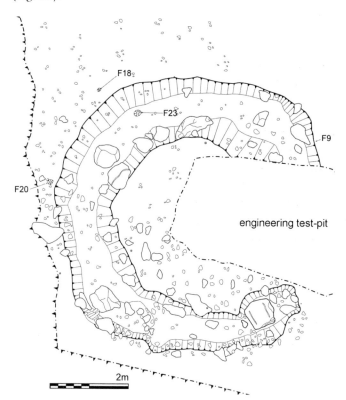

Fig. 8.2—Ballybronoge South: plan of ring-ditch and associated features (drawn by Katie O'Mahony, ADS Ltd).

The terminal of the southern arm was intact and was rounded in plan. A large subrectangular block of limestone was deeply embedded in the natural boulder clay in the base of this terminal. The opposing terminal had been destroyed prior to excavation. A post-hole (F23) was cut into the base of the ring-ditch; it had a maximum diameter of 0.15m and a maximum depth of 0.3m (Fig. 8.2). It was filled with gritty, light brown clay/silt with charcoal flecks (F22).

105

The earliest fills of the ring-ditch were two layers along the inner and outer edges of the cut (Fig. 8.4). A friable orange/mid-brown charcoal-flecked clay silt (F3) was found on the outer edge of the ditch. It had a maximum thickness of 0.1m. Small amounts of unidentified unburnt animal bone were found in this deposit. A layer of friable, greyish brown charcoal-flecked clay silt (F7) lay along the inner edge of the ring-ditch; it had a maximum thickness of 0.12m. These layers appear to have been deposited contemporaneously in the ditch. They were overlain by stony, friable, light mid-brown clay/silt (F6) containing lumps of charcoal. It had a maximum thickness of 0.2m. A naturally shed red deer antler (Nóra Bermingham, pers. comm.) was found in this layer close to the base of the ditch. This layer appeared to have been deposited into the ditch from its outer edge; it may therefore have derived from the destruction of an outer bank.

The main fill of the ring-ditch was a layer of friable black charcoal-rich silt (F5) with a maximum thickness of 0.3m. Fourteen discrete deposits of cremated bone were identified in this layer, as well as a number of pieces of unidentified unburnt animal bone (Fig. 8.3). One of the deposits of cremated bone (5:2) contained a fragment of a decorated bone panel (99E324:5:4). An unworked tubular shell of the marine mollusc species *Antalis entalis* was associated with another deposit of cremated bone (5:4), and a piece of a possible perforated bone object was associated with a third cremation deposit (5:3). A burnt flint pebble (99E324:5:3) and a

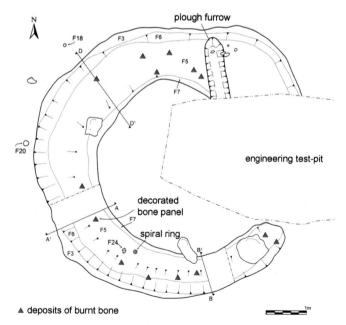

Fig. 8.3—Ballybronoge South: mid-excavation plan showing distribution of cremation deposits in F5 (drawn by Katie O'Mahony, ADS Ltd).

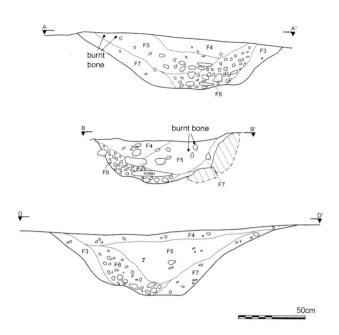

Fig. 8.4—Ballybronoge South: sections through ring-ditch (drawn by Katie O'Mahony, ADS Ltd).

fragmentary copper-alloy wire ring (99E324:5:1–2) were also found in this layer. Neither of these finds was directly associated with any of the deposits of cremated bone. It is important to note that while there was a considerable amount of burnt material in F5, this burning had not occurred *in situ*. As noted above, there was unburnt animal bone and none of the stones in this layer were obviously burnt.

A post-hole (F24) was identified in the southern sector of the ditch. It cut the main fill (F5) and had a maximum diameter of 0.12m and a maximum depth of 0.18m. It was filled with friable buff/light brown charcoal-flecked clayey silt (F12), identical to the upper fill. The upper fill of the ditch was compact light brown clay silt (F4) with charcoal flecks. This deposit had a maximum thickness of 0.15m and was very similar to ploughsoil.

External post-holes

Two post-holes were found on the north-western side of the ring-ditch (Fig. 8.2). The more easterly one (F18) had a maximum diameter of 0.05m and a maximum depth of 0.12m; it was filled by a friable, light orangey brown clayey silt with charcoal flecks (F17). The second one (F20) had a maximum diameter of 0.12m and a maximum depth of 0.15m; it was filled with friable mid-orangey brown clayey silt with charcoal flecks (F19). There was no stratigraphic relationship between these post-holes and the adjacent ring-ditch. It is worth noting that if these features pre-date the

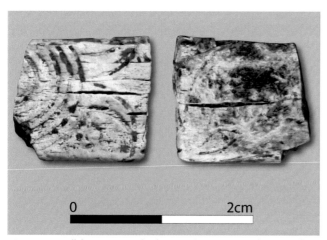

Fig. 8.5a—Ballybronoge South: decorated bone panel, face 1 (left) and face 2 (right) (ADS Ltd).

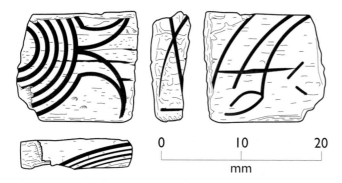

Fig. 8.5b—Ballybronoge South: decorated bone panel (drawn by Conor McHale).

postulated external enclosing bank they would have underlain it; on the other hand, they may post-date the destruction of that bank.

Finds

Decorated bone panel, incomplete (Fig. 8.5) (99E324:5:4): a square piece of greyish white burnt bone. Maximum length 13.4mm; maximum width 12.1mm; varies in thickness from 2.8mm to 3.6mm. The surface of the object is fissured and pitted owing to burning. All four original faces are decorated with incised motifs. The decoration was drawn with compass and ruler.

- *Face 1.* Six concentric circles. The outer circle is interrupted by two pairs of curving lines forming two semi-crescentic motifs; the complete motif terminates in a point at the surviving corner.
- *Face 2.* Decorated with a series of very faint compass-drawn incised lines. A vesica, 5mm long, is located close to the surviving corner. Three parallel curved lines (3mm apart) emanate from the corner and vesica.

- *Edge 1.* The motif is formed by two intersecting lines (one straight, the other slightly curved) forming an X. The surviving end of this edge is delineated by a deeply incised vertical line.
- *Edge 2.* Five oblique incised lines are located adjacent to the surviving corner.

Copper-alloy spiral ring (99E324:5:1–2): poorly preserved coil of copper-alloy wire, broken into two pieces. Maximum thickness of wire *c.* 1.5mm; maximum estimated diameter (external) of ring *c.* 16mm.

Shell (99E324:5:5): an unworked shell of marine mollusc *Antalis entalis* (commonly known as a tusk shell).[2] Curved tubular form open at both ends; 15mm long.

Bone (99E324:5:6): possible object, appears to have been burnt. Length 17mm; maximum width 4mm; tapers to 2mm, but this is probably the result of breakage. Surviving cross-section is an irregular C-shape; there is a possible eccentric perforation (diameter 2mm) along the length of the object. The external surface is marked with a number of linear fissures and striations.

Discussion

Excavation of this site revealed the remains of a truncated penannular ring-ditch. Ring-ditches, of both annular and penannular form, are predominantly associated with the later prehistoric period, though examples are known from the early Bronze Age, where they are associated with pottery of the vase tradition, and historical evidence suggests that such monuments may have been constructed into the middle of the first millennium AD. While examples are known that are associated with Beaker pottery (e.g. Doonmoon, Co. Limerick; Gowen 1988, 52–61) and there are historical references suggesting that ring-ditches could have been constructed up to Patrician times (O'Brien 1990, 41; Bhreathnach 2010), it has been recognised that such monuments are a particular feature of the Irish late Bronze Age and Iron Age (Raftery 1981; 1994, 188ff; Waddell 2010, 391–3). It has been argued that these monuments are a manifestation of the preference for circular forms of burial enclosure throughout Irish prehistory (Corlett 2005).

Ring-ditches are generally accepted to be the truncated remains of monuments that in their original design would have had an internal mound or bank and/or an outer enclosing bank. Where such features survive, these monuments can be subdivided into a variety of typological classes (see, for example, Newman 1997, 153–60). Penannular ring-ditches are rarely identified in field survey but they represent a significant subset of excavated Iron Age ring-ditches.

Form

The Ballybronoge South ring-ditch bears similarities as regards construction to seventeen other excavated examples with evidence for use in the Iron Age. In terms of size, it is important to remember that these sites are generally truncated to an unknown degree by ploughing, and therefore the maximum *recorded* dimensions have been analysed. The external diameters of these penannular ring-ditches range from 4m to 17m (average 7.78m), while the enclosing ditches range in width from 0.5m to 2m (average 1.22m) and in depth from 0.15m to 1.3m (average 0.5m). The internal diameters range from 3m to 13.4m (average 5.86m).

The material dug from the ditch would have provided sufficient material for the construction of a low-level earthen monument. A ring-ditch with an external diameter of 7.5m and 0.5m deep would have produced sufficient soil to build a mound approximately 0.3m high covering the entirety of the enclosed area, a 1m-wide internal bank approximately 0.65m high or a 1m-wide external bank approximately 0.5m high.

The digging of a ring-ditch creates a boundary and defines the enclosed space. This space is therefore physically separated or reserved from its surroundings. What is distinctive about penannular ring-ditches is the fact that their design incorporates an undug causeway providing access to the enclosed space defined by the ditch. There is considerable variability in the size of these gaps; they range in width from 0.2m to 3.5m (average 1.83m). One penannular ring-ditch at Ballydavis reportedly had a 'segmented' entrance with a short section of ditch or a linear pit between the terminals, thereby creating two narrower gaps (Keeley 1995). At Ask, a shallow subcircular pit was situated between the terminals of the ring-ditch closest to the western terminal (Stevens 2007). It can be assumed that the provision of an entrance indicates that the builders of these monuments intended to facilitate access to the internal area. The fact that such a narrow gap was maintained at Knockgraffon suggests that in some cases the occurrence of this design feature reflects the conceptual importance of access rather than the practicalities of access. Assuming there was no internal mound or bank, the area enclosed by even the smallest ring-ditch could have accommodated a restricted number of people.

The south-eastern orientation evident at Ballybronoge South is shared by five of the seventeen ring-ditches. The significance of this orientation should not be overstated, however, as a degree of variability is displayed by these

Table 8.1—Ballybronoge South: comparable penannular ring-ditches (all dimensions in metres).

Site	Internal diameter	External diameter	Ditch width (max.)	Ditch depth (max.)	Entrance orientation	Entrance width
Deerpark, Co. Galway	3.00	4.00	0.50	0.15	S	–
Lusk, Co. Dublin	4.00	5.00	0.75	0.60	W	0.75
Ask, Co. Wexford (site F)	3.36	5.35	1.20	0.30	N	1.95
Ballydowny, Co. Kerry	4.40	5.50	0.50	0.20	NE	3.50
Ballydavis, Co. Laois (site 4)	4.60	5.60	1.00	0.60	NW	2.20
Lehinch, Co. Offaly	4.27	6.19	0.90	0.60	SE	0.50
Coolnaveagh, Co. Wexford	4.80	6.30	1.00	0.30	N	2.40
Ballybronoge South, Co. Limerick	4.00	7.00	1.75	0.50	SE	–
Marlhill, Co. Tipperary	4.00	7.20	1.80	1.30	S	1.30
Ballydavis, Co. Laois (site 2)	6.00	7.60	1.50	0.70	SE	1.00
Ballydribbeen, Co. Kerry	6.50	7.80	0.85	0.16	SE	3.00
Knockgraffon, Co. Tipperary	5.40	8.20	1.90	0.70	NE	0.20
Knockcommane, Co. Tipperary	7.50	9.11	1.20	0.43	NE	0.70
Woodlands West, Co. Kildare (ring-ditch 1)	7.50	9.43	1.25	0.37	W	1.55
Burtown Little, Co. Kildare (ring-ditch A)	8.00	10.00	0.96	0.40	SE	0.43
Curraheen, Co. Cork	8.90	11.00	1.60	0.35	E	1.35
Ballydavis, Co. Laois (site 1)	13.40	17.00	2.00	0.91	SE	3.20

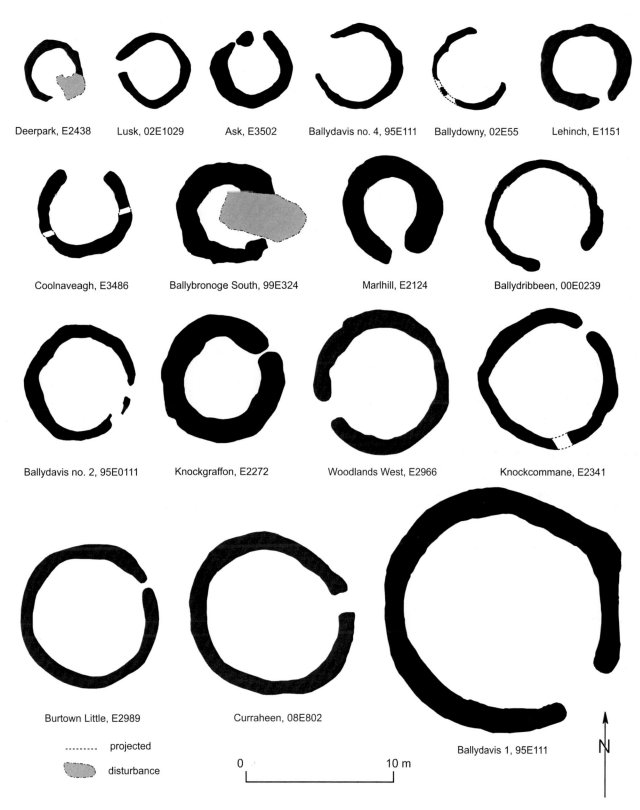

Deerpark, E2438　　Lusk, 02E1029　　Ask, E3502　　Ballydavis no. 4, 95E111　　Ballydowny, 02E55　　Lehinch, E1151

Coolnaveagh, E3486　　Ballybronoge South, 99E324　　Marlhill, E2124　　Ballydribbeen, 00E0239

Ballydavis no. 2, 95E0111　　Knockgraffon, E2272　　Woodlands West, E2966　　Knockcommane, E2341

Burtown Little, E2989　　Curraheen, 08E802　　Ballydavis 1, 95E111

.... projected

disturbance

0　　　　10 m

N

Fig. 8.6—Comparative plans of Iron Age penannular ring-ditches (after Dunne 2002; Hurley 2010; Keeley 1995; Kiely and O'Callaghan 2010; Clarke and Long, forthcoming; McCabe 2002; Molloy 2009a; 2009b; Moloney, forthcoming; Moriarty 2009; Ó Floinn 2011; Ó Mordha 2011; Stevens 2007; Wilkins et al. 2007).

monuments, with entrances facing north (2), north-east (3), east (1), south (2), west (2) and north-west (1). The predominant preference in entrance orientation is easterly.

The scale of the monuments and the provision of causewayed entrances indicate that these monuments could have been utilised to structure aspects of social practice. The size of the causeways suggests that those members of the community who were entitled to enter the enclosed space would have done so in single file (and would also have exited in the same fashion). While the ditch (and any associated bank) would have segregated off the small number of people who could be accommodated within the monument, they were not of such a scale that people outside could not witness and even participate indirectly in whatever activities were carried out internally. Indeed, if any of these sites originally had internal low mounds they would have elevated the participants in any activity above the surroundings.

The evidence indicates that the ultimate function of penannular ring-ditches was for the deposition of the cremated remains of deceased members of the community. It does not follow, however, that they had an exclusively funerary purpose. Indeed, the evidence from all these sites and from many annular ring-ditches suggests that the deposition of human remains generally took place as part of secondary rituals. At Ballybronoge South the cremations are associated with the deliberate filling up of the ditch, the effect of which would have been to render the site less visible in the landscape, presuming that there was no associated mound or enclosing bank. If the underlying layer (6) is associated with the destruction of an outer bank by the time the cremations were deposited, the site may have had a reduced monumental aspect.

Burials

A minimum of 44 deposits of cremated bone have been identified from eleven of the penannular ring-ditches. Fifteen of these deposits are from Ballybronoge South (see Appendix 8.1). Considering that between one and four deposits have been identified from the other sites, it can be seen that the number of deposits at this site is outside the norm. Thirty-eight of these deposits were found in the fills of the ring-ditch; three were in centrally located pits within the ring-ditch; two were in pits cut into the fill of the ring-ditch; and one was in a pit adjacent to the ring-ditch. Osteological reports are available for assemblages of cremated bone from nine of these sites. Analysis has confirmed the presence of human remains in 25 deposits, while it was not possible to positively confirm human remains in eight cremated bone deposits. Of these 25 deposits, 22 derived from adults, two from non-adults and one

could not be aged. Given that thirteen of the aged samples are from Ballybronoge South, it is doubtful that these figures are necessarily representative of wider patterns of deposition.

Artefacts

A decorated bone panel was found in one of the deposits of cremated bone (99E324:5:4) in the southern sector of the ditch. The closest parallel for this object, in form and style of decoration, is a bone panel from a deposit of cremated human bone buried in a small pit at the centre of tumulus 2 at Cush, Co. Limerick (Raftery 1981, 181). This object has been interpreted as a gaming piece (Ó Ríordáin 1940, 156; Raftery 1983, 227). Compass-drawn concentric circles, parallel arcs and semi-cresentic motifs are known from the large assemblage of decorated Iron Age bone flakes from Lough Crew (Raftery 1983, figs 187–200).

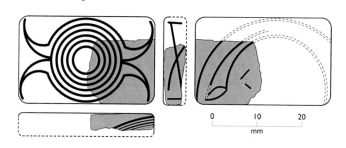

Fig. 8.7—Ballybronoge South: suggested reconstruction of decoration on bone panel; the shaded area indicates the extent of the surviving portion of the object (drawn by Conor McHale).

Bone objects have been recorded at comparable sites. Two carved bone or antler objects from Ballydribbeen (Dunne 2002) may be the heads of two pins or the terminals of a *c.* 40mm-long barbell-type object. It was previously reported that three decorated bone pieces were found in the ditch of Ballydavis site 3 (Keeley 1996; 1999), but more recent examination has shown that the suspected decoration was in fact fissures caused by the cremation process (Valerie J. Keeley, pers. comm.).

The fragmentary copper-alloy ring is also paralleled at a number of contemporary annular ring-ditches (McGarry 2008); most notably, three copper-alloy rings adorned the feet of a probable adult female crouched inhumation which was a secondary burial cut into the fill of a ring-ditch at Rath, Co. Meath (F. O'Carroll *et al.*, this volume).

The tubular tusk shell could have been strung on a necklace or sewn onto clothing. While glass beads have been recovered from seven comparable penannular ring-ditches and many annular ring-ditches, this is the first example of marine shell being found in such contexts.

The inclusion of artefacts in deposits of cremated bone distinguishes Iron Age funerary ritual from the preceding late Bronze Age practice. The artefacts deposited at Ballybronoge South were personal belongings; this pattern is replicated at contemporary burial sites, where glass beads, brooches, pins and rings were deposited with cremations. In many cases where objects are associated with cremation deposits they have been burnt, suggesting that they accompanied the corpse on the funeral pyre.

Animal bones

At Ballybronoge South, a naturally shed red deer antler and a number of deposits of unidentified unburnt animal bones were found in the basal fills of the ring-ditch. Unburnt animal bones were also associated with three deposits of cremated bone. The occurrence of unburnt animal bone has been noted at other penannular ring-ditches, such as Ballydavis 2, Knockgraffon, Lehinch, Lusk, Marlhill and Woodlands West. The deposition of animal bone has also been noted at contemporary annular ring-ditches. Animal bones are infrequently associated with Bronze Age burials or burial monuments (McCormick 1985/6); their occurrence in the fills of Iron Age ring-ditches appears to mark a change in depositional practice. The fact that these remains are unburnt, in contrast to the human remains, suggests that deposition of the animal remains represents a distinct aspect of activity at these sites. The final pattern of note with regard to the deposition of animal remains is the occurrence of cranial elements such as the antler at Ballybronoge South, a horse mandible at Lehinch and four cattle mandibles at Woodlands West.

The occurrence of animal bones at funerary monuments is often interpreted as evidence for feasting, but these apparently token deposits and the deposition of non-food elements of the animal suggest that this practice may have been symbolic. The deliberate deposition of animal remains at sites that were also used for the deposition of human remains may reflect a change in the way animals were perceived in the Iron Age. This might also be reflected in the depictions of animals and the use of zoomorphic ornament in contemporary art (Jope 2000, 105–20).

Distribution

The sites at which Iron Age penannular ring-ditches have been identified are all located in the southern half of the island of Ireland. Their distribution is an inversion of the distribution of La Tène metalwork and related material (Raftery 1983); it

fits well, however, with our developing awareness of the distribution of Iron Age settlement sites identified as a result of two decades of development-led archaeology (Becker *et al.* 2008).

Conclusion

The penannular ring-ditch at Ballybronoge South was constructed and used in the Iron Age, between the mid-third century BC and the first century AD. It is possible that originally this site had an enclosing bank and/or a central mound, which would place it in the class of monuments known as ring-barrows. The ditch may originally have enclosed a central burial; as this area was destroyed, however, it is not possible to prove or disprove this hypothesis. The evidence from comparable sites indicates that central burials are rarely found at penannular ring-ditches.

At Ballybronoge South the ditch was open for a period, during which soil that eroded from the edge of the cut or adjacent features, such as an internal mound or internal/external banks, accumulated in the base of the ring-ditch. This pattern has been noted at other ring-ditches of both annular and penannular form. The duration of the period over which the ditch remained open cannot be estimated with any certainty. At Ballybronoge South and some comparable sites, unburnt animal bone was deposited in these primary fills. Regardless of the length of time, it does indicate that these monuments could have been used for non-funerary or pre-funerary activity. This is particularly relevant in the case of the penannular ring-ditches, whose form displays a concern with providing access to the interior of the enclosed area.

The emerging evidence from the radiocarbon dating of samples associated with their construction and use, along with the small number of associated datable objects, such as the decorated bone panel from Ballybronoge South, suggests that activity at these monuments can be dated to the last two centuries BC, possibly continuing into the first century AD.

The cremation burials found in the upper fill of the Ballybronoge South ring-ditch are associated with the deliberate backfilling of the ditch. Similar patterns of deposition are replicated at other ring-ditches. This pattern is so frequent that it suggests that the deposition of human remains was associated with the symbolic 'closure' of these monuments.

Previous discussions of ring-ditches—whether annular or penannular—have not discriminated sufficiently between their architectural form and their use history. The evidence from Ballybronoge South indicates the importance of a careful reading of the sequence of construction or destruction and depositional activity at these small-scale sites. In his discussion

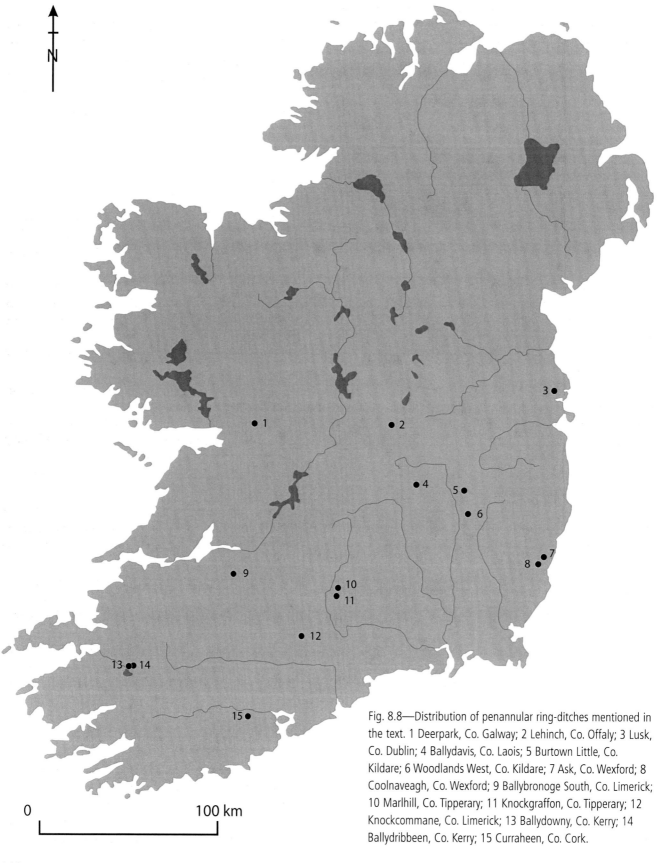

Fig. 8.8—Distribution of penannular ring-ditches mentioned in the text. 1 Deerpark, Co. Galway; 2 Lehinch, Co. Offaly; 3 Lusk, Co. Dublin; 4 Ballydavis, Co. Laois; 5 Burtown Little, Co. Kildare; 6 Woodlands West, Co. Kildare; 7 Ask, Co. Wexford; 8 Coolnaveagh, Co. Wexford; 9 Ballybronoge South, Co. Limerick; 10 Marlhill, Co. Tipperary; 11 Knockgraffon, Co. Tipperary; 12 Knockcommane, Co. Limerick; 13 Ballydowny, Co. Kerry; 14 Ballydribbeen, Co. Kerry; 15 Curraheen, Co. Cork.

0   100 km

of 'royal sites', Conor Newman has suggested that they represent regional or provincial ritual centres. He has also suggested that there are sites that fulfil some of the criteria for 'royal sites' but which are more modest in scale, and he considers that these may have operated as 'lower-order' ritual centres (1998, 132–3). While Newman only discusses two levels, the implication of this model of hierarchical ritual centres in the Irish Iron Age is that each local community would have had a site that was a focus of ritual activity (see R. Clutterbuck, this volume). According to the model, there should be a reduction in scale and complexity with each step down the hierarchical ladder, the corollary being that there should be a greater frequency of 'lower-' or 'lowest-order' ritual centres.

In their architectural form, in association with the evidence for their use for multi-stage non-funerary and funerary ritual, it seems that the penannular ring-ditch at Ballybronoge South and similar sites may represent the lowest order of formalised ritual centre in the Irish Iron Age between the mid-third century BC and the first century AD.[3]

Acknowledgements

I wish to thank Damian Finn, who supervised the excavation of this ring-ditch. I am grateful to Beth Cassidy and Eoin Halpin, of Archaeological Development Services (ADS) Ltd, for their support during and after the excavation. Katie O'Mahony and Cia McConway, also of ADS, provided significant assistance during the post-excavation phase. I am grateful to Nóra Bermingham and Laureen Buckley for identifying the animal and human remains. The excavation was funded by the National Roads Authority through Limerick County Council. I wish to acknowledge the on-site assistance of Sarah McCutcheon (archaeologist) and Charles Dendy (resident engineer) of Limerick County Council. I am grateful to very many people who have answered queries and provided me with copies of reports relating to ring-ditches over the past number of years: Maurice Hurley; Maeve Sikora (National Museum of Ireland); Valerie Keeley and Paul Stevens (Valerie J. Keeley Ltd); Trish Long and T.J. O'Connell (Rubicon Heritage Management Ltd); Jacinta Kiely (Eachtra Archaeological Projects); Stephen Johnston and Antoine Giacometti (Arch-Tech Ltd); Frank Coyne and Linda G. Lynch (Aegis Archaeology Ltd); Ed Danaher, Noel Dunne, Niall Roycroft, Jerry O'Sullivan and Kevin Martin (National Roads Authority). I would like to thank Michael Stanley for assistance with illustrations. I am particularly grateful to the editors for their invitation to participate in the original seminar and for their forbearance during the long process of delivering the final essay.

Bibliography

Becker, K., Ó Néill, J. and O'Flynn, L. 2008 Iron Age Ireland: finding an invisible people. Unpublished report prepared for the Heritage Council (project 16365).

Bhreathnach, E. 2010 From *fert(ae)* to *relic*: mapping death in early sources. In C. Corlett and M. Potterton (eds), *Death and burial in early medieval Ireland in the light of recent archaeological excavations*, 23–31. Bray.

Clarke, L. and Long, T. (forthcoming) Final report on archaeological investigations at Site E2966, in the townland of Woodslands West, Co. Kildare. Unpublished report by Rubicon Heritage Services Ltd for Kildare County Council and the National Roads Authority.

Corlett, C. 2005 Ring-barrows: a circular argument with a ring of truth. In T. Condit and C. Corlett (eds), *Above and beyond: essays in memory of Leo Swan*, 63–71. Bray.

Dunne, L. 2002 Archaeological excavation report. Ballydribbeen, Killarney, Co. Kerry. Unpublished report prepared by Eachtra Archaeological Projects for private client.

Eogan, J. 1997 Ballybronoge South. *Excavations 1996*, 65. Bray.

Gowen, M. 1988 *Three Irish gas pipelines: new archaeological evidence in Munster*. Dublin.

Hurley, M.F. 2010 Curraheen 1 ring-ditch. In M.F. Hurley, 'Ballynora to Lehanaghmore pipeline report', 15–27. Unpublished report for Bord Gáis Éireann.

Jope, E.M. 2000 *Early Celtic art in the British Isles* (2 vols). Oxford.

Keeley, V. 1995 Preliminary report: excavations at Ballydavis td, Portlaoise bypass, Co. Laois. Unpublished report by Valerie J. Keeley Ltd for Laois County Council and the National Roads Authority.

Keeley, V.J. 1996 Ballydavis. *Excavations 1995*, 51–2. Bray.

Keeley, V.J. 1999 Iron Age discoveries at Ballydavis. In P.G. Lane and W. Nolan (eds), *Laois: history and society*, 25–34. Dublin.

Kiely, J. and O'Callaghan, N. 2010 Archaeological excavation report 02E0055, Ballydowny, Killarney, Co. Kerry. *Eachtra Journal* 7 (1) on-line (http://eachtra.ie/index.php/journal/02e0055-ballydowny-co-kerry).

McCabe, S. 2002 Report on archaeological excavation at Lusk, Co. Dublin. Unpublished report by Arch-Tech Ltd for private client.

McCormick, F. 1985/6 Faunal remains from prehistoric Irish burials. *Journal of Irish Archaeology* 3, 37–48.

McGarry, T. 2008 Some exotic evidence amidst Irish late prehistoric burials. In O.P. Davis, N.M. Sharples and K. Waddington (eds), *Changing perspectives on the first millennium*, 215–34. Oxford.

McGarry, T. 2009 Irish late prehistoric burial ring-ditches. In G. Cooney, K. Becker, J. Coles, M. Ryan and S. Sievers (eds), *Relics of old decency: archaeological studies in later prehistory*, 413–23. Bray.

McQuade, M., Molloy, B. and Moriarty, C. 2009 *In the shadow of the Galtees: archaeological excavations along the N8 Cashel to Mitchelstown road scheme*. Dublin.

Molloy, B. 2009a Knockcommane, Co. Limerick: embanked ring-ditch. In M. McQuade, B. Molloy and C. Moriarty, *In the shadow of the Galtees: archaeological excavations along the N8 Cashel to Mitchelstown road scheme*, 163–5. Dublin.

Molloy, B. 2009b Marlhill, Co. Tipperary: ring-barrow. In M. McQuade, B. Molloy and C. Moriarty, *In the shadow of the Galtees: archaeological excavations along the N8 Cashel to Mitchelstown road scheme*, 166–9. Dublin.

Moloney, C. (forthcoming) Final report on archaeological investigations at Site E2989, in the townland of Burtown, Co. Kildare. Unpublished report by Rubicon Heritage Services Ltd for Kildare County Council and the National Roads Authority.

Moriarty, C. 2009 Knockgraffon, Co. Tipperary: ring-barrow. In M. McQuade, B. Molloy and C. Moriarty, *In the shadow of the Galtees: archaeological excavations along the N8 Cashel to Mitchelstown road scheme*, 170–2. Dublin.

Newman, C. 1997 *Tara: an archaeological survey*. Dublin.

Newman, C. 1998 Reflections on the making of a 'royal site' in early Ireland. *World Archaeology* **30** (1), 127–41.

O'Brien, E. 1990 Iron Age burial practices in Leinster: continuity and change. *Emania* **7**, 37–42.

O'Brien, E. and Bhreathnach, E. 2011 Irish boundary *ferta*, their physical manifestation and historical context. In F. Edmonds and P. Russell (eds), *Tome: studies in honour of Thomas Charles-Edwards*, 53–64. Woodbridge.

Ó Floinn, R. 2011 Lehinch, Co. Offaly. In M. Cahill and M. Sikora (eds), *Breaking ground, finding graves: reports on the excavations of burials by the National Museum of Ireland, 1927–2006* (vol. 2), 139–66. Dublin.

Ó Mordha, E. 2011 Final report on excavations at Coolnaveagh, Co. Wexford. Unpublished report prepared by Valerie J. Keeley Ltd for Wexford County Council and the National Roads Authority.

Ó Ríordáin, S.P. 1940 Excavations at Cush, Co. Limerick (1934 and 1935). *Proceedings of the Royal Irish Academy* **45**C, 83–181.

Raftery, B. 1981 Iron Age burials in Ireland. In D. Ó Corráin (ed.), *Irish antiquity: essays and studies presented to Professor M.J. O'Kelly*, 173–204. Dublin.

Raftery, B. 1983 *A catalogue of Irish Iron Age antiquities* (2 vols).

Marburg.

Raftery, B. 1994 *Pagan Celtic Ireland: the enigma of the Irish Iron Age*. London.

Stevens, P. 2007 Burial and ritual in late prehistory in north Wexford: excavation of a ring-ditch cemetery in Ask townland. In J. O'Sullivan and M. Stanley (eds), *New routes to the past*, 35–46. Dublin.

Waddell, J. 2010 *The prehistoric archaeology of Ireland* (2nd edn). Bray.

Wilkins, B., Bunce, A. and Lalonde, S. 2007 Final report on archaeological investigations at Site E2438, a ring-ditch with cremation deposits in the townland of Deerpark, Co. Galway. Unpublished report prepared by Headland Archaeology Ltd for Galway County Council and the National Roads Authority.

APPENDIX 8.1: CREMATION REPORT (LAUREEN BUCKLEY)

Introduction

Fourteen token deposits of cremated bone were found in a deposit (F5) filling the ring-ditch. Association with a decorated bone panel and a copper-alloy spiral ring suggests an Iron Age date for the deposition of the cremations.

Methods

Cremation is a type of funeral rite in which the body is burnt on a pyre, leaving only bone. There is evidence from early societies that this bone may have been collected as completely as possible from the pyre; alternatively, a token sample of the remains may have been taken. The remains were also deposited in various ways. When all that is left of the human remains are fragments of bone, it is important to derive as much information as possible from them in order to gain knowledge of the cremation ritual as well as of the individuals themselves.

During cremation the organic parts of the body, including the organic part of the bone, undergo a process of dehydration and oxidation. An efficient cremation is one in which all the organic content is burnt off and only the inorganic part of the bone remains. The inorganic part generally recrystallises to form a more stable structure, and so cremated remains survive for millennia in a well-preserved condition. Examination of cremated remains involves a description of the colour and texture of the bone, as this helps to determine the efficiency of the cremation. Efficiently cremated bone is white and usually has a chalky texture. Less well-cremated bone, where the temperature of the pyre was not high enough or where oxygen flow was restricted, or where the body was not burning for long enough, has a blue or a blue/black colour. Some studies on a limited number of bodies—or even on only a limited number of bones—have attempted to make a connection between the colour and warping of the bone and the temperature of the pyre. They have not considered, however, that the pyre only serves to ignite the body: it is the body fats that keep it burning and determine the temperature of cremation. The temperature attained, therefore, has more to do with the composition of the body, and in any case the temperature will not be maintained evenly across the body. In addition, bones can become fully cremated after burning at a lower temperature for longer and will look the same as those cremated at a higher temperature for a shorter time.

In analysis the bone fragments are graded by size in order to determine the degree of fragmentation. Although fragmentation of the bone occurs continuously after deposition, owing to compression, and also during the disturbance caused by excavation and processing, it is still possible to assess whether or not the bones were deliberately crushed as part of the cremation ritual. A high proportion of relatively large fragments suggests that the bones were not deliberately crushed after the cremation, whereas a small deposit of relatively small fragments indicates a ritually crushed token deposit. There are other factors to take into account, however, such as post-depositional disturbance, how the remains were discovered, and the treatment of the remains during the excavation, processing and post-excavation stages. Even storage of the material may affect the degree of fragmentation.

The process of grading the bone involves removing the obvious very large fragments and passing the remainder through a series of sieves. The bone from each sieving is stored separately and the fragments weighed. The weight of bone in each sample is used to determine the proportion of the various fragment sizes. The categories of fragment sizes used have been arbitrarily assigned to give the lay reader an impression of how crushed or not crushed the cremation was. The fragment sizes generally used are: <10mm; 10–15mm; 15–25mm; 25–40mm; >40mm. The overlap between the groups is deliberate, as it would not be possible to be exact about the size of every fragment.

Each fragment of bone is then examined and identified if possible. The degree of identification of fragments is generally dependent on fragment size. Larger fragments are usually easier to identify, although phalanges often are found intact among the smaller fragments. Successful identification depends on the number of distinguishing features present on the bone fragments, as well as knowledge of the thickness and expected cross-section of particular bones. Bones shrink and warp during the cremation process, however, and sometimes it

is not possible to specifically identify long-bone fragments. Bones of the skull, especially the petrous portions of the temporal bones, are easily identifiable and are therefore extremely useful in determining the minimum number of individuals and in distinguishing juveniles from adults.

The minimum number of individuals present can then be determined by the numbers of specific skeletal elements. It is possible to distinguish juveniles from adults by the thickness of the bone fragments, the presence or absence of unfused epiphyses and the fragmentation of the teeth. Adult tooth crowns tend to shatter during the cremation process but unerupted juvenile teeth tend to survive intact, as they are protected by the jaw bones. It is usually possible to age juveniles if enough teeth are present.

Results

The main fill of the ring-ditch (F5) consisted of black charcoal-rich silt to a maximum depth of 0.3m. It contained fourteen discrete deposits of burnt bone and five deposits of unburnt bone. The ring-ditch was divided into sectors on site and the separate deposits were numbered within these sectors.

Deposit 1, sector A

The total amount of bone recovered from this deposit was 54g. Most of the sample was white, indicating efficient cremation, with only a small proportion (6%) that was black or partially black where the organic portion of the bone had not been fully burnt off. Most of the bone had a chalky texture and the larger fragments had some fissure formation in the bone surface. The largest fragment was 37mm in length but the bone was highly fragmented, making identification difficult. Nevertheless, it was possible to identify 31% of the sample and the remains represented one adult individual.

Deposit 2, sector A/B

This sample consisted of 59.3g of cremated bone. The bone was basically white, although 15% was partially blue/black, indicating that there was still some organic part of the bone present. Most of the fragments had a chalky texture and the larger fragments had concentric and horizontal fissures in the bone surface. The largest fragment was 33mm in length and the bone was highly crushed, making identification difficult. Nevertheless, it was possible to identify 26% of the sample. The identified fragments included skull, clavicle and long bone from one adult individual.

Deposit 3, sector B

The total weight of bone recovered was 46.6g. The bone was mainly white with a chalky texture, although 29% consisted of fragments that were blue or black where the organic part of the bone had not been fully burnt off. The largest fragment was 33mm in length and the sample was highly crushed, making identification difficult, and it was only possible to identify 25% of the sample. The remains consisted of skull and long-bone fragments from one adult individual.

Deposit 4, sector C
The total amount of bone recovered was 49.9g. Although it was stained with charcoal, it was basically white, indicating efficient cremation. A considerable proportion (24%) was black or partially black, however, where the organic portion of the bone had not been fully burnt off. Most of the bone had a chalky texture and the larger fragments had some fissure formation in the surface. The largest fragment was 37mm in length and the bone was highly fragmented. The high fragmentation made identification difficult and it was only possible to identify 23% of the sample. The remains appear to represent one adult individual.

Deposit 5, sector D
This was the second-largest deposit from the ring-ditch, consisting of 117.7g of cremated bone. The bone was stained with charcoal but was basically white, although 12% was partially blue/black, indicating that there was still some organic part of the bone present. Most of the fragments had a chalky texture and the larger fragments had concentric and horizontal fissures in the bone surface. The largest fragment was 35mm in length but the sample was highly fragmented. It was possible to identify 23% of the sample and it consisted mainly of skull and long bones from one adult individual.

Deposit 6, sector D
This was a small sample consisting of 11.1g of highly fragmented, mainly efficiently cremated bone, although 15% was partially blue or black, indicating that there was still some organic part of the bone present. There was a moderate degree of crushing, with the largest fragment 31mm in length. It was possible to identify 64% of the sample and it consisted mainly of long-bone fragments as well as a small amount of skull from one adult individual.

Deposit 7, sector D
This was the largest deposit recovered from the ring-ditch and consisted of 128.9g of cremated bone. The bone was stained with charcoal but was basically white, although 15% was partially blue/black, indicating that there was still some organic part of the bone present. Most of the fragments had a chalky texture and there was some cracking of the bone

surface. The largest fragment was 41mm in length and the bone was only moderately crushed, making identification more straightforward. It was possible to identify 53% of the sample and it consisted mainly of skull and long-bone fragments. The remains represented one adult male individual. Two small samples were retrieved from soil samples from sector D but it is not known which deposits they were associated with, so they are not included with either deposit 6 or deposit 7.

Deposit 8, sector H
This was a small sample, consisting of 3.3g of efficiently cremated bone. Some of the fragments had a chalky texture and some appeared to be weathered. The largest fragment was 37mm in length; most of the sample, however, consisted of slivers of long bone only and could not be identified.

Deposit 9, sector H
This sample consisted of 39.6g of cremated bone. The bone was stained with charcoal but was basically white, although 21% was partially blue, indicating that there was still some organic part of the bone present. Most of the fragments had a chalky texture and the larger fragments had concentric and horizontal fissures in the bone surface. The largest fragment was 32mm in length and the sample was moderately fragmented, so it was possible to identify 41% of the bone. It consisted of skull and tooth fragments as well as long-bone fragments from one adult individual. A partially burnt animal tooth was present, along with a small quantity of non-burnt animal bone.

Deposit 10, sector H
This sample consisted of 67.7g of cremated bone. The bone was stained with charcoal but was basically white, although 27% was partially blue/black, indicating that there was still some organic part of the bone present. Most of the fragments had a chalky texture and the larger fragments had concentric and horizontal fissures in the bone surface. The largest fragment was 37mm in length and the sample was moderately fragmented. It was possible to identify 40% of the sample. It consisted of skull and long-bone fragments from one adult individual.

Deposit 11, sector E
This deposit consisted of 15.6g of cremated bone. The bone was stained with charcoal but was basically white, although 3% was partially blue, indicating that there was still some organic part of the bone present. Most of the fragments had a chalky texture and a weathered appearance. There was a slight amount of cracking and fissure formation on the surfaces of

the larger fragments. The largest fragment was 36mm in length and the bone was moderately crushed. It was possible to identify 27% of the sample and this included a small quantity of skull and fragments from the femur and tibia shafts from one adult individual.

Deposit 12, sector E
This deposit was very small and consisted of 8.1g of cremated bone only. Most of the bone was white, although 14% was partially blue or black where some of the organic part of the bone still remained. Most of the fragments had a chalky texture and the larger fragments had concentric and horizontal fissures in the bone surface. The largest fragment was 34mm in length and the sample was only moderately crushed, so it was possible to identify 56% of the bone. This consisted of fragments of femur and tibia shaft from an adult individual.

Deposit 13, sector G
This sample consisted of 44.7g of mainly white cremated bone, with only 11% consisting of fragments that still had some organic part of the bone remaining. The largest fragment was 30mm in length and the bone was moderately fragmented. It was possible to identify 43% of the sample and this consisted of skull and lower limb fragments from one adult individual.

Deposit 14, sector G
This deposit consisted of 15.9g of cremated bone. The bone was not efficiently cremated, with 56% consisting of fragments

that were blue or black where the organic part of the bone remained. The largest fragment was 35mm in length and there was a low degree of crushing of the bone, so it was possible to identify 63% of the sample. The identified bone included skull and femur shaft fragments from one adult.

Context 6
One further sample from context 6 was submitted for analysis. This layer was stratigraphically earlier than F5. The sample was very small and consisted of 4.7g of cremated bone. The bone was poorly cremated, with 66% still containing some organic part of the bone. The bone was moderately fragmented, with the largest fragment 20mm in length. It was possible to identify 79% of the sample, as it consisted of fragments of skull from an adult. A large fragment of non-burnt animal bone was present in the sample.

A summary of the results of analysis of cremated bone from F5 is given in Table 8.2. The total weight of bone recovered from all the deposits was 662.4g, which is still only about half of what would be expected from one adult cremation. The weight of bone in each deposit varied from 3.3g to 128.9g, although only two deposits had more than 100g. Five of the deposits were highly crushed, eight were moderately crushed and one had a low degree of crushing. Since they are token deposits, it is not possible to say whether they were deliberately crushed as part of the cremation ritual. It is possible that some crushing occurred after deposition, since

Table 8.2—Ballybronoge South: results from cremation deposits in F5.

Deposit	Weight (g)	Colour (% white)	Degree of crushing	% identified	MNI
1	54.0	94	High	31	1 adult
2	59.3	85	High	26	1 adult
3	46.6	71	High	25	1 adult
4	49.9	76	High	23	1 adult
5	117.7	88	High	23	1 adult
6	11.1	85	Moderate	64	1 adult
7	128.9	85	Moderate	53	1 adult male
8	3.3	100	Moderate	0	
9	39.6	79	Moderate	41	1 adult
10	67.7	73	Moderate	40	1 adult
11	15.6	97	Moderate	27	1 adult
12	8.1	86	Moderate	56	1 adult
13	44.7	89	Moderate	43	1 adult
14	15.9	44	Low	63	1 adult
Total	**662.4**				**13**

they were unprotected cremations.

The percentage of bone that could be identified varied according to the size of the sample and the degree of crushing, with over 40% of the bone identified in most of those that were low or moderately crushed but only around 25% being identified in the highly crushed samples. The identified bone was similar in most of the deposits, consisting mainly of skull and long bones, with the majority of the long bones being from the lower limb.

With the deposits being so small, the possibility that they represented one cremation ritually deposited around the ring-ditch has to be considered. The same piece from the occipital bone from the back of the skull was found in three different deposits, however, indicating that at least three individuals were present. Other fragments of skull were present in two different deposits, and fragments of femur and tibia were found in several of the deposits, making it more likely that these were separate token deposits, with the skull and long bones favoured over other bones.

Discussion

The analysis of the cremated bone from most ring-ditch sites has not been reported, so it is difficult to compare the results from Ballybronoge South. A report of a recent excavation of a ring-barrow at Kilmahuddrick, Co. Dublin, with evidence for Bronze Age as well as Iron Age activity (Doyle 2006), does contain a full report on the cremated bone (Buckley 2006, 64–6). The two cremations in the centre of the barrow were dated to the Bronze Age. One was identified as a single adult and the other was an adult, possibly with a juvenile. The cremations were token deposits, as was found at Ballybronoge South. Cremated bone was found in the ditch at Kilmahuddrick and thought to be Iron Age, but the deposits were so small that it could not be certain whether they were token deposits or disturbed fill from elsewhere.

One of the few Iron Age ring-ditches with a full cremation report available is the site at Knockcommane, Co. Limerick (McQuade et al. 2009, 163–9). This site had a central cremation as well as three separate token deposits in the ditch itself. The deposits ranged from 0.5g to 208g in the central burial. The central burial was that of an adult female, while one of the deposits in the ditch was a juvenile, one was an adult and the other could not be determined (Geber 2009, 221).

An example of a Neolithic passage grave being remodelled for an Iron Age barrow cemetery has been reported from Kiltierney, Co. Fermanagh (Hamlin and Lynn 1988, 24–6). Iron Age cremation deposits were inserted into the reconstructed mound of the passage tomb in shallow pits and also on the ground surface at the edge of the new ditch.

The deposits at the edge of the ditch were then mounded over. A total of nineteen Iron Age mounds were found. As they were not all excavated, it was not possible to determine whether this represented token deposits from one cremation burial or whether it indeed represented nineteen token deposits from individual burials.

Whether the Iron Age cremations were placed in reused Neolithic or Bronze Age monuments or whether they had a specially built ring-barrow, it seems that the most common feature of this period is the token deposit of cremation bone. At Ballybronoge it seems likely that the token deposits were from separate cremations, although it must be noted that they were not as highly crushed as at other sites (e.g. Kilmahuddrick) and identification was therefore much easier. Occasionally, however, single Iron Age cremations are found, such as at Loughey, Co. Down (Mallory and McNeill 1991, 173), where an Iron Age woman was cremated and her remains deposited in a pit with a bronze fibula, tweezers, ring, glass bracelets and glass beads. It seems that she came from southern Britain and was rich enough to be given a full separate burial.

Bibliography

Buckley, L. 2006 Appendix II: analysis of the human bone from Kilmahuddrick. In I. Doyle, 'Excavation of a prehistoric ring-barrow at Kilmahuddrick, Clondalkin, Dublin 22'. *Journal of Irish Archaeology* **14**, 64–6.

Doyle, I. 2006 Excavation of a prehistoric ring-barrow at Kilmahuddrick, Clondalkin, Dublin 22. *Journal of Irish Archaeology* **14**, 43–75.

Geber, J. 2009 The human remains. In M. McQuade, B. Molloy and C. Moriarty, *In the shadow of the Galtees: archaeological excavations along the N8 Cashel to Mitchelstown road scheme*, 209–40. Dublin.

Hamlin, A. and Lynn, C. 1998 *Pieces of the past: archaeological excavations by the Department of the Environment for Northern Ireland, 1970–1986*. Belfast.

Keane, M. 2009 Derroon. *Excavations 2006*, 469–70. Bray.

Keeley, V.J. 1996 Ballydavis. *Excavations 1995*, 51–2. Bray.

McQuade, M., Molloy, B. and Moriarty, C. 2009 *In the shadow of the Galtees: archaeological excavations along the N8 Cashel to Mitchelstown road scheme*. Dublin.

Mallory, J.P. and McNeill, T.E. 1991 *The archaeology of Ulster*. Belfast.

O'Sullivan, M. 1994 Haynestown, Co. Louth. *Excavations 1993*, 57–8. Bray.

Notes

1. Ballybronoge South townland, Killonahan civil parish, Pubblebrien barony, Co. Limerick, NGR 15110E/14840N. This site has been listed on the Records of Monuments and Places (LI021-167——). The townland name derives from the Irish *Baile na mBruthnóg*, meaning 'the town of the smelt-furnaces' (www.logainm.ie/31524.aspx; accessed 10 May 2012).

2. This marine species is native to Ireland: www.species.ie/search/species/detail/?species_id=4863 (accessed 10 May 2012).

3. It may be that the origins of the later *ferta* monuments are in these penannular ring-ditches, which appear to have been designed to facilitate entry, ceremony and burial (see O'Brien and Bhreathnach 2011). A number of penannular ring-ditches enclosing extended inhumations of fifth- to seventh-century date are known, e.g. Ardsallagh 1, Co. Meath, Castle Upton, Co. Antrim, and Corbally, Co. Kildare.

9. Mud hut redux: roundhouse vernacular at Coolbeg, Co. Wicklow, and Iron Age social organisation

William O. Frazer

Introduction

During archaeological monitoring of topsoil-stripping in advance of development, thirteen areas of archaeology were identified across 27.1ha of what was formerly a green-field site in the townland of Coolbeg *c.* 2km from the N11, near the Beehive pub (Fig. 9.1). Three of these areas were identified and excavated by Ellen OCarroll (licence 04E1633): a possible flat cremation cemetery at area 1 (preserved *in situ*), and a cluster of post-holes (area 2) adjacent to a small ring-ditch (area 3; Fig. 9.2) (see OCarroll, this volume). Eight further areas were identified and excavated in May–July 2006 and June 2007 by the writer (Fig. 9.2; Frazer and Eriksson 2008). Of those sites that were excavated, all but area 6—the area with which this essay is concerned—date from the Neolithic–Bronze Age (listed chronologically):

- Area 5 was a *fulacht fiadh* site that included a flattened burnt mound, a trough, a hearth and three post-holes (the latter possibly supporting a windbreak or similarly functioning apparatus alongside the trough). Activity on the site was radiocarbon-dated to 2460–2190 BC (at 95.4% probability and calculated to 2-sigma, as are other dates herein unless otherwise indicated).
- Area 4 was a *fulacht fiadh* site that included two burnt mounds, at least three hearths and six troughs (one lined with wooden planks), overlying a series of meandering palaeochannels. Flint tools were made on part of the site and approximately 200 lithics were recovered, as well as twenty sherds of prehistoric pottery. The site was used—probably episodically—over a long period of time, with the pottery and most of the flint deriving from the earliest, western part of the site (radiocarbon-dated to 2290–2030 BC). The south-eastern burnt mound, at the northern edge of a boggy area subject to flooding, was in use over a similar period (2210–2020 BC, 93.6% probability). Later, as the mound material obstructed the palaeochannel used to fill associated troughs, activity moved upslope along the same channel to a burnt mound in the north-east of the site (1980–1760 BC).
- Area 11 was a *fulacht fiadh* site that included a low burnt mound, two troughs (both with evidence of timber lining) and nine peripheral possible hearths, near to a palaeochannel. There was also evidence for water management near the troughs, and several series of stake-holes suggested a number of small timber structures, including a possible third above-ground trough and wattle fencing. A limited number of flint artefacts were recovered at area 11, along with a fragment from a burnt oak acorn cupule. On the basis of radiocarbon dates, activity on the site occurred between 2140–1940 BC (one date) and 1880–1680 BC (two dates), perhaps focused on the twentieth and nineteenth centuries BC.
- Areas 9 and 10 were a *fulacht fiadh* site that included a flattened burnt mound, a wood-lined trough and a hearth (area 10), close to a small post-medieval pond/marl-pit (area 9). A few flint artefacts were recovered from area 10, which yielded a radiocarbon date of 1890–1690 BC.
- Area 7 was a *fulacht fiadh* site that included a large burnt mound (15m by 20m), four troughs (two lined with wooden planks) and at least four hearths, adjacent to a prehistoric pond and palaeochannel. Several flint artefacts and a complete granite saddle quern were recovered here. The area was used—again probably episodically—over a lengthy period of time: early activity beneath the mound was radiocarbon-dated to 1770–1600 BC and the end of use of the mound was radiocarbon-dated to 1380–1120 BC.
- Area 8 was a small *fulacht fiadh* site near (30m) area 7 and alongside the same palaeochannel. It included two hearths and a trough, with no separate burnt mound, and yielded a radiocarbon date of 1210–970 BC.

Two final areas were identified by the writer during developer-funded monitoring of topsoil-stripping in June 2008 (Frazer 2008):

- Area 12 was an isolated pit filled with burnt mound material of uncertain date (but probably Bronze Age, considering its proximity to areas 7 and 8).
- Area 13, a location similar to area 6 discussed herein, was a settlement site consisting of at least one (apparently unenclosed) double-ring roundhouse of very shallow concentric post-holes, with a central hearth and a porch/vestibule to the south-east (*c.* 8.5m in diameter).

Area 6 was an unenclosed settlement site that included a

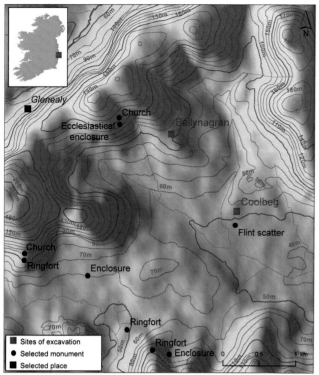

roundhouse (6.3–7.3m in diameter), a second probable roundhouse (on the same orientation and of similar size and build) that only partially survived, and a central oval pit/earth oven (Figs 9.3–9.9). The settlement was perched on a well-drained southerly slope surrounded by the aforementioned *fulachta fiadh*. Several flint artefacts were recovered at area 6, and the two buildings have unexpectedly yielded radiocarbon dates of 760–400 BC (but with a probability of 68.6% for the narrower range of 600–400 BC) and 380–160 BC (94%). On the basis of their similar location and orientation and identical build, a cogent argument may be made for their being nearly contemporaneous—that is to say, both dating from the fifth–fourth century BC.

Fig. 9.1 (left)—Coolbeg: site location.

Fig. 9.2 (below)—Coolbeg: plan of development, showing archaeology areas and the results of charcoal analysis.

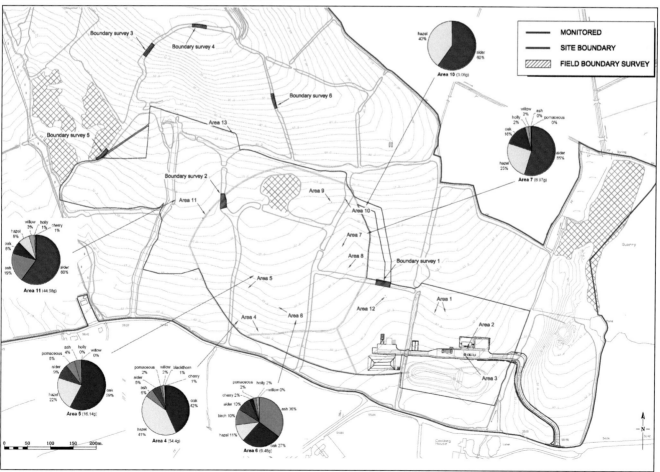

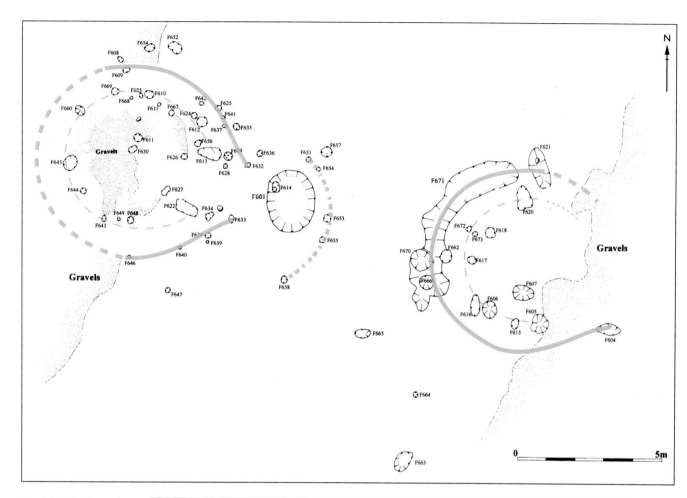

Fig. 9.3—Coolbeg: plan of area 6 after excavation.

Fig. 9.4—Coolbeg: view south-west of structure 1, with timbers added.

Setting: soil geology and preservation

Local soil geology appears to have been a significant factor in the survival of the archaeology at area 6. The regional soil geology is a zone of predominantly acid brown earths, with some gleys and brown podzolics, all derived from shale glacial tills. The area also lies near—perhaps 80–100m from—the northern limit of a zone of predominantly gleys, with some grey-brown podzolics, derived from glacial muds from the Irish Sea (National Soils Survey of Ireland 1980). A hydrogeological report in the EIS for the development indicates a significant north to south groundwater discharge (as distinct from the water-table) through the subsoil across the development toward the Three Mile Water (to the south) and the Long Ford Stream (a canalised mill-race to the south-east). The subsoil consists of 'highly impermeable' glacial drift boulder clay containing 'highly transmissive' (permeable) individual lenses of sands and gravels that 'tend not to be interconnected'.

Field observations and excavation indicate that these glacial sand and gravel lenses near the upper surface are frequently curvilinear and run north–south in accordance with the natural gradient, such that they canalise groundwater run-off into palaeochannels. In places where they are not interconnected, the groundwater spills up over the subsoil and flows downslope through the topsoil and across the upper surface of the boulder clay subsoil until it finds another sand/gravel lens. The effect, across the south-facing hillslope, is the (seasonal?) waterlogging of shallower lenses of sand/gravel and the formation of palaeochannels across areas of more impermeable boulder clay that lie downslope of those shallow lenses. In places—the location of area 7—this waterlogging has resulted in localised soil geologies of groundwater gleys (a process known as 'surface water gleying'). This variation in subsoil geology is important in understanding the location of the *fulachta fiadh* that appear to be sited in proximity to such palaeochannels (areas 4, 7–8 and 10). It is also significant in understanding the siting of Iron Age activity in area 6, which lies between two large gravel lenses (along the same contour) and would thus have been protected from flooding that might have occurred as a result of seasonal run-off.

The soil geology was fundamental to the extent of archaeological preservation on the site at the time of excavation. The western roundhouse, structure 1, was partly sited over the eastern edge of a large north-north-east/south-south-west gravel lens, with the consequence that its western half was much more poorly preserved. The eastern possible roundhouse, structure 2, was also built partially atop the western edge of a similar gravel lens such that its eastern half did not survive. The architecture of these structures, a point to

which we will return, evidently does not require significant 'earthfastness' for structural integrity; the footprint that the buildings leave is generally shallow and ephemeral in any soil geology, but particularly so over gravel. If such gravel lenses were being selected as preferred places for Iron Age settlement elsewhere in the neighbouring landscape, it may help to explain the dearth of surviving settlement archaeology from the era. Indeed, this point may have broader relevance to the survival of Iron Age settlement elsewhere in Ireland.

This is not to suggest, of course, that the choice of area 6 as a prehistoric building site was dependent on an assessment of soil geology, but rather on observations concerning the dryness of ground conditions and, perhaps, on the plants and trees growing in the immediate vicinity, which environmental data suggest were distinctive by the time of the settlement site.

Setting: past landscape

A reconstruction of the prehistoric palaeoenvironment may be instructive in relation to the latter point. In the accompanying Fig. 9.2, the writer has taken the results of Lorna O'Donnell's charcoal sample analysis (in which woody taxa were identified) and re-presented her data spatially. The amount (by weight) of charcoal analysed by O'Donnell is identified in grams below each pie chart, and the charts enumerate the different woody taxa, colour-coded for comparison between areas and listed from largest to smallest percentages, clockwise from the top. If we understand these to represent to some degree the available local flora at the time of use of each of the areas—with all the usual caveats about the possibilities of the skewing of such data by both the selective gathering of taxa for fuel or building by prehistoric people and the modern archaeological sampling process—several observations regarding the data are pertinent.

First, areas 7 and 10 demonstrate a clear dominance of first alder and then hazel. Area 11 is also dominated by alder, with a notable presence of hazel. It is likely that this flora is a consequence of the poorly drained ground conditions in the vicinity of these sites, with clearings free of a significant woodland canopy permitting the growth of hazel—and ash at area 11—around their perimeters. Particularly as the possible date range for area 10 overlaps with the possible range for the (in palaeoenvironmental terms) starkly different area 4, the writer is inclined to view the distinction between areas 5 and 4 and areas 11, 10 and 7 as illustrative of local variation in tree cover rather than as demonstrative of change through time in the Bronze Age. A partly preserved alder carr, contemporaneous with the use of the adjacent *fulacht fiadh*, was also identified alongside a palaeochannel in area 7.

Second, areas 5 and 4 demonstrate a remarkable

predominance of oak (canopy), followed by hazel (understorey). Even at areas 11 and 7, oak still forms a significant minority of the charcoal samples. A smaller component of alder, ash and pomaceous fruitwood (the latter is a catch-all term for rowan, hawthorn, crab-apple and pear) is also present at areas 5 and 4, as well as a smaller presence of holly, which also grows as an understorey in oak woodland. The latter taxa are likely to indicate the presence of numerous small clearings within mainly oak-canopied woodland.

Third, and most importantly for an understanding of the landscape surrounding the Iron Age buildings there, is the distinctiveness of the charcoal samples from area 6. A significant background presence of oak, hazel and alder—and, to a lesser extent, pomaceous fruitwood and holly—suggests the continuing importance of these taxa in the nearby landscape in the Iron Age. The remarkable predominance of ash and the presence of birch, however, both able colonisers of open areas (Lorna O'Donnell, pers. comm.), suggests significant clearance and perimeter regrowth. The key unanswered question is the extent to which this evidence is representative of the neighbouring landscape as a whole by this time. Does it indicate large-scale clearance and recolonisation around the start of the first millennium BC? On the basis of the continued background presence of oak, hazel and alder at area 6, and the substantial presence of ash at area 11, the writer is more inclined to view the existing data as indicating clearance related specifically to the building site itself. With this in mind, Fig. 9.8 depicts area 6 as it might have looked from the east.

The overall perspective regarding the prehistoric landscape of Coolbeg is admittedly one that is not especially diachronic: that is to say, it collapses several millennia into a snapshot representation of dominant woody vegetation, with the noteworthy exception that, by the time of the Iron Age, a certain localised setting had experienced more dramatic clearance, perhaps in relation to settlement. In places where the ground was particularly wet and poorly drained, alder carr, hazel and, to a lesser extent, willow seem to have been predominant. But elsewhere, across most of the hillside, the land was oak woodland, with hazel and some holly undergrowth. The oak canopy was interrupted by many clearings, around which biodiversity was especially evident, but with hazel and ash particularly prevalent. By the Iron Age, clearings like area 6, ringed by ash and birch regrowth, may have more frequently punctuated what continued to be oak-canopied woodland. In short, although many trees would undoubtedly have achieved significantly greater age and size than those we would generally find in Irish oak woodland today (for example, O'Donnell's analysis, in Frazer and

Eriksson 2008, of the wood lining of some of the *fulacht fiadh* troughs also indicates the presence of *very* mature ash and alder trees), the appearance of the landscape was something akin to the surviving woodland landscape in and near the Glen of the Downs in County Wicklow.

Excavation findings

Area 6 was identified by the writer during machine topsoil-stripping in advance of development just below the spur of a south-facing hillslope, at approximately 65m OD (Fig. 9.2). Some 900m² was cleaned by hand around the location of identified archaeology, although the archaeology in area 6 ultimately proved to extend across just 200m² (20m by 10m; Fig. 9.3). Soil descriptions may be found in Table 9.1; smaller feature descriptions are in Table 9.2.

Topsoil depth averaged 0.35–0.45m, thinner than further south and downslope on the hillside, a consequence of colluvial erosion aggravated by post-medieval and modern agriculture. A single prehistoric topsoil find (flint F600:1) was collected from topsoil over structure 1, but artefact recovery is likely to have been poorer than in the remainder of the excavation owing to the machine removal of topsoil and the lack of dry sieving.

The natural subsoil on the site contained secondary lenses of gravel at the eastern and western edges of area 6. A degree of mineral panning was visible in the upper surface of the gravels (although less so in area 6 than in other, wetter locations), generally of rust-coloured iron oxide.

Profiles suggest that almost all of the posts/stakes were sharpened and then driven into the ground, regardless of their diameter. The fills of many of the post-holes and stake-holes were similar across area 6 and have been grouped into four general categories (Table 9.1). None of these fills appear to represent the decomposition of wooden stakes/posts *in situ* but rather backfilling after a post or stake had been removed. Spatial analysis of the fill types yields no clear patterning. Instead, the fills appear to correspond to some extent to variations in the natural subsoil beneath—they reflect different post-depositional site-transformation processes according to the permeability of their immediately surrounding subsoil.

Stratigraphy on the site was sparse, except in a few instances where cut archaeological features overlapped. This has obliged interpretation to focus on the spatial patterning across the site, and the following descriptions are organised on this basis. Dimensions given for archaeological features are maximums.

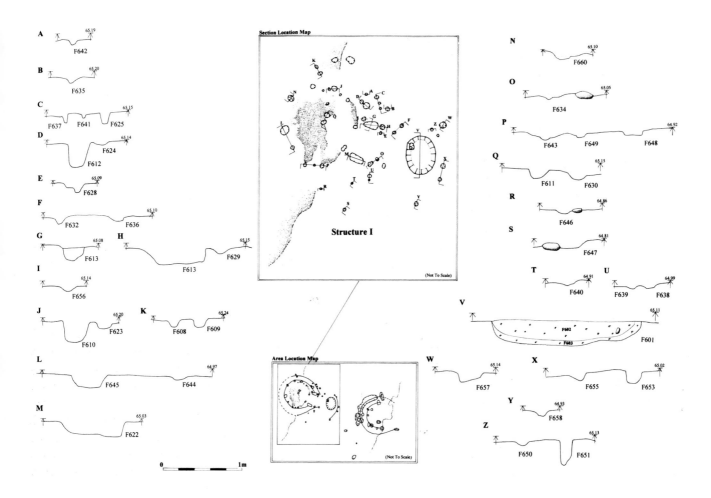

Fig. 9.5—Coolbeg: structure 1, sections and profiles.

Structure 1 (Figs 9.3–9.5 and 9.8)

Structure 1 was a roundhouse consisting of two nearly concentric oval rings of post-holes/stake-holes, with two central post-holes. The gravel surface of the subsoil in the building's centre, also oval in plan, appeared more compact than elsewhere and was probably formed partly as a consequence of the building's presence, although it was not a proper floor surface. There was little surviving evidence of an interior hearth, apart from the possible crazing of some of the central stones in the gravel subsoil. The inner oval of post-holes had a diameter of approximately 4.6–5.3m. The outer oval of stake-holes, 6.3–7.3m in diameter, was incomplete; the 'missing' stake-holes in the western portion of the building would have been atop gravel subsoil. Surviving post-holes and stake-holes in and near the gravel were shallower than at the eastern and north-eastern sides of the building, suggesting that the differential preservation in the ovals was due to the change in subsoil. Both concentric circles were splayed open to the east-south-east, indicating an entrance. In addition to an

incomplete secondary flint flake (F600:1) recovered from the topsoil over structure 1, two other structure 1 features yielded struck flint finds: a complete utilised secondary flake from inner ring post-hole F610 (F610:1), and a possible chip from a utilised flake from outer ring post-hole F633 (F633:1; Conor Brady, pers. comm.).

As noted, structure 1's inner oval of post-holes did not survive well to the south and south-west. The inner ring consisted of eight circular to subcircular post-holes (clockwise from the south: F648, F643, F644, F645, F660, F669, F610 and F612) that were quite regularly spaced, albeit perhaps closer together towards the rear north-west of the building (a not uncommon trait; see Guilbert 1981, 309, 315). These post-holes would have held load-bearing posts. Five of them (F610, F612, F644, F648 and F660) were similar in size, with F645 larger and F643 slightly smaller than the rest. F669 was shallow and at first thought to be non-archaeological, but its location between post-holes F610 and F660 suggests that it was part of the inner supporting oval ring of the structure. A further three stake-holes (F623, F624 and F649) appeared to relate to larger, adjacent post-holes in the oval; the northern two of these were angled up and towards the companion post-hole.

Two stake-holes (F631 and F668), a post-hole (F656) and a shallow depression (F667)—the latter not clearly archaeological—were recorded just inside the north-eastern inner ring. Post-hole F656 was possibly related to structure 1's entrance, considering its proximity to post-hole F613. Feature F667 was only a very shallow depression, with a fill slightly different from the surrounding subsoil.

The outer oval that formed the perimeter wall of structure 1 also survived best to the east and north-east, and had disappeared entirely to the west over the aforementioned gravel subsoil. The oval consisted of staggered stake-holes/small post-holes, positioned as if they were located on either side of an apparently lightweight (non-load-bearing) wall. They were not as regularly spaced as the inner oval, although that was probably due to poor preservation.

Fourteen small post-holes/stake-holes were recorded in the outer circle of structure 1. The best-preserved of these were the seven that formed the north-eastern part of the building (anticlockwise from the east: F632, F629, F635, F637, F641, F625 and F642).

Two oval post-holes also survived in the north-north-western part of the outer ring (F608 and F609). To the south and south-east were the final six surviving small post-holes/stake-holes in the outer oval (clockwise from the east: F633, F634, F638, F639, F640 and F646).

Two possible central post-holes were located within structure 1 (F611 and F630). These may have housed temporary uprights during the construction of the building (see below, and BBC 2007).

Five post-holes are considered to relate to the east-south-eastern entrance to structure 1. The distinction from surrounding parts of the building is somewhat arbitrary, and post-holes F634 and F629 (both described in the outer ring section) may also relate to the access way. Two main, large suboval/subrectangular post-holes (F613 and F622), aligned west-north-west/east-south-east, defined the entrance and its direction. Post-hole F613 was for the northern doorjamb and post-hole F622 for the southern doorjamb. Both of these differed from other post-holes/stake-holes in structure 1 in that they possessed flat bases. Both were also large enough that they may once have contained more than a single post, but there was no evidence for this apart from their shape in plan. Charcoal from post-hole F613 was used to obtain a radiocarbon date for structure 1.

Slightly further inside the building from these doorjamb post-holes were corresponding post-holes F626, to the north,

Fig. 9.6—Coolbeg: view east of oval pit 601.

and figure-of-eight-shaped F627, to the south. Double stake-hole F628 was positioned at the north-north-eastern side of the entry threshold.

Burnt, oval pit (Figs 9.3 and 9.5–9.6)
Just to the east-south-east of structure 1 was a large oval pit containing burnt mound-type material and burnt bone, ringed on the east by an arc of post-holes. The pit's proximity to structure 1 and its location directly before the latter's entrance might suggest that it is not contemporaneous with the occupation of that building. The nature of the fills surviving within the pit may, however, indicate its use as a clamp or 'earth' oven—also known as a 'roasting pit'—covered over during use, so that its nearness to a thatched structure 1 may not have posed a danger of fire (see below).

The oval pit F601 measured 1.85m north–south by 1.6m by 0.32m deep. It contained two fills: a basal one, just 0.07m deep, and a main, upper fill of burnt mound-type material. The base of the pit was oxidised to a reddish colour, demonstrating *in situ* burning. Jonny Geber's analysis of the minute undiagnostic fragments of burnt bone from the pit (and from nearby post-hole F653, see below) has indicated that they are mammalian.

There was a post-hole (F614) in the north-western base of pit F601. This was not necessarily earlier than the original cutting of pit F601, but it pre-dated the deposition of basal pit fill.

An arc of five post-holes flanked the oval burnt pit to the east (clockwise: F651, F654, F653, F655 and F658).

Structure 2 (Figs 9.3 and 9.7–9.9)
Archaeology at the eastern edge of area 6 has been interpreted as the remains of a second building, structure 2, a roundhouse of two concentric oval rings of similar dimensions to the other building. It did not survive as well as structure 1. The inner ring was made up of shallow post-holes, and the outer of a curvilinear gully and post-holes. The inner oval had a diameter

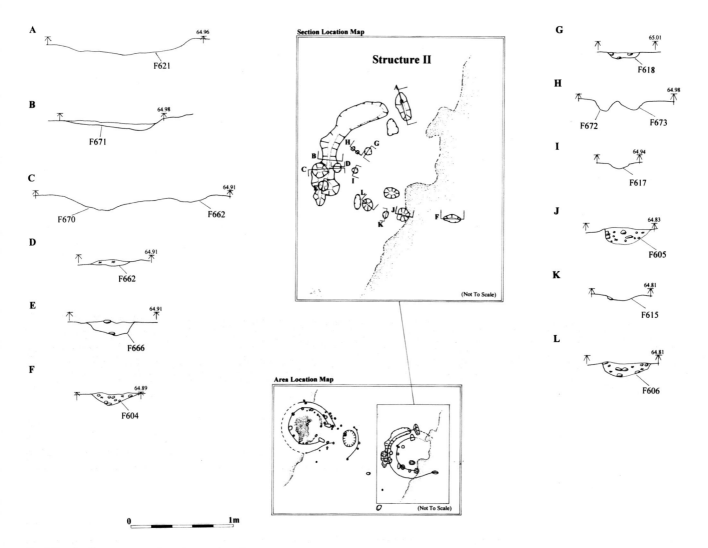

Fig. 9.7—Coolbeg: structure 2 sections and profiles.

of approximately 4.5m (north–south); the diameter of the outer circle was approximately 6.3–7.3m, with an apparent entrance to the east-south-east. As with structure 1, the differential preservation across the footprint of the building corresponded to changes in the subsoil: the remains of structure 2 mostly did not survive over the gravel subsoil to the east.

Eight post-holes survived in the inner ring, including four to the south-south-west (clockwise from the south: F605, F615, F606 and F616). Charcoal from F605 was sampled for radiocarbon dating. Three smaller post-holes were situated to the west and north-west (clockwise: F617, F673 and F672). In F673 the stones were positioned as packing material along the sides and base of the post-hole. The spacing of these post-holes was less regular than that of the southern four post-holes and they appear to represent only the survivors of this part of the inner ring.

The outer ring of structure 2 survived to the west, north-west and north as a gully containing post-holes, with an additional (double?) post-hole to the north and an isolated post-hole to the south-east. Such a gully, while distinct from the outer ring of structure 1, is increasingly understood as a characteristic of many late Bronze Age–Iron Age roundhouses in Britain and Ireland (see Cunliffe 1991, 213–311, *passim*; Becker *et al.* 2008, 26).

The gully (F671) measured 1.14m wide and 0.11m deep and contained a single fill. Three post-holes (F662, F666 and F670) were cut into the western part of gully F671, and an oval possible double post-hole (F621) was located in the northern part of the outer ring. Another post-hole (F604) also survived to the south-east.

Two possible post-holes (F607 and F618) were identified in the centre of structure 2. Possible post-hole F618 was

Fig. 9.8—Coolbeg: reconstruction of area 6 Iron Age roundhouses.

situated in the north-western interior of structure 2 and possessed a flat base. Pit/possible post-hole F607 was located just to the south.

Discussion

As noted, a charcoal sample from structure 2 (F605) yielded a radiocarbon date of 780–400 BC (95.4% probability), or more precisely 600–400 BC (68.6%), 760–680 BC (20.2%) and 670–630 BC (6.6%). A charcoal sample from structure 1 (F613) yielded a radiocarbon date of 380–110 BC (95.4%), or more precisely 380–160 BC (94.0%) and 140–110 BC (1.4%).

The two buildings in area 6 represent examples of a single prehistoric vernacular architectural tradition, constructed with locally exploited materials according to traditional methods. Anthropologically speaking, a characteristic of such 'practical' traditions of knowledge is a normative conservatism in the techniques employed. One consequence of this is a relative consistency of architectural form (albeit, as the writer has argued elsewhere, with the allowance for a remarkable degree of situational tactical improvisation in technical construction details; Frazer 2007a; 2007b). Another consequence is the persistence of such form across generations of builders.

Despite the latter point, the spatial proximity, extraordinary similarity of dimensions and identical orientation of the two buildings strongly suggest that they are contemporaneous. It is reasonable to suppose that the earlier of the two (structure 2) was still intact, in some manner, at the time of construction of structure 1. This is the supposition that has informed the eye-level reconstruction drawing (Fig. 9.8), in which structure 2 is being dismantled after structure 1 has been constructed. If the two radiocarbon date ranges for the two structures are cross-referenced, they yield a gap of just twenty years, or one generation, at the end of the fifth and start of the fourth century BC. This is the rationale for restricting the probable date of their occupation to the fifth–fourth centuries BC.

How the large oval pit F601 fits into this interpretive picture is less certain. It seems clearly contemporary with the settlement. In this interpretation and reconstruction (e.g. Fig.

Fig. 9.9—Coolbeg: view south of structure 2.

9.8) it is supposed that the pit may more likely be contemporaneous with structure 2, considering its apparent obstruction of structure 1's entry (and, insofar as it would have been a fire hazard, its proximity to structure 1's thatched roof). The evidence from the pit—its deep construction, the smallness and scarcity of its charcoal fragments, the relative largeness of its fire-cracked stones—suggests, however, that it served as a clamped cooking pit or 'earth oven' (also 'roasting pit'): a dry variant of a *fulacht fiadh* trough, in which stones were heated and then covered over to allow (in this case) the slow roasting of meat. Such a clamped pit may have been less of an obstacle and a fire hazard near structure 1. The eastern arc of post-holes around the pit has been interpreted as a windbreak, separate from structure 1, but there remains a possibility that the screen actually formed part of a south-eastern porch to that building. Other larger post-holes in the vicinity of the pit may have had a related function.

The purposes of the several scattered post-holes in area 6 are also difficult to determine. Those near structure 1 but outside the perimeter of the building may be temporary features related to the construction of the building, as suggested for central post-holes F611 and F630 (see below). The possible arc of F663–5 south-west of structure 1 may represent the last vestiges of a third building, but the surviving data are too insubstantial to be clear.

Anatomy of a small roundhouse
On the basis of the excavated data from Coolbeg, as well as comparative analysis of similar archaeological sites in Ireland and Britain and practical observations derived from experimental archaeology involving the rebuilding of roundhouses (primarily in Britain; see Pryor 2005; Bennet 2001; Drury 1982; Evans 1998; Romankiewicz 2004; Mytum 1986), a reconstruction of structures 1 and 2 is possible. While the term 'vernacular' is increasingly used by prehistorians to refer to routine or everyday activities, the actual scrutiny of prehistoric structures from a vernacular architectural perspective is rare. This does not relate to the potential

usefulness of such a perspective—after all, a defining aspect of vernacular building is its persistence and resistance to change—but rather to specialisation among archaeologists and the consequent relative lack of familiarity on the part of prehistorians with (mainly post-medieval) vernacular architectural studies.

A number of practical assumptions may be made concerning the building technique. While these are generally understood as 'common sense', it is worth outlining them explicitly. 'Common sense' is culturally specific, and while there are clear similarities between our own practical construction concerns and those of prehistoric builders, the case for such similarities benefits from their enumeration. First, as noted herein, it is reasonable to assume that the structures were built according to the broader archaeological evidence and practical concerns elicited during experimental archaeology reconstruction efforts. Second, it is reasonable to assume—at least for structures like those at Coolbeg, which appear humble both in scale and in the 'social location' of their inhabitants—that they were built as low to the ground as possible. The reasons for this relate not only to the conservation of resources and labour—more readily available (shorter) wood, ease of build etc.—but also to the structures' resistance to wind. Third, it is reasonable to assume a preference for simplicity in the build, namely that the wall-plate rested directly atop the supporting inner ring of load-bearing posts, and that a main 'spoked wheel' ring-beam and transverse timber tie-beam roof-support structure was either combined with or rested directly atop the wall-plate. This is despite the frequent reconstruction illustrations in archaeological literature that depict the *main* ring-beam as separate from the wall-plate and locate it well up towards the peak of the roof, resulting in a weaker roof and, as experimental archaeology has often demonstrated, an extraordinarily difficult construction. Fourth, it is reasonable to assume that builders sought to maximise uninterrupted interior space, i.e. that the inner ring of wall supports was located as close to the outer wall as possible (and that the central vertical support only extended to floor level during construction), so that the centre of the building was as free of posts as possible. Structure 1 had an approximate floor space of 145m², with some 52% of this within the inner load-bearing ring; compare Guilbert's (1981, 310) slightly larger examples, with 75–80% of the internal area within the inner ring. Finally, it is reasonable to assume that the level of the wall-plate/ring-beam was above average human head height, yet still low enough to be easily reachable during construction.

In analysing other criteria upon which a reconstruction may be based, there are several other constants:

- Plan dimensions derived from excavation data.
- The lowest roof pitch required for thatching to be effective in keeping out inclement weather is generally considered to be approximately 45° from the horizontal. Turf, or a weighty turf/reed combination with turf under-thatch (called 'scraw'; O'Reilly 2004, 24), is too heavy to have been used without the outer ring bearing the load also (see Pryor 2005, 87, 168), and there is no direct evidence for its use. Significantly, at least one reference links the effectiveness of a 45° pitch to the thickness of the thatch and argues that for a thinner layer of (combed longstraw) thatch to be effective against rain, an angle of 55° or greater is necessary (Wood 2004–7). Thinner thatch obviously makes a roof lighter (requiring a less substantial roof structure, less thatching material and making construction easier), but an additional benefit is the ease with which smoke can escape through the thatch (*ibid.*).
- Human height. Even understanding that the average height of humans has differed throughout history, an approximate average height (above which a wall-plate would be situated) of 1.55–1.83m is still sufficient for this reconstruction exercise.

The post-hole sizes indicate that the inner ring, less likely to suffer from damp, serves as the load-bearing supports for the building (Guilbert 1981, 310). A horizontal wall-plate (a perimeter of wood lintels around the ring) would have rested directly atop these posts, just high enough to allow clearance for humans standing within the building (c. 1.8m). In a structure like this, with a relatively narrow diameter to the load-bearing ring of posts, the wall-plate probably also served as the roof-supporting ring-beam, reinforced with horizontal timber tie-beams spanning the building interior. Together with the ring-beam, these reinforcing tie-beams resemble a spoked wooden wheel when viewed in plan (an observation that may prompt speculation as to whether there was a deliberate synecdochic analogue being made with a cart or chariot, considering the prevalence of ideas about warfare and horsemanship around this time; see Armit 2007, 136). The layout of structure 1's inner ring, in which individual load-bearing posts each had a companion directly opposite, just off-centre across the middle of the building interior, suggests that at least some of the horizontal tie-beams attached to the ring-beam were diameter-length rather than radius-length, a design attribute that would have strengthened the overall structure by forming a series of upright triangular trusses within the roof structure (with principal rafters forming two sides of each truss, there were perhaps as few as five; Fig. 9.2). These principal rafters, arranged in an inverted cone shape, were attached and supported at their upper end by a central post. While a central post support from the ground up was necessary during construction, once the roof was up the central post need only extend down to rest atop the horizontal tie-beams (akin to a king-post in rectangular buildings), freeing living space below from requiring a central, obstructive support (BBC 2007). The two central post-holes in structure 1 may indicate that companion central posts were employed during construction: one (F611) that was temporary (during construction) and extended all the way up to the roof peak, and a second (the more central F630) that was also temporary and supported the middle of the tie-beams, which in turn supported a separate, permanent central king-post that extended from the middle of the horizontal tie-beams up to the roof peak. It is worth noting that such an arrangement, with triangular principal trusses, a segmented ring-beam/wall-plate and slightly off-centre spoked wooden tie-beams to permit easy overlapping, could have relied almost entirely on wood joinery techniques for its affixing; Pryor (2005, 162) notes with caution the contradiction between our twine/cordage-heavy reconstructions and the lack of archaeological evidence for such binding material.

Details of the appearance of the south-eastern entrance of structure 1 are less straightforward: there is some uncertainty as to whether the outer perimeter wall curved out, as suggested in Figs 9.3 and 9.5, or continued in an oval. What is clear is the actual presence and location of the entrance, on an orientation that is commonly found in other similar buildings and that would have maximised light within (and, depending on surrounding tree cover, perhaps provided views down the valley and of the distant Irish Sea). In addition, there is a clear symmetry around an axis that extends from the centre of the building through the entrance (to form an internal vestibule rather than an external porch; see Guilbert 1981, 304): post-holes F627, F622, F634 and F633 to the south of the entry mirror, respectively, post-hole/stake-holes F626, F613, F628/629 and F632 to the north.

A reconstruction of the above-ground architecture allows a calculation of the height of the roof of structure 1 (and, by extension, structure 2). It also allows a calculation of the approximate height of the outer, non-load-bearing wall. Such information is important in understanding some aspects of the settlement, not least the use of interior space and the visibility of the site within the surrounding landscape (the latter is deliberately addressed in the eye-level perspective of Fig. 9.8). Surviving only as the remnants of cut features in plan, the buildings appeared unimpressive during excavation, but despite their restricted area (36.3m² each) they were

originally substantial structures that stood 4.9–5.6m high. Their roof peaks are nevertheless unlikely to have been visible from any great distance in most directions, considering the extensiveness of the surrounding woodland suggested by palaeoenvironmental data. The height calculation assumes an approximate thickness of thatch of between 0.3m and 0.6m, wherein thicker thatch is necessary with a lower roof pitch and thinner is only possible with a steeper pitch. The outer wall of structure 1—probably built of wattle supported by upright posts and stakes, and likely rendered with mud daub—stood 0.5–0.9m high. This meant that the perimeter aisle within the building, between the outer wall and the load-bearing inner ring of posts, was still of sufficient height to make it usable as living space. In the case of structure 2, the outer perimeter wall is demarcated by a gully (F671). Considering the other similarities between structures 2 and 1, the suspicion is that the gully of the former indicates a particular concern with water management beneath a similar wattle wall rather than a different build altogether (for example, one with a sill-beam/sleeper beam).

Two general equations for calculating the height of a roundhouse of similar architecture, and the height of its non-load-bearing perimeter wall, are presented below, where h = the height at the top of the conical roof, r_{inner} = the average radius of the inner *load-bearing* ring, θ = roof pitch (ranging from 45° to 55°), r_{outer} = the average radius of the outer *non-load-bearing* perimeter wall, t = thickness of thatch (inversely proportional to θ, ranging from 0.3m to 0.6m), w = the height at which the wall-plate was positioned (> average human height/max. headroom to prevent bumps on heads), and p = the height of the perimeter wall:

$$\text{Building height: } (\tan \theta_{shallow} \bullet r) + w + t_{thick} \leq h$$
$$\leq (\tan \theta_{steep} \bullet r) + w + t_{thin}$$

$$\text{Perimeter wall height: } w - (r_{outer} - r_{inner})\tan \theta_{steep} \leq p$$
$$\leq w - (r_{outer} - r_{inner})\tan \theta_{shallow}$$

This calculated height of the building indicates that there was a substantial amount of overhead space under the roof, an observation that has prompted varying interpretations in roundhouse design (such variation often appears to be a consequence of the licence afforded to reconstruction artists rather than deriving from excavator interpretation). One of these is the reconstruction of roundhouse roofs with domed or low conical roofs that descend to the ground, reducing the amount of overhead space. The difficulty with the former design in an Irish climate is the same as with low-pitched roofs: its relative ineffectiveness against inclement weather. It is worth noting the genius of a conical thatched roof more generally: a thatched roof requires maintenance and periodic repair, particularly along its ridge, and a roof design that minimises ridge area to a single point reduces the amount of necessary maintenance. The pre-eminent problem with thatching that extends to the ground is that in such circumstances the thatch gets wet, stays wet, rots, attracts more insects and other unwanted pests and is therefore very high-maintenance and lacking in longevity. At Coolbeg there was no evidence for the angled rafters of a conical roof extending to the ground, and such a reconstruction would result in a low building of distinctly small interior proportions (see Faegre 1979). Perhaps as robust a refutation of such reconstructions, barring specific archaeological evidence to make the case for them, is the absence of such vernacular designs—that is, ethnohistorical analogies—from more recent Irish architecture.

Evidence for central hearths was slight at Coolbeg (as were any internal occupation deposits), but this is perhaps a consequence of poor preservation; hearths seem an essential component in ensuring the habitability of such buildings and are a frequent feature of similar prehistoric structures. A roomy under-roof space would be useful in keeping smoke away from inhabitants; accepted wisdom considers that roundhouses probably lacked smoke-holes and instead relied on the slow dispersal of smoke through the thatch overhead. The roominess of overhead, under-roof space has also prompted considerations that such buildings may have had a first-floor loft, but scholars of more recent vernacular structures are well acquainted with the connection between the presence of a chimney and the existence of a loft or first floor: the former is required for the latter to be habitable (see Gailey 1987, 94). It seems more probable that overhead space was instead used for dry storage, perhaps particularly as a larder: foodstuffs and other items could readily be hung from principal rafters or stashed atop tie-beams, and even a slightly smoky environment there would help to prevent spoilage and to deter vermin.

At least one experimental archaeologist (Wood 2004–7) has noted that the smokiness of the interior space in such an arrangement is notably less pronounced with thinner thatch, prompting speculation concerning the latter's desirability. Perhaps of some relevance here are early modern accounts by visitors to Ireland of the overwhelming smokiness of vernacular cottage interiors, about which inhabitants seemed unconcerned (one seventeenth-century commentator even observes that cottage-dwellers associated smokiness with warmth and coziness and therefore sought to keep interiors as chokingly hazy as possible; see MacLysaght 1979, 106). As previously alluded to, however, the advantage of thinner

thatch, and consequently a steeper roof pitch of at least 55°, is perhaps more profound from the standpoints both of the conservation of labour (it required a much lighter load-bearing wooden timber framework, and less effort was needed to collect and prepare a lower volume of thatch) and of the conservation of resources (younger, more widely available timber would suffice, and less land would be needed to generate the necessary thatching material). Put another way, a thinner-thatch, steeper-pitched roof has a dramatic effect both on the trickiest and most difficult aspect of roundhouse construction (roof-raising) and on one of the most time-consuming aspects (thatching). Equally important, a lighter-framed, smaller-diameter building—particularly one that was structurally robust because of a low ring-beam/wall-plate and tie-beams that, together with principal rafters, formed a series of strong roof trusses—was less dependent on 'earthfastness' for structural integrity. Such structures would have a lower archaeological visibility today, since they did not need to be as deeply inserted into the ground.

A thick thatched roof with a lower (c. 45°) pitch disperses much of the rainfall that it receives via slow capillary action through the thatch. A steeper, thinner thatched roof, however, depends more significantly on run-off across its upper surface (Wood 2004–7), with a consequently greater need for water management below its eaves. This may be significant in relation to the growing number of known late Bronze Age–Iron Age roundhouses in Ireland and Britain possessing a perimeter gully. On the basis of the excavation data (the outer ring of structure 1 not least), structure 2's gully has been interpreted as a wall foundation gully (and it is worth noting that drainage features beneath, and parallel to, exterior walls in historic-era vernacular buildings are commonplace). Nevertheless, whether or not a given roundhouse gully is an eaves drip, a storm-water gully or a wall foundation gully is immaterial; *any* of these would have served to drain water away from the building and may therefore be particularly characteristic of smaller roundhouses with more steeply pitched roofs. The widespread coincidence of gullies with smaller buildings that also possessed less substantial evidence for earthfast, load-bearing posts—many of which, again, appear to date from the late Bronze Age–Iron Age (Becker *et al.* 2008, 25–7)—may therefore be a reflection of a widespread shift in the vernacular architecture of roundhouses to lighter building frames and steeper, more thinly thatched roofs.

Vernacular architecture: broader implications?
Why might such a change have occurred? If this explanatory interpretation is correct, then it is intriguing that the incidence of small-diameter Iron Age roundhouses with

perimeter gullies and shallow or non-existent load-bearing post-holes does not appear to be regionally restricted, as we might expect an innovation in vernacular architecture to be. In part, this lack of regional specificity must relate to the continuing scarcity of settlement evidence (Raftery 1994, *passim*; Becker *et al.* 2008, esp. 1, 63) and the consequent difficulty in discerning and defining structural traditions or recurrent patterning of domestic deposits (Armit 2007, 132, although further work building on Becker *et al.*'s project might yield more in this regard). The answer may lie in what such a shift meant in terms of labour and resource conservation.

A lighter building frame, shallower post-holes in the ground, a lesser quantity of thatch and a smaller number of withies and rods for a shorter perimeter wall are all attributes that save labour in the preparation of raw materials for the clearing of ground for, and the actual construction of, a roundhouse. Similar to this is a reduction in the resources necessary to build a roundhouse, the greater availability of thinner young–mature timber (especially fast-growing straight trees like ash and birch, so well represented in the charcoal samples from Coolbeg), the greater availability of (coppiced hazel?) rods and withies, and the decreased field size (or wetland access) needed to supply a sufficient amount of thatching material.

Combined with the relatively modest size of roundhouses like those at Coolbeg, what we may be seeing in the archaeology are changes to the vernacular building traditions that are a reflection of, but perhaps also contributed to, changes in social structure in the Irish Iron Age. While the impact of the radiocarbon plateau in the early Iron Age must not be overlooked (Becker *et al.* 2008, 51; van Geel *et al.* 1996), a significant drop in population and a major shift towards pastoral farming have both been posited as factors in the invisibility of routine, vernacular activities in the Iron Age generally, and particularly in the last two to three centuries BC (Armit 2007, 132–3; Weir 1995, 106–11). Both factors also relate fundamentally to the mobility of Iron Age people and the nature of their settlement (Raftery 1994, 112; Armit 2007, 135). Changes in vernacular building traditions may also feed into this mix, since there is a particular value on the conservation of house-building labour and raw material resources among smaller collectives leading a less sedentary existence.

It may be significant that the numbers of unenclosed scattered settlements appear to be growing over the course of the Iron Age, particularly in the years BC (Becker *et al.* 2008, 25–7), and that there is also an apparent lack of other 'local-scale' boundaries around not just houses but farms and fields as well (Armit 2007, 134). These shifts in the nature of settlement could be considered complementary to the changes in vernacular building traditions suggested here, and it is intriguing that there may be a correlation between unenclosed settlement and the incidence of post-built circular and subcircular houses with perimeter trenches or gullies (Becker *et al.* 2008, 25–6). Perhaps owing to necessity, smaller kin-groups (even nuclear families?) began to build more humble, dispersed—and possibly more numerous—dwellings.[1]

Further analysis at regional and national level may also eventually demonstrate that other dwellings like that at Coolbeg were located in 'practical' locations (near fresh water, on a south-facing slope, in an area protected from seasonal flooding, somewhat sheltered from the wind), but possibly less prominent, accessible or ostentatious locations than were 'typical' settlements of (often larger?) Bronze Age roundhouses. Such characteristics, in terms of their 'situatedness' within an Iron Age landscape, combined with the poor archaeological visibility that is likely to be partly a consequence of an architectural tradition not dependent on 'earthfastness' for the structural integrity of buildings, may support what many prehistorians have suspected for a long time: a lack of Iron Age settlement sites does not reflect merely a sparse population but perhaps a more scattered one too. Armit (2007, 132) has also suggested that the detection of Iron Age 'vernacular sites' may be masked by the density of early medieval settlement (see Becker *et al.* 2008, 63). Drawing upon the more limited resources available to a smaller 'collectivity'—smaller and less numerous cultivated fields, decreased territorial access to woodland and wetland, fewer strong backs to help raise a roof truss—Iron Age folk perhaps responded with architectural innovation.

The spread of shallow post-holes, perimeter gullies, smaller diameters and perhaps less prominent topographical settlement locations—all characteristics of the fifth- to fourth-century BC roundhouses at Coolbeg—may all be indicators of a change in vernacular building tradition that mirrored a social reorganisation involving a breakdown or dispersal of larger, extended kin-group collective settlement in favour of smaller, immediate families. These are grand conclusions from the limited evidence at Coolbeg and similar sites, but, as outlined, there are other aspects of Irish Iron Age archaeology that might be considered to provide complementary evidence for such change. Whatever the merit of such ideas, a broader consideration of Iron Age settlement patterns and their social implications would do well to engage in 'mud hut redux' and reconsider the minutiae of vernacular building evidence like that at Coolbeg, alongside broader landscape reconstruction and hypotheses seeking to explain their archaeological scarcity (see Armit 2007, 132–3; Becker *et al.* 2008, 1–3, 63–4).

Table 9.1—Coolbeg: soil descriptions.
Archaeological deposits and other soils are categorised using a terminology adapted from the Unified Soil Classification System (USCS): by compaction—loose/soft, moderately compact or hard; by colour—lightness (light/mid/dark), secondary tint and main hue; and by composition—sand/silt/clay/other. Descriptions are in ascending order, with the main hue and main soil type listed last (e.g. 'mid-grey brown sandy silt clay' is primarily brown clay). Where there is no secondary hue it is omitted. When compaction is moderate it is similarly omitted. Soil inclusions are described as occasional (<4% of content, by volume), moderate (5–7%) or frequent (8–10%): these are obviously estimates. Where inclusions make up more than 10% of a deposit, their percentage is described separately. Stones are described by shape—if shape is omitted, they are 'irregularly shaped', with no specific pattern—and by approximate size: tiny (<10mm across), small (10–50mm), medium-sized (50–200mm) and large (>200mm). Typical or average stone dimensions are also generally given, as is a compositional description. Most of the stone visible in the (glacial drift) subsoil was sedimentary—sandstone, fine siltstone/mudstone or shale—but occasional glacial erratics—e.g. granite—were also observed

Soil type	Compaction	Colour	Composition	Inclusions (by % of volume)				Inclusion details
				≤4%	5–7%	8–10%	>10%	
Topsoil	Loose–moderate	Mid-brown/mid-grey brown	Sandy silt clay	Stones				Tiny–medium-sized sand- and siltstones (avg. <50mm across)
Type 1	Moderate	Mid–dark grey brown	Sand clay	Stones, charcoal flecks				Tiny–small shale, mud- and siltstones (<50mm across)
Type 2	Moderate	Mid-grey brown	Clay sand	Stones, charcoal flecks				Tiny–small shale, mud- and siltstones (<50mm across)
Type 3	Moderate	Mid-brown/mid-grey brown	Silty sand clay	Charcoal flecks		Stones		Tiny–small shale, mud- and siltstones (<50mm across)
Type 4	Moderate	Mid–dark grey brown	Sand clay		Charcoal flecks		Stones (15–20%)	Tiny–small shale, mud- and siltstones (<50mm across)
Pit F601, upper fill F602	Moderate	Dark brown black	Clay silt	Burnt bone		Charcoal flecks	Stones (60%)	Small–medium-sized angular and subangular fire-cracked stones (siltstone, shale; avg. <90mm across)
Pit F601, basal fill F603	Moderate	Mid-yellow grey	Sandy silt clay	Charcoal flecks, burnt bone			Stones (25%)	Small–medium-sized angular and subangular fire-cracked stones (siltstone, shale; avg. <90mm across)
Post-hole F616	Compact	Mid-orange brown	Silt clay	Stones		Mineral pan (FeO)	Stones (≥75%)	Small–large packing shale, mud- and siltstones on S side (avg. 50–150mm across)
Gully F671 fill	Moderate	Mid-brown/mid-grey brown	Sand clay	Charcoal flecks			Stones (15%)	Tiny–medium-sized irregular, subangular and subround shale, mud- and siltstones (avg. 50mm across)
Subsoil	Moderate–compact	Mid-orange–grey brown	Sand clay					Small–medium-sized irregular, subround and subangular stones (avg. <100mm across)
Gravel subsoil	Loose–moderate	Mid-orange brown	Sandy clay gravel			Mineral pan (FeO)	Stones (≥75%)	Small subround and round stones (avg. 30mm across)

Table 9.2—Coolbeg: feature dimensions and fills.

Feature nos	Structure	Location	Feature type	Dimensions (maximums; metres)				Fill	Miscellaneous
				Diameter	Length	Width	Depth		
F648, F644, F660, F610, F612	1	Inner, load-bearing ring	Post-holes	0.23–0.35	–	–	0.06–0.34	Type 2 (most); type 1 (F610); type 4 (F612)	Listed clockwise from S (excluding those below)
F645	1	Inner, load-bearing ring	Post-hole	–	0.69	0.48	0.20	Type 2 (but with 20% stones)	Main orientation is N–S
F643	1	Inner, load-bearing ring	Post-hole	–	0.23	0.22	0.08	Type 2	Smaller than others in ring
F669	1	Inner, load-bearing ring	Stake-hole	0.25	–	–	0.04	Type 2	Very shallow
F623, F624	1	Inner, load-bearing ring	Stake-holes	0.12–0.20	–	–	0.05–0.10	Type 1	Relate to adjacent post-holes
F649	1	Inner, load-bearing ring	Stake-hole	0.10	–	–	0.07	Type 2	Relates to adjacent post-hole
F631, F668	1	Inner, load-bearing ring	Stake-holes	0.07–0.12	–	–	0.08–0.10	Type 3	Inside NE inner ring
F656	1	Inner, load-bearing ring	Post-hole	0.24	–	–	0.07	Type 1	Possibly related to entrance (proximity to F613)
F667	1	Inner, load-bearing ring	Shallow depression	0.20	–	–	0.03	Akin to surrounding subsoil	Inside NE inner ring; not clearly archaeological
F632, F635, F625, F642	1	NE outer, perimeter wall ring	Small post-holes	0.10–0.14	–	–	0.07–0.16	Type 1 (F625, F642); type 2 (F635); type 3 (F632)	Listed anticlockwise from the E (excluding those below)
F629	1	NE outer, perimeter wall ring	Post-hole	–	0.24	0.22	0.11	Type 2	Larger than others in ring
F637, F641	1	NE outer, perimeter wall ring	Stake-holes	0.05–0.07	–	–	0.06–0.10	Type 3	Smaller than others in ring
F608, F609	1	NW outer, perimeter wall ring	Post-holes	0.09–0.26	–	–	0.07–0.12	Type 1	Oval
F633, F634, F638, F639, F640, F646	1	S and SE outer, perimeter wall ring	Small post-holes/stake-holes	0.10–0.22	–	–	0.08–0.12	Type 2	Listed clockwise from the E
F611, F630	1	Central	Post-holes	0.22–0.28	–	–	0.05–0.11	Type 1	For temporary uprights during build
F613	1	Entrance	Post-hole	–	0.80	0.25	0.15	Type 1	N doorjamb; flat-based
F622	1	Entrance	Post-hole	–	0.80	0.30	0.21	Type 1	S doorjamb; flat-based
F626	1	Entrance	Post-hole	0.10	–	–	0.08	Type 1	N side of entry

Table 9.2 (cont.)—Coolbeg: feature dimensions and fills.

Feature nos	Structure	Location	Feature type	Dimensions (maximums; metres)				Fill	Miscellaneous
				Diameter	Length	Width	Depth		
F627	1	Entrance	Post-hole	–	0.26	0.12	0.08	Type 1	S side of entry; figure-of-eight-shaped; main orientation is NE–SW
F628	1	Entrance	Double stake-hole	0.14	–	–	0.13	Type 2	NNE side of entry
F652, F654	1	Vicinity	Post-holes	0.40–0.50	–	–	0.05–0.19	Type 1	N of str. 1; for temporary props during build?
F647	1	Vicinity	Post-hole	0.32	–	–	0.08	Type 2	S of str. 1; for temporary prop during build?
F636	1	Vicinity	Post-hole	0.22	–	–	0.06	Type 3	E of str. 1; for temporary prop during build?
F614	Oval pit F601	Base of pit	Post-hole	0.27	–	–	0.17	As basal fill F603 (but with 30% stones)	Pre-dates basal fill F603
F651, F656, F653, F655, F658	Oval pit F601	Arc around pit	Post-holes	0.15–0.22	–	–	0.08–0.32	Type 3 (most; more charcoal in F653); type 1 (F658)	Listed clockwise from NE; packing stones in F653
F657	Oval pit F601	NE of pit and arc	Post-hole	0.30	–	–	0.15	As main fill F602 (but with 20% tiny–medium stones)	Outside arc around pit
FF605, F615, F606, F616	2	Inner, load-bearing ring	Post-holes	0.27–0.71 (avg. 0.30)	–	–	0.06–0.13	Type 4 (most); F616 as Table 9.1	Listed clockwise from S
F617, F673, F672	2	Inner, load-bearing ring	Post-holes	0.19–0.25	–	–	0.07–0.12	Type 4 (packing stones in F673)	Smaller; listed clockwise from S
F620	2	Inner, load-bearing ring	Post-hole?	–	0.79	0.49	0.14	Type 4	To N
F662, F666	2	Outer, perimeter wall ring	Post-holes	0.45	–	–	0.06–0.13	Type 3 (but with 15–20% stones)	Cut into W end of gully F671
F670	2	Outer, perimeter wall ring	Post-hole	0.75	–	–	0.15	Type 3 (but with 15–20% stones)	Cut into W end of gully F671
F621	2	Outer, perimeter wall ring	Double post-hole?	–	1.34	0.65	0.08 (S); 0.15 (N)	Type 1	N outer ring
F604	2	Outer, perimeter wall ring	Post-hole	0.39	–	–	0.11	Type 3 (but with 15–20% stones)	SE outer ring
F607	2	Central	Post-hole?	0.29	–	–	0.08	Type 4	Flat-based; for temporary upright during build?

Table 9.2 (cont.)—Coolbeg: feature dimensions and fills.

Feature nos	Structure	Location	Feature type	Dimensions (maximums; metres)				Fill	Miscellaneous
				Diameter	Length	Width	Depth		
F618	2	Central	Post-hole?	0.60	–	–	0.13	Mid-orange brown silt clay, otherwise as type 4	Flat-based; for temporary upright during build?
F663, F664	Isolated	S part of area 6	Post-holes	0/65 (both)	–	–	0.24 (both)	Type 3 (but very silty)	Possible arc, with F665
F665	Isolated	S part of area 6	Post-hole	0.21	–	–	0.12	Type 3 (but very silty)	Possible arc, with F663, F664

Acknowledgements

The writer is grateful to editors Chris Corlett and Michael Potterton; colleagues at Margaret Gowen and Co. Ltd; Carina Eriksson, Katharina Becker and John Ó Néill for comments on drafts of this essay; Lorna O'Donnell, Nicki Whitehouse and Phil Barratt for critical perspectives on environmental interpretations; and John Tierney and Finn Delaney for discussing *fulachta fiadh*. Fieldwork described herein was directed by the writer and co-supervised by Carina Eriksson and Simon Dick, under licence 06E0552. Thanks also to the following: the excavation/post-excavation team, Deirdre Collins, Adam Collins and Arthur White; post-excavation specialists Jonny Geber and Lorna O'Donnell; and those involved in illustration production, Johnny Ryan, Simon Dick, Andrea Acinelli, Gary Devlin and Mario Sughi.

Bibliography

Armit, I. 2007 Social landscapes and identities in the Irish Iron Age. In C. Haselgrove and T. Moore (eds), *The later Iron Age in Britain and beyond*, 130–9. Oxford.

BBC 2007 Reconstructing an Iron Age roundhouse. BBC—history (www.bbc.co.uk/history/ancient/british_prehistory/launch_ani_roundhouse.shtml; accessed 28 May 2007).

Becker, K., Ó Néill, J. and O'Flynn, L. 2008 Iron Age Ireland: finding an invisible people. Unpublished report prepared for the Heritage Council (project 16365).

Bennet, P. 2001 (1 July) Reconstructing Iron Age buildings. BBC—history (www.bbc.co.uk/history/ancient/british_prehistory/ironage_roundhouse_01.shtml; accessed 28 May 2007).

Crumley, C.L. 1987 A dialectical critique of hierarchy. In T.C. Patterson and C.W. Gailey (eds), *Power relations and state formation*, 155–69. Washington.

Cunliffe, B. 1991 *Iron Age communities in Britain: an account of England, Scotland and Wales from the seventh century BC until the Roman conquest*. London and New York.

Drury, P.J. (ed.) 1982 *Structural reconstruction: approaches to the interpretation of the excavated remains of buildings*. British Archaeological Reports, British Series 110. Oxford.

Evans, C. 1998 Constructing houses and building context: Bersu's Manx round-house campaign. *Proceedings of the Prehistoric Society* **64**, 183–201.

Faegre, T. 1979 *Tents: architecture of the nomads*. London.

Frazer, W.O. 2007a Final report, archaeological excavation: Lidl site, Ashbourne Town Centre Development, Killegland townland, Ashbourne, Co. Meath. Unpublished report by Margaret Gowen and Co. Ltd for Lidl Ireland GmbH.

Frazer, W.O. 2007b Field of fire: evidence for wartime conflict in a 17th-century cottier settlement in County Meath, Ireland. *Journal of Conflict Archaeology* **3** (1), 173–96. [Article also published in T. Pollard and I. Banks (eds), *Scorched earth: studies in the archaeology of conflict* (Leiden, 2008), 173–96.]

Frazer, W.O. 2008 Archaeological monitoring, field boundary survey and mitigation impact statement: Phase 2, Ballynagran Landfill, Coolbeg townland, Co. Wicklow. Unpublished report by Margaret Gowen and Co. Ltd for Greenstar Ltd.

Frazer, W.O. and Eriksson, C. 2008 Archaeological excavation: Areas 4–11, Ballynagran Landfill, Coolbeg townland, Co. Wicklow. Unpublished report by Margaret Gowen and Co. Ltd for Greenstar Ltd.

Gailey, A. 1987 Changes in Irish rural housing, 1600–1900. In P. O'Flanagan, P. Ferguson and K. Whelan (eds), *Rural Ireland, 1600–1900: modernisation and change*, 86–103. Cork.

Ghey, E., Edwards, N., Johnston, R. and Pope, R. 2007 Characterising the Welsh roundhouse: chronology, inhabitation and landscape. *Internet Archaeology* **23** (intarch.ac.uk/journal/issue23/johnston_toc.html; accessed 21 October 2008).

Grogan, E., O'Donnell, L. and Johnston, P. 2007 *The Bronze Age landscapes of the Pipeline to the West: an integrated archaeological and environmental assessment.* Bray.

Guilbert, G. 1981 Double-ring roundhouses, probable and possible, in prehistoric Britain. *Proceedings of the Prehistoric Society* **47**, 299–317.

Larsson, E. 2006 Ballycullen Site 3, Oldcourt. *Excavations 2003*, 175–6. Bray.

Limbert, D. 1996 Irish ringforts: a review of their origins. *Archaeology Journal* **153**, 243–89.

McLaughlin, M. and Conran, S. 2008 The emerging Iron Age of south Munster. *Seanda* **3**, 51–3.

MacLysaght, E. 1979 *Irish life in the seventeenth century after Cromwell* (reprint of 2nd edn). Dublin.

Murray, C. 2005 Killoran 16. In M. Gowen, J. Ó Néill and M. Phillips (eds), *The Lisheen Mine Archaeological Project, 1996–8*, 296–8. Bray.

Mytum, H. 1986 The reconstruction of an Iron Age roundhouse at Castell Henllys, Dyfed. *Bulletin of the Board of Celtic Studies* **33**, 283–90.

National Soils Survey of Ireland 1980 *General soil map: second edition (1:575,000).* An Foras Talúntais.

Newman, C., O'Connell, M., Dillon, M. and Molloy, K. 2006 Interpretation of charcoal and pollen data relating to a late Iron Age ritual site in eastern Ireland: a holistic approach. *Vegetation History and Archaeobotany* **16** (5), 349–65.

O'Reilly, B. 2004 *Living under thatch: vernacular architecture in Co. Offaly.* Douglas.

Pryor, F. 2005 *Flag Fen: life and death of a prehistoric landscape.* Stroud.

Raftery, B. 1994 *Pagan Celtic Ireland: the enigma of the Irish Iron Age.* London.

Ralston, I. 2003 Scottish roundhouses: the early chapters. *Scottish Archaeological Journal* **25** (1), 1–26.

Romankiewicz, T. 2004 Building Iron Age roundhouses: an architectural view. *Scottish Archaeological News* **45**, 12–13.

Roycroft, N. 2007 Iron Age patterns: silent sites. *Seanda* **1**, 9.

Shaw, C. 2004 (3 February) Some pictures from around the farm: Butser ancient farm (www.butser.org.uk/bulletin15.html; accessed 28 May 2007).

Taylor, K. 2008 At home and on the road: two Iron Age sites in County Tipperary. *Seanda* **3**, 54–5.

Van Geel, B., Buurman, J. and Waterbolk, H.T. 1996 Archaeological and palaeo-ecological indications of an abrupt climate change in the Netherlands, and evidence for climatological teleconnections around 2650 BP. *Journal of Quaternary Science* **11**, 451–60.

Weir, D. 1995 A palynological study of landscape and agricultural development in County Louth from the second millennium BC to the first millennium AD: final report. *Discovery Programme Reports* **2**, 77–126.

Wood, J. 2004–7 The courtyard house roof structure: Saverock water archaeology (www.archaeologyonline.org/Courtyard%20Houses/Courtyard%20House%20Roof.htm; accessed 28 May 2007).

Note

1. Armit (2007, 137) has even suggested that Crumley's (1987) 'heterarchy' model of social organisation might be relevant for the Irish Iron Age: a model in which regional authority based around concepts of sacral kingship may have faded before more pressing quotidian and face-to-face social organisation dependent on immediate kinship obligation and local military intimidation.

10. An early Iron Age farmstead at Ballycullen, Co. Dublin

Ellinor Larsson

Introduction

This essay describes the results of the excavation of an early Iron Age roundhouse identified in 2003 during a programme of archaeological monitoring in Ballycullen, south Co. Dublin. The site was in the foothills of the Dublin Mountains within the townland of Oldcourt and bordering the townland of Ballycullen to the east (Fig. 10.1).[1]

Geographical context and topography

Ballycullen is on the north-facing foothills of the Dublin Mountains, with undulating fields of pasture and mature hedgerows lining the fields and country roads. The gentle slope is broken by small ridges and valleys created by streams carrying off the excess water from the mountains to the south. The highest point offers excellent views over extensive areas of land and sea, stretching far into north County Dublin, into Kildare to the west and overlooking the city of Dublin; Lambay and Howth can be seen to the north, and Killiney Hill to the east. The abundance of water sources is evident, with several springs, including a listed holy well (DU022-028), and many other small streams.

Archaeological background

There are two recorded monuments in the vicinity of the site. A levelled ringfort (DU022-020) in the townland of Scholarstown, over 500m north-east of the site, was excavated in 1985 by V.J. Keeley Ltd (Keeley 1985). The closest recorded monument (DU022-028), a holy well associated with St Columcille, is still venerated. It is in the townland of Oldcourt to the south-east of the site, directly east of Ballycullen Road and *c.* 50m from site 3. A multitude of stories and traditions relating to St Columcille's well can be found in the Irish Folklore Commission's Schools' Manuscripts (vol. 795, 1937, 24) for the parish of Tallaght:

> 'St Columcille's well at Ballycullen is situated at the foot of the Dublin Hills in a clump of trees close to the entrance of Orlagh College. It is told that one very hot summer's day St Columcille was journeying from his school in Drumcondra to visit another of his schools in Wicklow. He took the shorter way across the Dublin Mountains. Being tired and thirsty, he stopped for a while to rest. Finding a well, he drank of the water and then, having washed and rested, went on his way, blessing the well before he departed. The imprint of the saint's knees are still shown on the rock at that well and numerous cures have been effected. During the Great War, a pilgrimage was organised to this well to beg the saint's intercession to avert "conscription" in Ireland.'

Another interesting feature from the area is a late Bronze Age gold dress-fastener, dating from around 800–700 BC (NMI reg. 1988:070), which was found in topsoil during groundworks for the adjacent Woodstown Village housing development. Although the site was subsequently investigated, no other artefacts were recovered (NMI topographical files, Ballycullen townland).

Other sites identified

The additional sites identified during the different phases of the monitoring programme deserve a mention in this context, in order to show the spectrum of archaeological activity in an area

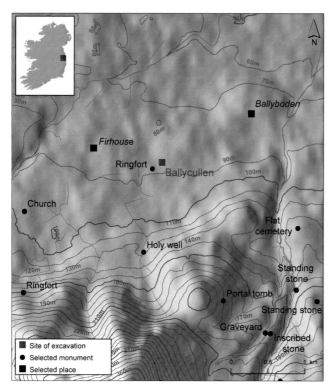

Fig. 10.1—Ballycullen: location map.

previously void of known prehistoric sites. The sites range from the early Bronze Age to the early medieval period and indicate intermittent settlement throughout this extended period.

Ballycullen site 1

Site 1 was preliminarily identified as a possible semicircular structure and was excavated in September 2002 under licence no. 02E1373. It was on the 100m OD contour in the lowest part of the development, on even, gently sloping ground, and extended over an area of 20m east–west by 11m. The most substantial element of the site consisted of a C-shaped feature, identified as a broken arc-shaped gully, which measured 10.2m east–west by 4.5m, with an average width of 0.5m and depth of 0.4m. The semicircular gully curved towards the south and had a gap in its centre, in which there was a large post-hole. There was no evidence for a continuation of the feature to the north, suggesting that the northern part of this potentially circular structure may have been built up with material rather than consisting of cut features. The gully was interpreted as a slot-trench for the support of posts or planks, and its fills contained charcoal and burnt and unburnt bone fragments. Seventeen post-holes were identified within the area enclosed by the gully, of which nine formed a regular pattern respecting the outline of the gully and may have held structural posts. Eight of the internal post-holes were associated with a possible hearth. To the east of the eastern terminal of the gully was a metalled surface with six associated post-holes and stake-holes, which has been interpreted as a possible entrance. Finds consisted of one lump of corroded iron recovered from a pit that truncated the eastern terminal of the gully, and flint débitage found mainly in association with the metalled surface. The site has been interpreted as a structure, possibly for habitation, and radiocarbon-dated to the late Iron Age, with a 2-sigma calibration date of AD 427–584 (cal. BP 1546±32, UB-7134). Although of Iron Age date and similar in shape, the structure differed from site 3 in terms of its low-lying location and size and is several centuries later.

Ballycullen site 2/2B

Site 2 was identified as a burnt spread, 20m in diameter, and was excavated in September 2002 (licence no. 02E1374). Excavation identified two phases of use, each associated with a trough, along with several associated post-holes, pits and areas of burning. The troughs were both wood-lined, although of different construction. The main spread was in a large natural depression, which resulted in an inverted mound with depths of up to 0.4m, and was partially capped by layers of natural silting, which separated the two phases. This deposit of heat-fractured sandstone and charcoal-rich soil was in the direct vicinity of a dried-up diverted stream bed/water channel; this appears to have been used for controlling the natural spring water source, which was still visible at the time of excavation and may explain the unusual elevated location of the site. The finds consisted mainly of undiagnostic flint flakes, although a date range of 2030–1870 BC (cal. 2-sigma, UB-7135 and UB-7136) has been confirmed from the two troughs.

Ballycullen site 4

Site 4, excavated in September 2003 (licence no. 03E1474; Larsson 2004), consisted of three areas of archaeological potential (areas K, L and P) containing negative features with evidence of *in situ* burning. Two of the features were confirmed as kilns of possibly early medieval date. One had a slight figure-of-eight shape, with a distinct bowl in its northern end, and its eight fills included various amounts of charcoal, burnt bone and lumps of scorched, oxidised soil. Area K consisted of a small pit and a possible post-hole; the pit contained frequent inclusions of charcoal, burnt bone fragments and sherds of undiagnostic prehistoric pottery, and was interpreted as the truncated base of a possible Bronze Age cremation pit.

Ballycullen site 5

Site 5 (area N) consisted of a solitary furnace pit excavated in September 2003 under licence no. 03E1475 (Larsson 2003d). The lack of associated features or datable material made further interpretation difficult, and this has been assigned a tentative prehistoric to early medieval date.

The early Iron Age habitation: site 3, area A

An early Iron Age habitation was identified in area A of site 3 and was excavated in late 2003 under licence no. 03E1473. The site comprised a large, circular gully enclosing a concentric circle of seventeen post-holes, several internal slot-trenches, a hearth and post-holes, stake-holes and pits (Fig. 10.2). The gully was not continuous, although nearly perfectly circular. A break towards the east-north-east may have been the entrance. The external features consisted of occasional pits and post-holes that appeared to respect the outline of the structure, as well as four kilns probably of a later date, two of which truncated features associated with the habitation phase. Two spreads were also identified within the area enclosed by the circular gully, although they cannot be confirmed as contemporary with the structure. Area A comprised 117 cut features, consisting of gullies, slot-trenches, post-holes, pits and stake-holes, with post-holes making up half of the total number of cuts. Evidence for stratification was identified in small numbers only.

Fig. 10.2—Ballycullen: the circular structure, looking south-east.

Geographical context

Site 3 was on the easternmost part of the crest of a prominent ridge that ran east–west and sloped down to the north, south and towards St Columcille's well (DU022-028) to the east. The flat surface of the crest was used for the circular structure (area A), which was situated approximately on the 120m OD contour. To the west of this were two groups of prehistoric features, including an area that contained a metalled surface and small cut features (area B) and a large pit with heat-fractured stones and associated small cuts (area E). Two solitary possible cremation pits (areas G and H) were located on the north-facing slope. Site 3 is the overall name of the above sites, although this essay deals only with area A, as this is a confirmed Iron Age settlement.

Circular gully/external wall-slot

The most substantial feature was a narrow, circular gully, which enclosed most of the features in this area. The discontinuous although perfectly circular gully had an external diameter of 15.2m (internal diameter 14.6m) and enclosed an area of

167.42m². It varied in depth and width, although only two post-holes and one stake-hole were identified in its southern part, associated with the terminals of segments of the gully. The northern half of the gully had more uniform, almost vertical sides and was also more substantial in width and depth than its southern counterpart; it consisted of one continuous arc, extending over 17.4m without interruption, with an average width of 0.3m and a maximum depth of 0.34m. In contrast, the southern part of the gully was subdivided into four segments and was more irregular in width and depth, and undercut sides were more prevalent. The southern half of the gully covered in total a distance of 18.8m and measured on average 0.22m in width and 0.18m in depth (max. depth 0.25m). It is possible that the segments were part of an originally continuous line and have been separated through later truncation, with only the deeper parts surviving. A smaller gap was also identified in the southern part of the gully, where a post-hole at the end of both the south-eastern and the south-western segments strongly suggested that this was an original feature. Two wider gaps in the gully were identified: to the west there was a gap of 7.6m between the southern and northern halves, while in the eastern side of the gully was a 3.4m-wide gap that has been identified as the entrance. The western gap may be the result of disturbance and there was no evidence for a cut. The eastern gap appeared more conclusive, with a terminal post-hole within the gully to the south of the gap. The northern part of the gap was obscured by the truncation of the gully by a kiln, and later features were located east of the entrance, making the interpretation of this area difficult. Several features appear to relate to a potential porch, including a short slot-trench aligned east–west, three post-holes and a shallow pit. The cut, both north and south, had steep sides with a U-shaped/flat base, although it had a blunted V-shape in places.

Four separate fills were identified in the northern half of the gully (C289, C290, C351 and C361). The primary fill (C361) was the most substantial and extended the full length of the cut. It yielded three iron fragments (03E1473:361:1–3). The fills all had a high sand/silt content, were similar to natural subsoil and were relatively sterile, with the exception of occasional charcoal flecks. They appear to be the result of silting. Fill C290, which lined the sides of the northern gully, has been interpreted as the *in situ* remains of the backfill supporting the structural elements of a wall of wooden logs, planks or wattle and daub. The southern half of gully C164 contained single fills in each of the four segments, consisting of silty clay with few inclusions of charcoal flecks, bone, unworked pieces of flint, quartz flakes and a possible bone point (03E1473:275:1). Very few stones were located in the gully, suggesting that stone packing was not used to support the wall materials. In all, very little domestic waste was identified in the gully, with only very occasional burnt bone fragments and one animal jawbone found.

Interpretation of the gully
The gully, originally believed to be a drip-gully, has been interpreted as a slot-trench for the external wall of the house, which may have consisted of vertical planks, slender posts or a wattle-and-daub screen, as in the case of several of the comparable excavated roundhouses from Britain. The small number of stones found in the fills did not give sufficient indication that posts had been used, as stone would almost certainly have been used as packing. The small amounts of burnt clay in the fills are not evidence enough to support the suggestion of wattle-and-daub construction. In addition, upstanding posts and stakes would most likely have left negative imprints at the base of the gully. This wall would have needed to be made of a material strong enough to hold the weight of the roof and yet thin enough to fit into the narrow

slot. The most likely explanation is that the gully was the footing for vertical planks, which may have been held in place with evenly spaced posts, stabilising each section, of which only two were detectable during excavation. The use of planks would explain the slender width and the flattish base of the gully. Given the very small amount of charcoal recovered, it is unlikely that the wall or any other structural feature of the house burnt down. Instead, the structural elements were probably removed or perhaps left to decay.

The roofing material was most likely straw/thatch, which necessitates an angle of pitch of 45° to ensure that rainwater does not leak through the roof.

Internal wall-slots
Two internal L-shaped slot-trenches (C164 and C167) were identified in the centre of the structure, mirroring one another and aligned with the east-facing entrance. The slots contained several post- and stake-holes set into their fills and have been interpreted as traces of dividers of the internal space, and perhaps also of roof supports in the eastern part of the structure. The features contained charcoal and both burnt and unburnt bone, including horse remains, interpreted as domestic debris.

Three smaller, linear cuts (C184, C223 and C270) were identified running at right angles from the gully in the eastern and southern parts of the structure. They were 1–1.75m long and 0.2–0.45m wide and appear to have been associated with the circular gully, not extending beyond this or the internal circle of post-holes. Their function is difficult to establish, although it is likely that they were also part of the additional support of this section of the structure, and perhaps dividers of the peripheral space within it. The central of the three linear cuts was located in the gap of the entrance, perpendicular to it and aligned with the southernmost internal slot-trench, suggesting that it was associated with the entrance and had a pivotal function.

Internal circle of post-holes
Seventeen post-holes were located internally and concentric with the circular gully, forming an almost perfect circle with a diameter of 10.2–10.44m (10.3m on average) and enclosing an internal area of 83.28m². The distance between the circle of internal post-holes and the inner edge of the gully ranged between 1.9m and 2.4m, averaging 2.07m. The area between the post-holes and the gully amounted to 84.14m². The largest gap between the post-holes (4.54m) was in the western part of the structure, where later disturbance may have obliterated additional post-holes. If this gap was factored out, the average distance between the post-holes would be 1.51m. The post-

holes were circular/oval (from 0.15m to 0.48m) in plan and 0.1–0.3m deep. The post-holes in the south-eastern quadrant were of slightly greater depth than average, and three of them also contained stone packing. The majority of the post-holes contained a single fill, although in several instances a lens of silt was detected lining the base. This has been interpreted as evidence for the silting up of the pre-dug post-holes prior to the insertion of the posts as part of the construction of the house. The fills consisted mainly of silty clay, while inclusions of burnt and unburnt bone fragments were identified in several of the post-holes. A varying quantity of charcoal inclusions was also identified, although in no instance was there evidence for a post having burnt *in situ*. The inclusions within the post-hole fills (76% of post-holes contained charcoal; 59% contained burnt bone) are indicative of domestic activity in the vicinity. Very few finds came from the post-holes, although a set of iron tweezers was found in one in the southern part of the structure, and three flint flakes were retrieved from another to the north-west. The concentric circle of posts is similar to those identified in other Iron Age houses. It was the spine of the construction, carrying most of the weight of the roof. The upper construction is not known, although it is likely to have had horizontal beams joining the posts and supporting the upper part of the roof. The two additional posts in direct proximity to those of the circle are likely to be secondary roof-support posts, inserted to increase stability and support after the original posts and the roof had been erected.

Internal features: secondary structural elements

A number of cuts were identified within the area enclosed by the circular gully, and respecting the outline of this and other structural features. These are most likely associated with the habitation. Several have been interpreted as secondary structural elements associated with the division of the internal space of the structure, or as additional support for the roof. The majority of these features were within the circle of post-holes associated with roof support, suggesting that the area between this and the gully was the secondary living space, as the angle of the roof would have made the height in this area too low for people to stand upright. This peripheral area, however, contained a small number of pits, mainly in the southern half of the structure, suggesting that it was used for storage.

Fourteen post-holes were identified within the circle of post-holes, which, together with a number of stake-holes, are likely to represent internal division of the space and/or superstructures associated with the habitation, such as benches or berths. Three post-holes were aligned east–west and in line with pit C231 and internal slot C167, suggesting that these were part of the division of the internal space of the structure. Similarly, a line of six stake-holes north of pit C140 may have been part of a flimsier internal superstructure, such as a bench, loom or screen. Two of the stake-holes were identified below one of the two internal spreads, suggesting that they were part of an earlier phase of the habitation. These post-holes were circular/oval in plan, 0.1–0.47m in diameter and 0.15–0.3m deep, and had a more V-shaped profile than the post-holes associated with the roof support. The vast majority of the post-holes within the circle had a single fill of generally silty clay or sandy silt with occasional inclusions of charcoal flecks and burnt and unburnt bone fragments. Two of the post-holes had packing stones and one post-hole, close to the hearth, was intentionally backfilled with a large stone. One of the smaller post-holes in the western part of the structure, in the vicinity of one of the hearths, was filled with heat-fractured stones and had inclusions of charcoal and burnt bone, suggesting that it was filled with habitation/occupation debris.

Three large post-holes (C98, C117 and C129) were located west of and in line with the southern internal slot-trench (C167). It is suggested that these post-holes were part of the main internal east–west division leading from the entrance. A smaller post-hole (C335) was also along this alignment but it is unclear whether it is part of this division or is associated with a group of stake-holes and small post-holes to the east of C167, which do not form any distinguishable pattern. Another large post-hole (C113) appeared to be in line with the opposing northern slot-trench (C194) and post-hole (C365). Some of the other post-holes appeared to be associated with internal pits and groups of stake-holes.

Five post-holes and one stake-hole were located between the concentric circle of roof-support posts and the circular gully, although not forming any discernible pattern and scattered across the space enclosed by the circular gully. Two of the post-holes were in close proximity to the roof-support posts and may have been secondary posts in this circle, possibly used for additional support and not part of the original design. These post-holes were circular/oval in plan and the majority had a V-shaped profile, unlike those of the roof-support posts, and they measured on average 0.23m in diameter and 0.23m in depth. None contained any packing stones and each contained a single fill with a high sand content (also contrasting with the silty clay of the post-holes directly associated with roof support), and only occasionally contained charcoal and burnt bone fragments. These were not as well dug as those of the circle of posts, which may indicate that they were secondary posts incorporated after the structure was already in place, possibly to house additional support posts.

Internal features associated with the habitation

A number of pits were identified within the area enclosed by the circular gully and were most likely related to the daily activities associated with the habitation. Of the seventeen pits found in area A, ten were within the area enclosed by the circular gully. The distribution of pits within the structure was relatively uneven. The south-western quadrant had the highest density, while the other quadrants had very few. The western part of the internal area also contained two spreads, which appear to respect the outline of the circular house and may be associated with it.

Of the ten internal pits identified, six were enclosed by the circle of post-holes associated with roof-support posts (C140, C144, C145, C160, C165 and C231), and four were in the area between this and the circular gully (C132, C197, C222 and C243). All but one of these were located in the southern part of the structure.

Pits within the circle of post-holes

The two largest pits (C231 and C140) were in the central part of the circular structure, directly north and south of the central passage and aligned respectively with the internal L-shaped slot-trenches C167 and C197, which may have been associated with the division of the internal space. The oval pits were 1.4m apart and between 0.65m and 1.7m west of the internal slot-trench; their size and morphology appear to mirror each other, and they seem to respect the central division of the internal space. The fills of the pits were, however, very different, suggesting that they may have had different functions. Pit C140 contained a single, relatively sterile, fill of brown sandy silt with rare inclusions of charcoal flecks, while pit C231 contained four separate fills, one of which contained frequent charcoal inclusions and lumps of burnt clay, and a small amount of burnt bone. The latter may possibly have been a hearth/fire-pit, based on its location in the centre of the circular structure and the abundance of charcoal and evidence of scorching, while C140 showed no signs of burning and may have been used for storage. Smaller cut features, such as post- and stake-holes, were identified in close proximity to these pits, in particular pit C140, which was situated east of an arc of stake-holes.

A small, shallow pit (C165) was identified in the very centre of the circular structure, where the only other feature was a stake-hole. The cut measured 0.49m in diameter and 0.14m in depth. It is likely that this feature played a part in the initial layout of the circular structure, as it is situated in the exact centre and crossing point of the paired post-holes of the inner circle of posts. The silty clay fill contained frequent charcoal inclusions and occasional burnt and unburnt bone

fragments, suggesting association with the habitation phase.

Three pits were located in the southern half of the area enclosed by the circle of post-holes. Two oval pits (C144 and C145), *c.* 0.25m apart, measured 0.65m by 0.6m and 0.13–0.25m in depth. Both contained two fills: the primary fills were redeposited natural and the secondary fills were of black silty clay with frequent charcoal inclusions and occasional inclusions of burnt bone and quartz. All the fills contained undiagnostic sherds of prehistoric pottery, comparable to that of the similarly twinned pits C222 and C197 some 3m to the east. Nine quartz flakes were also retrieved from pit C145. The association between the pits and the structure cannot be fully determined owing to a lack of stratigraphic relationships. A radiocarbon date of 3900–3600 BC was determined from the secondary fill of pit C145. The locations of the pits within, however, appear to respect the features associated with the structure, which may suggest contemporaneity. The similarity in size and content suggests that these may be of the same date and function, possibly associated with storage, refuse disposal or production. They also have similarities with the twin pits C222 and C197, suggesting that the southern half of the structure may have been used for a different purpose than the northern part.

A smaller pit (C160), which was circular in plan, 0.45m in diameter and 0.25m deep, was located 0.6m north-north-west of pit C144. The cut showed evidence of burning or deposition of a very hot fill, as scorching was evident along the edges and it contained three fills with frequent charcoal inclusions. The primary and tertiary fills contained very frequent inclusions of glass waste, making up *c.* 70% of the volume of the pit; they were separated by a dense charcoal layer with no glass waste. The slag-like glass waste from the primary fill differed from the larger, beige/light grey, irregular and porous lumps and droplets found in the tertiary fill, and consisted of smaller droplets of denser material. The pit may have been associated with glass production.

Pits located between the gully and the circle of post-holes

The four pits in the area outside the circle of roof-support posts were circular/oval in plan, 0.5–1.1m in diameter and 0.09–0.26m deep. Pit C243 was in the centre of the entrance and was cut by an internal slot-trench (C270) associated with the entrance, suggesting that it may be associated with, or even pre-date, the construction phase of the house. The remaining three pits in this zone showed no stratification confirming their association with the structure, although they appear to respect the internal features. All of the pits contained silty fills with various amounts of charcoal; pit C243 also contained occasional burnt bone fragments, and flint flakes were identified in the secondary fill of pit C197. The twin pits C197 and C222 were located only 0.06m apart in the southern part of the structure; they contained two and three fills of silty/sandy clay respectively, which all contained sherds of prehistoric pottery of two types (fine and coarse), although undiagnostic in nature. The similarity in fills and content between these pits suggests that they had the same function and were broadly contemporary; as pit C222 truncated the internal slot-trench C223, it is likely that these features post-dated the initial construction phase.

The function of these pits may be explained by their content as depositories utilised by the occupants of the structure, possibly for the storage of food or valuable articles, or as suggested by the finds, such as pottery sherds, flint and quartz flakes, burnt bone and charcoal. Therefore they may have functioned as depositories for refuse in the part of the house less favoured for daily activities, where the roof would have been low. It is worth noting that pottery was abundant in these features but less frequent in other pits in the area and not present at all in the remaining features of the site. The location of the pits mainly in the southern part of the structure may suggest that this half of the building functioned as an area of deposition/storage, or even industrial activity, while the northern half may have been used for habitation. It is, of course, possible that these pits pre-date the structure, although the density of features within the circular structure in comparison to the limited number of external features suggests that they had some association with the structure rather than being unassociated and coincidental.

Deposits
Only two spreads were identified within area A, both within the western half of the area enclosed by the circular gully. It is possible that these irregular shallow spreads were the remnants of accumulation layers associated with the habitation of the structure, although no finds or materials were detected to confirm this. It appeared that the larger of the two spreads respected the outline of the circular gully, which suggests that they may be contemporary. The larger deposit (C146) measured 5.5m by 4.4m and 0.17m in maximum depth and consisted of silty clay with occasional inclusions of charcoal and unburnt bone. The deposit was difficult to distinguish from natural, suggesting that it represents a deliberate deposition to make the ground surface even as part of the construction of the circular structure. A smaller irregular spread (C122), 0.96m by 0.82m, was identified in the north-western quadrant of the circular structure and consisted of brown/black silty clay with occasional charcoal flecks and fragments of bone. Evidence for stratification was identified as

this overlay two stake-holes (C118 and C120), and its location directly west of one of the two large central pits (C140) suggests that it may have been associated with this group of features.

External features
It is likely that several of these are contemporary and directly related to the activities associated with the Iron Age habitation phase.

External pits
A total of seven pits were identified in the area surrounding the circular structure. Their relationships with the structure remain uncertain and they were generally identified as solitary features, circular/irregular in plan with one to three fills. They range in size from 0.4m to 2.6m and in depth from 0.15m to 0.7m. The lack of finds and conclusive inclusions has made any attempts to explain their presence difficult. The largest of the cuts consisted of an irregular, slightly curvilinear pit (C201) with three fills, four post-holes and two stake-holes, located 15m to the south of the structure. The primary and tertiary fills, separated by a layer of redeposited natural, contained frequent charcoal inclusions and moderate inclusions of burnt and unburnt bone fragments. The post-holes and stake-holes were cut into the separate fills at different levels, confirming that this feature was reused several times, although its purpose is not clear.

Two pits were identified directly east of the east-facing entrance of the house. Pit C317 consisted of a wide but shallow cut in the centre of the gap for the entrance between the terminals of the circular gully and was truncated by kiln C258. This pit may be associated with a porch-like construction, as it appears to respect the features relating to the entrance of the house. It may also post-date the structure and be associated with later disturbance in this area. The smaller pit (C228) was located south of the entrance area; it contained fills with frequent inclusions of heat-fractured stones and charcoal and had an associated stake-hole cut into its base. This pit may constitute a roasting/burning pit or a dump for fire-affected material and may be contemporary with the activities associated with the habitation phase.

Kilns
Four kilns were found in area A. One was keyhole-shaped (C278) and three were figure-of-eight-shaped (C84, C258 and C76). They measured 1.57–2.55m by 0.66–1.4m and 0.25–0.67m in depth. The fills of the four kilns contained heat-fractured stones, charcoal and oxidised clay. Burnt and unburnt bone fragments were found in C76 and C258, and a

flint flake was retrieved from kiln C84. All four kilns displayed evidence for *in situ* burning in the deeper part of the cut. The morphology of the kilns suggests that they were used for corn-drying. Kilns C278 and C258 cut (and thus post-date) the gully of the Iron Age roundhouse and features associated with the entrance of the structure. The other two kilns were situated directly outside the circular gully that constitutes the outer limits of the circular structure, but the lack of stratigraphic relationship makes it difficult to confirm whether they were contemporary with this. Their proximity to the structure may, however, suggest that they were related to the habitation phase, although further analysis will be necessary to confirm their date.

Finds

A total of 68 finds were retrieved from a variety of features in area A. These consisted of sherds of prehistoric coarse undecorated pottery, a small assemblage of flint and quartz flakes, one object and three fragments of corroded ferrous metal and one elongated cylindrical blue glass bead. The finds were treated and conserved by conservator Aldara Rico-Rey and subsequently analysed by specialists.

Stone

The lithics, which consisted of a total of 55 items, were analysed by Claire Anderson. The majority of the worked lithics consisted of flint, although with a notable presence of quartz, and comprised mainly flakes and occasional chunks, suggesting that some manufacturing of tools had taken place in this location. Primary technology dominated the assemblage, although there were no cores or blades and débitage was scarce. The majority of the pieces displayed a medium to heavy patination and five were burnt, of which three were heavily burnt primary flakes from post-hole C92. In addition, an unstratified arrowhead was retrieved from this area during topsoil-stripping.

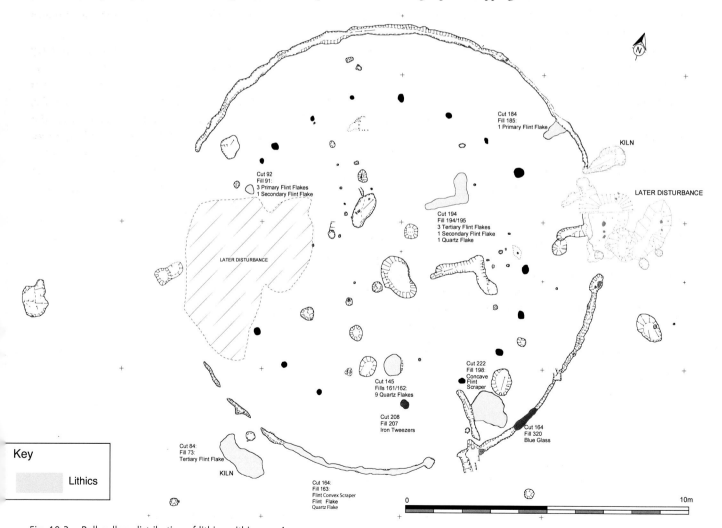

Fig. 10.3—Ballycullen: distribution of lithics within area A.

148

The lithic material was evenly divided between flint and quartz. A total of 28 flint finds were recovered from area A, including three scrapers, sixteen flakes, three pieces of débitage and six chunks. A total of ten flint finds came from unstratified contexts, including a concave flake scraper. Fifteen worked stratified flint finds were retrieved from a variety of features (Fig. 10.3). Two scrapers with abrupt retouch were identified in stratified contexts from the circular gully C164 and pit C222. Primary, secondary and tertiary flakes were identified from the circular gully C164, the internal slot-trench C194, post-holes C92 and C230, linear feature C184 and medieval kiln C84.

A total of 27 quartz finds were retrieved, consisting of sixteen flakes and eleven chunks, of which the latter category appeared mainly to be natural. The stratified quartz flakes were identified in four separate features: pit C145 contained eight flakes, gully C164 three flakes, and internal slot-trench C194 and post-hole C335 one each. Only two flakes of quartz showed evidence of working, one with a clear bulb of percussion and another with edge retouch on one side.

Anderson (2008) considers the lithics assemblage to be more characteristic of the late Neolithic/early Bronze Age than of the early Iron Age. It is possible that the lithics finds are residual pieces from an earlier phase of activity, although the concentrations in features associated with the structure suggest that these are likely to be contemporary with the habitation phase, and the lack of any distinguishable typological traits suggests that the technology may well have survived until this period and beyond.

Metal

Five finds of iron were retrieved from area A: four were from secure stratigraphic contexts (Fig. 10.6) and one L-shaped object was from topsoil and was modern. Three small unidentified fragments were retrieved from the primary fill of gully C164 (03E1473:361:1–3). A heavily corroded lump of iron, identified in conservation as a set of iron tweezers, was retrieved from the single fill of post-hole C208 (03E1473:207:64; Fig. 10.4). The tweezers measured 60mm in length and 8mm in width and were made from one plate of iron. They have a circular head and a diagonal line at the end. Analysis revealed that organic material was mineralised over the surface of the object, concentrated on the head and along the internal surfaces. This deposit was caused by exposure during the alteration process of the metal or as a result of being in contact with wood during storage/use (Rico-Rey 2008). The analysis suggests that the latter theory is the most probable and that this set was lost while in a wooden case, which later decayed and caused the organic deposit.

Ceramic

Ceramic finds from area A consisted mainly of pottery sherds, of which 27 were from secure archaeological contexts (Fig. 10.6). Six unstratified sherds were also retrieved, dating from the medieval to the modern period and consisting of Dublin Coarseware, Leinster Cooking Ware, earthenware and modern glazed crockery.

The remaining 21 sherds consisted of prehistoric pottery of two different types. The coarser pottery was originally believed to be Bronze Age but its date has not been established. The sherds were retrieved from four separate pits, C144, C145, C197 and C222 (Fig. 10.5), all located within the circular structure. Pits C144 and C145 were within the area enclosed by the circle of roof-support posts and only 0.26m apart, while pits C197 and C222 were in the area between the gully and the circle of posts, only 0.06m apart. No analysis of

Fig. 10.5—Ballycullen: pottery sherds from pit C222 (03E1573:220:3–8).

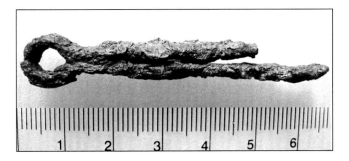

Fig. 10.4—Ballycullen: the set of tweezers (03E1473:207:64) found in post-hole C208, after conservation.

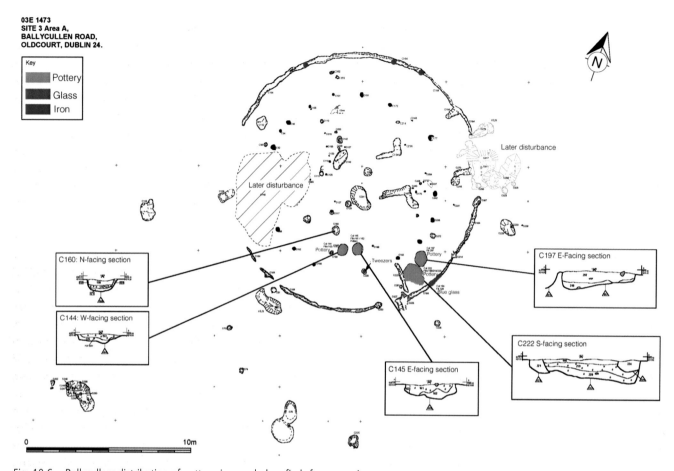

Fig. 10.6—Ballycullen: distribution of pottery, iron and glass finds from area A.

Fig. 10.7—Ballycullen: the cylindrical glass bead (03E1473:320:1) found in gully C164.

the pottery has yet been carried out to verify a date range contemporary with the habitation.

Glass

Two finds of glass were retrieved from the excavation of area A. One unstratified small glass flake (03E1473:1:1), which appeared to have been worked, was found during clearing, and one small glass bead was retrieved from fill C320 of gully C164 (Fig. 10.6). The glass bead was blue and had an elongated cylindrical shape with a rounded point; it was 29mm long, 7mm in diameter and weighed 2g (03E1473:320:91; Fig. 10.7). Analysis of the glass by conservator Aldara Rico-Rey showed this to be of poor manufacture from a rough manufacturing process, with slag and inclusions mixed in with the glass and with large bubbles visible on the surface and the interior.

Interpretation of the finds

The presence of ceramic material at an Iron Age site is significant. The distribution of the sherds within the structure suggests that they are related to this rather than to another phase of occupation. The lack of comparable ceramic material from this date makes the identification of the material difficult. The fabric is similar to that of the late Bronze Age vessels, and the sherds have no additional morphology or decoration that might suggest a specific or even general date range. It is likely, however, given the location of the features, that the pottery relates to the habitation phase of the structure. Until further analysis takes place, the date of the ceramic material cannot be confirmed. It is the belief of the present writer, however, that the pottery is contemporary with the structural evidence and the habitation phase of the site and is therefore of early Iron Age date.

Samples

A total of 134 samples of soil, bone, slag and charcoal were taken to optimise our understanding of the site through environmental analysis and for dating purposes. They have been used to retrieve further information on the nature, date and economy of the site. All of the soils from the negative features were sieved on site unless sampled, in which case they were later wet-sieved. After processing and selection, the samples were submitted to the respective specialists for analysis.

Soil

Soil samples taken during the excavation were analysed by Susan Lyons (Lyons 2009). The analysis showed low to high concentrations of charcoal from all features from area A, most likely representing the firing debris associated with the Iron Age habitation phase, from the fuel burnt within pits C144, C145, C222, C231 and C235, but also from the firing process associated with the possible early medieval kiln C84. Charcoal of oak was predominantly recorded from pits C160, C235 and C231 (Lyons 2009). Lyons suggests that the relatively high representation of charcoal from post-holes C92, C172 and C205 is indicative of a burnt structure, although it may also be the result of tree-felling or construction methods, such as felling by fire and charring of post bases. As very few features contained the amount of charcoal associated with fire, the

latter suggestion is the most likely.

Carbonised cereal remains were recorded from *c.* 50% of the samples, with the cereal representation from area A consisting of 73% barley (*Hordeum* sp.), 21% wheat (*Triticum* sp.), 5% oat (*Avena* sp.), 1% wild taxa and <1% emmer wheat (*Triticum diococcum*) (Fig. 10.8). The main type of wheat was bread/club wheat (*Triticum aestivum/compactum*), with emmer wheat being identified in a single feature in area A (pit C222). The presence of emmer wheat, generally recorded from the Neolithic and Bronze Age in Ireland, suggests that prehistoric arable agriculture was carried out at the site prior to the establishment of the Iron Age settlement.

Plant macrofossil remains were primarily recorded from kiln C84, post-hole C92 and pit C222, with a mix of prehistoric cereal grains (emmer wheat, wheat and barley) from pit C222 and a medieval crop assemblage from kiln C84 and post-hole C92, which contained the largest concentrations of cereal remains, including barley, wheat and oats. The high volume of carbonised cereal grain from C84 and C92 is indicative of medieval cereal-drying events. The volume of grain from C84 also indicates that the kiln was not properly cleaned out, suggesting that the kiln may have burnt down and been abandoned, or the accumulated material may have been left in the bowl for several uses of the kiln. Post-hole C92 had a similar composition of cereal grains and may have been utilised for disposing of residual charred debris from such drying events. This feature also contained the only evidence of cereal chaff from the site, identified as fragmented awns of possibly oat. Wild taxa were represented by 1% of the macrofossils retrieved from the samples and were found in very low concentrations in post-holes C92, C118 and C208. The plant assemblage contained species from arable fields and disturbed places, including knotgrass (*Polygonum* sp.), black bindweed (*Polygonum convolvulus*), dock (*Rumex* sp.) and goosefoot (*Chenopodium* sp.). The general absence of wild taxa and cereal chaff indicates that the material dried in the kilns at the site was essentially a clean or well-processed crop, with threshing having been carried out elsewhere. Carbonised hazelnut shells (*Corylus avellana*) were recorded from post-holes C92 and C110 and pits C144, C145, C243, C231 and C222.

Charcoal

Ten charcoal samples were taken from a selection of features in order to ascertain a date for the structure and to discern any potential phasing. Three samples were chosen for initial dating from three separate contexts: the primary fill of gully C164 (fill C320), and fills of pits C160 and C145, both located within the area encircled by the roof-support post-holes (Fig. 10.9). The analysis gave two separate date ranges, two from the early Iron

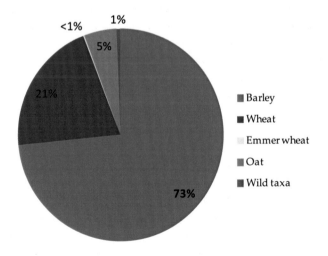

Fig. 10.8—Ballycullen: diagram showing percentage of plant remains from area A (based on information from Lyons 2009).

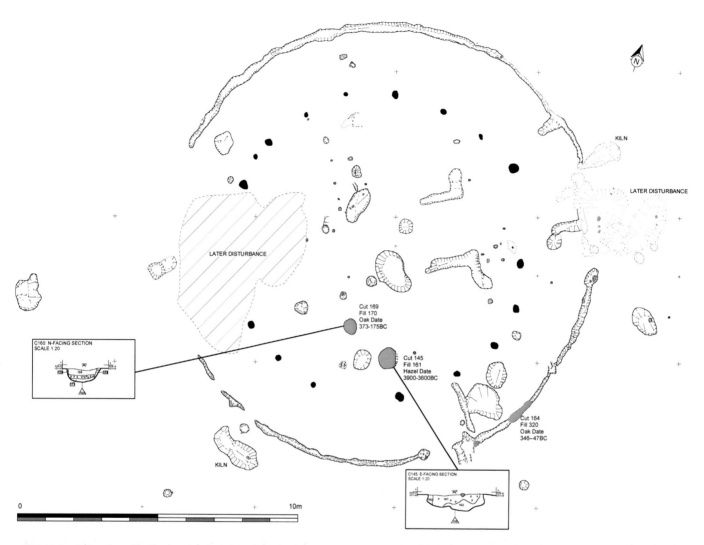

Fig. 10.9—Ballycullen: distribution of radiocarbon dates from area A.

Age and a third from the Neolithic. The samples from pit C160 and gully C164 were determined to be of oak and yielded dates of 375–175 BC (UB-7138) and 345–47 BC (UB-7139) respectively. The sample from pit C145, which also contained sherds of prehistoric pottery, was identified as hazel and returned a date of 3900–3600 BC (UB-7137). It is possible that the earlier date can be explained as a result of contamination from nearby prehistoric activity, such as area E, although it is also possible that activity took place in this location in prehistory. Further analysis will be required to confirm the date of the pottery, although the Iron Age dates concur with the limited yet distinct assemblage of iron and glass.

Bone

The bone material from the site was sampled in its entirety, resulting in a total of 63 bone samples from a variety of features within area A. These were analysed by osteologist Patricia Lynch and further examined by Siobhan Duffy. The material consisted of burnt and unburnt bone and teeth, all of animal origin. The preservation of the bone was poor and much of it was calcinated or singed. As a result, only 30% was identifiable.

The animals represented in the material from area A were horse, cattle, pig, sheep/goat and dog. Cattle had the highest representation, being found in ten samples from eight separate contexts, including the circular gully C164, one of the internal slot-trenches (C194) and post-holes C98, C180 and C293 (Fig. 10.10). Cattle bone, mainly from the extremities and the skull, was also identified in samples from pits C258 and C201, both outside the circular structure and possibly unrelated, and from kiln C76, which may be medieval. Sheep/goat bone was identified in samples from seven

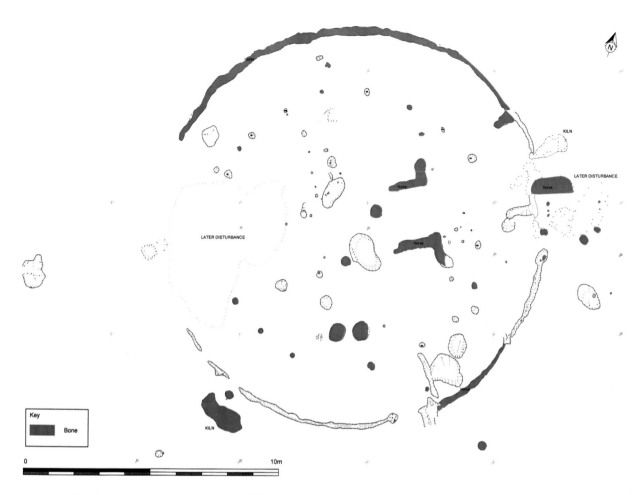

Fig. 10.10—Ballycullen: distribution of animal bone within area A.

contexts: the internal slot-trenches (C194), post-holes C98 and C293, pit C145 and kilns C258, C76 and C84. Only one of the bone fragments showed evidence for post-mortem trauma, in the form of twelve parallel cut-marks on a rib shaft, suggesting that the animal was butchered. Five samples contained horse bone and teeth; these were retrieved from the circular gully (C164), both of the internal slot-trenches (C194 and C167) and an internal pit (C317). The post-mortem trauma on a radius from gully C164 consisted of seven parallel cut-marks on its surface, indicative of skinning/butchering. Pig bones were found in four separate contexts: internal slot-trench C194, post-hole C208 and kilns C258 and C76. Of these only the post-hole and slot-trench are directly related to the structure. The samples derived from adult individuals and none of the fragments showed any sign of post-mortem trauma. Bone/teeth from dog were identified in three samples, of which two were from contexts associated with the structure. Upper leg fragments were found in the fills of roof-support post-hole C180 and circular gully C164.

Post-mortem trauma to the bone, consisting of parallel cut-marks, was identified in three samples from two animal groups (sheep/goat and horse). The cut-marks on the horse bones suggest that the horse was skinned, and possibly also

Fig. 10.11—Ballycullen: piece of glass slag from pit C160.

Fig. 10.12—Ballycullen: reconstruction of the structure of Ballycullen 3, by Michael Duffy.

consumed. Horseflesh was eaten in the Iron Age and later but became taboo with the introduction of Christianity.

Slag
Two samples of slag were taken from the fills of pit C161 within the circular structure. The pit contained a large amount of slag within a soil and charcoal matrix. One of the samples was taken to the National Museum of Ireland's in-house facilities and was confirmed to be glass slag (Fig. 10.11).

Conclusion
The excavations at Oldcourt have revealed a previously unknown prehistoric landscape, including evidence for Neolithic activity, a *fulacht fiadh* dating from the Bronze Age, evidence for habitation from both the early and the late Iron Age, and crop-processing from the medieval period. The well-drained and fertile land has been used for millennia, and the natural resources were used to create a suitable area for settlement.

The circular structure in area A bears resemblance to Iron Age structures in southern Britain and only a few examples from Ireland (Fig. 10.12). The size suggests that the construction required a substantial number of man-hours and material gathered from a wide area. Internal features suggest that there was a division within the structure, and clusters of small stake-holes indicate the presence of flimsier superstructures such as benches and beds. Internal storage pits would have been useful in protecting foodstuffs from scavenging animals and as temporary depositories. The hearth appears to have been placed in the centre of the circular structure, where the conical roof would have been at its highest and the risk of accidental fire the smallest. The east-facing entrance follows the pattern of previous periods, probably to maximise daylight. Although disturbed by later activity, it appears that the entrance consisted of a porch-like opening, as suggested by a number of post-holes and linear features.

The very limited finds assemblage from area A includes

lithics and iron as well as glass and pottery, and samples show that glass production is likely to have taken place in association with this habitation. The use of crops resembles that of earlier periods and the animal husbandry was varied, with the possibility that horseflesh was consumed. The evidence from the excavation indicates that this was a farmstead where animal husbandry and crop management were key to a healthy economy and where the inhabitants were used to a varied diet. The size of the house and the type of finds associated with this habitation suggest a certain control over the immediate area, as well as influences and contacts with areas beyond the region, and possibly the country.

Acknowledgements

Many thanks to the team of archaeologists who worked on site and in post-excavation, to Michael Duffy for the reconstruction drawing and to Stephen Johnston and Siobhan Duffy for the distribution maps.

Bibliography

Anderson, C. 2008 Lithics report: Ballycullen 3 (03E1473). Unpublished report for Ellier Developments Ltd.

Dehaene, G. 2002a Archaeological assessment report. Proposed Oldcourt Road/Ballycullen Road/Stocking Lane link road, Co. Dublin. Unpublished report prepared for Arch-Tech Ltd.

Dehaene, G. 2002b Report on archaeological monitoring of engineering test-pits at Ballycullen Road, Dublin 24. Unpublished report for Ellier Developments Ltd.

Keeley, V.J. 1985 The excavation of a ringfort in Scholarstown townland, Co. Dublin. Unpublished report prepared for V.J. Keeley Ltd.

Larsson, E. 2002a Report on Phases 2 and 3 of archaeological monitoring at Ballycullen Road, Dublin 24 (02E0190 Ext., Phases 2 and 3). Unpublished report for Ellier Developments Ltd.

Larsson, E. 2002b Report on Phase 4 of archaeological monitoring at Ballycullen Road, Dublin 24 (02E0190 Ext., Phase 4). Unpublished report for Ellier Developments Ltd.

Larsson, E. 2003a Report on Phase 5 of archaeological monitoring at Ballycullen Road, Dublin 24 (02E0190 Ext., Phase 5). Unpublished report for Ellier Developments Ltd.

Larsson, E. 2003b Report on Phase 6 of archaeological monitoring at Ballycullen Road, Dublin 24 (02E0190 Ext., Phase 6). Unpublished report for Ellier Developments Ltd.

Larsson, E. 2003c Report on Phase 7 of archaeological monitoring at Ballycullen Road, Dublin 24 (02E0190 Ext., Phase 7). Unpublished report for Ellier Developments Ltd.

Larsson, E. 2003d Report on archaeological excavation of Site 5 identified during Phase 7 of archaeological monitoring at Ballycullen Road, Dublin 24 (03E1475). Unpublished report for Ellier Developments Ltd.

Larsson, E. 2004 Report on archaeological excavation of Site 4 identified during Phase 7 of archaeological monitoring at Ballycullen Road, Dublin 24 (03E1474). Unpublished report for Ellier Developments Ltd.

Larsson, E. 2006 Preliminary report on archaeological excavation of Site 1 identified during Phase 3 of archaeological monitoring at Ballycullen Road, Dublin 24 (03E1373). Unpublished report for Ellier Developments Ltd.

Larsson, E. 2008 Report on archaeological excavation of Site 2 identified during Phase 3 of archaeological monitoring at Ballycullen Road, Dublin 24 (03E1374). Unpublished report for Ellier Developments Ltd.

Lynch, P. 2005 Animal osteological report for Ballycullen, Areas A, B, E and G–H, 03E1473. Unpublished report for Ellier Developments Ltd.

Lyons, S. 2009 Analysis of the plant macrofossil remains from Ballycullen 3, Co. Dublin, 03E1473. Unpublished report for Ellier Developments Ltd.

O'Curry, E. 1837 Ordnance Survey letters for Dublin. Unpublished typescript, Royal Irish Academy, MS 14 C. 23.

O'Kelly, M.J. 1993 *Early Ireland: an introduction to Irish prehistory*. Cambridge.

Raftery, B. 1994 *Pagan Celtic Ireland: the enigma of the Irish Iron Age*. London.

Rico-Rey, A. 2008 Conservation report on glass and metal finds from Ballycullen 2 (03E1473). Unpublished report for Ellier Developments Ltd.

Simington, R.C. 1945 *The Civil Survey, AD 1654–1656, 7: County of Dublin*. Dublin.

Note

1. The monitoring was carried out in advance of the Hunterstown residential development, on behalf of Ellier Developments Ltd, in seven separate phases in conjunction with the development and under an extension to excavation licence 02E0190 by the author. The initial phase comprised the monitoring of engineering test-pits by Goorik Dehaene (02E0190; Dehaene 2002a; 2002b).

11. An Iron Age ring-ditch at Ballynakelly, Co. Dublin

Ciara McCarthy

Introduction

An Iron Age ring-ditch was excavated during archaeological works (licence no. 07E0245) at the site of the proposed Lamberton Hotel in Ballynakelly, Newcastle, Co. Dublin, in 2007. The excavation was funded by Lamberton Properties Ltd. The ring-ditch comprised a circular ditch enclosing a single possible token cremation pit. It was on the edge of an earlier prehistoric flat cemetery on the plateau of a north-east/south-west-running ridge that also forms the boundary between Ballynakelly and Rathcreedon townlands (Figs 11.1 and 11.2). A significant prehistoric monument, a hilltop enclosure (RMP DU20–005), is located on Athgoe Hill to the north-east and is clearly visible from the cemetery. From the plateau there were also panoramic views to the north across the plain of the River Liffey and to the east to the Dublin Mountains (from Three Rock Mountain to Windmillhill). The extensive views from the cemetery to surrounding prehistoric monuments (such as on Athgoe Hill and the summits of the Dublin Mountains) were probably an important factor in the

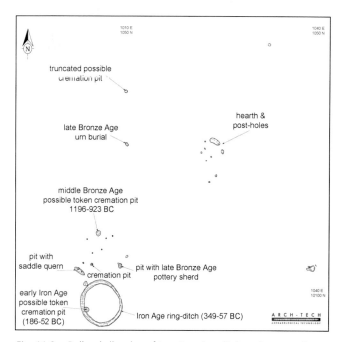

Fig. 11.2—Ballynakelly: plan of Iron Age ring-ditch and surrounding Bronze Age flat cemetery.

siting of this ring-ditch.

Unfortunately, the plateau had suffered severe truncation from long-term agricultural activity and, despite being positioned on a slight rise in what seemed to be the highest point on the plateau within the excavated area, the ring-ditch was so shallow in places as to be almost imperceptible. Evidence suggested that *c.* 0.4m of stratigraphy had been lost as a result of truncation.

The ring-ditch

The ditch

With an inner diameter of 5.46–5.74m and an outer diameter of 6.32–6.95m, the dimensions of the ditch are comparable with those of previously excavated examples (Fig. 11.3). Nothing remained of a bank either inside or outside the ditch, or of a central mound, and it is impossible to know whether one or other of these was constructed with the ditch. Charcoal from the main fill of the ditch was radiocarbon-dated to 349–57 BC (at two standard deviations), with an 84% probability of its dating from 208–89 BC (at two standard deviations), placing the infilling of the ditch in the Iron Age.

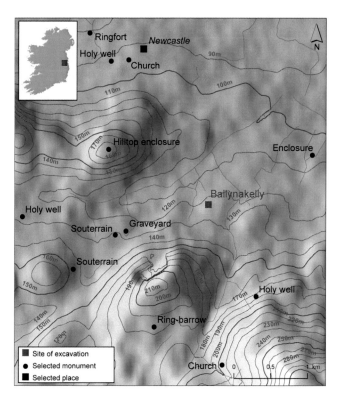

Fig. 11.1—Ballynakelly: site location.

Fig. 11.3—Ballynakelly: the ring-ditch after excavation, looking south-east. Possible token cremation pit visible on interior edge of ditch.

No burials were identified within the ditch but very occasional flecks of burnt bone were noted in its fill. These were too small to be effectively sampled. It is likely that the flecks of burnt bone were displaced from the cremation pit and entered the ring-ditch via local watercourses and rainwater over time. There was also evidence of the intentional deposition of additional material into the ditch. A piece of iron slag or corroded scrap iron and a fragment of burnt clay identifiable only as clay agglomerate were recovered from the fill of the ditch. This waste may have been deposited deliberately as a grave-offering. No other features or material relating to iron production during the Iron Age were recovered. Charcoal analysis identified a mixed wood assemblage, dominated by birch, blackthorn, fruit trees and ash. It was not clear whether the charcoal assemblage represented the remains of a single burning episode or several burning episodes; in either case, there did not appear to be a preference for a specific wood species to burn.

There was some evidence for burial in the area enclosed by the ditch; a broadly contemporary possible token cremation pit was identified immediately inside the inner south-eastern edge.

Token cremation pit
The token cremation pit was circular and notably deep (at 0.55m) in comparison with the ditch. The pit was almost funnel-shaped in section, loosely reflective of the shape of a

nearby upturned late Bronze Age urn, discovered as part of the adjacent flat cemetery. A very small quantity of burnt bone (2.9g) was recovered from the charcoal-rich basal fill. All of the bone fragments were small (measuring less than 10mm in length) and it was impossible to tell whether they were human or animal. Despite this, the presence of a small quantity of burnt bone and the nature and location of the pit suggest that it functioned as a token cremation pit, in which only a fraction of the cremated remains were buried. Charcoal from the pit was radiocarbon-dated to 186–52 BC (at two standard deviations), indicating that it was broadly contemporary with the surrounding ditch. A single-sided flint scraper was also recovered from the pit. Analysis of charcoal from the fills of this feature identified a mixed wood assemblage with a predominance of willow, fruit tree, cherry and birch. Again, there was no clear preference for a specific tree species and wood collection appears to have been indiscriminate.

The practice of token or partial deposition of cremated remains emerged in the middle Bronze Age and continued until the end of the Iron Age. It is not known why only partial remains of an individual were buried, although it has been suggested that the additional remains might have been kept for use in secondary funerary rites, for which no archaeological evidence remains (Lalonde 2008). Eoin Grogan (cited in Clarke and Carlin 2006) suggests that ring-ditches may have served as memorials to the dead and did not necessitate the inclusion of large quantities of human remains.

Discussion
The most interesting aspect of the ring-ditch was its position within the landscape. It was on the edge of an earlier prehistoric cemetery, which contained several burials in the form of cremation pits dating from the middle and late Bronze Age. The late Bronze Age urn was recovered from one of these burials. The ring-ditch was the only Iron Age feature identified within the vicinity of the cemetery and radiocarbon dating has indicated that it post-dated the Bronze Age burials by 500 years. Despite this long gap in activity, it seems likely that the Iron Age community was aware of the location of the Bronze Age cemetery and reused the site to bury their dead. Indeed, several posts were identified in and around the Bronze Age burials, and these may have acted as physical markers, visually identifying the area as distinctive. If this is the case, they may have been visible on the landscape for a considerable length of time.

Excavations at the base of the ridge below the Bronze Age cemetery and the Iron Age ring-ditch identified further ritual activity. This took the form of shallow, scorched irregular pits or depressions that may have marked the location of

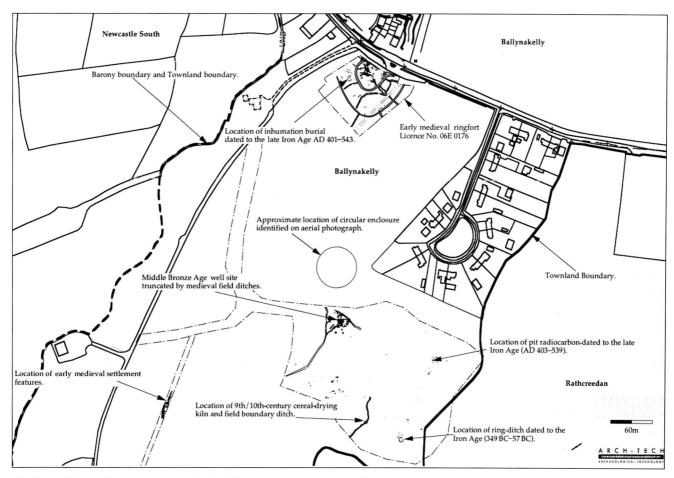

Fig. 11.4—Ballynakelly: location of ring-ditch within the wider archaeological landscape.

cremation pyres. Also identified here was a large well, interpreted as a ritual feature, from which a well-preserved middle Bronze Age palstave axehead and several enigmatic bundles of bound grass and wood were recovered. The lack of evidence for habitation on the crest and in the immediate vicinity suggests a deliberate division of the landscape into areas for the dead and for the living. It is likely that the occupants considered the ridge to be sacred ground, as it was chosen for the interment of the dead.

Additional Iron Age features in the vicinity of the ring-ditch have also been identified (Fig. 11.4). A single inhumation burial, dated to AD 401–543 (at two standard deviations), was identified on a neighbouring excavation (McCarthy 2009, 64) 320m to the north-west on lower ground below the ridge. In addition, a pit surrounded by a three-post structure, dated to AD 403–539, was located 120m to the north of the ring-ditch. This pit represents the final evidence of use of the sacred ridge. There were indications that the posts surrounding the pit had been burnt *in situ*, while all earlier posts seem to have rotted or been pulled out. The perhaps deliberate burning of this structure marks the final evidence of Iron Age (pagan) ritual at this site and preceded the change in land use here from funerary to settlement, with the coming of Christianity in the early medieval period. This represented a complete change of land use at Ballynakelly, with the introduction of domestic settlement and widespread agricultural activity in the form of a large double-ditched ringfort, a field system and several cereal-drying kilns.

Bibliography

Clarke, L. and Carlin, N. 2006 Life and death in Ardsallagh. *Seanda* **1**, 17.

Lalonde, S. 2008 Trade routes and grave goods: a unique Bronze Age burial in Co. Offaly. *Seanda* **3**, 46.

McCarthy, C. 2009 Final excavation report, residential development, Ballynakelly, Newcastle, Co. Dublin. Unpublished report prepared for Lamberton Properties Ltd.

12. Excavation of an Iron Age ring-ditch and associated features at Kerloge, Co. Wexford

Catherine McLoughlin with contributions by Meriel McClatchie, Ellen OCarroll and Maria B. O'Hare

Introduction

This essay outlines the results of an excavation carried out in 2002 at the site of a commercial development in the townland of Kerloge, Co. Wexford (Fig. 12.1), within what is now Kerloge Business Park. The archaeological sites were located *c.* 700m from the modern coastline of south-east County Wexford, at a height of 14–15m OD (NGR 305250/119200) and less than 2km south of Wexford town. Excavation revealed the remains of Neolithic pits and ard marks, an early Bronze Age ring-ditch, an Iron Age ring-ditch and linear features (gullies), and Early Christian grain-drying pits. This essay focuses on the Iron Age remains.

Archaeological setting

Ordovician and other rocks underlie the fertile lowland of County Wexford, renowned for its high-quality farming (Aalen *et al.* 1997, 14). The drift-covered lowland is extremely fertile and, coupled with the fact that the south-east receives low annual rainfall and Ireland's most frequent sunshine, this

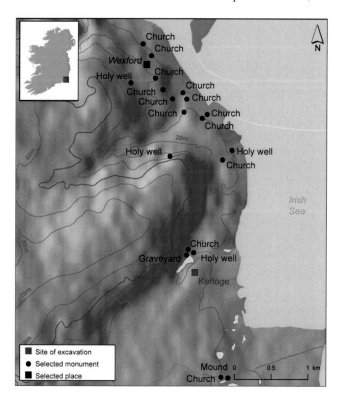

Fig. 12.1—Kerloge: location map.

means that the county has wide land-use capability with mainly well-drained soils. It is not surprising, then, that there is only one site listed for the townland of Kerloge in the archaeological inventory of County Wexford (Moore 1996), as intensive farming has probably resulted in the loss of many upstanding monuments.

Kerloge Church (RMP WX42:6) lies just to the north of the development site. Development in recent years has shown that there is also a wealth of prehistoric archaeology in this area. In 2002 the excavation took place of a burnt mound in the adjoining townland of Strandfield, at the location of the present waste-water treatment plant. An irregular spread of burnt stone was uncovered during topsoil-stripping. This sealed an unlined trough, and a collection of pits, post-holes and stake-holes were also uncovered. Among the discoveries were Bronze Age pottery, lithics and animal bone (McCarthy 2004, 521). In 2005, excavations took place at the site of a new car showroom in Strandfield and Kerloge townlands. Here the remains of a possible Bronze Age structure, a penannular ring-ditch and spreads of pits and post-holes were uncovered (MacManus 2006, 2).

The excavation

Archaeological excavation at Kerloge was undertaken during May and June 2002. The business park development was divided into a number of plots, and archaeological features were uncovered at four of these (Fig. 12.2). Excavation revealed the presence of an Iron Age ring-ditch at site 2 (which was initially thought to have been a Bronze Age roundhouse). Neolithic pits and a possible Iron Age gully were excavated at site 3 and multiphase activity was uncovered at site 4/5, including probable Iron Age gullies.

Site 2: ring-ditch and associated features

The ring-ditch (C1) was truncated by construction-related groundworks. It was circular in plan with an external diameter of 14.6m (Figs 12.3 and 12.4). It was not continuous; there was a 4.3m-wide entrance at the east. The ditch was mainly U-shaped in profile, with regular, steep sides along the northern portion and a narrow, rounded base. In the southern half the ditch was quite truncated, with shallow sides and a generally flat base. This truncation led to a difference in the width of the slot, from 0.32m at its narrowest to 0.6m at its

LIFE AND DEATH IN IRON AGE IRELAND IN THE LIGHT OF RECENT ARCHAEOLOGICAL EXCAVATIONS

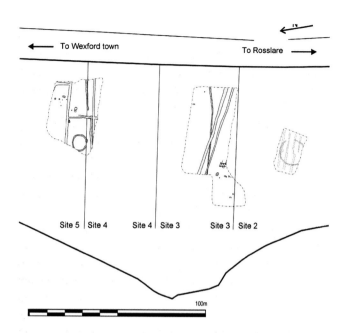

Fig. 12.2—Kerloge: location of sites 2, 3 and 4/5 within overall site layout.

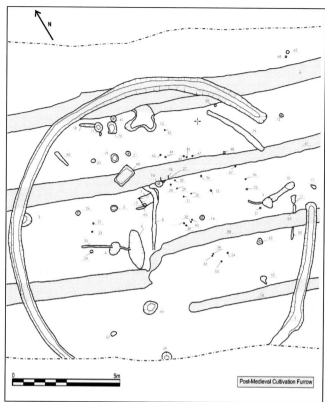

Fig. 12.3—Kerloge: plan of site 2 after excavation.

Fig. 12.4—Kerloge: overall view of site 2 after excavation.

162

Fig. 12.5—Kerloge: section of slot C1, cut by cultivation furrow C9.

Fig. 12.6—Kerloge: section through slot C1 at deepest point.

widest, and a difference in depth from 0.12m at its shallowest to 0.45m at its deepest. The terminals at either side of the entrance were of similar width and rounded profile.

The ring-ditch was filled by a variety of deposits, some of which suggested deliberate backfill (Figs 12.5 and 12.6). The basal fill from the southern terminal to the southern limit of excavation (C1e) was a moderately compacted orange/grey redeposited subsoil, up to 0.06m deep. This in turn was overlain by a moderately compact, dark greyish brown silty clay with frequent inclusions of burnt stone and charcoal (C1d), which was up to 0.38m deep. The upper fill throughout the eastern half consisted of a compact greyish brown sandy silt, which also contained burnt stone (C1a). The fills from the northern terminal were broadly similar. The basal fill (C1g) in this area consisted of soft, greyish brown clayey silt with frequent charcoal inclusions, up to 0.07m deep. It was overlain

by C1c, which consisted of soft greyish brown sandy silt with frequent well-packed burnt stones and high concentrations of charcoal (similar to C1d). Deposit C1c contained a small amount of burnt bone, but this could not be identified as either animal or human. Above C1c was a 0.1m-deep layer of redeposited subsoil (C1b), and this in turn was overlain by C1a. In the western portion of the ditch, where it became shallower, two fills were noted. The basal and main fill in this portion was a soft, mottled greyish brown clayey silt with frequent small stones and charcoal inclusions (C1f), which was 0.2m deep. C1f was overlain by C1b.

Samples from ditch deposits C1c and C1d were sieved and floated for macro-environmental remains. The resultant charcoal from C1c was identified as *Quercus* sp. (oak), *Prunus spinosa* (blackthorn) and *Salix* sp. (willow) (see Appendix 12.2). The oak was removed and a sample of blackthorn and willow was sent for radiocarbon dating. The resultant date, 2237±67 BP, puts the fill of the ring-ditch firmly in the Iron Age (Wk-15498, 410–110 cal. BC).

A wide variety of internal features, including possible post-holes, were excavated within the area enclosed by the ring-ditch. Owing to their morphology, thirteen features within this area may be interpreted as post-holes. Beginning at the northern end of the enclosed area, these were C41, C20, C19, C21, C26, C2, C16, C78, C57, C59, C63, C5 and C10.

Apart from the post-holes, a number of other features were present inside the area enclosed by the ring-ditch, including 38 stake-holes. Towards the centre of the ring-ditch several pits were excavated. C7 was a subrectangular pit, 0.98m east–west by 0.56m north–south and 0.22m deep, with a U-shaped profile and an even, regular base. It was filled with dark brown/black clayey silt, which contained inclusions of burnt stone, charcoal and a significant quantity of burnt bone. There was a stake-hole (C13) at the southern edge of this feature. The pit was cut by a linear slot (C8), running north-west/south-east, that was 3m long, 0.19m wide and 0.03–0.15m deep. This feature was cut at both ends by post-medieval furrows. Two shallow pits (C4 and C6) to the south-west of C7 may have functioned as storage pits. A small linear slot, which has been interpreted as a possible ard mark, connected the two pits but the relationship between them is unclear.

Samples taken from the pit were sieved and floated for macro-environmental evidence. The resultant charcoal was sent for identification. The sample, which weighed 154g, consisted solely of *Quercus* sp. (oak). A sample of this material was sent for radiocarbon dating and the resultant date, 2217±38 BP, is Iron Age (Wk-15497, 390–170 cal. BC), with a date range very similar to the blackthorn and willow charcoal from the fill of the ring-ditch.

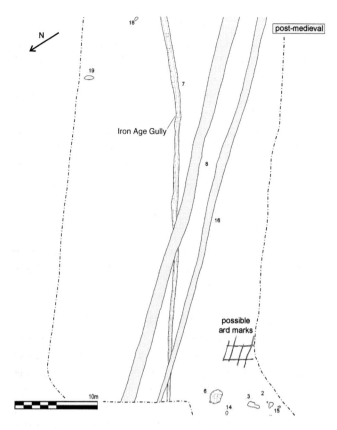

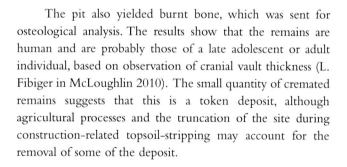

Fig. 12.7—Kerloge: plan of site 3 after excavation.

Fig. 12.8—Kerloge: gully C7 after excavation.

The pit also yielded burnt bone, which was sent for osteological analysis. The results show that the remains are human and are probably those of a late adolescent or adult individual, based on observation of cranial vault thickness (L. Fibiger in McLoughlin 2010). The small quantity of cremated remains suggests that this is a token deposit, although agricultural processes and the truncation of the site during construction-related topsoil-stripping may account for the removal of some of the deposit.

Site 3: gully
Site 3 contained a collection of Neolithic pits and a gully (C7) that may be of Iron Age date (Fig. 12.7). The gully ran roughly east–west and was excavated for a distance of 50m, although prior to the commencement of construction activity it had extended beyond the limit of the excavation at both ends (Fig. 12.8). The gully was characterised by two different sections and was not entirely straight, with a pronounced kink where the two sections joined. The western section consisted of a shallow, U-shaped cut with inward-sloping sides and a relatively flat base. This section was *c.* 32m long, with a general width of 0.5m and a depth of 0.2m. Around 32m to the east,

the gully kinked around slightly to the north and became substantially wider and deeper. The width increased to up to 0.8m and the depth to 0.5m. Some 7.5m to the east of where the deeper section began a small stone dump was excavated. It measured *c.* 2m in length and spanned the width of the gully. The stones were bedded on a layer of brown silty clay, identical to the fill of the remainder of the gully. The rounded east–west profile of the stone dump suggests that it was constructed when the gully was relatively free of debris and may therefore be contemporary with the original use of the feature. The fill of the gully also contained intermittent inclusions of charcoal and two pieces of flint. The gully was cut in several places by post-medieval field boundaries.

Site 4/5: gullies
Site 4/5 contained the remains of Neolithic pits, an early Bronze Age ring-ditch, three possible Iron Age gullies (C16, C17 and C19) and pits dating from the Early Christian period (Fig. 12.9). C16 ran east–west and was excavated for a length of 16m before continuing beyond the limit of excavation. It was 0.7–0.9m wide, with a maximum depth of 0.55m. In profile it was generally rounded with a flat base, filled by a

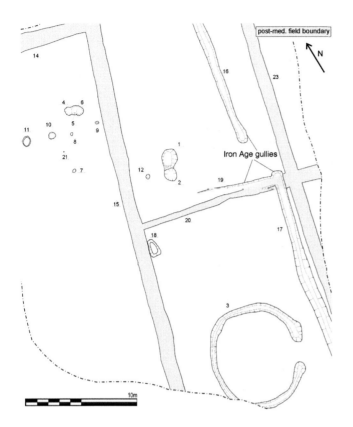

Fig. 12.9—Kerloge: site 4/5 after excavation.

single deposit of compact, dark brown silty clay, which contained a high percentage of heat-shattered stone and charcoal. C17 began to the west of the western terminal of C16, leaving a 3.2m gap between the terminals of the two features. It followed the same east–west direction as C16 and was situated 1.3m to its south. C17 was excavated for a length of 17m but had originally continued beyond the limit of excavation. It was slightly wider than C16, being up to 1.15m wide, and 0.4m deep. In profile C17 was very similar to C16, although its fill was dissimilar—compact, dark brown silty clay with moderate inclusions of charcoal, no burnt stone and a significant quantity of struck flint, some of which was retouched. One further possible prehistoric gully was excavated in this area. C19, a narrow gully running north–south, was largely obscured by a post-medieval ditch (C20). The relationship between C19 and C17 was unclear owing to the intersection of this post-medieval feature. Like C16, C19 contained significant quantities of burnt stone and charcoal.

Artefactual and environmental evidence

The excavations at Kerloge produced a range of material that was sent for specialist analysis. This included plant remains, cremated bone, lithics and charcoal from soil samples.

Plant remains (see Appendix 12.1)

Soil samples were taken from the ring-ditch and from numerous internal features at site 2. The plant remains from the ring-ditch deposits included grains of wheat and wheat/barley, a glume base of hulled wheat, a grass culm node and two grass culm fragments, as well as a small number of charred oat grains. Hazelnut shell fragments and knotgrass seeds were also recorded. Samples from three features also contained plant remains. Pit C7, which contained the cremated human bone, also contained wheat and barley grains, grass culm node fragments, hazelnut shell fragments and a cleaver seed. A post-hole (C2) contained a barley grain and a grass culm fragment, and another post-hole (C71) contained a wheat grain.

The gullies at sites 3 and 4/5 also contained plant remains broadly comparable to those recovered from site 2, indicating that they are indeed likely to be Iron Age.

Charcoal (see Appendix 12.2)

Charcoal was analysed from the fill of the ring-ditch and from the fill of the pit (C7) that contained the cremated human bone. This pit contained a large amount of oak, which was radiocarbon-dated to 2217±38 BP (Wk-15497, 390–170 cal. BC). A fill from the ring-ditch (C1c) contained oak, blackthorn and willow. The oak was removed from the sample and the blackthorn and willow were dated to 2237±67 BP (Wk-15498, 410–110 cal. BC).

Lithics (see Appendix 12.3)

Forty-seven pieces of flint were recovered from site 2, over a third of which were from subsoil or surface contexts and the remainder from cut features. Analysis showed a bipolar-on-anvil flint industry reflected in the predominance of split pebble/bipolar cores, which accounted for over 65% of the assemblage and 13% of scalar flakes. The ring-ditch, for example, contained nine bipolar cores, a scalar flake and a polishing stone, whereas various internal features (such as C6, C8 and C12) also contained bipolar cores. The assemblage appears to indicate that there was no major change in the nature of the lithic assemblage from the late Bronze Age to the Iron Age.

Gully 7 on site 3 contained two bipolar cores, while gully 17 on site 4/5 contained 41 pieces of flint, mostly bipolar cores, some scalar flakes and two thumbnail scrapers. Gully 19 of site 4/5 contained two bipolar cores and a scalar flake. The lithics from the gullies are similar to those recovered from site 2, again indicating an Iron Age date for these features.

Cremated bone

Cremated bone was recovered from a number of contexts at site 2 and was analysed by osteologist Linda Fibiger (Fibiger in

McLoughlin 2010). The ring-ditch (C1) and an internal feature (C8) contained deposits of cremated bone. The recovered samples were highly fragmented, however, and there were no fragments present which could be identified as either human or animal. Pit C7 contained a total of 31g of cremated bone, made up of cranium, radius and long bone, as well as unidentifiable fragments. The sample appeared to be that of a single individual, probably a late adolescent or adult, and represents a token deposit only.

Discussion

There is a paucity of dated Iron Age remains in County Wexford, as there is in much of the rest of the country. Two hillforts are listed in the RMP for the whole of the county (Moore 1996, 25), and until recent road-building schemes were undertaken there were few firmly dated remains.

Recent excavations along the route of the N11 Arklow–Gorey link road in north County Wexford have produced evidence for several Iron Age sites. A large multiperiod site at Ask produced a mixture of annular and penannular ring-ditches dating from the Bronze Age and Iron Age (Stevens 2010). None of the ring-ditches within this complex was as large as the Kerloge example. At Ask site 37, a burial area was uncovered that consisted of densely concentrated clusters of stake-holes, pits and post-holes (Martin 2008). Finds from the site, including blue glass beads, indicate that some of the excavated features may be Iron Age. At Coolnaveagh a ring-ditch and associated pits were also dated to the Iron Age (Flynn 2011).

At Bricketstown, to the west of Wexford town, two sites excavated as part of the N25 Rathsillagh–Harristown Little road scheme produced Iron Age dates. The first of these was a single pit and the second was a cremation cemetery (Elder 2002, 351). At Dungeer a burnt mound site was dated to the late Bronze Age/early Iron Age (NRA database; 00E474). At Ballyaddragh, close to Rosslare Harbour in south County Wexford, a complex of five intercutting ring-ditches and a series of gullies were excavated (McLoughlin 2010). While no radiocarbon dates have been obtained for this site, on the basis of comparative dating it is possible that all or parts of this site date from the Iron Age.

At Ballydavis, Co. Laois, an Iron Age funerary complex was excavated. The largest ring-ditch was similar in scale to the Kerloge example, with a 16m-diameter ring-ditch and a 3.2m-wide east-facing entrance. A central burial was uncovered, with a bronze box containing cremated bone and associated artefacts (Keeley 1999). A similar ring-ditch was excavated at Mountgorry, Co. Dublin. This feature, which measured 20m in diameter and had a 3m-wide entrance at the south-east, appears to date from the Bronze Age on the basis of artefacts uncovered (Giacometti 2007, 110).

The archaeological remains at Kerloge form part of a multiperiod complex that must be seen in conjunction with the other excavated sites in the immediate vicinity, specifically in the adjacent townland of Strandfield. There two circular structures were excavated, the smaller of which, based on morphology, is similar to the early Bronze Age ring-ditch of site 4/5. The larger one, with a diameter of 10.2m, has been interpreted by the excavator as a Bronze Age house (MacManus 2006). There are similarities between that feature and the Kerloge site 2 Iron Age structure.

Also at Strandfield, the remains of a truncated burnt mound with associated pits, post-holes and stake-holes were excavated (McCarthy 2004). Pottery recovered from the site suggests a Bronze Age date for some of the features, although there are no radiocarbon dates from the site. It is tempting to see some of the features as Iron Age, as burnt mound material was found infilling both the Kerloge site 2 ring-ditch and one of the gullies.

While a feature within the ring-ditch at Kerloge did contain cremated human bone, the structural evidence associated with it (the numerous internal post-holes) suggests that it may more properly be termed a 'structure', and indeed it may have functioned as a settlement site prior to its use as a funerary monument. While there are no immediate excavated parallels within County Wexford, a number of Iron Age settlement structures have been excavated throughout Ireland. At Ballinaspig More 5, Co. Cork, a slot-trench and associated post-holes were dated to 360–60 cal. BC, and at Ballycullen site 3, Co. Dublin, a large circular gully enclosed an area with a diameter of 14.5m. Internal features included post-holes for roof supports (Becker et al. 2008, 26).

The Kerloge ring-ditch or 'structure' is an intriguing set of features not neatly classifiable into either category. The monument, which is defined primarily by its encircling ring-ditch, may in fact be the surviving remnants of a roofed structure. Whether it was initially constructed for use as a domestic dwelling or as a funerary monument is unclear.

Acknowledgements

This excavation was funded by the developers of the Kerloge Business Park. Thanks are due to Meriel McClatchie, Ellen OCarroll and Maria O'Hare for permission to publish specialist reports, and to James Eogan for access to unpublished National Roads Authority site reports. Thanks also to the archaeological crew who took part in the excavation.

Bibliography

Aalen, F.H.A., Whelan, K. and Stout, M. 1997 *Atlas of the Irish rural landscape*. Cork.

Becker, K., Ó Néill, J. and O'Flynn, L. 2008 Iron Age Ireland: finding an invisible people. Unpublished report prepared for the Heritage Council (project 16365).

Elder, S. 2002 Bricketstown, Co. Wexford. *Excavations 2000*, 350–1. Bray.

Fibiger, L. 2007 Osteology report. In C. McLoughlin, 'Archaeological report, Kerloge, Co. Wexford'. Unpublished report for DoEHLG.

Flynn, C. 2011 Final report on the archaeological excavation by Eoghan Moore at Site 21 & 22, Coolnaveagh, Co. Wexford. Unpublished report by Valerie J. Keeley Ltd for Wexford County Council and the National Roads Authority.

Giacometti, A. 2007 Mountgorry Site B, Malahide Road, Drinan, Co. Dublin. *Excavations 2004*, 109–10. Bray.

Keeley, V.J. 1999 Iron Age discoveries at Ballydavis. In P.G. Lane and W. Nolan (eds), *Laois: history and society*, 25–34. Dublin.

McCarthy, M. 2004 Strandfield. *Excavations 2002*, 520–1. Bray.

McLoughlin, C. 2010 Ballyaddragh. *Excavations 2007*, no. 2065. Bray.

MacManus, C. 2006 Excavation report: Strandfield/Kerloge, Co. Wexford. Unpublished report by Stafford McLoughlin Archaeology.

Martin, K. 2008 Preliminary report: Site 37, Ask, Co. Wexford (E3497). Unpublished report by Valerie J. Keeley Ltd for Wexford County Council and the National Roads Authority.

Moore, M. 1996 *Archaeological inventory of County Wexford*. Dublin.

Stevens, P. 2010 Final report on the archaeological excavation of Sites 42–44, Ask, Co. Wexford (E3502). Unpublished report by Valerie J. Keeley Ltd for Wexford County Council and the National Roads Authority.

APPENDIX 12.1: THE PLANT REMAINS FROM IRON AGE DEPOSITS AT KERLOGE, CO. WEXFORD (02E0606) (MERIEL MCCLATCHIE)

Introduction

Archaeobotanical analysis was carried out on 29 soil samples from deposits at Kerloge, Co. Wexford, 22 of which contained charred non-wood plant macro-remains. Samples were taken from sites 2, 3, 4 and 5. Animal bone was not recorded in deposits at Kerloge, but charred cereal or possible cereal remains were found in deposits dating from the Neolithic, the Bronze Age, the Iron Age and the early Middle Ages (McClatchie 2007). Evidence for a narrow range of gathered foods and weeds was also recovered. This report focuses on the plant macro-remains recorded in ten soil samples from Iron Age deposits.

Methodology

The sampling strategy was systematic, whereby certain areas and feature types (such as pits) were targeted, with judgement sampling also being imposed in areas displaying concentrations of burning. Scatter sampling was also undertaken in some deposits, whereby a number of samples were taken from a single deposit. Processing of the soil samples was carried out by the excavators, following consultation with the author. Approximately eight litres of soil were processed from each sample, using the flotation method, with the minimum mesh size measuring 0.25mm.

Scanning, sorting and subsequent identification of the archaeobotanical material in all samples were carried out using a stereoscopic microscope, with magnifications ranging from x6 to x50. The material was identified on the basis of visual comparison of its morphological features to reference material in the UCC Archaeology Department collection of modern diaspores and the drawings from various seed keys (for example Beijerinck 1947; Katz *et al.* 1965; Berggren 1969; 1981; Anderberg 1994). The well-drained soils at the site resulted in the preservation of plant macro-remains by charring, and the taxa recorded are presented in Table 12.1. With the exception of cereals, botanical names are listed following the order and nomenclature of *Flora Europaea* (Tutin *et al.* 1964–83), and common names follow those provided in *New flora of the British Isles* (Stace 1991). The achenes and seeds of plants are referred to as 'seeds' throughout the text for convenience (see Table 12.1).

Site 2: Iron Age circular structure

A circular structure at site 2—comprising a slot-trench, an internal ring of post-holes and other interior features—was dated to the Iron Age. Three fills of the slot-trench (C1a, C1c

Table 12.1—Kerloge: plant taxa recorded in Iron Age deposits.

	Site	2	2	2	2	2	2	2	3	3	4/5
	Context	1a	1c	1d	2a/b	7a	7a	71b	7a	7a	16a
	Sample	*1*	*6*	*9*	*1*	*–*	*8*	*27*	*5*	*6*	*20*
Botanical name	**Common name**										
CORYLACEAE											
Corylus avellana L. (shell fragments)	Hazelnut	6	–	1	–	–	1	–	–	–	–
POLYGONACEAE											
Polygonum sp. (achenes)	Knotgrass	–	3	–	–	–	–	–	–	–	–
Cf. *Polygonum* sp. (achenes)	Cf. knotgrass	–	–	1	–	–	–	–	–	–	–
RUBIACEAE											
Galium cf. *aparine* L. (seeds)	Cleaver	–	–	–	–	–	1	–	–	–	–
GRAMINEAE											
Triticum sp. (glume bases)	Hulled wheat	–	1	–	–	–	–	–	–	–	–
Triticum sp. (grains)	Wheat	–	5	–	–	–	2	1	–	–	–
Triticum/Hordeum sp. (grains)	Wheat/barley	–	3	–	–	–	–	–	–	–	–
Triticum/Hordeum sp. (grain fragments)	Wheat/barley	–	3	–	–	–	–	–	–	–	–
Hordeum vulgare L. (grains)	Six-row hulled barley	–	–	–	–	–	–	–	–	–	1
Hordeum nudum L. (grains)	Naked barley	–	–	–	–	–	–	–	1	–	–
Hordeum sp. (grains)	Barley	–	–	–	1	–	–	–	2	–	–
Hordeum sp. (grain fragments)	Barley	–	–	–	–	–	2	–	1	–	–
Cf. *Hordeum* sp. (grains)	Cf. barley	–	–	–	–	–	–	–	–	1	–
Avena sp. (grains)	Oat	–	2	–	–	–	–	–	–	–	–
Avena sp. (grain fragments)	Oat	–	2	–	–	–	–	–	–	–	–
Cerealia (grain fragments)	Indeterminate cereal	–	–	1	–	–	1	–	–	–	–
Gramineae (culm node fragments)	Grass culm node	–	–	1	–	3	11	–	1	–	–
Gramineae (culm fragments)	Grass culm	–	–	2	1	4	14	–	–	1	–
	Total	*6*	*19*	*6*	*2*	*7*	*32*	*1*	*5*	*2*	*1*

and C1d) contained approximately ten charred cereal grains, including *Triticum* sp. (wheat) and *Triticum/Hordeum* sp. (wheat/barley), as well as a glume base of hulled wheat, a Gramineae (grass) culm node and two grass culm fragments. A small number of charred *Avena* sp. (oat) grains were also recorded in C1. It has been suggested that oat was not cultivated until the early medieval period in Ireland (Monk 1986), and its presence in late prehistoric deposits may therefore represent a wild variety that occurred as a weed of wheat and barley crops. *Corylus avellana* L. (hazelnut) shell fragments and *Polygonum* sp. (knotgrass) seeds were also recorded in C1, the latter representing a genus that can be found growing on disturbed ground and in arable fields. Hazelnuts may have been gathered as a seasonally available food resource. *Prunus spinosa* L. (blackthorn) and *Salix* sp. (willow) charcoal from C1 was radiocarbon-dated to 2237±67 BP (Wk-15498, 410–110 cal. BC).

The slot-trench (C1) enclosed a number of features, including pits and post-holes. C7a was a subrectangular pit that contained a small number of wheat and barley grains, in addition to grass culm node fragments and culm fragments. A hazelnut shell fragment and a seed of *Galium* cf. *aparine* L. (cleaver) were also recorded in C7a. Cleaver can be found growing in a range of habitats, including arable fields. *Quercus* sp. (oak) charcoal from C7 was radiocarbon-dated to 2217±38 BP (Wk-15497, 390–170 cal. BC). Fills of two interior post-holes (C2 and C71) also contained charred plant remains. C2a/b produced a barley grain and a grass culm fragment, while C71b contained a wheat grain.

Sites 3 and 4/5: possible Iron Age gullies
Possible Iron Age gullies were recorded at sites 3 and 4/5. The material remains in these gullies were similar to those uncovered at Iron Age site 2, and the plant remains were also broadly comparable. Two samples from C7a at site 3 contained a small number of barley grains, including *Hordeum nudum* L. (naked barley), in addition to a grass culm node fragment and a grass culm fragment. C16 at site 4/5 was also interpreted as a gully, and a sample from this deposit contained a grain of *Hordeum vulgare* L. (six-row hulled barley).

Discussion
The Iron Age plant remains from Kerloge are significant, as a relatively small number of Irish assemblages dating from this period have been published. It is hoped, however, that the excavation of significant numbers of Iron Age sites during the last decade (Becker *et al.* 2008; this volume) will enable clearer insights into plant use at a range of sites and in a variety of circumstances.

When considering the published evidence for Iron Age plant macro-remains in Ireland, we are largely reliant on a study carried out by Mick Monk (1986, 32) more than twenty years ago. Monk's overview indicated that a range of crops were cultivated during the Iron Age, with naked and hulled barley often predominant. A more recently excavated site provides a useful comparison for the Kerloge material, with a similar suite of remains being recorded. A ring-barrow at Kilmahuddrick, Co. Dublin, was constructed during the Bronze Age, but final infilling of the ring-barrow ditch and other nearby features did not take place until the Iron Age (Doyle 2005). The Iron Age deposits at Kilmahuddrick contained cremated human bone and small quantities of charred cereal remains, comprising barley and hulled wheat as well as oat. Hazelnut shell fragments and occasional weed seeds were also recorded.

The presence of cremated human bone in pits within the Iron Age circular structure at Kerloge similarly suggests that this area was the focus of ceremonial activities associated with disposal of the dead. Cereal foodstuffs may have been an integral part of such activities, being consumed by the living and perhaps accompanying the dead. While it is possible that the cereal remains recorded at Kerloge represent food waste, it should be noted that such material may have been accorded special treatment when being discarded (Brück 2000). Indeed, the deposition of cereal remains at Kerloge may not simply represent the disposal of waste but rather the placing of special deposits that recalled and commemorated people and events.

There is limited archaeobotanical evidence for plants growing in the local environment surrounding the site at Kerloge. Seeds of the knotgrass genus and cleaver were occasionally recorded, but these plants may have been growing alongside cereals in arable fields and their seeds inadvertently harvested. The value of any plant is, however, determined by the perceptions of its viewers. Many plants that we would consider to be weeds may have been considered useful in past societies, for example in contributing to food resources and medicines. Such plants may not have been prepared in the vicinity of fires, thus reducing their likelihood of being charred and preserved. Similarly, the absence of vegetable and fruit remains from Kerloge does not indicate that such foodstuffs were not utilised, as they may also have been consumed without coming into contact with fire.

Archaeobotanical analysis of deposits at Kerloge provided evidence for activities associated with arable agriculture over several millennia (McClatchie 2007). Changes can be observed in the types of cereals encountered over time, and also in the quantities of cereals preserved. When compared with the Neolithic remains at Kerloge, a wider range of cereals is represented in Iron Age deposits, possibly representing changes in agricultural techniques and strategies, including new farming tools, soil-improvement techniques and land management systems. This diversification in cereal types is accompanied by a dramatic reduction in the occurrence of hazelnut shell when compared with Neolithic deposits, suggesting that the gathering of this latter foodstuff had declined in importance by the Iron Age.

Further changes in agricultural evidence can be observed in early medieval deposits at Kerloge, which produced evidence for free-threshing wheat as well as an increased incidence of six-row hulled barley. Changes in crops grown during the early medieval period may have resulted from a range of factors, including improved soil management and harvesting techniques, climatic influences, market requirements and social constraints. The nature of activities on the site is also likely to have been influential. Smaller quantities of remains were recorded in Iron Age deposits associated with ceremonial activities at Kerloge, while significantly increased quantities were present in early medieval pits that may have been linked to more domestic pursuits.

Conclusions

Archaeobotanical analysis of Iron Age deposits at Kerloge produced evidence for a range of cereals and non-cultivated plants. Charred remains of naked barley, hulled barley and hulled wheat were recorded. The presence of charred oat remains may represent a wild variety, perhaps growing as a weed alongside barley and wheat crops. Other charred weed seeds recorded may represent additional plants growing in arable fields and inadvertently harvested. Charred hazelnut shell fragments were also recorded at Kerloge, possibly representing a seasonally available food resource. The presence of these plant remains alongside cremated human bone deposits suggests that they represent remnants of food incorporated into ceremonial activities. Foodstuffs may have been consumed by the living during ceremonies or placed alongside the dead. Given the relatively meagre published evidence for plant remains from Iron Age sites in Ireland, the Kerloge material provides an important insight into the use of plant resources during this period.

Bibliography

Anderberg, A.-L. 1994 *Atlas of seeds, part 4: Resedaceae–Umbelliferae*. Stockholm.

Becker, K., Ó Néill, J. and O'Flynn, L. 2008 Iron Age Ireland: finding an invisible people. Unpublished report prepared for the Heritage Council (project 16365).

Beijerinck, W. 1947 *Zadenatlas der Nederlandsche Flora*. Wageningen.

Berggren, G. 1969 *Atlas of seeds, part 2: Cyperaceae*. Stockholm.

Berggren, G. 1981 *Atlas of seeds, part 3: Salicaceae–Cruciferae*. Stockholm.

Brück, J. 2000 Settlement, landscape and social identity: the early–middle Bronze Age transition in Wessex, Sussex and the Thames Valley. *Oxford Journal of Archaeology* **19** (3), 273–300.

Doyle, I.W. 2005 Excavation of a prehistoric ring-barrow at Kilmahuddrick, Clondalkin, Dublin 22. *Journal of Irish Archaeology* **14**, 43–75.

Katz, N.J., Katz, S.V. and Kipiani, M.G. 1965 *Atlas and keys of fruits and seeds occurring in the Quaternary deposits of the USSR*. Moscow.

McClatchie, M. 2007 The study of non-wood plant macro-remains: investigating past societies and landscapes. In E.M. Murphy and N.J. Whitehouse (eds), *Environmental archaeology in Ireland*, 194–220. Oxford.

Monk, M.A. 1986 Evidence from macroscopic plant remains for crop husbandry in prehistoric and early historic Ireland: a review. *Journal of Irish Archaeology* **3**, 31–6.

Stace, C. 1991 *New flora of the British Isles*. Cambridge.

Tutin, T.G., Heywood, V.H., Burges, N.A., Valentine, D.H., Walters, S.M. and Webb, D.A. 1964–83 *Flora Europaea* (vols 1–6). Cambridge.

APPENDIX 12.2: IDENTIFICATION OF CHARCOAL DEPOSITS (ELLEN OCARROLL)

Introduction

Two charcoal samples from Kerloge site 2 were submitted for analysis. Prior to ^{14}C dating, the charcoal was sent for species identification to obtain an indication of the range of tree species that grew in the area, as well as the utilisation of these species for various functions. The Iron Age ring-ditch at site 2 (410–110 cal. BC) is the main subject of this report.

Wood used for fuel at prehistoric sites was generally sourced at locations close to the site and therefore charcoal identifications may reflect the composition of the local woodlands. Larger pieces of charcoal, if present, can provide information regarding the use of a species. The charcoal from Kerloge was excavated from the fill of a cremation feature (site 2, C7) and the tertiary fill (C1c) of the ring-ditch.

Methodology

The identification of wood, whether it is charred, dried or waterlogged, is achieved by comparing the anatomical structure of samples with known comparative material or keys

(Schweingruber 1990). The identification of charcoal material involves breaking the charcoal piece so that a clean section of the wood can be obtained. This charcoal is then identified to species under an Olympus SZ3060 x80 stereo-microscope as well as a metallurgical microscope with a transmitted light source at higher magnifications of x100–500. The species were determined by close examination of the micro-anatomical features of the samples, such as the vessels and their arrangement, the size and arrangement of rays, vessel pit arrangement and the type of perforation plates. All samples were suitable for species identification.

The samples comprised large fragments of charcoal, which were easily identified. The resultant identifications were bagged by weight.

Results

Table 12.2—Kerloge: results from charcoal identifications at site 2.

Feature	Sample	Species	Weight, comment, date
F7, cremation pit	8 (2 bags)	All *Quercus* sp.	Bag 1: 49g Bag 2: 105g
1C, slot-trench	2mm flot	*Quercus* sp. *Prunus spinosa* *Salix* sp.	*Quercus* sp. (1g), *Prunus spinosa* (3.4g) and *Salix* sp. (1.6 g) 2237±67 BP (Wk-15498, 410–110 cal. BC)
1C, slot-trench	1mm flot	All *Quercus* sp.	6.5g

Discussion

Wood use

The large quantities of oak may be related to the ritual funerary practices associated with this ring-ditch, as oak was nearly always used in connection with cremation rites and pyres in prehistory. Alternatively, the oak may have been selected for use as structural timbers within the slot-trenches. It is difficult to attribute a use or function to the willow and blackthorn.

Wood types identified

There are three taxa types present in the charcoal remains (Table 12.2). These represent large trees (oak) and smaller, scrub-type trees (blackthorn and willow). Oak and blackthorn are representative of dryland environments, while willow is normally associated with wetter areas. It is likely that there was a supply of oak in the surrounding environment. Oak also has unique properties of great durability and strength and was used throughout prehistory for structural timbers. Ireland has two native species of oak—pedunculate oak (*Quercus robur*) and sessile oak (*Quercus petraea*). The former prefers alkaline or neutral soils rich in minerals, particularly damp clay soils, and

is usually found in mixed woodland. The latter prefers acid and lighter, well-drained soils and is often found in pure stands. Both species are naturally distributed throughout Ireland. Oak charcoal was particularly important to activities that required heat, as it burned hotter and more cleanly than wood and was considered superior. Oak woods were valued for their natural resource of timber for many requirements, including raw material for metal-working activities. The heavier and denser the wood, the higher is its calorific value. Oak can burn for a considerable time and can reach the extremely high temperatures necessary for the production of metal objects and for smelting. It is also one of the only native taxa that can reach 650°C or even 850°C, the temperature required to efficiently cremate human bone (O'Donnell 2007). As such, oak is almost invariably associated with burial ritual during the prehistoric period. Oak timbers are often used to line troughs at burnt mound sites. There is also ethnographic evidence to suggest a connection between the deliberate selection of oak for the construction of domestic buildings and its use in burial ritual during the prehistoric period (Harding 2000, 108–9; Cooney and Grogan 1994).

Blackthorn (*Prunus spinosa*) is a very durable wood and is as strong as oak. It is a thorny shrub found in woods and scrub on all soil types. In a woodland situation it is more likely to occur in clearings and at the woodland edges.

A small amount of willow (*Salix* spp) charcoal was identified from the proposed carbon-dating sample and the 2mm flot sample. According to Webb (1977, 160–2), thirteen species of willow are found in Ireland, of which eight are certainly native. The wood of *Salix* trees and shrubs cannot be differentiated on the basis of anatomical characteristics. It is a strong wood and is commonly used for posts. All willows appear to favour wet conditions.

Summary and conclusions

Three taxa types were identified from the features (hearth and slot-trench) investigated. These were oak, blackthorn and willow in order of representation. The oak wood may have been selected and used in association with the cremation rites of the dead, as ring-ditches are generally associated with such activities. Oak may also have been selected for structural wood within the slot-trenches at site 2. The blackthorn may have grown locally in hedgerows or as scrub near the sites, while the willow may have been sourced from a wetter environment. The oak points to the presence of woodlands and indicates that open conditions did not prevail throughout some of the Kerloge area in the Iron Age.

Bibliography

Beckett, J.K. 1979 *Planting native trees and shrubs*. Norwich.

Cooney, G. and Grogan, E. 1994 *Irish prehistory: a social perspective*. Bray.

Harding, A.F. 2000 *European societies in the Bronze Age*. Cambridge.

Nelson, E.C. 1993 *Trees of Ireland*. Dublin.

O'Donnell, L. 2007 Wood and charcoal from the gas pipeline to the west. Unpublished technical report for Margaret Gowen and Co. Ltd.

Schweingruber, F.H. 1990 *Microscopic wood anatomy* (3rd edn). Birmensdorf.

Warner, R.B. 1990 A proposed adjustment for the 'old-wood' effect. In W. Mook and H. Waterbolk (eds), *Proceedings of the 2nd Symposium of C14 and Archaeology, Groningen, 1987*, 29, 159–72.

Webb, D.A. 1977 *An Irish flora*. Dundalk.

APPENDIX 12.3: LITHICS ANALYSIS (MARIA B. O'HARE)

Site 2 lithics analysis

This is a fairly small assemblage of 47 archaeological lithic pieces. The bulk of the lithic material was derived from contexts associated with structural features, such as hearth pits, slot-trenches and occasionally burnt mound material. Radiocarbon determinations indicate an Iron Age date. Although over a third of the lithic material came from subsoil/surface levels, the homogeneous nature of the collection indicates that it may all have belonged to the same cultural horizon.

There was a single coarse stone artefact, a fragmentary triangular portion of a possible whetstone or 'hone', which is in keeping with types described for the Irish Iron Age and Early Christian era by O'Connor (1991). The vast majority of lithic pieces were flint. The nature of the flint industry as a whole was bipolar-on-anvil, conforming to the criteria

outlined by Kobayashi (1975), Cotterell and Kamminga (1987), Ahler (1989), Shott (1989), Knight (1991), Kuijt *et al.* (1995) and Knarrström (2001). This is seen in the predominance of split pebble/bipolar cores, accounting for over 65% of the assemblage and 13% of scalar flakes (thinner and more flake-like than bipolar cores). There was just over 10% of micro-débitage (<10mm) pieces, mainly derived from sieved soil samples. The remainder of the flint assemblage consisted of a large nodule from which several flakes had been removed; although none of these originated from any discernible platforms or exhibited characteristics of a worked amorphous core, it does at least indicate that larger nodules were occasionally available for reduction. The primary technology accounted for 88% of the assemblage as a whole, and this ratio of primary to secondary technology (modified pieces) is reflected throughout the Irish Bronze Age assemblages, which are typically between 80% and 90% (O'Hare 2005; forthcoming). The only modified chipped stone tools (secondary technology) were in the form of flaked split-pebble scrapers (subcircular types), also characteristic of Bronze Age and later prehistoric lithic industries.

Comparanda and conclusion

The dimensional patterns for small flint pebbles from the same geological region as Kerloge, as described by Quinn (1984), and the lithic technology outlined for the Bally Lough regional study by Green and Zvelebil (1990) are fully applicable to the Kerloge lithics. For instance, although bipolar technology is predominant within lithic assemblages from the general prehistoric periods in this part of south-east Ireland (Green and Zvelebil 1990, 83), the bipolar reduction rather than platform technology is only an archaeological marker for later prehistoric activity—namely the Bronze Age—in the context of all the other regions in Ireland (O'Hare 2005; forthcoming).

It is perhaps significant that this small lithic collection from Kerloge, presumably belonging to the period indicated by the radiocarbon determinations (the Iron Age), does not deviate from the overall patterns of lithic technology established throughout the Irish Bronze Age by the present writer (O'Hare 2005; forthcoming) and, indeed, broadly conforms to other late prehistoric assemblages as indicated within a range of lithic studies emerging from several diverse regions, from Jordan to Sweden—a surprising, widespread continuation and similarity of highly expedient lithic technology of the later prehistoric period noted by Healy (2000, 13; 2004, 184). Furthermore, several studies within this emerging field of research show compelling evidence for a continuance of these same expedient industries into the Iron

Age, as demonstrated in studies from Scandinavia by Knarrström (2001) and Högberg (2009), and within Britain by Young and Humphrey (1999), Humphrey and Young (2003), Martingell (2003) and Humphrey (2004).

Not all scholars agree on the viability of these Iron Age lithics, however (see, for example, Saville 1981). More recently, Ó Drisceoil (2007, 21) has stated that 'in Ireland, flints do occur quite regularly on Iron Age sites, but none of the assemblages are chronologically clean and the use of flint after the early Bronze Age in Ireland remains unproven'. Finlay and Woodman (2001, 8), however, have proposed that the Irish post-Bronze Age lithics need to be considered, and certainly the research of the present writer has demonstrated the existence of fully viable lithic technology in Ireland well into the latest phases of the Bronze Age. Perhaps the lithic collection from Kerloge site 2 can be compared to many other late Bronze Age assemblages in Ireland and beyond, and may also reflect the contemporaneous Iron Age lithic collections not yet adequately assessed and still to be discovered.

Bibliography

Ahler, S.A. 1989 Experimental knapping with KRF and mid-continental cherts: overview and applications. In D.S. Amick and R.P. Mauldin (eds), *Experiments in lithic technology*, 199–234. British Archaeological Reports, International Series 528. Oxford.

Cotterell, B. and Kamminga, J. 1987 The formation of flakes. *American Antiquity* **52** (4), 657–708.

Finlay, N. and Woodman, P.C. 2001 Appendix III: Lithic assemblage from Chancellorsland Site A, Co. Tipperary. In M. Doody (ed.), 'Excavation report for Chancellorsland Site A, Co. Tipperary (92E0129)', 1–11. Unpublished report.

Green, S.W. and Zvelebil, M. 1990 The Mesolithic colonization and agricultural transition in south-east Ireland. *Proceedings of the Prehistoric Society* **56**, 57–88.

Healy, F. 2000 Lithic studies in the year 2000: lithic studies society conference, 8–10 Sept. 2000, Cardiff. *Past: the Newsletter of the Prehistoric Society* **36** (Dec. 2000); available on-line at www.ucl.ac.uk/prehistoric/past/past36.html #Lithics (accessed 24 Nov. 2006).

Healy, F. 2004 After hunter-gatherers: lithics in a crowd scene. In E.A. Walker, F.W.S. Healy and F. Healy (eds), *Lithics in action*, 183–4. Oxford.

Högberg, A. 2009 *Lithics in the Scandinavian late Bronze Age: socio-technical change and persistence*. British Archaeological Reports, International Series 1932. Oxford.

Humphrey, J. 2004 The use of flint in the British Iron Age: results from some recent research. In E.A. Walker, F.W.S.

Healy and F. Healy (eds), *Lithics in action*, 243–51. Oxford.

Humphrey, J. and Young, R. 2003 Flint use in later Bronze Age and Iron Age England? Some criteria for future research. In N. Moloney and M.J. Shott (eds), *Lithic analysis at the millennium*, 79–89. London.

Knarrström, B. 2001 *Flint: a Scanian hardware*. Lund.

Knight, J. 1991 Technological analysis of the the anvil (bipolar) technique. *Lithics* **12**, 57–87.

Kobayashi, H. 1975 The experimental study of bipolar flakes: lithic technology—making and using stone tools. In E. Swanson (ed.), *World anthropology*, 97–102. The Hague and Paris.

Kuijt, I., Prentiss, W.C. and Pokotylo, D.L. 1995 Bipolar reduction: an experimental study of debitage variability. *Lithic Technology* **20** (2), 116–27.

McLoughlin, C. 2002 Prehistoric remains at Kerloge, Co. Wexford. *Archaeology Ireland* **16** (3), 16–19.

Martingell, H.E. 2003 Later prehistoric and historic use of flint in England. In N. Moloney and M.J. Shott (eds), *Lithic analysis at the millennium*, 91–7. London.

Moloney, N. and Shott, M.J. (eds) 2003 *Lithic analysis at the millennium*. London.

O'Connor, L. 1991 Irish Iron Age and Early Christian whetstones. *Journal of the Royal Society of Antiquaries of Ireland* **121**, 45–76.

Ó Drisceoil, C. 2007 Life and death in the Iron Age at Carrickmines Great, Co. Dublin. *Journal of the Royal Society of Antiquaries of Ireland* **137**, 5–28.

O'Hare, M.B. 2005 The Bronze Age lithics of Ireland. Unpublished Ph.D thesis, Queen's University, Belfast.

O'Hare, M.B. (forthcoming) *The everyday chipped stone technologies of the Irish Bronze Age: a broad regional perspective*. British Archaeological Reports, International Series. Oxford.

Quinn, I. 1984 Distribution of flint erratics in parts of County Waterford. *Decies* **27**, 21–30.

Saville, A. 1981 Iron Age flint-working: fact or fiction? *Lithics* **1**, 16–20.

Shott, M.J. 1989 Bipolar industries: ethnographic evidence and archaeological implications. *North American Archaeologist* **10** (1), 1–24.

Walker, E.A., Healy, F.W.S. and Healy, F. (eds) 2004 *Lithics in action: papers from the conference, lithic studies in the year 2000*. Oxford.

Young, R. and Humphrey, J. 1999 Flint use in England after the Bronze Age: time for a re-evaluation? *Proceedings of the Prehistoric Society* **65**, 231–42.

13. Recent Iron Age discoveries in south County Tipperary and County Limerick

Melanie McQuade and Bernice Molloy

Introduction

Iron Age activity was identified on twelve sites uncovered during archaeological investigations along the 41km route of the N8 Cashel–Mitchelstown Road Improvement Scheme (Figs 13.1 and 13.2). These sites produced evidence for settlement, iron production and burial and they were dated by means of radiocarbon analysis (Table 13.1). Their discovery has added significant information to an area that was hitherto practically devoid of Iron Age evidence (Fig. 13.2). The only prior evidence for Iron Age occupation was a spearhead discovered in Ballydavid, north-west of Cahir (Cleary 2007, 49), and possibly also the undated barrows and hillforts in the wider area.

Distribution and siting

The evidence uncovered along the N8 road improvement scheme was confined to a linear corridor of investigation (averaging 60m in width) but nevertheless several trends can be observed. The settlements were located on south- and south-east-facing slopes, at altitudes of between 66m and

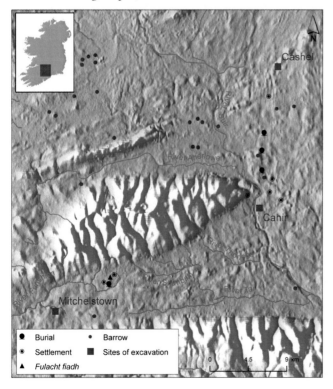

Fig. 13.1—Location map.

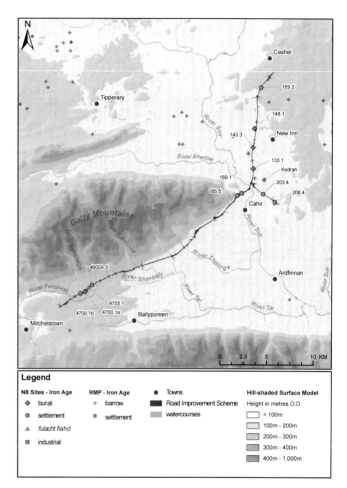

Fig. 13.2—Distribution of Iron Age sites discovered along the N8 road improvement scheme.

120m OD. They were all sited on well-drained fertile soils and were concentrated in the catchment areas of the River Funshion and the River Suir, with none of the settlements more than 1.2km from a watercourse. The burial sites were at similar altitudes and were in quite prominent positions in the landscape, providing clear views of the surrounding countryside. They were generally sited in isolation from the Iron Age settlement sites recorded on the scheme, with the exception of the ring-barrow at Knockcommane, Co. Limerick, which was identified in close proximity to a broadly contemporary settlement/iron production site and a late Bronze Age/early Iron Age *fulacht fiadh* (Fig. 13.2).

There was a notable dearth of occupation where the route passed along the southern flank of the Galtee Mountains in an area of poor boggy ground, which may formerly have been covered in dense, impenetrable scrub that would not have been suitable for settlement (Fig. 13.2).

Evidence for settlement and for iron production

Six Iron Age settlement sites were identified along the route of the road scheme (Fig. 13.2), and structural remains were uncovered on two of these. An enclosed circular building, which produced evidence for iron production, was excavated at Knockcommane, Co. Limerick (site 4700.1B), and three unenclosed subcircular structures were recorded at Ballydrehid, Co. Tipperary (site 185.5). Although no formal structure was recognised at Killemly, Co. Tipperary (site 203.4), a scatter of post-holes and pits characterised a large area of domestic occupation. Less substantial settlement evidence, in the form of hearths and pits, was uncovered at Shanballyduff (site 169.2) and Ballylegan, Co. Tipperary (site 206.4), and at Brackbaun, Co. Limerick (site 4602A.3). A *fulacht fiadh* dating from the late Bronze Age/early Iron Age transition was also identified at Brackbaun (site 4705.1) (cf. McQuade *et al.* 2009).

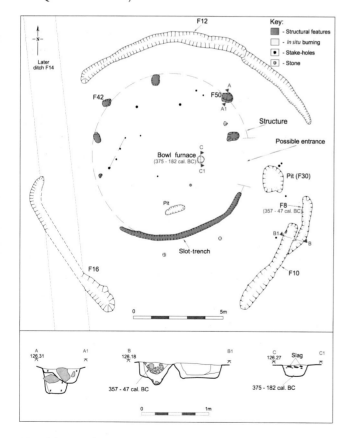

Fig. 13.3—Knockcommane: excavated structure.

Knockcommane settlement and iron production site

The Knockcommane structure was enclosed by a circular ditch and was defined by a curvilinear slot-trench and a semicircular arrangement of six post-holes (Fig. 13.3). The slot-trench, which was the foundation for the southern wall, was 6.8m long, 0.28m wide and 0.06–0.12m deep, and probably held plank walling. The northern wall of the structure may have been composed of wattle screens set between posts that ranged from 0.21m to 0.59m in diameter. Analysis of charcoal from two of the post-holes indicated that oak was used for the posts, while the screens were more than likely constructed mainly of hazel. The roof of this structure was probably constructed of sod or thatch and, since there was no evidence for an internal roof-support, it is likely that the roof was supported by the external wall. The entrance was in the eastern wall and measured 2.5m across. No traces of a floor surface or a hearth survived within the house, but internal furnishings were indicated by a line of stake-holes, 2m in length, at the western side of the structure. Also within the structure were a bowl furnace, which had been used for the production of iron, and a pit.

The enclosure around this structure was formed by a segmented ditch, the breaks in which indicate three possible entrance points (at the east, north-west and south). The ditch ranged from 0.35m to 0.7m in width and from 0.04m to 0.3m in depth and appeared to have silted up naturally. Hazel charcoal from the southern ditch segment was radiocarbon-dated to 357–47 cal. BC (UB-7842), indicating that this site dates from the early Iron Age.

The bowl furnace within the Knockcommane structure measured 0.42m in diameter and 0.15m in depth; it had steep sides and a flat base. Bowl furnaces such as this were used for reducing iron ore to iron. The ore was added to hot charcoal, which was then sealed by a clay dome. A constant temperature of 1100–1200°C was needed to consolidate the iron and form a bloom (O'Kelly 1989, 261). This temperature would have been maintained by pumping air into the furnace by means of a bellows inserted into a small hole towards its base. The furnace would then have been broken up and the bloom removed from the slag residue (*ibid.*) (the fragments from the bowl furnace at Knockcommane were found discarded in one of the enclosing ditch segments). The bloom was then hammered to weld the iron particles together and remove any remaining impurities (Raftery 1994, 149). Charcoal from the fill of the Knockcommane furnace was mostly identified as oak, but hazel was also present. Oak charcoal (sapwood) radiocarbon-dated this feature to 375–182 cal. BC (UB-7239), which is roughly contemporary with the date obtained for the enclosing ditch. Analysis of the slag recovered from the fill of that ditch indicated

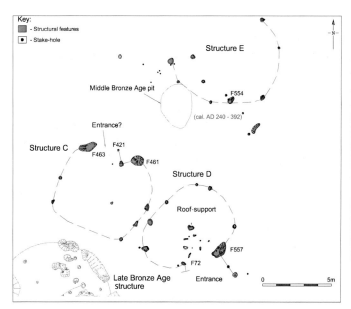

Fig. 13.4—Ballydrehid: excavated structures.

Fig. 13.5—Brackbaun: trough, hearth and stockpile of stone at *fulacht fiadh* (site 4705.1).

that only one smelt had taken place, perhaps representing an experimental attempt to produce iron (Photos-Jones 2007). O'Kelly (1989, 259) suggested that the slow spread of the use of iron was due to the difficulty of 'extracting the metal from its ores', and, indeed, experimental iron smelts within bowl furnaces have proved very inefficient, producing only small quantities of workable iron (Fairburn 2006).

Ballydrehid settlement site
The foundations of the three Ballydrehid structures were very different from that of the Knockcommane structure. They were defined by irregularly set post-holes (ranging from 0.1m to 0.31m in diameter and up to 0.28m in depth), with small slot-trenches (0.76–1.28m long by 0.49–0.7m wide and up to 0.26m deep) at the entrance to two of the structures (Fig. 13.4). Charcoal from one of the post-holes was almost exclusively oak, with some pomaceous fruitwood also identified, and it is likely that oak was used for the larger posts. Oak charcoal from one of the structures returned a date of cal. AD 240–392 (UB-7221), much later than the Knockcommane site. Given the proximity of the three structures at Ballydrehid, it is likely that they were broadly contemporary. Only one of the structures (structure D) had evidence for a central internal roof-support, and this suggests that the roofs of the other two structures probably rested on the walls. There was no clear preference for the location of the entrance to these structures, which had north-, north-west- and south-east-facing entrances that varied from 1.4m to 2.1m in width. Structure D may have had a porch, the remains of

which were indicated by two post-holes set outside the entrance. There was no evidence for a floor surface or hearth within any of these structures, but the absence of these features was probably due to later truncation on site.

Brackbaun fulacht fiadh
The *fulacht fiadh* at Brackbaun was on the eastern bank of a small tributary of the River Funshion and there was evidence for two phases of activity, separated by an episode of flooding. The first phase was represented by a large subrectangular trough located adjacent to the stream. The stone-lined trough was only partially exposed within the area of excavation but was at least 2.8m long by 1.5m wide and 0.6m deep. Two hearths lay adjacent to the trough, and a stockpile of stone, which appeared to have been gathered from the nearby stream, lay to the north (Fig. 13.5). The burnt mound, which sealed the aforementioned features, measured 17.5m by 12m and had a maximum depth of 0.35m. An episode of flooding was indicated by alluvial deposits that sealed the burnt mound material. These deposits were truncated by a trough, which represented a second phase of activity. That trough was only partially exposed within the limits of excavation but measured *c.* 1.6m wide and 0.5m deep. Hazel charcoal from the primary fill was radiocarbon-dated to 789–425 cal. BC (UB-7238). A second phase of flooding signalled the end of use of the site.

Finds
Artefacts recovered from the Iron Age settlement sites include a stone punch (Fig. 13.6), a possible pin-beater (Fig. 13.7) and a blue glass bead from Knockcommane, as well as a possible hammerstone from Brackbaun (site 4602A.3). The glass bead

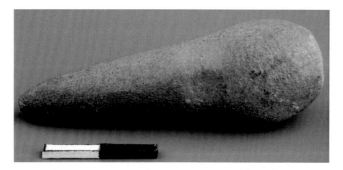

Fig. 13.6—Knockcommane: stone punch.

Fig. 13.7—Knockcommane: pin-beater.

was probably part of a necklace, but the other items recovered from Knockcommane indicate that craft activities such as weaving were being carried out. The hammerstone from Brackbaun was a more versatile implement that could have been used for a variety of tasks, such as producing stone tools or grinding grain.

Discussion
All of the structural remains identified along the scheme were circular or subcircular in plan and varied from 6m to 8.5m in diameter. These floor plans indicate a continuity of building style from the Bronze Age and also compare well with previously excavated examples of Iron Age buildings in Ireland and Britain, the majority of which are circular and typically range from 6m to 7m in diameter.

The Knockcommane structure, with its clear distinction between the northern post-built wall and the southern slot-trench foundation, differs from most recorded Iron Age buildings, which were typically defined by one or other of these foundation types, with additional post-holes occasionally representing roof-supports (see Murray 2000; Fegan 2006; Lennon 2002; Frazer 2007). The small enclosure (15m in diameter) around the Knockcommane structure is also

unusual, and the best Irish comparison comes from Ballycullen (site 3), Co. Dublin, where a post-built house was enclosed within a similarly sized gully (14.5m in diameter) (Larsson 2004; this volume). Another good structural parallel comes from an Iron Age settlement in Britain at Mingies Ditch, Oxfordshire, where four subcircular houses, defined by post-holes, were bounded by discontinuous curving gullies and there was evidence that iron-working was being carried out on a small scale (Allen and Robinson 1993, 20–69; Salter 1993).

The evidence for early iron production at Knockcommane is undoubtedly an important discovery and is part of a growing body of evidence for metal production sites in the earlier stages of the Iron Age. Among the sites recorded to date is Rossan, Co. Meath, where a bowl furnace and two smithing hearths produced radiocarbon dates ranging from 820–780 cal. BC to 370–50 cal. BC (Murphy 2004). Bowl furnaces dating from the Iron Age have also been identified at Marshes Upper, Co. Louth, Kinnegad, Co. Westmeath, and Mell, Co. Louth (Murphy 2003; Mossop 2004; McQuade 2005). A particularly large Iron Age industrial site excavated at Derrinsallagh, Co. Laois, had 42 furnaces and two hut structures (NRA 2006). These huts may have been workshops, as Crew and Rehren (2002) point out that some form of shelter would have been necessary to keep raw materials and metallurgical structures dry. Given the limited nature of the iron production activity at Knockcommane, however, it is unlikely that the structure at that site was specifically constructed as a workshop, but it may have functioned as such after it went out of use as a domestic building.

The three unenclosed subcircular post-built structures at Ballydrehid were less unusual in an Irish context than the Knockcommane structure. With diameters of between 6m and 7m, they were similar in size and plan to Iron Age structures excavated at Ballynagran, Co. Wicklow, Claristown, Co. Meath, and Cloongownagh, Co. Roscommon (Frazer 2007; Russell 2003; Lennon 2002). Their closest parallel, however, was a post-built structure from Muckridge, Co. Cork, which was also 6m in diameter and of comparable date (cal. AD 20–350, 2-sigma calibration; Noonan 2004).

Despite their differences in design, the structures on each of these sites were probably built from similar materials. The evidence indicates a preference for oak, which was a strong and durable wood, ideal for construction. Oak also appears to have been used for the Iron Age structures excavated at Maheraboy, Co. Sligo, and Ballinaspig More, Co. Cork, as well as at Mingies Ditch (Danaher 2007, 135, 204; Allen and Robinson 1993, 117).

The animal bones recovered during the excavations were

too fragmentary to be identified, either to species or anatomical element. However, they probably represent food waste, further evidence for which comes from the plant remains recovered.. These include a barley grain and indeterminate cereal grains from cooking pits at Killemly and Shanballyduff, and possible wheat and barley grains from the burnt spread at Brackbaun (site 4602A.3).

The *fulacht fiadh* at Brackbaun was one of twelve such sites identified along the scheme but was the only example with evidence for use during the Iron Age (see McQuade *et al.* 2009). The stockpile of stone uncovered on this site was an unusual feature not often recorded or preserved at such sites.

Burial evidence

Four Iron Age burial sites were identified along the road scheme (Fig. 13.2). Three of these were barrows and were situated in the townlands of Marlhill (site 148.1), Knockgraffon (site 143.3) and Knockcommane (site 4700.1A). An unenclosed cremation burial pit was identified in Knockgraffon (site 133.1).

Marlhill ring-barrow

The ring-barrow at Marlhill measured 4m in internal diameter and had a concave ditch that measured 1.9m in maximum width and 1.3m in maximum depth (Figs 13.8 and 13.9). A break in the ditch defined a south-facing entrance,

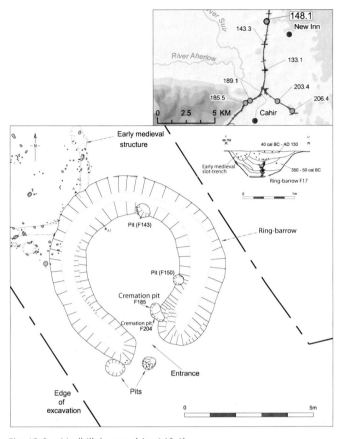

Fig. 13.8—Marlhill: barrow (site 148.1).

Fig. 13.9—Marlhill: barrow.

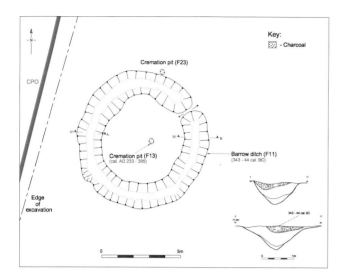

Fig. 13.10—Knockgraffon: barrow (site 143.3).

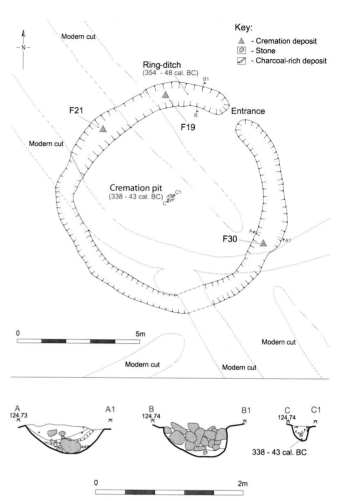

Fig. 13.11—Knockcommane: barrow (site 4700.1A).

1.3m wide. The upper fills of the ditch were charcoal-rich and contained cremated bone, which was evenly dispersed throughout the fills. Analysis of the cremated bone from both fills identified individuals aged 18–44 years, but the sex could not be ascertained. One of these fills was radiocarbon-dated by pomaceous fruitwood charcoal to 40 BC–AD 130. The bone from each deposit was white and very fragmented, indicating that it had been exposed to high temperatures. Two pits just inside the entrance of the ring-barrow and partially truncating the upper fills of the ditch also contained small amounts of cremated bone. Although the bone from both pits was identified as human, it was only possible to ascertain the age of one individual, who was between eighteen and 44 years of age at the time of death.

Knockgraffon ring-barrow
The ring-barrow at Knockgraffon was slightly larger than the Marlhill example, measuring 5.4m in internal diameter (Fig. 13.10). It had a V-shaped ditch, 2.1m in maximum width and 0.7m in maximum depth. A break in the ditch defined a north-east-facing entrance, 0.2m wide. A small amount of cremated bone was identified in the secondary fill of the ditch but, as at the Marlhill ring-barrow, the majority of the cremated bone was retrieved from the upper fill of the ditch and had been dispersed evenly throughout the fill. Analysis of the cremated bone from the upper fill identified the remains of at least one adult over 35 years of age. Hazel charcoal from this deposit was radiocarbon-dated to 343–44 BC (UB-7169). The cremated bone from the secondary fill was too fragmented to identify.

A small pit (0.3m in diameter), centrally located within the barrow, also contained deposits of cremated bone, which were too fragmented to identify to species or skeletal element but in all likelihood are human. Hazel charcoal from this fill yielded a radiocarbon date of AD 233–395 (UB-7170). A second small cremation burial pit (0.32m in diameter) was identified immediately to the north of the barrow and contained cremated remains, which were identified as those of an adult, possibly a female, aged between 34 and 64 years.

Knockcommane barrow
Knockcommane was the largest of the three barrows, with an internal diameter of 7m (Figs 13.11 and 13.12). The concave ditch measured 1.2m in maximum width and 0.48m in maximum depth. Three charcoal-rich deposits containing small amounts of cremated bone were identified in discrete locations around the ditch. Only two of these deposits could be identified as human and only one identified to age—an

Fig. 13.12—Knockcommane: ring-ditch.

individual aged less than eighteen years. Cremated bone from one of the deposits was radiocarbon-dated to 354–48 BC (UB-7514).

As at the ring-barrow at Knockgraffon, a small (0.3m in diameter) cremation burial pit was situated centrally within the barrow. It contained a small amount of cremated bone, which was identified as deriving from a female aged 18–44 years. A fragment of the cremated bone was radiocarbon-dated to 338–43 BC (UB-7515).

Knockgraffon cremation burial pit
The unenclosed burial pit at Knockgraffon (site 133.1) was situated among a cluster of pits. It measured 0.49m in maximum diameter and 0.15m in depth and contained a small amount of cremated bone, identified as that of an adult aged between 35 and 64 years at the time of death. A sample of ash charcoal from the cremation deposit was radiocarbon-dated to AD 40–250 (Beta-220335).

Fig. 13.13—Knockcommane: blue glass beads.

Fig. 13.14—Marlhill: blue glass beads and fragments of fused glass.

Finds

Blue glass beads, copper-alloy mounts, iron nails and ferrous slag were identified in association with the cremation deposits. At Knockcommane, nine blue glass beads (Fig. 13.13) and two pieces of fused glass were found in the upper fill of the ditch. Seven blue glass beads and fragments of fused glass were recovered from the upper fills of the ditch at Marlhill (Fig. 13.14), and two tiny blue glass beads were recovered from the upper fill of the ditch at Knockgraffon. Blue glass beads are often found in Iron Age barrows such as Ballydavis, Co. Laois, or Grannagh, Co. Galway (Keeley 1996; Rynne 1972), and were presumably personal ornaments. Other items of personal ornament included two copper-alloy mounts and a fragment of decorative inlay recovered from the Marlhill barrow. Iron nail shanks retrieved from the upper fills of the ditches at Marlhill and Knockgraffon may have been related to a pyre superstructure or a coffin stretcher (Tiernan McGarry, pers. comm.). Iron nails have been recovered from other ring-barrows, such as Ballydavis, Rathdoney Beg, Co. Sligo, and Ferns Lower, Co. Wexford (Keeley 1996; Mount 1995; O'Sullivan 1994). Iron slag was identified at the Knockgraffon barrow and may indicate that iron production was being carried out in the vicinity.

Discussion

The barrows at Marlhill and Knockgraffon had evidence for a central mound and outer encircling bank, indicating that they were ring-barrows, which are a common Iron Age burial site type known from sites such as Grannagh, Co. Galway, and Rathdooney, Co. Sligo (Rynne 1972; Mount 1995; Mount, this volume). They also compare closely with a number of recently excavated examples, such as sites 2–4 at Ballydavis, Co. Laois, Ferns Lower, Co. Wexford, and Ballybronoge, Co. Limerick (Keeley 1996; Ryan 2000; Eogan and Finn 2000; Eogan, this volume). The Knockcommane barrow was different in that it contained evidence for an encircling bank but no inner mound, suggesting that it could be an embanked ring-ditch (see Newman 1997, 157) rather than a ring-barrow. Examples of this site type are Oran Beg, Co. Galway, and Ballybronoge, Co. Limerick (Rynne 1970; Eogan and Finn 2000; Eogan, this volume). The positioning of the entrances into the barrows may be arbitrary but it could also be possible that the location of the entrance was influenced by the location of contemporary settlement sites or perhaps the rising sun.

Although barrows were the most common form of burial monument during the Iron Age, unenclosed burial sites similar to that at Knockgraffon are recorded at Manusmore, AR100 and AR102, Co. Clare (Hull 2006a; 2006b).

The burial rite at all of the sites was cremation, and the amount of bone from each site was quite small, varying from 0.8g to 518g, indicating that the cremation deposits were representative or 'token burials'. Most of the bone from each cremation deposit was highly fragmented, which may suggest that it was manually crushed prior to deposition. The majority of the burial deposits were identified as adult, with subadult remains at Marlhill and Knockcommane. Only two adults could be sexed (the central burial pit at Knockcommane and the unenclosed burial pit at Knockgraffon) and both of these were female. While all the deposits were of a 'token' nature, the manner in which they were deposited varied. At both Marlhill and Knockgraffon the cremated bone was dispersed evenly throughout the upper ditch fills, and the charcoal-rich nature of these fills suggests that the bone was deposited directly from a cremation pyre. At Knockcommane the cremated bone was deposited in three discrete locations around the ditch. Central burial pits were identified at both Knockcommane and Knockgraffon, while at Marlhill two cremation burial pits were found just inside the entrance of the barrow. The ring-barrow at Knockgraffon also had an external associated cremation burial pit.

Radiocarbon-dating evidence from Knockgraffon and Marlhill suggests that they were used over a prolonged period during the Iron Age. There is also evidence to suggest that the ring-barrow at Marlhill was visible over several hundred years or that its position was remembered in folk history, as the site was resettled in the medieval period and reused for burial (see McQuade *et al.* 2009).

Conclusions

The excavation of these sites has contributed a significant amount of information to what was known previously of Iron Age activity in the area. Nevertheless, there is a marked decrease in settlement and burial activity in the Iron Age in comparison to the evidence uncovered along the scheme for the Bronze Age (*ibid.*). Despite this, the evidence suggests that there was an established Iron Age community in the area, focused on the fertile areas around the River Suir and further south around the Funshion River.

Acknowledgements

The specialist analyses were completed by Jonny Geber (human and animal bone), Lorna O'Donnell (charcoal and wood identifications) and Sara Halwas (plant remains), and finds reports were prepared by Siobhan Scully. Full accounts of the specialist analyses can be found in the monograph on the archaeological excavations undertaken along the N8 Cashel to Mitchelstown road improvement scheme (McQuade *et al.* 2009).

Table 13.1—Radiocarbon dating for Iron Age sites excavated along the N8 road improvement scheme.

Townland	Site	NGR	Site description	^{14}C (2–sigma calibration range)
Brackbaun, Co. Limerick	4705.1 (E2306)	E 188384 N 116647	*Fulacht fiadh*	789–425 BC (UB-7238)
Knockcommane, Co. Limerick	4700.1B (E2342)	E187809 N116229	Settlement: enclosed circular structure with associated bowl furnace	375–182 BC (UB-7239), 357–47 BC (UB-7842)
Knockcommane, Co. Limerick	4700.1A (E2341)	E187898 N116311	Burial: embanked ring-ditch	354–48 BC (UB-7514), 338–43 BC (UB-7515)
Marlhill, Co. Tipperary	148.1 (E2124)	E206093 N133230	Burial: ring-barrow	350–50 BC (Beta-231089), 40 BC–AD 130 (Beta-232706)
Knockgraffon, Co. Tipperary	143.3 (E2272)	E205941 N131262	Burial: ring-barrow	343–44 BC (UB-7169), AD 233–395 (UB-7170)
Ballylegan, Co. Tipperary	206.4 (E2265)	E208320 N125600	Settlement: hearth	192–4 BC (UB-7211)
Killemly, Co. Tipperary	203.4 (E2126)	E207063 N126422	Settlement: pits and post-holes	190 BC–AD 20 (Beta-221187)
Brackbaun, Co. Limerick	4602A.3 (E2340)	E188634 N117000	Settlement: burnt spread	166 BC–AD 46 (UB-7513)
Shanballyduff, Co. Tipperary	169.2 (E2300)	E206807 N137442	Settlement: hearth, pits and associated features	160 BC–AD 51 (UB-7235)
Caherabbey Lower, Co. Tipperary	189.1 (E2266)	E204909 N126606	Charcoal production pit	AD 235–393 (UB-7385)
Ballydrehid, Co. Tipperary	185.5 (E2267)	E204290 N126280	Settlement: three circular structures and associated features	AD 240–392 (UB-7221)
Knockgraffon, Co. Tipperary	133.1 (E2270)	E205845 N130241	Burial: cremation pit	AD 40–250 (Beta-220335)

Table 13.2—Finds catalogue (by Siobhan Scully). D = diameter, DP = diameter of perforation, L = length, T = thickness, W = width.

Glass beads

Find	Type	Townland	Site	Description
E2124:9	Bead	Marlhill	148.1	Blue. Globular. Straight perforation. D 4.5mm. T 2.7mm. DP 0.7mm.
E2124:10	Bead	Marlhill	148.1	Blue. Annular. Straight perforation. D 3.7mm. T 1.6mm. DP 1.2mm.
E2124:11	Bead	Marlhill	148.1	Blue. Globular. Straight perforation. D 3.7mm. T 1.9mm. DP 0.9mm.
E2124:12	Bead	Marlhill	148.1	Blue. Annular. Straight perforation. D 3.6mm. T 1.7mm. DP 1mm.
E2124:13	Bead	Marlhill	148.1	Blue. Globular. Straight perforation. D 3.4mm. T 1.7mm. DP 0.8mm.
E2124:14	Bead	Marlhill	148.1	Blue. Globular. Straight perforation. D 2.8mm. T 1.8mm. DP 0.7mm.
E2124:15	Bead	Marlhill	148.1	Blue. Barrel-shaped. Straight perforation. D 2.5mm. T 2mm. DP 0.9mm.
E2124:22	Bead	Marlhill	148.1	Blue. Globular. Straight perforation. D 2.9mm. T 1.9mm. DP 0.6mm.
E2124:23	Bead	Marlhill	148.1	Blue. Barrel-shaped. Straight perforation. D 2.3mm. T 1.7mm. DP 0.7mm.
E2124:24	Bead	Marlhill	148.1	Blue. Globular. Straight perforation. D 2.4mm. T 1.7mm. DP 1mm.
E2124:31	Bead	Marlhill	148.1	Partial bead. Clear. Annular. Dull surface covered in glass corrosion. D 6mm. T 2.6mm.
E2272:1	Bead	Knockgraffon	143.2	Blue. Annular. Straight perforation. D 4.2mm. T 1.9mm. DP 2mm.
E2272:2	Bead	Knockgraffon	143.2	Green. Globular. Straight perforation. D 4.5mm. T 2.8mm. DP 2mm.
E2341:1	Bead	Knockcommane	4700.1a	Blue. Globular. Straight perforation. Surface pitted. Circumference not perfectly circular. D 8.5mm. T 5.5mm. DP 2.1mm.
E2341:2 (a)	Bead	Knockcommane	4700.1a	Blue. Globular. Straight perforation. D 5mm. T 4mm. DP 1.4mm.
E2341:2 (b)	Bead	Knockcommane	4700.1a	Blue. Annular. Straight perforation. D 4.9mm. T 2.2mm.
E2341:2 (c)	Bead	Knockcommane	4700.1a	Blue. Annular. Straight perforation. D 4.9mm. T 2.2mm.
E2341:2 (d)	Bead	Knockcommane	4700.1a	Blue. Annular. Straight perforation. D 4.9mm. T 2.2mm.
E2341:2 (e)	Bead	Knockcommane	4700.1a	Blue. Globular. Straight perforation. D 5.9mm. T 3.7mm.

Table 13.2 (cont.)—Finds catalogue (by Siobhan Scully). D = diameter, DP = diameter of perforation, L = length, T = thickness, W = width.

Find	Type	Townland	Site	Description
E2341:2 (f)	Bead	Knockcommane	4700.1a	Blue. Annular. Straight perforation. D 4.9mm. T 2.2mm. DP 0.9mm.
E2341:2 (g)	Bead	Knockcommane	4700.1a	Blue. Globular. Straight perforation. D 4.4mm. T 2.5mm. DP 1.5mm.
E2341:2 (h)	Bead	Knockcommane	4700.1a	Blue. Globular. Straight perforation. D 4.4mm. T 2.5mm. DP 1.5mm.
E2341:2 (i)	Bead	Knockcommane	4700.1B	Blue. Globular. Straight perforation. D 4.4mm. T 2.5mm. DP 1.5mm.
E2341:2 (j–k)	Fused glass	Knockcommane	4700.1A	Blue. Two small lumps. (1) 10.5mm by 8mm by 6mm. (2) 8mm by 6mm by 4.5mm.
E2342:3	Bead	Knockcommane	4700.1B	Green. Barrel-shaped. Straight perforation. Surface smooth and shiny. D 7.2mm. T 5.6mm. DP 2.2mm.
E2124:16	Fused glass	Marlhill	148.1	Blue. Globular head. L 7.3mm. D 3.4mm.
E2124:17	Fused glass	Marlhill	148.1	Blue. Vesicular lump, 15.5mm by 8mm by 5.6mm.
E2124:18	Fused glass	Marlhill	148.1	Blue. Vesicular lump, 8.2mm by 6.4mm by 5.4mm.
E2124:19	Fused glass	Marlhill	148.1	Blue. Sphere. D 2.9mm.

Metal finds

Find	Type	Site name	Site	Description
E2124:1	Ferrous nail	Marlhill	148.1	Shank. Rectangular in section. L 24mm. W 6mm. T 4.5mm.
E2124:2	Ferrous nail	Marlhill	148.1	Shank. Square in section. L 17mm. W 4mm. T 4mm.
E2124:3	Ferrous nail	Marlhill	148.1	Shank. Square in section. L 7mm. W 3.5mm. T 3.5mm.
E2124:4	Ferrous nail	Marlhill	148.1	Shank. L 23mm. W 6mm. T 6mm.
E2124:5	Ferrous nail	Marlhill	148.1	Shank of small nail or tack. Circular in section. L 13mm. D 1.5mm.
E2124:6	Mount	Marlhill	148.1	Possible mount. Six small pieces of copper-alloy sheet metal. Original form uncertain. (1) 12.5mm by 11.5mm by 1.5mm. (2) 10mm by 5.5mm by 4.8mm. (3) 8mm by 5.5mm by 2.5mm. (4) 5mm by 3.5mm by 0.5mm. (5) 5mm by 3mm by 0.5mm. (6) 4mm by 3mm by 0.5mm.

Table 13.2 (cont.)—Finds catalogue (by Siobhan Scully). D = diameter, DP = diameter of perforation, L = length, T = thickness, W = width.

Find	Type	Townland	Site	Description
E2124:7	Mount	Marlhill	148.1	Possible head of tack or mount. Small square piece of copper alloy. Has iron corrosion on one side. L 2.5mm. W 2.5mm. T 3mm.
E2124:8	Possible decorative inlay	Marlhill	148.1	Small copper-alloy cube, 2mm by 2mm by 2mm.
E2124:26	Ferrous nail	Marlhill	148.1	Shank. Rectangular in section. L 41mm. W 5mm. T 2.5mm.
E2124:31	Ferrous nail	Marlhill	148.1	Shank. L 34mm. W 3.5mm. T 2mm.
E2272:3	Ferrous nail	Knockgraffon	143.3	Shank. Rectangular in section. L 19mm. W 7.5mm. T 7mm.
E2272:4	Ferrous nail	Knockgraffon	143.3	Shank. Rectangular in section. L 29mm. W 9.5mm. T 8.5mm.

Stone finds

Find	Type	Site	Description
E2342:2	Possible pin-beater	4700.1B	Double-ended. Smooth surface. L 60mm. W 10.5mm. T 7mm.
E2340:1	Possible hammerstone	4602A.3	Pinkish-grey stone. Ovoid. Flattened at point of impact. 98mm by 87mm by 62mm.
E2342:1	Possible punch	F31	Fine-grained stone. Expanded at one end, tapering to a blunt point at the other. The widened end has a flattened surface which shows signs of wear. L 56.5mm. T 8–18mm.

Bibliography

Allen, T.G. and Robinson, M.A. 1993 *The prehistoric landscape and Iron Age enclosed settlement at Mingies Ditch, Hardwick-with-Yelford, Oxfordshire.* Oxford.

Cleary, K. 2007 The prehistoric landscape. In M. Doody (ed.), *Excavations at Curraghatoor, Co. Tipperary,* 39–51. Cork.

Crew, P. and Rehren, T. 2002 High-temperature workshop residues from Tara: iron, bronze and glass. In H. Roche, 'Excavations at Ráith na Ríg, Tara, Co. Meath, 1997'. *Discovery Programme Reports* **6**, 83–102.

Danaher, E. 2004 Ballinaspig More 5. *Excavations 2002,* 55–6. Bray.

Danaher, E. 2007 *Monumental beginnings: the archaeology of the N4 Sligo inner relief road.* Dublin.

Eogan, J. and Delany, F. 2000 New light on late prehistoric ritual and burial in County Limerick. *Archaeology Ireland* **14** (1), 8–10.

Eogan, J. and Finn, D. 2000 Ballybronoge South, Co. Limerick. *Excavations 1999,* 158–9. Bray.

Fairburn, N. 2006 Appendix 4: Assessment of industrial residues from excavations at Monganstown 1. In J. Lehane and P. Johnston, 'Final report, Monganstown 1. N6 Kinnegad to Kilbeggan, Co. Westmeath'. Unpublished excavation report by Eachtra Archaeological Projects for Westmeath County Council.

Fegan, G. 2006 Ballydavis. *Excavations 2003,* 284–5. Bray.

Frazer, W.O. 2007 Archaeological excavation Areas 4–11, Ballynagran Landfill, Coolbeg townland, Co. Wicklow, licence no: 06E0552. Unpublished report for Margaret Gowen and Co.

Hull, G. 2006a 04E0187, N18 Ennis bypass and N85 western relief, Site AR100, Manusmore, Clare. Unpublished report for TVAS Ireland.

Hull, G. 2006b 04E0189, N18 Ennis bypass, Site AR102, Manusmore, Co. Clare. Unpublished report for TVAS Ireland.

Keeley, V.J. 1996 Ballydavis. *Excavations 1995,* 51–2. Bray.

Larsson, E. 2004 Site 1, Ballycullen, Oldcourt. *Excavations 2002,* 180. Bray.

Lennon, A.M. 2002 Cloongownagh. *Excavations 2000,* 290–1. Bray.

McQuade, M. 2005 Archaeological excavation of a multi-period prehistoric settlement at Waterunder, Mell, Co. Louth. *County Louth Archaeological and Historical Journal* **26**, 31–66.

McQuade, M., Molloy, B. and Moriarty, C. 2009 *In the shadow of the Galtees: archaeological excavations along the N8 Cashel to Mitchelstown road scheme.* Dublin.

Mossop, M. 2004 Marshes Upper, Dundalk. *Excavations 2002,* 379. Bray.

Mount, C. 1995 New research on Irish early Bronze Age cemeteries. In J. Waddell and E. Shee Twohig (eds), *Ireland in the Bronze Age,* 97–112. Dublin.

Mullins, G. 2007 Pagan or Christian? Excavation of a hilltop cemetery at Cross, Co. Galway. In J. O'Sullivan and M. Stanley (eds), *New routes to the past,* 101–10. Dublin.

Murphy, D. 2003 Kinnegad 2: M4 Kinnegad–Enfield–Kilbeggan motorway. Unpublished report by ACS Ltd on behalf of Westmeath County Council.

Murphy, D. 2004 Rossan: M4 Kinnegad–Enfield–Kilbeggan motorway. Unpublished report by ACS Ltd on behalf of Westmeath County Council.

Murray, C. 2000 Killoran 16, Co. Tipperary. *Excavations 1998,* 199–200. Bray.

Newman, C. 1997 *Tara: an archaeological survey.* Dublin.

Noonan, D. 2004 Muckridge, Co. Cork. Unpublished report prepared for Dúchas: the Heritage Service.

O'Brien, E. 2003 Burial practices in Ireland: first to seventh centuries AD. In J. Downes and A. Ritchie (eds), *Sea change: Orkney and northern Europe in the later Iron Age, AD 300–800,* 62–72. Balgavies.

O'Kelly, M.J. 1989 *Early Ireland: an introduction to Irish prehistory.* Cambridge.

O'Sullivan, M. 1994 Haynestown, Co. Louth. *Excavations 1993,* 57–8. Bray.

Photos-Jones, E. 2007 One smelt man: metallurgical waste characterisation from Site 47001b, Knockcommane, Co. Limerick. Specialist report by SASAA (Analytical Services for Art and Archaeology (Scotland) Ltd) for Margaret Gowen and Co. Ltd.

Raftery, B. 1994 *Pagan Celtic Ireland: the enigma of the Irish Iron Age.* London.

Russell, I. 2003 Claristown 2, Co. Meath. *Excavations 2001,* 288–9. Bray.

Ryan, F. 2000 Ferns Lower, Ferns. *Excavations 1999,* 302. Bray.

Rynne, E. 1970 Oran Beg ring-barrow. *Excavations 1970,* 10. Belfast.

Rynne, E. 1972 Grannagh. *Excavations 1971,* 14. Belfast.

Salter, C. 1993 Metalworking. In T.G. Allen and M.A. Robinson, *The prehistoric landscape and Iron Age enclosed settlement at Mingies Ditch, Hardwick-with-Yelford, Oxfordshire,* 77. Oxford.

14. Created and appropriated continuity at Rathdooney Beg, Co. Sligo
Charles Mount

Introduction

Throughout history, people have built, copied and added to monuments according to the needs of the day. These alterations, emulations and additions draw on the histories and mythologies of the old monuments and the places and landscapes in which they are situated and recreate them to suit a new narrative. Cooney (1994) has discussed how Neolithic tombs and other sacred places continued as focuses of activity long after the Neolithic. In time, these monuments and associated landscapes were transformed and took on a mythic quality. The mythic landscape provided a medium for symbolism and for the manipulation and transformation of the past. Bradley (1987) drew on the ideas of Bloch (1977) concerning the use of the past in the present and Hobsbawm's (1983) concept of the invention of tradition, where practices of a ritual or symbolic nature seek to inculcate values and norms that imply continuity with a suitable past. Bradley argued that the use of the ritual past is one way in which groups establish their own political positions and put these positions beyond challenge. The past becomes a resource in the hands of the living. Using this resource, an élite may legitimate its position through the promulgation of origin myths (see, for example, Byrne 2001, 48–69, for the origin myths of the kingship of Tara). Bradley suggested that the past was also reused through the strategic use of old monuments that were incorporated into a different landscape. He called the appropriation of meaning held in the mythology of old monuments the 'creation of continuity'.

These processes can be seen at work in the development of the monument complex at Rathdooney Beg, Co. Sligo, and at other Iron Age sites. Rathdooney Beg is important to this discussion because it provides securely dated examples of both the copying and the physical conjoining of monuments and, through comparison, allows these strategies to be identified at a number of other Irish sites. To the idea of created tradition, this essay adds the concept of appropriated continuity. Appropriated continuity is a complementary strategy intended to forge a physical link to a dominant social group through the creation of conjoined monuments. In the oral tradition, appropriated continuity is paralleled by the promulgation of false genealogies intended to justify the position of one group by claiming lineal descent from another (see Byrne 2001, 3).

In the south-east County Sligo townland of Rathdooney Beg (Fig. 14.1), the summit of a prominent drumlin ridge rises to 128.5m OD with panoramic views of much of County Sligo, including the great cairn of Miosgán Meadhbha on Knocknarea to the north and the passage tomb cemetery of Carrowkeel to the south-south-east. The ridge is visible for many miles from the north-west, west and south, and the landscape setting provides a perfect platform to display symbolic activities and landscape monuments to a dispersed audience. The excavation at the site at Rathdooney Beg was intended to obtain environmental and dating information with which to place a group of monuments, including two conjoined barrows, into a chronological and cultural context.[1] Rathdooney Beg is only the second pair of conjoined barrows to be investigated in Ireland (see Raftery 1939; Raftery and Inkster 1940) and the only conjoined barrows to be scientifically dated to the Iron Age. Work took place over two seasons in March–April 1994 and August–September 1995. Reports of the excavation have appeared on a number of occasions, including a preliminary report (Mount 1995a;

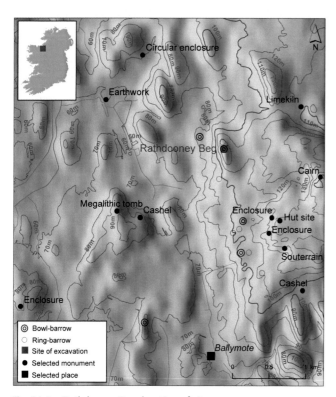

Fig. 14.1—Rathdooney Beg: location of site.

189

Fig. 14.2—Rathdooney Beg: aerial view of the monuments on the ridge, looking south (CUASI AVI 85.

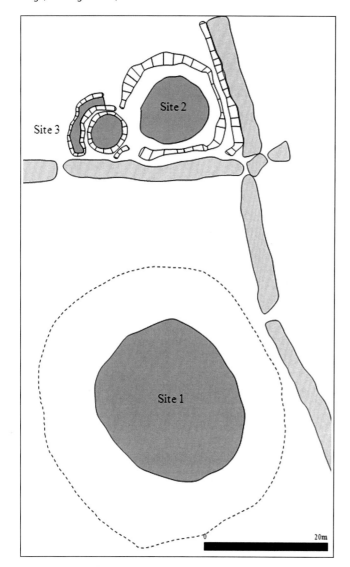

Fig. 14.3—Rathdooney Beg: plan of the monuments.

Fig. 14.4—Rathdooney Beg: view of the excavated section of the bowl-barrow, with the burnt old ground visible running into the section at right and the Neolithic mound visible in the background.

Fig. 14.5—Rathdooney Beg: ring-barrow during excavation, looking west.

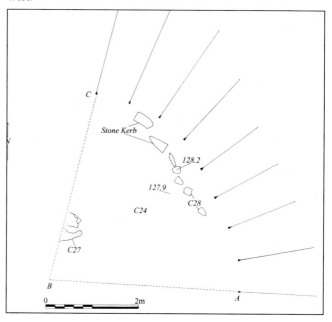

Fig. 14.6—Rathdooney Beg: plan of the excavated areas of the bowl-barrow.

1995b; 1996), a short illustrated article in *Archaeology Ireland* (Mount 1998) and a final report in the *Proceedings of the Prehistoric Society* (Mount 1999).

The monumental sequence at Rathdooney Beg

In the Neolithic, between 3930 and 3520 cal. BC, a large oval mound of earth, 6.1m high, with a basal diameter of 22m by 21m and enclosed by a wide and deep ditch, was constructed in a largely open area of grassland on the northern end of the ridge (Figs 14.2 and 14.3). This broad, conical mound was the sole monument on the ridge for more than 3,000 years.

During the period 380–120 cal. BC a funeral pyre was assembled and set alight on the old ground surface just 19m to the north of the Neolithic mound. The ridge-top was more open than in the Neolithic and the smoke from the pyre would have been widely visible. The cremation on the ridge-top may have been preceded by a range of funerary rituals of which no archaeological trace remains. Presumably, the deceased was removed from the place of death, prepared for the funeral and then carried to the top of the ridge, where the pyre was assembled. As the ridge-top was open grassland, the wood had to be collected; a wooden plank found in the ditch

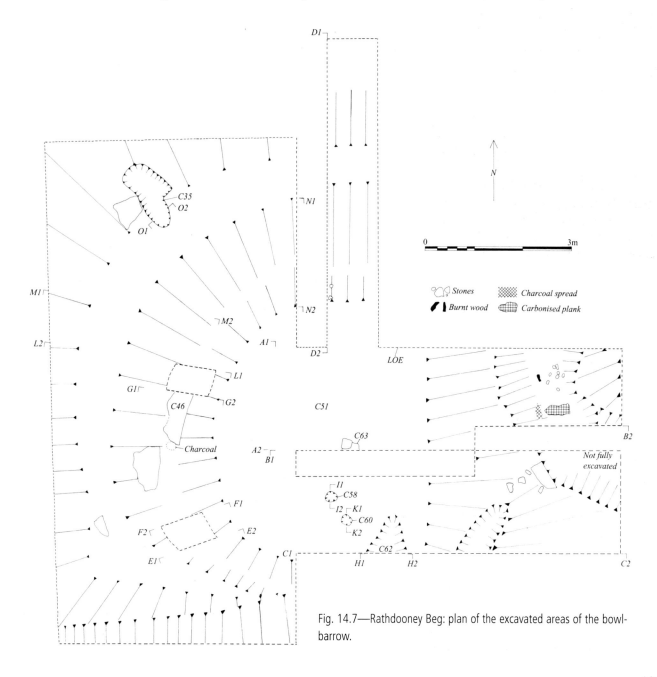

Fig. 14.7—Rathdooney Beg: plan of the excavated areas of the bowl-barrow.

Fig. 14.8—General location of the main sites mentioned in the text. (1) Rathdooney Beg, Co. Sligo. (2) Kiltierney, Co. Fermanagh. (3) Carrowjames, Co. Mayo. (4) Knockadoo-Brosna, Co. Roscommon. (5) Rathcroghan, Co. Roscommon. (6) Ardlow, Co. Cavan. (7) Slieve Breagh, Co. Meath. (8) Ardsallagh, Co. Meath. (9) Dunlever Glebe, Co. Meath. (10) Tara, Co. Meath. (11) Oranbeg, Co. Galway. (12) Lisnagloos, Co. Galway. (13) Grannagh, Co. Galway. (14) Ballydavis, Co. Laois. (15) Farneigh, Co. Tipperary. (16) Elton, Co. Limerick. (17) Cush, Co. Limerick. (18) Marlhill, Co. Tipperary. (19) Knockgraffon, Co. Tipperary.

(radiocarbon-dated to 380–120 cal. BC) was either part of the bier or part of a wooden structure that provided some of the pyre material.

After the cremation was complete, the pyre was cleared to one side, the area of a circular ditch was marked out and the burnt turves were dug from the top of the 2m-wide flat-bottomed ditch and stacked, burnt side up, into a low circular mound about 2m in diameter and 0.3m high. This turf stack probably covers a central cremation burial. An oval mound, 9.1m by 10.3m in basal diameter and 2.6m above the old ground surface, was then heaped up from the soil dug from the ditch and was retained by a small stone kerb, creating a bowl-

barrow (Figs 14.4 and 14.6). Fragments of unburnt human skull, rib and scapula were found in the base of the mound material and radiocarbon-dated to 370–50 cal. BC. The back of the skull had been cut with a sharp object and the body appears to have been deliberately disarticulated. The builders of the Iron Age barrow were careful that the new monument should be a scale copy of the Neolithic mound. The construction of the monument would have been visible throughout the local area. The funerary ritual and monument construction made an important statement about the identity and status of the individual or individuals buried and about the people who participated in the ceremony and built the barrow. They were commemorating a member of their community, but they did so in a way that looked back to a distant past that would have been known only through myth and legend.

Later, in the period 120 cal. BC–AD 80, the area to the west of the bowl-barrow appears to have been stripped of sod and a penannular U-shaped ditch, 1.6m wide at the top, enclosing a low oval mound 4.7m by 5.4m in diameter and 0.4–0.45m high above the old ground surface was constructed directly on its western side (Figs 14.5 and 14.7). An uncut section of ditch was left on the east side, where it faced the bowl-barrow. This was enclosed by an external bank, 1.7m wide and just 0.25m high above the old ground surface. The whole site has a maximum surviving diameter of 10.8m. This barrow was defined as a saucer-barrow in the excavation report (Mount 1999) and corresponds to what Newman (1997, 156–7) classifies as a ring-barrow. This essay will follow Newman's nomenclature. Three burial deposits were identified at this site. Two small pits in the southern part of the interior, 0.2m and 0.1m in diameter, were cut into the low mound. They contained charcoal and small unidentifiable fragments of cremated bone. The larger pit was radiocarbon-dated to 120 cal. BC–AD 80. In the western part of the base of the ditch, a deposit of cremated bone and charcoal associated with eleven iron artefacts, including nails, a riveted handle and an unburnt cattle tooth, were placed into the base of the ditch. The burial deposit was not covered at the time of deposition but became covered by the natural silting of the ditch. The iron objects appear to have been part of some wooden artefact that accompanied or contained the burial deposit when it was deposited in the ditch.

The barrows in context

Bowl-barrows are defined as having a relatively prominent circular mound enclosed by a fosse and sometimes an external bank (Newman 1997, 157). They are distributed throughout Ireland, with notable concentrations on the Hill of Tara, Co.

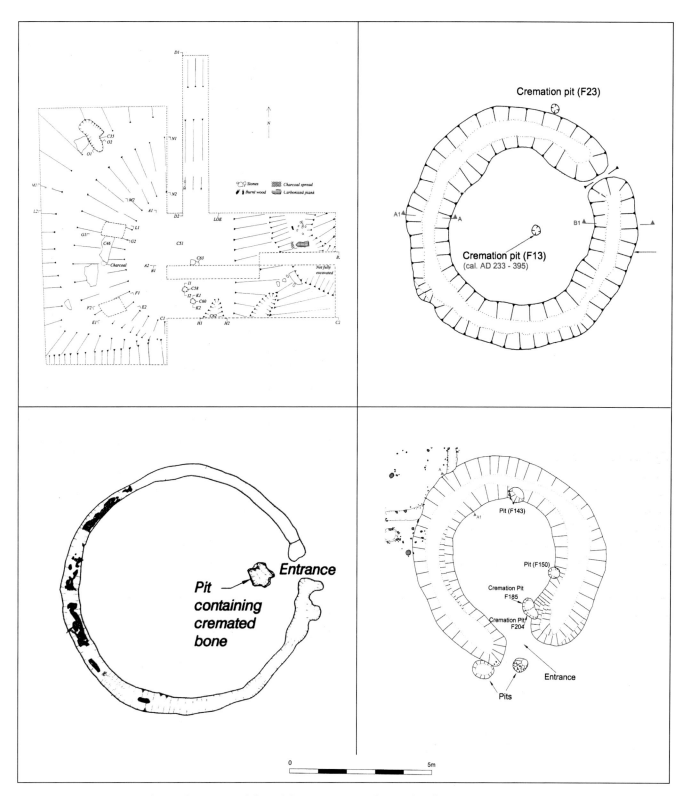

Fig. 14.9—Iron Age penannular ring-barrows. Top left: Rathdooney Beg; top right: Knockgraffon, Co. Tipperary; bottom left: Ardsallagh 2, Co. Meath; bottom right: Marlhill, Co. Tipperary.

Meath, where there are eleven broadly similar bowl-barrows (*ibid.*, 166). They also occur at Rathcroghan, Co. Roscommon, where four examples are referred to by Herity (1984, 129) as ditched tumuli (Fig. 14.8). To date, the only bowl-barrows that have been excavated and dated to the Iron Age are the two examples from Cush, Co. Limerick. These barrows are situated prominently on a west-facing slope of Slieve Reagh, with panoramic views over the Limerick plain to the west, and they were built at the site of an earlier Bronze Age barrow. Cush tumulus II, a wider and lower mound than Rathdooney Beg, is 13.7m in basal diameter and 1.8m high, and was also constructed on top of a pyre deposit with cremated bone and was enclosed by a ditch (Ó Ríordáin 1939–40, 137–9). It had a central pit containing cremated bone, charcoal and a burnt decorated bone plaque. Close by was tumulus III, which had a wider mound, 16.5m in diameter and 1.8m high above the old ground, and was enclosed by a ditch. This mound also overlay a layer of pyre material and cremated bone. The remaining excavated bowl-barrows at Carrowjames, Co. Mayo (Raftery 1939), and Carrowbeg North, Co. Galway (Willmott 1939), date from the Bronze Age. Newman (1997, 168) has suggested that, on the basis of these excavations, bowl-barrows date primarily from the middle Bronze Age. The Rathdooney Beg and Cush examples indicate that use of this monument type either continued into the Iron Age or was a monument tradition recreated in the Iron Age.

Ring-barrows are defined as low circular mounds built from the soil excavated from an enclosing fosse with an external bank (Newman 1997, 157). It is the presence of a mound and external bank that differentiates ring-barrows from ring-ditches, which have neither. They can be difficult to differentiate from ring-ditches without excavation, however. Some ring-ditches that have had their upper levels truncated through agricultural activities may originally have been ring-barrows. Like bowl-barrows, they are found throughout Ireland, with significant concentrations at Tara and Slieve Breagh, Co. Meath, and Rathcroghan, Co. Roscommon (Newman 1997; de Paor and Ó h-Eochaidhe 1956; Herity 1984). A number of excavated ring-ditches and ring-barrows date from the Neolithic and Bronze Age (see, for example, Waterman 1968; Ó Ríordáin 1948), so that Iron Age barrows cannot be definitively identified without excavation. The Rathdooney Beg ring-barrow has a penannular ditch. McGarry (2009, 416) noted that 40% of the excavated late Bronze Age to Iron Age ring-ditches in his survey had penannular ditches, and the entrances, as at Rathdooney Beg, were most often located on the eastern side. There are a number of similar ring-barrows that have also been dated to the Iron Age.

At Ardsallagh, Co. Meath, ring-ditch 1, radiocarbon-dated to 168 cal. BC–AD 52, is nearly contemporary with Rathdooney Beg (Clarke and Carlin 2006). This probable ring-barrow was 10.6m in diameter and consisted of a circular area enclosed by a penannular ditch with the opening at the east (Fig. 14.9). The central mound of this site appears to have been removed at a later date and the only internal burial was a pre-existing Bronze Age cremation pit. The primary fill of the ditch consisted of timber planks and the main fill contained a quantity of cremated bone and charcoal associated with an iron fragment, flint and chert. The wooden planks deposited in the ditch parallel the wood found in the ditch of the Rathdooney Beg bowl-barrow.

A similar Iron Age ring-barrow with deposits of cremated bone in the ditch has been excavated at Marlhill, Co. Tipperary, where the ditch also contained iron nails, fragments of bronze, glass fragments and a possible hone stone (McQuade *et al.* 2009, 166–8). At Knockgraffon, Co. Tipperary, the ditch contained two blue glass beads, two iron nails and two lumps of iron slag (*ibid.*, 170). At Grannagh, Co. Galway, four deposits of cremated bone were identified in the ditch, and at Oranbeg, Co. Galway, there were three deposits of cremated bone in the ditch, which also contained 80 glass beads, a bronze armlet and a bronze dumb-bell-shaped object (Raftery 1994, 189). Tumuli 4 and 8 at Carrowjames, Co. Galway, also date from the Iron Age and are discussed in detail below.

The possible use of a container for the burial in the ditch of the Rathdooney Beg ring-barrow may be paralleled by the central burial in ring-ditch 1 at the Ballydavis, Co. Laois, Iron Age barrow cemetery. The burial in this 16m-wide ring-ditch was contained in a cylindrical bronze box (Keeley 1999). Iron nails and other finds, including an iron knife, a bronze bracelet, a pin fragment, iron slag and crucible fragments as well as carbonised wood, were also found in the ditch of this site. Ring-ditches 3 and 4 had cremated bone and artefacts in the ditches too. The sequence at these sites suggests that after the primary burials were made in the central mounds the ditches were used to deposit additional secondary burials and artefacts. There are still very few published accounts of the Iron Age ring-barrows, but the emerging radiocarbon dating and stratigraphic succession at Rathdooney Beg may suggest that bowl-barrows are earlier in the Iron Age sequence and may have been replaced by ring-barrows as the period progressed.

The reuse of old sites in the Iron Age

Rathdooney Beg is one of a number of old landscape locations with prominent ancient monuments that were

Fig. 14.10—Conjoined barrows and earthworks. Left: Tara, Co. Meath; centre top: Rathdooney Beg, Co. Sligo; centre: Slieve Breagh, Co. Meath; centre bottom: Carrowjames, Co. Mayo; top right: Lismurtagh, Co. Roscommon; centre right: Knockadoo-Brosna, Co. Roscommon; bottom right: Kiltierney, Co. Fermanagh.

reused and recreated in the Iron Age. Cooney and Grogan (1994, 187) have drawn attention to the persistent reminder of the relevance of the past for understanding Iron Age developments and the deliberate location of Iron Age sites close to, within or surrounding existing monuments and landscapes already invested with significance. If we focus on barrows, we find that at Kiltierney, Co. Fermanagh, a Neolithic mound 20m in diameter and 1.5m high was remodelled into a barrow by the addition of an enclosing ditch in the Iron Age, and the dug material was used to heighten the mound and to seal cremations in pits (Foley 1988). Nineteen contiguous mounds averaging 3m in diameter and 1m in height were constructed next to the ditch on its external side, forming a sort of external bank, and a number of these covered cremations laid on the old ground surface (Fig. 14.10).

At Carrowjames, Co. Mayo, the construction of a barrow cemetery commenced in the Bronze Age with the construction of six bowl-barrows (sites 1–3, 6–7 and 9). Three

ring-barrows were added to the cemetery in the Iron Age (nos 4–5 and 8) and two of these were conjoined. At Cush, Co. Limerick, Iron Age bowl-barrows were located on the site of an early Bronze Age cemetery (Ó Ríordáin 1939–40). At Ardsallagh 2, Co. Meath, the location of an early Bronze Age flat cemetery was reused in the Iron Age with the addition of two ring-ditches (1 and 2). A third later ring-ditch (3) was placed next to the first two and its entrance faced the entrance to ring-ditch 1 (Clarke and Carlin 2006). It is also likely that some of the bowl- and ring-barrows at sites like Tara and Slieve Breagh, Co. Meath, and Rathcroghan, Co. Roscommon, were constructed and used during the Iron Age.

At Rathdooney Beg, a Neolithic monument that was over 3,000 years old and whose origins had probably entered the realms of mythology provided a medium for the manipulation and transformation of the past through the creation of a copy during the Iron Age. The reuse of old sites and ancient monuments in the Iron Age reflects more than simply a continuity of practice. It represents a conscious decision to use sites that would have had an established significance, mythological identity and landscape prominence. The occurrence of this reuse at a number of sites suggests an Iron Age preoccupation with forging links with the past, to draw on or recreate the past in order to support emerging social or political developments by creating a new continuity.

The construction of conjoined monuments

At Rathdooney Beg, the physical space of the Iron Age bowl-barrow monument was altered by the addition of a ring-barrow. Conjoined barrows are not characteristic of the Bronze Age, when burial took place either in single monuments, like Freestone Hill, or in a number of sizeable barrow cemeteries, like Mitchelstowndown West, Co. Limerick (Daly and Grogan 1993). The evidence now available indicates that conjoined barrows are mainly an Iron Age phenomenon that occurs at only a few significant locations. There are, for instance, no examples at Rathcroghan, Co. Roscommon (Herity 1984), or on the Curragh of Kildare (Ó Ríordáin 1950–1).

Conjoined barrows are known from a small number of sites, at the Hill of Tara, Slieve Breagh, Co. Meath, Carrowjames, Co. Mayo, Elton, Co. Limerick (Doody 2008, 124–6), and a handful of other sites (Fig. 14.10). At Carrowjames, Co. Mayo, barrow 5 was a ring-barrow with a mound (6m in diameter) and ditch (1.2m wide) but without an external bank. In the western part of the ditch, under a large limestone block, was a scattered cremation. Barrow 4, which was constructed partly over a Bronze Age pit burial, was later built onto the north-west side of barrow 5. It had a central low mound (8.7m in diameter) enclosed by a ditch (2.7–3.2m wide) and external bank. Within the mound were three scattered cremation deposits and two cremations in simple pits. Although there were no datable associations, Waddell (1990, 115) suggests that barrow 4 may be Iron Age.

The greatest concentration of conjoined barrows is found on the Hill of Tara, where they occur in five of the six main barrow groups (Newman 1997, 323–34; note that the sites are referred to as 'possible barrows', as none of the identifications has been confirmed through excavation). The Clóenfherta North group consists of two possible ring-barrows, four possible bowl-barrows and a possible barrow. The Clóenfherta South group consists of five possible bowl-barrows; the Ráith Gráinne group consists of two possible ring-barrows, a possible barrow and a possible ring-ditch; the Ráith na Senad group consists of a possible ring-barrow, a possible barrow and three possible ring-ditches; and the Ráith na Ríg group consists of two possible ring-ditches and a possible ring-barrow.

Elsewhere, the present writer has argued that three lineage groups can be identified among the early Bronze Age burials in the Mound of the Hostages at Tara (Mount, in press). The six main groups of barrows at Tara probably represent the continuation and elaboration of these lineage groups during the late Bronze Age and Iron Age. Cooney (2009, 379) has noted that, as the Tara barrow groups developed, lineages could be spatially and historically linked and these lineages could be seen at Tara to descend from remembered ancestors. The practice of physically conjoining a new barrow to an old one and encompassing old barrows into new monuments may have been intended to link lineages together or to emphasise an existing, a new or a falsely created lineal descent.

At Slieve Breagh, Co. Meath, there are two groups of conjoined barrows. The western group consists of seven ring-ditches with an eighth site just to the west. The eastern group consists of three ring-ditches conjoined with a pair of conjoined circular enclosures with internal banks and external ditches (de Paor and Ó h-Eochaidhe 1956).

Conjoined barrows are also known from sites like Lisnagloss, Co. Galway (McCaffrey 1955, 224), on the summit of an esker; Farneigh/Garraun, Co. Tipperary (Farrelly and O'Brien 2002, no. 155), on the top of a hill; Ardlow, Co. Cavan (O'Donovan 1995, no. 96), on the summit of a low drumlin; and at Dunlever Glebe, Co. Meath, where a cropmark ring-ditch cuts the outer two rings of a four-ringed cropmark ring-ditch (Moore 1987, no. 104).

There are other types of conjoined enclosures that bear comparison to Rathdooney Beg for which there is no independent dating evidence. On the Hill of Tara, within the Ráith na Ríg enclosure, are the conjoined enclosures of a multiphase monument known as the Forrad and Tech Cormaic (Newman 1997, 77–86). Three separate mounds, two of which are probably bowl-barrows, may have been constructed around a central flat-topped mound, or the mound could have been added in the next phase. The mounds were then incorporated into the bank of a large bowl-barrow, with the central flat-topped mound at its centre enclosed by an internal ditch and external bank. In the next phase, a second fosse and outer bank were constructed. Tech Cormaic was subsequently constructed on its south-eastern side, and the bank of Tech Cormaic was built over the outer bank of the Forrad and along the crest of the inner bank in an attempt to include both monuments in its circuit. Tech Cormaic is a circular enclosure with an internal bank and external fosse that has been interpreted as a ringfort.

At Rathcroghan, another conjoined earthwork (now

referred to as Dumha Selga) straddles the Lismurtagh/Carrowgarve townland boundary (FitzPatrick 2004, 64). The southern enclosure is a flattened or dished mound with a concave summit enclosed by an internal ditch and external bank 50m in diameter. The northern enclosure, which appears to have been built onto it, has an internal bank and external fosse 60m in diameter and is also interpreted as a ringfort. At Knockadoo-Brosna, Co. Roscommon, on the summit of a drumlin ridge, there is a large flat-topped mound (36.5m in basal diameter) enclosed by a ditch and external bank. On its western side, an oval enclosure (76m by 67m in internal diameter) enclosed by a bank has been constructed (Knox 1914).

Fig. 14.11—Rathdooney Beg: the excavation team.

Conclusion

The conjoining of barrows and other earthworks during and possibly after the Iron Age indicates that at times it was important to physically link a new monument to an existing one. This expressed a physical relationship between the new and old monument so that the new and old became one. In the case of barrows, this symbolically linked those commemorated by the later monument to the earlier one. The emergence of conjoined monuments and the Iron Age preoccupation with old sites and monuments are all related to the creation of continuity.

Emulating, reusing and recreating old monuments is characteristic of groups creating history to suit contemporary strategies. Building a barrow to resemble and emulate an ancient monument with associated mythology signals that a group is similar to or even descended from the mythological figures of old. Building a new monument that physically joins or encompasses another goes beyond emulation and represents the attempt to annex or appropriate the symbolic, familial or social associations of the earlier monument. The former

strategy looks to the formation of a new political or social order using the past as a frame of reference. The latter strategy is about establishing direct relationships within a political or social system and is connected with the creation of lineage and descent relationships. In lineal descent groups, conjoining monuments is a way of promoting a more distant relationship or supporting an entirely fictitious one and attempts to appropriate continuity with the earlier monument. This strategy, as one might expect, is most evident in the barrow groups at the 'royal site' of Tara, where the physical linking of one monument to another represents the creation and appropriation of élite lineages. The strategy of appropriating continuity is also evident at regional sites like Rathdooney Beg, Carrowjames and Slieve Breagh, where similar processes were at work.

Bibliography

Bloch, M. 1977 The past and present in the present. *Man* **12**, 278–92.

Bradley, R. 1987 Time regained: the creation of continuity. *Journal of the British Archaeological Association* **140**, 1–17.

Byrne, F.J. 2001 *Irish kings and high kings* (2nd edn). Dublin.

Clarke, L. and Carlin, N. 2006 Life and death in Ardsallagh. *Seanda* **1**, 16–18.

Cooney, G. 1994 Sacred and secular Neolithic landscapes in Ireland. In D.L. Carmichael, J. Hubert, B. Reeves and A. Schanche (eds), *Sacred sites, sacred places*, 32–43. London.

Cooney, G. 2009 Tracing lines across landscapes: corporality and history in later prehistoric Ireland. In G. Cooney, K. Becker, J. Coles, M. Ryan and S. Sievers (eds), *Relics of old decency: archaeological studies in later prehistory*, 375–88. Bray.

Cooney, G. and Grogan, E. 1994 *Irish prehistory: a social perspective.* Bray.

Daly, A. and Grogan, E. 1993 Excavations of four barrows in Mitchelstowndown West, Knocklong, Co. Limerick. *Discovery Programme Reports* **1**, 44–60.

de Paor, L. and Ó h-Eochaidhe, M. 1956 Unusual group of earthworks at Slieve Breagh, Co. Meath. *Journal of the Royal Society of Antiquaries of Ireland* **86**, 97–101.

Doody, M. 2008 The Ballyhoura Hills Project. *Discovery programme Reports* **7**. Bray.

Farrelly, J. and O'Brien, C. 2002 *Archaeological inventory of County Tipperary, 1: north Tipperary.* Dublin.

FitzPatrick, E. 2004 *Royal inauguration in Gaelic Ireland, 1100–1600.* Woodbridge.

Foley, C. 1988 An enigma solved: Kiltierney, Co. Fermanagh. In A. Hamlin and C. Lynn (eds), *Pieces of the past. Archaeological excavations by the Department of the*

Environment for Northern Ireland 1970–86, 24–6. Belfast.

Herity, M. 1984 A survey of the royal site of Cruachain in Connacht II. *Journal of the Royal Society of Antiquaries of Ireland* **114**, 125–38.

Hobsbawm, E. 1983 Introduction: inventing traditions. In E. Hobsbawm and T.O. Ranger, *The invention of tradition*, 1–14. Cambridge.

Keeley, V.J. 1999 Iron Age discoveries at Ballydavis. In P.G. Lane and W. Nolan (eds), *Laois: history and society*, 25–34. Dublin.

Knox, H.T. 1914 Dumha Brosna. *Journal of the Royal Society of Antiquaries of Ireland* **4** (4), 348–57.

McCaffrey, P. 1955 The Dunkellin barrow group. *Journal of the Royal Society of Antiquaries of Ireland* **85**, 218–25.

McGarry, T. 2009 Irish late prehistoric ring-ditches. In G. Cooney, K. Becker, J. Coles, M. Ryan and S. Sievers (eds), *Relics of old decency: archaeological studies in later prehistory*, 413–23. Bray.

McQuade, M., Molloy, B. and Moriarty, C. 2009 *In the shadow of the Galtees: archaeological excavations along the N8 Cashel to Mitchelstown Road Scheme*. NRA Scheme Monograph 4. Dublin.

Moore, M. 1987 *Archaeological inventory of County Meath*. Dublin.

Mount, C. 1993 Geophysical survey at Rathdooney Beg, Co. Sligo. *Irish Association of Professional Archaeologists Newsletter* **17**, 9–11.

Mount, C. 1994 Geophysical survey at Rathdooney Beg, Co. Sligo. *Excavations 1993*, 82. Bray.

Mount, C. 1995a Rathdooney Beg, barrow cemetery. *Excavations 1994*, 79. Bray.

Mount, C. 1995b Excavations at Rathdooney Beg, Co. Sligo, 1994. *Emania* **13**, 79–87.

Mount, C. 1996 Rathdooney Beg: Iron Age barrow cemetery. *Excavations 1995*, 78–9. Bray.

Mount, C. 1998 Ritual, landscape and continuity in prehistoric County Sligo. *Archaeology Ireland* **12** (3), 18–21.

Mount, C. 1999 Excavation and environmental analysis of a Neolithic mound and Iron Age barrow cemetery at Rathdooney Beg, County Sligo, Ireland. *Proceedings of the Prehistoric Society* **65**, 337–71.

Mount, C. (in press) The context of the early Bronze Age cemetery in the Mound of the Hostages, Tara, Co. Meath. In M. O'Sullivan, G. Cooney, C. Scarre and B. Cunliffe (eds), *Tara: from the past to the future*.

Newman, C. 1997 *Tara: an archaeological survey*. Dublin.

O'Donovan, P. 1995 *Archaeological survey of County Cavan*. Dublin.

Ó Ríordáin, S.P. 1939–40 Excavations at Cush, Co. Limerick. *Proceedings of the Royal Irish Academy* **45**C, 83–181.

Ó Ríordáin, S.P. 1948 Further barrows at Rathjordan, Co. Limerick. *Journal of the Cork Historical and Archaeological Society* **53**, 19–31.

Ó Ríordáin, S.P. 1950–1 Excavations of some earthworks on the Curragh, Co. Kildare. *Proceedings of the Royal Irish Academy* **53**C, 249–77.

Raftery, B. 1994 *Pagan Celtic Ireland: the enigma of the Irish Iron Age*. London.

Raftery, J. 1939 The tumulus-cemetery of Carrowjames, Co. Mayo: part i—Carrowjames I. *Journal of the Galway Archaeological and Historical Society* **18**, 157–67.

Raftery, J. and Inkster, R.G. 1940 The tumulus-cemetery of Carrowjames, Co. Mayo: part ii—Carrowjames II. *Journal of the Galway Archaeological and Historical Society* **19**, 16–87.

Waddell, J. 1990 *The Bronze Age burials of Ireland*. Galway.

Waterman, D. 1968 Cordoned urn burials and ring-ditch at Urbalreagh, Co. Antrim. *Ulster Journal of Archaeology* **31**, 25–32.

Willmott, G.F. 1939 Two Bronze Age burials at Carrowbeg North, Belclare, Co. Galway. *Journal of the Royal Society of Antiquaries of Ireland* **68**, 130–42.

Note

1. The excavation and post-excavation work was supported by an Archaeological Excavation Grant from the National Monuments Service on the recommendation of the National Committee for Archaeology of the Royal Irish Academy.

15. Stone circle or proto-cashel? An Iron Age enclosure in south-west Ireland
William O'Brien

Introduction

For many parts of Ireland, the Iron Age continues to be a poorly understood period of prehistory. This is partly because of low archaeological visibility, with few clearly recognisable monument types in comparison to the Bronze Age or the early medieval period. Many probable Iron Age monuments, such as funerary barrows, certain earthwork sites and hillforts, cannot be closely dated on surface evidence alone. The identification of settlements for this period is a particular problem, one that has been advanced in recent times by discoveries on road schemes in some parts of Ireland. These mostly comprise the subsurface remains of roundhouses and other habitation features, ring-ditches and cremation burials, burnt spreads and iron furnaces (see McLoughlin and Conran 2008 on recent finds in south Munster).

This paper draws attention to a new type of Iron Age monument recently identified in the Beara Peninsula, Co. Cork. It consists of a small, stone-walled, circular enclosure, built by a local farming community in the Barrees Valley in the early centuries AD (Fig. 15.1). The significance of the site and the range of associated activities remain enigmatic, with both ceremonial/assembly use and residential function possible. There is reason to believe that similar Iron Age enclosures occur elsewhere in Beara, but the wider distribution of this monument type is uncertain, as no excavated parallels are known elsewhere in Ireland.

The Beara Project

The excavation of the Barrees monument was part of a project established in 2001 to investigate the history of human settlement in upland areas of the Beara Peninsula, Co. Cork (O'Brien 2009). Archaeological and palaeoenvironmental investigations were undertaken in selected hill valleys to examine patterns of settlement and farming activity during the period c. 2000 BC–AD 1000. These valleys have well-preserved settlement features and ritual monuments, with ancient field patterns partly covered by blanket peat or fossilised within later agricultural landscapes.

One of these early farmscapes is the Barrees Valley, located on the northern side of a hill ridge that extends east from Eyeries village at the western end of the peninsula (Fig. 15.2). Excavations in this valley in 2002–3 identified a *longue durée* of settlement, beginning in the Bronze Age with several sites dating from c. 1500–1000 BC. These include two *fulachta fiadh* (sites B and C), a copper mine (site J) and a standing stone pair (site H). This settlement evidence may be connected to a palaeoecological record for Bronze Age farming in the valley c. 1400–450 BC. The pollen record indicates continued agriculture during the Iron Age, which intensified in the early centuries AD. This is supported by the discovery of a large field stockade and an adjacent enclosure (site A), both of which date from the late Iron Age.

Farming in the Barrees Valley continued into the early

Fig. 15.1-Pre-excavation view of site A enclosure, Barrees Valley.

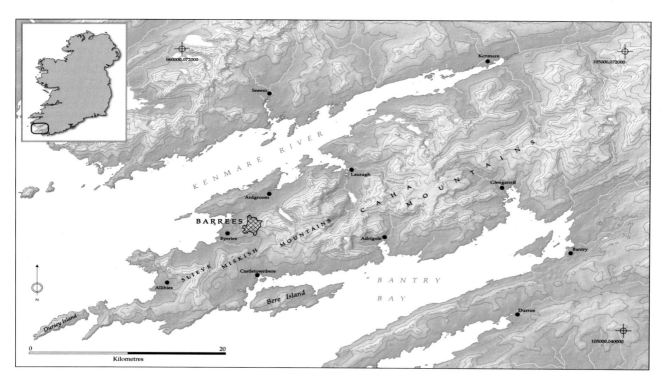

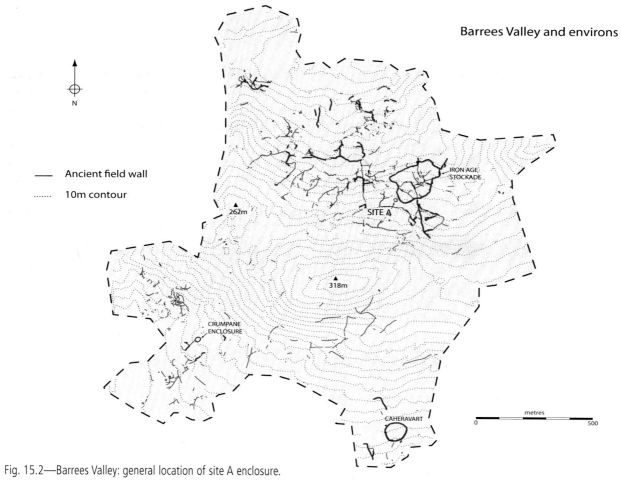

Barrees Valley and environs

—— Ancient field wall

...... 10m contour

Fig. 15.2—Barrees Valley: general location of site A enclosure.

Fig. 15.3—Barrees Valley: excavation of site A enclosure.

medieval period, expanding *c*. AD 700–1200 to include both pastoralism and cereal-growing. Several sites of that period are recorded in the valley, including two excavated huts (sites E and F), two souterrain locations, an ogham stone and a number of excavated field walls. There may also have been a connection with an early ecclesiastical site at Caheravart, on the southern side of the Barrees ridge.

Site A: Barrees

This enclosure is located on a narrow shelf on the upper north-facing slopes of the Barrees Valley (226–230m OD), in an area of intermittent rock outcrop and blanket bog growth (Fig. 15.2). There is a panoramic view from the site, covering the entire valley and the coastal lowland to the north, with Kenmare Bay and the mountainous Iveragh Peninsula of County Kerry visible in the distance (Fig. 15.3). The enclosure itself has a low visibility within the valley owing to its small size.

The Archaeological Survey of Ireland recorded the site in 1990 (Cork RMP CO102–03010), following earlier references by local historians. Prior to excavation in 2002–3, the outline of a circular stone-walled enclosure with a single entrance gap was visible. The interior was covered by blanket peat, with only the inner boulder face of the enclosing wall exposed.

Excavation confirmed that site A comprises a circular enclosure, defined by a low stone wall with an entrance opening on the south-eastern side (Fig. 15.4). The internal diameter is 14.1m (north–south) by 14.8m, with a wall width of 1.2–1.5m. The enclosure wall is L-shaped in cross-section, consisting of an inner face of upright slabs and an outer kerb of lower recumbent boulders, with an intervening fill of loose smaller stones (Fig. 15.5). The surviving wall height is generally less than 1m along its extent and is intact except for collapse on the north-eastern side. The original entrance to the enclosure was a narrow opening on the south-eastern side, defined by opposing pairs of upright boulders, with an entrance passage measuring 1.6m long, narrowing inwards from 2.4m to 1.4m (Fig. 15.6).

The inner wall face comprises low, upright slabs placed contiguously in a circular arrangement. These are mostly rough boulders of local sedimentary geology, 0.5–0.9m in height and 0.5–1.4m in width. The largest stone, 1.56m high by 1.84m wide, is located on the eastern inner side of the entrance passage. They were originally set upright, but examples on the south-western side have fallen inwards. The wall on the north-eastern side survives as a single line of low recumbent boulders, 0.08–0.26m in height, placed directly on an exposed rib of bedrock.

201

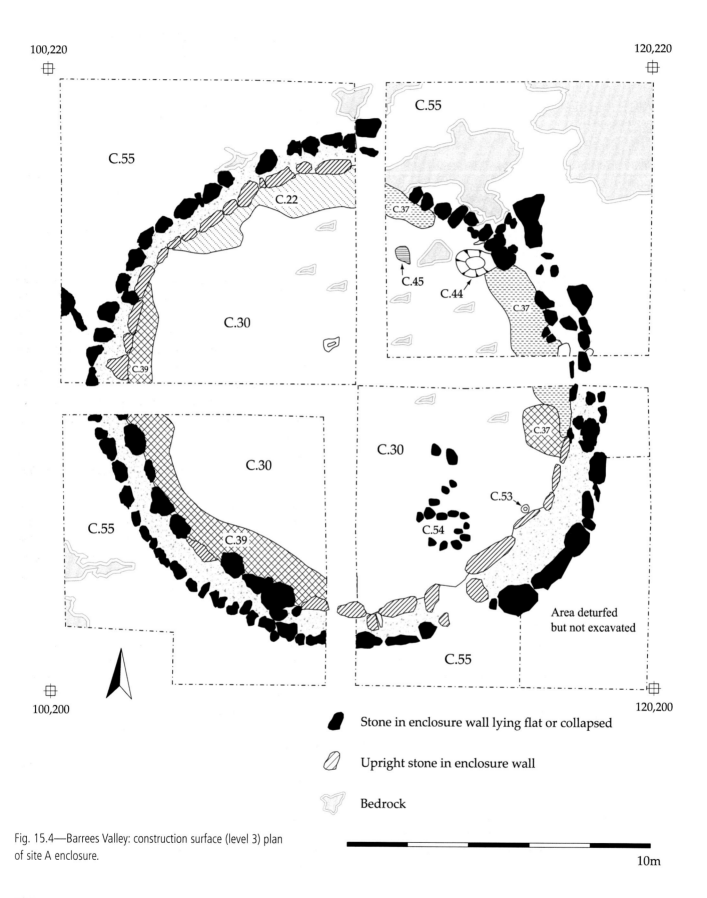

Fig. 15.4—Barrees Valley: construction surface (level 3) plan of site A enclosure.

Stone in enclosure wall lying flat or collapsed

Upright stone in enclosure wall

Bedrock

10m

Fig. 15.5—Barrees Valley: detail of enclosure wall, site A.

Fig. 15.6—Barrees Valley: entrance passage (looking inwards), site A.

The slabs were placed directly on the old ground surface, with some in shallow sockets and occasionally supported by wedge stones. The majority stayed upright owing to their contiguous arrangement and low, squat form, with support provided by the wall core. Smaller stones were used to fill gaps between these upright boulders in some places. Additional support was provided by thin deposits of stony sediment dumped against the base of the inner wall stones. This debris included angular stone fragments that were produced by rough tooling and breaking of stones during wall construction.

The outer wall face consists of a circular arrangement of contiguous boulders placed horizontally on the old ground surface. These subrounded boulders measure 0.5–1.05m in length, 0.4–0.7m in width and 0.15–0.34m in height. The space between the inner slab face and the outer boulder kerb

of the enclosure wall was filled with loose irregular stones measuring 0.05–0.15m, with some larger examples up to 0.4m.

The Iron Age stockade at Barrees

Site A lies 7m outside the south-western corner of a large, stone-walled field enclosure, located at 170–212m OD on a broad shelf in the mid-slope section of the Barrees Valley (Fig. 15.7). This has an irregular curving shape, defined by a collapsed stone wall that was originally *c*. 1m wide by 1.5m high. The interior measures 160–204m (east–west) by 95–150m, with a wall perimeter of 710m enclosing an area of 2.8ha.

This enclosure can be interpreted as a large field stockade of single-period construction. A number of partly exposed field walls in the interior may have divided the stockade into smaller field units but could also be earlier. The original entrance consists of a 2.5m-wide opening on the north-eastern side, where a small hut site served either as a gatehouse or a herdsman's shelter. Outside the entrance a 3–3.5m-wide trackway leads to the enclosure from lower in the valley. The collapsed remains of a further four stone huts are visible adjoining the stockade wall on the inside, two of which are dated to the early medieval period.

The dating of the stockade itself is based on radiocarbon results from an excavation trench on its north-western side. The enclosure was built in or around the first century AD, a time when pollen studies indicate substantial agricultural activity in the valley (Overland and O'Connell 2009). This included pastoralism and cereal cultivation, both of which required careful animal management using the stockade in combination with external fields and open grazing on the valley slopes.

Site A history

Excavation has provided much information on the history of the site A enclosure from its initial construction to its final abandonment. Radiocarbon dating indicates that it was built some time between the first and fourth centuries AD (Table 15.1). There is no clear evidence for its immediate use, though there are radiocarbon-dated contexts and a small number of finds connected to activity in the period *c*. AD 340–620. The enclosure appears to have been entirely abandoned by the seventh century, if not earlier.

Pre-enclosure activity

There is only slight evidence of human activity at this location prior to construction of the enclosure. This takes the form of a small pit (C33) and a cattle tooth (02E914:A51) found in the

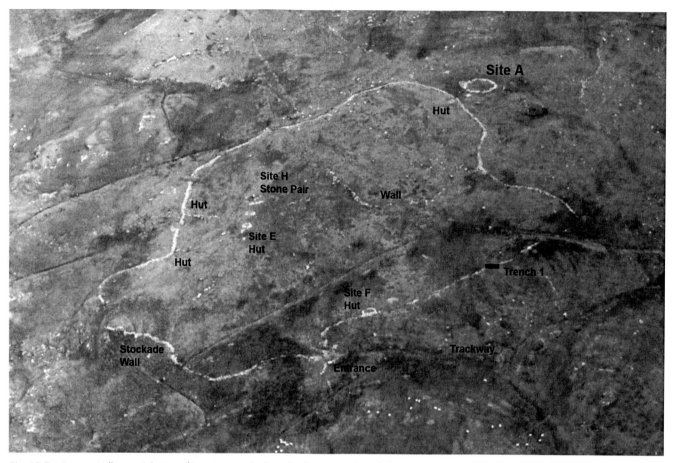

Fig. 15.7—Barrees Valley: aerial view of Iron Age stockade and adjacent site A enclosure.

Table 15.1—Barrees Valley: radiocarbon dates from site A (all AMS dates, except for conventional date GrN-28301, with calibration after OxCal v.3.10).

Site history	Sample	Context	Context type	14C result BP	Lab	1-sigma cal.	2-sigma cal.
Pre-enclosure							
	Charcoal	32	Fill of pit C33	2830±40	GrA-22611	1040–920 BC	1130–890 BC
	Cattle tooth	51	Stony deposit	2485±35	GrA-27496	760–530 BC	780–410 BC
Construction?							
Terminus post quem	Charcoal	48	Under wall	1835±40	GrA-22609	AD 130–230	AD 70–320
Terminus ante quem?	Hazelnut	45	Hearth	1965±40	GrA-22610	20 BC–AD 80	50 BC–AD 130
Use							
Early use	Charcoal	10	Layer	1620±40	GrA-22613	AD 390–540	AD 340–550
	Charcoal	35	Layer	1610±40	GrA-22616	AD 400–540	AD 340–550
	Charcoal	09	Burnt deposit	1590±40	GrA-22614	AD 420–540	AD 390–570
Later use							
	Charcoal	34	Burnt deposit	1555±40	GrA-22617	AD 430–550	AD 420–600
	Charcoal	24	Burnt deposit	1525±40	GrA-22619	AD 440–600	AD 420–620
Abandonment							
	Peat	02	Peat layer	800±30	GrN-28301	AD 1220–1260	AD 1180–1275

interior. The pit contained charcoal of late Bronze Age date (*c.* 1130–890 BC). This is significantly older than the construction date range for the enclosure, as is a radiocarbon date range of 780–410 BC for the cattle tooth, which was found in construction rubble (C51) piled against the inner face of the enclosure wall on the south-eastern side. The significance of the pit is unknown, but the presence of charcoal and a covering stone suggest a deliberately dug feature. The cattle tooth is likely to be residual from final Bronze Age farming in the site area.

Enclosure construction (level 3)

In the absence of diagnostic artefacts, we are reliant on radiocarbon analysis to date the construction and earliest use of the site A enclosure (Table 15.1). The dating of charcoal flecks from beneath one of the exterior wall stones (C48) provides a *terminus post quem* of AD 70–320 (GrA-22609) for the construction event. A date range of 50 BC–AD 130 (GrA-22610) for a hazelnut fragment, recovered from a small hearth (C45) on the construction surface, may be contemporary with the building of this enclosure. A resolution of these

radiocarbon results at 2-sigma calibration suggests that this may have occurred some time in the first or early second century AD. It is possible, but less likely, that both the pre-wall charcoal and the C45 hearth pre-date the construction of this enclosure, which may have occurred as late as the fifth century AD.

The construction of the enclosure was a single event carried out to a clear design concept, where a circular shape was accurately laid out on a carefully chosen shelf of level ground in the upper valley slopes. Care was taken in the selection of wall stones of suitable size and in their contiguous and concentric arrangement. The stones used are mostly grey sandstones and siltstones of local Devonian geology, probably sourced from surface scree on the surrounding valley slopes. Rough tooling was undertaken in some cases to achieve desired sizes or shapes, but this was minimal.

A significant feature is the low height of the enclosure wall, which does not exceed 1m along most of the perimeter (Fig. 15.5). There is no evidence that the wall was originally higher or was reduced by later robbing. As mentioned, the wall has a continuous L-shaped profile in cross-section, except on

Fig. 15.8—Barrees Valley: excavation of interior of site A enclosure, north-west quadrant.

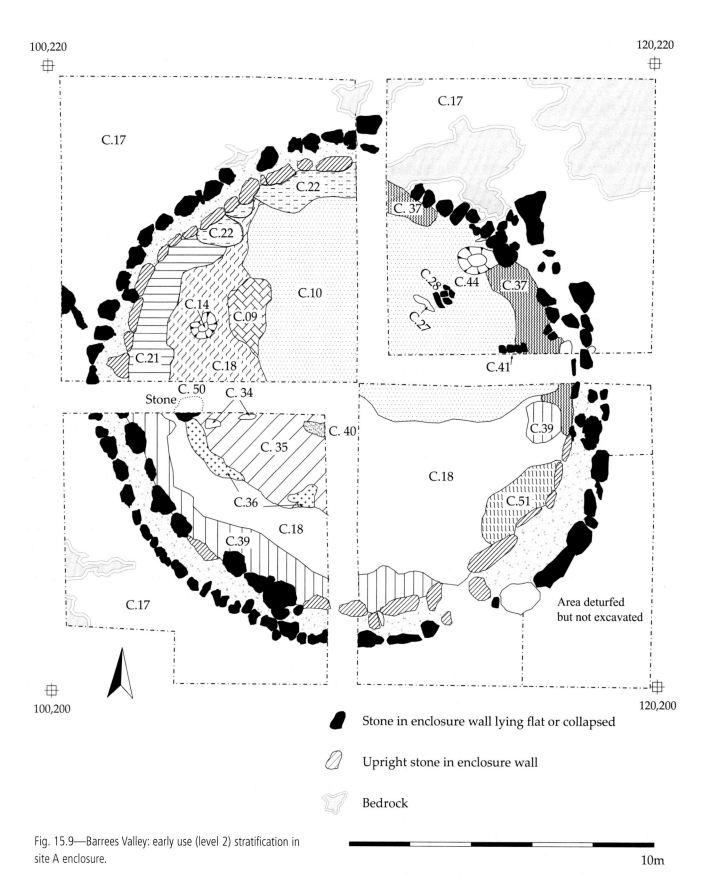

Fig. 15.9—Barrees Valley: early use (level 2) stratification in site A enclosure.

100,220

120,220

C.17

C.17

C.22

C.22

C.37

C.10

C.28 C.44 C.37

C.14

C.09 C.27

C.21

C.18 C.41

C. 50 C. 34

Stone

C.39

C. 35

C. 40

C.18

C. 36

C.51

C.18

C.39

C.17

Area deturfed but not excavated

100,200

120,200

Stone in enclosure wall lying flat or collapsed

Upright stone in enclosure wall

Bedrock

10m

the north-eastern side, where surface bedrock probably necessitated a different construction method. The use of low recumbent boulders instead of vertical slabs on this side demonstrates a concern with maintaining a circular shape rather than with building a strong enclosing wall.

The enclosure was originally built on a hard, stony B-horizon surface covered by a thin organic soil (Fig. 15.8). In addition to the C45 hearth, another feature from the construction level was a small pit (C53) found beneath construction rubble (C51) piled against the inner wall on the south-eastern side of the enclosure (Fig. 15.4). This pit was filled with dark sediment containing charcoal flecks (C52). Excavation of the enclosure entrance did not uncover any post-holes or other features that might indicate a gate. A small spread of slabs (C54) inside the entrance may represent crude paving, but there is no indication that this extended along the passageway or across the enclosure interior.

Early use (level 2)
Excavation of the enclosure interior uncovered a thin sequence of stony silt deposits with occasional charcoal concentrations and surface boulders, all sealed beneath blanket peat growth (Fig. 15.9). Following some fires on the construction surface, the earliest use of the enclosure is represented by a series of compact sediment spreads across the interior (level 2). These include an extensive spread of dark brown silt (C10) across the northern and north-eastern side, as well as small deposits of sandy silt (C18, C21 and C35) in the western area. These are consistent with open-air silting on the stony B-horizon surface, which incorporated material residues of human activity. Though stratigraphically early in the history of this site, radiocarbon dates for contexts 9, 10 and 35 place these deposits in the fifth or sixth century AD.

Excavation of the level 2 surface inside the enclosure exposed a small number of discrete features, both on and within the general silt spreads. Indications of fires were found in three places, including a small deposit of dark silt (C40) with frequent charcoal flecking near the centre of the enclosure. A second concentration of charcoal (C9) was identified as part of a larger spread of brown/grey silt (C8) on the north-western side of the interior. Charcoal from C9 is radiocarbon-dated to AD 390–570. A small deposit of charcoal-rich sediment (C27) was identified in the north-eastern part of the interior. These charcoal deposits indicate the lighting of fires at different times during the early use of the enclosure. The amount of charcoal present and the absence of surface reddening and formal hearth settings suggest that these fires were once-off events.

There are no artefact finds from the early use horizon in this enclosure, apart from some rounded stones of questionable significance. No post-holes, stake-holes or foundation trenches were found to indicate the presence of structures, and no graves or bone deposits were found. Some large boulders and two small arrangements of flat stones (C28 and C41) were identified, although their significance is unknown.

Later use (level 1)
The level 2 deposits were overlain by a similar sequence of surface sediments, charcoal deposits and occasional large boulders (Fig. 15.10). This level 1 surface was marked by a general spread of mid/dark brown silt (C4) across most of the central enclosure area, bordered by a compact spread of stone-free silt (C5 in quadrant 2; C23 in quadrant 1). This relates to open-air silting of the interior in the fifth or sixth century AD. The degree of overlap with radiocarbon dates for the level 2 surface suggests a broad continuum of activity in the fourth to sixth centuries AD. Once again there is no evidence for structures but charcoal evidence suggests the continued lighting of occasional fires, though no formal hearths.

Five large boulders were found lying flat on the level 1 surface, including three examples (C6, C6A and C29) below the C4 and C23 sediment spreads and two boulders (C20 and C50) overlying these deposits. These ranged from 0.52m to 0.84m and were probably derived from local ORS scree. They had no obvious function or use wear, although some may have been used as crude seats. One example (C29) occurred at the centre of a charcoal-rich spread (C24) radiocarbon-dated to AD 420–620. A second concentration of charcoal (C34), identified under the C23 spread in the south-western part of the enclosure, was radiocarbon-dated to AD 420–600.

Importantly, there are some artefact finds from these later use contexts, including stone objects, a small collection of glass beads and an iron point (Fig. 15.11). The stone finds comprise three hammer-stones, two stone discs (one part-perforated) and a hollowed stone. A small number of rounded stones, both broken and complete, and cobble spalls were also recovered, some of which may have been introduced by human agency. Interestingly, a near-complete hammer-stone (02E914:A44) found directly below the C2 peat layer inside the enclosure bears haft marks indicating that it may originally have been used in the Bronze Age copper mine (site J) in Crumpane townland. This implement may have been collected from surface mine spoil during the Iron Age and brought to site A for use in some activity.

Other finds include a heavily corroded iron object (02E914:09) from the north-western interior. This object has a hollow cylindrical shape, measuring 61mm long by 8–10mm in diameter, with a rounded end and a 4–5mm-wide opening

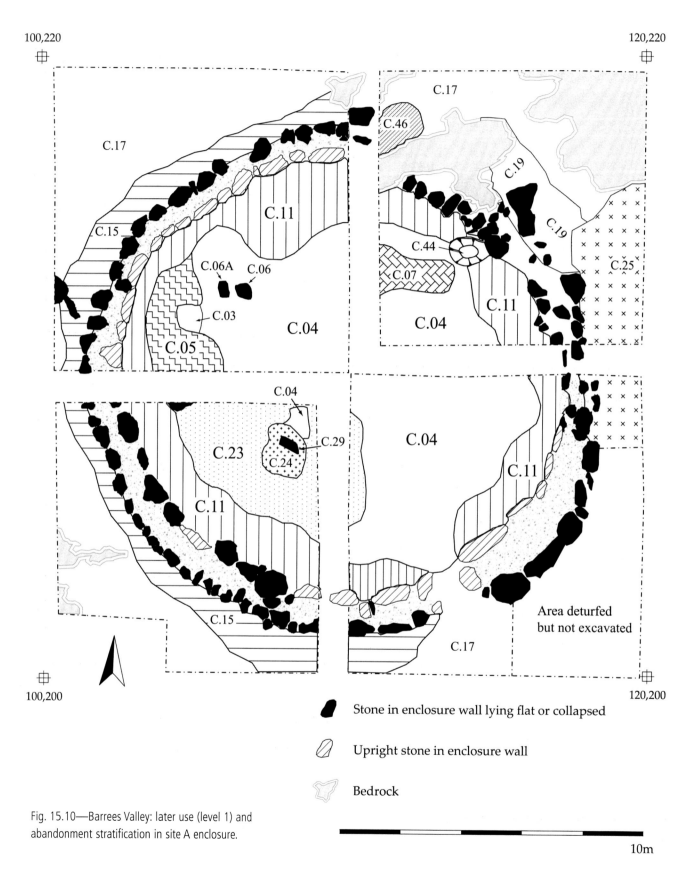

Fig. 15.10—Barrees Valley: later use (level 1) and abandonment stratification in site A enclosure.

Stone in enclosure wall lying flat or collapsed

Upright stone in enclosure wall

Bedrock

10m

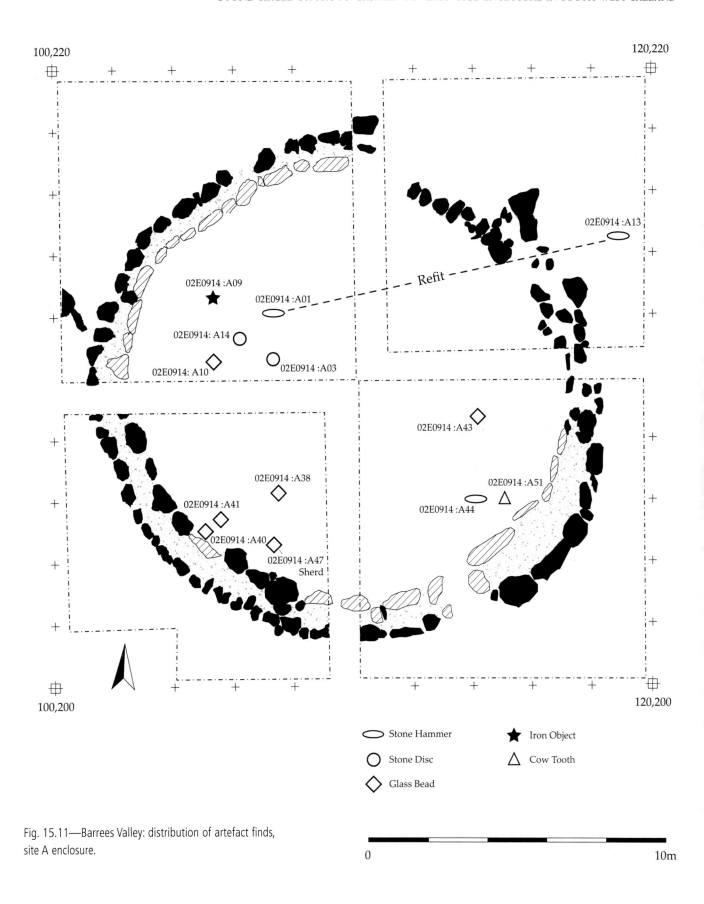

100,220

120,220

02E0914 :A13

Refit

02E0914 :A09

02E0914 :A01

02E0914: A14

02E0914: A10

02E0914 :A03

02E0914 :A43

02E0914 :A51

02E0914 :A44

02E0914 :A38

02E0914 :A41

02E0914 :A40

02E0914 :A47
Sherd

100,200

120,200

Stone Hammer   Iron Object

Stone Disc   Cow Tooth

Glass Bead

Fig. 15.11—Barrees Valley: distribution of artefact finds, site A enclosure.

0

10m

running down one side. An exact date is uncertain but the find context suggests an association with later use of the enclosure, *c.* AD 420–620.

Five glass beads were also found inside the enclosure. These include a small amber bead (E914:A10), a plain blue spherical glass bead (E914:A43) and three dumb-bell or toggle glass beads of different colours (E914:A38, A40, A41). A sherd of pale blue glass (E914:A47) was also found. These glass finds belong to the later use of the enclosure. This is consistent with the radiocarbon chronology, as dumb-bell beads are considered to date from the Iron Age into the early historic period (Raftery 1994).

Site abandonment

The site A enclosure appears to have fallen into disuse by the early seventh century AD, if not earlier. This is marked archaeologically by collapse of the enclosing wall on the north-eastern side, and by the initiation of blanket peat growth across the site. Excavation revealed an early layer of peat (C26) immediately outside the enclosure on the eastern side. This was overlain by a deposit of large stones (C46), as part of the initial collapse of the enclosure wall. Minor wall collapse is also recorded on the south-western, western and north-western sides of the enclosure. The most significant collapse occurred on the north-eastern side, where a large deposit of wall stones (C19) was discovered at the base of a bedrock exposure. A large oval pit (C44), dug into the construction levels, was filled with loose stony sediment (C11) that probably derived from this wall collapse. The significance of this pit is uncertain, but it was dug around the time the site was abandoned. This is finally marked by the uninterrupted growth of blanket peat across the site, ranging in thickness from <0.1m over the enclosing wall up to 0.4m in the interior. Radiocarbon dating of basal peat growth in the interior indicates that the site was effectively abandoned by *c.* AD 1180–1275, if not several centuries earlier.

Site A interpretation

There are no close parallels for Barrees site A in the known range of Iron Age sites in Ireland. The identification of similar sites is problematic, as there are large numbers of unclassified stone-walled enclosures in different parts of Ireland, few of which have been excavated. For example, some 134 unclassified enclosures, mostly circular in plan, are recorded in the west Cork region (Power 1992, 258–70). Without excavation, it is not known whether the distinctive wall profile of the Barrees enclosure is present at any of these sites.

A recent survey in the Beara Peninsula identified some 69 unclassified enclosures of possible prehistoric date,

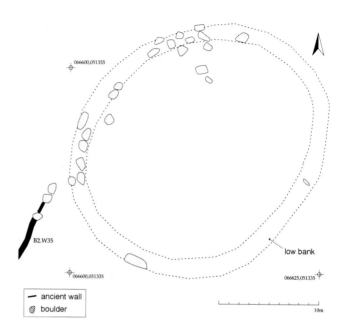

Fig. 15.12—Crumpane, Beara, Co. Cork: plan of enclosure (CO102-021; see Fig. 15.2).

occurring in proximity to ancient field walls, hut sites and *fulachta fiadh* (Murphy 2009). Circular enclosures are the most common, with 53 known examples that range from 5m to 16m in internal diameter. They include examples built with a low earthen bank or a wall of small stones and/or boulders. Some of these may be similar to Barrees site A, but again this cannot be confirmed without excavation.

One of these unclassified enclosures is on the southern side of the Barrees ridge, in the northern part of Crumpane townland (Fig. 15.2). It comprises a subcircular enclosure, measuring 24.7m (east–west) by 24m (RMP CO102–021). The interior is roughly flat with no visible features and is overgrown. The enclosing element appears to consist of a low bank, averaging 2.2m in width, with no apparent entrance opening (Fig. 15.12). A number of large boulders are exposed along the bank, but it is not clear whether the latter is entirely of stone construction. A comparison with the Barrees site A enclosure in terms of dating or morphology is not possible without excavation.

The site A enclosure at Barrees can also be considered in relation to the widespread occurrence of early medieval ringforts in the Beara Peninsula, and elsewhere in Ireland. A recent survey identified some 44 ringfort settlements at the western end of the peninsula (Comber 2009). These include nine stone-built (cashels) and 35 earthen (raths) examples, including sites of composite construction and some with souterrains. While none have been excavated, the majority of Irish ringforts were built *c.* AD 600–900, and in some cases continued in use into the high medieval period (Stout 1997).

The origin of the ringfort is a long-standing research question, as there is no definite background in the late Iron Age to the emergence of the extraordinary number of these sites in the early medieval period (see Waddell 1998, 319). No cashels of early medieval type are dated to the prehistoric period in Ireland, although examples of small, circular or oval, stone-built enclosures are known from the late Bronze Age. These include sites at Lough Gur, Co. Limerick (Cleary 2003), Aughinish, Co. Limerick, and Carrigillihy, Co. Cork (Waddell 1998, 210, 268). These all had internal house structures and artefact records consistent with habitation but are significantly different from cashels in form and size.

Site A at Barrees is also different from late Bronze Age settlement enclosures, and from ringforts of the early medieval period. Cashels are generally much larger, and have enclosing walls that are more substantial and of different construction. A typical example may be seen at Bofickil (CO102-016) on the western side of the Barrees Valley, where a cashel with an internal diameter of 25–27m and a 2m-wide enclosing wall of drystone construction has a souterrain in the interior. These cashels typically had one or more houses in the interior, as well as other features and material culture connected to domestic habitation.

The original function and use history of the Barrees site A enclosure is a matter for some speculation. The excavation record is consistent with the use of an open-air enclosure for activities other than human habitation or animal containment. While the early history of this enclosure is unclear, radiocarbon dates indicate a pattern of more intensive use *c.* AD 340–620. Charcoal deposits suggest the occasional lighting of fires, though no actual hearths were identified. The purpose of these fires is unclear, as they cannot be connected to either domestic or industrial activity. The artefact finds from site A are not particularly helpful in respect of site function, though they do indicate a history of episodic human use as opposed to permanent occupation. The low incidence of these finds, together with their haphazard occurrence, points to casual loss rather than deliberate deposition. The glass beads might be taken as status signifiers, but the site certainly cannot be regarded as high-status based on the finds record.

The enclosure is unlikely to have been used as a stockade for animals, given its morphology and the evidence of internal fires and glass bead finds. There is no evidence to indicate that it was roofed, nor would the enclosing wall have afforded enough shelter from prevailing winds to be useful for human habitation. There were no structural features to indicate the presence of houses or other built structures inside the enclosure. Instead, the site appears to have functioned as an open-air enclosure during its entire history of use.

Iron Age stone circles?

With no clear evidence of human habitation or specialised craft activity, it is necessary to consider the possibility that the Barrees site A enclosure was used for ceremonial assembly. The primary intention of the builders appears to have been to create a circular enclosure of symbolic meaning rather than a domestic or agricultural enclosure. This is suggested by the height and unusual structure of the enclosing wall. The use of a very low, internal slab facing suggests that the primary intention was to create a setting for certain activities rather than to physically enclose, defend or restrict access. The emphasis may have been on enclosing and framing certain actions and performances connected to ceremonial space used by a local community. No graves were found, so funerary ritual may be excluded, unless the deceased were interred elsewhere. No material deposits of a ritual character were discovered at the site. There is no indication that deliberate alignment, either with heavenly bodies or landscape features, was a consideration in the design or aspect of this enclosure.

Though there are no direct parallels for Barrees site A, some reference may be made to other ritual monuments and sacred landscapes from the Iron Age in Ireland. The 'royal sites' of Tara, Navan and Rathcroghan illustrate the importance of ritual in this period, representing great ceremonial complexes where past and present converge in a highly mythologised setting. There are also individual monuments of a largely funerary and/or commemorative nature, including ring-barrows, standing stones and burial grounds. The Iron Age is also marked by the continued use of and reverence for older monuments on the landscape—for example, in patterns of deposition in wedge tombs of south-west Ireland (O'Brien 2002). Other expressions of religious belief are evident in votive deposition of metalwork in wet contexts and in the use of an iconic sculpture, wooden idols and other cult artefacts (Raftery 1994, 178–99).

Ceremonial monuments of a non-funerary character were also built during the Iron Age in Ireland. These include a timber post enclosure recently discovered at Lismullin, Co. Meath, comprising two concentric rings of post-holes with an overall diameter of 80m (O'Connell 2007). These sites, and monuments such as ring-barrows, reveal the continued importance of the sacred circle motif in ritual monuments of the late prehistoric period in Ireland. This was a legacy from older Neolithic and Bronze Age cults of sun worship and reflects the enduring nature of religious belief in prehistoric Ireland. While Barrees site A may be an entirely unique monument, it does raise interesting questions in respect of the large number of unclassified enclosures in Ireland. Like the Lismullin example, this monument is another physical expression of the sacred space created by different regional groups in the indigenous Iron Age.

Acknowledgements

Many thanks to Michelle Comber, Liam Hickey, Nick Hogan, Madeline O'Brien and other members of the excavation team for help with this project.

Bibliography

Cleary, R. 2003 Enclosed late Bronze Age habitation site and boundary wall at Lough Gur, Co. Limerick. *Proceedings of the Royal Irish Academy* **103**C, 97–189.

Comber, M. 2009 Beara in the first millennium AD. In W. O'Brien, *Local worlds: early settlement landscapes and upland farming in south-west Ireland*, 58–68. Cork.

McLoughlin, M. and Conran, S. 2008 The emerging Iron Age of south Munster. *Seanda* **3**, 51–3.

Murphy, C. 2009 The prehistoric archaeology of the Beara Peninsula. In W. O'Brien, *Local worlds: early settlement landscapes and upland farming in south-west Ireland*, 27–58. Cork.

O'Brien, W. 2002 Megaliths in a mythologised landscape: south-west Ireland in the Iron Age. In C. Scarre (ed.), *Monuments and landscape in Atlantic Europe*, 152–76. London and New York.

O'Brien, W. 2009 *Local worlds: early settlement landscapes and upland farming in south-west Ireland*. Cork.

O'Connell, A. 2007 Iron Age enclosure at Lismullin, Co. Meath. *Archaeology Ireland* **21** (2), 10–13.

Overland, A. and O'Connell, M. 2009 Palaeo-ecological investigations in the Barrees valley. In W. O'Brien, *Local worlds: early settlement landscapes and upland farming in south-west Ireland*, 285–322. Cork.

Power, D. 1992 *Archaeological inventory of County Cork, i: west Cork*. Dublin.

Raftery, B. 1994 *Pagan Celtic Ireland: the enigma of the Irish Iron Age*. London.

Stout, M. 1997 *The Irish ringfort*. Dublin.

Waddell, J. 1998 *The prehistoric archaeology of Ireland*. Galway.

16. An Iron Age ring-ditch at Coolbeg townland, Ballynagran, Co. Wicklow

Ellen OCarroll with a contribution by Jonny Geber

Introduction

Monitoring of soil-stripping at Coolbeg townland, Ballynagran, Co. Wicklow, conducted as part of a landfill project for Greenstar Recycling Holdings Ltd, uncovered several archaeological features, one of which was a small ring-ditch dated to 112 BC–AD 56 (2-sigma, 95.4% probability). It was an annular enclosure with an overall diameter of 5.2m. The ditch yielded a copper-alloy artefact, as well as a small amount of cremated animal bone and fragments of charcoal. The charcoal was mainly oak and alder, with smaller quantities of hazel, ash, cherry and birch. These taxon types are inconsistent with the species normally identified from cremated human deposits, where oak or Pomoideae was generally used almost exclusively (OCarroll 2010).

Site location

The Iron Age ring-ditch was located on a gently sloping south-facing field on a low rise. The main concentration of Bronze Age activity excavated by Frazer was located on higher

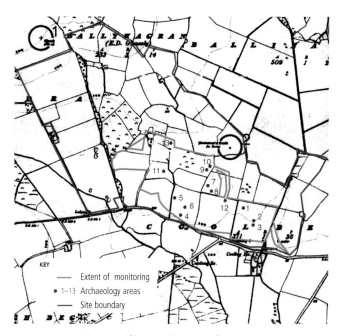

Fig. 16.2—Coolbeg: landfill site with areas of archaeological activity numbered (1–13).

ground to the north and west of the Coolbeg ring-ditch (Frazer, this volume). The siting of this ring-ditch on a low rise is consistent with other excavated sites, such as the small ring-ditches at Mitchelstowndown West, Co. Limerick (Daly and Grogan 1993, 57–8).

Archaeology in the local landscape

In April 2006, three small areas with archaeological potential were identified by the author within a zone measuring approximately 105m by 20m; these were numbered as areas 1, 2 and 3 (Fig. 16.2). Area 1, deemed not at risk and comprising some charcoal-rich pits and some possible kilns and cremation burials, was preserved *in situ*. Areas 2 and 3 were located within the footprint of the proposed administration complex and it was agreed that these should be preserved by record. The excavation revealed a small cluster of pits and smaller possible post-holes (area 2) and a small subcircular ring-ditch (area 3). A fragment of ash charcoal from the lower fill of the ditch has been dated to 112 BC–AD 56, the middle of the Iron Age.

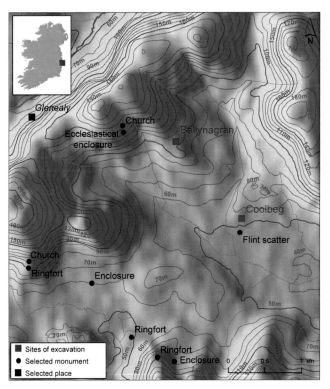

Fig. 16.1—Coolbeg: location of site.

213

Description of archaeological remains

Area 2, 10m by 6m, was located 17m north of area 3. It consisted of a cluster of eleven subcircular features of varying sizes, which were all cut directly into the natural subsoils (Fig. 16.3). The more substantial of these features were three closely grouped subcircular hole-cuts, which varied from 0.45m to 0.6m in width and were approximately 0.6m deep. The other features, scattered indiscriminately around the larger ones, were generally smaller and shallower, averaging 0.25m in width and 0.15m in depth. A date has not been obtained for this cluster of pits and post-holes, and therefore their association with the ring-ditch excavated in area 3 is unknown.

Area 3 comprised a small, circular ditch, 5.2m in overall diameter and 3m in internal diameter, with no evidence for an entrance. The ditch was 0.8–1.1m wide and 0.6–0.8m deep (Figs 16.3 and 16.5). It was filled with intermittent deposits of sand, silt and gravel or combinations thereof. Some of the deposits notably contained, or were composed almost entirely of, flecks of charcoal and included some cremated remains (Figs 16.6 and 16.7). The amount of cremated bone was small and has been identified as animal bone (Geber 2008).

A subcircular deposit, initially deemed to be a possible pit associated with a primary burial, was noted on its south-eastern side. This deposit (0.6m by 0.85m by 0.16m deep) underlay the natural subsoil and contained a layer of stones, filling a natural depression. The deposit contained no charcoal or archaeological inclusions. Cutting this feature at its south-eastern side was the main cut of the ring-ditch (Figs 16.3 and 16.4). The cross-section of the ditch had both a U- and V-profile. The V-shape was most noticeable on the western side and the U-shape on the eastern side. There was also a marked change in cross-section between the southern and northern sides of the ditch. The southern side, where it was generally narrowest and shallowest, was at least 0.5m deep and 0.85m wide, increasing to 1.2m in width and 0.9m in depth on the northern side.

The stratigraphy within the ring-ditch was fairly simple. Some layers may represent infilling episodes, possibly from a levelled mound or enclosing bank that may once have characterised the monument as a positive feature in the landscape. Six deposits were recorded within the ring-ditch, some of which could be found all the way around the ditch (Fig. 16.4). The earliest deposit was loose, gravelly silty sand with occasional charcoal flecks. This occurred on the base of the ditch to varying depths along the sides. Charcoal from this layer consisted mainly of *Alnus glutinosa* (alder) and small fragments of *Corylus avellana* (hazel) and *Fraxinus excelsior* (ash). The ash charcoal was dated to 112 BC–AD 56 (2-sigma,

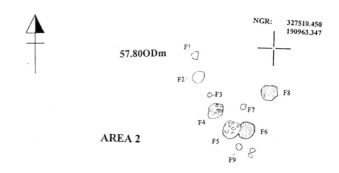

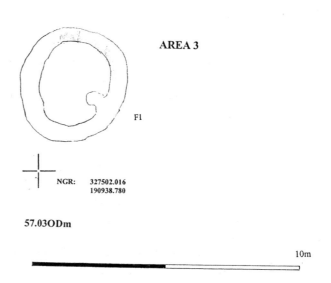

Fig. 16.3—Coolbeg: plan of ring-ditch (area 3) and pits and post-holes (area 2).

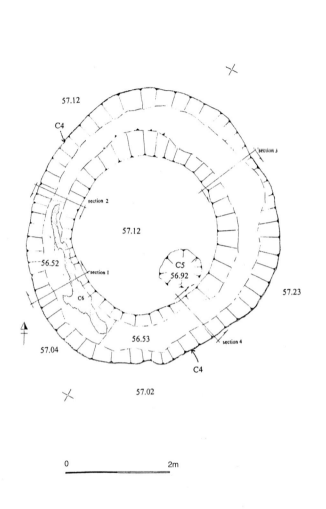

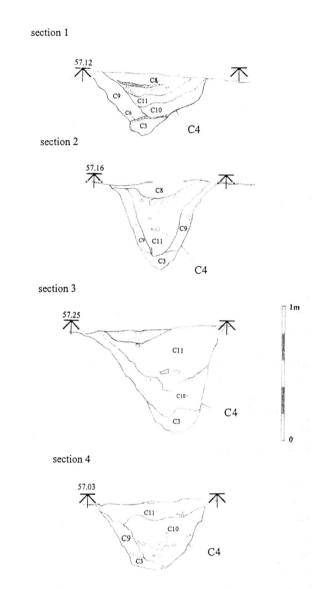

Fig. 16.4—Coolbeg: plan and sections of ring-ditch.

95.4% probability). Overlying this material, on the southern side, was a substantial charcoal and cremated bone deposit consisting of nearly pure charcoal with small concentrations of burnt animal bone (Fig. 16.7). The deposit was 3.2m long, 0.1–0.45m wide and 0.01–0.03m deep. A copper-alloy object, which was in an advanced state of degradation, was recovered from within this deposit. Its function has not been established. The object measured 45mm in length and 4mm in maximum diameter. There were some degraded and consequently unidentifiable wood remains attached to the artefact.

Three deposits were excavated over the natural silt layer and the main charcoal lens/cremated remains layer. These may represent infilling from the mound and bank which would have been created by the initial excavation of the ring-ditch (Fig. 16.4). The deposit recorded most frequently along the

Fig. 16.5—Coolbeg: pre-excavation photograph of post-hole and pit arrangements in area 2.

215

Fig. 16.6—Coolbeg: post-excavation photograph of ring-ditch.

inner edge of the ditch consisted of brown-yellow sand that reached a maximum depth of 0.3m and width of 0.2m. The next deposition layer was mid-brown sand with moderate gravel, 0.7m in maximum width and 0.3m in depth. This was present through most of the ditch, with the exception of the western side. It sealed the charcoal deposit. Mid-brown sandy gravel overlay the lower sand and gravel layer. This was present throughout the ditch, although it varied substantially in depth from a maximum of 0.55m at the northern end to a minimum of 0.18m elsewhere.

The final recorded ditch fill, which represents a second episode of charcoal and bone deposition, was only present in the northern half of the ring-ditch (Fig. 16.8). It consisted of mid- to dark brown sandy silt with a high concentration of charcoal within. The depth varied from 0.05m to 0.18m, increasing towards its western end. Occasional fragments of burnt bone were recorded within this material.

Discussion

A ring-ditch is generally classified as a flat area defined by an annular or penannular ditch. The area enclosed by the ditch is 'unenhanced' (i.e. no redeposited material was placed on top of this central area to form a mound) and is approximately the same height as the external ground level. In general, ring-ditches provide burial evidence from the ditches and occasionally from the internal area, although recent excavations have shown that evidence for formal burial is not always present. They may, however, be considered as part of the funerary rite. The ring-ditch excavated at Coolbeg is of particular importance in the study of Iron Age culture and associated monuments in that it is one of only a handful of Iron Age monuments to be excavated in this area of County Wicklow. The Coolbeg ring-ditch was not recognised prior to topsoil-stripping, and may indeed be a ploughed-out or a heavily denuded barrow—an earthen burial mound, generally dating from the Bronze Age and Iron Age. The layers of infill within and at the edge of the ditch may represent infilling from a possible mound and outer bank which once presented themselves as positive elements of the monument.

Ring-ditches excavated to date suggest a long tradition for this type of monument. Certainly, they are shown to be in use throughout the Bronze Age and into the Iron Age, as seen at recent excavations along the M3 at Ardsallagh, Co. Meath (Deevy and Murphy 2009). Although there are several ring-ditches in the surrounding area of County Wicklow, they are larger than the example at Coolbeg and their dates are unknown. Other ring-ditches recorded in County Wicklow include a series in Kilpoole Upper, measuring on average 12m in diameter. They remain unexcavated but are located approximately 3.5km west of Coolbeg, close to the coastal terrain of County Wicklow.

In recent decades several smaller ring-ditches have been excavated in different areas of the country. Some of these are Iron Age. An annular ring-ditch at Cloncurry, Co. Meath, measured between 6.4m and 7m in total diameter and contained no evidence of cremated remains in the fills (Carlin et al. 2008). This ring-ditch has been dated to the Bronze Age, 2470–2140 BC (2-sigma), but the date is from a cremation burial outside the ditch and may not be related to the actual use of the ring-ditch. Similar parallels as regards monument size and morphology can be seen at excavations in Rath townland, Co. Meath (Schweitzer 2005). This annular ring-

Fig. 16.7—Coolbeg: charcoal and bone layer at base of ditch.

ditch measured 3m in diameter. It appears that several phases of burial had taken place within the northern side of the ditch. Of most interest at this site was the discovery of a copper-alloy decorated toe-ring on a crouched inhumation at the southern side of the ditch. Although the crouched inhumation remains undated, Schweitzer has found direct parallels for this toe-ring in Britain, from Iron Age contexts mainly dating from the last century BC and first century AD (ibid., 97). These dates coincide with the date of the ring-ditch at Coolbeg. Barrow 4 at Chancellorsland, Co. Tipperary, was late Bronze Age/early Iron Age (790–410 BC) and measured 4.4m in overall external diameter (Doody 2008). As at Rath, Cloncurry and Coolbeg, there was no evidence of any internal features associated with the ring-ditch and there were no entrance features. There were small quantities of cremated bone in the ring-ditch at barrow 4 and, as at Coolbeg, the bone has been identified as animal rather than human.

An Iron Age complex at Ballydavis, Co. Laois, consisted of four ring-ditches ranging between 6m and 16m in diameter and contained a wealth of artefactual remains in the ditch fills. These included a bronze box, bronze fibula, beads, iron blades and fragments of stone bracelets (Keeley 1995). Site 2 at Ballydavis and barrow 4 at Chancellorsland may provide parallels for the site at Coolbeg, as animal bone was uncovered in the ditch fills of all three sites.

The phenomenon of the burial of animal bone within ring-ditches at Chancellorsland, Ballydavis and Coolbeg is an interesting aspect of these small Iron Age ring-ditches. It is tempting to suggest an Iron Age ritual. Cremated bone from the ditches of these monuments is generally presumed to be human when not assessed scientifically by an osteoarchaeologist. Is it possible that some of the unanalysed cremated bone from many of the previously excavated ring-ditch sites is from animals rather than humans?

The environmental evidence from the charcoal analysis points to the presence of oak and alder trees in the surrounding environment (OCarroll 2008). These oak and alder trees were used as a source of firewood for burning rituals associated with the animal bone in the ditch. Although oak trees are generally associated with primary woodlands, the presence of alder suggests a slightly more wetland landscape. The significance of water and river settings in association with ring-ditches and barrows has been noted elsewhere at Mitchelstowndown and in the floodplain of the Morningstar River, Co. Limerick (Daly and Grogan 1993).

The nearly equal quantities of oak and alder identified in one charcoal lens, and the presence of oak, ash, birch and cherry in a second lens from the ring-ditch, may point to a different ritual process, associated with the cremated animal bone

Fig. 16.8—Coolbeg: profile of fills in the ring-ditch.

to human cremations.

The lack of internal features and human burials indicates that this ring-ditch functioned as a ceremonial or sepulchral site, possibly associated with animals, as evidenced by the cremated animal bones in the ditch fills. It is possible that these small annular ring-ditches were constructed as ceremonial gathering places associated with ritual aspects of animal deities as opposed to the rite of human burials, as is generally presumed.

Acknowledgements

I would like to dedicate this essay to the memory of Simon Dick, who was supervisor on the excavations and who completed all the plans, photographs and stratigraphic reports. I would also like to thank James Eogan and Fiona Maguire for drawing my attention to parallels and for commenting on the text. I would like to acknowledge Bill Frazer, who produced Fig. 16.2. This excavation was funded by Greenstar Ltd, through Margaret Gowen and Co. Ltd.

Bibliography

Carlin, N., Clarke, L. and Walsh, F. 2008 *The archaeology of life and death on the Boyne floodplain: the linear landscape of the M4.* Dublin.

Daly, A. and Grogan, E. 1993 Excavations of four barrows in Mitchelstowndown West, Knocklong, Co. Limerick. *Discovery Programme Reports* **1**, 44–60.

Danaher, P. 1964 A prehistoric burial mound at Ballyeskeen, Co. Sligo. *Journal of the Royal Society of Antiquaries of Ireland* **94**, 145–58.

Deevy, M. and Murphy, J. (eds) 2009 *Places along the way: first findings on the M3.* Dublin.

Doody, M. 2008 *The Ballyhoura Hills Project.* Bray.

Eogan, J. and Finn, D. 2000 New light on late prehistoric ritual and burial in County Limerick. *Archaeology Ireland* **14** (1), 8–10.

Frazer, B. 2006 Excavation summaries: Ballynagran Landfill, Co. Wicklow. Unpublished summary prepared for Margaret Gowen and Co. Ltd.

Geber, J. 2008 Report on the burnt bone from Ballynagran (04E1163). Unpublished report prepared for Margaret Gowen and Co. Ltd.

Keeley, V. 1995 Excavation of Iron Age ring-ditches at Ballydavis, Co. Laois. Available at www.excavations.ie.

Newman, C. 1997 *Tara: an archaeological survey.* Dublin.

OCarroll, E. 2008 Analysis of charcoal remains from an Iron Age dated ring-ditch at Coolbeg, Co. Wicklow. Unpublished report prepared for Greenstar Recycling Holdings Ltd.

deposits rather than the cremation ritual associated with human remains, in which oak is nearly always the source of fuel.

Conclusions

The ring-ditch at Coolbeg provides evidence of an Iron Age population in east Wicklow around the beginning of the first millennium AD. The evidence for Iron Age societies in the area is scarce when compared to the Bronze Age culture that preceded it. Although no trace of a mound was evident in the central area of the ring-ditch, the ditch fills present along either side of the fosse may relate to the remains of the denuded mound and/or bank. The annular ring-ditch at Coolbeg is one of the smaller examples of this monument type excavated in Ireland, although parallels can be found from recent excavations elsewhere in the country. There were two deliberate depositions of charcoal and bone within the ring-ditch. The small quantities of bone examined point to the cremation of animals rather than humans. The charcoal types also suggest a different ritual associated with animal as opposed

OCarroll, E. 2010 Ancient woodland use in the midlands: understanding environmental and landscape change through archaeological and palaeo-ecological techniques. In M. Stanley, E. Danaher and J. Eogan (eds), *Creative minds: production, manufacturing and invention in ancient Ireland*, 47–56. Dublin.

Pilcher, J. and Hall, V. 2001 *Flora Hibernica*. Cork.

Raftery, B. 1981 Iron Age burials in Ireland. In D. Ó Corráin (ed.), *Irish antiquity: essays and studies presented to Professor M.J. O'Kelly*, 173–204. Dublin.

Raftery, B. 1994 *Pagan Celtic Ireland: the enigma of the Irish Iron Age*. London.

Schweitzer, H. 2005 Iron Age toe-rings from Rath on the N2 Finglas–Ashbourne road scheme, Co. Meath. In J. O'Sullivan and M. Stanley (eds), *Recent archaeological discoveries on national road schemes, 2004*, 93–8. Dublin.

Stout, G. 1994 Wicklow's prehistoric landscape. In K. Hannigan and W. Nolan (eds), *Wicklow: history and society*, 1–40. Dublin.

APPENDIX 16.1: SPECIES IDENTIFICATION AND ANALYSIS OF CHARCOAL SAMPLES
(ELLEN OCARROLL)

Introduction

Five charcoal samples from archaeological investigations at Coolbeg, Ballynagran landfill, Co. Wicklow, were analysed in respect of suitability for dating and species selection in association with the excavated features. The excavated features consisted of a ring-ditch which contained various fills in its ditch, including two deliberately deposited charcoal lenses. The ring-ditch has been dated to the Iron Age (112 cal. BC–cal. AD 56).

The charcoal was sent for species identification prior to ^{14}C dating, and also to obtain an indication of the range of tree species that grew in the area, as well as the utilisation of these species for various purposes. Wood used for fuel at prehistoric sites would generally have been sourced at locations close to the site, and therefore charcoal identifications may (although not necessarily) reflect the composition of the local woodlands. Larger pieces of charcoal, when identified, can provide information regarding the use of a species.

Methodology

The process of identifying wood, whether it is charred, dried or waterlogged, is carried out by comparing the anatomical structure of wood samples with known comparative material or keys (Schweingruber 1990). The identification of charcoal material involves breaking the charcoal piece so that a clean section of the wood can be obtained. This charcoal is then identified to species under an Olympus stereo-microscope with a magnification of x100 and a compound transmitted light microscope at magnifications of x500. By close examination of the micro-anatomical features of the samples the species were determined. The diagnostic features used for the identification of charcoal are micro-structural characteristics such as the vessels and their arrangement, the size and arrangement of rays, vessel pit arrangement and also the type of perforation plates.

The identifications are represented by weight and fragment counts. The charcoal fragments from similar species were grouped together and then counted and weighed (Table 16.1). In most cases, 50 charcoal fragments from each sample were identified.

Results

Table 16.1—Coolbeg: species present in the samples. *Weight in grammes/fragment count.

Context number	Sample number	Context type	Identifications
6	4	Charcoal deposit	Oak (14g,★ 50f★), alder (1.3g, 8f)
3	10	Primary ring-ditch infill. Date: 112 cal. BC–cal. AD 56	Alder (0.5g, 10f), oak (0.8g, 12f), ash (0.1g, 2f), hazel (0.8g, 12f)
6	2	Charcoal and cremated bone deposit	Alder (9g, 50f)
8	9	Charcoal and cremated animal bone deposit	Ash (0.2g, 10f), oak (1.2g, 35f), birch (0.1g, 2f), cherry (0.05g, 3f)
2	1	Subsoil	Alder (0.8g, 25f), oak (0.01g, 1f), ash (0.1g, 10f), birch (0.01g, 1f)

Table 16.2—Coolbeg: wood species identified.

Botanical name	Species	Weight
Alnus glutinosa	Alder	11.6g
Corylus avellana	Hazel	0.8g
Fraxinus excelsior	Ash	0.3g
Quercus spp	Oak	16.1g
Prunus avuim/padus	Cherry	0.05g
Betula sp.	Birch	0.11g

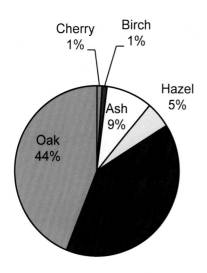

Fig. 16.9—Coolbeg: species represented in the identified samples (based on fragment count).

Discussion

There were six taxon types identified from the charcoal remains (Table 16.1; Fig. 16.9). These were oak (*Quercus* sp.), alder (*Alnus glutinosa*), ash (*Fraxinus excelsior*), hazel (*Corylus avellana*), cherry (*Prunus avuim/padus*) and birch (*Betula* sp.) in order of representation (Table 16.2). The range of species identified from the excavated features analysed includes dryland trees (hazel, oak, cherry and ash) as well as wetland species (alder and birch). There were large trees (ash and oak), medium-sized trees (alder and birch) and smaller, scrub-like trees (cherry and hazel) present in the assemblage. The wood types identified are most likely associated with firewood used at the sites during the period of the Iron Age.

Oak and alder were by far the most dominant taxa identified from the wood remains associated with the ring-ditch (Fig. 16.9). Oak is a dense wood and is very suitable for charcoal production. It also makes good firewood when dried and will grow in wetland areas when conditions are dry. Oak has unique properties of great durability and strength. The oak identified suggests that there was a supply of oak in the surrounding environment at the time of use of the site. Sessile oak (*Quercus petraea*) and pedunculate oak (*Quercus robur*) are both native to and common in Ireland. The wood of these species cannot be differentiated based on its micro-structure. Pedunculate oak is found on heavy clays and loams, particularly where the soil is of alkaline pH. Sessile oak is found on acid soils, often in pure stands, and although it thrives on well-drained soils it is also tolerant of flooding (Beckett 1979, 40–1). Both species of oak grow to be very large trees (30–40m) and can live to an age of about 400 years.

Alder was nearly as dominant as oak in the analysed

assemblage identified; this is unusual, as alder is generally not the normal taxon type identified from ritual monuments associated with the dead, where oak generally predominates. Alder is a widespread native tree and occurs in wet habitats along streams and riverbanks. Alder also grows regularly on fen peat. It is an easily worked and split timber and does not tear when worked. Alder is commonly identified from wood remains associated with wet/boggy areas and is one of the main species identified from *fulacht fiadh* material.

Other taxa present were birch, hazel, ash and cherry, albeit in smaller quantities. Hazel was very common up to the end of the seventeenth century and was used for the manufacture of many wooden structures, such as wattle walls, posts, trackways and baskets. McCracken (1971, 19) points out that 'it was once widespread to a degree that is hard to imagine today'. With the introduction of brick, steel and slate, the crafts associated with hazel became obsolete and today the woods that supplied hazel have diminished rapidly. Hazel is normally only about 3–5m in height and is often found as an understorey tree in deciduous woods dominated by oak. It also occurs as pure copses on shallow soils over limestone, as in the Burren in County Clare, and survives for 30 to 50 years. Its main advantage is seen in the production of long, flexible, straight rods through the process known as coppicing.

Ash is a native species preferring lime-rich, freely draining soils. It is not a very durable timber in waterlogged conditions but has a strong elastic nature. It is easily worked and lends itself well to a range of different requirements, such as the turning of wooden bowls.

Wild cherry is more common in Ireland than bird cherry. There is very little archaeological evidence for the use of cherry wood in Ireland, although the wild cherry tree is commonly found in many hedgerows (Nelson 1993, 167). It is a very durable wood and is as strong as oak.

Hairy birch (*Betula pubescens* Ehrh.) and silver birch (*Betula pendula* Roth.) cannot be distinguished microscopically. Silver birch requires light and dry soil, while hairy birch grows on wet marginal areas. Birch more often occurs on wet marginal areas and is one of the first trees to establish itself on raised bogs. The wood from birch trees is strong but it rots quickly when exposed to outdoor conditions.

Comparative material

Charcoal and wood were analysed from the Bronze Age sites excavated by B. Frazer near this ring-ditch (L. O'Donnell, unpublished post-excavation report for Margaret Gowen and Co. Ltd). The overall results show that ten taxa were identified within the charcoal, and were dominated by oak, hazel and alder. In contrast, only four wood taxa were identified within the wood samples, including oak, alder, ash and hazel. O'Donnell concludes that the site lay where wetland and dryland environments met, which is a typical location for *fulachta fiadh*.

Charcoal analysed from the roundhouses dated to the Bronze Age/Iron Age at Ballynagran and excavated by Frazer shows that ash, oak, hazel, birch and alder dominate the assemblage, with smaller fragments of Pomoideae and cherry also present. Charcoal from an early Iron Age barrow at Balregan 1 and 2, Co. Louth, showed that oak, ash and hazel were identified more frequently within these features (OCarroll 2008). This is in slight contrast to the results here, where oak and alder are the more dominant taxa.

Summary and conclusions

Five taxa were identified from the charcoal remains: oak (*Quercus* sp.), alder (*Alnus glutinosa*), hazel (*Corylus avellana*), ash (*Fraxinus excelsior*), birch (*Betula* spp) and cherry (*Prunus avium/padus*). The assemblage was dominated by oak and alder charcoal.

It is difficult to interpret the results, although the charcoal present in the ditch could represent firewood associated with the process of cremating animal bone. Oak and Pomoideae are nearly always identified and dominant in charcoal analysis from cremation burials and pyres associated with human cremation (Grogan *et al.* 2007). The occurrence of the alder charcoal in such high quantities along with oak may therefore be symptomatic of different ritual processes and the selection of alternative wood types associated with the burning of the animal bone.

It is clear from the results that the local environment of the site in the Iron Age included dryland trees such as oak, ash, hazel and cherry as well as wetland taxa such as alder and birch.

The wood types and selection of trees for use at the ring-ditch site do not differ extensively from the wood types identified by O'Donnell from the earlier Bronze Age at the Ballynagran landfill. Similar tree types were therefore available to the inhabitants of Ballynagran during both the Bronze Age and the Iron Age. There does not appear to have been any deliberate selection policy, particularly in relation to ritual uses.

Bibliography

Beckett, J.K. 1979 *Planting native trees and shrubs*. Norwich.

Grogan, E., O'Donnell, L. and Johnston, P. 2007 *The Bronze Age landscapes of the Pipeline to the West: an integrated archaeological and environmental assessment*. Bray.

Irish Archaeological Wetland Unit 1993 *Excavations at Clonfinlough, County Offaly*. Dublin.

McCracken, E. 1971 *The Irish woods since Tudor times*. Belfast.

Nelson E.C. 1993 *Trees of Ireland*. Dublin.

OCarroll, E. 2002a The analysis of charcoal remains from Cherryville, Co. Dublin. Unpublished report for V.J. Keeley Ltd.

OCarroll, E. 2002b The analysis of charcoal remains from Crabbsland, Co. Limerick. Unpublished report for Aegis Archaeology Ltd.

OCarroll, E. 2004a The analysis of charcoal remains from Kilgobbin, Co. Dublin. Unpublished report for Margaret Gowen and Co. Ltd.

OCarroll, E. 2004b The analysis of charcoal remains from Lughill and Site 5, Celbridge, Co. Kildare. Unpublished report for V.J. Keeley Ltd.

OCarroll, E. 2004c The analysis of charcoal remains from Morett, Co. Laois. Unpublished report for V.J. Keeley Ltd.

OCarroll, E. 2005 The analysis of charcoal remains from Ballybrowney Lower, Fermoy Bypass, Co. Cork. Unpublished specialist report for Archaeological Consultancy Services Ltd.

OCarroll, E. 2008 Iron Age barrow at Balregan 1 and 2, Co. Louth. Unpublished report prepared for Irish Archaeological Consultancy Ltd.

Pilcher, J. and Hall, V. 2001 *Flora Hibernica*. Cork.

Schweingruber, F.H. 1990 *Microscopic wood anatomy* (3rd edn). Birmensdorf.

Warner, R.B. 1990 A proposed adjustment for the 'old-wood' effect. In W. Mook and H. Waterbolk (eds), *Proceedings of the 2nd Symposium of C14 and Archaeology, Groningen, 1987*, 29, 159–72.

Webb, D.A. 1977 *An Irish flora*. Dundalk.

APPENDIX 16.2: THE BURNT BONE (JONNY GEBER)

Two small samples of burnt bone from two contexts (F6 and F7) were analysed (Table 16.3). Both samples contained less than 1g of burnt animal bone from unknown species. The bones could not be identified to element. The fragments were bright white.

Table 16.3—Coolbeg: identified burnt bone in contexts F6 and F7.

Feature	Sample	NISP	Weight (g)	Species	Element	Colour
F6	S2	8	0.53	Animalia sp.	Indet.	Bright white
F7	S4	9	0.21	Animalia sp.	Indet.	Bright white

17. Rath, Co. Meath: of beads and burials

Fin O'Carroll, Alison Sheridan and Katherine Eremin

Introduction

In 2004, excavations were carried out in the townland of Rath, Co. Meath, directed by Holger Schweitzer (Schweitzer and O'Carroll 2009), as part of the N2 road realignment between Finglas, Co. Dublin, and Ashbourne, Co. Meath (now the M2 motorway). This essay briefly describes the main findings on this important site but focuses on an unusual find of faience beads.

The excavation area was *c.* 500m north of Ashbourne (Figs 17.1 and 17.2) on gently sloping terrain. From the highest point of the site, the ground slopes down imperceptibly to the north and east and more steeply to the south-west, towards a stream at the base of the hill. The higher, northern end of the site commands excellent views in all directions, though the elevation in real terms is slight (Fig. 17.3).

Extensive archaeological remains were recorded, ranging in date from the late Neolithic to the modern period. The site was most intensively used during the Bronze Age and Iron

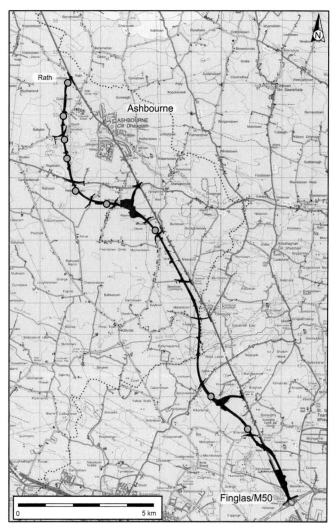

Fig. 17.2—Rath: map showing the position of the site in relation to Ashbourne, Co. Meath.

Age (from about 1200 BC to AD 100; Table 17.1) and evidence ranged from ritual/burial to industrial and settlement activity. Although the total area excavated was almost 300m in length, the archaeology was concentrated within several discrete pockets.

Different kinds of activity on the site were contained within discrete zones. Continuity from the Bronze Age to the Iron Age was a notable feature and was seen in all parts of the site, where individual areas appeared to have been used for

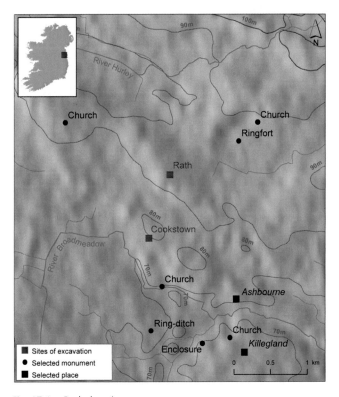

Fig. 17.1—Rath: location map.

Fig. 17.3—Low-level aerial shot of the site at Rath, looking south-west (photo: Hawkeye).

specified functions over centuries. The nature of the activities was partly determined by location: for example, the sweat-lodges were close to the stream at the southern end, which was also the townland boundary, while the majority of the ring-ditches were on the higher ground to the north.

The site was divided into six areas prior to excavation, with area 1 at the townland boundary at the southern end of the site and area 6 lying across the N2 at the northern end (Fig. 17.4). The site is being published as part of the overall N2 road scheme archaeological excavations (O'Carroll *et al.*, forthcoming).

While the site produced a number of unique finds, predominantly of Iron Age date, perhaps the most unusual were also the smallest. A total of fifteen tiny faience beads, plus fragments of two more, were recovered from the primary fills of a ring-ditch. Their form and composition are most unusual, while the dating evidence, which is not clear-cut, suggests either a late Bronze Age or (more possibly) an early Iron Age date, making them unique so far in the record. They have been examined in detail and this work is presented below.

Overview of the site from south to north

The southern end of the site was bounded by a stream, partly canalised to form a field boundary, which is one of the tributaries of the Broad Meadow River. This stream forms the townland boundary between Rath and Cookstown. It is likely that its original bed encroached a little further into the site at Rath and that its presence was a major factor in the utilisation of this area over a number of centuries.

In area 1 (Fig. 17.5), adjacent to this stream, a group of related Bronze Age features included a sweat-lodge and nearby water-hole, while a more elaborate sweat-lodge was in operation in the Iron Age. The Iron Age complex was located to the east of the earlier features and incorporated a sophisticated water management system, channelling water from the nearby stream alongside the sweat-lodge and out through the top of the now silted-up water-hole, presumably back to the stream. The earlier features were dated by their relationship to the later ones and by the presence of artefacts of Bronze Age date, including a sherd of an early Bronze Age bowl food vessel and a late Bronze Age disc-headed pin. A La

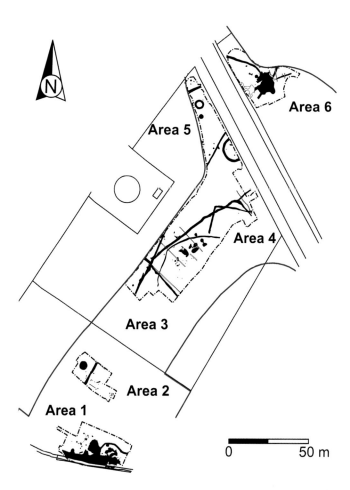

Fig. 17.4—Rath: overall plan of the excavations, showing the location of areas 1–6.

industrial in character; these included a possible kiln or roasting pit, a grain store and associated pits, metalled surfaces, a hearth and a trough. A possible kiln or roasting pit yielded a date of 1050–840 cal. BC from its primary fill, while a bowl furnace associated with metal-working processes, as indicated by its extremely high iron slag content, was dated to 50 cal. BC–cal. AD 80 using a sample of alder recovered from its fills.

Two ring-ditches (F557 and F691) and one ring-barrow (F692; Fig. 17.5) were excavated in area 5. Cremated human remains were recovered from ring-ditches F557 and F692. The southern half of one ring-ditch (F557) was located at the northern part of area 5 and was cut almost perfectly in half by the existing N2. The ditch was U-shaped in profile and enclosed an area measuring 15.8m east–west. There were no traces of an internal mound or enclosing bank. The primary fills appeared to be the result of siltation processes and contained occasional inclusions of burnt bone and charcoal. The ditch was subsequently recut, respecting its original line. The majority of finds came from the upper fills of the recut ditch, which contained charcoal, animal bone and small quantities of cremated human bone. Finds included three hammer-stones, a stone ard point, a flint blade, a potential stone mould, lumps of slag and fragments of iron, including ring or loop fragments. While most of the finds suggest a Bronze Age date, some of these objects may also reflect later activity, perhaps unrelated to funerary functions. Two small internal pits contained fragments of burnt bone that were too fragmented for identification. Interestingly, internal pits were not a feature of any other ring-ditches or barrows, possibly simply reflecting the effects of intensive agriculture, although in all cases the surrounding ditches survived to a reasonable depth.

Ring-ditch F691 was a small annular ditch with an internal diameter of 2.15m. There was no evidence for burial and no dating evidence was forthcoming. Ring-ditch F692 enclosed an area measuring 6m east–west by 5.8m, and the width of the ditch ranged from 1m to 1.2m. The feature was originally constructed as a ring-barrow, consisting of a central mound enclosed by a ditch, and possibly an external bank. Evidence for the mound is implied by the presence of slump material in the ditch. The area in the centre was devoid of any features and all deposits recovered were within the ditch, which had silted up and been recut a number of times. Deposits containing human bone were recorded lying above the basal deposits in the northern half of the ditch; some time later, the mound appears to have slumped into the ditch. Subsequently, three further episodes of burial activity occurred within recuts on the northern side. Much later, a body was interred in the fully silted-up ditch on its southern side and

Tène fibula of a type not previously found in Ireland, with a distinctive bowl at the spring and with chevron ornament on its bow, was recovered from a terrace adjacent to the Iron Age sweat-lodge and may have been lost by someone who was using the lodge. Similar fibulae with springs of four coils, thin bars and domed tops are relatively common in Britain and on the Continent and are usually dated to c. 75–25 BC (Farwell and Molleson 1993). The solid catch-plate of the Rath fibula appears to place it relatively late within this series and, as there is no known parallel for it in Ireland, it may well have been imported. The base of the associated furnace, which lay immediately outside the sweat-lodge structure, was filled with a deposit of burnt-mound-like material and returned a ^{14}C date of 370–110 cal. BC.

In area 2 (Fig. 17.5), on a slight terrace overlooking the activity adjacent to the stream, fragmented faience beads were recovered from a small ring-ditch (F24) and these are described in detail below. Features in areas 3 and 4 were

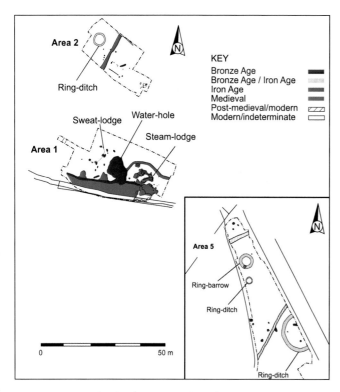

KEY

Bronze Age	▬
Bronze Age / Iron Age	▬
Iron Age	▬
Medieval	▬
Post-medieval/modern	▨
Modern/indeterminate	▭

Fig. 17.5—Rath: details of areas 1 and 2 (left) and area 5 (right).

this marked both a change in burial rite—inhumation, not cremation—and the reuse of what must by now have been an ancient burial ground.

The burial, a crouched inhumation that dates from the Iron Age, contained the badly decomposed skeletal remains of a young female aged between 21 and 25. The body was aligned north–south, with the head at the north and the hand tucked underneath the jaw. She was buried wearing copper-alloy rings, two on the right foot and one on the left. Two almost identical rings were found on each foot. They were undecorated and were shaped in a flat coil similar to modern key-rings. Their rather plain and identical make could suggest that they were part of some sort of footwear. Given the presence of the third ring, which featured incised herringbone decoration, it could be assumed that the footwear was some kind of sandal that would allow the decorated ring to be seen. Attempts to date the burial by radiocarbon analysis failed owing to the extremely low collagen content in the remaining bone. Although so far unique in Ireland, similar burials have been found at late La Tène sites in Britain, where they usually date from the first century BC/first century AD. A burial with toe-rings excavated at Poundbury in Dorset has been dated to *c.* 50 BC–AD 50 (O'Brien 1999). Two Scottish Iron Age burials with toe-rings have been excavated at Mine Howe,

Orkney (Card and Downes 2004), and an Iron Age cist burial at Alloa, Clackmannanshire, was also recorded with toe-rings (Mills 2003). In the light of these examples, it is probable that the burial from Rath is of Iron Age date.

These burial monuments are located on the highest point of the site. The ground is virtually level to the north and east, but the site was divided here by the N2, which had cut through one of the ring-ditches and separated this area from area 6 to the north-east.

Two large and complex wood-lined water-holes were among the features excavated in area 6. Post-and-wattle subdivisions and linings were identified within the pits and these formed internal chambers or containers. Platforms (in one case with a very fine cobbled surface) were set within the pits beside their lowest points, presumably to provide access to the water at the bottom of the pits and a level surface to stand on while working. A wooden bowl, a bentwood box, a ladle, a losset (an object rather like a tray) and withies, which were twisted hazel or willow rods and were probably used as ropes, were recovered from these water-holes, which had been shaped and reshaped over time. Dates ranging from 390 to 160 cal. BC were returned for these features, similar indeed to the date from the sweat-lodge in area 1. A swan's-neck-type pin of early Iron Age date, similar to pins described by Raftery (1984, 14), was recovered from an associated linear ditch. These features lay on the flatter ground at the higher end of the site and it is likely that there are further features in the fields outside the footprint of the new road. No houses were identified within the area excavated but it is possible that they were situated nearby, perhaps on the south-facing slopes, which were not investigated.

It is clear that there was longevity of use and of function at the settlement at Rath. The southern area next to the stream continued to be used to access and heat water and probably served a variety of mundane (washing) and ritual (purification) purposes. Industrial processes were carried out in the area upslope of this but below the barrows that lay across the ridge. The water-holes at the furthest end may have been closest to where settlement activity took place. So there was an intermingling of all aspects of life—work, leisure, ritual, death and day-to-day living in close proximity. In the middle of all of this, however, was one seemingly isolated barrow, set apart from those on the higher ground though on a slight elevation close to the stream, which may also have had a long history.

Ring-ditch and faience beads
Ring-ditch F24, in the western half of area 2 (Fig. 17.5), enclosed an area 3.9m in diameter internally. The ditch itself was 0.5–0.65m wide, with an average depth of 0.5m and a

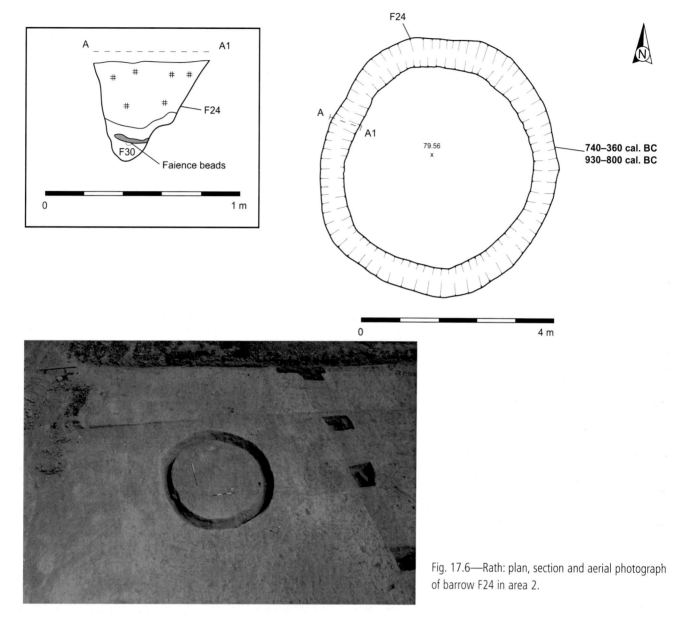

Fig. 17.6—Rath: plan, section and aerial photograph of barrow F24 in area 2.

steeply U-shaped profile. Two fills were recorded within the ditch (Fig. 17.6). The primary fill was a silt layer (F30), which contained a rich seam of charcoal *c.* 0.05m above the base of the ditch cut; this extended for *c.* 1.5m along the north-western quarter of the ditch and was up to 0.04m deep.

What initially appeared to be six fragmented faience beads (03E1214:030:007; 008; 009; 010; 023) were found embedded within the charcoal deposit (Fig. 17.7). Lithic artefacts recovered from the fill included a flint awl (03E1214:030:031), a piece of worked quartz (03E1214:030:026) and a quantity of flint débitage. An early Bronze Age date was suggested for the flint awl, and this appeared to tie in with the presence of faience beads. Their form and composition, however, does not place them within

the known canon of faience beads from Ireland. Charcoal from this deposit has been ^{14}C-dated to 930–800 cal. BC and 740–360 cal. BC, indicating a later Bronze Age/Iron Age date. The earlier date relates to a sample of oak that may have had a long lifespan; the latter was from short-lived species. This deposit was sealed by a silty fill that contained little or no charcoal.

If the flint awl and other lithic items date from the early Bronze Age and do not represent residual material, this implies that this monument had a long use-life, originating in the Bronze Age and with activity continuing into the Iron Age. Such a sequence of activity is known from other sites, such as Kilmahuddrick, Co. Dublin (Doyle 2005), and, more locally, the cemetery further upslope at Rath. Glass beads of similar form to the faience beads were recovered from a barrow at Knockcommane, Co. Tipperary, in the upper ditch fill. Cremated remains from within the barrow were dated to 338–43 cal. BC (McQuade *et al.* 2009, 165).

This activity at the ring-ditch (F24) and the inhumation in the ditch of the ring-barrow (F692) signal another type of continuity and cultural transformation at Rath, which goes beyond the simple continuity of features such as the sweat-lodges and creates a narrative of ancestry and belonging. It is now well established that some ring-ditches had no formal associated burial (Grogan 2004). The monument itself could be the focus for depositional activity, including in some cases deposits of cremated bone, to express a link between the living and the land. This ties in with the recognition that cemeteries, like the small one at Rath, could be about defining both territory and ancestry (Newman 1997; Grogan 2005; Cooney 2009). The high degree to which the landscape surrounding Rath townland was utilised indicates a well-populated and organised community, involved in farming as well as industrial activities. A series of large Bronze Age ritual enclosures (Byrnes 2002) only *c.* 500m to the north-east of the site, and coincidentally on the eastern townland boundary, further highlight how the landscape surrounding Rath townland was utilised, organised and populated from at least the Bronze Age onwards.

The faience beads from the Rath ring-ditch

The beads found within the charcoal deposit at the bottom of the ring-ditch consist of fourteen tiny, roughly cylindrical faience beads (plus traces of two further beads attaching to one of the others), each around 2.5mm in diameter and around 1.5mm wide, with thread-holes ranging between 0.7mm and 1.7mm in diameter (Fig. 17.8). Several had fused together to form irregular 'segmented beads', with the individual 'segments' slightly misaligned in some cases (Fig. 17.9). This misalignment, together with the fact that the individual beads do not appear to have been broken from larger beads, makes it clear that the beads had originally been formed as discrete

entities rather than as genuinely segmented beads. In other words, we are not dealing with a tube of faience paste that had been rolled against a mould, or else scored or crimped, to create a segmented appearance (as was the case with early Bronze Age segmented faience beads, as at Tara, Co. Meath; O'Sullivan 2005, fig. 146).

The beads' surface colour ranges from a bright medium blue or turquoise to pale blue, with the whitish or cream-coloured core material showing through (Fig. 17.10). The core also has brownish speckles, relating to impurities in the sand used as the beads' main constituent. The surfaces range from smooth to slightly rough, and where they are smoothest—where the sand grains had fused to form a thin surface glaze—the surface has a low sheen; otherwise they are matte.

The identification of the material as faience—a glass-like material, made by firing a silica-rich paste (see below)—has been confirmed non-destructively through X-ray fluorescence spectrometry and through examination and microprobe analysis using a scanning electron microscope (SEM). This work was undertaken by Katherine Eremin at National Museums of Scotland, and an example of one of the SEM images is shown in Fig. 17.11. Faience is made by grinding sand (or another source of silicon; sand was used here), mixing

Fig. 17.7—Rath: faience beads before conservation (photo: CRDS Ltd).

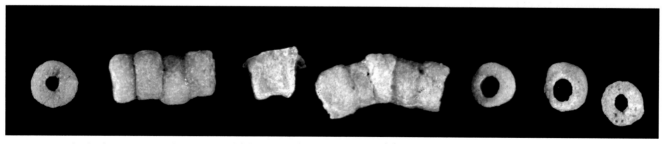

Fig. 17.8—Rath: the faience beads after conservation (photo: National Museums of Scotland).

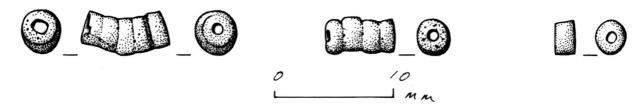

Fig. 17.9—Rath: drawing of some of the faience beads: 03E1214:030:23.1 on left, 03E1214: 030:10.1 in centre and 03E1214: 030:9 on the right (Marion O'Neil, National Museums of Scotland).

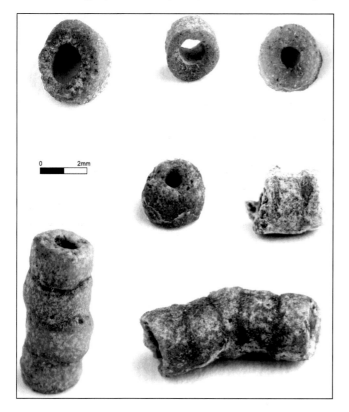

Fig. 17.10—Rath: detail of the beads (John Sunderland).

it into a paste with an alkali such as plant ash—whose function was to lower the melting point of the constituent quartz grains—and firing it (Sheridan *et al.* 2005). The turquoise/blue colour results from the use of a glaze containing a copper-based colourant; the glaze also contains the same materials as the body of the bead. Glazing can be done in various ways (Tite and Bimson 1986), but in the present case it was either applied to the surface or mixed in with the core material prior to firing. Where the firing has succeeded in fusing the surface grains together, the glaze appears as very thin, smooth but discontinuous patches with a glassy finish; elsewhere the glaze appears just as a turquoise colour towards the surface of the

beads. Under the SEM, the granular texture of the incompletely fused quartz grains in the body of the beads can be seen, along with smoother patches of glaze where the grains have fused (Fig. 17.11). Not only did the firing lead to the fusing of individual quartz grains but it may also have been responsible for the fusing together of several of the individual beads.

The analysis showed that the beads were weathered, with chemical leaching having occurred during their long burial in the ground; the copper that had coloured the glaze was depleted, but the presence of small amounts of tin alongside the copper suggests that the colourant had also contained tin. A tiny amount of lead was noted in one bead, and this, together with the tin, raises the question of whether the colourant had come from recycling bronze that contained lead rather than from using copper ore (for suggestions as to the source/s of glaze colourant used in European Bronze Age faience see Aspinall *et al.* 1972; Henderson 1988; Sheridan and Shortland 2004).

The consolidation of the beads during conservation had trapped particles of extraneous sediment on the surface; these showed up analytically as areas high in aluminium. Occasional specks rich in iron, chromium, nickel and aluminium may represent impurities in the sand used to form the beads. The alkali material had contained some potassium and some sodium; it might have come from a sodium-rich plant, but the degree of weathering makes it impossible to tell exactly what had been used and whether it had been a mixed alkali, as was the case for early and middle to late Bronze Age European faience (Henderson 1988). Occasional specks of calcium were noted, but whether these represent impurities in the sand or are the result of contact with human remains is impossible to tell (no definite traces of human remains were found in the ring-ditch fill; some flecks of material found near the beads had originally been thought to be cremated bone but this was not subsequently corroborated).

The beads may originally have belonged to a necklace or bracelet, but clearly only a fraction of the object is represented, since the beads' overall length, when laid end to end, comes to

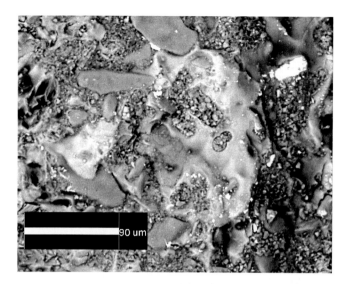

Fig. 17.11—Rath: scanning electron microscope image, at high magnification, showing the surface of one of the beads, with areas of fused glaze and other areas where individual quartz grains of the paste are visible (National Museums of Scotland).

only *c.* 22.5mm. There could theoretically have been additional organic beads that disintegrated, but no traces of any such material were found. Likewise, no trace of any thread was found; if the beads had been strung when buried, this indicates the use of an organic thread. How the beads came to be deposited in the ring-ditch is unclear: were they buried on their own—perhaps as a token deposit—or as grave-goods accompanying a now-disappeared deposit of human remains? (And, if that was the case, might the charcoal have belonged to a funeral pyre?) Simple loss seems unlikely, given the specific location of their discovery.

Discussion

The discovery of faience beads in what appears to be a first-millennium BC context in Ireland is remarkable and, apparently, unique. The seeming ambiguity posed by the radiocarbon-dating evidence from the associated charcoal layer makes it hard to be certain whether they were deposited during the early first millennium BC (in the late Bronze Age), as is suggested by the AMS date of 930–800 cal. BC at 2-sigma from oak charcoal, or later during that millennium, as suggested by a standard date of 740–360 cal. BC at 2-sigma from a mixed sample of short-lived species charcoal (Pomoideae and hazel). The former date is potentially problematic since, as noted above, the oak charcoal may have been from old wood, and the fact that the latter date has been obtained from a mixed sample, rather than a single-entity sample, means that its reliability is not guaranteed. Whatever

the date, it is remarkable to find faience in a post-early Bronze Age context in Ireland; the latest date for early Bronze Age faience in Ireland is the sixteenth century BC (from Kilcroagh, Co. Antrim: Brindley 2007, 314), and it is clear that the Rath beads constitute a late reappearance of this type of material, unconnected with the earlier period of faience use.

The closest Irish comparanda for the beads are the tiny beads of glass and glass paste that have been found with Iron Age deposits—often token deposits (Waddell 1998, 367)—of cremated human bone, placed either in ring-ditches (as at Grannagh, Co. Galway: Raftery 1981, 180) or in pits inside ring-ditches (as at Carrowjames, Co. Mayo: *ibid.*, 181). While none of these beads has been found to be of faience, several characteristics of these finds offer parallels with Rath (in addition to the fact that they have been associated with ring-ditch monuments). Simple, tiny beads made of blue glass—as at Oranbeg, Co. Galway (*ibid.*, 190, no. 511), and Pollacorragune, Co. Galway (*ibid.*, 191)—and of yellow opaque glass paste (at Oranbeg, Co. Galway: Raftery 1983, 190, no. 510) resemble the Rath beads in size and shape, as indeed do the bone beads found with an unburnt female buried in a ring-ditch at Carrowbeg North, Co. Galway (*ibid.*, 194 (no. 525), fig. 155), and in a settlement at Oranbeg (*ibid.*, 195 (no. 528), fig. 155). In more than one instance glass beads seem to have been through the funeral pyre with the corpse, so that individual beads fused together (as at Oranbeg; see also Carbury Hill, site A, Co. Kildare: Raftery 1981, 186). This offers a further point of similarity with the Rath beads, although with the latter the fusing could have occurred during their manufacture; as noted above, there is no proof that the beads had been deposited with human remains.

In discussing the chronology of these Iron Age beads, however, Raftery (1981, 195–9) places them not earlier than the first century BC (while acknowledging that the practice of constructing ring-ditch funerary monuments extends back many centuries; see also McGarry 2009)—in other words, several centuries later than the latest date associated with the Rath beads. Raftery's dating of the Irish Iron Age beads is consistent with our understanding of the chronology of yellow glass paste use in Britain and Ireland (F. Hunter, pers. comm.); and if we look across the water to Roman Britain, numerous parallels exist (in glass, bone, jet and faience) for the use of tiny annular beads (for example in York: Allason-Jones 1996, fig. 15 and no. 9). This poses the question: might the Rath beads be later than the charcoal in which they were embedded, and might they be contemporary with the tiny beads discussed above? If not, how is their presence to be explained?

One possible clue is offered by the activities that are known to have occurred at Rathgall, Co. Wicklow, where both

Table 17.1—Rath: radiocarbon dates from the excavations (03E1214).

Lab no.	Feature	¹⁴C			Archaeological period
		BP date	1σ date	2σ date	
Wk-16316	Fill of water-hole, area 6	2203±36	360–200 BC	380–180 BC	Iron Age
Wk-16317	Ring-ditch, area 2	2353±41	510–380 BC	740–360 BC	Bronze Age–Iron Age
Wk-16320	Hurdle structure in water-hole, area 6	2190±35	360–190 BC	380–160 BC	Iron Age
Wk-16824	Fill of water-hole, area 6	2217±36	370–200 BC	390–190 BC	Iron Age
Wk-17942	Fill of hearth/ furnace, area 1	2170±32	360–170 BC	370–110 BC	Iron Age
Wk-17943	Ring-ditch, area 2	2716±38	900–825 BC	930–800 BC	Bronze Age
Wk-18204	Hearth assoc. with metal-working, area 3/4	2534±31	800–550 BC	800–520 BC	Bronze Age
Wk-18205	Fill of bowl furnace F89, area 4	1985±28	40 BC–AD 55	50 BC–AD 80	Iron Age
Wk-18206	Primary fill of roasting pit/kiln, area 3/4	2812±31	1000–920 BC	1050–840 BC	Bronze Age
Wk-18207	Fill of trough F1189, area 6	2897±53	1210–990 BC	1260–920 BC	Bronze Age
Wk-18208	Fill of pit F9, area 4	1029±36	AD 980–1030	AD 890–1160	Early–high medieval
Wk-18209	Pit/hearth, area 4	2403±61	760–390 BC	770–380 BC	Bronze Age–Iron Age

glass and glazed ceramic beads were being produced during the ninth and eighth centuries BC, arguably as a result of contacts with continental Europe (Henderson 1988; Raftery 1973; 1976). While no beads were found in the late Bronze Age grave containing cremated remains found inside a ring-ditch at Rathgall (Raftery 1973; see also Raftery 1981), nevertheless the fact that 71 greenish-turquoise annular beads were found elsewhere at Rathgall demonstrates an interest in producing beads of a turquoise colour during the early first millennium BC. Furthermore, the discovery there of a fragmentary bead featuring a fired clay core and a turquoise surface glaze (Henderson 1988, 442) demonstrates an interest in experimenting with technology that is not unrelated to faience manufacture—technology that was already in place in northern Italy and Switzerland, the areas of Europe that are

believed to have been the inspiration for activities at Rathgall and elsewhere in Ireland (ibid.). From Rathgall, therefore, comes an interest in glass and related technology and an interest in the same colour of bead as found at Rath. Thus the conditions existed for true faience to be produced in Ireland during the early first millennium BC.

In conclusion, the Rath beads constitute a very significant find, although the uncertainty about their date raises more questions than can easily be answered. In terms of potential for future investigation, there may be scope for further investigation of the faience beads' composition (for comparison with that of Continental late Bronze Age and Roman faience) through electron microprobe analysis of a section cut through one of the better-preserved beads or through other analytical techniques including isotope analysis.

This would be a slightly risky undertaking, however, since the weathered nature of the beads makes it uncertain whether significantly more information would emerge from destructive analysis. The question of whether the beads had been made locally cannot currently be addressed, although analysis of sand deposits in the area might reveal whether similar impurities to those seen in the beads are present.

Bibliography

Allason-Jones, L. 1996 *Roman jet in the Yorkshire Museum.* York.

Aspinall, A., Warren, S.E., Crummett, J.G. and Newton, R.G. 1972 Neutron activation analysis of faience beads. *Archaeometry* **14**, 27–40.

Brindley, A. 2007 *The dating of food vessels and urns in Ireland.* Galway.

Byrnes, E. 2002 Gas pipeline to the west: section 1a, preliminary report, site 1A/12/1, licence 02E0638. Unpublished report prepared on behalf of Bord Gáis Éireann.

Card, N. and Downes, J. 2004 An Iron Age burial on Orkney. *Current Archaeology* **194**, 58–9.

Cooney, G. 2009 Tracing lines across landscapes: corporality and history in later prehistoric Ireland. In G. Cooney, K. Becker, J. Coles, M. Ryan and S. Sievers (eds), *Relics of old decency: archaeological studies in later prehistory*, 375–88. Dublin.

Doyle, I.W. 2005 Excavation of a prehistoric ring-barrow at Kilmahuddrick, Clondalkin, Dublin 22. *Irish Journal of Archaeology* **14,** 43–75.

Farwell, D.E. and Molleson, T.I. 1993 *Excavations at Poundbury, 1966–80, ii: the cemeteries.* Dorchester.

Grogan, E. 2004 Middle Bronze Age burial traditions in Ireland. In H. Roche, E. Grogan, J. Bradley, J. Coles and B. Raftery (eds), *From megaliths to metals: essays in honour of George Eogan*, 61–71. Oxford.

Grogan, E. 2005 *The North Munster Project, Vol. 2. The later prehistory of north Munster.* Bray.

Henderson, J. 1988 Glass production and Bronze Age Europe. *Antiquity* **62**, 435–51.

McGarry, T. 2009 Irish late prehistoric burial ring-ditches. In G. Cooney, K. Becker, J. Coles, M. Ryan and S. Sievers (eds), *Relics of old decency: archaeological studies in later prehistory*, 413–23. Bray.

McQuade, M., Molloy, B. and Moriarty, C. 2009 *In the shadow of the Galtees: archaeological excavations along the N8 Cashel to Mitchelstown road scheme.* Dublin.

Mills, S. 2004 Alloa: a Bronze Age woman and an Iron Age warrior. *Current Archaeology* **191**, 486–9.

Newman, C. 1997 *Tara: an archaeological survey.* Dublin.

O'Brien, E. 1992 Pagan and Christian burial in Ireland during the first millennium AD: continuity and change. In N. Edwards and A. Lane (eds), *The early church in Wales and the West: recent work in early Christian archaeology, history and place-names*, 130–7. Oxford.

O'Brien, E. 1999. *Post-Roman Britain to Anglo-Saxon England: burial practices reviewed.* British Archaeological Reports. Series 289. Oxfrod

O'Carroll, F., Seaver, M., Clutterbuck, R. and Fallon, D. (forthcoming) The archaeology of the N2 road scheme: travels through time from Finglas to Ashbourne.

O'Sullivan, M. 2005 *Duma na nGiall: the Mound of the Hostages, Tara.* Bray.

Raftery, B. 1973 Rathgall: a late Bronze Age burial in Ireland. *Antiquity* **47**, 293–5.

Raftery, B. 1976 Rathgall and Irish hillfort problems. In D.W. Harding (ed.), *Hillforts, later prehistoric earthworks of Britain and Ireland*, 339–57. London.

Raftery, B. 1981 Iron Age burials in Ireland. In D. Ó Corráin (ed.), *Irish antiquity: essays and studies presented to Professor M.J. O'Kelly*, 173–204. Dublin.

Raftery, B. 1983 *A catalogue of Irish Iron Age antiquities* (2 vols). Marburg.

Raftery, B. 1984 *La Tène in Ireland: problems of origin and chronology.* Marburg.

Schweitzer, H. 2005 Iron Age toe-rings from Rath, County Meath, on the N2 Finglas–Ashbourne road scheme. In J. O'Sullivan and M. Stanley (eds), *Recent archaeological discoveries on national road schemes 2004*, 93–8. Bray.

Schweitzer, H. and O'Carroll, F. 2009 Report on Site 27, Rath, Co. Meath. Unpublished report prepared for the National Roads Authority.

Sheridan, J.A. and Shortland, A. 2004 '… beads which have given rise to so much dogmatism, controversy and rash speculation': faience in early Bronze Age Britain and Ireland. In I.A.G. Shepherd and G.J. Barclay (eds), *Scotland in ancient Europe*, 263–79. Edinburgh.

Sheridan, J.A., Eremin, K. and Shortland, A. 2005 Understanding Bronze Age faience in Britain and Ireland. In P.B. Vandiver, J.L. Mass and A. Murray (eds), *Materials issues in art and archaeology, vii*, 217–29. Warrendale.

Tite, M.S. and Bimson, M. 1986 Faience: an investigation of the microstructure associated with the different methods of glazing. *Archaeometry* **28** (1), 69–78.

Waddell, J. 1998 *The prehistoric archaeology of Ireland.* Galway.

18. Stars in their eyes: the ceremonial complex at Lismullin, Co. Meath

Aidan O'Connell

Introduction

Located about halfway between the towns of Dunshaughlin and Navan in County Meath, the townland of Lismullin is on the eastern bank of the River Gabhra, roughly 2.1km to the north-east of the Hill of Tara (Figs 18.1 and 18.2). In 2007 a major archaeological complex was excavated here in the course of advance archaeological investigations along section 2 of the M3 Clonee–North of Kells motorway scheme. This archaeological site sat on a plateau overlooking the Gabhra Valley, within a natural saucer-shaped depression surrounded on all sides by a ridge of higher ground (Fig. 18.3). This distinctive hollow and the surrounding higher ridge had the appearance of a mini-amphitheatre. Much of the human activity at Lismullin for which evidence was recorded in the course of the excavations appears to have been focused on this natural topography. This paper focuses on the Iron Age ceremonial complex (Fig. 18.4).

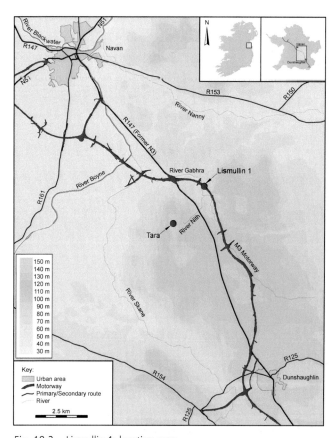

Fig. 18.2—Lismullin 1: location map.

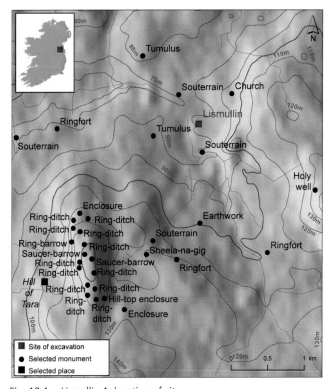

Fig. 18.1—Lismullin 1: location of site.

A square building

A square timber building (12m by 12m) was located towards the south-western boundary of the excavated area. It comprises the first stage in the development of the ceremonial complex. The walls were defined by a series of small post-holes (0.13–0.19m in diameter by 0.12–0.15m in depth) that extended beyond the excavated area (most of the southern wall lay outside the limit of excavation). There was an entrance, aligned to the east and comprising two parallel lines of larger post-holes (0.13–0.19m in diameter by 0.12–0.15m in depth) extending both to the exterior and to the interior of the structure. Although burnt bone (not identifiable) was recovered from the majority of the entrance post-holes, none was recovered from those on the walls. The small charcoal assemblages from these post-holes were very similar to each other and were dominated by ash, hazel and Maloideae, with

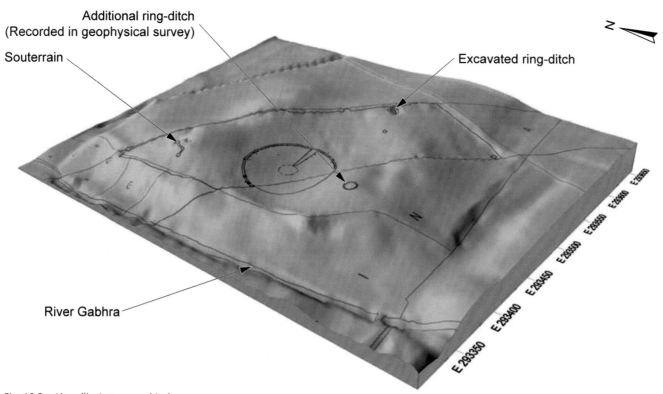

Fig. 18.3—Lismullin 1: topographical survey.

a few fragments of alder and cherry. The main structural timber in this building was probably ash, and lengths of hazel were woven between the upright timber posts to form a wall facing. The relatively high quantities of Maloideae (part of the rose family) may indicate that flower-bearing branches were suspended from the wall facing for aesthetic or symbolic purposes (O'Brien *et al.* 2009, appendix 5; see also Newman *et al.* 2007). Five radiocarbon dates indicate the construction and use of the building in the early Iron Age, between the early eighth and early sixth centuries BC.

There was no indication of hearths or domestic debris in the interior of the structure. Furthermore, its location within the poorly drained hollow might have rendered this structure unsuitable for occupation. Perhaps its most striking feature was the elaborate east-facing entrance and the deposition of burnt bone in all of its constituent post-holes. There are no obviously comparable structures in Ireland, although two late Bronze Age buildings of similar shape and size were found at Ballinderry 2 crannog, Co. Offaly (Hencken 1942; Newman 1991), where a build-up of settlement debris suggests that they were associated with domestic habitation (Newman 1991, 97). The Lismullin structure may, however, have served a different

purpose, and Walsh (2011; this volume) has recently identified a possible rectangular shrine, dating from the late Iron Age, at Kilmainham, Co. Meath. It is possible, therefore, that this building was a shrine or temple, with the main focus on a monumental east-facing entrance. This suggests that the base of the hollow had, by the late Bronze Age/early Iron Age, become a focus for religious structures. The formal use of sacred space evolved over subsequent centuries, with the construction of a series of exceptional timber structures.

Post-enclosure

The enclosure complex is represented by three principal elements:

- an outer enclosure, roughly 80m in diameter, formed by two concentric rings of posts;
- a central inner enclosure, 16m in diameter, defined by a single ring of closely spaced post-holes;
- an avenue of stakes extending from an entrance structure defined by four substantial upright posts located at a gap on the eastern side of the outer enclosure and leading to the inner enclosure (Fig. 18.4).

Fig. 18.4—Lismullin 1: post-excavation plan.

Fig. 18.5—Lismullin 1: elevated view of the site, with team members standing on the outer edge of the enclosure (John Sunderland).

Outer enclosure: inner ring

The inner ring of the outer enclosure was 76.7m in diameter, represented by 131 post-holes within the footprint of the road. Analysis of the excavation evidence estimated the original number of posts in the complete ring at 258 (including the area outside the proposed roadway, which was not excavated). The average surviving dimensions of a typical post-hole were approximately 0.2m in diameter by 0.16m in depth. The individual posts were between 0.41m and 1.74m apart (average 0.93m).

Outer enclosure: outer ring

The outer ring was 80.5m in diameter, with 85 post-holes (of an estimated total of 242) identified through excavation (Fig. 18.5). The average dimensions of the posts were 0.18m in diameter by 0.14m deep, and they were typically placed 0.47–1.68m apart (average 1.04m). Of these post-holes, 76% (or 65/85) had a single fill, suggesting that these had been simply driven into position.

The inner enclosure

The inner enclosure, which was located at the lowest part of the hollow, was 15.82m in diameter and consisted of 62 closely spaced post-holes (average dimensions 0.32m in diameter by 0.21m in depth; Fig. 18.6). It was the only one of the three rings fully exposed during the excavation. The individual posts were 0.57–1.17m apart (average 0.82m). Importantly, the prehistoric topsoil into which many of these posts was inserted survived, probably because the lowest point of the hollow was not as disturbed by ploughing as elsewhere.

Entrance

An entrance to the complex was defined by a gap in the two outer post-rings flanked by a rectangular arrangement of four large post-holes (0.75–0.9m in diameter) enclosing a space approximately 6m east/west by 4m north/south. The size of these post-holes indicates that the timber uprights in the entrance structure were substantially larger than those in the enclosing rings.

236

Fig. 18.6—Lismullin 1: elevated view of the inner enclosure and elongated pit, from the east (John Sunderland).

This formal entrance was aligned with an avenue formed by two parallel lines of stake-holes (average dimensions 0.09m in diameter by 0.09m deep). These extended from the entrance towards the inner circle but terminated at an elongated pit 4m away from it. There were nine stake-holes in the northern row and fourteen in the southern; the avenue had a uniform width of 3.96m and extended between the entrance and the elongated pit.

Internal features

A cluster of eleven pits and nine post-holes were recorded within the inner enclosure. These can be broadly grouped into three stratigraphical phases, the earliest of which comprises a single post-hole, located roughly 0.5m from the centre point of the complex. Six of the remaining internal features have been radiocarbon-dated, indicating that they were broadly contemporary with the remainder of the complex.

Elongated pit

A narrow linear pit was set at right angles to the entrance avenue at a distance of 4m from the inner enclosure (Fig. 18.6). The fill contained large quantities of charcoal (mainly ash, with hazel and Maloideae also frequently recorded), in addition to burnt and unburnt (animal) bone fragments and a significant quantity of hazelnut shell fragments. Radiocarbon dating indicated that this pit was contemporary with the enclosure complex. At first glance, the pit appears to have hindered access to the inner enclosure, perhaps representing the remains of a screen or fence erected for such a purpose. Yet excavation of the pit yielded no indications that it was intended to support a structure of any kind. The recovered charcoal did not appear to have been burnt *in situ*, nor was there any evidence for the existence of posts or stone packing to support a screen or fence. In contrast, the primary function of the pit was for deposition.

Fig. 18.7—Lismullin 1: computer-generated reconstruction of the enclosure.

Enclosure design

Lismullin 1 takes the form of three circular concentric enclosures integrated by an easterly aligned avenue and set in a distinctive natural hollow (Fig. 18.7). Effectively, the activities taking place within the enclosure, at the base of the hollow, could well have been viewed from the external ridge of high ground. Charcoal analysis indicates that ash and hazel were the most common wood species. Ash was possibly the main structural timber, and it was faced with woven hazel rods or hazel panels. The dimensions of the post-holes recorded during the excavation were similar to the size of timber posts that can be seen in modern post-and-wire fences. This suggests that the timber uprights at Lismullin would have reached somewhere between waist and chest height, allowing people situated outside the enclosure, on the external ridge of higher ground, to see into the internal space.

The regularity of the enclosures is immediately apparent, especially their rigid circularity. A geospatial dataset was generated from the coordinates of individual post-holes. Statistical analysis of these data (Prendergast 2009) indicates that a specific unit of measurement was used in the construction. This unit was recognisable in the dimensions of the following elements:

- the radii of the three principal circular enclosures;
- the gap between the two outer enclosure rings;
- the entrance avenue width;
- the distance between each post-hole (the post-hole pitch) in the external ring of the outer enclosure;
- the gap between the inner enclosure and two separate internal arcs of post-holes;
- the distance between the inner enclosure and the elongated pit.

The template unit, which was based on either the radius of the inner enclosure (7.97m) or the width of the entrance avenue (3.94m), was either positively or negatively scaled in order to set out the monument.

Analysis of the orientation of the entrance avenue also indicates that it was aligned towards the Pleiades, a visually distinctive grouping and the nearest star cluster to earth (Prendergast 2009). This cluster is visible to the naked eye for a period of roughly three months in an annual cycle that coincided with the end of harvest and the onset of winter. The cluster would have risen in the east above the entrance avenue at roughly 9pm before moving across the night sky (Fig. 18.8).

238

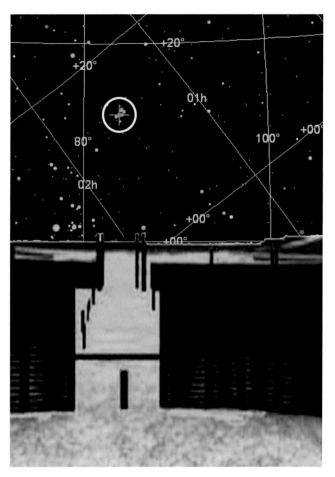

Fig. 18.8—Lismullin 1: view from enclosure interior, showing alignment of the entrance to the Pleiades star cluster.

Enclosure chronology

A comprehensive programme of radiocarbon dating was undertaken across the site in order to establish its precise chronology. Five separate architectural components of the enclosure complex were dated: the three enclosure rings, the entrance structure and the entrance avenue. Sample material was retrieved from calibrated radiocarbon dates, which were then subjected to Bayesian analysis. This involves analysing 'known likelihoods' about a problem (radiocarbon dates) in the context of existing experience and knowledge about that problem (the archaeological sequence as recorded during an excavation) to produce a set of 'posterior beliefs' (the probable dates of each event in the archaeological sequence) in order to provide more precise age estimates for events represented in the archaeological sequence (Faulkner 2007).

The results of the extensive dating programme (Fig. 18.9) suggest that the enclosure complex was erected on a phased basis, with the inner ring of the outer enclosure

constructed in the period 455–400 BC (68% probability), followed by the construction of the outer ring of the outer enclosure in the period 415–385 BC (68% probability). Finally, the inner enclosure was erected in the period 405–365 BC (56% probability) or 285–265 BC (12% probability). Use of the monument was estimated to cease *c.* 370–330 BC (38% probability) or 270–220 BC (32% probability). This suggests a duration of use of between 45 and 115 years (36% probability) or 140–225 years (32% probability). The probability that the inner ring of the outer enclosure was the earliest part of the monument to be built was estimated at 86.7%, casting doubt over the initial interpretation of the monument being constructed in a single event.

Parallels

The best Irish comparisons for the circular timber structures at Lismullin 1 are to be found at the major Iron Age regional centres, collectively called 'royal sites'. These are Tara, Co. Meath, Navan Fort (Emain Macha), Co. Armagh, Dún Ailinne (Knockaulin), Co. Kildare, Rathcroghan (Cruacháin), Co. Roscommon, Uisneach, Co. Westmeath, and Raffin Fort, Co. Meath (Newman 1997; Grogan 2008; Waterman 1997; Johnston and Wailes 2007; Waddell *et al.* 2010; Schot 2011; Newman 1993). Additionally, the late Bronze Age ceremonial enclosure at Lugg, Co. Dublin (Kilbride-Jones 1950; Roche and Eogan 2007), although not part of a wider ritual landscape or associated with a 'royal' site, is worthy of comparison. Here, a burial site comprising numerous cremation pits and funerary pyres was succeeded by a complex of earthworks consisting of a central flat-topped mound with enclosing ditches and banks. An avenue of large, free-standing wooden posts was laid out between the north-eastern side of the outer enclosure and the eastern side of the inner enclosure. This formed a routeway and entrance to the central raised platform, with obvious comparisons to the entrance avenue at Lismullin.

The remaining comparable timber structures comprise successive enclosures. The most pertinent of these, in part owing to their proximity to Lismullin, are to be found at the Rath of the Synods (Ráith na Senad), Tara, Co. Meath, where large palisade enclosures, up to 30m in diameter, were defined by upright posts set into bedding trenches. They were conjoined with smaller (16.5m) timber enclosures on the southern side and replaced by secondary circular structures, *c.* 40–42m wide. This occurrence of figure-of-eight timber structures succeeded by circular ones is replicated at Navan Fort and Dún Ailinne. Comparable circular structures are to be found at Raffin Fort.

Some parallels for the Lismullin enclosure can be noted further afield. For example, at Thwing, Yorkshire, a 23m-wide

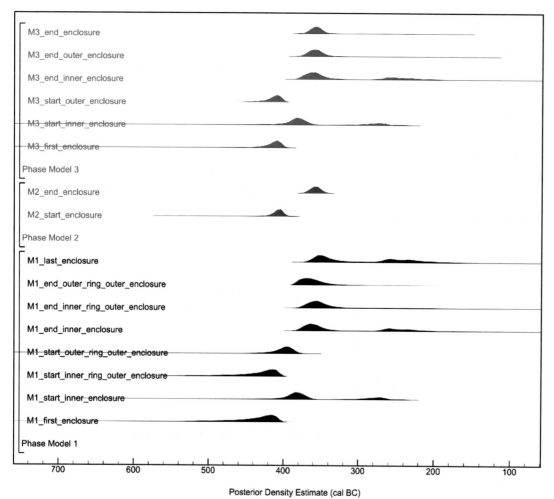

Fig. 18.9—Lismullin 1: the radiocarbon chronology of the enclosure.

timber building (950–750 BC) was set inside a 120m-wide earthwork enclosure (Manby *et al.* 2003, 76). In southern England there is a corpus of small timber temples and shrines dated to the late Iron Age, albeit with a striking variation in form, with round, oval, square and rectangular examples recorded (Webster 1995, 455–8). In northern France there is a group of rectangular palisaded earthwork enclosures known as 'Belgic sanctuaries'. These are associated with large numbers of votive deposits and sacrificial remains and, most importantly, internal religious buildings (Brunaux 1988, 11–31).

Circular arguments and sacred groves

Religious structures, like those outlined above, are a physical manifestation of the ideas and beliefs of the communities that built them. The concept of the circle must have been of primary importance to the people who built Lismullin, when one considers the care taken here to achieve perfect, concentric enclosures. The circle is a recurring element in the design of both domestic and ritual prehistoric monuments (Gibson 2004; Corlett 2005) and understanding the symbolism of this form is of primary importance for our interpretation of the site.

On the one hand, the circular form is the easiest to set out accurately and the result can be aesthetically pleasing. On the other, however, archaeologists in recent years have attempted to explain this form as representing the sun and its motions (Parker-Pearson and Ramilisonina 1998, 322) or as symbolic of the surrounding circular horizon and, consequently, creating a miniature model of the known world (Richards 1996, 203–6).

The timber used in the construction of the enclosure may also have been a metaphor for the sacred grove or *nemeton* of Celtic religious practices. Many Greek and Roman writers, including the historian Strabo, have noted the veneration of trees (and other topographical features) among Iron Age peoples. It is therefore envisaged that Lismullin and comparable sites were conceived as a means of reconstructing

Table 18.1—Lismullin: radiocarbon dates from post-enclosure.

Inner ring of outer enclosure

Lab no.	Sample	BP	Cal. date range (95% probability)	Modelled ^{14}C (95% prob.)
NZA-30407	Charcoal, ash	2440±25	390–200 BC	400–340 (89%) or 305–245 (8%) BC
NZA-30399	Charcoal, Maloideae	2292±55	410–205 BC	425–340 (91%) or 310–240 (4%) BC
NZA-30408	Charcoal, willow/poplar	2392±20	520–395 BC	480–395 BC
NZA-30391	Charcoal, ash	2327±20	405–380 BC	410–380 BC
NZA-30403	Charcoal, willow/poplar	2243±20	390–205 BC	395–345 (89%) or 295–250 (6%) BC
NZA-30404	Charcoal, blackthorn	2452±55	790–390 BC	495–385 BC
NZA-30405	Charcoal, ash	2241+20	390–205 BC	395–315 (89%) or 295–250 (6%) BC
NZA-30397	Charcoal, willow	3803±20	2295–2145 BC	–
Beta-230460	Charcoal, ash and hazel	2360±40	520–380 BC	480–370 BC

Outer ring of outer enclosure

Lab no.	Sample	BP	Cal. date range (95% prob.)	Modelled ^{14}C (95% prob.)
NZA-30393	Charcoal, hazel	2253±20	395–205 BC	395–350 BC
NZA-30392	Charcoal, ash	2279±20	400–235 BC	400–360 BC
NZA-30401	Charcoal, hazel	2324±20	405–380 BC	405–375 BC
NZA-30398	Charcoal, ash	2895±20	1190–1005 BC	–
NZA-30402	Charred blackthorn fruit stone	2235±25	390–200 BC	400–340 BC
Beta-230461	Charcoal, ash and hazel	2340±40	510–230 BC	415–360 BC

Inner enclosure

Lab no.	Sample	BP	Cal. date range (95% prob.)	Modelled ^{14}C (95% prob.)
NZA-30400	Charcoal, ash	2240±40	400–190 BC	395–340 (62%) or 305–225 (33%) BC
NZA-30390	Charred barley grain	1414±20	AD 600–660	–
NZA-30406	Charcoal, Maloideae	2881±45	1260–920 BC	–
SUERC-23519	Charred monocot stems	2275±30	400–210 BC	400–345 (47%) or 310–210 (48%) BC
SUERC-23520	Charcoal, ash	2450±30	770–400 BC	–
SUERC-23529	Charcoal, ash	2265±30	400–200 BC	395–350 (64%) or 290–230 (31%) BC
SUERC-23530	Charcoal, *Prunus* sp.	3635±30	2130–1910 BC	–
SUERC-23532	Charcoal, ash	2240±30	400–200 BC	395–345 (63%) or 300–230 (32%) BC
SUERC-23533	Charred hazelnut shell	2225±30	390–190 BC	395–340 (62%) or 305–225 (33%) BC
SUERC-23534	Charred false oat-grass tuber	2270±30	400–200 BC	395–350 (65%) or 290–235 (30%) BC
SUERC-23558	Charcoal, ash	2320±30	410–370 BC	400–355 (67%) or 285–235 (28%) BC

Enclosure entrance

Lab no.	Sample	BP	Cal. date range (95% prob.)	Modelled ^{14}C (95% prob.)
SUERC-23544	Charcoal, ash, from post-hole in entrance structure	2220±30	390–190 BC	380–205 BC
SUERC-23548	Charcoal, ash, from post-hole in entrance structure	2260±30	400–200 BC	400–345 (41%) or 315–210 (54%) BC
SUERC-23543	Charcoal, ash, from entrance avenue	2295±30	410–230 BC	410–350 (72%) or 295–230 (23%) BC
SUERC-23549	Charcoal, hazel, from entrance avenue	2350±35	510–380 BC	540–365 BC
SUERC-23550	Charcoal, oak, from entrance avenue	4195±30	2900–2670 BC	2890–2845 (12%) or 2815–2660 (81%) or 2650–2635 (2%) BC

a symbolic model of the sacred grove.

The Lismullin 1 post-enclosure was constructed in a location set apart from the surrounding landscape by its unusual topography. Within this distinctive and carefully chosen physical setting, a simple yet elegant circular building was laid out and constructed in such a way as to carefully segregate the internal space into distinctive zones of activity. The inner enclosure was probably set aside for religious activities, and access to the central sacred space may have been restricted to a specialised priestly class who moved in procession through the avenue. The elongated pit, situated at the end of the avenue, was intended to augment the entrance, with burnt offerings apparently deposited therein before entry to the inner sanctum. This activity may have been viewed by the populace from the relative safety of the ridge of higher ground surrounding the enclosure. The physical boundaries of the inner enclosure, the outer enclosure and the external high ground may thus have marked the separation of different functional spheres associated with different modes of behaviour (Smith 2001, 17).

The alignment of the entrance avenue with the Pleiades suggests that ceremonies and rituals undertaken at Lismullin were centred on autumn harvest. The ceremonies would have taken place at night, when the Pleiades alignment was visible. The Lismullin excavations thus facilitate the creation of a vivid picture of religious activity in the Irish Iron Age, suggesting processions and ceremonies undertaken by firelight for the benefit of the massed spectators gathered on an external viewing platform. Whatever the precise nature of the beliefs represented by the monument, they have provided us with evidence for a set of ceremonies differing in scale and prominence from the great regional gatherings at the major royal centres—perhaps the petitions or thanksgiving of one particular community for a successful harvest.

Bibliography

Brunaux, J.L. 1988 *The Celtic Gauls: gods, rites and sanctuaries* (trans. D. Nash). London.

Corlett, C. 2005 Ring-barrows: a circular argument with a ring of truth? In T. Condit and C. Corlett (eds), *Above and beyond: essays in memory of Leo Swan*, 63–71. Bray.

Faulkner, N. 2007 The new radiocarbon dating revolution. *Current Archaeology* **209**, 9–20.

Gibson, A. 2004 Round in circles: timber circles, henges and stone circles—some possible relationships and transformations. In R. Cleal and J. Pollard (eds), *Monuments and material culture: papers in honour of an Avebury archaeologist: Isobel Smith*, 70–82. Salisbury.

Grogan, E. 2008 *The Rath of the Synods, Tara, Co. Meath: excavations by Seán P. Ó Ríordáin*. Bray.

Hencken, H. O'Neill 1942 Ballinderry Crannog no. 2. *Proceedings of the Royal Irish Academy* **47**C, 1–76.

Johnston, S.A. and Wailes, B. 2007 *Dún Ailinne: excavations at an Irish royal site, 1968–1975*. Philadelphia.

Kilbride-Jones, H.E. 1950 The excavation of a composite early Iron Age monument with 'henge' features at Lugg, Co. Dublin. *Proceedings of the Royal Irish Academy* **53**C, 311–32.

Manby, T.G., King, A. and Vyner, B.E. 2003 The Neolithic and Bronze Ages: a time of early agriculture. In T.G. Manby, S. Moorhouse and P. Ottaway (eds), *The archaeology of Yorkshire: an assessment at the beginning of the 21st century*, 35–116. Leeds.

Newman, C. 1991 Ballinderry Crannog no. 2, Co. Offaly: pre-crannog early medieval horizon. *Journal of Irish Archaeology* **11**, 99–123.

Newman, C. 1993 Sleeping in Elysium. *Archaeology Ireland* **7** (3), 20–3.

Newman, C. 1997 Ballinderry Crannóg No. 2, Co. Offaly: the later Bronze Age. *Journal of Irish Archaeology*, **8**, 91–100.

Newman, C., O'Connell, M., Dillon, M. and Molloy, K. 2007 Interpretation of charcoal and pollen data relating to a late Iron Age ritual site in eastern Ireland: a holistic approach. *Vegetation History and Archaeobotany* **16**, 349–65.

O'Brien *et al.* 2009 Lismullin 1, M3 Motorway, Co. Meath, Ireland; plant macrofossil, charcoal, cremated bone and mollusc analysis. Unpublished report 2204, Archaeological Services Durham University.

Parker-Pearson, M. and Ramilisonina 1998 Stonehenge for the ancestors: the stones pass on the message. *Antiquity* **72**, 308–26.

Prendergast, F. 2009 A study of the morphology, metrology and archaeoastronomy of the Iron Age enclosure, Lismullin, Co. Meath. Unpublished report for Archaeological Consultancy Services Ltd and Meath County Council on behalf of the School of Spatial Planning, Dublin Institute of Technology, and the School of Archaeology, UCD.

Richards, C. 1996 Monuments as landscape: creating the centre of the world in late Neolithic Orkney. *World Archaeology* **28** (2), 190–208.

Roche, H. and Eogan, G. 2007 A reassessment of the enclosure at Lugg, County Dublin, Ireland. In C. Gosden, H. Hamerow, P. de Jersey and G. Lock (eds), *Communities and connections: essays in honour of Barry Cunliffe*, 154–68. Oxford.

Schot, R. 2011 From cult centre to royal centre: monuments,

myths and other revelations at Uisneach. In R. Schot, C. Newman and E. Bhreathnach (eds), *Landscapes of cult and kingship*, 87–113. Dublin.

Smith, A. 2001 *The differential use of constructed sacred space in southern Britain from the late Iron Age to the 4th century AD.* British Archaeological Reports, British Series 318. Oxford.

Waddell, J., Fenwick, J. and Barton, K. 2010 *Rathcroghan: archaeological and geophysical survey in a ritual landscape.* Bray.

Walsh, F. 2011 Seeking sanctuary at Kilmainham, Co. Meath. *Archaeology Ireland* **96**, 9–12.

Waterman, D.M. 1997 *Excavations at Navan Fort, 1961–71* (ed. C.J. Lynn). Belfast.

Webster, J. 1995 Sanctuaries and sacred places. In M. Green (ed.), *The Celtic world*, 441–64. London.

19. An Iron Age ring-ditch at Donaghmore, Co. Louth

Brian Ó Donnchadha and Shane Delaney

Introduction

This excavation at Donaghmore was carried out in October 2002 as part of the excavations in advance of the construction of the Dundalk Western Bypass. It was undertaken by Irish Archaeological Consultancy Ltd under the direction of Brian Ó Donnchadha. The excavation revealed a prehistoric ring-ditch or barrow.

Location

The site was in the townland of Donaghmore, *c.* 3km west of Dundalk at NGR 302020/307125 (Fig. 19.1). It was in an agriculturally productive area that surrounds Dundalk town and undulates between *c.* 20m and *c.* 33m OD. Archaeological excavations associated with the road construction revealed that the Donaghmore area is part of a prehistoric and early historic landscape, with material recovered from associated excavations dating from the Neolithic and continuing into the early medieval period. Five excavations were undertaken in Donaghmore townland, spread out over a distance of 250m,

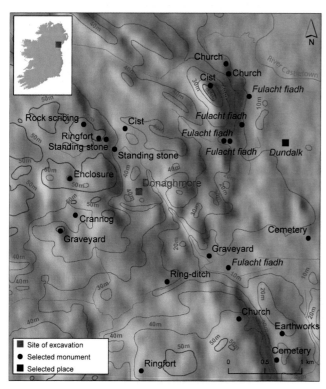

Fig. 19.1—Donaghmore: location of site.

with an average distance of 30m separating the sites.

Donaghmore 7 was located on a well-drained, north-east-facing gentle slope. While an outcrop of bedrock to the north-west of the site afforded some protection from the elements, it was largely exposed to the northern and eastern winds from the Cooley Mountains and the Irish Sea. The ring-ditch was discovered during the supervised topsoil clearance that occurred as part of the excavation phase of archaeological exploration.

There is a marked lack of known Iron Age activity within the surrounding area, and the ring-ditch was one of the few Iron Age sites identified from the Dundalk Western Bypass excavations (the others being one phase of a hilltop habitation at Fort Hill (02E1326), a cereal-drying kiln at Balriggan 1 (02E1325) and limited domestic activity at Balregan 1 and 2 (03E0157)).

Site description

The site consisted of a small ring-ditch with one cremation pit on the interior (Figs 19.2–19.4). The interior of the enclosure measured 6m in diameter. The ditch cut was 0.35–0.6m wide and survived to a depth of 0.28–0.5m. It was shallowest along the southern edge. The interior of the ring-ditch contained a single pit burial (0.45m by 0.32m by 0.14m) close to the internal eastern edge of the ditch.

This oval pit contained only a small quantity of burnt bone and charcoal and may represent a token funerary deposit. It is possible that the pit originally contained considerably more bone but was truncated by later agricultural activity. The bone was in very poor condition and weighed only 0.5g. None of the bone fragments could be identified to species (Lofqvist 2007). The white colour and high level of fragmentation of the bones indicated intense heat during burning, and the degree of fragmentation suggests that the bones were disturbed while still hot and/or that they were exposed to weathering and trampling before being placed in the pit.

The ditch was filled with two layers of loose brown silty sand. The base of the ditch may have silted up naturally but was sealed by the deliberate deposition of a darker fill that contained charcoal and fragments of burnt timber and probably represents the deliberate deposition of pyre material within the ditch. The burnt timber was identified as oak

Fig. 19.2—Donaghmore: aerial view of ring-ditch.

Fig. 19.3—Donaghmore: plan of ring-ditch.

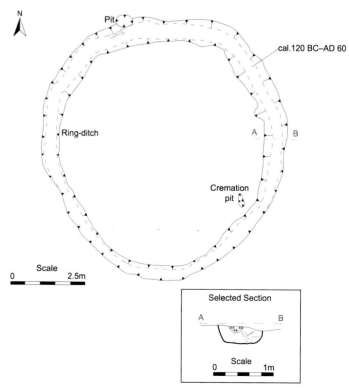

(*Quercus* sp.) and returned a date of 2030±36 BP (WK-18564). The 2-sigma calibrated results produced an Iron Age date of 120 BC–AD 60. It is not surprising that oak was the dominant species identified from the ring-ditch, as oak was a favoured timber for cremation pyres, owing to its burning qualities. The analysis of charcoal from other cremation sites, including Bettystown, Co. Dublin (98E0072), Ballybrowney Lower 1 (03E1058), Ballynapark, Co. Wicklow (A022–33), and Hermitage, Limerick (01E0319), has revealed oak to be the dominant species within cremation features (O'Carroll 2006).

A later pit appears to have been cut into the upper fill of the ring-ditch, but no finds or any other datable material were retrieved from the fill to indicate either a date or a function.

Fig. 19.4—Donaghmore: the ring-ditch after excavation, looking north.

Conclusion

The excavation at Donaghmore 7 identified an Iron Age ring-ditch in an area where little evidence for Iron Age activity had been previously identified. Although the cremated remains recovered on site were minimal, they still represented the deliberate and ceremonial burial of an individual who lived in the larger, as yet unidentified, Iron Age landscape of the area.

Acknowledgements

The archaeological excavation at Donaghmore 7, Co. Louth, was carried out on behalf of Louth County Council and the National Roads Authority in advance of the construction of the M1 Dundalk Western Bypass.

Bibliography

Lofqvist, C. 2007 Osteological report of animal bone from Dundalk western bypass: Donaghmore 7, County Louth. Unpublished report by Moore Group for IAC Ltd.

O'Carroll, E. 2006 Species identification of charcoal samples from Donaghmore 7 (02E1583), Co. Louth. Unpublished report for IAC Ltd.

Ó Donnchadha, B. 2009 Site Donaghmore 7 (licence 02E1583): final report. Unpublished report prepared by IAC Ltd for Louth County Council.

20. Invisible people or invisible archaeology? Carrickmines Great, Co. Dublin, and the problem of Irish Iron Age settlement[1]

Cóilín Ó Drisceoil and Emma Devine

Introduction

The absence of evidence for domestic habitation during the millennium between *c.* 500 cal. BC and cal. AD 500 has been without question the major issue dogging the study of late prehistoric Ireland. It must surely be one of the supreme ironies of Irish archaeology that it is possible to stare into the leathered face of an Iron Age bog body but at the same time know virtually nothing of the place he/she called home. This 'settlement problem' famously led Barry Raftery to coin the term 'the invisible people' to describe the inhabitants of Iron Age Ireland, but a host of new archaeological discoveries made over the past two decades can now provide a window into the everyday lives of these people. Before any conclusions are drawn from the new evidence, however, it is imperative that the emerging corpus is critically assessed, and one of the purposes of this paper is to highlight some of its inherent problems. The other intention of the essay is to describe one of the more recent discoveries, an Iron Age settlement at Carrickmines Great, Co. Dublin, which was excavated in 2002 by the authors.

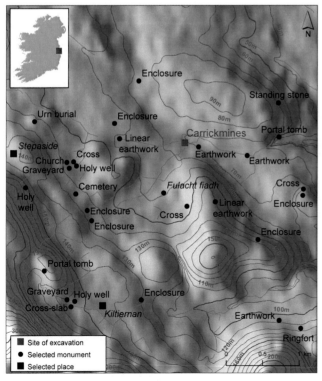

Fig. 20.1—Carrickmines Great: site location.

Location and find circumstances

Carrickmines Great is a townland between Kiltiernan and Cabinteely in the northern foothills of the Dublin Mountains, overlooked by the prominent peaks of Two Rock and Three Rock mountains (Figs 20.1–20.3). The excavation site was improved grassland beside a reclaimed wetland known locally as 'Tracy's Bog' prior to its discovery during archaeological monitoring of the topsoil strip for the M50 south-east motorway. Within the 155m by 40m excavation area, a sequence of prehistoric activity was documented that ranged over a period of four millennia, from the Neolithic to the late Iron Age. Five archaeological phases were defined (Fig. 20.3):

- early–middle Neolithic: pit with disc-bead necklace (Ó Drisceoil 2006);
- early Bronze Age: flint-knapping shelter;
- late Bronze Age: possible sweat-house/*fulacht fiadh*;
- early Iron Age: farmstead;
- late Iron Age: pit cremation and water-hole.

The Iron Age settlement at Carrickmines Great

The settlement was concentrated within a 40m by 30m L-shaped area of flat ground in the south-east of the excavation site (Fig. 20.6). A roundhouse, a hut, a post alignment, pits and an iron-smelting furnace were documented. A full report on the Iron Age archaeology of Carrickmines Great has already been published (Ó Drisceoil 2007), and the following is a summary of the key findings.

Roundhouse (structure 1)

Eight post-pits and a stake-hole formed a 3.3m-diameter ring, from which a 0.95m-wide 'porch' of six post-pits projected to the south-west (Figs 20.7 and 20.8). Reconstructing the building's original form is not without problems because the site was quite badly damaged by ploughing. The most straightforward reconstruction, however, presents the post-ring supporting a ring-beam onto which the roof rafters were set. The four largest post-pits would have been the main roof-supports. Any evidence for an outer wall had been removed, but a wigwam-type construction is possible for the simple reason that it maximises the space available—this produces a building with a maximum diameter of *c.* 4.75m and an area of 17.7m² (Fig. 20.9). No finds were recovered from the

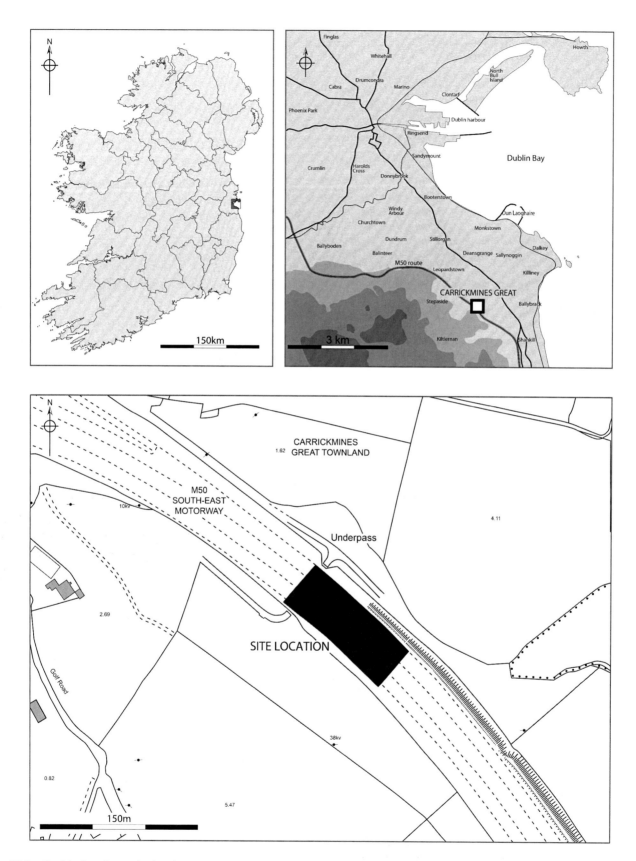

Fig. 20.2—Carrickmines Great: site location map.

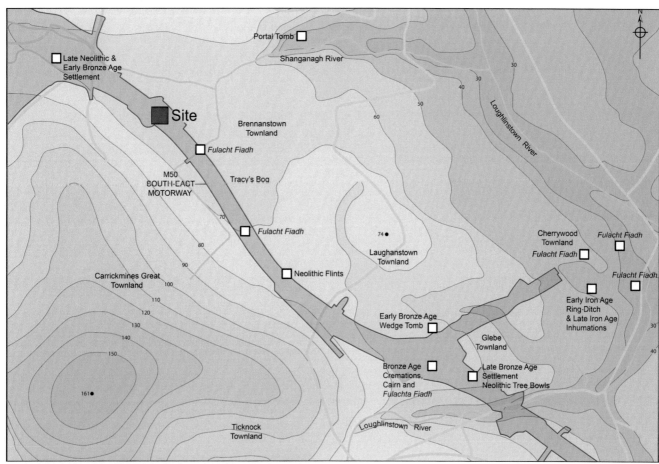

Fig. 20.3 (above)—Carrickmines Great: excavation area and environs with known prehistoric archaeological sites marked. The bulk of these sites were uncovered during the archaeological interventions that occurred in 2000–3, prior to the construction of the M50 south-east motorway.

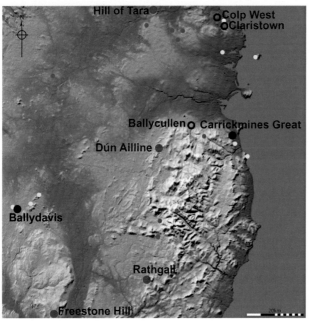

Fig. 20.4—Iron Age archaeology of east central Ireland (sources: Raftery 1994; Warner et al. 1990).

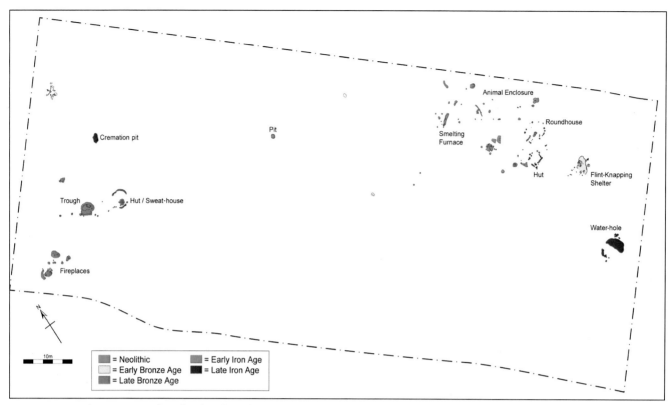

Fig. 20.5—Carrickmines Great: plan of archaeological area.

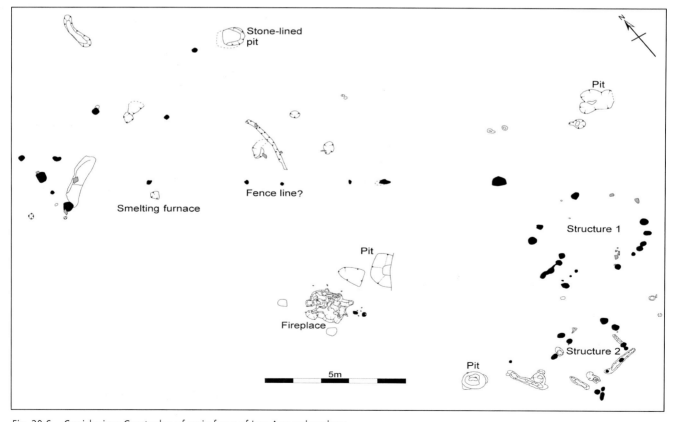

Fig. 20.6—Carrickmines Great: plan of main focus of Iron Age archaeology.

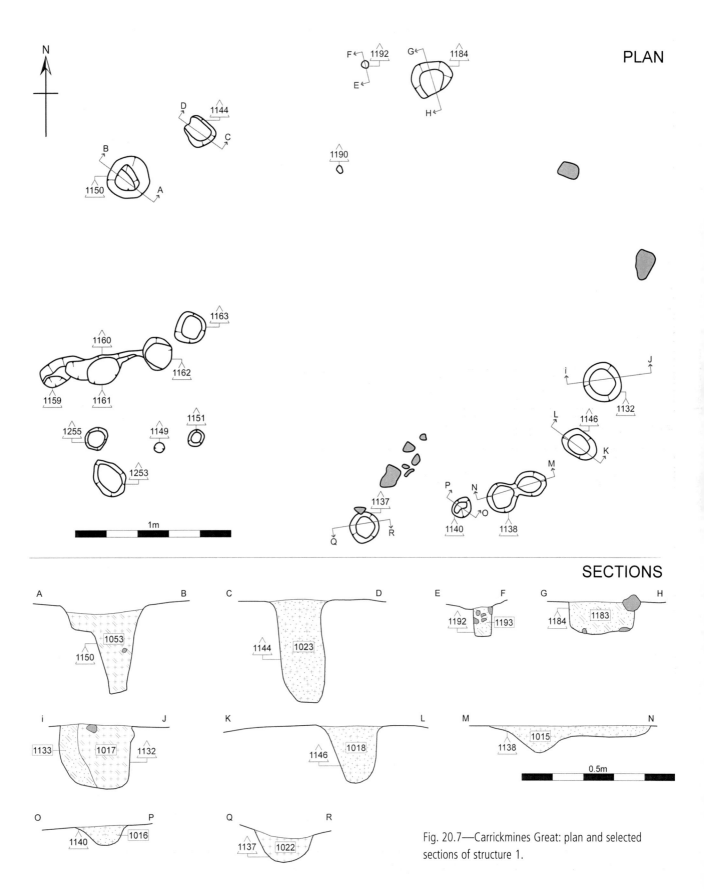

PLAN

SECTIONS

Fig. 20.7—Carrickmines Great: plan and selected sections of structure 1.

Fig. 20.8—Carrickmines Great: structure 1 (right) and structure 2 (left), from east.

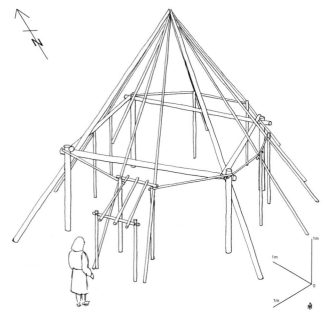

Fig. 20.9—Carrickmines Great: suggested reconstruction of structure 1 (Phelim Manning).

structure. A sample of the sloe (*Prunus spinosa*) charcoal from the backfill of one post-pit produced a radiocarbon date of 380–180 cal. BC, and the charred grain of wheat, presumably the result of cereal-processing, from the same context was dated to 180 cal. BC–cal. AD 10 (^{14}C dates 1 and 4; Table 20.3). Neither sample was primary (beyond doubt directly associated with the structure), and the fact that they only barely overlap means that neither can strictly be held to date the building's construction or use. The radiocarbon dates for the site are discussed further below.

Hut (structure 2)

Adjacent to structure 1 were the footing trench and post-pits for a roughly square hut/shed (2.3m by 2m across), termed structure 2 (Fig. 20.10). A series of stake- and post-holes and sections of a footing trench to the north of the building may have formed an annexe or shelter. A charred twig of *Prunus spinosa* (sloe) from the silted fill of structure 2's slot-trench produced a radiocarbon date of 360–50 cal. BC (^{14}C date 3). Again, because this was a secondary sample, its correlation with the structure's period of use is uncertain.

Features outside the buildings

A series of post-pits, pits and truncated slot-trenches were recorded to the north-west of structures 1 and 2 (Fig. 20.11). Though few clear patterns presented themselves, the arrangement of the posts on the south was suggestive of a fence line. At the northern edge of the site was a bell-shaped, stone-lined pit. It was 0.8m in diameter by 0.6m in depth and contained flint chips, a possible core and a retouched flint piercer in a dump of fire-scorched soil, ash and charcoal.

Iron-smelting furnace and charcoal production

The truncated base of a small iron-smelting furnace was found 15m from structure 1 (Fig. 20.12). It was circular (0.34m by 0.3m across and 0.11m deep). The base was scorched and its fills were chiefly of charcoal and slag-rich debris that represented the furnace's final use. The furnace pit was steep-sided and flat-bottomed and was blown from the side. Its slag type was 'tabular cakes filling most of the area of the furnace, showing flowage down the blowing wall', which indicates that it was not a 'bowl furnace' but rather a 'slag-pit furnace', one of the few recorded Irish examples of Iron Age date and similar to those at Tullyallen, Co. Louth, and Celbridge, Co. Kildare (Young 2003).

All of the charcoal, presumably remnant fuel, was of oak (*Quercus*), a sample of which produced a radiocarbon date of 360–100 cal. BC (^{14}C date 2). Immediately to the south of the smelting furnace, a sunken fireplace was at the centre of a series of stake-holes and pits (Fig. 20.13). Large lumps of charred wood were found at its base and it was probably used primarily to produce charcoal for the furnace. This would have required the construction of a clamp of regularly sized timbers. The logs at the base of the clamp were fired and a thick layer of damp soil was used to seal it. This produced the oxygen-free environment that generated charcoal over a period of a day or so.

An Iron Age habitation at Carrickmines Great?

It is solely on the basis of its radiocarbon dates that

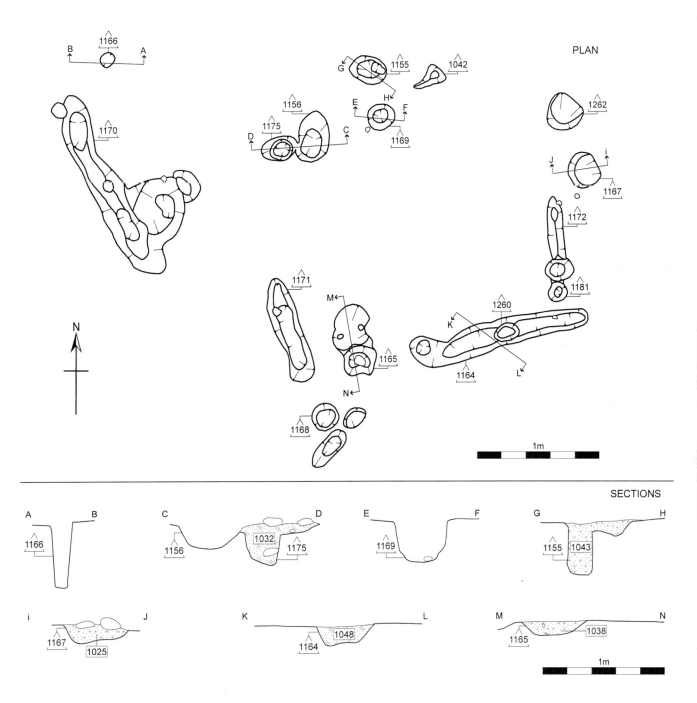

Fig. 20.10—Carrickmines Great: plan and selected sections of structure 2.

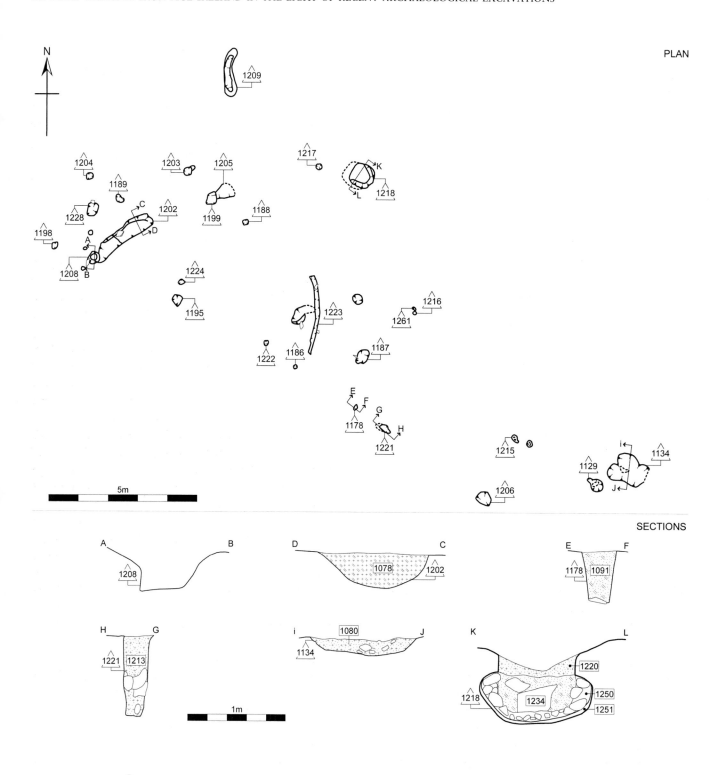

Fig. 20.11—Carrickmines Great: plan and selected sections of pit and possible fence line.

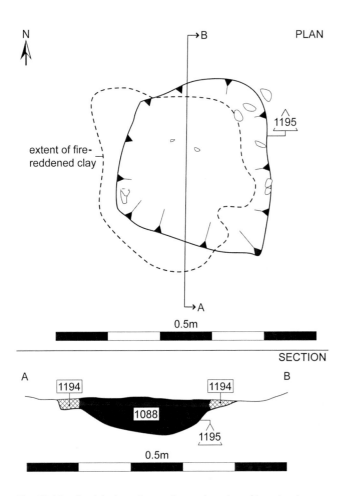

N

→B   PLAN

extent of fire-
reddened clay

1195

→A

0.5m

SECTION

A   B

1194   1194

1088

1195

0.5m

Fig. 20.12—Carrickmines Great: plan and section of Iron Age iron-smelting furnace.

Carrickmines Great can be characterised as belonging to the Iron Age. But, given the problems of connecting the radiocarbon dates from structures 1 and 2 (¹⁴C dates 1, 3 and 4) with their construction and/or use, can the dates be firmly associated with these buildings and by extension facilitate interpretation of the site as an Iron Age habitation? In short, the answer is 'no', but what can be stated with some confidence is that the radiocarbon dates show 'domestic' activity—including cereal-processing and iron-smelting—taking place in the area of the buildings in the first half of the Iron Age, at some time between 380 cal. BC and cal. AD 70. While it cannot be proven that structures 1 and 2 were in use at the same time as this activity was occurring, the three Iron Age radiocarbon dates obtained from them indicate that in all probability this was the case.

The archaeological evidence thus indicates that Carrickmines Great was an open (unenclosed), small-scale single-household farmstead of the first half of the Iron Age

(Fig. 20.14). The people who lived here were experimenting with iron-working, producing charcoal, and cultivating and processing wheat and perhaps other cereals. The habitation was surrounded in the main by woodland with oak, alder, hazel, ash and apple trees. The impression—and because of the limited evidence it is only that—is of a small family unit living a rather deprived existence within a landscape dominated by woodland. There is nothing to suggest that life was comfortable here in the Iron Age.

Discussion

Emerging from the shadows? Iron Age settlement in 2012
Prior to the advent of large-scale rescue archaeology in Ireland, there were just two sites that could be cited as putative examples of Irish Iron Age settlements—Scrabo, Co. Down, and a 'hut' associated with Roman glass and pottery at the Rath of the Synods, Tara, Co. Meath (Owens 1972; Raftery 1994, 113, 212; Grogan 2008, 81–92).[2] Both of these have always been problematic, however. Scrabo was interpreted as an Iron Age settlement on the basis of two radiocarbon determinations with large standard deviations that were obtained in 1972 on unidentified bulk charcoal and cannot therefore be considered reliable. The Rath of the Synods structure was classified as an Iron Age house on the basis of associated finds. Given its location within a major Iron Age ceremonial and ritual site, however, it is difficult to conceive of this as a domestic habitation; instead, it is more in keeping with the ritual structures from Dún Ailinne, Co. Kildare, and Raffin, Co. Meath (Raftery 1994, 113; Grogan 2008, 81–92).

In recent years Iron Age archaeology has been documented on some 400 Irish excavations. The vast majority of these sites remain unpublished, but many of the 'raw' data have been collated by the Heritage Council-funded 'Iron Age Ireland: finding an invisible people' project (Becker et al. 2008; Becker 2009; this volume), which has identified around 200 sites with evidence for settlement and/or industry (Becker 2009, 354). Within this group, just 30 buildings of 'habitational [*sic*] or workshop character' were identified. All but a handful of these have been characterised, as was the case with Carrickmines Great, on the basis of their attendant radiocarbon dates.

The sites with buildings are obviously of the utmost importance, because they present the best available evidence for settlement. The total is probably substantially less than 30, however, as it is evident that the project did not undertake any critical 'quality control' of the corpus of radiocarbon dates (Becker et al. 2008, 18). It is well recognised that unless dating samples are short-life single entities that had a demonstrable association with the archaeological event in question the

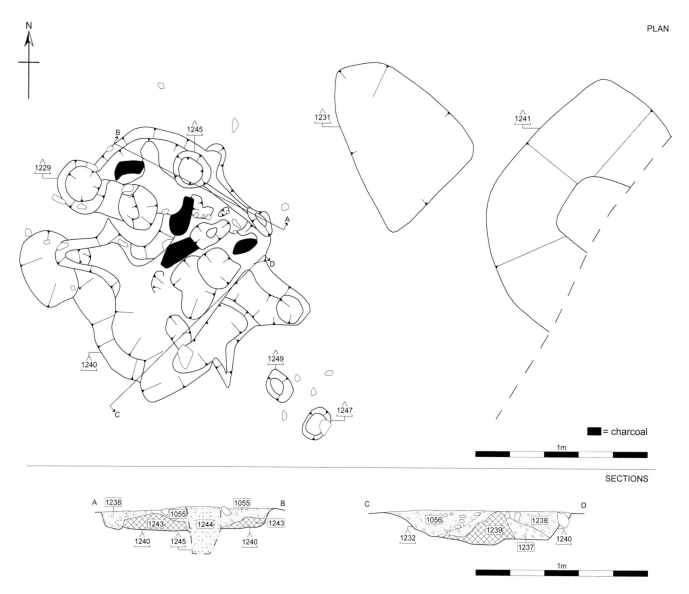

Fig. 20.13—Carrickmines Great: plan and section of Iron Age charcoal-producing pit/fireplace.

interpretation must be treated with considerable caution (Ashmore 1999; 2004; Lanting and van der Plicht 1993–4; and see Becker *et al.* 2008, 18). These criteria are not met in the case of the vast bulk of the 30 structures that have been identified. To take some examples, at Ballinaspig More 5, Claristown, Cloongownagh, Colp West and Lislackagh, sample material was not identified and therefore the age of the material that was dated is unknown (Tables 20.1 and 20.2); furthermore, at Lislackagh the artefacts from an enclosing ditch around a pair of purported Iron Age roundhouses were of early medieval rather than Iron Age date. At Magheraboy and Ballycullen, the dated samples were oak and there is a possibility of the 'old wood effect'. At Killoran 16, the date for

the roundhouse has a standard deviation of ±130 years and must therefore be considered unsafe. Balriggan produced a single determination from two charcoal samples that may not be from secure contexts (Niall Roycroft, pers. comm.). In view of the absence of due diligence on the radiocarbon dates, it is not possible at this stage to come to any conclusions about the numbers of sites that contain Iron Age houses/structures, though what is clear is that the final number is likely to be far fewer than the 30 suggested.

Invisible people?

A reversion to nomadism, a way of life that would leave little or no discernible archaeological trace, has been suggested

Fig. 20.14—Carrickmines Great: suggested reconstruction, *c.* 200 BC.

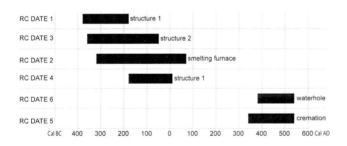

Fig. 20.15—Carrickmines Great: graph showing Iron Age calibrated date ranges. All dates are AMS and have been calibrated using OxCal Program v.3.10; IntCal04 Calibration Data (Bronk Ramsey 1995; 2001; Reimer *et al.* 2004).

before to explain the meagre settlement evidence of the Irish Iron Age (Lynn 2003; and see Becker 2009, 356). While this could be at least part of the explanation, it is belied somewhat by what is ostensibly a 'sedentary' site at Carrickmines Great. Vast quantities of ground have been opened and examined by archaeologists over the years of the 'Celtic Tiger' and yet settlements of the Iron Age remain elusive. For instance, Carrickmines Great was the only Iron Age site excavated

along the 10km-route of the M50 south-east motorway and the period has, in general, been rather poorly represented on virtually all other motorway projects. Moreover, where it has been possible to investigate long-term settlement patterns over wide areas, such as at Derryville Bog, Co. Tipperary/Co. Kilkenny, a marked decrease in human activity can be demonstrated to have occurred in the Iron Age (Gowen *et al.* 2005, 68, 73). It is hard to escape the conclusion that if a settlement record of substance existed it would have been found by now.

Invisible archaeology?
Recent studies have also drawn attention to the possibility that, because of an absence of diagnostic finds such as pottery and metalwork, evidence for Iron Age occupation could be archaeologically anonymous within the sites of other periods (Cooney 2000, 30). This was certainly the case at Carrickmines Great, where radiocarbon dating was the key to distinguishing Iron Age horizons that would otherwise have been impossible to date. It is also worth noting that the Iron Age features at this site were quite ephemeral and required the right weather conditions and much patient trowelling before they came to light. If both these factors are typical of settlements of the Iron Age, it is possible that many such sites

259

Table 20.1—Preliminary list of Iron Age domestic settlement sites with house structures (both definite and possible sites).

Site	Brief description	Date range	References
Ballinaspig More, Co. Cork	Unenclosed single-ring roundhouse (structure 1) defined by a subcircular arrangement of post-holes (dimensions unknown). A small hut structure (structure 3) (4m by 0.4m) was also excavated 60m from the roundhouse and returned a late Bronze Age/early Iron Age determination.	260–50 cal. BC	Danaher 2004; 2007, 136; this volume; NRA leaflet, *Archaeological discoveries on the N22 Ballincollig Bypass Scheme, Co. Cork*; Ken Hanley, pers. comm.
Ballycullen site 3, area A, Co. Dublin	Unenclosed, single-ring roundhouse, 14.5m in diameter, defined by a gully with internal post-circle; fire-pits. Undecorated 'coarse' pottery, ferrous objects, slag and flints.	380–40 cal. BC	Larsson 2006; this volume; Stephen Johnston and Ellinor Larsson, pers. comm.
Ballydavis, Co. Laois	Unenclosed, single-ring roundhouse outside ditch of major ceremonial/ritual site. House was a 9m-diameter circular 'post-built structure' defined by fifteen post-holes. Adjacent large pit contained burnt seeds and grain. One unidentified ferrous object recovered. Some evidence for ancillary structures adjacent to main roundhouse.	390–190 cal. BC	Fegan 2006; Grace Fegan, pers. comm.
Balriggan, Co. Louth	Found beneath medieval motte; partially excavated (unenclosed?) roundhouse, 7–8m in diameter with external drip-gully and north-facing entrance. House was associated with butchered animal bone and horn-working. An adjacent burial may be contemporary. Radiocarbon determination was obtained from material in drip-gully and may not be secure.	Cal. AD 250–430	Roycroft 2006; Niall Roycroft, pers. comm.
Claristown 2, Co. Meath	Unenclosed, 6m-diameter 'hut site' defined by semicircular post-circle with entrance to east. Pits, external hearths and 'structures' adjacent (Russell 2004). Animal bone the only 'find'. Possibly an additional roundhouse, though this is not clear. Site covered by late Iron Age funerary barrow and within multiphase site of Neolithic–post-medieval date.	370 cal. BC–cal. AD 10	Russell 2003; 2004, 66; this volume; Niall Roycroft, pers. comm.
Cloongownagh, Co. Roscommon	Unenclosed late Iron Age 'industrial area on the periphery of a larger settlement ... preserved under the ringfort bank and extended 4–5m into the interior of the site' (Henry 2001, 11, 47). Seven structures, large pits and stone surfaces recorded. Structure 3b was only building that produced Iron Age radiocarbon determinations. Two other structures were subrectangular and five circular (including 3b). Small quantity of animal bone found, representing cattle, sheep/goat and pig. Cereals from pits and foundation trenches were barley, oats and wheat/rye. Main phase of Iron Age activity from first century BC to fourth century AD, but preceded by possible late Bronze Age/early Iron Age activity. *Fulacht fiadh* nearby also produced late Iron Age dates.	Phase 1: 820–360 cal. BC; phase 2: 180 cal. BC–cal. AD 440	Henry 2000; Henry 2001; Lennon 2002; Mary Henry and Sebastian Joubert, pers. comm.

Table 20.1 (cont.)—Preliminary list of Iron Age domestic settlement sites with house structures (both definite and possible sites).

Site	Brief description	Date range	References
Colp West, Co. Meath	Unenclosed, subcircular 'hut structure' *c.* 5m in diameter, truncated by sixth/seventh-century AD ringfort ditch. Associated with kiln, and possibly a ditched enclosure 25m to south. Within early medieval enclosure complex.	40 cal. BC–cal. AD. 220	Clarke and Murphy 2003; Linda Clarke, pers. comm.
Killoran 16, Co. Tipperary	Unenclosed roundhouse, slightly oblong in plan, 14.88m in maximum diameter, defined by a central post, wall posts and a south-east-facing doorway formed by four post-holes. Two shallow wall-slots also defined. No associated finds. Succeeded by limited early medieval activity.	200 cal. BC–cal. AD 240	Gowen *et al.* 2005, 296–8
Lislackagh, Co. Mayo	Three circular houses within an early medieval circular ditched enclosure (Walsh 1995). Smelting furnaces and iron objects, including nails, hooks and a knife, recovered, along with a decorated blue glass bead, a polished lignite bracelet fragment, a bronze stick-pin and lithics. Bone assemblage of cattle, horse, sheep and pig. Six animal jawbones found in one of the trench foundations (Walsh 1993). How many of the finds relate to the Iron Age activity is not stated, though most are clearly of early medieval date. Likewise, the relationship between the houses and the enclosure ditch is unknown.	200 cal. BC–cal. AD 220	Waddell 1998, 319; Walsh 1993; 1995; Gerry Walsh, pers. comm.
Magheraboy, Co. Sligo	Small isolated, unenclosed circular 'store, shelter or hut', *c.* 4m in diameter, defined by a wall-trench with *in situ* charred timbers.	350–80 cal. BC	Danaher 2007, 135–6
Scrabo, Co. Down	Enclosed hilltop settlement, 35m by 32m, within which were 'several groups of hut circles' (O'Kelly 1989, 309). A *c.* 10m-diameter circular structure with associated pits and 'coarse' pottery (*ibid.*). Warner lists a single radiocarbon date for the site; O'Kelly also notes just one determination, though this differs from Warner's (*ibid.*; Warner *et al.* 1990, 48). Relationship between the enclosure and houses is not known.	550 BC–AD 350	*Radiocarbon* (1971), 451–2; Owens 1972; O'Kelly 1989, 308–9; Mallory and McNeill 1991, 150; Mallory and Hartwell 1997, 27–8; Warner *et al.* 1990; Cooney 2000, fig. 1.12

Table 20.2—Iron Age radiocarbon determinations of possible and definite domestic settlement sites with structures.

Site	Radiocarbon dates
Ballinaspig More 5, Co. Cork	Beta-178205: charcoal (ash?) from fill of post-hole, structure 1, roundhouse (02E1033:F12:S29); 2150±40 BP; 260–50 cal. BC.
	Beta-178205: charcoal (ash?) from fill of post-hole, structure 1, roundhouse (02E1033:F12:S29); 2150±40 BP; 260–50 cal. BC.
	Beta-178209: charcoal (*Quercus*)[3] from plank wall, structure 3, hut (02E1033:F1121:S143); 2440±60 BP; 770–400 cal. BC.
Ballycullen site 3, area A, Co. Dublin	UB-7138: *Quercus*, 3.59g, from fill of post-hole (03E1473:170:S42); 2194±34 BP; 380–170 cal. BC.
	UB-7139: *Quercus*, 7.19g, from fill of gully containing iron, glass (03E1473:320:S95); 2117±33 BP; 210–40 cal. BC.
Ballydavis, Co. Laois	SUERC-9019 (GU-13732): charred alder from post-hole in roundhouse (group 1) (03E0151:631:S#275); 2210±35 BP; 390–190 cal. BC.
Balriggan, Co. Louth	WK-18560: *Prunus spinosa* and *Fraxinus excelsior* from drip-gully (C60); 1679±33 BP; cal. AD 250–430.
Claristown 2, Co. Meath	Beta-159642: charred material (unid.) from primary fill of pit F158, adjacent to hut; 2170±40 BP; 370–100 cal. BC.
	Beta-159643: charred material (unid.) from primary fill of pit F267, adjacent to hut; 2110±60 BP; 260 cal. BC–cal. AD 20.
	Beta-159649: charred material (unid.) from fill of stake-hole F346 of hut; 2080±40 BP; 210 cal. BC–cal. AD 10.
Cloongownagh, Co. Roscommon	UCD-000114: charred material (unid.) from fill of pit C363 beneath ringfort bank; 2460±106 BP; 820–360 cal. BC.
	UCD-000143: charred material (unid.) from pit C1228 at south of main settlement; 1980±80 BP; cal. AD 180–230.
	UCD-9966: charred material (unid.) from foundation trench of structure 3b; 1976±60 BP; 170 cal. BC–cal. AD 140.
	UCD-000110: charred material (unid.) from pit fill C118; 1860±80 BP; 40 cal. BC–cal. AD 350.
	UCD-00144: charred material (unid.) from *fulacht fiadh*; 1720±60 BP; cal. AD 130–440.
Colp, Co. Meath	UB-4669: charcoal (unid.) from fill of foundation trench of hut structure; 1927±53 BP; 40 cal. BC–cal. AD 220.
Killoran 16, Co. Tipperary	Beta-117551: charcoal (unspecified) from roundhouse post-hole; 1890±130; 200 cal. BC–cal. AD 450.
Lislackagh, Co. Mayo	UB-3764: charred material (unid.) from wall-trench C106, house 1; 2071±36 BP; 200 cal. BC–cal. AD 10.
	UB-3765: charred material (unid.) from wall-trench C131, house 2; 1996±81 BP; 200 cal. BC–cal. AD 220.
	UB-3766: charred material (unid.) from wall-trench C237, house 3; 2050±49 BP; 200 cal. BC–cal. AD 60.
Magheraboy, Co. Sligo	Beta-186485: charcoal (*Quercus*) from charred wooden plank in foundation trench for circular building; 2140±60 BP; 380–40 cal. BC.
Scrabo, Co. Down	UB-414A: charcoal (unid.) from wall-slot of round 'hut'; 1925±100 BP; 250 cal. BC–cal. AD 350.
	UB-414E: charcoal (unid.) from wall-slot of round 'hut'; 2305±70; 550–150 cal. BC.

Table 20.3—Carrickmines Great: radiocarbon dates. All dates obtained are AMS and are calibrated using OxCal Program v.3.10; IntCal04 Calibration Data (Bronk Ramsey 1995; 2001; Reimer *et al.* 2004).

[14]C no.	Lab no.	Mean ±sd	Sample	Context	Context description	Material	AL	Cal. 95%
1	Poz-17955	2200±35	S41A	1017	Fill of structure 1 post-pit	Charred sloe twig (*Prunus spinosa*)	0	380–180 BC
2	Poz-11607	2165±30	S211	1088	Fill of smelting furnace	Oak (*Quercus*) charcoal	250	360–100 BC
3	Poz-17956	2150±35	S112	1050	Fill of slot for structure 2, 'shed'	Charred sloe twig (*Prunus spinosa*)	0	360–50 BC
4	Poz-11605	2065±30	S41	1017	Fill of structure 1 post-pit	Single charred wheat grain	0	180 BC–AD 10
5	GrA-29944	1625±35	S3	111	Calcined human bone from cremation pit	Fragment of human femur	0	AD 340–540
6	Poz-17957	1625±30	S32	1123	Secondary fill of 'water-hole'	Charred bark, species unknown	0	AD 380–540

have simply been overlooked.

Is there also a possibility that habitation evidence remains unseen because excavated remains have been misinterpreted? This is especially relevant with regard to the ubiquitous smaller, circular ditched enclosures that are generally termed 'ring-ditches'. Though hundreds of these sites have been excavated in recent years, with many more identified through field and aerial surveys, there has been a tendency automatically to assume that they represent the remains of funerary monuments. While this is certainly the case with many, if not most, examples, there may be a significant cohort that are in fact the remains of house structures. There are two main instances in which this could have been the case. As a result of attrition to the upper levels, deep circular gullies are often all that remain of a roundhouse. These rings could be the drip-trenches that drained water off the roundhouse roof. Alternatively, they could also be the bedding trench for the timber wall, the 'ring-ditch' or 'ring-groove' houses of northern England and Scotland having been thus constructed (Harding 2004, 68–9, 96–8; Armit 2005, 31–3). To complicate matters further, drip-trenches often had their bank upcast on the *outside* of the ditch (to place it on the inside would have prevented water from flowing off the house and into the gully), making them identical in every way to many of the funerary 'ring-ditches' where no burial evidence is known.

Conclusion

The critique offered above suggests that, despite claims to the contrary, a very modest settlement record characterises the Irish Iron Age. In particular, domestic settlements with houses of the period remain rare in the extreme, marking a complete severance with the extensive and flourishing settlement record of the late Bronze Age. Indeed, the statement that 'there is now a considerable body of dated Iron Age sites which can inform us about where and how people lived during this period' would seem somewhat premature (Becker *et al.* 2008, 63). In many ways Carrickmines Great, a site that was difficult to find in the ground and whose characterisation relied completely on a suite of somewhat frustrating radiocarbon dates, encapsulates the problems that confront the newly acquired evidence. To understand better the nature and extent of Iron Age settlement in Ireland, greater scrutiny of radiocarbon dates is required, problematic sites need to be re-dated using 'gold-standard' samples (if available), and structures with uncertain chronologies within multiperiod sites should be targeted for dating. A closer examination of those 'ring-ditch' sites that have produced secure Iron Age dates, 'domestic' finds and no human remains could also pay dividends.

Acknowledgements

The excavations at Carrickmines Great were funded by the National Roads Authority and Dún Laoghaire–Rathdown County Council. I am grateful to the excavation team: Christina Bennett, Morgan Bolger, Noel Carroll, Mary Chesham, Julia Crimmins, Emma Devine (supervisor), Orla Egan (supervisor), Fernando Fernandez, Brendan Fitzpatrick, Clare Gray, Michael Healy, Ed Lyne, Kevin Martin, Brian McConway, John O'Brien, Declan Quinn, Nora Thornton, David Timbs and Deirdre Walsh. I am also indebted to Gary Conboy, who discovered the Carrickmines Great site during archaeological monitoring for V.J. Keeley Ltd. A charred seeds report was produced by Penny Johnston, charcoal identifications by Ingelise Stuijts and Ellen OCarroll, a metal slags report by Tim Young and the lithics report by Torbin Ballin. Figures were digitally rendered by Philip Kenny and the house reconstruction was drawn by Phelim Manning. Information pertaining to reported Iron Age settlements was very kindly offered prior to publication by the following: Ian Russell (Archaeological Consultancy Services Ltd)—Claristown 2, Co. Meath; Niall Roycroft (National Roads Authority Project Archaeologist)—Balriggan, Co. Louth; Mary Henry and Sebastian Joubert—Cloongownagh, Co. Roscommon; Ken Hanley (National Roads Authority Project Archaeologist)—Ballinaspig More 5, Co. Cork; Stephen Johnston (Arch-Tech Ltd) and Ellinor Larsson—Ballycullen Site 3, Co. Dublin; Linda Clarke (Archaeological Consultancy Services Ltd)—Colp West, Co. Meath; Gerry Walsh (National Roads Authority Project Archaeologist)—Lislackagh, Co. Mayo; Grace Fegan—Ballydavis, Co. Kildare.

Bibliography

Armit, I. 2005 *Celtic Scotland*. London.

Ashmore, P.J. 1999 Radiocarbon dating: avoiding errors by avoiding mixed samples. *Antiquity* **279** (73), 124–30.

Ashmore, P.J. 2004 Absolute chronology. In I.A. Shepherd and G.J. Barclay (eds), *Scotland in ancient Europe*, 125–38. Edinburgh.

Becker, K. 2009 Iron Age Ireland: finding an invisible people. In G. Cooney, K. Becker, J. Coles, M. Ryan and S. Sievers (eds), *Relics of old decency: archaeological studies in later prehistory*, 353–62. Bray.

Becker, K., Ó Néill, J. and O'Flynn, L. 2008 Iron Age Ireland: finding an invisible people. Unpublished report prepared for the Heritage Council (project 16365).

Bronk Ramsey, C. 1995 Radiocarbon calibration and analysis of stratigraphy: the OxCal program. *Radiocarbon* **37** (2), 425–30.

Bronk Ramsey, C. 2001 Development of the radiocarbon program OxCal. *Radiocarbon* **43** (2A), 355–63.

Clarke, L. and Murphy, D. 2003 Colp West. *Excavations 2001*, no. 952. Bray.

Cooney, G. 2000 Reading a landscape manuscript: a review of progress in prehistoric studies in Ireland. In T. Barry (ed.), *A history of settlement in Ireland*, 1–49. Oxford.

Danaher, E. 2004 Report on the archaeological excavation of a multi-phased site at Ballinaspig More 5, Ballincollig, Co. Cork. Unpublished report prepared for Archaeological Consultancy Services Ltd.

Danaher, E. 2007 *Monumental beginnings: the archaeology of the N4 Sligo inner relief road*. Bray.

Fegan, G. 2006 Ballydavis. *Excavations 2003*, 284–5. Bray.

Gowen, M., Ó Néill, J. and Phillips, M. (eds) 2005 *The Lisheen Mine Archaeological Project, 1996–8*. Bray.

Grogan, E. 2008 *The Rath of the Synods, Tara, Co. Meath: excavations by Seán P. Ó Ríordáin*. Bray.

Harding, D.W. 2004 *The Iron Age in northern Britain: Celts and Romans, natives and invaders*. London and New York.

Henry, M. 2000 Cloongownagh. *Excavations 1999*, no. 765. Bray.

Henry, M. 2001 Archaeological excavation at Cloongownagh, Co. Roscommon. Unpublished report prepared by Mary Henry Ltd.

Lanting, J.N. and van der Plicht, J. 1993–4 ^{14}C-AMS: pros and cons for archaeology. *Palaeohistoria* **35–6**, 1–12.

Larsson, E. 2006 Ballycullen Site 3, Oldcourt. *Excavations 2003*, 175–6. Bray.

Lennon, A.M. 2002 Cloongownagh. *Excavations 2000*, 290–1. Bray.

Lynn, C. 2003 Ireland in the Iron Age: a basket case? *Archaeology Ireland* **17** (2), 20–3.

Mallory, J.P. and Hartwell, B. 1997 Down in prehistory. In L. Proudfoot (ed.), *Down: history and society*, 1–32. Dublin.

Mallory, J.P. and McNeill, T. 1991 *The archaeology of Ulster*. Belfast.

Ó Drisceoil, C. 2006 A Neolithic disc bead necklace from Carrickmines Great, Co. Dublin. *Journal of the Royal Society of Antiquaries of Ireland* **136**, 141–57.

Ó Drisceoil, C. 2007 Life and death in the Iron Age at Carrickmines Great, Co. Dublin. *Journal of the Royal Society of Antiquaries of Ireland* **137**, 5–28.

O'Kelly, M.J. 1989 *Early Ireland: an introduction to Irish prehistory*. London.

Owens, M. 1972 Scrabo. *Excavations 1970*, no. 16. Dublin.

Raftery, B. 1994 *Pagan Celtic Ireland: the enigma of the Irish Iron Age*. London.

Reimer, P.J., et al. 2004 IntCal04 radiocarbon age calibration, 24000–0 cal. BP. *Radiocarbon* **46**, 1029–58.

Roycroft, N. 2006 Iron Age patterns: silent sites. *Seanda* **1**, 11–12.

Russell, I. 2003 Claristown 2, Co. Meath. *Excavations 2001*, 288–9. Bray.

Russell, I. 2004 Final report on the archaeological excavation at Claristown 2, Co. Meath (01E0039). Unpublished report prepared by Archaeological Consultancy Services Ltd.

Stuijts, I. 2006 Charcoal identification for Carrickmines, Sites 59–62. Unpublished report prepared for Kilkenny Archaeology.

Waddell, J. 1998 *The prehistoric archaeology of Ireland*. Galway.

Walsh, G. 1993 Lislackagh. *Excavations 1992*, no. 146. Bray.

Walsh, G. 1995 Iron Age settlement in County Mayo. *Archaeology Ireland* **9** (2), 7–8.

Warner, R.B., Mallory, J.P. and Baillie, M.G.L. 1990 Irish early Iron Age sites: a provisional map of absolute date sites. *Emania* **7**, 46–51.

Weir, D. 1995 A palynological study of landscape and agricultural development in County Louth from the second millennium BC to the first millennium AD. *Discovery Programme Reports* **2**, 77–126.

Young, T. 2003 Is the Irish iron-smelting bowl furnace a myth? A discussion of new evidence for Irish bloomery ironmaking. Unpublished report prepared for GeoArch.

Notes

1. This paper is dedicated to the memory of Emma, whose expertise led to the discovery of the Iron Age archaeology.

2. A scatter of radiocarbon dates that had been recorded on non-structural settlement traces in the form of occupation debris, pits, hearths and post-pits had also been documented by Warner *et al.* (1990).

3. The sample material is described as 'ash' in the radiocarbon dating report, but Danaher (2007, 136) records it as 'a sample of the oak plank'.

21. The excavation of an Iron Age site at Claristown, Co. Meath

Ian R. Russell

Introduction

The site was identified as a low mound beneath an upstanding sycamore tree in the townland of Claristown, Co. Meath (NGR 31410, 26775) (Fig. 21.1). There are commanding views over the surrounding landscape, particularly to the east and south. The site was partially excavated in advance of the development of the Gormanston section (Contract 6) of the northern motorway (M1), Co. Meath.[1] The earliest activity on the site was dated to the Neolithic. This was followed by an Iron Age ring-ditch with a central inhumation burial, and two areas of subsequent burials that are provisionally dated to the Iron Age/Early Christian transition (Fig. 21.2).

Early prehistoric features

Neolithic activity was represented by a metalled surface and a possible circular ring-ditch or structure. An infant burial (burial 15) may also date from this phase. The Neolithic ring-ditch was identified below an Iron Age stone cairn and other layers, and had been cut into the natural boulder clay. It did not make up a complete circle but rather consisted of four

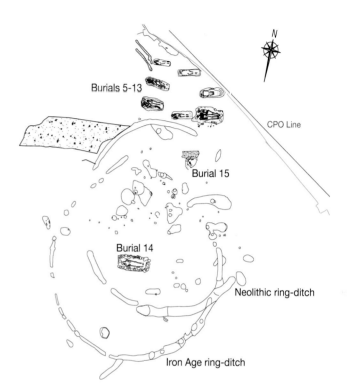

Fig. 21.2—Claristown: plan of two ring-ditches and fifteen burials.

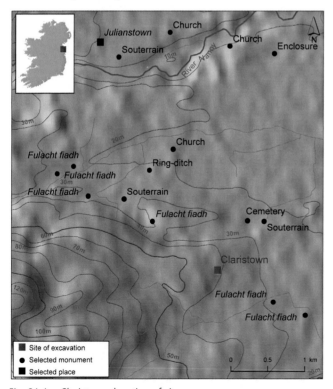

Fig. 21.1—Claristown: location of site.

large sections of a curved narrow ditch surviving at the south, south-west and north. No ditch sections were identified at the east or west. The ditch sections varied in width from 0.3m to 0.45m and were filled with brown silty clay, charcoal flecks and burnt bone. A sample of the fill returned early Neolithic dates of 3710–3620 cal. BC and 3580–3530 cal. BC. In addition, a total of eighteen pits, six spreads and three post-holes were identified outside the area enclosed by the ring-ditch. Although some of these features may be associated with

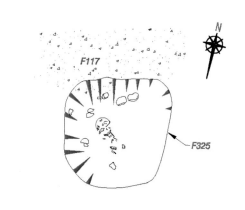

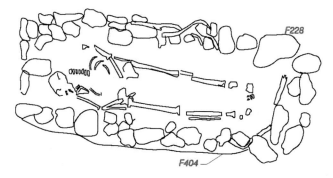

Fig. 21.3—Claristown: plan of burial 15 (F307; top) and burial 14 (F401; bottom).

the earliest Iron Age phase (phase 1, described below), at least one pit returned a radiocarbon date of 2650–2340 cal. BC, indicating that activity at the site continued into the late Neolithic. In addition, a number of pieces of flint débitage were recovered from at least four other pits, as well as a sherd of possible prehistoric pottery (01E039:021:1).

Burial 15 was just inside the northern edge of the Neolithic ring-ditch (Fig. 21.3). It consisted of the poorly preserved remains of a crouched infant burial within a subrectangular pit measuring 0.85m north–south, 0.59m east–west and 0.18m deep. A jawbone of a pig within the fill of the grave may have been placed there deliberately. A large stone within the upper fill was provisionally identified as a grave-marker. It is possible that this burial of an infant relates to the Neolithic ring-ditch, but no date could be obtained for the burial owing to its poor state of preservation and it is equally possible that it relates to the Iron Age or later activity on the site.

Iron Age activity
The earliest phase of Iron Age activity (phase 1) appears to be represented by a large number of spreads and pits, as well as post-holes and stake-holes that may have formed the framework of a circular structure. Following the disuse or

abandonment of this structure, an adult male was buried in a subrectangular grave topped by a small stone mound (phase 2). The grave was centrally placed within a circular ring-ditch (phase 3) containing a number of pits and paired post-holes, possibly representing a timber structure or henge. The ring-ditch was subsequently covered by a large stone cairn (phase 4).

Phase 1: possible structure
The first Iron Age activity was identified as a series of spreads, pits, post-holes and stake-holes appearing to represent the remains of a circular or oval structure. In total, six spreads, nineteen pits, twelve post-holes and 46 stake-holes were identified, mostly within the area defined by the earlier Neolithic ring-ditch. All of the features had been cut through the natural orange clay.

The largest spread was roughly oval and measured 1.96m north–south, 2.02m east–west and up to 0.04m in thickness. The smallest spread measured 0.52m north–south, 0.31m east–west and 0.03m in thickness. All of the spreads consisted of brown silty clay containing occasional charcoal flecks. The largest pit was subrectangular (1.93m long by 0.97m wide with a maximum depth of 0.19m) and was filled with brown silty clay containing stone and charcoal flecks. The smallest pit (0.44m across and 0.18m deep) had been filled with dark brown silty clay containing occasional charcoal flecks and burnt animal bone. The contents of these pits may be consistent with domestic activity at the site. Radiocarbon dates were obtained from charcoal sampled from three of the pits:

- pit F128: 370–100 cal. BC;
- pit F288: 360–280 cal. BC/240 cal. BC–cal. AD 20;
- pit F327: 370–10 cal. BC.

Of the sixteen post-holes, the largest measured 0.6m by 0.4m by 0.33m deep and was filled with dark brown silty clay containing moderate flecks of charcoal and animal bone. The smallest identified stake-hole measured 0.05m across and 0.07m deep, while the largest measured 0.18m by 0.12m by 0.13m deep. All of the stake-holes were filled with a brown silty clay and charcoal. Several of the post-holes and stake-holes appeared to form a semicircular arc and could be the remains of a hut site *c.* 6m in diameter, with an entrance at the east.

Phase 2: adult burial and possible stone mound
The second Iron Age phase was represented by the burial of an adult male (burial 14) to the south of the earlier settlement. The well-preserved remains were found beneath the roots of a well-established sycamore tree planted in the nineteenth century. The man was buried within a stone-lined,

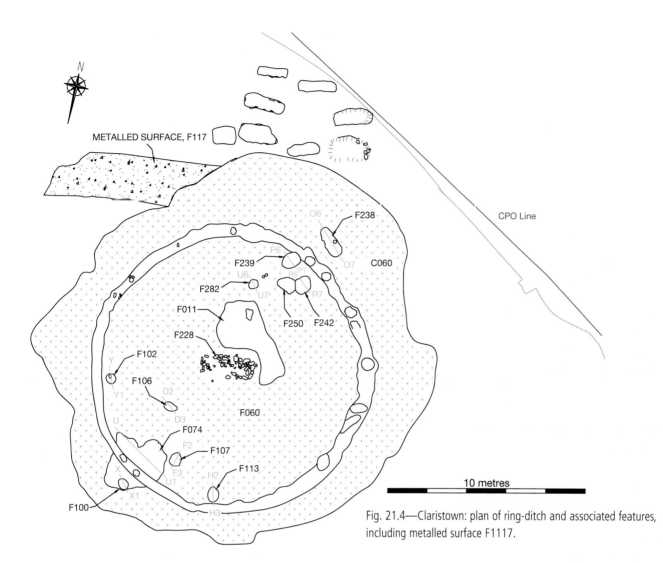

Fig. 21.4—Claristown: plan of ring-ditch and associated features, including metalled surface F1117.

subrectangular grave (2.84m east–west, 1.1m north–south and 0.19m deep) and was aligned north-east/south-west, with the head to the south-west. A number of large, medium and angular stones in the fill were interpreted as the remains of a small stone mound erected above the burial following interment. Either by coincidence or, more likely, by design, this burial was in the centre of a later ring-ditch (phase 3) that was erected around the grave.

Phase 3: silt layer, ring-ditch and associated features
The area surrounding burial 14 appears to have been deliberately sealed by a layer of grey sandy clay, which formed a spread that extended over a roughly circular area or low mound and measured 30m across and 0.05–0.12m deep. Associated with this layer were nine pits, two spreads and one stake-hole. The largest pit measured 1.54m north-west/south-east, 0.76cm north-east/south-west and 0.17m deep, and was filled with brown silty clay containing charcoal flecks, burnt

bone and heat-shattered stone. The smallest pit measured 0.5m in diameter and 0.05m deep and was filled with grey clay. Two spreads appeared to have been deposited above the grey sandy clay layer to the south. The first measured 3m by 3.25m across and 0.06m thick. The second measured 0.69m by 0.58m across and 0.07m thick. Both consisted of spreads of brown silty clay and charcoal flecks.

The grey sandy clay layer, the ring-ditch (Fig. 21.4) and its associated features lay below a layer of burnt black sandy clay, charcoal flecks and burnt animal bone. A sample obtained from this layer returned a date of 370 cal. BC–cal. AD 30. This layer was associated with four spreads and one pit. The largest spread measured 1.2m north–south, 0.55m east–west and 0.05m thick, and the smallest measured 0.55m north–south, 0.45m east–west and 0.01m thick. All four spreads consisted of black silty clay, stone, charcoal flecks and burnt bone. The pit measured 0.55m in diameter by 0.1m deep and had been filled with grey silty clay and charcoal.

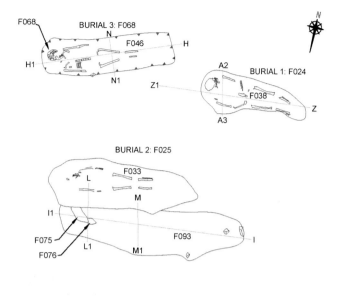

Fig. 21.5—Claristown: plans of burials 1–4.

A large, circular ring-ditch or slot-trench was cut through the grey sandy clay layer and appeared to have been excavated deliberately to enclose burial 14 at its centre. The ditch was roughly circular and measured 14m in diameter, a maximum of 0.4–0.5m in width and 0.21m in depth. The fill consisted of two deposits: a basal fill comprising brown sandy clay with small stones, charcoal flecks and animal bone, and an upper fill consisting of brown silty clay and stone. A sample obtained from the basal fill returned a date of 360–80 cal. BC. Eighteen post-holes were identified at the base of the ring-ditch—eight at its northern and north-eastern edge, three at its western edge, four at its eastern edge and three at its southern edge. The largest post-hole measured 1.2m north–south, 0.62m east–west and 0.46m deep, while the smallest was 0.2m in diameter and 0.18m deep. All had been filled with brown sandy clay. There were varying amounts of charcoal flecks but no evidence of *in*

situ burning of the wooden posts. The post-holes, with two exceptions, were found in pairs or in close association with each other. The post-holes within each pair were approximately 1m apart, and the pairs were approximately 1.9m apart. The structure appears to have had an entrance facing south-west. There was no evidence for any internal posts to indicate the presence of a roof or superstructure. The function of this ring-ditch and the associated structure represented by the post-holes is unclear, but it may have formed some type of wooden henge. After use, it was sealed by two layers of burnt silt and orange silty clay.

Phase 4: stone cairn
The fourth and final Iron Age phase was the erection of a stone mound or cairn over the ring-ditch and the central burial (burial 4). This mound, *c.* 30m in diameter and 0.34m thick, was constructed from a large number of angular and round stones.

Early medieval features
In addition to the two burials described above, a further thirteen burials were identified. These formed two separate cemeteries, one to the north and the other to the south of the stone cairn. The southern group consisted of four inhumations (burials 1–4) some 10m south of the cairn (Fig. 21.5). These were all poorly preserved and were aligned west–east. Burial 4 showed traces of possible stone lining. It appears that these graves belong to the early medieval period.

The northern group consisted of the remains of nine extended inhumations (Fig. 21.6), all aligned north-east/south-west and placed within relatively deep graves, some with stone linings. Five of the inhumations were in single graves, while four were in stone-lined double graves. Burials 5 and 6, interred together in a subrectangular grave measuring 2.25m in length and 1.1m in width, consisted of the well-preserved remains of two adult males, one aged 25–40 years and the other a young adult. Both were buried with their heads to the west and facing north, with the right elbow of burial 5 slightly overlying the left elbow of burial 6. Burials 12 and 13 were interred in a second subrectangular grave, 1.96m long by 0.94m wide. Burial 12 consisted of the remains of an adult male and burial 13 the remains of a juvenile. Burial 12 was lying on its left side, looking north, and burial 13 lay on its right side, looking south. Interestingly, burial 8 comprised the poorly preserved remains of a juvenile aged between twelve and fifteen years, while burial 11 represented the remains of a young female aged around sixteen years. This cemetery may have continued to the east and north-east beyond the limits of the excavation. At the time of writing the

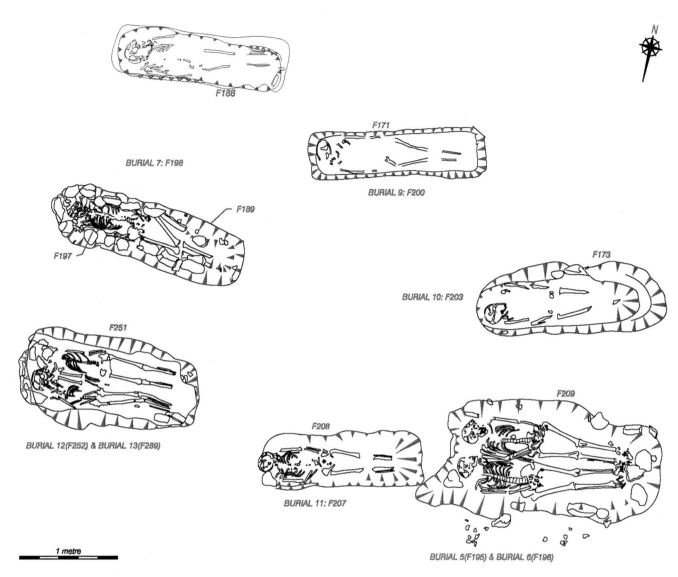

Fig. 21.6—Claristown: plans of burials 5–13.

remains have not yet been dated, but it is suggested that they date from the period of the Iron Age/Early Christian transition.

Conclusion

The earliest activity on the site consisted of a metalled surface, which must be of early Neolithic date or earlier, given that it is cut by an early Neolithic interrupted ring-ditch. It is possible that several pits, post-holes or stake-holes cut into the natural subsoil are contemporary with this early Neolithic phase and that further Neolithic evidence was removed by intensive Iron Age activity. The Neolithic ring-ditch may represent the remains of a foundation trench for a subcircular structure of some sort. No definite entrance was discernible, but large gaps between the ditch sections facing slightly south of west and slightly north of east could have served as entrances. It is difficult to determine the type or function of such a structure owing to the extensive disturbance by the later Iron Age activity. It is possible that the burial of an infant (burial 15) within the area defined by the interrupted ring-ditch could relate to this phase of activity, but no date could be obtained for the burial owing to its poor state of preservation and therefore it could equally be associated with the Iron Age activity.

The next phase post-dates the ring-ditch by nearly a thousand years, though it still represents Neolithic activity. This phase was represented by a collection of seven pits and two deposits to the south-west of the ring-ditch. The pits

271

appear to represent cooking activities, given the amount of animal bone and cremated bone within the fills.

The earliest Iron Age activity was represented by a semicircular arc of posts ending in post-pits, which could be the remains of a hut site *c*. 6m in diameter. Associated with the arc of post-holes were two hearths (outside the structure) and various pits. The butchered animal bone, charcoal and hazelnuts indicate some sort of domestic cooking activities. Following the concentration of activity around this area of the site, the focus appears to have shifted both spatially and functionally.

At roughly the same time as the abandonment of these structures, a burial took place (burial 14) and a small mound was raised over it. The burial was aligned north-east/south-west, with the skull to the west, and appeared to be of an adult male (35–45 years old); it was laid within a stone-lined grave, topped with a cairn mound, followed by the deliberate raising of an earthen mound over the grave. This burial, whether by accident or design, was interred within (though not centrally in) the area enclosed by the Neolithic ring-ditch.

The next phase of Iron Age activity, which may have taken place shortly after the interment of burial 14, involved the construction of a ring-ditch 14m across and containing eighteen post-holes within the ditch. The post-holes were arranged in pairs. The structure appears to have had an entrance facing the south-west. There was no evidence for a roof or any superstructure and there do not appear to have been any internal posts. The ring-ditch and its associated structure enclosed a subcircular area of approximately 286m², with burial 14 roughly at the centre. The pits associated with this phase exhibit evidence of cooking. It appears that the structure was then dismantled and subsequently a deposit of burnt silt and orange silty clay was laid down, maybe as a result of the burning of the superstructural elements. As a final act, the whole mound was covered with a cairn of stones.

After the construction of the cairn the site continued to function as a focus for burial, with the formation of two small separate cemeteries on the perimeter of the cairn. The southern one contained the poorly preserved remains of four individuals. The northern one consisted of nine individuals, including two double burials in stone-lined graves. These are probably late Iron Age or Early Christian.

It appears that the significance of the site as a burial ground was subsequently lost or forgotten. A medieval date obtained from the cairn seems to relate to a period of field clearance and agricultural activity in the thirteenth to fourteenth century. It also seems likely that the large ditch to the south-east of the cairn may be a field boundary associated with this phase of activity. In post-medieval times, stones from the cairn were used in the construction of field drains and the cairn was ploughed down to a low mound. The most recent event at Claristown 2 was the planting of a sycamore tree some 150 years ago, roughly in the centre of the low mound.

Note

1. The excavation was carried out by the writer, under licence no. 01E0039, on behalf of Archaeological Consultancy Services Ltd.

22. Excavation of a late Iron Age ring-ditch at Ferns Lower, Co. Wexford

Frank Ryan with a contribution by Laureen Buckley

Introduction

Location

The site is in the townland of Ferns Lower, in the parish of Ferns and barony of Scarawalsh, Co. Wexford (OS 6in. sheet 15; 55.3cm from west; 28cm from south). It is on the eastern outskirts of Ferns town, approximately 500m south-east of St Aidan's Cathedral, 150m south of the Ferns–Milltown road, near the northern corner of the reed-bed area of the town's sewerage scheme. The River Bann flows north–south 500m to the east of the site and joins the River Slaney 7km south of Ferns. Although low-lying, the site has clear views all round (Fig. 22.1).

History

A monastery was founded in Ferns by St M'Aodhog (Mogue), alias Aidan, at the end of the sixth century on land allotted by a recently converted Hy Kinsella ruler. The monastery became the principal church of southern Leinster. Diarmait MacMurrough resided in Ferns on the site of the present

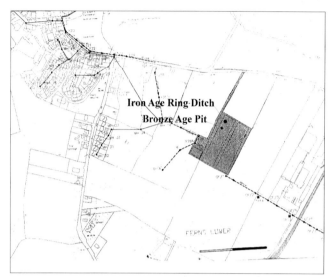

Fig. 22.2—Ferns Lower: location of site within reed-bed area.

castle (which was built in the early thirteenth century) and founded St Mary's Abbey for the Canons Regular of St Augustine. After Diarmait's death, Ferns passed to his son-in-law Strongbow and subsequently to his heirs until it was reclaimed by the MacMurrough family in the fourteenth century. The castle was dismantled in 1641 by the Parliamentarian Sir Charles Coote, who slaughtered the inhabitants of the town. The see of the Catholic diocese was moved to Enniscorthy, after which Ferns became a quiet village on the Gorey–Enniscorthy road (Killanin and Duignan 1969).

Discovery of site

The site was uncovered during archaeological monitoring of the upgrading of the sewerage scheme in Ferns by Wexford County Council, whereby a reed-bed system was installed on the east side of the town (Ryan 2000). The surface of the four-acre reed-bed area was scraped level by a bulldozer in order to accommodate the growing of reeds to filter the 'outflow' from the septic tanks. Two archaeological features were revealed during the levelling of the site. The first was a large pit, 3m in diameter and 1m deep, which was excavated under the monitoring licence 98E0132 and was dated by radiocarbon analysis to the middle Bronze Age (Fig. 22.2). The second feature was a ring-ditch, which is the subject of this paper. It

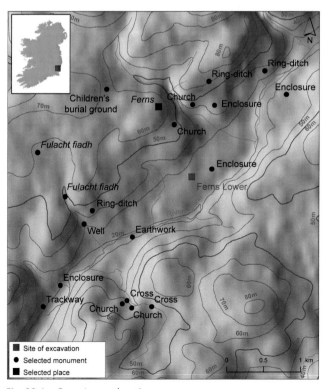

Fig. 22.1—Ferns Lower: location map.

273

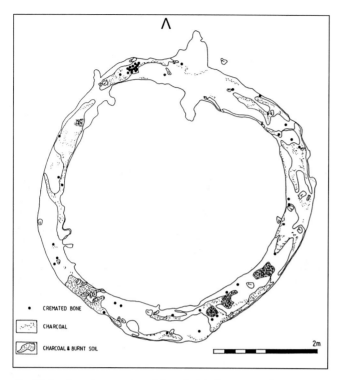

Fig. 22.3—Ferns Lower: plan of ring-ditch before excavation.

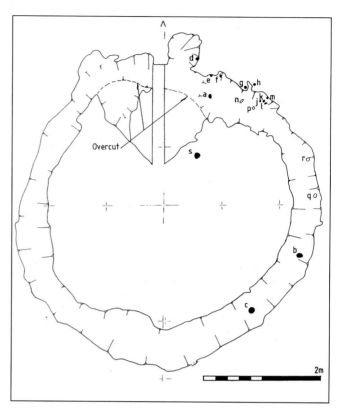

Fig. 22.4—Ferns Lower: plan of ring-ditch after full excavation.

was 20m to the north of the pit and comprised a narrow circle of charcoal-rich clay, approximately 5m in diameter, which contained fragments of burnt bone and oxidised clay. This ring-ditch was excavated by the writer under licence no. 99E0450 for Mary Henry Archaeological Services Ltd, which was commissioned by Wexford County Council to carry out the monitoring of the sewerage scheme.

Situated on flat ground, no surface indications of the site existed prior to removal of the topsoil. The only feature within the internal edge of the fosse was a small stake-hole in the north-east quadrant. The area beyond the outer edge of the ring-ditch contained no evidence of archaeological activity. It was evident that the surface layer had been displaced and that the original structure above subsoil level had been completely removed. The northern end of the fosse had been further disturbed prior to excavation, as a result of which the fosse was over-cut during the excavation where the line of the original cut was difficult to trace (Fig. 22.3).

Excavation
The fosse of the ring-ditch was roughly circular (Fig. 22.4), ranging from 3.6m to 4.25m in internal diameter and from 4.9m to 5.38m in external diameter. Its width varied from 0.28m at the north-east to 0.9m at the south, averaging approximately 0.5m. The depth ranged from 0.21m in the

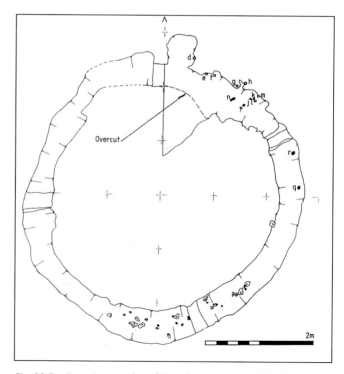

Fig. 22.5—Ferns Lower: plan of ring-ditch at upper silt level.

south-south-west to 0.38m in the south-south-east and tended to be shallower in the north and west than in the south and east. The profile of the fosse was U-shaped, with shallow vertical sides and a round base.

An oval stake-hole ('S'), measuring 0.12m by 0.1m across and 0.15m deep, was located 1m north-east of the centre of the ring-ditch. Three stake-holes were uncovered at the base of the fosse at the north-north-east and south-east. Stake-hole 'A' was oval in plan, measuring 0.065m by 0.04m across by 0.1m in depth. Stake-hole 'B' at the east-south-east was also oval, 0.1m by 0.08m across and 0.16m deep, while 'C' was 0.12m in diameter and 0.15m deep.

A group of nine stake-holes (D–M), 0.04–0.06m in diameter and up to 0.15m deep, were located between the north-eastern and northern outer edge of the ditch. A further four stake-holes (N, P, Q, R) exposed at this level were visible at the base of the fosse.

The only evidence that there may have been a bank on the inside and outside of the ditch was provided by the layer of fill that completely covered the base of the fosse (Fig. 22.5). The silt layer averaged almost 0.1m in depth but was as much as 0.15m deep in places. The soil, which contained charcoal flecks, was mid-brown and crumbly with a silty, slightly sticky texture, with small stone inclusions that made it gritty.

Timber layer

Evidence for substantial timbers was provided by the thick layer of charcoal that extended clockwise from the north-north-western side of the fosse, covering the eastern side and continuing as far as the south-west (Fig. 22.6).

A layer of charcoal-rich soil, measuring approximately 1.1m by 0.3m in maximum width, was found near the western side, indicating that timbers were used on this side too and probably originally extended across the entire enclosing fosse feature. The upper layer comprised mostly decayed silty fill. A continuous, 2.3m-long stretch of timbers was still somewhat intact, though completely charred, in the south-east quadrant of the ring-ditch, immediately below the charcoal silty fill (Fig. 22.7). The grain of some of the timbers was still visible along this stretch. It was possible to discern overlapping of timbers along a length of 0.86m. The best-preserved piece was 2.15m long and 0.4m wide.

The thickness of this timber varied from 7mm to 30mm. It was evident that the timber was not completely burnt through, though it was extensively burnt on the underside as well as on top. It was pitted with grey silt where it had rotted *in situ*, indicating that complete combustion had not been achieved. A section through the timber showed that the centre remained unburnt and was completely surrounded by charcoal

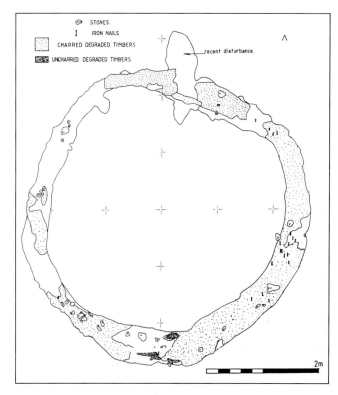

Fig. 22.6—Ferns Lower: plan of ring-ditch at timber level.

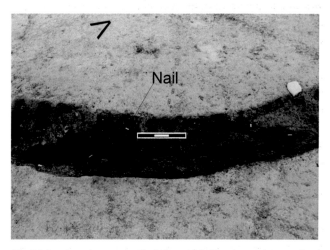

Fig. 22.7—Ferns Lower: detail of charred timbers in south-east of fosse.

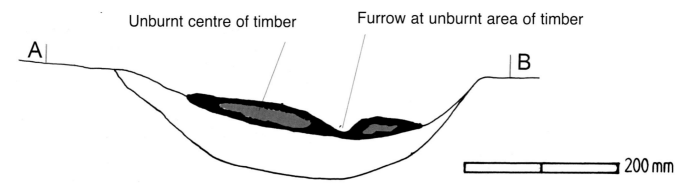

Fig. 22.8—Ferns Lower: section A–B of charred timber.

Fig. 22.9—Ferns Lower: timber layer in south-east of fosse.

(Fig. 22.8). The unburnt and decayed timber caused pocking of the charred surface during excavation, which made the surface appear uneven (Fig. 22.9).

The remains of regular-shaped small block timbers could also be seen at both the northern and southern ends of the fosse. On the northern outer edge, a length of charred timber, 0.5m long by 0.1m wide, appeared to be indented into the ditch surface (Fig. 22.10). This timber may have been placed on its edge along the outer face of the fosse.

The remains of an unburnt piece of timber (0.3m by 0.075m by 0.06m) were also excavated from the southern exterior side of the fosse (Fig. 22.11). Opposite this, on the inner edge, was another subrectangular piece (0.2m by 0.17m). The surface of this piece was burnt all round, while the core was filled with grey silt, indicating that the unburnt centre had decayed *in situ* after burning.

A total of 27 samples of timber were examined from

Fig. 22.10—Ferns Lower: block of charred timber at northern end of fosse.

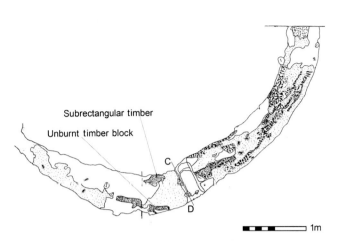

Fig. 22.11—Ferns Lower: timber layer in south-east quadrant below burial 1.

thirteen contexts. Of these, fourteen were associated with burials 2 and 3 and from beneath burial 4. The remaining thirteen samples were chosen at random from the layer associated with the timbers between the burials, with the exception of one unidentified sample from a stake-hole. The timbers identified were oak, birch and ash.

It might be expected that, because of its durability, structural timbers would be of oak, which accounted for 50% of the assemblage. A surprisingly large amount of the sample (40%) was identified as birch, which was found for the most part in association with the oak. This is not to say that 40% of the timber used on the site was birch and 50% was oak. It may, however, indicate that large quantities of birch were collected as firewood, placed beneath a platform of structural oak timbers and set alight. Ash occurred in two of the samples, both of which were associated with burial 3 and probably represented the remains of wooden artefacts.

Iron nails

A total of 39 nail fragments were associated with the timber layer (Figs 22.6 and 22.7). The remains of two nails were found still lodged horizontally in the timber. Most others were found on the surface of the timber or within the fill of the degraded charcoal in the south-east quadrant of the fosse. Others were located in the west and south-west of the fosse. A few were found within the fills of the burials, where pits were dug through the timber prior to interment. The nails were heavily corroded for the most part and appeared to have been no more than 3mm or 4mm square in section. Individual pieces were up to 39mm in length when found. The timbers had been disturbed by subsequent activity when pits were dug for the insertion of burials 2 and 3.

Burials (Fig. 22.12)

A total of four separate cremation deposits were placed into the fosse after these timbers were burnt. No sedimentary build-up occurred above the timbers prior to interment. Burial 1 was the most elaborate because of the manner in which the cremated remains were deposited and the quality of the grave-goods. It was located at the southern end of the ring-ditch, spread over a 2.5m length. An area of fire-reddened

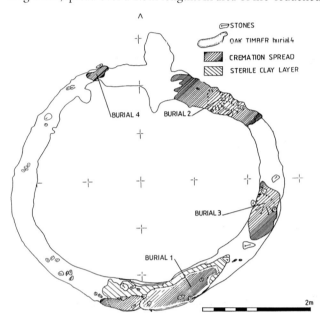

Fig. 22.12—Ferns Lower: plan of ring-ditch at burial level.

clay at the base of the timber layer contained some cremated bone. This timber layer was covered by sterile clay, upon which was laid a 1.6m length of oak timber that supported a large deposit of cremated bone. Burial 2 was partly placed into a pit that was dug through the charred timber layer in the north-east of the ring-ditch and was spread over a 1.9m length within the ditch fill above the timber layer. The burial 3 cremation deposit was also partly placed into a pit, which was dug through the charred timber layer at the east-south-east of the ditch and was spread over a 1.26m length above the timber. Cremated animal bone was also recorded from the deposit. Burial 4 was a small deposit of cremated bone placed on top of the charred timber in the north-north-western end of the fosse (Fig. 22.6). No grave-goods were deposited in burial 4.

Cremated bone analysis (see Appendix 22.1). Analysis of the cremated remains revealed that the burials represented seven individuals. The bones appeared to have been well burnt for the most part but were not subsequently crushed, which allowed positive identification to be made.

Burial 1. A sterile layer of clay was spread across the southern end of the ditch over an area of 2.4m by up to 0.5m, to a maximum depth of 0.15m above the timber layer. A flat piece of oak (1.52m in length by 0.43m in maximum width) overlay the sterile layer of clay east of the southern line of the ditch. The oak timber was completely charred, so that only a thick bed of charcoal remained (Fig. 22.13). The cremated bones were spread on top of the charred oak, extending beyond the limit of the timber at both ends. A total of 1,374 fragments of cremated bone, weighing 255g, were examined. The longest bone measured 40mm and the range included the skull, femur, tibia, radius, vertebrae, hand and foot from an adult male, as well as a skull fragment of a juvenile.

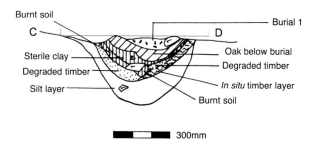

Fig. 22.13—Ferns Lower: section C–D of fosse facing south-west at burial 1.

Removal of the sterile layer below the oak revealed an area of burnt soil below the lower layer of timbers, which extended under burial 1 (Fig. 22.13). The area was marked by heavy *in situ* scorching of the surface clay layer to a depth of 0.08m over a 1.2m by 0.65m area. Above the oxidised clay layer were 125 cremated bone fragments weighing 15g, including the skull, radius and vertebrae of an adult and skull bones of a juvenile. It appeared that some attempt was made to separate the juvenile from the adult burial, as the bones of the juvenile were placed below the sterile layer of soil, while the adult remains were placed on an oak stretcher above the sterile layer.

Burial 2. This burial was deposited in a rough figure-of-eight-shaped pit that was 0.7m in maximum length by 0.4m in maximum width and was cut through the charcoal layer. The upper bone layer was spread over a 1.9m length and across the full width of the north-eastern end of the fosse. The pit was 0.12m deep on its western side but 0.28m deep on the eastern side, where the size of the pit was reduced to 0.25m by 0.2m

(Fig. 22.12). A total of 1,637 fragments (weighing 464g) of well-cremated bone were examined. The largest fragment measured 58mm. The remains were of an adult male and included the skull, long bones, pelvis, vertebrae and foot bones. A juvenile was represented by long bones, ribs and scapula fragments.

Burial 3. As in burial 2, a pit was cut through the timber prior to insertion of the cremated remains, which were also spread over a 1.2m by 0.5m area of the eastern side of the ditch. It measured 0.4m in diameter by 1.8m in depth (Fig. 22.12). A total of 1,689 fragments of bone were examined, the majority of which were well cremated. Some, however, were not well cremated, indicating less efficient burning, especially in the area of the skull. They weighed 378g. The longest bone measured 38mm. The bones of an adult included the skull, vertebrae, tibia, femur, patella, rib, ulna, foot, humerus and scapula. In addition, fragments of skull, tibia and radius of a juvenile were present.

Burial 4. This directly overlay the extreme north-north-western end of the timber layer and was contained within a 0.45m by 0.2m area. It comprised a dense, small pocket of some 49 fragments (9g) of cremated bone of an adult within a silty clay layer (Figs 22.3 and 22.12). While this was a small amount compared to the other burials, it did contain evidence of well-cremated fragments of long bone, ilium, mandible and vertebra. No artefacts were recorded with this deposit. It is likely that the main deposit of bone was removed prior to excavation of the site.

Finds
Grave-goods were deposited with burials 1, 2 and 3. No finds were recorded with burial 4.

Burial 1
The finds associated with burial 1 (Fig. 22.14) included the remains of composite objects that were deliberately deposited with the cremated remains. These comprised:

- a metal tack in a good state of preservation, 15mm long, shaft 3mm square, with a flat head (Fig. 22.14:1); the point of the tack was bent, indicating that it probably protruded through a wooden or leather object 12mm thick and was deliberately bent to hold the tack in place;
- a flat piece of folded sheet iron in six fragments, 120mm in length by 5mm by 2.5mm, that contained evidence of wood remains (Fig. 22.14:3);
- a flat copper-alloy mount or escutcheon, with a retaining

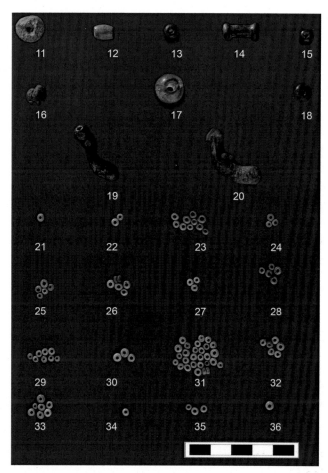

Fig. 22.14—Ferns Lower: finds from burial 1. (1) Iron tack, 17mm by 3mm by 3mm, reduced to 2mm by 1mm, hooked at pointed end; flat head, 8mm by 6mm, at other end. (2) Iron nail fragment, 18mm by 3mm by 3mm, very corroded. (3) Hollow U-shaped iron object (in six fragments), 55mm by 6mm by 2mm. (4) Iron point, 20mm by 1.5mm by 1mm, with some corrosion, and nail head fragment, very corroded. (5) Copper-alloy object, 40mm by 19mm max. by 2.2mm max. (escutcheon fragment), with one rivet, one rivet hole and linear indentations on one side. (6) Copper-alloy coil, 12mm long by 10mm by 8mm, oval with ridge. Hollow, probably made of 2mm-diam. wire, partially melted. (7) Flint flake scraper, 30mm by 32mm with central ridge. (8) Flint flake, patinated. (9) Pottery fragment, coarseware, 20mm by 15mm max. width by 8mm thick. Dark brown body and coarse white grainy interior, light brown slip surface on one side; other surface light brown and bumpy; mica on both surfaces. Identified as early Neolithic or possibly Beaker. (10) Light grey-brown stone cube, 17mm by 15mm max. by 12mm, with six flat surfaces; straight hole (5mm diam.) through two sides with 1mm-diam. iron fragment in the hole. Scale in centimetres.

Fig. 22.15—Ferns Lower: finds of beads from burial 1. (11) Glass bead, flat, weathered, of undetermined type. (12) Bone bead, barrel-shaped, 10mm by 7.5mm in diam. with 2.5mm-diam. hole, burnt. (13) Round amber bead, 7mm in diam. with 4.5mm-diam. hole. (14) Dumb-bell amber bead, 16.5mm by 5mm, expanded to 8mm at either end. (15) Round amber bead, 6mm in diam. by 3mm with 2mm-diam. hole. (16) Two dark green translucent glass beads, congealed, 5–7mm in diam. (17) Light blue/green translucent glass bead. (18) Dark green translucent glass bead. (19) Four or five dark green translucent glass beads, vitrified. (20) Five–eight dark green translucent glass beads, melted. (21–36) Ninety-three yellow annular glass beads, 1.5–3.5mm in diam. by 0.7–2mm in height with 0.5–1.5mm perforations. Scale in centimetres.

pin attached to the back of the narrow, rounded end and a pair of rivet holes, one containing a rivet, in the centre of the wide end (Fig. 22.14:5), and a copper-alloy tube (Fig. 22.14:6) that appeared to have been made with 2mm-diameter round wire;

- a stone bead with flat sides and a straight hole that was drilled through two of the sides, which were at right angles to each other; the hole contained a piece of iron rod (Fig. 22.14:10).

A single small fragment of coarseware pottery was also found in the grave fill (Fig. 22.14:9). This was identified as probably of early Neolithic date or possibly from an early Bronze Age Beaker pot. These objects were found mainly in the centre and at the southern end of the oak timber, with a few scattered examples at the eastern end beyond the confines of the oak.

A total of 117–127 glass beads were recorded with the cremated remains, as well as a bone bead (Fig. 22.15:12) and three beads of amber, two of which were round (Fig. 22.15:13 and 15) while the third was dumb-bell-shaped (Fig. 22.15:14). The glass beads comprised mainly 93 individual yellow beads of annular type, 1.5–3.5mm in diameter (Figs 22.15:21–36), of Guido's (1978) class 8. The remaining glass beads were of Guido's class 7. These included eight–eleven translucent dark green beads, 6–8mm in diameter, that were fused together and melted in two bunches (Fig. 22.15:19–20), a single light blue/green bead, 11.5–12mm in diameter (Fig. 22.15:17), and a further three beads that were badly burnt (Fig. 22.15:16 and 18).

Below burial 1
The finds from below burial 1 (Fig. 22.16) comprised three iron fragments, each 19mm by 15mm by 1.5mm, and another 65mm by 5mm by 5mm with a piece of timber attached (Fig. 22.16:37); a small, flat segment of flat sheet metal containing three 13mm-long tacks (Fig. 22.16:40); three translucent dark green beads, 7mm in diameter (Fig. 22.16:44), two of which had been fused together by heat; the charred remains of what was probably the base of a small wooden vessel (Fig. 22.16:43); a melted glass bulbous droplet, 19mm long by 8mm thick, that may have represented up to three beads (Fig. 22.16:46); and a single melted glass droplet, 10mm by 8mm, that was badly discoloured by heat (Fig. 22.16:45). These items had percolated down through gaps in the timber layer and lodged on the surface of the silt layer.

West side of fosse
A single piece of iron, 27mm long, contained a broad, flat, hooked end, 15mm wide, with a serrated edge and tapered to

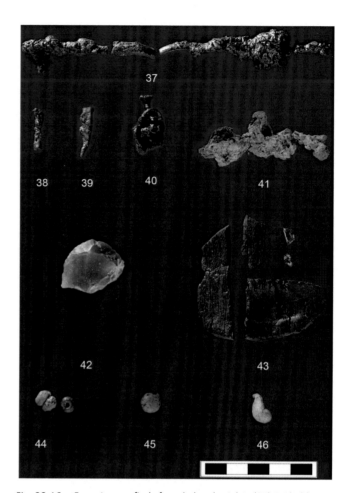

Fig. 22.16—Ferns Lower: finds from below burial 1. (37) Probable 1mm-thick sheet-iron strap (hollow), 120mm by 4mm by 2mm, expanded to 13mm at one end and containing a 17mm-long tack at other end, very corroded; also one fragment, 17mm long, very corroded. (38) Iron nail fragment, 18mm by 2mm in diam., corroded. (39) Iron nail, 24mm by 3mm, tapering to a point, with a 5mm by 4mm head at other end. (40) Flat oval sheet-iron fragment, 20mm by 15mm, with three iron tacks (one is flat-headed, 15mm long). (41) Two iron fragments with wood attached, 40mm and 20mm long, very corroded. (42) Flint flake scraper with pointed end. (43) Four wood fragments, birch; probable circular base of object. (44) Three dark green translucent glass beads, 7mm in diam., two fused together. (45) Glass bead of uncertain colour, 10mm by 8mm. (46) One–three glass beads, melted droplet, badly discoloured, 19mm by 8mm. Scale in centimetres.

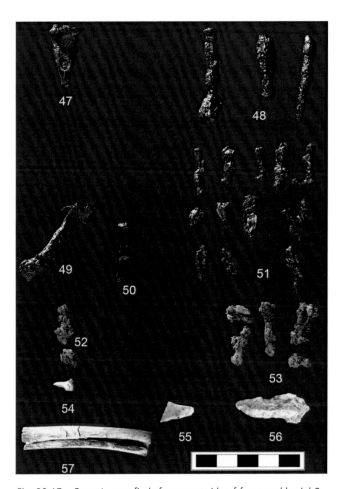

Fig. 22.17—Ferns Lower: finds from west side of fosse and burial 2. (47) Piece of iron, 27mm long, max. width 15mm, tapering to a point at other end. (48) Three nails: 29mm by 3mm by 2.5mm, fragment with bulbous corrosion; 38mm by 3mm by 2.5mm with tapering shaft; 38mm by 3mm by 3mm with flat head and bulbous corrosion at end. (49) Five nail fragments; four wire fragments, each 22mm long; two wire fragments 15mm and 13mm long. (50) Flat strip of iron with iron rivet and broken rivet hole, 45mm by 8–11mm by 1–2mm. (51) Iron nail, 25mm by 1.5mm by 1.5mm. (52) Three corroded iron fragments; two wire pins, 15mm and 13mm long. (53) Corroded iron fragment, 17mm by 3mm. (54) Flint flake, 9mm by 6mm max. width, pointed. (55) Flint fragment, 10mm long by 13mm wide with retouched edge. (56) Limestone flake, 34mm by 14mm max. width, reducing to a point. (57) Hollow bone cylinder, burnt, 119mm long by 21mm in diam., split along its length; hole, 5mm sq., at one end, other end partially frayed, both ends cut square. Scale in centimetres.

a point at the other end (Fig. 22.17:47). It may have been the remains of a tool. It was found in the west side of the fosse and was not directly associated with any of the burials.

Burial 2

Burial 2 contained a variety of finds (Fig. 22.17). There was a total of thirteen corroded fragments of iron nails, some of which indicated damage to underlying timbers when the pit was dug; the incomplete nail fragments were up to 27mm in length, while other examples looked more like complete tacks 20mm in length (Fig. 22.17:48 and 49). A corroded flat strip of iron, 52mm by 10mm by 2mm (Fig. 22.17:50), was shaped into a slight curve. One end contained a rivet hole and a metal pin attachment not unlike that attached to the escutcheon found with burial 1. Also deposited with the remains were a flint fragment, a broken flint blade and a limestone flake (Fig. 22.17:54–56). A bone handle, 59mm long by 9mm across, was split along its length and the ends cut square (Fig. 22.17:57). No beads were found with the cremation deposit, which represented the remains of an adult male and a juvenile.

Burial 3

The finds from burial 3 (Fig. 22.18) included eleven fragments of iron nails that probably belonged to the underlying timbers; these were up to 33mm in length and a maximum of 4mm by 4mm in section (Fig. 22.18:58–64). Minute flecks of copper staining occurred in the fill, as well as a fragment of a copper-alloy ring, 20mm long by 3mm across (Fig. 22.18:66). Fragments of amber, probably the remains of a bead, were also found, along with fourteen–eighteen dark green translucent glass beads of Guido's (1978) class 7, some of which were fused together during the cremation process. These included a bead measuring 11–12mm across with a perforation that was distorted during the cremation process, perhaps by the string that held it (Fig. 22.18:71). Another badly burnt and flattened bead measured 21mm by 11mm by 2mm (Fig. 22.18:69). A group of five–eight beads were also fused together (Fig. 22.18:68). This conglomeration measured 40mm long by 4–8mm thick. Another two groups of five and three fused beads were also found together (Fig. 22.18:70). Each bead measured 6.5–7mm in diameter by 4mm in thickness. It is likely that these beads were deposited intact with the cremated remains and became distorted in the fire that followed. Burnt animal bone fragments were also contained within the cremation.

Timber layer

Finds at the timber layer (Fig. 22.19) included at least 24 nail fragments, some with wood attached. Also worthy of note was

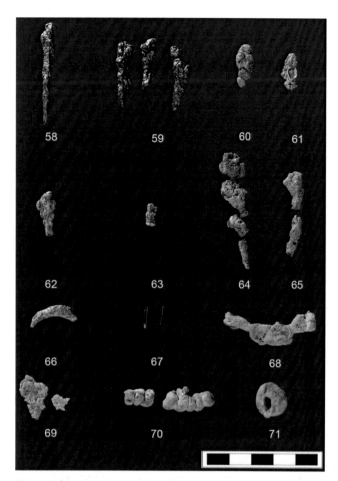

Fig. 22.18—Ferns Lower: finds from burial 3. (58) Iron nail, 43mm by 3mm by 3mm, tapering to a point, with a 4mm squared head. (59) Three iron nails, bottom half, all pointed, 27mm, 27mm and 21mm long. (60) Iron fragment, 14mm long, very corroded. (61) Iron fragment, 15mm long, very corroded. (62) Iron fragment, 18mm by 2.5mm by 2.5mm, very corroded. (63) Iron fragment, 15mm long. (64) Iron nail in three fragments, 40mm by 2mm by 2mm, tapering, very corroded. (65) Iron nail, incomplete, in fragments, 25mm by 2.5mm by 2.5mm, very corroded. (66) Copper-alloy ring fragment, 22mm by 3mm in diam., probably from a ring 25–30mm in diam. (67) Probable fish bone, 10mm by 1mm, hollow. (68) Five–eight glass beads, badly burnt, melted and heat-fused. (69) Flat fragment of dark green glass, badly burnt, 21mm by 11mm by 2mm. (70) Three and five dark green translucent glass beads, congealed, 6.5–7mm in diam. (71) Light blue/green translucent glass bead, partially melted, 11–12mm in diam. Scale in centimetres.

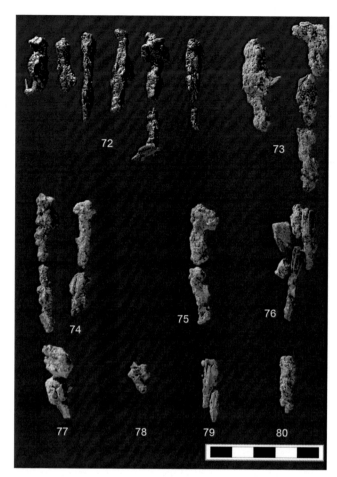

Fig. 22.19—Ferns Lower: finds from timber layer. (72) Seven iron nail fragments: 40mm by 3mm by 3mm, pointed at one end and very corroded; 38mm by 3.5mm by 3.5mm, very corroded; 33mm long and very corroded; 28mm, 24mm, 20mm and 10mm long, very corroded. (73) Four iron nails: 40mm, 30mm, 26mm and 20mm long, max. section 4mm by 4mm, very corroded. (74) Five iron nails, bottom fragments: 30mm, 30mm, 28mm, 18mm and 8mm long, max. section 2.5mm by 2.5mm. (75) Two iron nail fragments, 27mm and 25mm long, very corroded. (76) Two iron nail fragments, over 40mm long when joined. (77) Two iron fragments, 20mm and 15mm long, very corroded. (78) Iron fragment, 14mm long, very corroded. (79) Nail point, 22mm long, very corroded. (80) Nail point, 26mm long, very corroded. Scale in centimetres.

the presence of small fragments of natural quartz in burials 2 and 3, above the timber layer at the southern end of the fosse and again at the base of the fosse on the west and north-west.

Dating

The site was dated by radiocarbon analysis to 2090±65 BP and 2190±65 BP from two samples of charcoal supplied to the University College Dublin laboratory. The first sample was taken from the fill of burial 3; the second was from beneath the sterile clay of the primary burial. This date range was supported by the chronology of the glass beads.

Recent activity

Subsequent activity on the site obliterated any evidence of what the area may have looked like in antiquity above surface level. There was no evidence of features above subsoil level to indicate the presence of a bank. The only possible evidence that the soil was built up on both sides of the fosse was provided by the sedimentary fill at the base of the fosse, which may have slipped in from either side before the timbers were ignited.

Discussion

The village of Ferns is known to have been occupied from the Early Christian period, when a monastic foundation was set up by St Aidan in the late sixth century (Killanin and Duignan 1969). Indications of earlier occupation came to light during the monitoring of trenches dug for the Ferns Sewerage Scheme, when evidence of Bronze Age activity was uncovered. A pit, 3m in diameter and containing four distinct layers of intense burning, was dated by radiocarbon analysis to 3180±65 BP. It was located at the south-east of the town near the River Bann (Ryan 2000).

The ring-ditch was found within 20m of the pit and contained a sherd of pottery dated to the early Neolithic, indicating the likelihood that the district of Ferns was occupied from between 3900 and 3650 BC. Measuring little over 5m in diameter, the ring-ditch was one of the smallest of its type excavated in the country.

The fosse of the ring-ditch appeared to have been allowed to remain open for some time after it was initially dug, as evidenced by the build-up of silt at the bottom of the fosse. This fill was evenly distributed, indicating perhaps that an inner and outer bank were heaped up from the ditch fill. It is also likely that the fosse was considerably deeper than indicated by the surviving evidence and was subsequently truncated, since no surface evidence of banks, either internal or external, remained. Silting of the base of the fosse occurred also at Knockgraffon (Moriarty 2007) and at Cappakeel (Ó

Maolduín 2006), where it was suggested that the fosse remained open for some time, allowing bank material to erode back into it.

Stake-holes found both at the level of the silt layer and hidden by silt on the eastern side of the fosse indicated possible structural activity at an initial digging stage and again associated with structural work relating to the phase when timbers were laid in the ditch.

The timbers that covered most of the fosse circumference from the inside edge to the outside edge were charred on the bottom as much as on the top. This indicated that air may have been allowed to pass under the timbers to achieve the degree of combustion evident in the charred remains of the timber structure that subsequently collapsed into the fosse. It was clear that complete combustion had not been achieved, as the centre of some of the timbers was charred on the outside and decayed on the inside. Similarly, the external surface of these timbers contained areas that appeared to have rotted *in situ*. Similar *in situ* burning of structures was less evident on other sites, such as at Ballydavis 1 (Keeley 1999), where extensive areas of burning were revealed at the base of the fosse, and at Rathdooney Beg (Mount 1996; this volume), where carbonised wood, including oak planking, was found within the fosse fill.

The excavation did not conclusively reveal that planking was the form of timber used. The upper layer was so degraded as to reduce the charred timber to powder. The timber was well enough preserved so that the grain was recognisable over a length of 2.15m by a width of 0.4m along the south-east of the fosse, however, and one length of timber overlay a second 0.85m length. Evidence of the direction of the grain was also picked up at intervals along the fosse surface, especially at the northern outer fosse edge and the north-north-eastern inner edge, showing that the grain was oriented tangentially with the fosse, whereas it appeared that the timbers ran in line with the fosse. It might reasonably be assumed that each timber was no more than a couple of metres in length, that they were overlapped and perhaps tacked into place with nails. There was no evidence of mortises or tenons. A large number of iron nail fragments were associated with the timber layer. These were heavily corroded and the original size of the nails remains uncertain. The cross-sections indicated that the nails were no more than 4mm by 4mm originally, and perhaps were as long as 100mm. Though the quantity of fragments was high compared to other sites, some of these could be grouped to make one nail, thus reducing the actual number of nails found. In addition, the level of corrosion was high and it is possible that other nails completely disappeared over time.

The indications were that the nails may have been used

to tack timbers together but were perhaps not large enough to support a heavy permanent structure, particularly as heavy oak timbers were used (Figs 22.6, 22.7 and 22.19). Nails of similar size were found on other sites of the period, including Haynestown (O'Sullivan 1994) and Rathdooney Beg (Mount 1996), where they were found in the ditch fills, as well as Cappakeel (Ó Maoldúin 2006), Knockgraffon (Moriarty 2007) and Marlhill. Large nails with a square section above 5mm and longer than 100mm do not seem to have been used on Iron Age sites in Ireland.

The occurrence of nails with two of the cremation deposits indicated disturbance of the lower timbers when pits were dug to inter the cremations. The quantity of bone associated with burial 4 was very small compared to the other deposits, perhaps because the upper layer was removed prior to excavation. This may also explain why there was a shallower depth of timbers in this western side of the fosse.

The deposition of pairs of cremations, as in burials 1, 2 and 3, occurred also on other sites from the early Bronze Age and inhumed burials of the later Iron Age. It perhaps suggests that the practice of interring an adult burial with a juvenile was one that continued uninterrupted during the early Iron Age. There may have been many reasons for double burials of this nature, including the possibility of human sacrifice (Raftery 1994). The formal laying out of burial 1, at the southern end of the fosse, where the cremated remains of an adult were laid out on a stretcher above the sealed interment of a juvenile, may also be a feature unique to this site. At Ballydavis site 1 (Keeley 1999), however, there was evidence of the placing of artefacts, bone and charcoal, interspersed with sterile clay layers.

While the grave-goods for the most part were typical of what might have been expected in a late Iron Age context, few sites recorded the range of artefacts found at Ferns. Most of these were associated with burial 1 and the cremation layer below. It was evident that the cremated remains represented token deposition with which the artefacts were deposited. The most numerous artefact type was glass beads, of which there were two main categories: the yellow annular beads and those of dark green translucent glass. The small yellow annular beads fit into Guido's class 8, which are found on sites mainly of the third to first century BC. There was a concentration of these beads in the Meare district of Somerset and the Culbin Sands area in Moray (Guido 1978, 75). The dark green translucent beads fit into Guido's class 7. Plain green translucent beads of natural glass, both dark green and light blue-green, annular and globular, are usually found in Roman contexts, though they are known from pre-Roman sites in Britain, such as Glastonbury and Meare in Somerset.

Most prehistoric Iron Age glass beads from Ireland derive from burial sites (Raftery 1984, 200). Examples include Grannagh, Co. Galway (Hawkes 1982, 60), Mullaghmore, Co. Down (Mogey and Thompson 1956), and Ballydavis, Portlaoise (Keeley 1999), which were all ring-ditch cremation sites. The Loughey, Co. Down, burial (Jope and Wilson 1957), which produced yellow annular glass beads comparable to those from Ferns, may also have been a ring-ditch cremation, though there was no record of this, except that the artefacts are stated to have been found in 'black slimy clay'.

A total of 144 glass beads were found at Loughey, including 71 small yellow beads of Guido's class 8, similar to the Ferns beads, 65 small blue beads and eight large globular examples set with spirals. They are likely to represent one necklace. Raftery (1984, 201) dated the Loughey burial by the bronzes, notably the Nauheim-derivative fibula, to the years around the birth of Christ. The Loughey beads compare with those found at Grannagh and Portlaoise as well as Ferns. At the ring-barrow at Grannagh, a number of glass beads, including Meare spiral beads, were found in the cremation deposits and the mound. The assemblage, including a number of bronzes, is likely to date from before the first century AD (Hawkes 1982, 59–60). During the excavation of four ring-ditches at Ballydavis, Portlaoise, glass beads were found with cremation burials and a number of bronzes, including a Nauheim-type fibula and a box with an enamelled mounting and other artefacts of the Iron Age. The beads, including Oldbury and Meare parallels, had parallels in the Grannagh and Kiltierney assemblages (Keeley 1999, 52), suggesting that they belonged to the same type of period as the assemblages above. A single Guido class 8 bead was also recorded from the late Bronze Age site at Kilmahuddrick, Co. Dublin (Doyle 2005). McGarry (2008) has suggested that the dating of artefacts found on Irish sites is often based on typological sequences from abroad and may not be strictly reliable.

Finds of decorated glass beads are rare in Ireland, as indeed are beads made of other materials, such as stone, bone and amber, three of which were found at Ferns. Flint flakes, although found on other sites, were rarely associated with burials (Tiernan McGarry, pers. comm.). At Ferns, burials 1 and 2 contained worked flint. Quartz was also found in several parts of the fosse at Ferns, as at Haynestown (O'Sullivan 1994), Claureen (Hull 2007) and Balrothery 1 (Ryan, forthcoming), where a quartz crystal was found in the fill of the fosse.

Bronze artefacts occur on 20% of Iron Age burial sites, as well as at Ferns, where a bronze escutcheon and wire coil were found with burial 1 (Fig. 22.14:30 and 31) and a ring fragment with burial 3 (Fig. 22.18:66). These and the fragmented remains of objects made of sheet iron, sometimes with tacks, wood or rivets attached, indicate that composite wooden boxes and other receptacles were also deposited with the burials. These vessels may have housed more fragile offerings, which did not survive. The charred remains of the base of a wooden vessel (Fig. 22.16:43) was a case in point, as were the fragments of flat sheet iron found below burial 1 (Fig. 22.16:37 and 40). Evidence for the deposition of tools was likewise scarce, apart from the flint fragments (Figs 22.14:7, 22.16:42 and 22.17:54–5) and the iron tool found in the western side of the fosse (Fig. 22.17:47).

The perforated cube-shaped stone containing a fragment of iron (Fig. 22.14:10) was also an unusual item, as was the single fragment of early Neolithic pottery (Fig. 22.14:9), which, if not incidentally lodged, may have been a keepsake deliberately deposited with the primary cremation. Sherds of flat-bottomed pottery were also recorded at Haynestown (O'Sullivan 1994).

Conclusion

It is likely that the original site was a ring-barrow with perhaps a raised internal surface or mound and a low external bank. There was no evidence of a central burial. All burials were located within the fosse. Juveniles and adults were buried in pairs, a practice found with inhumed burials of the later Iron Age but which may have been carried through from the early Bronze Age.

The size of the monument at Ferns was modest compared to other Iron Age burial sites although the ritual associated with the burials was well defined, with four separate cremation deposits, three of which produced grave-goods. The primary burial was distinctive in that the juvenile cremation was separated from that of the adult, which was placed on a stretcher or platform, as well as in the quality and range of the grave-goods deposited with the remains, indicating that this was a high-status burial.

Acknowledgements

I would like to thank Mary Henry and Bob Withers for their support during the excavation, and the team of archaeologists (Mairead McLoughlin, Mark Rylands, Maureen McAllister and Siubhan O'Neill) whose combined skills were responsible for the wealth of information recovered from the site. I extend my thanks also to Colm Morris, who promoted a lot of local interest in the site. I am indebted to Wexford County Council, who funded the excavation, and to Michael Jones, the site engineer, in particular, for the backup he provided. The machine diggers and pipe-layer also deserve credit for their patience and interest. I am grateful to Rachel Barrett in the National Monuments Archive Section of the Department of the Environment, Heritage and Local Government. I would like to take this opportunity to thank the Department for permission to consult the relevant excavation reports in its possession, as well as the archaeologists who allowed me to use the information contained in those reports. My thanks also to specialist contributors: Laureen Buckley (bones), Ellen OCarroll (wood identification), Eddie McGee of the Experimental Physics Department, UCD (carbon dates), Judith Carroll (glass beads), Eoin Grogan (pottery identification), Susanna Kelly (conservation), Brenda Moran (typing), Nick O'Neill (photography) and particularly Michael McGee (graphic arts) for his patience in producing the final images. Finally, I would like to thank Tiernan McGarry for proofreading the report and for his helpful suggestions.

Bibliography

Beckett, J.K. 1979 *Planting native trees and shrubs.* Norwich.

Buckley, L.A. 1993 Human skeletal report. In C. Mount, 'Early Bronze Age cemetery at Edmondstown, County Dublin'. *Proceedings of the Royal Irish Academy* **93**C, 64–79.

Buckley, L.A. 1998 Human skeletal report. In C. Mount, 'Five early Bronze Age cemeteries at Brownstown, Graney West, Oldtown and Ploopluck, County Kildare, and Strawhall, County Carlow'. *Proceedings of the Royal Irish Academy* **98**C, 69–97.

Cooney, G. and Grogan, E. 1994 *Irish prehistory: a social perspective.* Bray.

Doyle, I.W. 2005 Excavation of a prehistoric ring-barrow at Kilmahuddrick, Clondalkin, Dublin 22. *Journal of Irish Archaeology* **14**, 43–75.

Guido, M. 1978 *The glass beads of prehistoric and Roman Britain and Ireland.* London.

Hawkes, C.F.C. 1982 The wearing of the brooch: early Iron Age dress among the Irish. In B.G. Scott (ed.), *Studies on early Ireland: essays in honour of M.V. Duignan*, 51–73. Belfast.

Hull, G. 2007 Excavation of a ring-ditch at Claureen, Co. Clare (04E0026). *Excavations 2004*, 35. Bray.

Jope, E.M. and Wilson, B.C.S. 1957 A burial group of the first century AD near Donaghadee, Co. Down. *Ulster Journal of Archaeology* **20**, 73–95.

Keeley, V.J. 1999 Iron Age discoveries at Ballydavis. In P.G. Lane and W. Nolan (eds), *Laois: history and society*, 25–34. Dublin.

Killanin, Lord and Duignan, M.V. 1969 *Shell guide to Ireland.* London.

McCracken, E. 1971 *The Irish woods since Tudor times.* Belfast.

McGarry, T. 2007 Irish late prehistoric burial practices:

continuity, developments and influences. *Trowel* **11**, 7–25.

McGarry, T. 2008 Some exotic evidence amidst Irish late pre-historic burials. In O.P. Davis, N.M. Sharples and K. Waddington (eds), *Changing perspectives on the first millennium*, 215–34. Oxford.

McKinley, J. 1989 Cremations: possibilities and limitations. In C. Roberts, F. Lee and J. Bintliff (eds), *Burial archaeology: current research, methods and developments*. British Archaeological Reports, British Series 211. Oxford.

Mogey, J.M. and Thompson, G.B. 1956 Excavation of two ring-barrows in Mullaghmore townland, Co. Down. *Ulster Journal of Archaeology* **19**, 11–28.

Moriarty, C. 2007 Final report on excavations at Knockgraffon, Co. Tipperary. N8 Cashel–Mitchelstown ministerial directive A035/000; registration no. E2272. Unpublished report prepared by Margaret Gowen and Co. Ltd.

Mount, C. 1996 Rathdooney Beg: Iron Age barrow cemetery. *Excavations 1995*, 78–9. Bray.

Nelson, E.C. 1993 *Trees of Ireland*. Dublin.

O'Brien, E. 1990 Iron Age burial practices in Leinster: continuity and change. *Emania* **7**, 37–42.

Ó Maoldúin, R. 2006 Cappakeel. *Excavations 2003*, 289. Bray.

O'Sullivan, A. 1996 Neolithic, Bronze Age and Iron Age woodworking techniques. In B. Raftery, *Trackway excavations in the Mountdillon Bogs, Co. Longford, 1985–1991*, 291–342. Dublin.

O'Sullivan, M. 1994 Haynestown, Co. Louth. *Excavations 1993*, 57–8. Bray.

Raftery, B. 1984 *The La Tène in Ireland*. Marburg.

Raftery, B. 1994 *Pagan Celtic Ireland: the enigma of the Irish Iron Age*. London.

Ryan, F. 2000 Ferns Lower, Ferns. *Excavations 1999*, 302. Bray.

Ryan, F. (forthcoming) Excavation of Iron Age ring-ditches, cist burials and features relating to habitation at Glebe South.

Schweingruber, F.H. 1990 *Microscopic wood anatomy* (3rd edn). Birmensdorf.

Stephens, P. 2006 Preliminary report of archaeological excavations at Ask, Co. Wexford: Sites 42–44 (A003/020). Unpublished report prepared by Valerie J. Keeley Ltd for the DEHLG.

Warner, R.B. 1990 A proposed adjustment for the 'old-wood' effect. In W. Mook and H. Waterbolk (eds), *Proceedings of the 2nd Symposium of C14 and Archaeology, Groningen, 1987*, 29, 159–72.

Webb, D.A. 1977 *An Irish flora*. Dundalk.

APPENDIX 22.1: CREMATION REPORT (LAUREEN BUCKLEY)

Introduction and methodology

The site was not seen during excavation nor was a stratigraphic report provided to the osteoarchaeologist. The site archaeologists processed some of the samples and some were processed by the osteoarchaeologist, with all fragments of bone being collected.

The bone was first checked for colour and texture. Generally, a very white colour and chalky texture indicate a very efficient cremation with high temperatures in the pyre. A grey or blue colour indicates less efficient cremation, either because there is insufficient body fat around the bone for burning (for example, the skull) or because oxygen cannot get around the body or part of the body because it is lying close to the ground.

The sample was then checked for fragment size and each subsample was weighed. The proportion of large to small fragments gives an indication of whether a cremation was deliberately crushed or not before deposition. Some fragmentation occurs naturally over time and during excavation, but if there are enough larger fragments it can be assumed that the deposit was not deliberately crushed. Each fragment of bone was then examined to identify which bone it belonged to, whether it was adult or juvenile and whether there were any distinguishing features or pathology present. In this report, the bones are adult human remains unless otherwise stated.

Results

There were four main deposits of bone. Burial 1 (the main burial) was divided in two. The upper half was separated from the lower half by a sterile layer. The upper half consisted of 243g of white, chalky, well-cremated bone. The bone was moderately crushed and it was possible to identify 19%. It consisted mainly of one adult individual, although there was a fragment of juvenile skull. The lower half of the deposit contained only 28g of well-cremated bone and it was possible to identify 32% of it. It consisted mainly of a juvenile, although there was also a small amount of adult long bone. It is possible that there was some attempt to separate two cremations here, with the juvenile being placed in the lower half and the adult being placed in the upper half, but there was some stray bone in each half.

Burial 2 was the largest sample, with a total weight of 456g. The bone was white and well cremated. It was not highly crushed and contained a high proportion of larger fragments. This enabled easier identification and it was possible to identify 50% of the bone. There was a minimum of one adult male and one juvenile present in this cremation.

Burial 3 was also a relatively large sample, containing 348g of bone. Most of the bone was white with a chalky texture, but a number of fragments were blue/grey, indicating less efficient cremation. The fragments were of moderate size and it was possible to identify 25% of the bone. There was a minimum of one adult and one juvenile in this cremation.

Burial 4 was a token deposit of well-cremated crushed bone weighing only 9g. Fragments of one adult individual were identified.

Summary and conclusions
Three of the deposits on this site contained moderate-sized samples of bone, although by no means enough to represent full adult cremations. One was a token deposit containing evidence for one adult only. The other three pits contained at least one adult and one juvenile and it was possible to determine that the adult in burial 2 was a male. There appeared to be some attempt to separate the adult and juvenile in burial 1. It is not unusual to find mixed adult and juvenile cremations, and they have been reported from Bronze Age contexts in Ireland (Buckley 1993; 1998).

Inventory
A description of each sample is given below, under the label that was on the sample bag. There were four main deposits: C15/C19 (burial 1), C24 (burial 2), C28 (burial 3) and C16 (burial 4). There are a number of samples from each deposit, apart from C16, which was a single sample. In two of the deposits the samples are taken from the top to the bottom of the pit, which should help to determine whether there was any differentiation of the bones when they were buried. A summary of the whole deposit is then given and the minimum number of individuals present is noted.

Burial 1
Upper layer C15/C19
Although not an exact count of the smaller fragments, Table 22.1 gives a summary of the fragmentation of all samples from the upper half of this pit.

There were no very large fragments (>40mm), but two-thirds of the cremation consisted of fragments over 10mm in length, which suggests only a moderate degree of crushing. A full adult cremation should yield between 1,600g and 3,600g of bone (McKinley 1989). Although this is rarely obtained, some Bronze Age cremations in which there has been careful collection of all bones from the funeral pyre have come close to this minimum weight (Buckley 1998).

Table 22.1—Ferns Lower: cremated bone from the upper half of burial 1.

Size (mm)	No. of fragments	Weight (g)
<5	294	13
5–10	678	80
10–15	275	72
15–25	22	70
25–40	7	8
Total	1,376	243

The upper half of this burial pit obviously does not contain a full cremation, but the identified fragments were mainly skull and long bones of an adult as well as some vertebrae and phalanges. As there was no repetition of skeletal elements, it must be assumed that only one adult was present. Since most of the identified bone consisted of the skull and leg bones, it must be assumed that the bones were not carefully collected from the pyre, with only the main larger bones being collected and many of the smaller bones ignored. One fragment of juvenile skull was identified, but this is not sufficient to state with certainty that a juvenile was buried in the upper half of the pit. It could well be a stray bone from the pyre.

Lower layer C33/43
The lower layer of burial 1 was separated from the upper layer by a sterile layer, C27/29. The total sample size is very small (28g). The identified bone consisted mainly of juvenile skull fragments, although there were some adult long-bone fragments also. If the burial is considered as one entity, then the minimum number of individuals present was two, one adult and one juvenile. The adult was mainly in the upper half of the fill and the juvenile was in the lower half. If they are considered as two separate burials, then the lower half contained fragments of an adult and juvenile and the upper half contained another adult burial. Considering the very small sample from the lower half, it is unlikely to be a full adult and juvenile burial. It is more likely that an adult and juvenile were buried at the same time and that an attempt was made to separate the juvenile and adult deposits with a sterile layer, but that some stray bone from each individual ended up in each half.

Burial 2, pit deposit C24
Summary of upper layer (NE19, C24 above C24A)
This sample consisted of 58 fragments of white, well-cremated bone, weighing a total of 6g. The largest fragment was 31mm in length, but most of the bones were less than 10mm. The

majority of the bone (5g) consisted of skull bone, including a large piece of parietal bone.

Summary of middle layers

Since the pit deposit (C24) was not excavated in layers, nothing can be said about the deposition of bone within the pit. It is best to combine all the samples from this pit and to consider it as one cremation deposit.

It can be seen from Table 22.2 that over half the cremation consists of fragments over 15mm in length and that there are several fragments greater than 25mm; therefore the bones do not seem to have been severely crushed as part of the cremation ritual.

Table 22.2—Ferns Lower: fragmentation of cremated bone from burial 2.

Size (mm)	Number of fragments	Weight (g)
<5	236	2
5–10	417	40
10–15	550	28
15–25	358	85
25–40	59	76
>40	6	25
Total	626	456

Identification

It was possible to identify 228g of bone, which is 50% of the sample. This is a very high identification rate, which is probably a reflection of the relatively large pieces of bone in the sample. A full breakdown of the identified bone is given in Table 22.3.

It can be seen from Table 22.4 that, although all parts of the skeleton are represented, the proportion of skeletal parts recovered is not typical of one adult cremation. The skull is slightly higher than expected and the axial skeleton is slightly lower than expected. The axial skeleton, consisting mainly of the vertebrae, ribs and pelvis, is often underrepresented, possibly because vertebrae are difficult to extract from the funeral pyre. The percentage of lower limb bones recovered is much higher than expected, and this seems to be at the expense of the upper limbs. It is much easier to identify fragments of femurs and tibiae than the arm bones, however, and this might account for the difference.

The identified bone is described in more detail below.

Skull: fragments included the frontal bone with the left supraorbital ridge, a left orbit, parietal bone, zygomatic bone,

Table 22.3—Ferns Lower: cremated bone identified in burial 2.

Bone	No. of fragments	Weight (g)	% of identifiable bone
Femur	46	75	33
Skull	136	58	25
Tibia	29	33	14.5
Pelvis	15	15	6.5
Humerus	16	11	5
Ulna	4	4	2
Radius	3	3	1
Fibula	3	1	0.5
Vertebrae	38	19	8
Ribs	12	4	2
Tarsals/ metatarsals/ phalanges	12	4	2
Hand phalanges	5	1	0.5
Total	319	228	100

Table 22.4—Ferns Lower: summary of the percentages of the various regions of the skeleton.

	Obtained	Expected
Skull	25%	18.2%
Axial skeleton	16.5%	23.1%
Upper limb	8.5%	20.6%
Lower limb	50%	38.1%

temporal bone including the petrous part and the mastoid process, occipital bone, sphenoid and the mandible and some teeth fragments.

Femur: fragments of shaft, some showing the linea aspera, and fragments of the distal joint surface.

Tibia: shaft fragments only.

Fibula: shaft fragments only.

Pelvis: fragments of the acetabulum and the wing of the ilium, including a sciatic notch.

Vertebrae: numerous fragments of bodies and articular surfaces, including at least three lumbar, two thoracic, fragments of sacrum and an axis.

Ribs: fragments of body and sternal end.

Humerus: fragments of shaft, neck, distal end.

Ulna: shaft fragments.

Radius: shaft fragments.

Tarsal/metatarsals: two first metatarsals, two other metatarsals, four foot phalanges.

Hand phalanges: one proximal phalange.

Since there was no repetition of skeletal elements, the minimum number of adults present is one.

Juvenile bones

These included an infant femur, infant scapula and rib fragments.

Burial 3, pit deposit C28

Summary of upper layers (Table 22.5)

The total sample size is not large enough to represent a full cremation, although identified fragments suggested that one adult individual was present.

The total weight of the sample is higher than for any other layer from this site, although it is still not a full cremation. Most of the sample consisted of fragments greater than 10mm and there was a significant proportion higher than 15mm. This indicates that the samples were not highly crushed.

There appears to have been efficient collection of the bones from the pyre, as all elements of an adult skeleton were present, including skull, vertebrae, ribs, upper and lower limbs and hand and foot phalanges. There was no repetition of skeletal elements, however, so the number of adults was one. There was also no repetition of any elements recovered from the upper layers. As well as the adult burial, some juvenile skull was recovered.

Table 22.5—Ferns Lower: size and weight of bone fragments from upper layers of burial 3.

Size (mm)	No. of fragments	Weight (g)
<5	96	1
5–10	70	5
10–15	41	6
15–25	29	15
25–40	1	2
Total	237	29

Table 22.6—Ferns Lower: size and weight of bone fragments from middle layers of burial 3.

Size (mm)	No. of fragments	Weight (g)
<5	60	2
5–10	320	} 36
10–15	496	110
15–25	277	137
25–40	17	19
Total	1,170	304

Summary of lower layers

Since only 15g of bone was recovered from the lower layers of C28, it does not add significant information to the burial, apart from the fact that skull, long bones and vertebrae were present in the lower levels as well as the middle and upper levels, so there does not seem to have been any differentiation of the bone within the pit.

Summary of burial 3

A total of 348g of bone was recovered from this pit. Although this does not represent a full adult cremation, identification of fragments indicates that only one adult was present. All elements of the skeleton were recovered: skull, vertebrae, ribs, long bones and hand and foot phalanges. The cremation was not crushed to a high degree, although the fragments were mainly of a moderate size. There was no differentiation of the bone within the pit, that is to say, there is no evidence to suggest that long bones were placed in before the skull or vice versa. Some fragments of juvenile skull were found in the middle layers, indicating that this was a mixed cremation of a juvenile and an adult.

Burial 4, deposit C16

This consisted of 49 fragments of bone, weighing a total of 9g (Table 22.7). The bone was white and well cremated. The fragmentation is shown in Table 22.7, with the largest fragment being 25mm in length.

The bone consisted mainly of fragments of long bone which were too small to identify, but there was also one fragment of ilium, one fragment of mandible and one fragment of vertebra. The sample is a token deposit containing part of the remains of one adult only.

Table 22.7—Ferns Lower: size and weight of bone fragments from burial 4.

Size (mm)	No. of fragments	Weight (g)
<5	11	–
5–10	10	1
10–15	15	3
15–25	13	5
Total	49	9

23. An Iron Age timber causeway in Annaholty Bog, Co. Tipperary

Kate Taylor

Introduction

A large number of archaeological investigations were carried out in 2006–7 in advance of construction of the N7 Nenagh to Limerick High-Quality Dual Carriageway, including monitoring of road-building in Annaholty Bog. A substantial timber causeway (Annaholty site 8, E3530) was discovered during monitoring and was dated by dendrochronology to approximately 40 BC. Several finely worked wooden artefacts were recovered from within the causeway. A separate collection of disturbed wood that probably represented another trackway or platform was recovered nearby and this was also Iron Age, being radiocarbon-dated to the fourth to first centuries BC. The sites were excavated by TVAS (Ireland) Ltd and the work was funded by the National Roads Authority (NRA) through Limerick County Council. The preliminary results of these investigations are discussed here and the final results of all the excavations on the scheme will be published in an NRA monograph in due course.

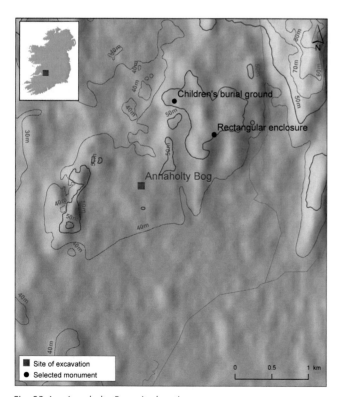

Fig. 23.1—Annaholty Bog: site location.

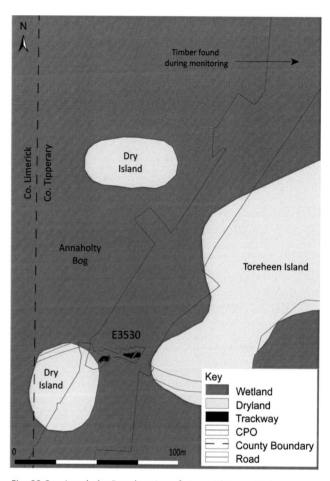

Fig. 23.2—Annaholty Bog: location of sites within road-take.

Location, topography, geology

The route of the new road traverses a gently undulating landscape of lowland pasture broken only by raised mire (Annaholty Bog) that straddles the border between counties Limerick and Tipperary. The region is overlooked by the Silvermines Mountains to the east and by the Arra Mountains to the north and west.

Annaholty Bog is a large raised mire and, although subject to peat-cutting, retains much of its natural form and extent. The mire evolved from a pre-existing fen that was surrounded by gravel slopes covered with woodland (Carter *et al.* 2006) to the south-west of the excavated sites. A dry peninsula extends into the northern edge of the bog and is named Toreheen Island where it protrudes through the peat. The two Iron Age sites lay 425m apart, just to the west of the south-western tip of Toreheen Island. The sites both lay at approximately 40–45m OD. Annaholty site 8 (E3530) was centred on NGR 168385 163535 and the disturbed wood was recovered during monitoring (E3462) at NGR 168630 163900, both in Annaholty townland, parish of Kilcomenty, barony of Owney and Arra, Co. Tipperary (Figs 23.1 and 23.2).

Archaeological and historical background

Annaholty Bog is indicated on the Down Survey maps of Owney and Arra and Clanwilliam baronies (*c.* 1656) and is named on the latter as 'The Red Bog in Common', with 'A Causy way' through its narrowest crossing, south-east of the excavated site. A scrub-covered dry island in the bog is indicated in Annaholty on the 1843 first-edition 6in. Ordnance Survey map and later revisions, and is named 'Toreheen Island' (Fig. 23.3).

According to local tradition, the bog was known as 'the moving bog' (Tuohy 1997). The name derives from 1880, when uncut bog flowed forward as a result of the internal build-up of water, burying existing cutaway bog. A report from the summer of 1924, one of the wettest on record, indicates that the bog flowed for a second time.

The association of Annaholty with wetland is preserved in the townland name, which translates as *Eanach Abhlta* (*Eanach* meaning 'marsh' or 'fenland' and *Abhlta* containing *abh* for 'river'), although an alternative translation is 'the Ulsterman's march'. Toreheen Island probably derives its name from *tuar*, meaning a bleach-green.

The topographic files of the National Museum of Ireland contain records of finds from Annaholty townland. They include fragments of two stone axeheads (1944:257 and 258), a stone spearhead (1943:133), the blade of a bronze spearhead (1947:228) and a leather shoe (1941:1042). All of these finds were discovered in the 1940s in the course of turf-cutting. The find-spot of the bronze spearhead was recorded as Tooreen, thought to be Toreheen Island. The find-spots of the other artefacts are unknown.

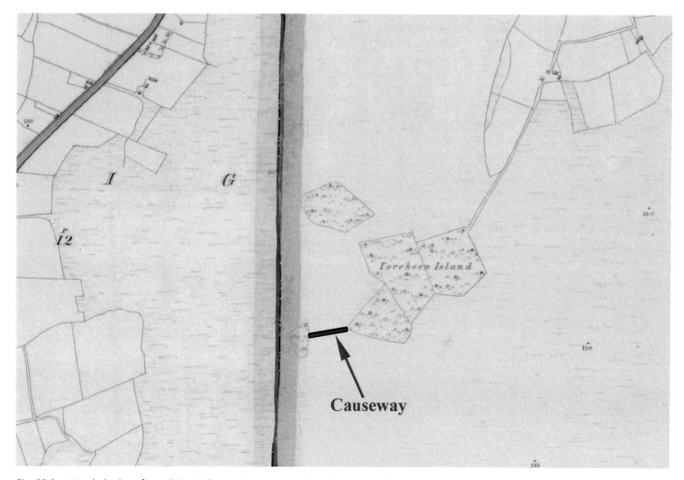

Fig. 23.3—Annaholty Bog: first-edition Ordnance Survey map, 1843, showing site location.

A section of wooden trackway was discovered in the bog during resurfacing of the Dublin to Limerick road in 1950 (Hanrahan 1950). This togher, located approximately 1km north of the excavated site, is described as consisting of

'whole trees or branches, 6in to 1ft in diameter, laid side-by-side. The length of each unit varied from about 5 to 7ft. The ends showed evidence of having been half cut with an axe-like instrument and then broken by bending. In some cases the ends were roughly pointed. In most instances the bark had been stripped or rotted away, but traces still adhered to a few of the smaller-diameter units. The timbers were soft and waterlogged when removed and bore no discernible marks of wheels. A number of other small pieces of timber were removed including wedges and pegs . . .' (*ibid.*).

The investigations carried out in advance of the N7 road construction have added to the story of the exploitation of Annaholty Bog, with a number of (principally Bronze Age) *fulachta fiadh* being excavated on its margins.

The causeway: discovery and excavation methodology

Given the known archaeological potential of the bog, and because it had not been possible to excavate test-trenches in the deep peat, construction work was subject to archaeological monitoring (McCooey *et al.* 2010). Peat was excavated by large mechanical excavators and removed from site, to be replaced by stone to form a solid base for the new carriageway; this work was observed, where it was safe to do so, by an archaeologist.

Annaholty site 8 was discovered during the monitoring and was excavated under ministerial directions with the record number E3530. The fieldwork took place between June and August 2007 and was directed by this author.

The causeway had been damaged in a number of places by a bog road, turf-cutting, drain-digging and construction activity and only survived in short sections, 0.4–0.8m below the modern surface of the bog. The worked wood technology was reported on by Caitríona Moore (2010a) and the wood was identified to species by Susan Lyons (2010a). Nóra Bermingham advised on the interpretation of the excavation results.

The causeway: excavation results

The excavation revealed the remains of a wooden causeway, which overlay two earlier episodes of trackway construction in this location. The causeway was aligned approximately east–west between Toreheen Island and another small gravel island, essentially connecting two areas of dry ground (Fig. 23.4). Unfortunately, neither end of the causeway was found, both having been destroyed by construction work. It is possible, however, to estimate that the causeway would have been 65–70m long in order to reach dry ground at both ends. The surviving portion was 55m long (with sections missing within this length).

Deposits below the causeway
All archaeological deposits were located in peat (Fig. 23.5). The underlying peat deposits were up to 2m thick, but the total depth was not recorded as the peat was truncated at its deepest point.

A small trackway or platform
The earliest site was a small, rough trackway at the south-western end of the excavation area, at the edge of the small gravel island. The platform was made up of 142 pieces of split wood, brushwood, roundwood and one artefact, the end of a forked branch. The assemblage was dominated by hazel. Included in this deposit was a piece of honeysuckle-impressed hazel, natural in origin but striking to look at and probably deliberately collected and prized. The elements were fairly jumbled but were broadly aligned south to north and south-west to north-east, covering an area of approximately 9.1m by 5.2m. The surviving elements did not form a level surface but could have been a crude trackway or platform providing solidity in soft peat.

Roundwood and brushwood trackway
The first attempt to build a trackway to connect the two islands was represented by discontinuous deposits of wood up to 8m wide, most clearly visible at the ends but poorly represented and truncated in the centre of the mire, in the deepest area of peat. At the south-western end these deposits occurred up to 0.2m above the earlier structure. The deposits were typically a single layer of casually laid roundwoods, brushwood and split timbers, generally aligned north–south and mostly consisting of oak, birch and hazel, with significant amounts of ash and alder.

Within these deposits were several artefacts, including a possible cart fragment and another composite object. Nearby, but not part of the trackway, was part of a wooden tub with a carefully finished surface.

In places where the ground may have been wetter and softer, a different deposit was recorded. This layer was composed mostly of worked birch, hazel and oak brushwood and woodworking waste; it yielded one artefact, a carved piece with a perforated end, possibly a flail handle.

Fig. 23.4—Annaholty Bog: the causeway, looking north-east, with Toreheen Island in the background (based on Hawkeye photograph).

Fig. 23.5—
Annaholty Bog:
section through
causeway and peat
layers. Scales 1m
and 2m (TVAS
(Ireland) Ltd).

Fig. 23.6—Annaholty Bog: causeway, looking south-west; runners visible beneath planks in foreground (Hawkeye).

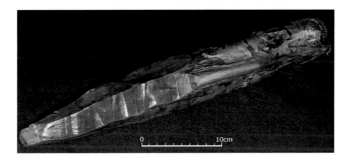

Fig. 23.7—Annaholty Bog: one of the stakes used in causeway construction (John Sunderland).

The causeway

Substructural runners, mostly birch and oak roundwoods, were aligned west–east and acted as a support for the superstructure of oak planks. The runners were recorded on the western and eastern parts of the site.

In the wetter central part, where the runners were absent, was a deposit of mixed-species brushwood that included a number of artefacts. These items included broken pieces from two tubs and possibly three other different vessels.

The causeway superstructure consisted mostly of long, narrow oak planks, reaching a maximum length of 7.9m, with brushwood and roundwoods inserted as fillers between them (Fig. 23.6). In some places pegs were also seen holding down the ends of the planks. A fragment of a yoke was placed among the roundwood fillers within the plank layer.

There were 97 stakes and posts set in vertical or angled positions (Fig. 23.7). Some of these were set through the sockets in planks; others were found along the edges of the causeway and may originally have been similarly placed through sockets that have since rotted away.

The finds and samples

All the finds from the site were of wood. A total of 1,113 pieces were recorded and lifted from the site. Of these, over 350 were obviously worked. The worked pieces included socketed planks, pegs with finely sharpened points, numerous cut roundwoods and logs, and fifteen wooden artefacts. The artefacts included several vessel fragments, a broken yoke and a number of larger items, including part of a possible cart.

Fig. 23.8—Annaholty Bog: portion of trough or losset (John Sunderland).

Fig. 23.9—Annaholty Bog: part of a tub handle (John Sunderland).

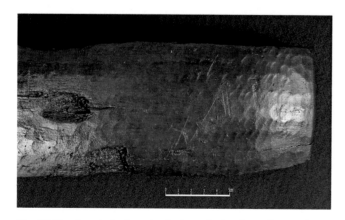

Fig. 23.10—Annaholty Bog: the finely worked surface of a vessel (John Sunderland).

Woodworking

The woodworking details given here are taken from Caitríona Moore's report (2010a). The types of pieces are summarised in Table 23.1.

Table 23.1—Annaholty Bog: overview of examined wooden finds from Annaholty site 8.

Element type	Number of pieces
Bark fragment	2
Woodworking waste	26
Post	42
Stake	55
Split wood	128
Worked end	173
Split timber	259
Unworked wood	427
Wooden artefact	15

Many pieces were unworked and were incorporated into the trackways and causeway during construction. The split timbers and split wood (differentiated on the basis of size) included the superstructural planks as well as numerous smaller pieces throughout the site. Where a piece was still in the round and had one or both ends cut, it was described as a worked end if found lying horizontally and as a post or stake if in a vertical or angled position; posts were defined as larger than 55mm in diameter and stakes as smaller than that.

At least twelve of the split timbers showed evidence of joinery, including the end sockets, one lap joint and a possible bare-faced tenon. The latter two joints were not used in the causeway construction, indicating that these were reused structural timbers.

Some of the posts and stakes were especially finely worked; torn, chisel, wedge and pencil points were evident, with up to 145 facets on one post (Fig. 23.7). Almost all the facets were flat, with rare slightly concave examples. Occasional partial jam curves indicated axes that had generally straight edges and sides with sharp 90° corners, and a number of pieces showed tool signatures caused by flaws in the blades. The angles of the facets and the small number of jam curves indicate that the tools were sharp and well maintained and that those using them were skilled in their jobs.

Fig. 23.11 (opposite page)—Annaholty Bog: yoke fragment. Complete collar in the centre and partial collar at left (John Sunderland).

Table 23.2—Annaholty Bog: wooden artefacts from site 8 (from Moore 2010a).

Find	Description	Species	Condition	L (cm)	W (cm)	D (cm)	Diam. (cm)
55:10	Fragment of a wooden vessel, likely a trough or losset	Alder	Moderate	29.50	7–9.10	2.5–80	N/A
55:22	A dressed peg	Hazel	Good	16.10	N/A	N/A	2.10–3.20
90:247	Fragment of an animal yoke	Ash	Very good	61.50	N/A	N/A	7.80–9.70
97:1 & 97:2	Two fragments of a wooden tub which fit together, comprising part of the vessel wall and a carved handle	Alder	Very good	12.60	8.10	0.90–2.80	N/A
97:18	Fragment of a wooden vessel, comprising part of the vessel wall and a carved handle	Alder	Very good	10.50	4	0.90–2.70	N/A
97:19 & 97:20	Two fragments of a wooden tub which join together and a short section of the croze	Alder	Very good	19.50	10.80	0.80–2.20	N/A
97:21	A small fragment of split wood, possibly part of a wooden vessel	Alder	Good	5.10	2.60	0.40	N/A
97:22	A small fragment of split wood, possibly part of a wooden vessel	Alder	Good	6.10	2.30	0.50	N/A
189:1	Portion of a wooden vessel comprising a long, narrow section of the vessel wall with an intact rim and base	Alder	Excellent	76.10	8.10–8.80	1.60–4.20	N/A
255:1	Possible cart fragment	Timber: alder. Dowel: ash	Poor	55.20	5.50–6	8.20–8.50	N/A
255:2	Wooden object with three dowels/dowel holes	Round-wood: willow. Dowels: hazel	Moderate	150.50	N/A	N/A	6.20–7.50
262:3	Wooden object with a carved shaft and perforated head	Ash	Good	40	5	4	N/A
298:133	Wooden object consisting of a forked branch with carved termini	Hazel	Moderate	13	7	2.50–3.90	N/A

Table 23.3—Annaholty Bog: dendrochronological dates.

QUB no.	Find	No. of rings	Start year	End year	Felling date range
Q11040	90:60	155	255 BC	101 BC	After 69 BC
Q11041	90:117	152	251 BC	100 BC	After 68 BC
Q11042	90:131	103	171 BC	69 BC	40 BC ± 9 years
Q11043	255:5	151	277 BC	127 BC	After 95 BC
Q11044	282:7	132	233 BC	92 BC	After 60 BC
Q11045	297:33	87	202 BC	116 BC	After 84 BC

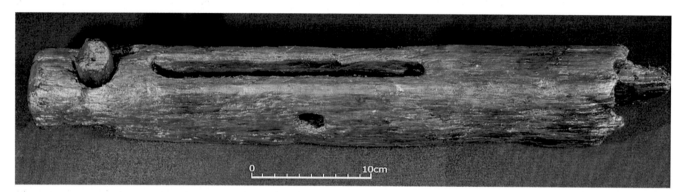

Fig. 23.12—Annaholty Bog: cart fragment (John Sunderland).

Some of the woodworking waste showed evidence of the use of smaller woodworking tools, such as chisels or gouges, and may have been by-products of artefact manufacture.

Artefacts
In addition to the timbers making up the causeway, there were fifteen carefully crafted artefacts (Table 23.2). Seven definite and two possible wooden vessel fragments were recovered, representing at least three different vessels, all carved from alder. A portion of a small trough or losset (a trough for kneading dough) was fairly crudely made, and tool marks suggested the use of a small chisel and a gouge (Fig. 23.8). Five pieces, including two co-joining pairs, are probably part of a cylindrical vessel with a separate base. The retrieved fragments are from the vessel wall, including part of the croze (the slot into which the base fitted) and the rim, and parts of two lug handles with everted rounded rims and perforations that would probably have held a rod to secure a separate lid (Fig. 23.9). Two other pieces of alder may also be part of the wall of the same vessel. This type of vessel is occasionally found containing bog butter and appears to have been developed during the later Iron Age (Earwood 1997, 28). The third vessel is represented by a piece that survives to the full height of the

vessel wall, with the upper and lower rims intact. This vessel was 76.6cm tall and was narrower at the top than at the base. The outer surface of the vessel is exquisitely finished and is completely covered with tiny shallow, oval tool marks created by a skilled woodworker with a very sharp, fine tool, probably a knife (Fig. 23.10).

The yoke fragment is broken at both ends but has one complete and one partial collar (Fig. 23.11). The close spacing of the collars and the small size of the intact example suggest that this is part of a head yoke that would probably have sat behind the horns of the animal, requiring the animals to lower their heads and push forward. Several animal yokes have been found in Irish bogs, including one of suggested Iron Age date from Erriff Bog, Co. Mayo (Fenton 1986, 43). In 2001 a yoke of late Bronze Age date was found in a bog at Toberdaly, Co. Offaly (Stanley *et al.* 2003), and was also made of ash, a strong, elastic and shock-resistant wood—ideal for this type of implement.

A broken composite item is thought to be part of a cart (Fig. 23.12). This piece is a rectangular timber of alder perforated by an *in situ* dowel of ash, with a rectangular slot or mortise cut through the central portion and crossed, at right angles, by a circular dowel hole. At the broken end of the object are the remains of either a dowel hole or a second mortice. This item is similar to an object found at Corlea, Co. Longford (Raftery 1996, 273–5), which had the broken ends of planks in position in its slots. It is likely that the Annaholty piece held planks which formed either the side or base of a cart or slipe (a simple sled) and was attached to a frame by way of the dowels. A finely carved peg and an item with a carved shaft and perforated head might also potentially have been part of the same vehicle.

A second composite item was a roundwood with three dowel holes, two of which contained *in situ* dowels. The roundwood is quite crude, with bark still intact, but the dowels are finely worked, indicating that care was taken in construction. Presumably this piece was part of a frame but the exact function is unknown.

The final artefact is part of a forked branch with carved termini. It is possible that this is the top of a walking stick or some other implement in which the natural forking of a branch was utilised because of its shape.

Together these artefacts demonstrate fine woodworking skills, access to a range of tools and craftspeople aware of the differing properties of the wood they selected.

Dendrochronological dates
Six dendrochronological dates were obtained from oak timbers from the site by David Brown (2010) at the Palaeoecology Centre at Queen's University, Belfast (Table 23.3).

There was a strong correlation between the timbers and other known Irish sequences, including Corlea, Co. Longford. Two of the pieces from the upper plank layer proved to be from the same tree. Although there was no definite sapwood present, one of the timbers had three possible crushed sapwood rings and it is on that basis that a felling date of 40 BC ± 9 years is given for this tree. This date makes Annaholty causeway the latest dendrochronologically dated causeway in the prehistoric period.

Three of the timbers are from the causeway superstructure (90:60, 90:117 and 90:131), while three derive from earlier structures and deposits (255:5, 282:7 and 297:33). There is little difference in date between the samples and, although no definite felling dates could be established for five of the pieces, it would appear that all the trees were felled within one or two generations, indicating that the different episodes of trackway construction at least were carried out within a fairly short period of time. It should also be noted that find 255:5 is one of the pieces that showed evidence of joinery and appeared to be reused from an earlier structure. This indicates that the structure cannot have stood for very long before being dismantled and the timber reused in the platform.

Palynology
A column sample was taken through the causeway, stretching from the base of the peat to the modern surface of the bog. This sample was analysed at Durham University (O'Brien 2010) and the results are summarised here.

Five local pollen assemblage zones were identified within the column. The earliest level of peat was radiocarbon-dated to the early Bronze Age, 2300–2040 cal. BC (3775±35 BP; SUERC-26437 (GU-20140)). In this zone the pollen indicates a mixed woodland environment at the site, dominated by birch, oak and alder. Lesser concentrations of ash, elm and pine were recorded, which may derive from small local stands of these trees, or woodland at some distance from the site. There are sporadic occurrences of cereal-type pollen, which may reflect some localised arable farming, but the high percentages of arboreal pollen suggest that large areas of woodland were not being cleared for farming at this time.

The next zone contained pollen indicative of a change to wetter conditions, shown by a significant reduction in woodland cover and expansion of wetland taxa. In this zone sedges begin to rise, there is a peak in *Sphagnum* (bog moss) and grasses form a significant component of the more open local environment. Human activity may have contributed to the decline in woodland, and there is an increase in the pastoral-indicating herb *Plantago lanceolata* (ribwort plantain), although cereal-type pollen is absent from this zone.

The third zone shows a return to drier conditions with dominance of hazel and heather, although sedges continue to be an important component of the local vegetation. There are few indications of farming activity in this zone, which is consistent with evidence from other early Iron Age sites in Ireland.

At the level of the causeway (*c*. 40 BC) changes in the pollen assemblage are indicative of human activity. There is an expansion of herb taxa, including increases in grass pollen and various meadow types, accompanied by significant reductions in heather pollen, considered to reflect the expansion of grass following grazing of heather shrubs. Many of the herbaceous taxa present are associated with pasture, and spores of a fungus obligate on dung would also indicate grazing animals. A few cereal-type pollen grains might indicate nearby arable agriculture in addition to pastoral farming. Also noteworthy is the elevated level of a fungal spore that reflects a wet local depositional environment, presumably the reason that the causeway was constructed.

Above the causeway the pollen indicates continued drier conditions with heather increasingly common. There is little evidence of any farming in the first half of this zone, with cereal-type pollen not seen, presumably indicating an

Table 23.4—Annaholty Bog: radiocarbon dates from disturbed wood.

Sample material	Find	Lab	Radiometric age	Calendrical cal. 2-sigma (95%)
Betula sp. (birch), waterlogged	E34662:50:6	Beta-249828	2200±60 BP	390–90 BC
Betula sp. (birch), waterlogged	E3462:50:33	UBA-13257	2135±22 BP	348–317 BC, 207–91 BC, 71–60 BC

agricultural decline for some time in the late Iron Age. Later in the zone, sporadic increases in herb taxa may reflect episodic human activity and management of the bog. A radiocarbon determination from the top of the sequence gave a date of cal. AD 890–1120 (1035±35 BP; SUERC-26436 (GU-20139)), indicating that the last millennium or so of peat growth had been removed by turf-cutting.

Additional archaeological wood
During the monitoring of road groundworks pieces of worked wood were observed in an area of cracking and subsiding peat to the west of Toreheen Island. It was considered unsafe to attempt to excavate in the collapsing bog and so the peat from this location was separated and spread out for artefact retrieval. The spoil was sorted by hand and a total of 49 pieces of worked wood were recovered, comprising 48 worked ends and a single wood chip. Of the worked ends, 31 were identified as chisel points, eleven as wedge point and four as pencil points, with two pieces too damaged to identify (Moore 2010b). Most of the pieces appeared to have been cut with iron axes and several different-shaped blades were identifiable. The assemblage was dominated by birch, with hazel and willow making up most of the rest (Lyons 2010b). It is likely that some of these pieces at least represent a trackway or platform that broke apart when the peat collapsed. Although not recovered, as no evidence for woodworking was seen, there were a number of large pieces of wood observed within the spoil from this area which might perhaps have been planks for a substantial causeway.

Radiocarbon determinations were obtained from two of the pieces of wood and both are dated to the fourth to first centuries BC (Table 23.4). It would appear that the collapsed structure was constructed earlier in the Iron Age than the causeway at Annaholty site 8.

Also discovered during the hand-sorting of the peat from the same area was a leather shoe. This was a left shoe; the sole was made from tanned cowhide and the upper was made from deerskin (Nicholl 2010). There are a number of possible parallels for this shoe from urban sites in Dublin, Cork, Waterford, York and London, and it can be dated to the early twelfth century. Although considerably later than the dates obtained from the wood, the presence of the shoe might indicate that the narrow gap between Toreheen Island and the dry land to the west continued to be used as a crossing point through the medieval period. It remains to be seen whether this shoe matches that found in the same bog in the 1940s.

Discussion
Iron Age sites were revealed in two locations in Annaholty Bog, Co. Tipperary, during a road development. The most substantial, at Annaholty site 8, E3530, was a wooden causeway spanning a peat basin between two dry islands. The larger of the islands, Toreheen Island, lay to the north-east of the site. In addition, a collection of archaeological wood found during monitoring (E3462) to the west of Toreheen Island probably represents another structure.

The causeway was preceded by two trackways, although the dendrochronological dating suggests that the gaps between phases were not long. The first site was characterised by a brushwood trackway located against the edge of the smaller island, and this was followed by discontinuous deposits of wood that may originally have spanned the space between the two islands. The final structure to be built, the large causeway, was constructed by putting down timber runners and overlaying these with planks. Some of the planks were secured with pegs inserted through sockets, and many other posts and stakes were used within the structure. The causeway was clearly designed in advance and the builders knew what they were aiming to achieve. Although the carpentry techniques used were not unusual, they demonstrated great skill on the part of the builders and the use of a variety of sharp, well-maintained tools.

In looking for comparative sites for the oak plank causeway, the most obvious starting point is Corlea, Co. Longford, the best-known and most extensively recorded trackway in Ireland, first discovered in 1984 and subsequently excavated by Barry Raftery and the Irish Archaeological Wetland Unit (IAWU). Corlea 1, of which 120m was examined, was 2.5–4.2m wide, with a superstructure of large planks and a substructure of roundwood runners (Raftery 1996, 7–54). Socketed ends were observed on some of the planks with pegs through them, and many other pegs were used to secure the runners in position. Brushwood, branches and waste wood were used under the superstructure to stabilise wetter areas, and broken wooden artefacts were also deposited in these wet spots. The similarities between this site and Annaholty, both in construction technique and artefact deposition, are striking; the sites are also of a comparable date, as Corlea 1 was constructed in 148 BC, just one century earlier than Annaholty.

Another significant trackway was recorded in Mountdillon Bog at Derraghan More by Etienne Rynne in 1957 and was then revisited by the IAWU (Raftery 1996, 94–104). This trackway was of similar construction to Corlea 1, consisting of planks on roundwood runners underlain with brushwood in places, and was probably built a few years earlier than Corlea.

Further investigations at Mountdillon Bog in 2001–2 uncovered an additional fourteen Iron Age sites at Derrycolumb and Begnagh: six toghers, seven platforms and one platform with associated toghers (Whitaker 2009). These sites were smaller examples than those excavated by the IAWU and were mostly constructed of roundwood and brushwood, producing a date range of 400–200 BC.

A number of other Iron Age sites have been excavated in Irish bogs, including a causeway in Derryville Bog, Co. Tipperary, discovered during the Lisheen Mine project. This site, Cooleeny 31, is dated to 778–423 BC (Gowen et al. 2005, 224–6) and crossed the southern part of Derryville Bog, bridging the mouth of Cooleeny Bog and running from one glacial ridge to another. The causeway was constructed in four phases: brushwood was first laid down to level the area, then three lines of pegs marked out the route, and sand was used to level the area once again before roundwood and planks were laid transversely.

Other Iron Age sites recorded in Derryville Bog include fifteen trackways, three platforms, a roundhouse, a destroyed structure, a stake row and archaeological wood. At the Derryfadda 13 trackway the excavator suggests that artefacts were intentionally deposited within the structure; even though it was not substantial, it formed part of the Iron Age route through the bog (ibid., 229–31).

The construction technique seen at Annaholty is not unique to Irish sites and the causeway also resembles northern European examples, such as in Dievenmoor/Schweger Moor,

Germany, dated to 190–170 BC, and the Valtherbrug, Netherlands, dated to 345±50 BC (Raftery 1996, 224–6).

As the entire Annaholty causeway lay within the excavated area it is not clear whether it was part of a wider network of roads through the bog, using the islands as 'stepping stones', or whether it merely connected Toreheen Island with the smaller island. The western side of the small island was not investigated but a small gravel track, still in use today, spans the shortest distance from this island to the dry ground to the south-west and could potentially overlie an earlier wooden road. The width of the Annaholty causeway is unprecedented in Ireland and would have allowed two carts to pass comfortably or a large herd of cattle to be driven with ease. If a road of this size was built across the entire bog it would have been an enormous undertaking and would have greatly exceeded what was required for simple cross-bog traffic.

It is possible, however, that the small island was the intended destination. The previous discoveries of artefacts from the Toreheen Island area indicates that it was a focus of activity earlier in the prehistoric period and it could well have been occupied during the Iron Age. Indeed, the pollen evidence indicates pastoral and arable farming taking place nearby at this time. The small island would then have protruded from the bog a little more than it does today, and would have been a distinctive and recognisable location. If the causeway was constructed specifically to reach this island, it must have had a special significance to require such a substantial entrance. Approximately half of the island was stripped of topsoil during road construction but no evidence of any archaeological features was revealed and there are no visible features above the ground outside the excavated area.

The motive for the construction of the causeway, be it pragmatic or less practical, is unknown, but its substantial size indicates the organised effort of a community or a localised power directing the labour, and there can be no doubt that it was, in part at least, an ostentatious expression of that power.

The other question surrounding the Annaholty causeway is the significance of the artefacts found within its construction layers. It is not uncommon for wooden artefacts to be deposited in this fashion in platforms and trackways, but there is little agreement as to the relevance of this practice. The artefacts found in these circumstances are almost always broken and could simply have been regarded as waste and used along with other scrap wood; it is equally possible, however, that they retained some residual meaning from their former functions in the home or the field and were placed, for example, as foundation deposits. Raftery (1996) regarded the vessels and cart fragment at Corlea as discarded waste material, but recent work at Edercloon, Co. Longford (Moore 2007), has shown that at that site the artefacts were not distributed randomly, suggesting that careful thought was put into their positioning. Unfortunately the truncation of a large part of the Annaholty causeway limits artefact distribution analysis and it is unlikely that it will be possible to determine whether there was deliberate intent behind the deposition.

Bibliography

Brown, D. 2010 Dendrochronological dates. In K. Taylor, 'N7 Nenagh to Limerick high quality dual carriageway (E3530)—Annaholty Site 8, Co. Tipperary: preliminary archaeological excavation report'. Unpublished report prepared by TVAS (Ireland) Ltd.

Carter, S., Tipping, R., McCulloch, R. and Tisdall, E. 2006 N7 Nenagh to Limerick: archaeological assessment of deep sediment at Drominboy and Annaholty. Unpublished report prepared by Headland Archaeology Ltd (project NNL05).

Earwood, C. 1997 Bog butter: a two thousand year history. *Journal of Irish Archaeology* **8**, 25–42.

Fenton, A. 1986 Early yoke types in Britain. In A. Fenton (ed.), *The shape of the past 2. Essays in Scottish ethnology*, 35–46. Edinburgh.

Gowen, M., Ó Néill, J. and Phillips, M. (eds) 2005 *The Lisheen Mine Archaeological Project, 1996–8*. Bray.

Hanrahan, E.T. 1950 Note on old timber road, Annaholty, Co. Limerick. *North Munster Antiquarian Journal* **6** (2), 64.

Lyons, S. 2010a Wood species identification. In K. Taylor, 'N7 Nenagh to Limerick high quality dual carriageway (E3530)—Annaholty Site 8, Co. Tipperary: preliminary archaeological excavation report'. Unpublished report prepared by TVAS (Ireland) Ltd.

Lyons, S. 2010b Wood species identification. In J. McCooey, E. Ruttle and K. Taylor, 'N7 Nenagh to Limerick high quality dual carriageway (E3462): monitoring of wetlands, Cos Limerick and Tipperary'. Unpublished report prepared by TVAS (Ireland) Ltd.

McCooey, J., Ruttle, E. and Taylor, K. 2010 N7 Nenagh to Limerick high quality dual carriageway (E3462): monitoring of wetlands, Cos Limerick and Tipperary. Unpublished report prepared by TVAS (Ireland) Ltd.

Moore, C. 2007 Right on track at Edercloon. *Seanda* **2**, 20.

Moore, C. 2010a Worked wood. In K. Taylor, 'N7 Nenagh to Limerick high quality dual carriageway (E3530)—Annaholty Site 8, Co. Tipperary: preliminary archaeological excavation report'. Unpublished report prepared by TVAS (Ireland) Ltd.

Moore, C. 2010b Worked wood. In J. McCooey, E. Ruttle and K. Taylor, 'N7 Nenagh to Limerick high quality dual carriageway (E3462): monitoring of wetlands, Cos Limerick and Tipperary'. Unpublished report prepared by TVAS (Ireland) Ltd.

Nicholl, J. 2010 Leather shoe. In J. McCooey, E. Ruttle and K. Taylor, 'N7 Nenagh to Limerick high quality dual carriageway (E3462): monitoring of wetlands, Cos Limerick and Tipperary'. Unpublished report prepared by TVAS (Ireland) Ltd.

O'Brien, C. 2010 Pollen analysis. In K. Taylor, 'N7 Nenagh to Limerick high quality dual carriageway (E3530)—Annaholty Site 8, Co. Tipperary: preliminary archaeological excavation report'. Unpublished report prepared by TVAS (Ireland) Ltd.

Raftery, B. (ed.) 1996 *Trackway excavations in the Mountdillon Bogs, Co. Longford, 1985–1991*. Dublin.

Stanley, M., McDermott, C., Moore, C. and Murray, C. 2003 Throwing off the yoke. *Archaeology Ireland* **17** (2), 6–8.

Tuohy, P. 1997 The moving bog. *An Caisleán: The Castleconnell, Ahane, Montpelier Journal* (1997), 72–4.

Whitaker, J. 2009 *Peatland excavations, 2001–2002: Mountdillon group of bogs, Co. Longford*. Dublin.

24. Iron Age sanctuary enclosure, boundary ditch and kilns at Kilmainham, Co. Meath[1]

Fintan Walsh

In the seventh to eighth centuries AD, the increasing influence of the Church led to the firm establishment of standardised 'Christian' burial in Ireland (O'Brien 2009). Prior to this, in the early centuries AD, as inhumation burial practice replaced that of cremation, it was common for pagans and Christians to be buried together in ancestral burial plots (*ibid.*). There is also increasing evidence that foreign influences, from the Roman world, had an impact on the attitude of the people in the Iron Age–early medieval period regarding burial rites. Tentative evidence of this influence has recently been unearthed at Kilmainham (site 1C:E3140), south of Kells, Co. Meath. A large rectangular structure (structure 8) directly associated with two inhumation burials was unearthed. It is possible that this structure was an indigenous interpretation of the La Tène, Romano-Celtic and Anglo-Saxon sanctuary enclosures found in continental Europe and Britain.

Kilmainham 1C was located in the townland of Kilmainham, *c.* 2.5km south-east of Kells town and *c.* 1km south of the N3. The topography varied sharply across the site

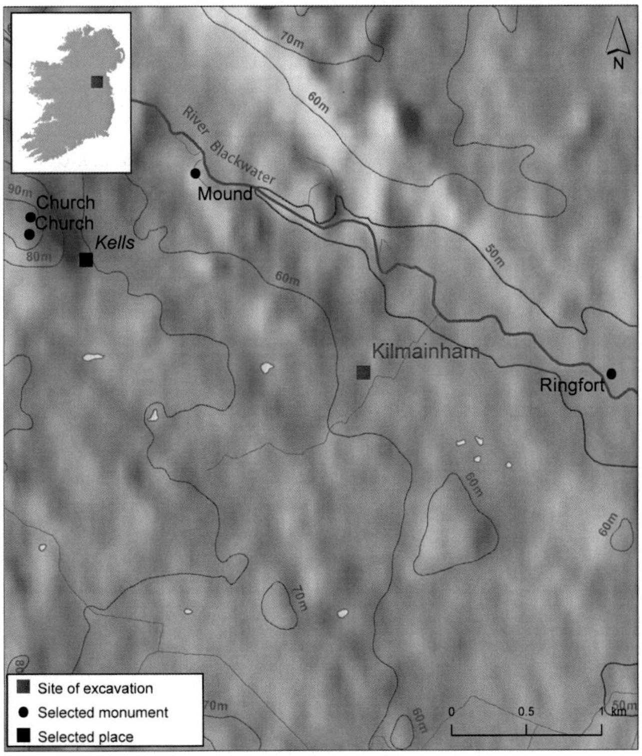

Fig. 24.1—Kilmainham: location of site.

and was characterised by a large, crescent-shaped ridge (*c.* 63m OD) that traversed the centre and east of the site, while gravel outcrops/banks were evident to the west. This ridge formed natural high points in the site's topography, coupled with a corresponding gravel bank to the west. The natural geology varied across the site, but gravel and sands were most prominent.

Excavations at Kilmainham 1C revealed extensive evidence of settlement, ritual and industrial activity dating from the early Neolithic through to the Middle Ages. Ten phases of archaeological activity, including six Neolithic/Bronze Age phases, Iron Age/early medieval activity and a medieval and post-medieval phase, were recorded across an area measuring *c.* 21,330m².

Numerous Neolithic and Bronze Age structures were identified, including at least three early Neolithic houses, a Bronze Age stone platform, stake-hole 'fences', pits, hearths, burnt mounds, a pond and boundary ditches. The Iron Age/early medieval phase was primarily concerned with agriculture and industry, while there was burial and possible ritual activity dating from this period too. A series of eleven cereal-drying kilns, plus one possible additional kiln, were in use at this time, while a long boundary ditch (ditch A), which traversed the entire site, partially enclosed the entire eastern half of the site. Two Iron Age/early medieval burials, positioned on the cusp of a gravel ridge in the centre of the site, appear to have been associated with a large rectangular structure, tentatively interpreted as a sanctuary enclosure or shrine. A number of large medieval pits and numerous post-medieval furrows represented the later phases.

Boundary ditch A

The Iron Age activity was demarcated by a 180m-long boundary ditch that bordered a large area including eleven kilns, structure 8 and the burials. This ditch extended across the entire length of the site in a south-west/north-east direction. It was on average 2m wide and 0.5m deep, though this varied considerably throughout its length. The primary fill at its western end included a fragment of holly (*Ilex* sp.) charcoal, which returned an AMS result of 2117±26 BP (UBA-12915). The 2-sigma calibrated result for this was 203–51 BC, indicating a date in the Iron Age for this ditch.

Fig. 24.2—Kilmainham: aerial view of site (Studio Lab).

Kilns

Eleven cereal-drying kilns (plus one possible example) were identified. Of these, three were Iron Age. Kiln C81 was distinctively different from the others; it was an oval-shaped cut feature (0.91m long, 0.41m wide and 0.22m deep) aligned north-east/south-west. The majority of the burning appeared to have taken place in the centre of the feature. Charcoal from the backfilling of the kiln was found to consist of hazel (*Corylus avellana*), oak (*Quercus* sp.), alder (*Alnus* sp.) and holly (*Ilex aquifolium*). Samples of the fills contained 35 barley (*Hordeum* sp.) grains and two indeterminate cereal grains. The date of the kiln was established from a single barley grain (0.1g) from one of the primary fills, which returned an AMS result of 1924±20 BP (UBA-12927). The 2-sigma calibrated result for this was AD 27–127.

Kiln C689 was located in the low-lying gravel outcrop and was surrounded by four other kilns that were dated to the Iron Age/early medieval transition. This 'early' kiln was, like the other kilns in the area, roughly figure-of-eight in plan

(2.35m long, 1.25m wide and 0.6m deep), but, unlike the others, the fire-bowl appeared to have been at the southern end. This kiln was also considerably deeper than the others around it. The primary deposit was a level of *in situ* burning, covered by a charcoal-rich deposit. The remaining three contexts appeared to represent post-abandonment backfilling of the kiln and contained a large quantity of stone, which may be the remains of the kiln's superstructure. On the basis of the fill/deposit sequence, it is deduced that this kiln had only one working cycle. Charcoal analysis of a sample of the primary *in situ* burning deposit identified a single fragment of hazel (*Corylus avellana*) and a fragment of elm (*Ulmus* sp.). Samples taken from the two working levels of the kiln were found to contain a combined total of 63 grains of spelt wheat (*Triticum* cf. *spelta*), 87 wheat (*Triticum* sp.) grains, 186 barley (*Hordeum* sp.) grains, 28 oat (*Avena* sp.) grains and a single grain of rye (*Secale cereale*). A large number of further indeterminate grains were recorded from both contexts. The date for the kiln was established from a single barley grain (0.1g) identified from a sample of the primary fill (C888). The grain returned an AMS result of 1750±20 BP (UBA-12929). The 2-sigma calibrated result for this was AD 235–376.

Kiln C13 was also figure-of-eight in plan (1.75m long, 0.8m wide and 0.28m deep) and was located north of centre of the site on the crest of the gravel ridge. It was aligned north-north-west/south-south-east, with the wider, deeper part (the fire-bowl) at the northern end. The primary fill at the northern end was a charcoal-rich material that was covered by yellow-orange burnt clay. The primary fill of the southern end of the kiln was a yellow brown clay. Covering both of these contexts was a charcoal-rich deposit that appeared to be the final context from the working life of the feature. Analysis of this deposit found that it contained mainly hazel (*Corylus avellana*), with oak (*Quercus* sp.), ash (*Fraxinus* sp.) and pomaceous fruitwood (Maloideae sp.) also present. A second sample, from C14, was found to contain oak, hazel and birch (*Betula* sp.). This suggests that these taxa were among those used as fuel in this kiln. Plant remains analysis of the primary fills identified a total of over 1,000 barley (*Hordeum* sp.) grains.

A total of 282 oat (*Avena* sp.) and 21 wheat (*Triticum* sp.) grains were also identified. The date for this kiln was established from a single barley grain (0.2g) from the charcoal-rich deposit. The grain returned an AMS result of 1654±21 BP (UBA-12926). The 2-sigma calibrated result for this was AD 269–432.

A further eight kilns, all figure-of-eight forms, were also excavated and produced transition dates that spanned the fifth to seventh centuries.

Structure 8

The most interesting Iron Age feature was structure 8. This was positioned in the centre of the site, on the crest of a crescent-shaped gravel ridge, overlooking lower-lying areas to the east and west. This location, a high point in the local topography, afforded commanding views of the wider area, including Kells to the north-west. Structure 8 was defined by a foundation trench forming three sides of a rectangular area measuring 16.2m south-south-east/north-north-west by 14.1m west-south-west/east-north-east. The northern, eastern and southern elements were present, but it was open to the

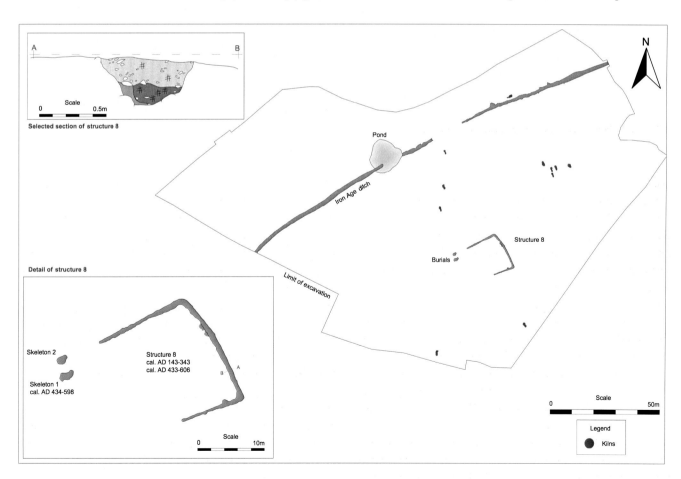

Fig. 24.3—Kilmainham: Iron Age/early medieval phase at Kilmainham 1C, with detail of structure 8 and burials (IAC).

Fig. 24.4—Kilmainham: ditch A, looking south-west (IAC).

Fig. 24.5—Kilmainham: kiln C81 (IAC).

Fig. 24.6—Kilmainham: kiln C689 (IAC).

Fig. 24.7—Kilmainham: kiln C13 (IAC).

west. Terminals were recorded at the western end of the northern and southern sections of the foundation trench. The cut of the foundation trench averaged 1.2m in width and ranged from 0.31m to 0.51m in depth at the northern corner. The trench narrowed and became significantly shallower towards its two western termini.

A small number of post-pipes and post settings were recorded. These survived primarily in the southern section of the foundation trench. The projected sizes of the posts varied greatly, ranging in diameter from 0.07m to 0.41m, with depths ranging from 0.05m to 0.25m. The fills of these post-holes/post-pipes consisted of dark grey or brown clay/silts. The level of preservation of the shape of the post-pipes, combined with the dark organic fills, suggests that the posts were left to rot *in situ* rather than being removed, especially in the southern foundation trench section, whereas the disturbed nature of the eastern section suggests that the posts here were removed. The clearest evidence for these posts was found mainly at the corners of the structure.

Of the earliest fills in the slot-trench that were not

Fig. 24.8—Kilmainham: elevated view of structure 8 after excavation, looking north-west (Hawkeye).

packing fills, the most distinctive was a very soft, dark brown silty clay, which was recorded throughout the length of the northern half of the eastern section of the foundation trench. Charcoal analysis carried out on a sample of this fill identified oak (*Quercus* sp.), pomaceous fruitwood (Maloideae sp.) and hazel (*Corylus avellana*). These species were presumably burnt in the vicinity while this silt deposit was accumulating. Unidentifiable burnt animal bone (1.8g) from a sample of this fill was chosen for AMS dating. It returned a result of 1769±23 BP (UBA-15488), for which the 2-sigma calibrated result was AD 143–343. A secondary charcoal-rich deposit, or disturbed level of *in situ* burning, at the western terminal of the southern foundation trench contained birch charcoal that was dated to 1523±30 BP (cal. AD 433–606). This indicates that the structure was built in the late Iron Age and was still in use during the Iron Age–early medieval transition.

Twelve fills in the foundation trench produced a total of 148 bones, most of which were tiny fragments of indeterminate burnt bone. The only identified specimen was a cow tooth. One bone fragment may have derived from a medium-sized mammal, probably sheep/goat or pig.

Very few artefacts were associated with this structure, but the fills of the slot-trench yielded a spindle-whorl (Fig. 24.10) and an ammonite bead (similar to that found associated with skeleton 2). The bead measured 4mm in diameter and 1mm in thickness and the perforation was 1.5mm wide. The spindle-whorl was circular in plan and disc-shaped in section. The stone was 37mm in diameter and 9mm thick. The perforation was very slightly off-centre and worked from both faces, giving the classic hourglass profile in section. The perforation was 8mm in diameter, while the splay of the perforation was 14mm wide.

Interestingly, despite the fact that it was contemporary with the Iron Age/early medieval kilns, there was no evidence of any charred seeds in any of the soils sampled from the foundation trench. Samples from thirteen contexts were processed by flotation, including soils from post-hole fills, silted deposits, disturbed packing fills, possible post-pipes and settings and the backfilled deposits. None of these samples produced charred or uncharred seeds, despite many being very charcoal-rich. This implies that structure 8, although contemporary, was not related to the agricultural/industrial activity at Kilmainham 1C. This structure is unlikely to have been a domestic building, as it was too large and did not have

Fig. 24.9—Kilmainham: structure 8, southern foundation trench with *in situ* packing, looking south-west (IAC).

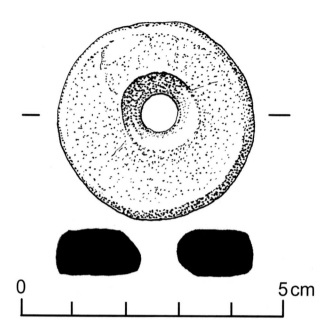

Fig. 24.10—Kilmainham: spindle-whorl (E3140:2262:1) from structure 8 (Alva Mac Gowan).

the structural components for roofing. It is suggested, therefore, that structure 8 was a religious building/structure, such as a sanctuary enclosure.

Inhumation burials

Two burials were identified, immediately west of structure 8 on the crest of the large gravel ridge. The burials were extremely fragmented, with only tiny elements of each surviving. It was clear from the remains, however, that they were extended inhumations in the Christian tradition (extended, with head to the west). There was no indication of any other burials in the immediate area, but as the burials were obviously severely truncated, and specifically exposed to truncation on top of the gravel ridge, it is possible that other burials did at one time exist but were completely removed by modern agriculture.

Skeleton 1 was contained within a suboval grave-cut (2.2m long, max. 2m wide and 0.2m deep) with sloping sides and a flat base. The skeleton was very fragmentary and survived only as the poorly preserved remains of the right and left legs, left foot and a very small number of pelvic fragments of an individual. The position of the legs within the grave-cut suggests that this individual was buried in a supine and extended position and was aligned west–east.

Skeleton 2 was also very fragmentary and survived as only a small number of skull and vertebral fragments. The skull fragments were identified in the western end of the grave, indicating that the burial was aligned west–east. A single bead was recovered from the grave fill. This had been fashioned

Fig. 24.11—Kilmainham: detail of skeleton 1 (IAC).

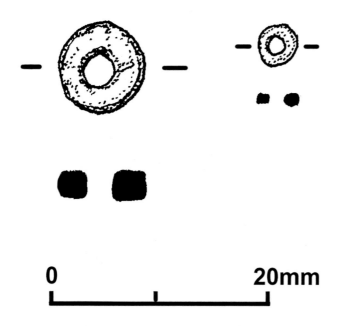

Fig. 24.12—Kilmainham: ammonite beads associated with skeleton 2 (left) and from structure 8 (right) (Alva Mac Gowan).

from ammonite and measured 8mm in diameter by 2mm in thickness; the perforation was 3mm wide.

The date for skeleton 1 was established through an AMS determination of a sample of the right tibia (1529±22 BP; cal. AD 434–598). There was no suitable dating material from skeleton 2, but it is assumed that it is roughly contemporary, by association. Both individuals were determined to be adult, but neither could be assigned a more specific age category. Sex could not be determined for either. Of interest was a stone (ammonite) bead found associated with skeleton 2, which was similar to a bead found in the foundation trench of structure 8 (Fig. 24.12).

These two isolated related burials may have been part of an ancestral/familial burial plot dating from the late Iron Age/earlier part of the early medieval period. It was not until the seventh century AD that the increasing power and influence of the Church provided the impetus for burial in cemeteries attached to the major ecclesiastical sites rather than in ancestral or familial burial plots (Edwards 1999; O'Brien 2003). The Kilmainham 1C burials pre-date this change in burial practice. It is interesting to note that there is a clear view to the centre of Kells to the north-west from this high point in the site.

Discussion

Kilmainham 1C was a large, multiperiod site, from the Neolithic through to the medieval and post-medieval periods. It was positioned within an extensive, recently identified prehistoric landscape that includes at least seven newly discovered early Neolithic structures, late Neolithic ritual structures, Bronze Age structures, pits and habitation deposits and Iron Age/early medieval kilns distributed across a wide area in the hinterland of Kells town (McLoughlin and Walsh 2008).

The key components of the Iron Age at Kilmainham 1C were a series of kilns, a long boundary ditch (ditch A), a large rectangular structure (structure 8) and two inhumation burials. This marks a distinct 'jump' in the chronological sequence at Kilmainham, where there is a hiatus in activity from the late Bronze Age to the start of the Iron Age, which seems to be signified by boundary ditch A. Ditch A 'demarcates' the main body of Iron Age–early medieval activity and may have been established to create a physical boundary for the industrial and/or perhaps the funerary element of these phases at Kilmainham. Ditch A traversed the site and continued outside the limits of excavation to the east and south-west into adjacent site Kilmainham 1A. It partially enclosed the entire south-eastern portion of the site, which included the majority of the kilns, structure 8 and the burials.

Eleven Iron Age/early medieval kilns (plus one possible example) were identified. Kilns C13, C81 and C689 were clearly part of an earlier phase (or phases) of kilning, while the remainder sit firmly within the Iron Age/early medieval transition period. It should be noted that kiln C81 was the earliest in the sequence (AD 27–127). Kiln C689 was characteristically different, in that the fire-bowl was at the southern end rather than towards the north, which was the norm for the Kilmainham kilns. The presence of spelt wheat (*Triticum* cf. *spelta*) grain in this kiln also set it apart from the others.

As discussed above, structure 8 is unlikely to be a domestic building, as it was too large and probably unroofed. Two dates were established: one from animal bone in a primary deposit of the eastern foundation trench (1769±23 BP; AD 143–343), and one from birch charcoal in a secondary deposit at the western terminal of the southern foundation trench (1523±30 BP; AD 433–606). These dates indicate that the structure was extant, or perhaps built, in the late Iron Age and was in use in the Iron Age–early medieval transition. Interestingly, despite the fact that it was contemporary with the Iron Age/early medieval kilns, there was no evidence of any charred seeds in any of the soils sampled from the foundation trench. This implies that structure 8, although

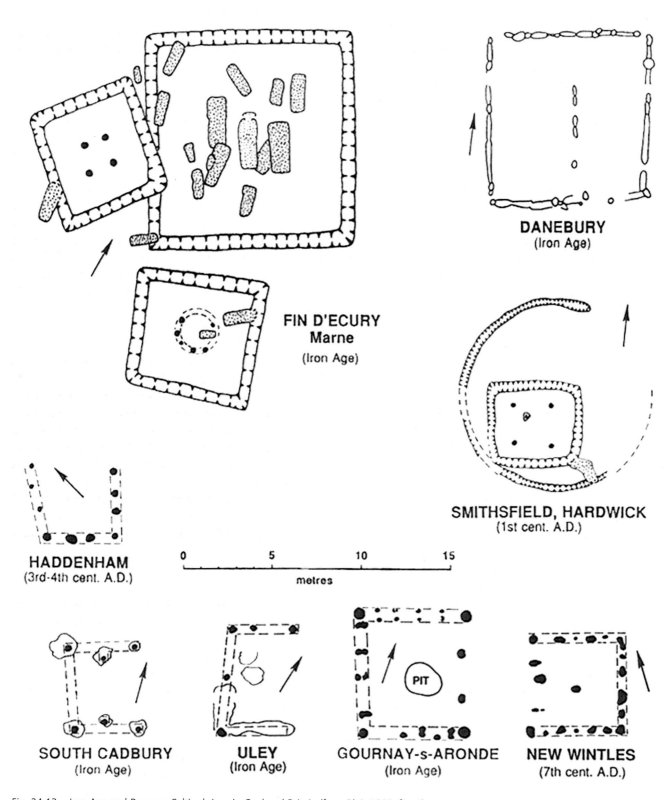

Fig. 24.13—Iron Age and Romano-Celtic shrines in Gaul and Britain (from Blair 1995, fig. 1).

contemporary, was not related to the agricultural/industrial activity at Kilmainham 1C.

As the later date (cal. AD 433–606) is comparable with that obtained for skeleton 1, it is probable that structure 8 was directly related to the two inhumation burials immediately to the west. With this in mind, it can be suggested that structure 8 was an enclosure that delineated a ritual or ceremonial area—that is, a form of sanctuary.

Sanctuary-type sites are essentially areas marked out as sacred space (Powell 1980). The demarcation of space is present in the archaeological record on Celtic, pre-Roman and La Tène ritual/burial sites. It is likely, however, that sanctuary sites are in general influenced by Roman examples. These include the Romano-Celtic temples, in which a (predominantly) square or rectangular area was demarcated by a ditch within which small buildings (shrines) were located. It has been suggested that worshippers remained outside the shrine but that the portico, within the enclosed space, provided an area to which the sacred contents could be brought out for exposure and veneration (*ibid.*). Ritual deposition was common at sanctuary sites and this included weaponry and coins, while animal sacrifice and feasting has also been noted (Fitzpatrick 2009, 393). The feasting and animal sacrifice would result in the deposition of animal bone within the ditches associated with these monuments. At Kilmainham, however, the artefacts recovered from the foundation trench do not suggest ritual deposition and, unfortunately, the animal bone was too fragmentary and poorly preserved to provide any further evidence.

Few examples, or variations, of this site type can be identified in Ireland, although components of a recently excavated site at Marlhill, Co. Tipperary, can tentatively be identified as inspired by the sanctuary sites of the Roman world, or perhaps even by some Anglo-Saxon cemeteries. This site included a rectangular structure (cal. AD 540–650) and two slightly later inhumation burials (cal. AD 690–900 and cal. AD 650–780) at the site of an earlier Iron Age ring-barrow (McQuade *et al.* 2009, 187, fig. 5.4). One of these burials was positioned at the entrance to the structure and the other was a short distance outside and to the north of the entrance. It is possible that this may in fact be a 'mortuary house' similar to that of Capel Eithin on the Isle of Anglesey, north-west Wales. Central to this site in Wales was a rectangular structure, which has been interpreted as supporting upright posts and planks with a narrow entrance to the east (Williams 2006, 151). Two graves were positioned centrally within the structure, while at a later date a third grave was added to the doorway, respecting the position of the still-standing mortuary house, perhaps to 'seal' the doorway (*ibid.*, 152). This arrangement may be

mirrored at the Marlhill site.

Similar examples have also been excavated in England at, to name but a few, Heathrow (Middlesex), New Wintles (Eynsham), Uley (Gloucestershire) and Danebury (Hampshire), and at Écury-le-Repos in north-eastern France (Powell 1980; Woodward and Leach 1993; Blair 1995). This phenomenon was not uncommon in England, however, as by the late first century BC there was a well-established tradition of ritual sites that included square enclosures and shrines demarcated by ditches or post settings (Blair 1995, 3).

Although the Kilmainham structure lacks any internal features (and therefore evidence for a shrine), the shape in plan of the foundation trench of structure 8, the association with burial and the date of this archaeological find do share some notable characteristics with these English and French examples. It may offer an intriguing insight into some aspects of burial and ritual in the latter stages of the Iron Age in Ireland.

Acknowledgements
Grateful thanks to Eoin Grogan, Katharina Becker and Bernice Molloy. Ciara McCarthy, Antoine Giacometti, Elizabeth O'Brien, Neil Carlin, Shane Delaney, Rob Lynch and Tim Coughlan made valuable comments on drafts of this text. Kieron Goucher and Graeme Kearney prepared Fig. 24.3. This site was part of the M3 Contract 4 excavations, which were managed by Mary Deevy and funded by the National Roads Authority and Meath County Council. Lorna O'Donnell and Susan Lyons analysed the charcoal and environmental remains. Jennie Coughlan analysed the skeletal remains. Richard O'Brien analysed the beads and spindle-whorl.

Bibliography
Blair, J. 1995 Anglo-Saxon pagan shrines and their prototypes. *Anglo-Saxon Studies in Archaeology and History* **8**, 1–28.

Coughlan, J. 2011 Appendix 2.9: Human skeletal remains report. In F. Walsh, 'Site E3140 Kilmainham 1C final report'. Unpublished report prepared for the National Monuments Service, DEHLG, Dublin.

Edwards, N. 1999 *The archaeology of early medieval Ireland*. London.

Fitzpatrick, A. 2009 'The Champion's Portion': feasting in the Celtic pre-Roman Iron Age. In G. Cooney, K. Becker, J. Coles, M. Ryan and S. Sievers (eds), *Relics of old decency: archaeological studies in later prehistory*, 389–404. Bray.

McCarthy, M. 2011 Appendix 2.7: Faunal assemblage report. In F. Walsh, 'Site E3140 Kilmainham 1C final report'.

Unpublished report prepared for the National Monuments Service, DEHLG, Dublin.

McLoughlin, G. and Walsh, F. 2008 A slice through time: prehistoric settlement and ritual near Kells, Co. Meath. *Seanda* **3**, 20–2.

McQuade, M., Molloy, B. and Moriarty, C. 2009 *In the shadow of the Galtees: archaeological excavations along the N8 Cashel to Mitchelstown road scheme*. Dublin.

O'Brien, E. 2003 Burial practices in Ireland: first to seventh Centuries AD. In J. Downes and A. Ritchie (eds), *Sea change: Orkney and northern Europe in the later Iron Age 300–800*. Angus.

O'Brien, E. 2009 Pagan or Christian? Burial in Ireland during the 5th to 8th centuries AD. In N. Edwards (ed.), *The archaeology of the early medieval Celtic churches*, 135–54. London.

O'Brien, R. 2011 Appendix 2.4.2: Worked stone report. In F. Walsh, 'Site E3140 Kilmainham 1C final report'. Unpublished report prepared for the National Monuments Service, DEHLG, Dublin.

Powell, T.G.E. 1980 *The Celts*. London.

Williams, H. 2006 *Death and memory in early medieval Britain*. Cambridge.

Woodward, A. and Leach, P.E. 1993 *The Uley shrines: excavation of a ritual complex on West Hill, Uley, Gloucestershire, 1977–9*. London.

Note

1. The archaeological excavation at Kilmainham 1C was located on the route of the M3 Navan–Kells and Kells Bypass (Archaeological Services Contract 4) of the M3 Clonee–North of Kells motorway scheme, Co. Meath. The excavation was undertaken by Fintan Walsh of Irish Archaeological Consultancy Ltd on behalf of Meath County Council and the National Roads Authority. The work was carried out under ministerial direction A029/022 and National Monuments Service (NMS) excavation registration E3140, which were received from the DEHLG in consultation with the National Museum of Ireland. The fieldwork took place between 25 September 2006 and 24 March 2007.

This paper is an extension of the following paper: Walsh, F. 2011 Seeking sanctuary at Kilmainham, Co. Meath. *Archaeology Ireland* **25** (2), 9–12.

25. An Iron Age ring-ditch complex at Holdenstown 1, Co. Kilkenny

Yvonne Whitty with a contribution by Jennie Coughlan

This essay presents the results of the archaeological excavation of a ring-ditch complex at Holdenstown 1, Co. Kilkenny. The excavation was undertaken by the writer for IAC, on behalf of Kilkenny County Council and the NRA, under ministerial direction A058, as part of the archaeological mitigation programme of the N9/N10 Kilcullen to Waterford Road Scheme that extends between Knocktopher, Co. Kilkenny, and Powerstown, Co. Carlow.

Holdenstown 1 occupied a commanding position on gently rising ground (60–80m) above the valley of the River Nore (Figs 25.1–25.3). Holdenstown 2, an early medieval secular cemetery, was *c.* 300m to the north. There is an early church site immediately north-west of the cemetery at Holdenstown 2. The Holdenstown landscape provides a glimpse of burial practices from the Iron Age through to at least the tenth century AD. The earliest focus of burial activity was found at Holdenstown 1 and consisted of three ring-ditches, eight inhumations and a large penannular enclosure, ranging in date from the middle Iron Age to the late Iron Age/early medieval transition.

Fig. 25.2—Holdenstown 1: aerial view of site before excavation.

Ring-ditch 1

Ring-ditch 1 was located on flat ground and measured 16.65m in diameter. The ditch was 0.4m in maximum depth and 1.3m in average width, widening to 1.5m across at either side of an undug entrance causeway (2.3m wide) at the west. There was no surviving evidence for either an associated internal mound or an external bank. The primary fill has been interpreted as a natural silting layer once the ditch had been excavated for the first time, indicating that the ditch had been left open for some time before it was backfilled. Animal bone (240.6g) was recovered from this basal fill.

A loose, mid-yellowish brown sandy silt was backfilled above the natural siltation layer. This layer contained twelve antler fragments, which had been carefully deposited in the southern part of the ditch. All of the fragments derive from red deer (*Cervus elaphus* L.). Most display evidence of having been chopped into lengths with an axe and of having been crudely broken, and therefore appear to be waste from antler-working. Also found in this layer was one half of a sandstone spindle-whorl (021:1) with a central perforation. It may have been used subsequently as a hone stone. A small quantity of burnt bone, hazelnut and charcoal was also recovered from this fill. A sample of hazel charcoal (0.5g) was chosen for AMS dating and returned a result of 2119±25 BP. The 2-sigma calibrated date for this was 203–53 BC, dating this feature to the Iron

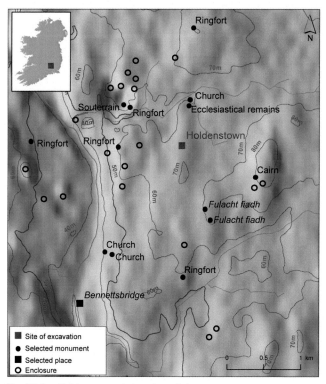

Fig. 25.1—Holdenstown 1: location of site.

Fig. 25.3—Holdenstown 1: aerial view of site (Gavin Duffy, Airshots).

Age. The uppermost backfilled layers contained similar inclusions to the above-mentioned fills, and analysis of these inclusions indicates that these layers were not pyre material related to the cremation process.

The south-western area of ring-ditch 1 was recut on two occasions, possibly to redefine the ditch. The primary recut had a length of 12m, a width of 1.05m and a depth of 0.4m, and respected the original cut of the ring-ditch (Figs 25.5 and 25.6). This recut contained a single fill, which included a small amount of charcoal and minimal burnt bone (2g). A sample of willow charcoal (1.1g) was chosen for AMS dating and returned a result of 1567±23 BP. The 2-sigma calibrated date for this was AD 426-546, dating this feature to the late Iron Age/early medieval transition. A secondary recut was identified within the primary recut. It respected the original recut in length and width, and two fills were identified within

it. The primary one was a backfill and the second was a deliberate backfill with frequent charcoal fragment inclusions (138.9g) and burnt bone (11.2g).

Charcoal was retrieved from several of the ring-ditch fills. The fragments were identified as alder (*Alnus glutinosa*), ash (*Fraxinus excelsior*), pomaceous woods (Pomoideae spp), oak (*Quercus* sp.), cherry-type (*Prunus* sp.) and birch (*Betula* sp.). Ring-ditch 1 was the only feature to contain a notable quantity of ash charcoal, which may relate to the recut or reuse of the ditch. Plant remains were also recovered and identified from several of the ring-ditch fills. These included hazelnut shell fragments (*Corylus avellana* L.), wild radish (*Raphanus raphanistrum* L.) capsules and indeterminate cereal grains. A moderate quantity of animal bone was retrieved from the fills of ring-ditch 1, representing sheep/goat, pig and, in particular, cattle, some of which displayed evidence for butchery.

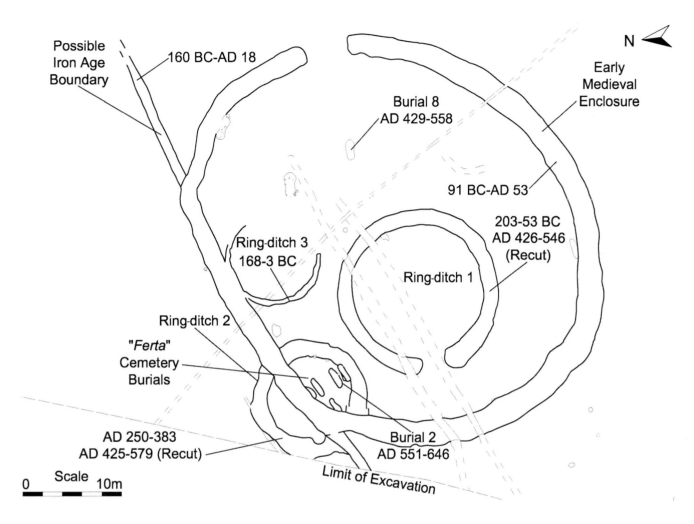

Fig. 25.4—Holdenstown 1: sketch-plan based on aerial photograph.

Fig. 25.5—Holdenstown 1: recut of southern part of ring-ditch 1.

Fig. 25.6—Holdenstown 1: fill of recut of ring-ditch 1.

Ring-ditch 2

Ring-ditch 2 was located on flat ground at the western limit of excavation. It was circular and had an external diameter of 11.9m. The maximum depth of the ditch was 0.3m and it had an average width of 1m. The primary fill has been interpreted as collapsed material from the sides of the ditch soon after its original excavation. The lower fill contained 66 fragments of bone, from which a total of six species were identified: cow, sheep/goat, deer, horse, pig, mouse and possibly partridge. The secondary fill was perhaps the remains of an external or internal bank, which had either eroded naturally into the ring-ditch cut or had resulted from intentional backfilling (the subsequent sequence of silting and/or backfilling was destroyed when the ring-ditch was recut (described below), so it is not possible to state with absolute certainty whether or not a bank had ever existed). A possible limestone hone stone (E3681:056:1) was recovered, along with seeds and charred hazelnut, animal bone, charcoal and a very small quantity of burnt bone. The uppermost fill of ring-ditch 2 was redeposited from elsewhere on the site and included four antler fragments. One is a shed antler with a ruptured burr, while others have chop-marks. A significant quantity of animal bone (829.8g), seeds and hazelnut, charcoal (15.2g), shell and burnt bone (5.4g) was recovered and is perhaps indicative of feasting or cooking. A sample of alder charcoal (1g) was chosen for AMS dating and returned a result of 1728±22 BP. The 2-sigma calibrated date for this was AD 250–383, implying a late Iron Age date for the ring-ditch; this date may be too late, however, and it is likely that it was constructed sometime earlier (see below). Plant remains were also recovered from the lower ring-ditch fills. These were identified as hazelnut shell fragments (*Corylus avellana* L.), pear/apple pips (*Pyrus* L./*Malus* Mill.), naked barley grains (*Hordeum vulgare* L. var. *nudum*), barley grains of indeterminate species (*Hordeum* sp.) and indeterminate cereal grains.

The entire circumference of ring-ditch 2 was recut. This recut respected the original cut of the ditch in general, although at the southern part of the ring-ditch it extended to the south of the original line. This recut contained three fills (Fig. 25.7). The primary fill was a deliberate deposit and contained a significant quantity of animal bone (1,352.3g), as well as seeds, charred hazelnut, charcoal, shell and burnt bone (2g). A small fragment of jet was also recovered from this fill. The jet fragment is triangular (L 3mm; W 2.8mm; T 1.9mm). It is polished along its curving edge and is possibly tooled on its two other faces, suggesting that it may have been a decorative inset. Five pieces of non-diagnostic possible iron slag (3.2g) were recovered. Three of the fragments were magnetic, while a single piece with drippy morphology was

Fig. 25.7—Holdenstown 1: section of recut of ring-ditch 2.

also noted. The primary fill of the recut produced 48 fragments of bone, primarily of cow and horse. Some of the cow bone and unidentified bone displayed evidence of burning.

The two uppermost layers within the recut were contemporary. An area of sterile yellow clay, 4m in length, was only contained within the south-eastern area of the recut and appeared to be a sealing layer. The main upper fill contained a significant amount of charcoal, as well as seeds, burnt bone (31.8g) and animal bone (541.1g). A red deer antler shaft (one antler broken in two parts) with a burr attached was also retrieved. The burr, although well developed, does not appear to be naturally ruptured, and the cornet appears to have been cut below the burr. It is likely to be from a mature stag (c. 6–11 years) that was slaughtered in the autumn/early spring, when antlers were fully grown. A small quantity of animal bone was retrieved from the main upper fill of the recut. Of the identified bone, pig was most often noted and the majority of the bones displayed evidence of burning. A fragment of bone was chosen for AMS dating and returned a result of 1550±32 BP. The 2-sigma calibrated date for this was AD 425–579, implying a late Iron Age/early medieval transition date for the recut of the ring-ditch.

Charcoal was retrieved from the ring-ditch fills; the fragments were identified as alder (*Alnus glutinosa*), cherry-type (*Prunus* sp.), pomaceous woods (Pomoideae spp), oak (*Quercus* sp.), willow (*Salix* sp.), ash (*Fraxinus excelsior*) and holly (*Ilex aquifolium*). A mixed wood assemblage such as this suggests that a variety of species were burnt at the site and it is likely that this material was redeposited or dumped into this open feature over time. A small quantity of plant remains recovered from the recut fills of the ring-ditch included hazelnut shell fragments (*Corylus avellana* L.) and barley/wheat grains (*Hordeum/Triticum*).

The date of the construction of ring-ditch 2 remains unclear. Stratigraphically it is earlier than a linear ditch (described below) from which a sample of cherry charcoal produced a date of 160 BC–AD 18. Conversely, alder charcoal from the original cut of ring-ditch 2 produced a date of AD 250–383, and a fragment of bone from the recut produced a date of AD 425–579. Clearly these dates contradict the stratigraphy The date returned from a sample of bone in the recut of the ring-ditch is less likely to be intrusive, however, and may be more reliable than the charcoal samples from the original cut of the ring-ditch or the linear ditch. If so, the recut of the ring-ditch may be related to the reuse of the site and the placement of five inhumation burials within the southern half of ring-ditch 2. They all had a south-west/north-east alignment, with their feet towards the north-east. These burials represent a subsequent reuse of ring-ditch 2.

Burial 1 consisted of the remains of a well-preserved adult skeleton (Fig. 25.8). It was the most southerly of the five

Fig. 25.9—Holdenstown 1: burial 2.

graves and it cut ring-ditch 2. Charcoal was retrieved from the grave fill and all of the fragments were identified as pomaceous woods (Pomoideae spp). A total of five fragments of burnt ceramic material (10–12mm thick) were retrieved from the grave of burial 1. It was evident that these fragments had been subject to heat and therefore possibly represented hearth lining, burnt pottery or clay mould fragments. Two fragments of unidentified animal bone were also retrieved from the grave. A sample of Pomoideae charcoal (0.4g) from the grave was chosen for AMS dating and returned a result of 2418±31 BP. The 2-sigma calibrated date for this was 748–400 BC, dating this feature to the early Iron Age. This has been interpreted as disturbed charcoal from the fill of ring-ditch 2.

Burial 2 consisted of the remains of a young middle adult female (Fig. 25.9). Strontium analysis was undertaken to investigate the geographical origins of burial 2, and the results imply that this woman was an incomer to the area. This contrasts with the individual in burial 8, who appears to have had local origins. A human tooth (canine) from burial 2 was chosen for AMS dating and returned a result of 1464±30 BP. The 2-sigma calibrated date for this is AD 551–646, placing this feature in the early medieval period.

Burial 3 was the most north-westerly of these five and lay parallel to burials 1, 2 and 4. It was also heavily truncated by the penannular enclosure ditch (described below) and less than half of the skeleton remained. A total of six fragments of burnt ceramic material were retrieved from the grave. It was evident that these fragments had been subject to heat and thus possibly represented hearth lining, burnt pottery or clay mould fragments.

Burial 4 consisted of a young adult male skeleton (Fig. 25.10). Burial 5 consisted of the truncated remains of an old

Fig. 25.8—Holdenstown 1: burial 1.

Fig. 25.10—Holdenstown 1: burial 4.

adult male (Fig. 25.11). The head, left shoulder and upper arm of this burial were truncated by the penannular enclosure ditch (described below).

Ring-ditch 3

Ring-ditch 3—the most poorly preserved of all three ring-ditches—was crescent-shaped, with a projected external diameter of 8.5m. It was truncated by a large penannular enclosure and a linear ditch (described below). It was also badly truncated by later agricultural practices, making it impossible to conclude whether it was originally completely circular.

Ring-ditch 3 had a maximum depth of 0.2m and an average width of 0.5m. The primary fill represented a layer of natural silt, demonstrating that the ditch had been left open for some time. The secondary fill contained a small quantity of burnt bone, charcoal and hazelnut. A small number of fragments of animal bone were also retrieved. Only two of these were positively identified to species: a cow molar and a fragment of sheep/goat. The only plant remains identified were hazelnut shell fragments (*Corylus avellana* L.). A sample of ash charcoal (0.1g) was chosen for AMS dating and returned a result of 2068±22 BP. The 2-sigma calibrated date for this was 168–3 BC, dating this feature to the middle Iron Age.

At the western part of this ring-ditch a third fill was identified. It contained cremated bone, seeds, charcoal, animal bone and shell. A total of 27 fragments of animal bone were retrieved from this fill, representing cow, sheep/goat and pig. The charcoal fragments were identified primarily as oak (*Quercus* sp.), with lesser amounts of alder (*Alnus glutinosa*), ash (*Fraxinus excelsior*) and pomaceous woods (Pomoideae spp).

Linear ditch

The shallow, north-east/south-west linear ditch spanned the entire width of the site, skirting the perimeter of ring-ditch 3 and cutting through the middle of ring-ditch 2. The fills within the ditch indicated that it had been left open for some time before it was eventually backfilled. The primary fill has been interpreted as collapsed material from the sides of the cut. Above this layer, a natural siltation layer was visible throughout the length of the ditch. Animal bone, seeds, shell and a small quantity of charcoal were recovered from this layer. Nine fragments of animal bone were retrieved, of which five fragments were positively identified as cow bone and some displayed evidence of butchery and exposure to heat. The majority of the charcoal fragments were identified as alder (*Alnus glutinosa*), with smaller amounts of oak (*Quercus* sp.), pomaceous woods (Pomoideae spp) and cherry-type (*Prunus* sp.). A sample of cherry charcoal (0.5g) was selected for AMS

Fig. 25.11—Holdenstown 1: burial 5.

dating and returned a result of 2046±23 BP. The 2-sigma calibrated date for this was 160 BC–AD 18, dating this feature to the Iron Age. As noted already, however, this date is questionable and it is possible that the ditch is somewhat later than these dates suggest.

The precise function of this ditch is unknown; its length and the fact that no return was identified suggest, however, that it may have been a boundary ditch. It is therefore likely that the burials associated with ring-ditch 2 were deliberately and consciously aligned on this boundary.

Penannular enclosure

A large penannular enclosure was formed by a ditch and incorporated the earlier linear ditch; this relationship resulted in a D-shaped enclosure 40m across. The enclosure ditch truncated ring-ditch 2 as well as burials 3 and 5. The ditch had an average width of 2.6m and was 1.15m deep. The enclosure

had an undug entrance causeway (4.5m across) at the east. There was no evidence of an internal or external bank associated with this enclosure. The ditch appeared to have been left open once it had been excavated, as demonstrated by the primary silt fills. Although this site was located on elevated ground, naturally occurring springs ensured that the ditch filled with water.

The primary fill was a layer of silt that accumulated once the ditch had been constructed. Animal bone (2,201.4g; cow, sheep/goat, horse and pig), seeds and shell, as well as small quantities of burnt bone and charcoal, were recovered from this fill. The charcoal fragments were identified as alder (*Alnus glutinosa*), oak (*Quercus* sp.), pomaceous woods (Pomoideae spp) and cherry-type (*Prunus* sp.). A sample of hazel charcoal (0.4g) was chosen for AMS dating and returned a result of 2019±25 BP. The 2-sigma calibrated date for this was 91 BC–AD 53, implying an Iron Age date for this feature. It

Fig. 25.12—Holdenstown 1: section of penannular enclosure ditch.

should also be noted, however, that the enclosure ditch cut burials 3 and 5 (associated with ring-ditch 2) and that burial 5 has been AMS-dated to AD 425–579. This indicates that the penannular enclosure could not date from 91 BC–AD 53 and instead must post-date burial 5.

The secondary sequence of silting was present throughout the entire length of the ditch. This layer contained a considerable quantity of animal bone (*c.* 8kg) as well as an iron blade (E3681:005:6). It was not possible to identify a large quantity of the bone to species, but among the identified material five species were noted: cow, sheep/goat, horse, pig and deer. Three fragments of antler were also present, one of which was burnt. A number of the cow and deer bones displayed evidence of butchery.

A large quantity of plant remains were recovered from one of the ditch fills, including hazelnut (*Corylus avellana* L.) shell fragments, wild radish (*Raphanus raphanistrum* L.) capsules, over twenty oat (*Avena* L. sp.) grains, thirteen possible barley (cf. *Hordeum vulgare*) grains, almost 40 probable free-threshing wheat (*Triticum* cf. *aestivum* L./*turgidum* Desf./*durum* L.) grains, and over 100 indeterminate cereal grains.

A post-hole at the centre of the penannular enclosure truncated ring-ditch 1. It measured 0.59m by 0.47m across by 0.33m deep and contained stone packing. This post-hole may have supported a 'marker' post. The absence of any structures within the enclosure and the paucity of occupational debris (other than in the fills of the enclosure ditch) suggest that it may have had a ritual rather than a domestic function.

The ritual purpose of the enclosure is also suggested by the presence of three burials within its eastern part. Burials 7 and 8 were both lined with sub-rounded cobbles and were

Fig. 25.13—Holdenstown 1: burial 7.

placed 5.8m apart, with an east–west alignment. Burial 6 was adjacent to the southern edge of the penannular enclosure and was in a poor state of preservation. Osteological analysis identified the individual in burial 6 as an adult of undetermined sex. This burial was the most poorly preserved inhumation on site. Burial 7 (Fig. 25.13) has been identified as an old middle adult of undetermined sex, whereas burial 8 (Fig. 25.14) has been identified as a young middle adult male. Strontium analysis was undertaken to investigate the geographical origins of burial 8 and the results suggest that this

man was a local. This contrasts with the woman in burial 2, who seems to be an incomer to the area. A fragment of human bone (left tibia, 4.4g) from burial 8 was chosen for AMS dating and returned a result of 1556±23 BP. The 2-sigma calibrated date for this was AD 429–558, dating this individual to the late Iron Age/early medieval period.

Discussion

The site at Holdenstown 1 consisted of three ring-ditches, a linear boundary ditch, a penannular enclosure and eight inhumation burials, all of which have been dated to the Iron Age and the late Iron Age/early medieval transition. Holdenstown 1 is situated on the crest of a hill with commanding views of the surrounding countryside. The ring-ditches have been dated to the Iron Age and appear to have been associated with funerary activity. Ring-ditch 1, the largest one (16.65m in external diameter), contained the only surviving evidence of an undug causeway, which faced west. There was no evidence that any internal cremations or other features were contained within this ring-ditch. The southern part of ring-ditch 1 was recut on two occasions. It contained approximately twice as much animal bone as any of the other ring-ditches. Hazel charcoal from the secondary fill of the ring-ditch produced a date of 203–53 BC, whereas willow charcoal from the primary fill of the recut yielded a date of AD 426–546.

Ring-ditch 2 was located at the western limit of the excavation. It was not possible to determine whether a causeway had ever been present owing to the degree of truncation by later features. Alder charcoal from the secondary fill produced a date of AD 250–383. Ring-ditch 2 was subsequently recut the whole way around its circumference, and bone from the upper fill of the recut was dated to AD 425–579. Both dates stratigraphically contradict an earlier date produced from material in the linear ditch that cut ring-ditch 2. The ring-ditch was subsequently reused, with the placement of five inhumation burials within its southern portion. Burial 2 was dated to AD 551–646. Ring-ditch 3 was the most poorly preserved of the three. Ash charcoal from the secondary fill of the ditch returned a date of 168–3 BC.

Evidence for burials associated with the primary construction of the three ring-ditches at Holdenstown 1 was not forthcoming. This is not an uncommon feature of later prehistoric ring-ditches elsewhere in the archaeological record. Compared to Iron Age ring-ditch excavations elsewhere, however, the ring-ditches at Holdenstown 1 contained quite a large amount of animal bone. It is certainly tempting to suggest that this animal bone represents ritual feasting associated with funerary or other ritual activities at

Fig. 25.14—Holdenstown 1: burial 8.

these sites, but it is also possible that they are related to domestic activities at the site.

The linear ditch appears to have served as a boundary. Cherry charcoal from the main siltation fill produced a date of 160 BC–AD 18, though it has been noted that there is reason to be suspicious of this date. This ditch cut the perimeter of ring-ditch 3 and cut through the centre of ring-ditch 2. A large penannular enclosure (40m across) was built onto this linear boundary ditch. Hazel charcoal from the primary fill of this enclosure ditch produced a date of 91 BC–AD 53. This is quite similar to the date suggested for the linear ditch itself; the enclosure must be later than this, however, on the grounds that it truncates burials 3 and 5. Given that burial 5 has been dated to AD 425–579, the enclosure must post-date this burial. Three burials (6, 7 and 8) were within the penannular enclosure; burial 8 has been dated to AD 429–558. This is broadly contemporary with burial 5, which can be shown to pre-date the enclosure. Therefore it seems possible that these three burials also pre-date the enclosure, though that is not to say that the enclosure was not related in some way to the funerary activities at this site.

Clearly the site developed over a long period, starting with the construction of ring-ditch 1 in the mid-third century BC, followed by the construction of ring-ditch 3 sometime later. Ring-ditch 2 probably dates from about this time also. Subsequently, a boundary ditch was constructed across the site, skirting the perimeter of ring-ditch 3 and cutting through ring-ditch 2. This event may mark the beginning of a new development in the evolution of the site, whereby it was felt necessary to construct a physical boundary across it—a boundary that may have had a significant symbolic meaning, which in turn created a new symbolic meaning for the site as a boundary cemetery. The site continued to be used as a cemetery as late as the end of the Iron Age and the beginning of the early medieval period, with the reuse of ring-ditch 2 for inhumation burials, all aligned on the linear boundary ditch. The penannular enclosure represents the final phase of activity at the site, yet the precise function of this enclosure is not clear. The fact that the penannular enclosure incorporated several already ancient monuments and what may have been a symbolic boundary, as well as a number of broadly contemporary inhumations, strongly implies that this enclosure served a ritual purpose. O'Brien has suggested that Holdenstown 1 in its later form represents an ancestral boundary *fert* and has suggested that it continued in use for a time even after the fifth- or sixth-century foundation nearby of a familial cemetery (Holdenstown 2) that served the broader family or community. Eventually, both sites were abandoned as burial

sites in favour of an early church site adjacent to Holdenstown 2 (O'Brien and Bhreathnach 2011, 58).

Bibliography

O'Brien, E. and Bhreathnach, E. 2011 Irish boundary *ferta*: their physical manifestation and historical context. In F. Edmonds and P. Russell (eds), *Tome: studies in honour of Thomas Charles-Edwards*, 53–64. Woodbridge.

APPENDIX 25.1: OSTEOLOGICAL ANALYSIS OF THE HUMAN SKELETAL REMAINS FROM HOLDENSTOWN 1 (JENNIE COUGHLAN)

Introduction

This report discusses the results of the osteological analysis of eight inhumations recovered during archaeological investigations in the townland of Holdenstown, Co. Kilkenny. Analysis of the skeletal remains was undertaken to determine basic demographic information and to identify skeletal and/or dental changes that could be linked to occupational, nutritional or pathological stresses.

Burial 1

Burial 1 comprised the relatively complete skeleton of a young adult female. Age estimation was based on the auricular surface, dental attrition and fusion of the sacrum. Both the skull and pelvis exhibited strongly female morphological traits. Although all skeletal elements were represented in this burial, the majority were fragmented and incomplete, with the ribs and vertebrae particularly poorly preserved. Despite the overall fragmentation of the remains, the dentition survived relatively complete, with a total of 29 sockets and 31 teeth recovered. Post-mortem loss affected one tooth position. There was very little dental pathology affecting this individual. Slight to moderate calculus deposits were observed on all surviving teeth, with the buccal, lingual, mesial and distal tooth surfaces all affected. Dental attrition was scored as slight to moderate (stage 1–4) throughout, with the most severe level of wear (stage 4) affecting the mandibular central incisors. Although there was very little pathology noted through the dentition, both the right and left maxillary central incisors did exhibit an unusual and distinctive wear pattern. The occlusal surfaces of both teeth were affected by slight attrition only (stage 3), but the enamel on both lingual surfaces was worn. This resulted in the lingual surface taking on a 'vertical' appearance, as opposed to the more normal 'concave' look, with the wear facets terminating in a 'shelf' of enamel superior to the CEJ. No other unusual wear patterns were observed through the dentition and it seems likely that this wear was associated with some form of habitual occupational or cultural use of the teeth, and probably resulted from running material across the back of the maxillary incisors.

Skeletal pathology was limited to an area of barely discernible scattered porosity extending along the sagittal suture and barely discernible striations along the posterior femoral and medial and later tibial shafts. The cranial porosity is indicative of healed porotic hyperostosis, suggesting that this individual had suffered a period of iron-deficiency anaemia but that this had been fully resolved at time of death. The lesions on the femora and tibiae represented healed periostitis, associated with non-specific infection. As with the cranial lesions, the periosteal lesions were in an advanced stage of healing, indicating that the infection had not been active at time of death.

Burial 2

Burial 2 was a young middle adult female located immediately to the north-west of burial 1. Ageing of this individual was based on dental attrition, and sex assessment was based on the morphology of the skull. Both preservation and completeness were scored as 'moderate' for this individual, and although the majority of skeletal elements were represented all were in an incomplete and fragmented state.

The dental remains were affected by post-mortem damage and only four maxillary sockets and thirteen mandibular sockets survived. Of the 24 teeth recovered with this individual, only 22 could be identified, with the remaining two too severely worn to identify. Slight to moderate calculus deposits affected a total of seventeen of the 24 surviving teeth. Four of the affected teeth had calculus deposits on the roots, indicating that this individual had also suffered from periodontal disease. Periodontal disease is normally identified through resorption of the margins of the alveolar bone but can only be confirmed when the socket margins survive undamaged. In this example, only one of the sockets survived complete. This single undamaged socket was affected by severe periodontal disease.

Two small caries were visible on the mesial and distal surfaces of the left mandibular molar, with a further two large caries on the occlusal surface of the right mandibular first molar and right mandibular second premolar. Buccal abscesses were observed in association with the two right mandibular caries.

Dental attrition was variable, ranging in severity from stage 2 through to stage 8. The relatively young age of this individual, combined with the very slight wear affecting a number of the teeth, suggests that the more severe wear was associated with specific cultural or occupational activities. There was a notable difference in severity of wear between the left and right sides of the jaw, with the most severe levels of attrition affecting the left maxillary incisors and first premolar, the left mandibular lateral incisor and canine and the right mandibular central incisor. This suggests preferential use of this side of the mouth.

The only skeletal pathology affecting this individual was extreme bilateral upper limb asymmetry. On-site records describe an unusual body position for this burial, with the lumbar region of the spine strongly curved and the right ribs extending lower in the thoracic region than the left ribs. On-site interpretation suggested that this individual may have suffered from scoliosis, as evidenced by the lateral curvature of the spine. Unfortunately, both the vertebrae and ribs were very poorly preserved and only a small number of vertebral fragments were recovered. As such, the diagnosis of possible scoliosis could not be confirmed osteologically. The position of the arms in the burial also appeared different to the other burials on site, where the normative position was arms by the side. In this burial, both arms were crossed over the thoracic region, with the hands appearing strongly flexed.

Although both arms were very fragmented and incomplete, it was apparent during analysis that the right arm and hand bones were significantly more gracile than those of the left side. The right arm was represented by a fragment of the spine of the scapula, the mid-lateral third of the clavicular shaft, the distal third of the humeral shaft, the middle two-thirds of the ulnar shaft and the middle two-thirds of the radial shaft. The right hand survived as four incomplete and unidentified metacarpal shafts and three incomplete proximal phalanges. The left arm survived as a small fragment of the spine of the scapula, the distal third of the humeral shaft, the proximal third of the ulnar shaft and the mid-third of the radial shaft. Very small fragments of the humeral and radial proximal articular facets were also recovered. The left hand survived as two incomplete and unidentified metacarpal shafts, three incomplete proximal phalanges and one complete distal phalanx.

All bones in this skeleton appeared relatively gracile, but the right arm was significantly smaller than the left. Unfortunately, as the bones were so poorly preserved and incomplete, no site-specific metrical data were available. A comparative measurement taken at the distal humeral shaft of both the right and left bones indicated that there was a difference of up to 6.2mm between the widths of the shaft at this point. The disparity between the sizes of the radii and ulnae was less extreme but still significant. Measurements at the mid-right and left radial shafts identified a 2.2mm difference between the bones, while measurements taken at the proximal ulnar shafts identified a 2.6mm difference. Although the skeleton of this individual was gracile throughout, observations suggest that the right arm was more comparable in size to that of an older child or adolescent than that of an adult. There was no further asymmetry identified through the skeleton.

The disparity in size between the left and right arm bones suggests atrophy or hypotrophy of the entire right arm. There are a number of varying factors or conditions that can affect limb use, some of which would not appear on the skeleton. Analysis of a case of marked upper limb bilateral asymmetry in an Upper Palaeolithic skeleton from Barma Grande, Italy, led the authors to suggest a range of differential diagnoses for this condition (Churchill and Formicola 1997). These included, among others, direct trauma to the shoulder region, glenohumeral joint instability, soft-tissue trauma to the shoulder muscles and brachial plexus palsy.

Brachial plexus palsy describes paralysis of the arm after injury to the brachial plexus, a network of spinal nerves that originate in the back of the neck and give rise to nerves to the upper limbs. Nerve damage can occur as a result of trauma to the shoulder, tumours or inflammation. It can also be caused by injury to the shoulder region during birth (congenital brachial plexus palsy) and can lead to long-term muscle damage/weakness. Commonly, brachial plexus palsy affects one arm only (University of Michigan Motor Control Laboratory: on-line resource) and, although the affected individual can recover, persistent muscle weakness can also occur. It is possible that the bilateral asymmetry of the upper limbs in burial 2 relates to brachial plexus palsy, although it is also possible that there was an additional pathology or trauma that would have prevented use of the right arm but that the signs of this did not survive the burial process.

Notably, there was a second case of bilateral upper limb asymmetry in the cemetery population from the nearby site of Holdenstown 2 (Coughlan and Tobin 2009). Although burial 74 there (an older middle adult of undetermined sex) was in a fragmented and incomplete state, there was a very visible discrepancy in size and robustness between the right and left arms. In contrast to burial 2, in this example the left arm was significantly more gracile than the right. As with burial 2, no additional skeletal changes could be identified as factors contributing to this asymmetry.

Burial 3

Burial 3 was identified as an old middle adult male. This burial had been truncated by the medieval enclosure ditch (C7) and survived as fragments of the maxilla, mandible, right arm, right and left hands, right pelvis and right leg only. Ageing was based on patterns of dental attrition and the incomplete remains of the right auricular surface. Sex estimation was based solely on the mandible, although the overall size and robustness of the surviving bones also supported a male determination.

A total of 24 sockets and 24 teeth were recovered with this individual, with a total of five teeth lost post-mortem. Ante-mortem tooth loss affected the left first mandibular molar (4.2% of sockets). The adjacent second and third molars had been lost post-mortem. Although ante-mortem loss is commonly found to increase with age, there are a number of additional dental conditions and/or external factors that can contribute to premature loss of teeth. These include periodontal disease, severe dental caries, severe dental attrition and trauma. Additional dental conditions affecting this individual included a single small carious lesion on the mesial surface of the left maxillary second molar and three small buccal abscesses associated with the right maxillary premolar, the left mandibular second molar and the right mandibular first premolar. Although the two mandibular teeth had been lost post-mortem and the dental conditions associated with the development of the abscesses could not be determined, it is argued that, given the severity of attrition throughout the jaw, these abscesses were most likely associated with exposure of the tooth pulp through wear, as evidenced with the right maxillary premolar. Slight to moderate calculus deposits affected seven teeth, with sub-gingival calculus identified on the roots of three of these. Slight to moderate periodontal disease affected all eight undamaged socket margins.

Most of the teeth were affected by severe (stage 7–8) wear. In the maxilla, all but the left canine and left third molar displayed total/almost total loss of enamel, and the right lateral incisor survived as the partial crown only. The tooth crown appears to have been broken ante-mortem, possibly resulting from some form of occupational/cultural activity. Although the wear on the mandibular teeth was not as severe as that affecting the maxillary teeth, a number of mandibular teeth, including the right first and second molars and right lateral incisor, were severely worn, with significant loss of crown height.

Although very fragmented and incomplete, the vertebrae did exhibit evidence for mild to moderate degenerative changes. In the cervical region, mild osteophytes were observed on three incomplete vertebrae. An additional two unidentified left cervical articular facets were affected by severe degenerative changes, with extensive irregularity of both the joint surface and the joint margins. Although the thoracic region was very fragmented, there were a small number of central and articular facets that had been affected by moderate osteophytes and severe porosity. None of the surviving lumbar articular facets were affected. In addition to spinal joint disease, this individual also displayed changes indicative of degenerative joint disease at a number of extra-spinal joints. These included the right elbow, which was affected by mild osteophytes, porosity and eburnation, and the right knee, which was affected by both mild porosity and eburnation. In addition to these degenerative changes, this individual also exhibited fusion between the right first proximal and distal phalanges. There were no associated degenerative changes and this fusion may have been traumatic in origin.

Burial 4

Burial 4 was a young adult male. Age estimation was based on a combination of the auricular surface and dental attrition. Sex determination was based on the morphology of the skull and the sciatic notch. In this instance, the sciatic notch appeared strongly male, but the characteristics of the skull were slightly more ambiguous. Both the mental eminence and the orbital margins appeared strongly male, but both the mastoid processes appeared small and were scored as 'female'. As the supraorbital margins and nuchal crest were scored as 'probable male', the overall suggestion is that this individual was male. Fragmentation was common throughout the skeleton.

Twenty-one sockets and ten teeth were recovered, with nine teeth lost post-mortem. There was very little dental pathology, which may be related to the young age of this burial. Ante-mortem loss affected two (9.5%) of the 21 surviving tooth positions, with both left mandibular premolars lost prematurely. Attrition was slight (stage 1–4) throughout the dentition and slight calculus was identified on six of the ten surviving teeth. Moderate periodontal disease was observed affecting the only undamaged socket (left mandibular canine), and it is possible that periodontal disease played a contributory role in ante-mortem loss.

There was very little pathology through the skeletal remains. In the cranial region there was an area of barely discernible porosity extending from the posterior aspect of the frontal bone through the medial parietals and terminating at the nuchal crest on the superior occipital bone. These lesions are indicative of well-healed porotic hyperostosis, indicating that this individual had suffered a period of iron-deficiency anaemia but that this had been resolved by the time of death. No corresponding lesions were observed on the orbits. In addition to these cranial lesions, both the right and left mastoid processes had visible grooves extending in a superior–inferior direction through the centre of the bone. These may relate to stresses caused to the

sternocleidomastoideus muscles, which aid in flexion and torsion of the neck. Notably, the groove in the left mastoid was more pronounced than that in the right, perhaps indicating that the left muscle was under more stress than the right.

Burial 5

Burial 5, an old middle adult male, was partially truncated by the large early medieval enclosure, with resulting loss of the skull and left shoulder. Slight surface erosion affected all bones, and the vertebrae and ribs were poorly preserved. Both the age and sex determination were based on the pelvis. There were no visible skeletal pathologies and/or abnormalities affecting this individual.

Burial 6

Burial 6 was the most poorly preserved inhumation on site. Located at the southern boundary of the penannular enclosure, this burial consisted of the fragmented remains of the right humerus, right and left legs and feet and a single fragment of vertebral neural arch only. Poor preservation limited the information retrievable during analysis and this individual could only be given the broad age determination of 'adult'. Sex could not be established. There was no visible skeletal pathology.

Burial 7

Burial 7 was an old middle adult of undetermined sex. Although the skull survived relatively complete, it displayed both probable male and probable female traits and thus could not be used to determine sex. Age estimation was based on dental attrition. Although this skeleton survived mostly complete, all recovered elements were fragmented and incomplete, with the vertebrae and pelvis surviving as a very small number of fragments only; no rib fragments were recovered.

Four maxillary sockets and all sixteen mandibular sockets survived, with a total of 28 teeth recovered. One tooth was lost post-mortem. Calculus deposits affected nineteen (67.9%) of the 28 surviving teeth. The majority of calculus deposits were classed as slight to moderate, although severe deposits were noted on the lingual surfaces of the right mandibular first premolar and left mandibular first and second premolars. Calculus deposits were also observed adhering to the tooth roots (sub-gingival calculus) of seven of the affected teeth. The sub-gingival calculus indicated that that the tooth roots were partially exposed in the jaw through periodontal disease. Although a number of the sockets were too damaged to score for periodontal disease, six survived intact. All were affected by periodontal disease. The majority were affected by moderate periodontal disease, although slight periodontal disease affected the left mandibular third molar socket and severe disease affected the left maxillary first premolar. Rates of calculus were lower through the maxillary dentition (4/12 teeth: 33.3%) than the mandibular dentition (15/15 teeth: 100%).

The right maxillary second molar had a small carious lesion on the mesial surface. A medium carious lesion was visible on the mesial surface of the right mandibular third molar, while the left maxillary second molar displayed total destruction of the crown through carious activity. There were no associated abscesses.

Burial 7 was affected by moderate levels of attrition (stage 4–5) through most of the mandible, although both first molars and the right second molar displayed more severe wear (stage 6–7). The most severe levels of wear (stage 7–8) affected a number of maxillary teeth, including the incisors, where only fragments of the buccal and lingual enamel survived, and the right mandibular third molar. Through the maxilla teeth were worn along a lingual or lingual-mesial plane of wear.

Skeletal pathology was limited to barely discernible scattered porosity along the surviving portions of the sagittal suture, indicative of non-active iron-deficiency anaemia.

Burial 8

Burial 8, a young middle adult male, was well preserved, although, as was common on this site, the vertebrae and ribs were fragmented and incomplete. Ageing was based on patterns of dental attrition and sex estimation was based on the morphology of the skull.

Twenty-five sockets and 30 teeth were recovered with this individual. Visible calculus deposits affected all surviving teeth. As with burial 7, the majority of deposits were slight to moderate, although severe deposits were observed on the lingual surface of the left mandibular third molar. There were no other dental pathologies, and attrition was scored as slight to moderate throughout (stage 1–5). This individual also displayed an unusual root anomaly, with two left maxillary roots, identifiable as probable premolar roots, protruding from the alveolar bone adjacent to the mesial and distal aspects of the second premolar. A similar angled development of the tooth roots was also observed in the skeletal remains from Holdenstown 2. This latter example (burial 66), a young middle adult female, displayed similar development of the lateral incisor roots, although in this instance this appears to have affected tooth development and the permanent canines were congenitally absent. This condition appears congenital and, while it may not have impacted on the affected persons, it may suggest a link between the individuals in the two burial sites.

Identifiable skeletal lesions comprised healed cribra orbitalia and porotic hyperostosis. There was also very slight eburnation along the anterior margin of the left radial head, indicative of very mild osteoarthritis. There were no corresponding changes at the distal humerus. A small number of Schmorl's nodes, indicative of degenerative disc disease, were identified through the fragmented remains of the vertebrae.

Discussion

Excavations at Holdenstown 1 uncovered the remains of a range of archaeological enclosure features that have been given provisional dates ranging from the Iron Age through to the early medieval period. Five inhumation burials were identified within ring-ditch 2, with a further three within the eastern part of a penannular enclosure. The eight burials appear to represent two distinct phases of Early Christian/early medieval burial activity.

All five burials identified within the limits of the ring-ditch were inhumed in simple graves in a supine and extended position and shared the same south-west/north-east orientation. The three burials identified within the penannular enclosure shared the same west-east orientation and all were supine and extended. Two of the burials (7 and 8), both of which were in stone-lined graves, were near the eastern entrance to the enclosure. The third burial (6) was in a simple grave adjacent to the southern boundary ditch.

Osteological analysis identified a range of dental and pathological conditions commonly encountered in the study of past populations. These included evidence for joint disease, nutritional deficiencies and infection. None of the identified pathological changes appeared to have an unusually high occurrence in this group. There was a single example of bilateral upper limb asymmetry, which may have been related to brachial plexus palsy. Although interesting in itself, more notable was the identification of a second case of upper limb bilateral asymmetry in the nearby cemetery site of Holdenstown 2 (Coughlan and Tobin 2009).

Bibliography

Churchill, S.E. and Formicola, V. 1997 A case of marked bilateral asymmetry in the upper limbs of an Upper Palaeolithic male from Barma Grande (Liguria), Italy. *International Journal of Osteoarchaeology* **7**, 18–38.

Coughlan, J. and Tobin, M. 2009 Osteological analysis of the human skeletal remains from Holdenstown 2, Co. Kilkenny. Unpublished report prepared by IAC Ltd for Kilkenny County Council.

26. Iron Age ring-ditch at Commons of Lloyd, Kells, Co. Meath

Yvonne Whitty

Introduction

A portion of an Iron Age ring-ditch was excavated in the townland of Commons of Lloyd as part of the M3 Clonee–North of Kells motorway scheme (Archaeological Services Contract 4). The excavation was carried out by the present writer for Irish Archaeological Consultancy Ltd on behalf of Meath County Council and the National Roads Authority. The work was carried out under ministerial direction A029 and excavation registration no. E3157 in March 2006.

Location

The site was 66m above sea level within an irregular-shaped, gently sloping field of rough pasture (NGR 272901, 276686). The first-edition OS map of the area (1837) shows two small ponds *c.* 30m to the south-east of the site. There is no intervisibility between the Commons of Lloyd ring-ditch and any known contemporary site in the area, with the exception of the late prehistoric hillfort at the Hill of Lloyd, *c.* 550m to the west-south-west (Fig. 26.1).

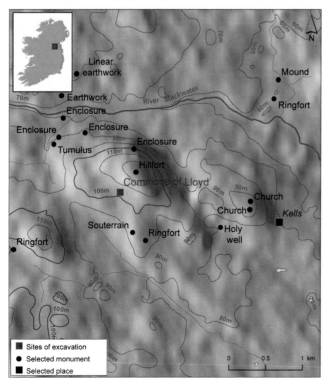

Fig. 26.1—Commons of Lloyd: location of site.

The ring-ditch

Approximately a third of the ring-ditch was exposed within the excavation cutting and it extended outside the limit of excavation to the south-west (Figs 26.2 and 26.3). Based on the excavated remains, the diameter of the ring-ditch is projected to be *c.* 20m. The ditch cut varied between 0.2m and 0.63m in depth and was deepest at the south-east. The exposed length of the ditch was 18.75m and the average width was 0.85m. The sides were steeply sloped; the break of slope at the base was gradual and the shape of the base was concave.

Primary fill

The primary fill of the ditch (C8) was a grey sandy clay that contained burnt/cremated bone and charcoal inclusions. This fill was consistent throughout the entire excavated length of the ditch and contained a large sample of burnt indeterminate bone fragments. Two cattle teeth were identified, as well as a small quantity of pig bones from an animal slaughtered at less than one year of age. The remainder of the sample consists of 54 medium mammal fragments and 89 indeterminate fragments. No cremated human remains were conclusively identified within the assemblage, but it is possible, although unfounded, that some of the unidentifiable fragments are human. A fragment (3.3g) of unidentifiable burnt bone from the primary fill of the ditch was chosen for AMS dating. It returned an AMS result of 2233±22 BP (UBA-12938). The 2-sigma calibrated result for this was 384–207 BC, indicating an Iron Age date for the ring-ditch. Hazel (*Corylus avellana*), ash (*Fraxinus excelsior*), *Prunus*, oak (*Quercus* sp.) and willow (*Salix* sp.) charcoal were all identified in samples from the ditch fill. The presence of oak within this context may be relevant, as this species was often selected as pyre fuel in prehistoric Ireland.

Two hulled barley grains were also identified from the primary fill of the ditch. One returned an AMS result of 1427±22 BP (UBA-12112). The 2-sigma calibrated result for this was AD 593–655. This is an early medieval date and is inconsistent with the Iron Age date from burnt bone in the ring-ditch. It is likely that this barley seed is intrusive, or was 'washed in' from a later deposit, and must be discounted.

A small fragment of an antler spindle-whorl (E3157:8:1) was found in the primary fill (Fig. 26.5). It was cut from the burr area of a red deer antler and has traces of cortile tissue on

327

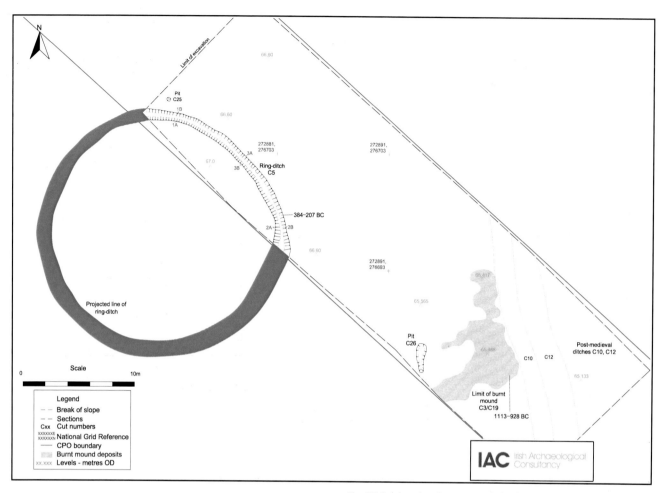

Fig. 26.2 (above)—Commons of Lloyd: site plan.

Fig. 26.3—Commons of Lloyd: view of ring-ditch.

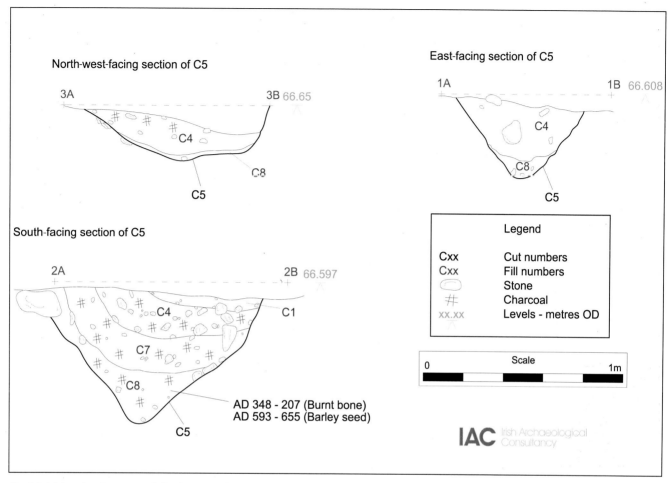

North-west-facing section of C5

3A   3B 66.65
            C4
                    C8
        C5

East-facing section of C5

1A   1B 66.608
            C4
        C8
            C5

South-facing section of C5

2A   2B 66.597
            C4   C1
        C7
        C8
                    AD 348 - 207 (Burnt bone)
                    AD 593 - 655 (Barley seed)
        C5

Legend	
Cxx	Cut numbers
Cxx	Fill numbers
⬭	Stone
#	Charcoal
xx.xx	Levels - metres OD

Scale
0   1m

IAC Irish Archaeological Consultancy

Fig. 26.4 (above)—Commons of Lloyd: section drawings.

Fig. 26.5—Commons of Lloyd: spindle-whorl from ring-ditch.

0mm   10mm

one side. It has been lathe-turned and includes a rounded section with an indented area on the upper face, defined by a deeply cut groove. The estimated diameter of the whorl is 33mm and its estimated weight is 5–35g. It has characteristics comparable with known early medieval examples, tying it in well with the late sixth/seventh-century date established for a barley grain from the fill of the ditch.

Secondary fills

A localised secondary fill (C7) was recorded within the deeper, south-eastern, portion of the ring-ditch. This consisted of a light brown sandy clay with a moderate amount of charcoal flecking and a small quantity of burnt bone. This fill extended for an approximate length of 2.75m. The burnt bone assemblage from this context comprised six medium mammal fragments and seventeen indeterminate pieces. The bones are all burnt to varying degrees, from blue/grey to black to chalky white. None of these bones could be conclusively categorised as human. Seeds identified in a sample from fill C7 included uncarbonised wild taxa such as bramble (*Rubus* sp.) as well as carbonised seeds including oat (*Avena* sp.), barley (*Hordeum* sp.) and wheat (*Triticum* sp.) grains. Above this layer was a mid-brown silty clay (C4), which was consistent throughout the excavated section of the ditch. It produced 24 burnt bone fragments, most of which were totally calcined from being in contact with fire. Just four bones were identified—two teeth, a portion of a scapula and the distal end of a tibia—all of which were from sheep/goat. The teeth were not burnt but the two post-cranial fragments were totally calcined. The remainder of the assemblage consisted of eighteen fragments from a medium-sized animal, probably sheep/goat, and a single fragment from a large mammal, either a horse or a cow.

Samples from this context produced a number of seeds from wild plants. Pale persicaria (*Polygonum lapathifolium*), knotgrass (*Polygonum* sp.) and persicaria (*Fallopia persicaria*) were all present, as well as oat (*Avena* sp.) and bedstraw (*Galium* sp.) grains and a number of other unidentifiable grains.

Conclusion

The ring-ditch (384–207 BC) was only partially excavated. Approximately two-thirds of it extended outside the excavation area to the south-west. The projected size of the ring-ditch was 20m. Although none of the burnt bone from the fills could be identified conclusively as human, the incidence of charring and burning on the bone was quite high, suggesting that the remains are probably linked to some form of ritual activity associated with burial. The antler spindle-whorl from the primary ditch fill is characteristically early medieval and does not fit with the Iron Age date of the ring-ditch; there is evidence of early medieval activity in the immediate area, however, as a charred barley seed from the primary fill also returned an early medieval date (AD 593–655). The presence of this seed in the supposed Iron Age horizon was interpreted as a later intrusion, possibly a result of material washing down through the soils from later levels. The whorl was not identified during the excavation; it was recorded as part of the burnt bone assemblage and was submitted for analysis as part of the faunal report. As a result, the exact provenance of this find cannot be determined. It is possible that it was from an interface between the primary and secondary fills of the ditch. If this was the case, then there is a possibility that this object was deposited within the ring-ditch fill at a later period, possibly in an intrusive cutting not identified during the excavation.